T0190293

# Communications
# in Computer and Information Science

**2152**

Editorial Board Members

Joaquim Filipe ⓘ, *Polytechnic Institute of Setúbal, Setúbal, Portugal*
Ashish Ghosh ⓘ, *Indian Statistical Institute, Kolkata, India*
Lizhu Zhou, *Tsinghua University, Beijing, China*

## Rationale

The CCIS series is devoted to the publication of proceedings of computer science conferences. Its aim is to efficiently disseminate original research results in informatics in printed and electronic form. While the focus is on publication of peer-reviewed full papers presenting mature work, inclusion of reviewed short papers reporting on work in progress is welcome, too. Besides globally relevant meetings with internationally representative program committees guaranteeing a strict peer-reviewing and paper selection process, conferences run by societies or of high regional or national relevance are also considered for publication.

## Topics

The topical scope of CCIS spans the entire spectrum of informatics ranging from foundational topics in the theory of computing to information and communications science and technology and a broad variety of interdisciplinary application fields.

## Information for Volume Editors and Authors

Publication in CCIS is free of charge. No royalties are paid, however, we offer registered conference participants temporary free access to the online version of the conference proceedings on SpringerLink (http://link.springer.com) by means of an http referrer from the conference website and/or a number of complimentary printed copies, as specified in the official acceptance email of the event.

CCIS proceedings can be published in time for distribution at conferences or as post-proceedings, and delivered in the form of printed books and/or electronically as USBs and/or e-content licenses for accessing proceedings at SpringerLink. Furthermore, CCIS proceedings are included in the CCIS electronic book series hosted in the SpringerLink digital library at http://link.springer.com/bookseries/7899. Conferences publishing in CCIS are allowed to use Online Conference Service (OCS) for managing the whole proceedings lifecycle (from submission and reviewing to preparing for publication) free of charge.

## Publication process

The language of publication is exclusively English. Authors publishing in CCIS have to sign the Springer CCIS copyright transfer form, however, they are free to use their material published in CCIS for substantially changed, more elaborate subsequent publications elsewhere. For the preparation of the camera-ready papers/files, authors have to strictly adhere to the Springer CCIS Authors' Instructions and are strongly encouraged to use the CCIS LaTeX style files or templates.

## Abstracting/Indexing

CCIS is abstracted/indexed in DBLP, Google Scholar, EI-Compendex, Mathematical Reviews, SCImago, Scopus. CCIS volumes are also submitted for the inclusion in ISI Proceedings.

## How to start

To start the evaluation of your proposal for inclusion in the CCIS series, please send an e-mail to ccis@springer.com.

Lorna Uden · I-Hsien Ting
Editors

# Knowledge Management in Organisations

18th International Conference, KMO 2024
Kaohsiung, Taiwan, July 29 – August 1, 2024
Proceedings

 Springer

*Editors*
Lorna Uden ⓘ
Staffordshire University
Stoke-on-Trent, UK

I-Hsien Ting
National University of Kaohsiung
Kaohsiung, Taiwan

ISSN 1865-0929          ISSN 1865-0937 (electronic)
Communications in Computer and Information Science
ISBN 978-3-031-63268-6          ISBN 978-3-031-63269-3 (eBook)
https://doi.org/10.1007/978-3-031-63269-3

© The Editor(s) (if applicable) and The Author(s), under exclusive license
to Springer Nature Switzerland AG 2024

This work is subject to copyright. All rights are solely and exclusively licensed by the Publisher, whether the whole or part of the material is concerned, specifically the rights of translation, reprinting, reuse of illustrations, recitation, broadcasting, reproduction on microfilms or in any other physical way, and transmission or information storage and retrieval, electronic adaptation, computer software, or by similar or dissimilar methodology now known or hereafter developed.
The use of general descriptive names, registered names, trademarks, service marks, etc. in this publication does not imply, even in the absence of a specific statement, that such names are exempt from the relevant protective laws and regulations and therefore free for general use.
The publisher, the authors and the editors are safe to assume that the advice and information in this book are believed to be true and accurate at the date of publication. Neither the publisher nor the authors or the editors give a warranty, expressed or implied, with respect to the material contained herein or for any errors or omissions that may have been made. The publisher remains neutral with regard to jurisdictional claims in published maps and institutional affiliations.

This Springer imprint is published by the registered company Springer Nature Switzerland AG
The registered company address is: Gewerbestrasse 11, 6330 Cham, Switzerland

If disposing of this product, please recycle the paper.

# Preface

The 18th International Conference on Knowledge Management in Organisations (KMO 2024) took place at the Garden Villa Hotel, Kaohsiung, Taiwan from July 29 – August 1, 2024. The conference was preceded by one day of free tutorials for participants who wished to learn the state of the art of research relating to the topics of KMO and LTEC. The tutorials were held on the 29th of July 2024. The conference itself commenced on the 30th of July 2024.

There are opportunities and challenges to managing knowledge in Industry 4.0. These include theoretical and empirical contributions on how Industry 4.0 technologies allow firms to create and exploit knowledge. Industry 4.0 technology provides a large amount of data and information, and knowledge management ensures that this information can be effectively collected, organized, and applied. Together, they help enterprises improve competitiveness, reduce risks, and achieve sustainable development, while also promoting innovation and continuous improvement.

Knowledge management (KM) solutions are now more powerful and offer advanced capabilities to help employees access knowledge and share it easily. Team collaboration tools have made it more challenging to automatically consolidate information shared between different team members from different applications and make it accessible in one single repository. Automating knowledge management (AKM) is becoming a key element in knowledge management trends because it allows organizations to improve efficiency and effectiveness in their daily operations.

The KMO 2024 conference brought together leading academic researchers and research scholars to exchange and share their experiences and research on all aspects of Knowledge Management challenges. This conference provided an interdisciplinary platform for researchers, practitioners, and educators to present and discuss their most recent work, trends, innovation, and concerns as well as practical challenges encountered, and solutions adopted in the fields of Knowledge Management and Industry 4.0 in Organisations.

These proceedings consist of thirty-three papers covering various aspects of Knowledge Management, from 72 submissions. All published papers have undergone a rigorous double-blind review process involving at least four reviewers. Authors of these papers come from 15 different countries including Australia, Austria, China, Colombia, Finland, Germany, India, Japan, Malaysia, Poland, Slovenia, South Africa, Taiwan, Thailand and the UK.

The papers are organised into the following topics:
Knowledge Transfer & Sharing
Knowledge in Business & Organization
Innovation & Knowledge Creation
KM and Education
KM Process and Model
Information & Knowledge Management Systems
AI, IT & New Trends in KM
Healthcare

Besides the papers, we also had invited keynote speakers and tutorials. We would like to thank our authors, reviewers, and program committee for their contributions and the National University of Kaohsiung, Taiwan for hosting the conference. Special thanks to the authors and participants at the conference. Without their efforts, there would be no conference or proceedings.

We hope that these proceedings will become a useful reference tool and that the information in this volume will be used for further advancements in both research and industry in Knowledge Management.

We hope you enjoyed the 18th KMO conference in Kaohsiung, Taiwan

Lorna Uden
I-Hsien Ting

# Organization

## Conference Chair

Lorna Uden — Staffordshire University, UK

## Program Chair

Derrick I-Hsien Ting — National University of Kaohsiung, Taiwan

## Conference Secretary

Ming-Jun Chen — National University of Kaohsiung, Taiwan

## Local Chairs and Organizing Team

| | |
|---|---|
| Reinhard C. Bernsteiner | MCI Management Center Innsbruck, Austria |
| Elvis Eduardo Gaona | Universidad Distrital Francisco José de Caldas, Colombia |
| Victor Hugo Medina Garcia | Universidad Distrital Francisco José de Caldas, Colombia |
| Marjan Heričko | University of Maribor, Slovenia |
| Gan Keng Hoon | Universiti Sains Malaysia, Malaysia |
| Akira Kamoshida | Hosei University, Japan |
| George Karabatis | University of Maryland, Baltimore County, USA |
| Mariusz Kostrzewski | Warsaw University of Technology, Poland |
| Eric Kin-Wai Lau | City University of Hong Kong, China |
| Dario Liberona | Universidad Santa Maria, Chile |
| Furen Lin | National Tsing Hua University, Taiwan |
| Magdalena Marczewska | University of Warsaw, Poland |
| Jari Kaivo-Oja | University of Turku. Finland |
| Luka Pavlič | University of Maribor, Slovenia |
| Christian Ploder | MCI Management Center Innsbruck, Austria |
| Stephan Schlögl | MCI Management Center Innsbruck, Austria |
| Dai Senoo | Tokyo Institute of Technology, Japan |
| Derrick I-Hsien Ting | National University of Kaohsiung, Taiwan |

| Lorna Uden | Staffordshire University, UK |
| Kamoun-Chouk Souad | Manouba University, ESCT, Tunisia |
| Iraklis Varlamis | Harokopio University of Athens, Greece |
| Remy Magnier-Watanabe | University of Tsukuba, Japan |
| William Wang | University of Waikato, New Zealand |

The CIPPI Saen Saeb Canal Model for Community Planning
and Improvement ...................................................... 248
    *Thanakhom Srisaringkarn, Suppanunta Romprasert,*
    *Polpat Kotrajarras, and Wichuta Adulwattanakul Khunrath*

## Information and Knowledge Management Systems

Building a Sustainable Knowledge Management System from Dark Data
in Industrial Maintenance ............................................. 263
    *Keyi Zhong, Tom Jackson, Andrew West, and Georgina Cosma*

Product-Service System for the Foundry Sector ......................... 275
    *Mariusz Salwin, Dominika Strycharska, and Andrzej Kraslawski*

The Design of AI-Enabled Experience-Based Knowledge Management
System to Facilitate Knowing and Doing in Communities of Practice ......... 292
    *Wen-Cheng Shen and Fu-Ren Lin*

Digital Decarbonization in Manufacturing Supply Chains: Addressing
the Environmental Impact of the Data Industry .......................... 304
    *Marios Georgiou, Thomas Jackson, Ian R. Hodgkinson, Lisa Jackson,*
    *Steve Lockwood, and Keyi Zhong*

## AI, IT and New Trends in KM

Increasing Interpretability in Outside Knowledge Visual Question
Answering ........................................................... 319
    *Max Upravitelev, Christopher Krauss, and Isabelle Kuhlmann*

Application of Open AI in Small and Medium-Sized Enterprise (SME)
Risk Assessment and Financial Analysis System ......................... 331
    *Chia-Chun Kang, Li-Jie Zhang, Jie-Mie Wang, and Chi-Hsu Lin*

An Initial Insight into Measuring Quality in Cloud-Native Architectures ....... 341
    *Vasilka Saklamaeva, Tina Beranič, and Luka Pavlič*

KP-Cartographer: A Lightweight SLAM Approach Based on Cartographer .... 352
    *Linjie Li, Ran Tao, Xiaohui Lu, and Xin Luo*

Artificial Intelligence to Elevate Knowledge Management in Malaysian
Public Sector: An Overview ........................................... 363
    *Rohaizan Daud, Norasyikin Shaikh Ibrahim, and Min Hui Leow*

A Study on the Factors Affecting the Use of Smartphone Payment Services
in Japan ............................................................ 378
    *Kazunori Minetaki and I.-Hsien Ting*

The Use of Web Scraping to Explain Donation Behavior .................... 394
    *Christian Ploder, Johannes Spiess, Stephan Schlögl, Thomas Dilger,
    Reinhard Bernsteiner, and Markus Gander*

Knowledge Management and Web 3.0 ................................... 404
    *Eric Kin Wai Lau*

## Healthcare

Predictive Analytics a Silver Bullet for a Pandemic – A Systematic
Literature Review ...................................................... 415
    *George Maramba and Hanlie Smuts*

Covid and Emotional Intelligence – Doctors' Reflections .................... 430
    *Chun Wai Wong and Benjamin Sutton*

**Author Index** ...................................................... 445

# Knowledge Transfer and Sharing

# Telework Frequency, Media Use and Knowledge Sharing in the USA During COVID-19

Remy Magnier-Watanabe(✉)

Graduate School of Business Sciences, University of Tsukuba, Tokyo, Japan
magnier-watanabe.gt@u.tsukuba.ac.jp

**Abstract.** This study investigates the interplay between telework frequency, communication media, and knowledge sharing during telework brought about by COVID-19 in the United States. Analyzing data from 614 participants with prior telework experience, the research unveiled nuanced associations between these variables. While higher telework frequency positively correlated with increased phone calls, chat, and virtual meetings, face-to-face interactions and email frequency remained unaffected. Furthermore, phone calls, chat, and virtual meetings exhibited positive links with knowledge sharing, confirming a mediation effect of these 3 communication media between telework frequency and knowledge sharing. This emphasizes the pivotal role of technology-based synchronous communication tools in mediating knowledge exchange within remote work contexts. The findings underscore the need for organizations to foster dynamic communication strategies, prioritizing interactive channels to optimize collaboration and information dissemination in remote work environments. Understanding these dynamics presents crucial insights for shaping effective communication frameworks and maximizing knowledge sharing in contemporary remote work scenarios.

**Keywords:** Telework · Knowledge sharing · Communication medium · United States

## 1 Introduction

The COVID-19 pandemic, caused by the novel coronavirus SARS-CoV-2, has brought about a seismic shift in various aspects of daily life across the globe. One of the most significant and enduring changes has been the transformation of work environments, with telework emerging as a central feature of the "new normal" (BLS, 2022). In the United States, the period from 2020 to 2022 witnessed a remarkable evolution in work practices and a reevaluation of the role of telework, which, in turn, significantly impacted the modes of communication and knowledge sharing. This article delves into the intricate relationship between the COVID-19 pandemic, telework, media use (including face-to-face interactions, phone calls, emails, chats, and virtual meetings), and knowledge sharing in the U.S.

The first cases of COVID-19 in the United States were confirmed in January 2020. To ensure business continuity and safeguard employee health, many U.S. companies and

© The Author(s), under exclusive license to Springer Nature Switzerland AG 2024
L. Uden and I.-H. Ting (Eds.): KMO 2024, CCIS 2152, pp. 3–15, 2024.
https://doi.org/10.1007/978-3-031-63269-3_1

organizations expedited the adoption of telework policies. The shift to telework significantly transformed how employees communicated. The absence of physical proximity meant that interactions, which were once face-to-face, had to be facilitated through various media channels. This transformation had far-reaching effects on media use, including face-to-face interactions, phone calls, emails, chats, and virtual meetings. The temporary measures adopted in response to the pandemic have had long-lasting effects on knowledge sharing. The transition to telework compelled employees and organizations to explore new avenues for sharing knowledge, expertise, and information.

The purpose of this paper is to examine how telework frequency, communication media, and knowledge sharing are interconnected during telework resulting from the COVID-19 pandemic in the United States. The study aims to understand the relationships between these variables and how they affect knowledge sharing among individuals who have prior experience with telework.

## 2 Literature Review and Hypotheses Development

### 2.1 Telework from Home

Telework from home, often referred to as home-based teleworking or home-working, is characterized by regular salaried employment conducted by employees from their homes. The frequency of telework can range from a few days a month to 5 days a week (Aguilera et al., 2016). Extensive research has explored the factors influencing the adoption of home-based telework, primarily related to the nature of the job, perceived benefits and drawbacks, and alignment with the company or national cultural norms (Peters and Batenburg, 2015; Aguilera et al., 2016).

It is widely recognized that telework from home is most suitable for highly skilled and autonomous workers who perceive it as advantageous for their professional and personal lives (De Graaff and Rietveld, 2007). Furthermore, the frequency or intensity of telework plays a pivotal role in employee satisfaction, performance, relationships with colleagues, as well as its implications for employees who do not engage in teleworking (Allen et al., 2015).

The U.S. government has recognized both advantages and drawbacks associated with telework, as outlined in several government materials (OPM, 2020; GSA, 2021). In terms of benefits, telework is seen as a means of ensuring continuity of operations for federal agencies, especially during emergencies like natural disasters or public health crises such as the COVID-19 pandemic. It allows government services to continue even when traditional office settings are disrupted. Additionally, telework is viewed as an attractive option for recruiting and retaining talented employees, as it provides a flexible work arrangement that appeals to those seeking better work-life balance. Employees benefit from greater work-life balance, with reduced commute times and more time for personal and family activities. There are also cost savings, both for employees who save on commuting expenses and time, and for the government, which can reduce costs associated with office space and utilities. Moreover, when implemented effectively, telework is believed to enhance productivity by allowing employees to work in environments conducive to concentration and with fewer distractions.

On the downside, teleworking employees might experience feelings of isolation and loneliness due to reduced in-person interactions with colleagues, which can result in social isolation. Communication challenges, such as delays in getting quick answers or discussing complex issues, can arise in remote work settings. Establishing clear work-life boundaries can be difficult, potentially leading to longer working hours as employees find it challenging to "log off" from work. Some employees might not have access to the necessary resources or technologies for effective telework, creating a barrier to success. There are also security concerns, especially for government agencies handling sensitive information, requiring a focus on data security and confidentiality. Lastly, supervisors might face challenges in supervising and holding remote employees accountable, ensuring that teleworking employees meet performance expectations (GSA, 2021).

## 2.2 Communication Modes

Daft and Lengel (1984, 1986) introduced the media richness theory at the onset of the electronic communication era. This theory postulates that the effectiveness of a communication channel or medium hinges on its ability to emulate the richness of the original medium. Richness is gauged by various factors, including immediate feedback, the presence of multiple cues, linguistic diversity, and individual focus. When opting for a communication medium for a specific message or meeting, the foremost objective is to curtail equivocality or the potential for misinterpretations and manifold interpretations of the message.

In situations where a message is intricate and arduous to decipher, a greater array of cues and data is necessary to ensure a correct understanding. As elucidated by Suh (1999), "a lean medium (e.g., a memo) is adequate for exchanging an unequivocal message (e.g., routine communication), while a rich medium (e.g., a face-to-face meeting) is recommended for resolving an equivocal situation (e.g., negotiation)" (p. 296). In addition to the original four richness criteria, Carlson and Zmud (1999) introduced social influence and experience as supplementary factors to consider when selecting a communication channel, taking into account the specific topic, communicator, and organizational context.

Face-to-face communication is categorized as the richest medium, succeeded by phone conversations, written addressed documents, and unaddressed documents (e.g., bulk emails, flyers). Nonetheless, over the nearly four decades since the theory's inception, novel communication methods have emerged and garnered widespread acceptance. Virtual meetings conducted through platforms like Zoom, Microsoft Teams, and Webex are recognized as rich media, one step below face-to-face communication. These virtual meetings provide a level of richness but still lack certain elements, such as the ability to manipulate objects collectively, physical contact, and a comprehensive grasp of non-verbal cues, especially when video is activated (Reed and Allen, 2021). In contrast, instant messaging, while facilitating real-time interaction, is deemed much leaner due to its limited support for nonverbal cues (Tang and Bradshaw, 2020).

## 2.3 Knowledge Sharing

Knowledge sharing represents a pivotal phase within the domain of knowledge management, encompassing creation, storage, application, and sharing (Heisig, 2009). Among the knowledge management processes, knowledge sharing stands out as the most frequently scrutinized, followed by knowledge acquisition and knowledge application (Al-Emran et al., 2018). This sharing of knowledge entails the flow of information among organizational actors (Kianto et al., 2018) and can manifest in formal or informal contexts. Knowledge donation involves the act of imparting one's knowledge to others, while knowledge collection revolves around receiving knowledge from another unit or actor. True knowledge sharing is recognized when knowledge is voluntarily given and received (Van Den Hooff and De Ridder, 2004).

The foundation of knowledge sharing hinges on several critical factors: trust, intrinsic and extrinsic motivation, job satisfaction, organizational norms and values, and support from leadership (Van Den Hooff and De Ridder, 2004). It's important to acknowledge that not all knowledge can be effortlessly verbalized or transmitted. In this regard, Polanyi introduced a fundamental distinction between two types of knowledge (1966). Tacit knowledge comprises highly individual cognitive knowledge that defies easy expression through language or numbers, encompassing beliefs, perspectives, technical expertise, and practical know-how. On the contrary, explicit knowledge is characterized by its objectivity and rationality, rendering it expressible through words or numerical representations. This category includes texts, equations, specifications, and manuals and is notably straightforward to identify, store, and retrieve (Wellman, 2009).

## 2.4 Hypotheses and Research Model

Various studies, such as the work of Bélanger and Allport (2008), have demonstrated that communication patterns are significantly influenced by collaborative technology, leading to an increase in explicit knowledge sharing but a decrease in the transfer of tacit knowledge. Telework has been found to affect knowledge sharing in organizations, especially between teleworkers and non-teleworkers (Taskin and Bridoux, 2010). This phenomenon aligns with the concept of media richness theory, which underscores the importance of selecting an appropriate communication medium based on the nature of the knowledge to be conveyed. Generally, richer media are deemed more effective for the exchange of tacit knowledge, while leaner media are better suited for the transfer of explicit knowledge, a principle corroborated in prior research (Murray and Peyrefitte, 2007). In essence, the choice of communication media within organizational settings hinges on the medium's richness and the type of knowledge intended for transmission.
*Telework frequency and Communication Media*
Hypotheses H1a to H1e are centered around the impact of telework frequency on various communication modes.

Telework reduces the opportunities for face-to-face interactions among employees, as they are physically separated and rely more on technology-mediated communication (Golden and Gajendran, 2019) (H1a). Telework increases the need for synchronous communication, such as phone calls, to coordinate tasks, share information, and maintain social ties (Magnier-Watanabe, 2023) (H1b). Telework also increases the need for asynchronous communication, such as email, to document work processes, provide feedback, and exchange knowledge (Yang et al., 2022) (H1c). Telework also creates a demand for instant and informal communication, such as chat, to facilitate collaboration, problem-solving, and social support (Faraj and Azad, 2012) (H1d). Telework also requires a mode of communication that can simulate face-to-face interactions and convey rich information, such as body language, facial expressions, and tone of voice, such as that offered by virtual meetings (Hinds and Bailey, 2003) (H1e). Therefore, we hypothesize the following:

H1a: Higher telework frequency is related to lower face-to-face frequency.
H1b: Higher telework frequency is related to higher phone call frequency.
H1c: Higher telework frequency is related to higher email frequency.
H1d: Higher telework frequency is related to higher chat frequency.
H1e: Higher telework frequency is related to higher virtual meeting frequency.

*Communication and Knowledge Sharing*
H2a to H2e focus on the relationship between communication modes and knowledge sharing, among workers with prior telework experience.

Face-to-face communication is associated with higher knowledge sharing due to the richness of non-verbal cues, immediate feedback, and relationship (Dennis and Valacich, 1999) (H2a). Phone call communication allows for synchronous and verbal interactions, moderate levels of trust and rapport, and clear and concise information (Srikanth and Puranam, 2010) (H2b). Email is effective for sharing explicit knowledge, documents, and information (Malhotra et al., 2001) (H2c). Chat communication Chat and instant messaging platforms are valuable for quick exchanges and informal knowledge sharing among teams (Faraj and Azad, 2012) (H2d). Virtual meetings provide a middle ground between face-to-face and digital communication, enabling remote teams to collaborate effectively (Gibson and Gibbs, 2006) (H2e). Therefore, we hypothesize the following:

H2a: Higher face-to-face frequency is related to higher knowledge sharing.
H2b: Higher phone call frequency is related to higher knowledge sharing.
H2c: Higher email frequency is related to higher knowledge sharing.
H2d: Higher chat frequency is related to higher knowledge sharing.
H2e: Higher virtual meeting frequency is related to higher knowledge sharing.

## 3 Methodology

### 3.1 Survey and Sample

In October 2023, a survey was carried out using the services of an Internet survey company. The participants in the survey were exclusively full-time employees with at least 2 years of seniority based in five major US metropolitan areas. By design, all respondents had telework experience of at least 1 full day per week prior to COVID-19 and they all engaged in some degree of telework during the period of interest.

In this sample of 614 respondents, we have about equal numbers of men and women, most are in their 30s (49%) with a university degree or higher (79%), having subordinates (96%), employed in companies with more than 500 employees (37%), with an average commute one-way between 30 and 60 min (40%) (Table 1). During the health emergency, most respondents teleworked 4 days (22%) or 5 days (35%) a week.

A single question was used to assess knowledge sharing ("we spent time to share ideas and experiences with each other"), based on Kianto et al. (2018) on a 7-point scale. During the public health emergency related to COVID-19, respondents teleworked on average between 3 and 4 days a week, and used face-to-face communication once a week, and phone, email, chat, and virtual meetings all once a day. Correlations, all below 0.6, reveal no issues with collinearity (Table 2).

**Table 1.** Sample demographics

| Indicator | N | % | Indicator | N | % |
|---|---|---|---|---|---|
| Gender | | | Company size | | |
| Men | 327 | 53.3 | 0–10 | 14 | 2.3 |
| Women | 287 | 46.7 | 10–49 | 64 | 10.4 |
| Age | | | 50–249 | 168 | 27.4 |
| 20–24 | 27 | 4.4 | 250–499 | 142 | 23.1 |
| 25–29 | 77 | 12.5 | Over 500 | 226 | 36.8 |
| 30–39 | 300 | 48.9 | Subordinates | | |
| 40–49 | 137 | 22.3 | 0 | 26 | 4.2 |
| 50–59 | 56 | 9.1 | 1–5 people | 89 | 14.5 |
| 60+ | 17 | 2.8 | 6–10 people | 144 | 23.5 |
| Education | | | 11–30 people | 206 | 33.6 |
| High school | 60 | 9.8 | Over 31 people | 149 | 24.3 |
| Vocational school | 15 | 2.4 | Prior telework exp | | |
| Junior College | 50 | 8.1 | 1 day a week | 119 | 19.4 |
| University | 187 | 30.5 | 2 days a week | 132 | 21.5 |
| Master degree | 180 | 29.3 | 3 days a week | 93 | 15.1 |
| PhD degree | 120 | 19.5 | 4 days a week | 140 | 22.8 |
| Other | 2 | .3 | 5 days a week | 130 | 21.2 |
| Position | | | Telework frequency | | |
| Entry level | 45 | 7.3 | 1–3 days a month | 21 | 3.4 |
| Intermediate | 90 | 14.7 | 1 day a week | 50 | 8.1 |
| First-level mgt | 83 | 13.5 | 2 days a week | 103 | 16.8 |
| Middle mgt | 164 | 26.7 | 3 days a week | 92 | 15.0 |
| Senior mgt | 232 | 37.8 | 4 days a week | 136 | 22.1 |
| Commute (one-way) | | | 5 days a week | 212 | 34.5 |
| 0–30 min | 156 | 25.4 | | | |
| 31–60 min | 245 | 39.9 | | | |
| 61–90 min | 146 | 23.8 | | | |
| 91–120 min | 50 | 8.1 | | | |
| Over 120 min | 17 | 2.8 | | | |

**Table 2.** Means, standard deviations and correlations of survey variables

| | Mean | SD | 1 | 2 | 3 | 4 | 5 | 6 | 7 | 8 | 9 | 10 | 11 | 12 | 13 | 14 | 15 |
|---|---|---|---|---|---|---|---|---|---|---|---|---|---|---|---|---|---|
| 1. Gender | 1.47 | 0.499 | 1.000 | | | | | | | | | | | | | | |
| 2. Age range | 3.28 | 1.032 | 0.016 | 1.000 | | | | | | | | | | | | | |
| 3. Education | 4.27 | 1.447 | -0.044 | .105** | 1.000 | | | | | | | | | | | | |
| 4. Position | 3.73 | 1.299 | -.112** | 0.025 | .349** | 1.000 | | | | | | | | | | | |
| 5. Subordinates | 3.59 | 1.128 | -0.066 | -0.056 | .217** | .303** | 1.000 | | | | | | | | | | |
| 6. Company size | 3.82 | 1.110 | -0.075 | .162** | .318** | .233** | .241** | 1.000 | | | | | | | | | |
| 7. Commute time | 2.23 | 1.008 | -0.032 | -0.058 | .191** | 0.028 | .261** | .113** | 1.000 | | | | | | | | |
| 8. Telework freq. prior | 5.05 | 1.437 | 0.034 | .086* | .079* | 0.061 | 0.028 | 0.069 | 0.045 | 1.000 | | | | | | | |
| 9. Telework freq. | 5.48 | 1.476 | .112** | .190** | 0.065 | .118** | 0.013 | .135** | -.082* | .253** | 1.000 | | | | | | |
| 10. F2F freq. | 4.61 | 1.770 | -0.072 | -.122** | .167** | .121** | .193** | -0.020 | .242** | .113** | -0.029 | 1.000 | | | | | |
| 11. Phone freq. | 5.73 | 1.411 | .084* | 0.078 | .115** | .124** | 0.074 | .172** | -0.049 | .160** | .389** | .112** | 1.000 | | | | |
| 12. Email freq. | 5.79 | 1.383 | 0.068 | .089* | .163** | .109** | 0.011 | .190** | -0.055 | .134** | .415** | 0.025 | .497** | 1.000 | | | |
| 13. Chat freq. | 5.74 | 1.508 | .082* | 0.019 | .147** | .082* | -0.027 | .138** | -0.059 | .165** | .323** | .087* | .443** | .521** | 1.000 | | |
| 14. Virt. Meet. freq. | 5.56 | 1.400 | 0.012 | 0.000 | .209** | .168** | 0.076 | .156** | 0.042 | .092* | .266** | .145** | .369** | .423** | .467** | 1.000 | |
| 15. K. sharing | 5.49 | 1.463 | -0.021 | -0.035 | .185** | .165** | .139** | .123** | 0.065 | .154** | .185** | .198** | .301** | .213** | .279** | .323** | 1.000 |

Age range: 1 = under 25; 2 = 25–29; 3 = 30–39; 4 = 40–39; 5 = 50–59; 6 = over 60.

Education: 1 = High school; 2 = Prof. School; 3 = Associate degree; 4 = University; 5 = Master degree; 6 = PhD; 7 = Other.

Position: 1 = entry level; 2 = intermediate; 3 = first-level mgt.; 4 = middle mgt.; 5 = senior mgt.

Subordinates: 1 = 0; 2 = 1–5; 3 = 6–10; 4 = 11–30; 5 = 31 +

Company size: 1 = < 10; 2 = 10–49; 3 = 50–249; 4 = 250–499; 5 = 500 +

Commute time (1-way): 1 = 0–30 min.; 2 = 31–60 min.; 3 = 61–90 min.; 4 = 91–120 min.; 5 = over 120 min.

Telework freq.: 1 = none: 2 = 1–3 days a month; 3 = 1 day a week; 4 = 2 days a week; 5 = 3 days a week; 6 = 4 days a week; 7 = 5 days a week.

Comm. Freq.: 1 = never; 2 = once a year; 3 = once a month; 4 = once a week; 5 = 2–3 times a week; 6 = once a day; 7 = several times a day.

Knowledge sharing: 7-point Likert scale.

*p < 0.05; **p < 0.01.

## 4 Results and Discussion

### 4.1 Results

The subsequent statistical analyses utilize SPSS in conjunction with PROCESS, a readily accessible computational tool designed for SPSS that specializes in conducting mediation, moderation, and conditional process analyses (Hayes, 2018). The outcomes are visually represented in Table 3 and Fig. 1.

After controlling for gender, age, position, number of subordinates, company size, and prior telework experience, the indirect effects of telework frequency on knowledge sharing through communication mode frequencies remain the same as without the control variables; the total effect is significant, the direct effect is not significant, and the indirect effects through phone, chat, and virtual meeting frequencies are significant.

Certain control variables have a significant effect on communication modes, but those effects were much weaker than those from telework frequency. F2F frequency is higher among those who are younger ($-0.182$, p = 0.009), with more subordinates (0.272, p = 0.000), or with higher prior telework frequency (0.159, p = 0.002). Phone frequency

**Table 3.** Regression coefficients, standard errors, and model summary information for respondents with prior telework experience (n = 614), with control variables

| Antecedent | M1 (F2F) | | | M2 (Phone) | | |
|---|---|---|---|---|---|---|
| | Coeff. | SE | P | Coeff. | SE | P |
| X (TW Freq) | −0.044 | 0.050 | 0.376 | 0.333 | 0.038 | **0.000** |
| Gender | −0.197 | 0.141 | 0.163 | 0.165 | 0.106 | 0.119 |
| Age range | −0.182 | 0.069 | **0.009** | −0.015 | 0.052 | 0.773 |
| Position | 0.106 | 0.057 | 0.066 | 0.057 | 0.043 | 0.184 |
| Subordinates | 0.272 | 0.066 | **0.000** | 0.036 | 0.049 | 0.472 |
| Company size | −0.112 | 0.067 | 0.092 | 0.138 | 0.05 | **0.006** |
| TW freq. Prior | 0.159 | 0.050 | **0.002** | 0.058 | 0.037 | 0.121 |
| constant | 3.995 | 0.498 | **0.000** | 2.548 | 0.375 | **0.000** |
| | R2 = 0.277; F(7,606) = 7.203, p = 0.000 | | | R2 = 0.177; F(7,606) = 18.578, p = 0.000 | | |

| Antecedent | M3 (Email) | | | M4 (Chat) | | |
|---|---|---|---|---|---|---|
| | Coeff. | SE | P | Coeff. | SE | P |
| X (TW Freq) | 0.024 | 0.364 | 0.503 | 0.293 | 0.041 | **0.000** |
| Gender | 0.359 | 0.036 | **0.000** | 0.171 | 0.116 | 0.141 |
| Age range | 0.104 | 0.103 | 0.309 | −0.099 | 0.057 | 0.085 |
| Position | −0.016 | 0.051 | 0.748 | 0.054 | 0.047 | 0.254 |
| Subordinates | 0.050 | 0.042 | 0.233 | −0.101 | 0.054 | 0.064 |
| Company size | −0.050 | 0.048 | 0.299 | 0.157 | 0.055 | **0.004** |
| TW freq. Prior | 0.175 | 0.049 | **0.000** | 0.091 | 0.041 | **0.027** |
| constant | 2.930 | 0.036 | **0.000** | 3.299 | 0.411 | **0.000** |
| | R2 = 0.195; F(7,606) = 20.952, p = 0.000 | | | R2 = 0.132; F(7,606) = 13.194, p = 0.000 | | |

| Antecedent | M5 (Virt. Meet.) | | | Y (Knowledge sharing) | | |
|---|---|---|---|---|---|---|
| | Coeff. | SE | P | Coeff. | SE | P |
| X (TW Freq) | 0.233 | 0.039 | **0.000** | 0.041 | 0.043 | 0.341 |
| M1 (F2F) | | | | 0.093 | 0.032 | **0.004** |
| M2 (Phone) | | | | 0.157 | 0.047 | **0.001** |

(*continued*)

**Table 3.** (*continued*)

| Antecedent | M5 (Virt. Meet.) | | | Y (Knowledge sharing) | | |
|---|---|---|---|---|---|---|
| | Coeff. | SE | P | Coeff. | SE | P |
| M3 (Email) | | | | −0.030 | 0.051 | 0.557 |
| M4 (Chat) | | | | 0.102 | 0.045 | **0.025** |
| M5 (Virt. Meet.) | | | | 0.184 | 0.046 | **0.000** |
| Gender | 0.017 | 0.110 | 0.876 | −0.080 | 0.11 | 0.464 |
| Age range | −0.091 | 0.054 | 0.091 | −0.069 | 0.054 | 0.205 |
| Position | 0.121 | 0.045 | **0.007** | 0.068 | 0.045 | 0.128 |
| Subordinates | 0.012 | 0.051 | 0.816 | 0.083 | 0.052 | 0.112 |
| Company size | 0.132 | 0.052 | **0.011** | 0.037 | 0.053 | 0.485 |
| TW freq. Prior | 0.020 | 0.039 | 0.604 | 0.076 | 0.039 | 0.054 |
| constant | 3.458 | 0.388 | **0.000** | 1.764 | 0.436 | **0.000** |
| | **R2 = 0.103; F(7,606) = 9.973, p = 0.000** | | | **R2 = 0.192; F(12,601) = 20.967, p = 0.000** | | |

Total effect 0.151, p = 0.000, direct effect 0.041, p = 0.341

| Indirect effects | Effect | BootSE | BootLLCI | BootULCI |
|---|---|---|---|---|
| TOTAL | 0.110 | 0.025 | **0.064** | **0.159** |
| F2F freq. | −0.004 | 0.005 | −0.016 | 0.005 |
| Phone freq. | 0.052 | 0.019 | **0.017** | **0.093** |
| Email freq. | −0.011 | 0.019 | −0.050 | 0.027 |
| Chat freq. | 0.030 | 0.015 | **0.003** | **0.064** |
| Virt. Meet. freq. | 0.043 | 0.015 | **0.016** | **0.075** |

is higher among those who work in larger firms (0.138, p = 0.006). Email frequency is higher among those with higher prior telework frequency (0.175, p = 0.000).

Chat frequency is higher among those who work in larger firms (0.157, p = 0.004), or with higher prior telework frequency (0.091, p = 0.027). Virtual meeting frequency is higher among those in higher positions (0.121, p = 0.007), or those who work in larger firms (0.132, p = 0.011). Control variables had no significant associations with knowledge sharing.

H1a, whereby higher telework frequency is related to lower face-to-face frequency (−0.044, p = 0.376), and H1c (higher telework frequency related to higher email frequency) (0.024, p = 0.503), are not supported. H1b (higher telework frequency related

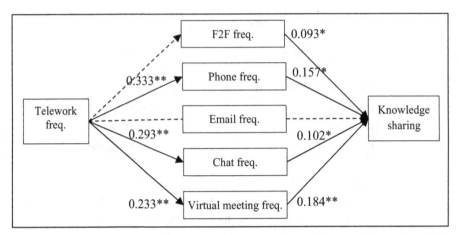

**Fig. 1.** Empirical model for respondents with prior telework experience, with control variables (n = 614)

to higher phone call frequency) (0.333, p = 0.000), H1d (higher telework frequency is related to higher chat frequency) (0.293, p = 0.000), H1e (higher telework frequency is related to higher virtual meeting frequency) (0.233, p = 0.000) are all supported.

H2a (higher face-to-face frequency related to higher knowledge sharing) (0.093, p = 0.004), H2b (higher phone call frequency related to higher knowledge sharing) (0.157, p = 0.001), H2d (higher chat frequency related to higher knowledge sharing) (0.102, p = 0.025), and H2e (higher virtual meeting frequency related to higher knowledge sharing) (0.184, p = 0.000) were supported, while H2c (higher email frequency related to higher knowledge sharing) (−0.030, p = 0.051) was not.

In the model, the total effect (0.151, t(606) = 3.682, p = 0.000) is significant while the direct effect is not significant (0.041, t(606) = 0.953, p = 0.341). However, several indirect effects are significant, as indicated by the asymmetric bootstrap confidence intervals which do not contain zero (Hayes, 2018): through phone call frequency (0.052, bootstrap confidence interval between 0.017 and 0.093), through chat frequency (0.030, bootstrap confidence interval between 0.003 and 0.064), and through virtual meeting frequency (0.043, bootstrap confidence interval between 0.016 and 0.075).

## 4.2  Discussion

*Telework Frequency and Communication Media*

Embracing Diverse Communication Channels: Organizations should acknowledge the shift towards remote work by encouraging and supporting diverse communication tools, since all channels besides face-to-face proved to be highly and equally used. Prioritizing phone calls, chat, and virtual meetings is essential for remote collaboration.

Reconsidering Email and Face-to-Face Interactions: While not significantly influenced by telework frequency, these communication modes remain valuable. However, the findings suggest that their frequency might not change significantly with increased remote work, contrary to past research (Yang et al., 2022). Strategies for optimizing these interactions rather than increasing their frequency might be beneficial.

*Communication Media and Knowledge Sharing*

Encouraging Interactive Communication: Platforms fostering real-time, interactive conversations (phone calls, chats, virtual meetings) seem more conducive to knowledge sharing. Encouraging their use for discussions and brainstorming sessions might enhance knowledge exchange.

Rethinking Email's Role: While still important for formal communication, especially documentation and archiving, its role in facilitating knowledge sharing might be limited, in contrast to past results (Malhotra et al., 2001). Encouraging more interactive media for knowledge dissemination and collaboration might be more effective.

*Mediation of Telework Frequency and Knowledge Sharing through Communication Media*

Significant Indirect Effects: Despite the direct effect not being significant, several indirect effects are significant, indicating the importance of media-rich technology-based synchronous communication channels in mediating the relationship between telework frequency and knowledge sharing.

Focus on Indirect Pathways: While direct telework frequency might not directly impact knowledge sharing, the indirect effects through phone calls, chat, and virtual meetings are noteworthy. Emphasizing and fostering these indirect pathways could be vital for promoting knowledge sharing in remote work environments.

These results suggest a nuanced understanding of communication dynamics in remote work settings. Embracing and encouraging effective communication channels while understanding their varying impacts on knowledge sharing could significantly benefit organizational practices in remote work scenarios.

# 5 Conclusion

In this study, the relationships between telework frequency, communication media, and knowledge sharing were examined. Findings indicate that increased telework frequency positively correlates with heightened phone calls, chat, and virtual meeting frequency, but not with face-to-face interactions or email frequency. Moreover, while phone calls, chat, and virtual meetings positively impact knowledge sharing, email frequency does not show a significant relationship. Although the direct effect of telework frequency on knowledge sharing was not significant, indirect effects through communication media such as phone calls, chat, and virtual meetings were substantial. These results underscore the importance of media-rich technology-based synchronous communication channels in facilitating knowledge sharing in remote work environments, highlighting avenues for optimizing communication strategies to enhance collaboration and information exchange.

While this research was conducted among employees with prior telework experience in the United States, future work should compare it to workers with no prior remote work experience in other countries and investigate whether experience and training, as well as location and culture affect the relationships between telework frequency, communication media, and knowledge sharing.

# References

Aguilera, A., Lethiais, V., Rallet, A., Proulhac, L.: Home-based telework in france: characteristics, barriers and perspectives. Transport. Res. Part A: Policy and Practice **92**, 1–11 (2016)

Al-Emran, M., Mezhuyev, V., Kamaludin, A., Shaalan, K.: The impact of knowledge management processes on information systems: A systematic review. Int. J. Inf. Manage. **43**, 173–187 (2018)

Allen, T.D., Golden, T.D., Shockley, K.M.: How effective is telecommuting? Assessing the status of our scientific findings. Psycholog. Sci. Pub. Interest **16**(2), 40–68 (2015)

Bélanger, F., Allport, C.D.: Collaborative technologies in knowledge telework: An exploratory study. Inf. Syst. J. **18**(1), 101–121 (2008)

BLS: Ability to telework available to 10.6 percent of civilian workers in 2022. Bureau of Labor Statistics, U.S. Department of Labor (2022). Available at: https://www.bls.gov/opub/ted/2022/ability-to-telework-available-to-10-6-percent-of-civilian-workers-in-2022.htm

Carlson, J.R., Zmud, R.W.: Channel expansion theory and the experiential nature of media richness perceptions. Acad. Manag. J. **42**(2), 153–170 (1999)

Daft, R.L., Lengel, R.H.: Information richness: A new approach to managerial behavior and organizational design. Res. Organizat. Behav. **6**, 191–233 (1984)

Daft, R.L., Lengel, R.H.: Organizational information requirements, media richness and structural design. Manage. Sci. **32**(5), 554–571 (1986)

De Graaff, T., Rietveld, P.: Substitution between working at home and out-of-home: The role of ICT and commuting costs. Transport. Res. Part A: Policy and Practice **41**(2), 142–160 (2007)

Dennis, A.R., Valacich, J.S.: Rethinking media richness: Towards a theory of media synchronicity. In: Proceedings of the 32nd Annual Hawaii International Conference on Systems Sciences (HICSS-32). IEEE (1999)

Faraj, S., Azad, B.: The materiality of technology: an affordance perspective. Material. Organiz. Soc. Interact. Technol. World **237**(1), 237–258 (2012)

Gibson, C.B., Gibbs, J.L.: Unpacking the concept of virtuality: The effects of geographic dispersion, electronic dependence, dynamic structure, and national diversity on team innovation. Adm. Sci. Q. **51**(3), 451–495 (2006)

Golden, T.D., Gajendran, R.S.: Unpacking the role of a telecommuter's job in their performance: Examining job complexity, problem solving, interdependence, and social support. J. Bus. Psychol. **34**(1), 55–69 (2019)

GSA: Telework: A Handbook for Managers. U.S. General Services Administration (2021). Available at: https://www.telework.gov/guidance_and_legislation/telework_toolkit/Handbook_for_Managers.pdf

Hayes, A.F.: Introduction to mediation, moderation, and conditional process analysis: A regression-based approach, 2nd edn. Guilford Press, New York, NY (2018)

Heisig, P.: Harmonisation of knowledge management – comparing 160 KM frameworks around the globe. J. Knowl. Manag. **13**(4), 4–31 (2009)

Hinds, P.J., Bailey, D.E.: Out of sight, out of sync: Understanding conflict in distributed teams. Organ. Sci. **14**(6), 615–632 (2003)

Kianto, A., Shujahat, M., Hussain, S., Nawaz, F., Ali, M.: The impact of knowledge management on knowledge worker productivity. Balt. J. Manag. **14**(2), 178–197 (2018)

Magnier-Watanabe, R.: Communication media as mediators of telework frequency and knowledge sharing in japan under COVID-19. Int. J. Web Eng. Technol. **18**(1), 62–79 (2023)

Malhotra, A., Majchrzak, A., Carman, R., Lott, V.: Radical innovation without collocation: A case study at Boeing-Rocketdyne. MIS Quarterly, 229–249 (2001)

Murray, S.R., Peyrefitte, J.: Knowledge type and communication media choice in the knowledge transfer process. J. Manag. Issues **19**(1), 111–133 (2007)

OPM: Fact Sheet: Telework in the Federal Government. U.S. Office of Personnel Management (2020). Available at: https://www.telework.gov/policies_and_guidance/fact_sheets_and_faq/fact-sheet-telework-in-the-federal-government.pdf

Peters, P., Batenburg, R.: Telework adoption and formalisation in organisations from a knowledge transfer perspective. Int. J. Work Innov. 1(3), 251 (2015)

Polanyi, M.: Tacit Dimension. Gloucester, MA: Peter Smith (1966)

Reed, K.M., Allen, J.A.: Suddenly Virtual: Making Remote Meetings Work. John Wiley & Sons (2021)

Srikanth, K., Puranam, P.: Integrating distributed work: comparing task design, communication, and tacit coordination mechanisms. Strateg. Manag. J. 32(8), 849–875 (2010)

Suh, K.S.: Impact of communication medium on task performance and satisfaction: an examination of media-richness theory. Information & Management 35(5), 295–312 (1999)

Tang, C.M., Bradshaw, A.: Instant messaging or face-to-face? How choice of communication medium affects team collaboration environments. E-learning and Digital Media 17(2), 111–130 (2020)

Taskin, L., Bridoux, F.: Telework: a challenge to knowledge transfer in organizations. The Int. J. Human Res. Manage. 21(13), 2503–2520 (2010)

Van Den Hooff, B., De Ridder, J.A.: Knowledge sharing in context: the influence of organizational commitment, communication climate and CMC use on knowledge sharing. J. Knowl. Manag. 8(6), 117–130 (2004)

Wellman, J.L.: Organizational Learning: How Companies and Institutions Manage and Apply Knowledge, 1st ed., Palgrave Macmillan, Ltd. (2009)

Yang, L., et al.: The effects of remote work on collaboration among information workers. Nat. Hum. Behav. 6(1), 43–54 (2022)

# Knowledge Management in the Gig Economy

Dario Liberona[1]([⊠]), Dona Layani Thirimanna[1], and Aravind Kumaresan[2]

[1] Seinajoki University of Applied Sciences, Seinäjoki, Finland
{Dario.liberona,Dona.thirimanna}@seamk.fi
[2] Optimists Healthcare, Chennai, India
ak@optimists.in

**Abstract.** Remote working and home office has been increasing rapidly during the last decade, among other factors enhanced by the Covid pandemic. These new modern workers that normally work as freelancers, are not part of formal organizations and have been spreading around the world, are the pillars of the new so called gig economy. The digital gig economy has undergone substantial growth in the past decade, powered by internet platforms like Fiverr and Upwork [1]. This study explores the relationship between technology, knowledge management, and the development of the gig economy It analyses the dynamics of learning and sharing information among its participants. Building on existing literature which highlights the importance of both factors, this research seeks to further understand the relative influence of technology and knowledge management on Gig economy. Utilizing a quantitative approach, the study employed a survey to collect data from 78 individuals who are operating within the gig economy. The survey instrument measured participants' knowledge and skill sets, preferred learning methods, and platform usage.

**Keywords:** Knowledge Management · Technology · Gig Economy · Freelancing platforms

## 1 Introduction

The gig economy has grown drastically in the last few years, and number of gig workers has expanded worldwide. In the United States, 14–20% of employees were working in the gig economy in 2014, and it was increased up to 35% by 2021 [2]. According to [3], gig economy can provide 90 million jobs for people in India in non-agriculture sectors and has the potential to contribute to GDP in 1.25%. Further, there are about 163 million freelancer profiles registered on digital gig platforms worldwide, approximately 19 million of them have found employment through these platforms [4]. The rise of the gig economy has changed the way people work, leading to a higher number of individuals to choose freelancing work over traditional employments. The gig economy is consisted with short-term projects and the work is carried out through digital platforms, which is significantly different from traditional employment. This transformation has made considerable changes to the knowledge management and to the way knowledge is applied

© The Author(s), under exclusive license to Springer Nature Switzerland AG 2024
L. Uden and I.-H. Ting (Eds.): KMO 2024, CCIS 2152, pp. 16–31, 2024.
https://doi.org/10.1007/978-3-031-63269-3_2

at work. To effectively handle and disseminate the knowledge among freelancers, independent contractors, and platform-based workers, it is essential to explore knowledge management in relation to the gig economy. As the gig economy keeps developing, it is essential to understand the dynamics of knowledge management within the gig economy context.

As the gig economy has transformed the nature of employment, the need for freelancers to have a wide range of expertise and abilities to survive this changing professional setting has increased [5], emphasized three categories of gig works, app work, crowd work and platform work. Further, importance of understanding algorithmic management in the gig economy was highlighted. They emphasized the significance of understanding those effects for employment relations and human resource management. This highlights the importance of researching different types of knowledge required for freelancers to succeed in the gig economy.

Furthermore, the platforms that freelancers use have a significant impact on their access to opportunities and resources. According to [6] although freelancing platforms have a focus on individual work, there is a need for collaborative work involves interdependent contributions from multiple workers. The study by [7] found evidence of bias in two online freelance marketplaces, Task Rabbit and Fiverr, with gender and race significantly correlated with worker evaluations. This highlight researching on the different needs of choosing the ideal platforms for freelancers and comprehending the factors that influence their motivation and engagement in the gig economy.

The emergence of gig economy represents a dynamic relationship with different factors including technology and professional knowledge management practices. Technology has a significant influence on the development of the gig economy and it is identified as a prominent factor. On the other hand, people with specialized knowledge have greater ability to take advantage of the opportunities provided by the gig economy. Being capable of marketing a person's skills online is vital. It emphasizes the importance of competent knowledge management when entering the gig economy. Therefore, there is a dynamic relationship between technology and professional knowledge management in the development of the gig economy, with both factors playing crucial roles in its growth and success. Accordingly, the objectives of this research are as follows.

- To explore the type of knowledge required by freelancers
- To identify the best platforms for freelancers
- To examine whether the gig economy is a result of better professional knowledge management, technology or both.

The objectives are determined by the necessity to fill gaps in the literature and enhance comprehension of knowledge management in the gig economy.

This research is important because it has the potential to assist in establishing strategies for effective knowledge management in the gig economy. This study intends to provide significant information on policymaking, platform design, and human resource management which are unique for freelancers and independent workers. By addressing the outlined research objectives this research can provide practical implications for improving career prospects of freelancers in the gig economy.

## 2  Literature Review

### 2.1  Knowledge Management

Within the gig economy, knowledge management refers to the proficient acquisition, utilization, and dissemination of information and expertise by freelancers to successfully navigate their professional environment. The main emphasis is on how freelancers acquire, utilize, and distribute knowledge within the gig economy, hence improving their professional skills and overall achievements. The rise in online freelancing has led to comprehensive research highlighting the specialized expertise and dedication needed to succeed in this ever-changing field [8].

Nowadays, freelancers are required to develop distinct professional skills. Prior study emphasizes the importance of freelancers proactively utilizing platform features to reduce hazards associated with the online freelancing environment [9]. As per [10] continuously developing skills is essential to ensure an uninterrupted flow of business, and freelancers are encouraged to acquire new self-presentation and impression-management abilities in order to establish trust in remote settings. These developing skills are essential for freelancers to succeed in an environment which has a higher uncertainty, influenced by mismatches in information and managed through analytics.

Studies have explored the nature of the freelancers' experiences, showing the conflict between the freedom and disappointments provided by online freelance platforms and the lack of control over job results. Research, such as the qualitative analysis conducted by [8] on freelancing Reddit boards, emphasizes the challenges that freelancers face. Furthermore, recent studies conducted on platforms such as Upwork and Fiverr has revealed a range of unique financial, reputational, relational, and emotional challenges experienced by freelancers, as well as prospects for professional growth [1]. Although previous studies have shed light on the possible disadvantages and advantages of online freelancing, as well as the specific skills needed, there is a significant lack of knowledge regarding how these aspects specifically impact the difficulties individuals come across and the help they seek when moving to online freelance platforms. This gap highlights the necessity for a comprehensive study of the relationship between specialized knowledge, expertise, and the difficulties that freelancers face in the changing gig economy environment.

Within the field of online on-demand labor platforms that facilitate knowledge work, there is a fundamental difference in the nature of jobs performed by freelancers [11] emphasis on macro-tasks done on platforms such as Upwork and Fiverr, as well as micro-tasks frequently observed on platforms like Amazon Mechanical Turk and Appen. Macro-tasks, which are known for requiring a high level of knowledge and competence, require specialized abilities and tend to take a longer time to complete. However, micro-tasks are limited in duration and are usually regarded as divided and lacking in skill requirements. As per [12], micro-task platforms and macro-work platforms do not include automated matching systems. Instead, they rely on 'algorithmic management,' which primarily involves the use of ratings and reputation. This situation establishes the conditions for a highly competitive atmosphere, necessitating freelancers to swiftly submit bids for jobs. Therefore, freelancers who are using these platforms must have a thorough awareness of the technological characteristics and guidelines that regulate them.

In the gig economy, freelancers must possess a diverse skill set beyond basic computer literacy. They must possess strong financial knowledge, showing proficiency in managing their income and making prudent financial decisions [11]. Having an awareness of entrepreneurship expertise, which involves understanding how to operate a business, is equally important [13]. Freelancers assume the role of being their own superiors, thus it is vital for them to comprehend the art of self-promotion and maintaining client satisfaction. Proficiency in language is also important as it enables freelancers to effectively communicate with clients and carry out their tasks with success [14]. Although freelancers operate independently, possessing teamwork abilities is especially important since they frequently engage in collaborative efforts with others on various projects.

## 2.2   Digital Freelancing Platforms

Online platforms play a significant role in facilitating knowledge management among freelancers by providing a centralized space for collaboration and knowledge sharing. Some platforms enable freelancers to connect with each other, share their expertise, and learn from one another, thereby enhancing their overall knowledge base. Specific platform features, such as discussion forums, project collaboration tools, and knowledge repositories, contribute to the success of freelancers by promoting effective communication, information exchange, and access to relevant resources [15]. The availability of project management tools on these platforms helps freelancers in organizing their work, tracking progress, and ensuring timely delivery of projects. Moreover, platforms provide a rich information environment where freelancers can showcase their skills, work history, and experience, which serves as a credible signal of their quality to potential clients. These platform features impact on freelancer success including improved efficiency, increased opportunities for networking and collaboration, enhanced learning and skill development, and access to a wider range of projects and clients [16].

However, platforms can enhance elements that promote efficient learning and utilization of knowledge, taking into account the needs of freelancers. Understanding the technological obstacles that freelancers come across, such as algorithmic management, can assist platform designers in developing interfaces that are clear and easy to use. The influence of technology also emphasizes the significance of functionalities that enhance freelancers' technological abilities, guaranteeing a smooth and supportive environment. By incorporating knowledge management ideas into platform design, an environment is created where freelancers can utilize technology to further their professional development. As per [17] findings, Platforms such as Upwork and Fiverr provide freelancers specific, scheduled assignments instead of offering them long-term employment. The characteristics of these platforms shape the nature of the activities that freelancers undertake, with macro-tasks necessitating specialized expertise and abilities for a longer period of time [12] state that the analytical thinking, through the use of ratings and reputation systems, has a significant impact on macro-work platforms by influencing the visibility and assignment of jobs for freelancers. Therefore, a competitive environment is created where it is essential to uphold a high ranking in order to obtain additional assignments. Freelancers have difficulties such as adjusting to algorithmic management methods and acquiring the necessary skills to efficiently navigate the marketplace. A study by [6], revealed although freelancing platforms have a focus on individual work, there is a need for collaborative work which involves interdependent contributions from multiple workers.

## 2.3 Driving Forces of Gig Economy

[18] conducted a study to identify the reasons driving the development of gig economy synthesizing scientific publications related to the gig economy phenomenon. According to his study, the Gig economy is a result of the platformization of the economy, which involves optimizing business processes through the development of digital platforms. As researched by [19], the Gig economy is the result of technological, social and economic and political environments. Technology plays an important role in influencing the experiences and achievements of freelancers in the gig economy. As per [20] findings, the emergence of new technologies has drastically changed the environment, presenting both prospects and difficulties for persons participating in online freelancing platforms. The influence of technology is broad affecting how freelancers obtain, employ, and show their skills in the digital domain. The growing presence of online freelancing platforms requires freelancers to continuously enhance and adjust their technological skills [8] emphasize that being proficient in utilizing platform features is essential for reducing the risks of the online freelancing environment. Regular updates and skillful use of technology resources are essential for maintaining competitiveness in the gig economy. According to [10], it is crucial for freelancers to have skills in self-presentation and impression management. In remote settings, when face-to-face encounters are limited, technology acts as the medium via which freelancers establish trust. Possessing the capacity to properly showcase oneself online is a significant expertise that aids in obtaining commercial prospects and nurturing professional connections. Challenges and opportunities arising from the influence of technology have been examined in studies undertaken by [11] on sites such as Upwork and Fiverr. As per [8], freelancers face financial, reputational, relational, and emotional difficulties as they navigate the details of these platforms. Nevertheless, technology also provides opportunities for career advancement and transparency, highlighting the two-sided nature of its influence.

The conceptual framework for the study is provided below (Fig. 1).

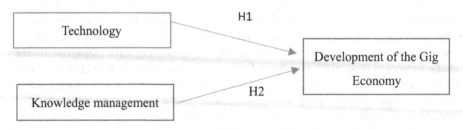

**Fig. 1.** Conceptual framework

The study's conceptual framework proposes two main hypotheses that are based on the existing literature on the gig economy. The initial hypothesis (H1) propose that technology has a significant effect on the establishment and development of the Gig Economy. As per the findings of [17] and [11], it is clear that the impact of technology in the gig economy is broad and has multiple aspects. Online freelancing sites, such as Upwork and Fiverr, utilize technology to facilitate the connection between freelancers and specific, prearranged jobs, hence influencing the types of tasks performed by gig workers [13]. Moreover, the use of analytical on these platforms, which involves the use of ratings and reputation systems, has a substantial impact on the visibility and distribution of projects for freelancers, resulting in a competitive atmosphere. This supports the argument that technology not only plays an essential part in shaping the gig economy, but also significantly influences the experiences of freelancers in it.

**H1:** Technology has a significant impact on the emergence of Gig Economy

Hypothesis 2 (H2) suggests that Knowledge Management plays an essential part in the development of the Gig Economy. The conceptual framework recognizes the significance of freelancers' capacity to obtain, employ, and distribute knowledge within the gig economy, based on the research conducted by [8, 10], and [12]. Specialized knowledge and ongoing skill enhancement are highlighted as essential requirements for freelancers to effectively manage the complexities of the internet freelancing landscape. Moreover, the wide range of activities available on gig platforms, which can vary from complex projects that require extensive knowledge and expertise to simple tasks that just require basic skills, highlights the different knowledge requirements that freelancers face. This hypothesis states that Knowledge Management serves an essential part in determining the skill sets and capacities of freelancers, therefore impacting the overall dynamics of the Gig Economy.

**H2:** Knowledge Management has a significant impact on the emergence of Gig Economy

## 3  Research Methods

This research adopts a quantitative approach to gather data from individuals participating in the gig economy. The target population for this study comprises individuals actively participating in the gig economy as freelancers, independent contractors, or platform-based workers. A convenience sampling technique was employed due to the difficulty in accessing a comprehensive list of all gig workers. This technique involves recruiting participants readily available and accessible to the researchers, potentially through online platforms or social media groups frequented by gig workers. A structured questionnaire was developed to collect data from participants combining both multiple questions and likert scale questions. The collected data was analyzed using appropriate statistical methods, such as descriptive statistics, correlation analysis and multiple regression analysis.

## 4   Results and Analysis

The analysis was done to answer the three research questions which were developed initially. The survey was answered by 78 individuals. The demographic analysis of the research is as follows (Table 1).

**Table 1.** Gender distribution

| Gender | Respondents | Percentage |
|--------|-------------|------------|
| Male   | 39          | 50%        |
| Female | 39          | 50%        |

The analysis of the gender distribution shows that there is an equal number of male and female respondents, each accounting for 50% of the sample (Table 2).

**Table 2.** Age distribution

| Age      | Respondents | Percentage |
|----------|-------------|------------|
| Under 18 | 0           | 0%         |
| 18–24    | 5           | 6.41%      |
| 25–34    | 40          | 51.28%     |
| 35–44    | 26          | 33.33%     |
| 45–54    | 6           | 7.69%      |
| 55–64    | 1           | 1.28%      |
| 65+      | 0           | 0%         |

Most respondents (51.28%) fall within the 25–34 age range, indicating this age group is the most represented in the gig economy. This could be due to several factors, such as this age group being more likely to be active in the gig economy and more comfortable with technology. The second largest group (33.33%) belongs to the 35–44 age range, followed by the 45–54 age range (7.69%). This suggests a gradual decrease in participation as age increases, potentially due to factors like individuals being less likely to participate in the gig economy. There is a very low representation of individuals under 18 (0%) and over 65 (1.28%). This might be because these age groups are closer to their retirement age and they might not be as prevalent in the gig economy. Overall, the data suggests that the survey participants are primarily young to middle-aged adults, with the 25–34 age group being the most prominent (Fig. 2).

Based on the data depicted in the chart, it appears that the most prevalent profession among freelancers is Administration, constituting approximately 22.99% of respondents. This is closely followed by Accounting, at 11.49%, and Creative Designing,

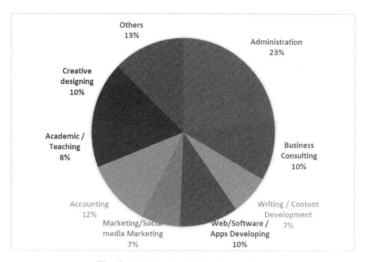

**Fig. 2.** Profession of the respondents

Business Consulting, and Web/Software/App Developing, all at 10.34%. Respondents had the option to select multiple freelance professions, revealing a diverse range of roles they engage in. The "Others" category emerges as the second most commonly selected profession, suggesting a wide range of alternative occupations among freelancers.

### 4.1 Research Objective 1: To Explore the Type of Knowledge Required by Freelancers

To find out the answer for the first research objective we asked in the questionnaire that What does the respondent think are the most important Knowledge that they need to become a successful freelancer in the gig economy. The respondents were allowed to choose more than one option (Fig. 3).

A majority of respondents (80%) highlights most critical knowledge is digital skills in the gig economy. Many gig jobs involve online work and utilizing digital tools, necessitating proficiency in areas like designing tools, project management software, communication platforms, and potentially industry-specific digital tools. Entrepreneurial knowledge is deemed highly important (68%). Freelancers essentially operate as individual businesses, requiring them to market themselves, secure clients, and manage their finances effectively. Understanding business fundamentals like marketing, sales, and basic business management becomes crucial for success. Nearly half (49%) of respondents recognize the value of language skills. This can be particularly beneficial for freelancers aiming to work with international clients or expand their reach beyond geographical boundaries. 43% of respondents consider sales and promotional skills crucial. Freelancers need to market themselves effectively to attract clients and secure projects, highlighting the importance of communication, persuasion, and personal branding skills. These findings are consistent with the findings of [21] which states that most individuals state the utmost importance of the critical digital skills knowledge for their career efforts.

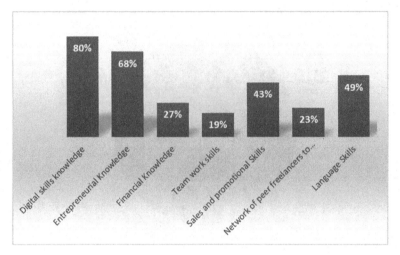

**Fig. 3.** The knowledge required

Although not as highly rated as the above skills, financial knowledge (27%) remains significant. Freelancers need to track income and expenses, set competitive prices, and plan for the future, making financial literacy essential for financial stability and long-term success. Building a network of peers (23%) is viewed as moderately important. Connecting with other freelancers can provide valuable resources through shared experiences, advice, and potential collaboration opportunities. Even though freelancers may not work in traditional teams, teamwork skills (19%) hold value. They might need to work with clients or other freelancers on projects, requiring effective communication and collaboration abilities. Accordingly, Freelancers believe digital skills, Entrepreneurial knowledge, language skills and sales and promotional skills are highly important to be success in the gig economy. Although the data analysis findings of do agree with the little importance of having the financial knowledge, the findings of [22] states that having the financial knowledge plays a key role in being successful; in the gig economy.

Freelancers were asked that what is the best way to learn for their freelancer activities. The answers gave insights on knowledge gaining and sharing practices of freelancers (Fig. 4).

Learning while working (60%) is the most preferred method, which suggests that experience is highly valued for acquiring the necessary skills and knowledge for freelance work. Online courses (58.67%) and independent learning (57.33%) using various resources like videos are popular options, offering flexibility and accessibility for busy freelancers. Learning from other freelancers (46.67%) is viewed as a valuable approach, highlighting the potential benefits of mentorship, networking, and peer-to-peer learning. Artificial intelligence (18.67%) is emerging as a potential learning tool, although it is still not as widely adopted as other methods. Traditional university courses (6.67%) are the least preferred, possibly due to factors like cost, time commitment, and potentially not being tailored to the specific needs of freelance work. These findings emphasize that many prefer to learn a skill while working and learning through online courses while least prefer taking traditional university courses.

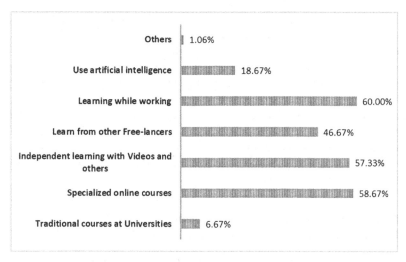

**Fig. 4.** The best way to learn for freelancer activities

## 4.2 Research Objective 2: To Identify the Best Platforms for Freelancers

The respondents were asked which platforms they use for their gig works (Table 3).

**Table 3.** Platform usage

| Platform | Respondents | Percentage |
| --- | --- | --- |
| Upwork | 12 | 15.38% |
| Fiverr | 25 | 32.05% |
| People per hour | 2 | 2.56% |
| Freelancer | 8 | 10.25% |
| I do not use a platform | 29 | 37.17% |
| Others | 2 | 2.56% |

Fiverr (32.05%) emerges as the most popular platform, potentially due to its focus on offering specific services for set prices, which might appeal to some freelancers. Upwork (15.38%) comes in second, known for its broader project marketplace connecting free-lancers with clients. PeoplePerHour (2.56%) and "Others" (2.56%) represent a smaller portion of platform users, suggesting these platforms may cater to more niche markets or cater to specific regional preferences. Freelancer.com (10.25%) holds a smaller but established presence in the platform landscape. Nearly 37.2% of respondents reported not using any platforms, indicating a significant portion of the gig economy operates independently of these platforms. This could be due to various reasons, such as free-lancers having established clientele and not needing platform assistance for finding work, preference for direct client relationships and avoiding platform fees and focus on niche markets not well-represented on major platforms.

Upwork and Fiverr are well-known platforms in the gig economy. Upwork is particularly recognized for its comprehensive project marketplace, which connects freelancers to a wide range of clients seeking different skills and services [24]. Conversely, Fiverr has become popular due to its emphasis on distinct services provided at fixed costs, attracting freelancers who value transparent pricing systems and specialized offerings [8] Freelancer.com, an established platform, has a wide-ranging presence in multiple project categories [24]. The popularity of these platforms is typically credited to their user-friendly interfaces, safe payment mechanisms, and the capability to demonstrate talents through thorough profiles [14].

### 4.3   Research Objective 3: To Examine Whether the Gig Economy is a Result of Better Professional Knowledge Management, Technology or Both

To achieve the third objective, researchers used the likert scale responses collected from the survey. The likert scale questions were categorized in to three variables; Technology, knowledge management and Gig economy. Technology variable had eight questions, knowledge management variable five questions and Gig Economy six questions respectively. Before proceeding to Pearson Correlation analysis and regression analysis, the reliability of the questionnaire was assessed using Cronbach's alpha test. As the Cronbach's alpha values for all three variables were above 0.7 the reliability of the questionnaire was ensured (Table 4).

**Table 4.** Reliability analysis

| Variable | Cronbach's alpha |
| --- | --- |
| Technology | 0.832 |
| Knowledge Management | 0.893 |
| Gig Economy | 0.792 |

The Pearson Correlation analysis was carried out to understand the relationship between technology and Gig Economy and Knowledge management and Gig economy (Table 5).

The correlation coefficient for Technology is .769 with a p-value of .000. This indicates a strong positive correlation between technology and the gig economy. This suggests that as technology usage and adoption increase, the gig economy also tends to grow. The correlation coefficient for Knowledge Management is .684 with a p-value of .000. This indicates a moderately strong positive correlation between knowledge management and the gig economy. This suggests that effective management of knowledge and skills plays moderate a role in the development of the gig economy.

As per the findings of [12] knowledge management includes a wide range of skills and abilities that contribute to efficient performance and achievement. Within the field

**Table 5.** Pearson Correlation analysis

| Independent Variables | | Gig Economy |
|---|---|---|
| Technology | Pearson Correlation | .769[**] |
| | Sig. (2-tailed) | .000 |
| | N | 78 |
| Knowledge Management | Pearson Correlation | .684[**] |
| | Sig. (2-tailed) | .000 |
| | N | 78 |

of freelancing, knowledge management involves knowledge of finance which means the understanding and management of finances, entrepreneurial expertise which are the skills related to operating a business, language proficiency for effective communication and teamwork skills for the ability to collaborate effectively. Freelancers must effectively handle a wide range of skills in order to effectively move through the challenges of the gig economy [22]. Agreeing to the data analysis findings [22], states the significant impact of these fields of knowledge management highlights their combined impact on the effective operation and expansion of the gig economy (Table 6).

**Table 6.** Model summary

| Model Summary | | | | |
|---|---|---|---|---|
| Mode | R | R Square | Adjusted R Square | Std. Error of the Estimate |
| 1 | .794[a] | .631 | .621 | .41550 |

a. Predictors: (Constant), Knowledge Management, Technology

R value of 0.794, represents the correlation coefficient between the predicted and actual values of the dependent variable (Gig Economy). It indicates a strong positive linear relationship between the independent variables (Knowledge Management and Technology) and the dependent variable. R-Squared value, 0.631, represents the proportion of variance in the dependent variable (Gig Economy) that is explained by the linear regression model. In this case, 63.1% of the variance in the Gig Economy can be explained by the combined effects of Knowledge Management and Technology.

F-statistic value, 64.158, is used to test the overall significance of the model. The p-value (0.000) associated with the F-statistic is less than 0.05, indicating that the model is statistically significant, meaning the combined effects of Knowledge Management and Technology significantly predict the Gig Economy.

This data suggests that both Knowledge Management and Technology are statistically significant predictors of the Gig Economy. The model explains 63.1% of the variance in the Gig Economy, suggesting a moderately strong association between the variables (Table 7).

**Table 7.** Regression coefficients

Coefficients[a]

| Model | | Unstandardized Coefficients | | Standardized Coefficients | t | Sig |
|---|---|---|---|---|---|---|
| | | B | Std. Error | Beta | | |
| 1 | (Constant) | .408 | .301 | | 1.353 | .180 |
| | Technology | .640 | .111 | .570 | 5.756 | .000 |
| | Knowledge Management | .252 | .088 | .282 | 2.851 | .006 |

a. Dependent Variable: Gig Economy

Based on the above regression coefficients, regression function of this study can be developed as follows.

Gig Economy = 0.408 + 0.640 * Technology + 0.252 * Knowledge Management + 0.301.

The B value, 0.640, represents the average change in the Gig Economy for a one-unit increase in Technology, holding Knowledge Management constant. Accordingly, for every unit increase in Technology, the Gig Economy is predicted to increase by 0.640 units on average. The associated p-value (0.000) is less than 0.05, indicating that the relationship is statistically significant, meaning Technology has a significant effect on the Gig Economy. While certain scholars [26] had counter arguments on that technology alone cannot impact the economy, the data analysis findings are in line with the findings of scholars [21] and [8], who claim that technology has a direct positive relationship with the gig economy. Accordingly, we can accept the first hypothesis.

**H1:** Technology has a significant impact on the emergence of Gig Economy

The B value, 0.252, represents the average change in the Gig Economy for a one-unit increase in Knowledge Management, holding Technology constant. For every unit increase in Knowledge Management, the Gig Economy is predicted to increase by 0.252 units on average. The p-value (0.006) is less than 0.05, indicating a statistically significant relationship between Knowledge Management and the Gig Economy. These findings are in line with the findings of the scholars [22] who stated that Knowledge management has a positive correlation with the gig economy. Therefore, we can accept the second hypothesis.

**H2:** Knowledge Management has a significant impact on the emergence of Gig Economy

Based on the regression coefficients, both Technology and Knowledge Management have statistically significant positive relationships with the Gig Economy. However, the impact of Technology (Beta = 0.640) is stronger than the impact of Knowledge Management (Beta = 0.252), suggesting that Technology plays a more substantial role in the growth of the Gig Economy in this model. These findings agree with the findings of authors like [2] which state that technology has a stronger impact towards gig economy.

# 5 Conclusion

The gig economy, characterized by short-term projects and independent work arrangements, has grown rapidly in recent years. This study explored the relationship between knowledge management, technology, and their contributions to the development of the gig economy. Our findings highlight the diverse knowledge and skill sets required by freelancers in this highly competitive gig economy. Digital skills, entrepreneurial knowledge, language skills, and sales and promotional skills emerged as the most critical competencies for success. Freelancers prioritize learning through hands-on experience while working, alongside online courses and independent learning resources. However, a significant portion of the gig economy operates independently, although there are popular platforms such as Fiverr and Upwork, but there are many emerging platforms that will help the development of these free lancers economy such as DoorDash, Contently, 99Designs and Toptal. Through statistical analysis, the research established statistically significant positive correlations between both technology and knowledge management with the gig economy. However, technology displayed a stronger influence compared to knowledge management. This suggests that technological advancements not only facilitate the connection between freelancers and projects but also shape the overall dynamics of the gig economy.

In general, Knowledge Management has been incorporated insight organization and very recently outside the scope of organizations, freelance workers are basically independent knowledge workers and their ability to use knowledge management is crucial for their development, also the way the companies interact and exchange knowledge with them on this new emerging type of economy will be of great importance in the future, has it now the upwork research institute conducted a survey and estimated that more than these independent workers already contribute more than 1.27 trillion dollars for the US economy.

However, this study did not extensively explore the role of online platforms in knowledge management, further research could be done in this matter. Investigating the impact of specific platform features and functionalities on freelancer knowledge management and success could offer valuable insights. Analyzing how platforms facilitate knowledge sharing, collaboration, and access to resources could provide crucial information for platform designers and policymakers.

In conclusion, this research has highlighted the crucial roles of both technology and knowledge management in the development of the gig economy. Recognizing these key factors is essential for stakeholders, including platform developers, policymakers, and freelance workers themselves, to work towards fostering a more sustainable gig economy. By empowering individuals through knowledge development and fostering collaboration within this growing ecosystem, the gig economy can continue to grow and contribute to the broader economy.

# References

1. Faster capital: Exploring the Gig Economy's Impact on Employment. Faster capital (2024). Online. Available: https://fastercapital.com/topics/exploring-the-gig-economys-impact-on-employment.html. Accessed 11 March 2024

2. Ray, S., Hermann, N., Sen. I.: Disruptive transformation fueling gig economies. In: 2021 IEEE Technology & Engineering Management Conference-Europe (TEMSCON-EUR) (2021)
3. Subbiah, R.: Gig Economy. IJFMR-International J. Multidiscipl. Res. **5**(1) (2023)
4. Paul, O.: The gig economy. The IZA World of Labor (2020)
5. Duggan, J., Sherman, U., Carberry, R., McDonnel, A.: Algorithmic management and app-work in the gig economy: A research agenda for employment relations and HRM. Hum. Resour. Manag. J. **30**(1), 114–132 (2020)
6. Reidl, C., Fulker, R.C.: Who wants to cooperate-and why? Attitude and perception of crowd workers in online labor markets. Human-Computer Interaction (2023)
7. Hannák, A., et al.: Bias in online freelance marketplaces: evidence from task rabbit and fiverr. In: Proceedings of the 2017 ACM conference on computer supported cooperative work and social computing (2017)
8. Blaising, A., Dabbish, L.: Managing the transition to online freelance platforms. Proce. ACM Human-Comp. Interact. **6**(2), 1–26 (2022)
9. Nierling, L., Krings, B., Küstermann, L.: IT freelancers as knowledge workers: shifts. J. Labor and Soc. 480–509 (2023)
10. Gandhi, A., Sensuse, D., Sucahyo, Y.: Knowledge sharing model for competitive ecosystem on gig economy. In: SPBPU IDE'19: Proceedings of Peter the Great St. Petersburg Polytechnic University, New York (2019)
11. Wilkins, D., Muralidhar, S., Meijer, M., Lascau, L., Lindley, S.: Gigified knowledge work: understanding knowledge gaps when knowledge work and on-demand work intersect. Proce. ACM on Human-Comp. Interact. 1–27 (2022)
12. Wagner, G., Prester, J., Paré, G.: Exploring the boundaries and processes of digital platforms for knowledge work: a review of information systems research. The J. Strat. Info. Sys. 2–7 (2021)
13. Galpaya, H., Senanayake, L.: Online freelancing: potential for digital gig work in India, Sri Lanka and Myanmar. Seoul, Korea (2018)
14. Silva, B., Moreira, A.: Entrepreneurship and the gig economy: A bibliometric analysis. Management Letters 23–44 (2022)
15. Kozica, A., Bonss, U., Kaiser, S.: Freelancers and the absorption of external knowledge: practical implications and theoretical contributions. Knowl. Manag. Res. Pract. **12**, 421–431 (2014)
16. Claussen, J., Khashabi, P., Kretschmer, T.: Knowledge work in the sharing economy: What drives project success in online labor markets? (2018). SSRN 3102865
17. Seppänen, L., Spinuzzi, C., Poutanen, S., Alasoini, T.: Co-creation in macrotask knowledge work on online. Nordic J. Work. Life Stud. 77–92 (2021)
18. Bucos, T.: Economia GIG–rezultat al platformizării pieţei muncii. Economica **124**, 25–42 (2023)
19. Graham, M., Woodcock, J.: The gig economy: a critical introduction. Polity 54 (2019)
20. Griep, A., Vranjes, L., Madelon, M.: Technology in the Workplace: Opportunities and Challenges. Tilburg University, Tilburg (2021)
21. Czerwinska, K., Moore, M.: Understanding the use of digital technology in the career development sector. The University of Derby, Derby, International Centre for Guidance Studies (2019)
22. Milam, B.: Exploring financial literacy of independent musicians in the gig economy. Aquila Digital Community 3–39 (2019)
23. Zappa, P., Tonellato, M., Tasselli, S.: Multiple identities and multiple relationships: an exploratory study of freelancers' knowledge-seeking behavior. Unders. Workp. Relations. **26**(2), 225–260 (2023)
24. Gertenbach, E.: Fiverr vs. Freelancer: Full Guide For 2024. Upwork **17**, 1 (2024). Online. Available: https://www.upwork.com/resources/fiverr-vs-freelancer. Accessed 12 March 2024

25. Green, D., McCann, J., Vu, T., Lopez, N., Ouattara, S.: Gig Economy and the future of work: a fiverr.com case study. Manage. Econo. Res. J. **4**, 281 (2018)
26. Branstetter, L.: The online gig economy's impact is not as big as many thought. Peterson Ins. Int. Econo. Policy Brief 9–22 (2022)
27. Kost, D., Fieseler, C., Wong, S.: Boundaryless careers in the gig economy: An oxymoron?. Human Res. Manage. J. 100–113 (2019)

# Sustainability Practices in Higher Education Enhanced by University Rankings and Knowledge Management

Dario Liberona[1]([✉]), Roberto Ferro[2], Vishmi Madduma Patabendige[1], and Marcel Rother[3]

[1] Department of Business Administration, Seinajoki University of Applied Sciences (Seamk), Seinäjoki, Finland
{Dario.liberona,vishmi.maddumapatabendige}@seamk.fi
[2] Universidad Distrital Francisco Jose de Caldas, Bogota, Colombia
rferro@udistrital.edu.co
[3] Vaasa University, Vaasa, Finland
Marcel.Rother@th-ab.de

**Abstract.** Sustainability has been a mayor concern over the last three decades since in 1988 James Hansen Former director of Nasa declared about green gas emissions and its impact in changing the climate, in a testimony to the US senate. Declaring for the first time the possibility of human race extinction impact; since then there has been a lot of work, controversy, and research on the matter. This paper is related to the importance of Sustainability in Higher Education institutions has part of the core skills and competences that new professionals need and about the main role Universities must have to be part and contribute to society. The case analyzed the methodologies of the current only two Sustainability University rankings, compares them and proposed a Knowledge Management strategy to implement and enhance sustainability practices in higher education institutions.

The application of a SECI model approach should be implemented at the University, however the sustainability knowledge is still very basic among the community of students who are not very aware of the University efforts, programs, or related policies. Socialization within the SECI model encourages the sharing of tacit knowledge related to sustainability practices among students and the community in general, some aspects of Circular Economy have been reviewed. The use of sustainability rankings helps in creating a shared understanding and commitment to sustainable goals in the community and validates the use of a Knowledge Management approach to enhance sustainability in higher education institutions.

**Keywords:** SECI Model · Sustainability · Sustainability practices · University Rankings · Knowledge transfer · Circular Economy

© The Author(s), under exclusive license to Springer Nature Switzerland AG 2024
L. Uden and I.-H. Ting (Eds.): KMO 2024, CCIS 2152, pp. 32–50, 2024.
https://doi.org/10.1007/978-3-031-63269-3_3

# 1 Introduction

## 1.1 About Sustainability in Higher Education

Regarding Sustainability in Higher Education there are three important areas in the field are reviewed, Sustainability concepts, Circular Economy Strategies and the Sustainability Development Goals, this will be covered, then how Sustainability University rankings and a Knowledge Management approach could enhance and collaborate with higher education institutions is discussed.

According to an Article by Santander Universidades (Santander, 2022) Sustainability consists of fulfilling the needs of current generations without compromising the needs of future generations, while ensuring a balance between economic growth, environmental care, and social well-being (Fig. 1). Furthermore, sustainability can be defined as the practices of meeting the needs of the present without compromising the ability of future generations to meet their own needs. It is a holistic and forward-thinking approach that seeks to balance economic, social, and environmental considerations to create a harmonious and enduring system. In the broadest sense, sustainability refers to the ability to maintain or support a process continuously over time, the concept of sustainability is very old, referred has Nachhaltigkeit in German, can be traced back to Hans Carl von Carlowitz (1645–1714), and was applied to the forestry industry.

There is an agreement in Contemporary society that considers Sustainability and UN Sustainable Development goals has the best way to address the vast, complex and interrelated environmental and development issues for the sake of current and future human well-being and for the integrity of the planet (Waas et al., 2011, Sustainable Development Networks, 2015, OECD, 2016; Andreoni and Miola, 2016).

Sustainable practices strive to minimize the detrimental effects on the environment, foster social justice, and guarantee enduring economic sustainability. This involves responsible resource management, the reduction of carbon footprints, and the development of strategies that foster resilience and adaptability in the face of global challenges such as climate change. By embracing sustainability, universities, individuals, businesses, and societies contribute to a more equitable and resilient world, in an attempt to protect both current and future generations wellbeing.

According to Viqueira (2023) emphasizes the critical role of higher Education in fostering sustainable development. Also, the author describes that while higher Education has the potential to be a powerful force for sustainability, there exists a prevalent issue where graduates often perpetuate unsustainable behaviours and contribute to environmental damage due to a lack of awareness and understanding of sustainability principles or problems. Despite some institutions recognizing the importance of sustainability, Viqueira contends that many academic institutions have yet to fully integrate sustainability into their curriculum and more research could be done on the matter.

Universities must have a relevant role in shaping the future by educating leaders, professionals, and citizens to support and understand sustainability, institutions could include eco-friendly topics in their courses, adopt green practices on campus, and engage in research for renewable energy, conservation, and social justice for example. There are different and multiple aspects to the role of universities in sustainability, in the last ten years at least two Higher Institutions world rankings have developed a methodology to portrait some of these aspects and key process indicators for sustainability in higher education, helping and supporting Universities with a global benchmarking of this indicators, initially the Green Metric Global ranking was an initiative of academics that realized that the vast amount of available University Rankings developed globally since 2003 have not consider the Sustainability measures. This ranking started in 2010 and was followed by Times Higher Education Impact ranking (Sustainability Impact) in 2019.

By the end of 2022 QS ranking has launched a new version of a Sustainable University rankings, since is on its pilot stage will not be part of this research but indicates the recent concern about these aspects in Higher education, they are launching a 2$^{nd}$ version this 2024 that is in working progress.

**Fig. 1.** Sustainability model. (OECD, 2001, Dalay Cleyton, 1994)

## 1.2 About Circular Economy

Circular Economy strategies are being implemented has one of the main strategies towards a more sustainable economy and has been gaining momentum has a relevant tool to tackle the climate change and biodiversity challenges contributing to a more ecofriendly consumption in our society (Europarl Topics, 2023).

A circular economy is a model of production and consumption that optimize processes and business models, is a systemic approach to economic development designed to benefit businesses, society, and the environment. (Ellen MacArthur Foundation, 2024) In contrast to the 'take-make-waste' linear model, a circular economy is regenerative by design and aims to gradually decouple growth from the consumption of finite resources. (Ellen MacArthur Foundation, 2024) So, the circular economy is about making our economic actions work smoothly with the environment. It believes that using resources efficiently is not just the right thing to do but also makes economic sense. This means keeping materials in a continuous loop to reduce waste and save energy. The idea is to design things to last, encourage reuse, and promote recycling.

Furthermore, according to the Ellen MacArthur Foundation (2024) a key supporter of circular economy ideas, this new way of thinking is a shift from the old 'take-make-waste' pattern. In-stead, it wants to create a system where products last longer, materials get reused, and the impact on the environment is lessened. This move towards circularity aims to disconnect eco-nomic growth from using up limited resources, showing a smart change in how we approach sustainability.

When we consider about Circular Economy, it is like diving into an economic app-roach that aims to restore and regenerate. It is all about making sure our economic activities contribute positively to the entire system, whether it's big businesses, small enterprises, or individuals, both globally and locally.

Based on the information by Ellen MacArthur Foundation (2024), It is based on three principles:

- Eliminate waste and pollution: This involves addressing issues like the emission of greenhouse gases and dangerous substances, pollution of the air, land, and water, and even problems like traffic congestion. The goal is to design a system that minimizes these negative impacts.
- Circulate products and materials: This involves designing products for durability and encouraging practices like reuse, remanufacturing, and recycling to ensure that products, components, and materials continue circulating within the economy. Cir-cular systems also maximize the use of bio-based materials by promoting multi-ple applications for these materials as they cycle between the economy and natural systems.
- Regenerate nature: The goal is to steer clear of non-renewable resources and instead safeguard or improve renewable ones. This involves actions such as returning valuable nutrients to the soil to facilitate regeneration or opting for renewable energy sources in-stead of relying on fossil fuels.

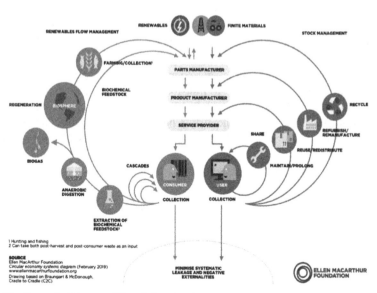

**Fig. 2.** The Butterfly Diagram: Visualizing the circular economy (Ellen MacArthur Foundation, 2019)

This butterfly diagram illustrates a visual representation of the circular economy, a system that aims to minimize waste and pollution, circulate products and materials at their highest value, and regenerate natural systems. It is based on the concept of the circular flow of materials, in contrast to the linear flow of the traditional economy, which takes resources from the Earth, makes products, and then throws them away as waste. Furthermore, this cycle is divided in to main two cycles as,
Biological Cycle and Technical Cycle.

- The Biological Cycle: The processes -such as composting and anaerobic digestion - that together help to regenerate natural capital. The only materials suitable for these processes are those that can be safely returned to the biosphere. (Ellen MacArthur foundation, 2023). In the Biological cycle the concept of regeneration is considered as the heart of the cycle, and this is the third principle of the circular economy.
- The Technical Cycle: This cycle focuses on products and materials that are not consumed during use, such as metals, plastics, and wood. The goal of the technical cycle is to keep these materials in circulation as long as possible by using them again and again. This can be done through a variety of methods, including reuse, repair, remanufacture, and recycling.

So, the butterfly diagram is a powerful tool for visualizing and understanding the circular economy. It can be used by businesses, governments, and individuals to identify opportunities to reduce waste, conserve resources, and create a more sustainable future.

Furthermore, if we consider CE, Morseletto (2020) defends that Circular Economy (CE), when viewed as an economic framework, can be considered an effective strategy for optimizing re-source utilization by minimizing waste and promoting a closed-loop system for products. This not only contributes to environmental preservation but also yields social advantages. The primary focus is on mitigating the adverse effects of the linear economy by fostering long-term business resilience and economic opportunities, thereby delivering both environmental and social benefits. Moreover, based on the information provided by Giannoccaro et al. (2021) the transition toward a CE is gaining momentum in the policy plans of several countries. The European Commission, for instance, has strategically committed to transforming the EU economy into a circular one, launching the first CE Action Plan in 2015 and a subsequent plan in 2020, integral to the European Green Deal. Simultaneously, China has embraced the concept by incorporating the Development Plan for the Circular Economy into its 14th Five-Year Plan Period (2021–2025).

Some Circular economy basis strategies are:

Re-Use,
Re-Cycle
ReFurbish
Reduce
Refill
Repurpose
Repair
Redesign

### 1.3    Circular Economy and Education

Education plays a pivotal role in increasing public awareness and understanding of the Circular Economy, demanding the acquisition of new skills and knowledge (European Environment Agency, 2016). So, through education, individuals gain awareness about the significance of sustainable practices, enabling them to make informed choices in daily life. Learning opportunities extend to the development of skills related to waste management, eco-design, and the principles of a circular economy. Moreover, education empowers consumers to support businesses aligned with sustainable values. It acts as a catalyst for innovation and entrepreneurship, encouraging the creation of products and business models that prioritize environmental responsibility.

### 1.4    United Nations Sustainable Development Goals (SDGs)

When discussing sustainability and the circular economy, it is important to have a firm understanding of the UN Sustainable Development Goals (SDGs). According to an article by Slight Savers (2024) Sustainable development goals were outlined by the UN in 2015 and Sustainable Development Goals (SDGs) aim to eradicate extreme poverty, improve healthcare for all, and promote gender equality.

Furthermore, According to United Nations Department of Economic and Social Affairs (n.d.), the SDGs are a set of 17 global goals adopted by the United Nations in 2015 as a universal call to action to end poverty, protect the planet, and ensure that all people enjoy peace and prosperity by 2030. The goals are integrated, recognizing that action in one area will affect outcomes in others, and that development must balance social, economic, and environmental sustainability. (United Nations Department of Economic and Social Affairs, n.d.) They tackle a range of pressing global issues, including widespread destitution, unfair distribution of re-sources, climate instability, environmental destruction, maintaining peace, and upholding jus-tice.

**Fig. 3.**  Sustainable Development Goals. (United Nations, n.d.)

The short titles of the 17 SDGs are:

No poverty (SDG 1), Zero hunger (SDG 2), Good health and well-being (SDG 3),

Quality education (SDG 4), Gender equality (SDG 5), Clean water and sanitation (SDG 6),

Affordable and clean energy (SDG 7), Decent work and economic growth (SDG 8), Industry, innovation and infrastructure (SDG 9), Reduced inequalities (SDG 10), Sustainable cities and communities (SDG 11), Responsible consumption and production (SDG 12),

Climate action (SDG 13), Life below water (SDG 14), Life on land (SDG 15),

Peace, justice, and strong institutions (SDG 16), and Partnerships for the goals (SDG 17).

So, exploring sustainable development reveals a powerful collaboration between the Circular Economy and Sustainable Development Goals (SDGs). The Circular Economy's focus on cut-ting waste, supporting regenerative systems, and efficient resource use aligns seamlessly with the diverse aims of the SDGs. By encouraging responsible consumption, prioritizing environ-mental care, and promoting social fairness, the Circular Economy offers a practical route to achieve SDGs' goals. This partnership not only addresses global challenges but also highlights the need for comprehensive, systemic approaches. Embracing the Circular Economy within the SDGs framework encourages us to rethink societal and economic systems, contributing to a world where prosperity is intertwined with environmental sustainability and social balance an essential step toward a lasting future.

## 1.5 Sustainable Development Goals (SDGs) and Higher Education

The connection between Sustainable Development Goals (SDGs) and Higher Education is a crucial intersection where academic institutions, including Seinäjoki University of Applied Sciences, play a vital role. The SDGs, consisting of 17 interconnected goals addressing pressing global issues, provide a significant framework for SeAMK's com-mitment to higher Education that promotes sustainability and societal impact. SeAMK's aspiration to achieve a strong position in the THE Impact Rankings highlights the impor-tance of aligning with the SDGs. This alignment not only demonstrates the University dedication to making a positive impact but also positions it as a catalyst for global change. In this context, the thesis aims to evaluate a benchmark among universities, in order to identify areas for improvement, and suggest customized strategies for better alignment.

At the core of SeAMK's mission are the SDGs, an ambitious agenda covering a wide range of social and environmental objectives. Among these, SDG 17, which highlights global partnerships, plays a pivotal role in driving progress. As SeAMK strives for a prominent position in the esteemed THE Impact Rankings, the convergence of the SDGs and THE Rankings becomes exceptionally important. The SDGs not only emphasize SeAMK's commitment to sustainability and societal impact but also serve as a guiding beacon on its path to recognition in the higher education sector.

Furthermore, when universities actively integrate SDGs into their teaching, research, and campus operations, they play a vital role in catalyzing significant societal change. This potential for transformation is not limited to SeAMK alone it highlights the shared responsibility of higher Education to empower students with the knowledge, abilities, and values needed to make positive changes in a world dealing with intricate global challenges. As SeAMK strives for recognition in the Times Higher Education Impact Rankings, the SDGs serve as a guiding force, showing the way to a future that's more sustainable, fair, and impactful, not only for the institution itself but also for the broader realm of higher Education (Fig. 4).

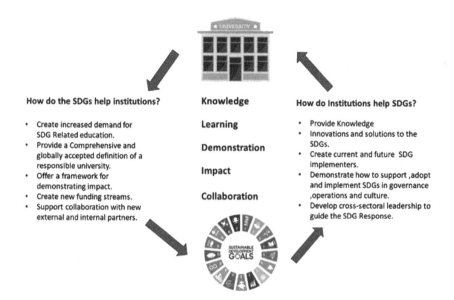

How do the SDGs help institutions?                Knowledge                How do Institutions help SDGs?

• Create increased demand for                     Learning                 • Provide Knowledge
  SDG Related education.                                                    • Innovations and solutions to the
• Provide a Comprehensive and                      Demonstration             SDGs.
  globally accepted definition of a                                        • Create current and future SDG
  responsible university.                           Impact                    implementers.
• Offer a framework for                                                    • Demonstrate how to support ,adopt
  demonstrating impact.                             Collaboration            and implement SDGs in governance
• Create new funding streams.                                              ,operations and culture.
• Support collaboration with new                                           • Develop cross-sectoral leadership to
  external and internal partners.                                            guide the SDG Response.

**Fig. 4.** Relationship between Educational Institution VS SDGs (EAUC - The Alliance for Sustainability Leadership in Education.)

According to a report by EAUC (n.d.) The relationship between the Sustainable Development Goals (SDGs) and institutions is reciprocal. Also, as this figure above states SDGs could help institutions in different ways such as, SDGs offer a framework for universities to define what it means to be a responsible institution. This framework can help universities to make decisions about their operations, research, and teaching that are aligned with the SDGs. Furthermore, SDGs provide a framework for institutions to measure their progress in achieving the goals. This reason can help institutions to track their progress and identify areas where they can improve.

On the other hand, Universities or the higher educational institutions could help to achieving the SDGs as institutions have the expertise, resources, and reach to address the complex challenges that the SDGs address, such as climate change, poverty, and inequality. By working together, institutions can develop and implement innovative solutions that can make a real impact on the world.

So, as SeAMK aspires to achieve recognition in the prestigious THE Impact Rankings, the interplay between SDGs and higher Education becomes pivotal. The 17 interconnected SDGs serve as a guiding framework for institutions like SeAMK, fostering a sense of responsibility and providing a roadmap to integrate sustainability into their core missions. This reciprocal relationship, as illustrated in Fig. 3, highlights how institutions can leverage their expertise and resources to contribute meaningfully to the SDGs, while simultaneously utilizing the SDGs as a benchmark to measure and enhance their societal impact. By actively engaging with the SDGs, SeAMK and other higher education institutions play a vital role in shaping a more sustainable, fair, and impactful future, not only within their campuses but also in the broader landscape of global Education and societal transformation.

## 1.6   Most Sustainable and Circular Economy Universities in the World

We are very aware of the sustainable problems in the world (Hansen, 1997; Morseletto, 2020, OECD, 2016; Conrad, 2013), then what should be the role of universities on the solutions or awareness, which are the most sustainable universities in the world, which ones are the ones with the best education on this regard and further on, how can universities embrace and improve their performance in sustainability and circular economy.

A simple diagnostic will be to rely on the current sustainability related rankings that are currently available, then best practices, and using a simple Knowledge Management model for the improvement on the situation.

**Table 1.** Time Higher University Impact ranking 2023 (Own elaboration base on the ranking)

| Rank Position 2022-2023 | University | | SDG | SDG | SDG | SDG |
|---|---|---|---|---|---|---|
| 1 | Western Sydney University | Australia | 5 | 12 | 15 | 17 |
| 2 | University of Manchester | United Kingdom | 11 | 12 | 15 | 17 |
| 3 | Queens University | Canada | 2 | 11 | 16 | 17 |
| 4 | Universiti Sains Malasya | Malasya | 1 | 2 | 16 | 17 |
| 5 | University of Tasmania | Australia | 13 | 14 | 15 | 17 |
| 9 | Aalborg University | Denmark | 4 | 10 | 14 | 17 |
| 14 | Yonsei University | South Korea | 8 | 9 | 12 | 17 |
| 32 | National Autonomos University | Mexico | 3 | 7 | 9 | 17 |
| 46 | KTH Royal Institute of Technology | Sweden | 9 | 11 | 12 | 17 |
| 67 | National Taiwan University | Taiwan | 2 | 9 | 12 | 17 |
| 79 | University of Liverpool | United Kingd | 10 | 11 | 16 | 17 |
| 101-200 | University of Barcelona | Spain | 9 | 11 | 16 | 17 |
| 201-300 | Charles University | Check R. | 3 | 8 | 16 | 17 |
| 301-400 | Aalto University | Finland | 9 | 11 | 12 | 17 |
| 301-400 | University Of Eastern Finland | Finland | 3 | 13 | 16 | 17 |

## 1.7   University Sustainable Rankings Methodologies

### Green Metric Ranking

Although UI GreenMetric ranking was not based on any existing ranking system, it was developed with the awareness of several existing sustainability assessment systems and academic university rankings. Sustainability systems that were referred to during the design phase of UI GreenMetric included the Holcim Sustainability Awards, GREEN-SHIP (the rating system recently developed by the Green Building Council of Indonesia which was based on the Leadership in the Energy and Environmental Design (LEED)

**Table 2.** Green Metric university ranking 2023 (Own elaboration base on the ranking)

| Rank 2023 | University | Country | Total Score | Setting & Infrastructure | Energy & Climate Change | Waste | Water | Transportation |
|---|---|---|---|---|---|---|---|---|
| 1 | Wageningen University & Rese | Netherlands | 9500 | 1350 | 1825 | 1800 | 1000 | 1750 |
| 2 | Nottingham Trent University | United Kingdom | 9475 | 1375 | 1850 | 1800 | 950 | 1700 |
| 3 | Umwelt-campus Birkenfeld (tr | Germany | 9450 | 1275 | 1925 | 1800 | 1000 | 1700 |
| 4 | University of Groningen | Netherlands | 9450 | 1325 | 1775 | 1800 | 1000 | 1800 |
| 5 | University of California, Davis | USA | 9425 | 1400 | 1900 | 1800 | 1000 | 1575 |
| 6 | University College Cork | Ireland | 9425 | 1250 | 1875 | 1800 | 1000 | 1700 |
| 7 | University of Nottingham | United Kingdom | 9425 | 1375 | 1825 | 1800 | 1000 | 1750 |
| 8 | Universidade De Sao Paulo Us | Brazil | 9425 | 1450 | 1775 | 1800 | 950 | 1700 |
| 12 | Universita Di Bologna | Italy | 9300 | 1325 | 1675 | 1800 | 900 | 1800 |
| 32 | Universidad del Rosario | Colombia | 8835 | 1160 | 1750 | 1725 | 1000 | 1725 |
| 35 | Universidad Complutense De I | Spain | 8800 | 1075 | 1900 | 1725 | 1000 | 1500 |
| 46 | Istanbul Technical University | Turkiye | 8635 | 1275 | 1585 | 1575 | 900 | 1575 |
| 70 | Politecnico Di Milano | Italy | 8560 | 760 | 1550 | 1800 | 950 | 1750 |
| 218 | Universidad de Salamanca | Spain | 7680 | 980 | 1575 | 1500 | 800 | 1275 |
| 322 | Sumy State University | Ukraine | 7160 | 950 | 1485 | 1275 | 700 | 1325 |
| 360 | Hochschule Weihenstephan-tr | Germany | 7010 | 1100 | 1035 | 1725 | 350 | 1350 |

system used in the U.S. and elsewhere), the Sustainability, Tracking, Assessment and Rating System (STARS) and the College Sustainability Report Card (also known as the Green Report Card).

For the year 2023, 1.182 universities participated in the ranking, in Table 1. There is a sample of the results for some universities (Table 2 and Fig. 5).

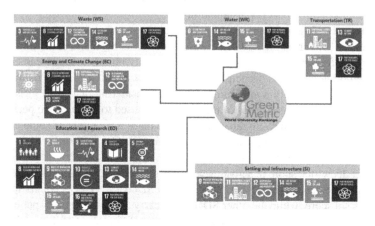

**Fig. 5.** Relationship between green metric indicators and its relationship with SGDs. (Green Metrics Rankings, 2021).

The UI GreenMetric evaluates university's policy and perfomance on the basis of six categories; Setting and Infrastructure (SI), Energy and Climate Change (EC), Waste (WS), Water (WR), Transportation (TR), and Education and Research (ED). Each category has a weighting of points as shown in the following table (Table 3).

**Table 3.** Categories use in the ranking and their weighting

| No | Category | Percentage of Total Points (%) |
|----|----------|-------------------------------|
| 1 | Setting and Infrastructure (SI) | 15 |
| 2 | Energy and Climate Change (EC) | 21 |
| 3 | Waste (WS) | 18 |
| 4 | Water (WR) | 10 |
| 5 | Transportation (TR) | 18 |
| 6 | Education and Research (ED) | 18 |
|  | TOTAL | 100 |

## Times Higher Education Impact (Sustainability Ranking)

The Times Higher Education Impact Rankings are the only global performance tables that assess universities against the United Nations' Sustainable Development Goals. It uses calibrated indicators to provide comprehensive and balanced comparisons across four broad areas: research, stewardship, outreach and teaching.

Definitions of areas covered in the ranking.

Research: Is the traditional way that a university might help to deliver the SDGs is by creating research in relevant topics related to the SGDs.

Stewardship: universities are custodians of significant resources; not just physical resources, but also their knowledge, employees, faculty and students. How they act as stewards is one of the key factors in delivering the SDGs.

Outreach: place an important role in higher education, and the work that universities do with their local, regional, national and international communities is another keyway that they can have an impact on sustainability.

Teaching: teaching plays a critical role, it could ensure that there are enough skilled practitioners to deliver on the SDGs and sustainability matters, and in making sure that all alumni take forward the key lessons of sustainability into their future careers.

The methodology allows participant universities to submit data on as many of these SDGs as they are able with a minimum of fourth, considering that SDG 17 is the only mandatory. Each SDG has a series of metrics that are used to evaluate the performance of the university in that SDG, in table number one there is a sample of some university results for the 2023 ranking considering their best fourth SDG performances, in this year 1.705 universities from 115 countries participated.

A university's total score in a given year is calculated by combining its score in SDG 17 with its best three results on the remaining 16 SDGs. SDG 17 accounts for 22 per cent of the total score, while the other SDGs each carry a weighting of 26 per cent. This means that different universities are scored based on a different set of SDGs, depending on their focus. The score for the overall ranking is an average of the last two years' total scores.

The score from each SDG is scaled so that the highest score in each SDG in the overall calculation is 100 and the lowest score is 0. This is to adjust for minor differences in the scoring range in each SDG and to ensure that universities are treated equitably whichever SDGs they have provided data for. It is these scaled scores that we use to determine which SDGs a university has performed in most strongly; they may not be the SDGs in which the university is ranked highest or has scored highest based on unscaled scores.

## 2 Methodology

### 2.1 The SECI Model

In order to enhance the process of sustainability and circular economy adoption in universities, we proposed a Knowledge Management approach by using an initial SECI model approach for knowledge acquisition and transfer, there are many applications for the model inside universities and organizations, but not previous attempts to use it related to sustainability and circular economy. The SECI model was selected since is one of the fundamental models in Knowledge Management theory [14], and since the main goal of this work is to identify the status and diagnostic of Sustainability Knowledge and practices inside the organization culture, to propose an implementation plan for universities.

Our research based on the SECI Model [17,14], as can be seen on Fig. 2, consist of applying the model to transfer Knowledge through a sequence of tacit and explicit processes involving Socialization, externalization, combination and internalization.

The first one, **Socialization**, is about an informal sharing of experience (e.g. between master and apprentice), for this process a general survey was conducted among current students to identify general knowledge. Also, a diagnostic process was aimed in terms of sharing and basic information that was used for participating in one of the sustainability impact ranking.

During this stage we evaluated the general knowledge of students in these matters and if it was acquired on the university or somewhere else, the general knowledge of concepts and policies were prompted to have a general diagnostic, general material or contents about Sustainability and Circular economy were reviewed.

The second key process in the model, **Externalization**, is about the formalization of tacit knowledge, here a series of interviews were conducted, the interviews helped to identify documents posted, and general process related to the Sustainability and Circular economy practices. In this case the results of the surveys interviews were built into a first report on Sustainability, a list of policies, and general information was gathered, then was use on the submission of the Times Higher Education Sustainability Impact Ranking. A Web Site regarding sustainability was updated in order to connect the academic and students' community and share some of the findings and information.

The third process in the SECI model implemented was **Combination**, related to the construction of explicit knowledge from tacit knowledge, a series of practices were identified, and a series of surveys with the participation of about 100 students, this permitted to validate and weighted some practices that were identified during the socialization and externalization process.

The combination process was considered by the team has the most complex since it requires that new knowledge will be created from previous findings and the combination of a series of process and knowledge, during this process there were the combination of the information gathered and the Seci model, during this stage the recognition of different competences and knowledge were identify and structured, for example previous to the launching of the a project, in the stage of preparation it is important to define and establish the correspondent participation of founders, generally founders lack of experience and usually only divide the company among them in equal participations, this often end up has a problem among them, with investors, and potential partners since does not recognized the contributions of each founder, and the possible participation of future partners in the ownership, here the combination of knowledge for example with the Slicing Pie methodology [16] is a set of knowledge that should be tough previous to the launching of the startup.

The fourth one, **internalization**, is the transformation of explicit knowledge into tacit knowledge through the creation of a documents, information and practices, the idea is to implement an updated of important information, include courses in the curricula and formalize some initiatives among students. Later with the development of a public data base of general and important indicators and initiatives for the community (Fig. 6).

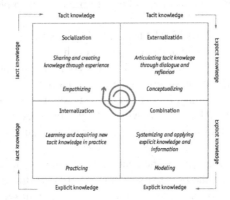

**Fig. 6.** "SECI MODEL for entrepreneurial knowledge transfer" (own elaboration)

## 3   Findings and Discussion

### 3.1   Sustainability Related Knowledge

One of main findings was the recognition of the little knowledge about sustainability practices and initiatives on the University. Students are not very knowledgeable about sustainability or circular economy, and what they have learnt about SGDs, was mostly outside the university on their own initiatives. Students basically do not participate in sustainable initiatives even though they have somehow hear about them.

We recognized five stages for an emerging Startup, there are four initial stages, the time in which the companies pass through these stages varies among different industries and different Startups, but we consider that sixty months is the normal period of startup development and in some cases up to seventy-two months since the beginning of the operations. This time frame will fairly represent the initial stages of the projects in Latin America. In the case of develop economies the startup genome report [15] defines a period that varies between thirty-six to forty-eight months, so Latin American startups takes one or two extra years to scale up or find and exit (Merge, sale, or other growth strategy). One of the reasons to explain this is the venture capital development in this develop economies is scarce.

Proposed Knowledge Management Implementation plan

a.- Diagnostic stage (Socialization)
Prepare the information for participating in any of the Sustaibility Rankings.
Asses about Website, writing information and related policies.
Meet the Sustainability or related committee at the Organization and present the project.

b.- Develop explicit knowledge (Internalization)
Make a general survey to gain more information and reach to university organizations.
Meetings with responsible of initiatives teams (Campus management, sustainability committee, academic and energy and other related responsible people.
Develop pending policies, review them and update.

c.- Increasing Knowledge (Combination)
Develop sustainability, SDGs, and Circular Economy reports.
Review academic programs and propose new courses for all the programs.
Evaluate sustainable projects – Renewable energy, recycling, suppliers,
Evaluate permanent practices with students' community.
Propose related research.

d.- Promotion and Recognition (Externalization)
- Develop, increase, update Websites and Intranet
- Develop permanent content and Sustainability related news in all media
- Develop seminars, congress or workshop on the matter
- Collaborate with other organizations

## 3.2  Survey Results

A survey was conducted among students, with around 100 answers this are some of the results (Figs. 7, 8, 9, 10, 11, 12, 13 and 14).

Have you heard about sustainability initiatives on SeAMK?

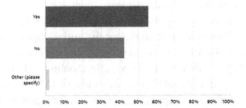

**Fig. 7.** Students' Sustainable initiatives familiarity knowledge

Please rate your level of knowledge about sustainability policies and practices on campus.

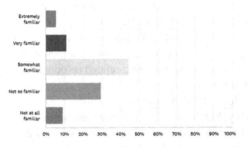

**Fig. 8.** Student's Sustainable policies and practices knowledge

Are you familiar with the term "Sustainable Development Goals" (SDGs)?

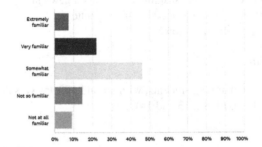

**Fig. 9.** Students Sustainable Development Goals knowledge

Have you learned about the SDGs at SEAMK University?

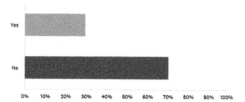

**Fig. 10.** Have Students learn about SDGs at the University

Have you actively participated in any sustainability-related projects, research, or volunteer activities at SEAMK University focused on SDGs ?

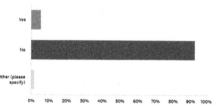

**Fig. 11.** Have Students learn about SDGs at the University

Are you aware that SEAMK is ranked in the Green Metric Ranking for sustainable campuses?

Answered: 53   Skipped: 1

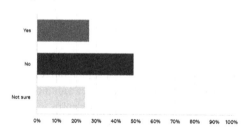

**Fig. 12.** Students Knowledge about Green Metric ranking and University participation

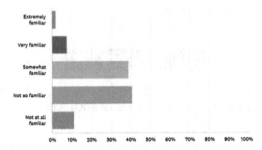

Are you aware of SEAMKs sustainability plan and goals
(Carbon neutrality, supplier policies, others)

**Fig. 13.** Students' Knowledge about the Carbon neutrality and sustainable goals at the University

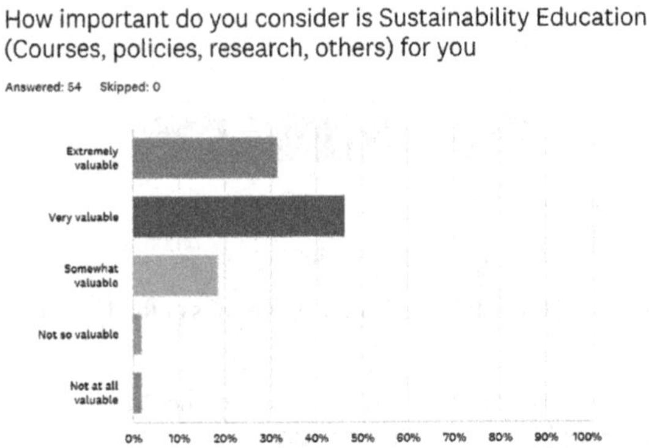

How important do you consider is Sustainability Education
(Courses, policies, research, others) for you

**Fig. 14.** Students' evaluation of the Importance of Sustainable Education

## 4   Conclusions

Universities should address societies most important and relevant challenges and opportunities, Sustainability is among one of the most relevant nowadays, Sustainability principles and its underlying problems are being currently tackled by Circular Economy strategies and United Nations sustainable development goals.

The Green Metrics international university rankings and the Impact Times Higher University rankings are useful tools for universities to embark and advance in the adoption of good sustainability practices allowing to benchmark with other institutions in the world and expedite the related processes.

These adoption process could be enhanced by utilizing a knowledge management approach for the adoption of sustainability practices, awareness and cultural development in the academic community and society at large.

Usually, the SECI model approach has been use inside companies, and has been related to internal organizational culture, in this case we have use a SECI model approach to enhance knowledge transfer related to Sustainability in a University considering benchmarking and the methodologies included in external ranking, so external knowledge has been incorporated has part of the socialization process and allows to expedite the incorporation and development of an internalization process.

Since the spiral of knowledge or the amount of knowledge so to say, grows all the time when more rounds are done in the model, we can expect an increase in the learning curve in the organization and its community, however it requires a communication systems and shared indicators to be implemented. There are also incentives that could be developed to support the learning spiral.

Students are willing to participate in sustainability initiatives, also consider that implement and academic program that has mandatory sustainable core through all the carriers. Even in an academic environment it draws attention the fact that there is not much information shared in relation to Circular Economy or Sustainability, both being of big interest for the students.

In the case of Circular economy practices there are tremendous opportunities, and a specific implementation plan needs to be developed.

By utilizing the SECI model, organizations can create a continuous cycle of learning and improvement in sustainability efforts. This approach not only enhances the effectiveness of sustainability initiatives but also contributes to the development of a culture that values and prioritizes environmental and social responsibility. The SECI model's emphasis on knowledge creation, sharing, and integration aligns well with the multifaceted nature of sustainability, where diverse perspectives and insights are essential for addressing complex challenges.

# References

Andreoni, V., Miola, A.: Competitiveness and Sustainable Development Goals. JCR Technical Reports, European Comission (2016). ISBN 978-92-79-64533-4, ISSN 1831-9424, https://doi.org/10.2788/64453. Retrieved on 10 December 2023

Hansen, J., Sato, M., Ruedy, R.: Radiative forcing and climate response. J. Geophys. Res. **102**(D6) (1997). 6831. Bibcode:1997JGR...102.6831H. https://doi.org/10.1029/96JD03436. Retrieved from https://ui.adsabs.harvard.edu/abs/1997JGR...102.6831H/abstract

Bath, S.: Infrastructure, Industrialization, and Innovation: Why SDG 9 matters and how we can achieve it. IISD (2018). https://www.iisd.org/articles/infrastructure-industrialization-and-innovation-why-sdg-9-matters-and-how-we-can-achieve-it

Bautista-Puig, N., Orduña-Malea, E., Perez-Esparrells, C.: Enhancing sustainable development goals or promoting universities? an analysis of the times higher education impact rankings. Int. J. Sustain. High. Educ. **23**(8), 211–231 (2022). https://doi.org/10.1108/IJSHE-07-2021-0309

Conard, B.: Some challenges to sustainability. Sustainability. **5**, 3368–3381 (2013). https://doi.org/10.3390/su5083368

Daniel, K.: Goal 11—Cities Will Play an Important Role in Achieving the SDGs. UN Org (2015). https://www.un.org/en/chronicle/article/goal-11-cities-will-play-important-role-achieving-sdgs

Dalal-Clayton, D.B.: The History of the Sustainable Development Concept. EC Aid and Sustainable Development Briefing Paper No.2. January 1995, IIED (1994)

Ellen Macarthur Foundation: The circular economy in detail. Ellen Macarthur Foundation (n.d.). https://www.ellenmacarthurfoundation.org/the-circular-economy-in-detail-deep-dive

Ellen Macarthur Foundation: The biological cycle of the butterfly diagram. Ellen Macarthur Foundation (2022). https://www.ellenmacarthurfoundation.org/articles/the-biological-cycle-of-the-butterfly-diagram

European Environment Agency: Circular economy in Europe. Developing the knowledge base, EEA Report, 2, Publications Office of the European Union, Luxembourg (2016). available at: https://eco.nomia.pt/contents/documentacao/thal16002enn-002.pdf. Accessed 18 August 2019

Europarl: Circular economy: definition, importance and benefits, European Parliament topics (2023). Retrieved on 13 November 2023 at https://www.europarl.europa.eu/topics/en/article/20151201STO05603/circular-economy-definition-importance-and-benefits

Giannoccaro, I., Ceccarelli, G., Fraccascia, L.: Features of the Higher Education for the Circular Economy: The Case of Italy. Sustainability 13, 11338 (2021). https://doi.org/10.3390/su1320 11338

Green Metrics Rankings: Detail Rankings 2021 - Seinäjoki University of Applied Sciences. UI Green Metric (2021). https://greenmetric.ui.ac.id/rankings/overall-rankings-2021/seamk.fi

Green Metrics Rankings: UI Green Metric World University Rankings: Background of The Ranking. UI GreenMetric (2024). https://greenmetric.ui.ac.id/about/welcome

Morseletto: Targets for a circular economy. Resources, Conservation and Recycling 153, 104553 (2020)

OECD: Better Policies for 2030 An OECD Action Plan on the Sustainable Development Goals (2016). Retrieved on January 5th 2024 at https://www.oecd.org/dac/Better%20Policies%20for%202030.pdf

OECD: Sustainable development strategies What are they and how can development co-operation agencies support them?. Policy Brief. Retrieved on December 21st, 2023 (2001). at https://www.oecd.org/dac/environment-development/1899857.pdf

Santander Universidades: Santander (2022). Rerieved on January 3rd at https://www.santander openacademy.com/en/blog/what-is-sustainability.html

Stensaker, B., Hermansen, H.: Global, Nordic, or institutional visions? An investiga-tion into how Nordic universities are adapting to the SDGs, Higher education (2023). https://doi.org/10.1007/s10734-023-01047-3

Slight Savers: What are the Sustainable Development Goals? Slight Savers (n.d.). https://www.sightsavers.org/policy-and-advocacy/global-goals/?gad_source=1&gclid=CjwKCAiA4 4OtBhAOEiwAj4gpOfVrcO3MsaQ9AeWA0SecZ3idGVhwK4JOl2kdR3mWhiz6CD_we66 TLRoCL08QAvD_BwE

Sustainable Development Network: Getting Started with the Sustainable Development Goals (2015). Retrieved from: https://sustainabledevelopment.un.org/content/documents/2217Ge tting%20started.pdf

Times higher education: Impact Rankings 2023. Times higher Education (2023). https://www.tim eshighereducation.com/impactrankings

Viqueira, P.: Why Does Sustainability Matter in the Higher Education Sector? Odgersberndt-son (2023). https://www.odgersberndtson.com/en-us/insights/why-does-sustainability-matter-in-the-higher-education-sector

# Trust as a Determining Factor in Tacit Knowledge Sharing Among Academics in Higher Education Institutions

Rexwhite Tega Enakrire[(✉)] [iD] and Hanlie Smuts[iD]

Department of Informatics, School of Information Technology, University of Pretoria, Pretoria, South Africa
rexwhite.enakrire80@gmail.com, hanlie.smuts@up.ac.za

**Abstract.** Trust plays a pivotal role in contemporary higher education settings. Trust is an intangible asset that is cultivated and maintained among individuals. However, there is concern regarding certain academics within higher education institutions (HEIs) who demonstrate unfaithfulness by appropriating others' insights or tacit knowledge for their research papers, projects, innovations, grant writing, and career advancement, as outlined by the authors. This behaviour raises questions about the perception of such actions among academics, who are intellectuals capable of developing their tacit knowledge through diligent research and exploration. This concern underscores the need for this study to examine trust as a determinant in tacit knowledge sharing among academics in HEIs. Two research objectives were used to address the study, namely: to establish the role of trust in tacit knowledge sharing, and to explore factors that may hinder not having trust in tacit knowledge sharing among academics. The study employed qualitative content analysis and phenomenological research approaches. Findings from the empirical literature harvested and the researchers' experiences revealed that trust significantly impacts tacit knowledge sharing among academics, particularly when issues such as jealousy, rivalry, and competition are set aside. Findings further reveal that tacit knowledge emerges as beneficial, especially when academics collaborate for professional growth and institutional advancement. Various factors, including limited time of interaction among colleagues, job insecurity, the dominance of explicit knowledge over tacit knowledge sharing, educational and experiential disparities, poor communication skills, age and gender discrepancies, lack of social networks, and cultural differences, can impede trust in tacit knowledge sharing among academics in HEIs. The study recommends fostering thought-provoking discussions and continuous engagement among academics from diverse backgrounds to enhance trust and facilitate more effective tacit knowledge sharing in the future within HEIs.

**Keywords:** Trust · Tacit · Knowledge · Sharing · Higher Education Institutions · productivity · interpersonal skills

© The Author(s), under exclusive license to Springer Nature Switzerland AG 2024
L. Uden and I.-H. Ting (Eds.): KMO 2024, CCIS 2152, pp. 51–60, 2024.
https://doi.org/10.1007/978-3-031-63269-3_4

# 1 Introduction

Higher Education Institutions (HEIs) have evolved into enterprises where the dissemination of information and knowledge is vital for societal transformation and development. The acknowledgement of the significance of information and knowledge in societal advancement has led academics to recognize its importance, resulting in a reluctance to share tacit knowledge with colleagues within HEIs. Academics within HEIs are apprehensive that sharing their tacit knowledge could be exploited by colleagues for personal gain, such as developing research papers/projects, innovations, course materials, securing grants, or advancing their careers. The apprehension stems from concerns about potential betrayal, where colleagues might appropriate ideas for their benefit. The authors of this paper question why colleagues, who are also academics with extensive training and experience, cannot cultivate their tacit knowledge through ongoing exploration and discovery. Drawing from their combined experience of over ten years in HEIs, the authors have observed instances where sharing thoughts, innovations, and ideas with other academics has led to those ideas being claimed by colleagues in published research papers or seminars. This phenomenon may arise from a lack of time or motivation to implement the ideas, prompting this study to explore methods of fostering trust among academics for the sharing of tacit knowledge within HEIs.

The study by [1] indicates that the activities surrounding teaching learning and research in HEIs are essential roles that require certain knowledge and skills before academics can dominate in the tasks given to them. Therefore, since the tasks of teaching-learning, and research in HEIs are complex and uncertain as stipulated by [1], guiding tacit knowledge with the attribution of trust becomes significant. The thought of the authors in this regard is that it takes years, rigorous study, and experiences to build tacit knowledge and the essence of sharing it is to enhance organisational productivity and career growth among academics. The ownership of any tacit knowledge is willing and prepared to share if it is not going to be stolen or used for other selfish purposes. [1] note that Tacit knowledge has proven to be the panacea to organizational problems [2], because of hidden expertise in the human brain/mind. The hidden know-how in the human brain/mind is unveiled when activities take place in HEIs. Tacit knowledge sharing is an enabler that results in quality service delivery in HEIs [1].

[3] notes that tacit knowledge comprises insights, innovations, human behaviour, intelligence, and fresh ideas that are products of organizational sustainability. The insights, innovations, human behaviour, intelligence, and fresh ideas cannot work in isolation, but rather through human effort. Trust is an intangible asset that is created, developed, and sustained by and among people [4]. Trust is an antecedent to knowledge sharing [4]. Trust is a key factor when it comes to building relationships. Without trust among academics, it would be difficult to work together as team members, how much more sharing tacit type of knowledge (hidden treasure). Therefore, for academics to share tacit knowledge there is a need to build relationships. Building a relationship among academics is crucial because it would help to strengthen the part to follow whenever academics want to share the tacit type of knowledge for their work practices.

While academics display their trust, it becomes much easier to share tacit knowledge when executing any tasks in HEIs. Tacit knowledge application is significant in the actualisation of work performance in the HEIs. The accomplishments made thus far among academics, especially in their teaching and learning, research, attending workshops and conferences and other extracurricular activities within HEIs result in employing tacit knowledge for proper planning, and decision-making among academics. The tacit type of knowledge that resonates for the success of events in HEIs is predictable and valued based on the trust that academics have for each other in their job performance [4]. This trust has given birth to a resounding and informative renovation and expansion within the HEIs circle. The focus of this paper therefore investigates trust as a determining factor in tacit knowledge in enhanced quality service delivery in organizations.

The paper applied the qualitative content analysis and the phenomenological research approaches using the authors' lived experiences and expositions in their careers in developing this paper. The adopted research approaches have helped to address the role of trust that tacit knowledge has played in knowledge sharing among academics. The paper reflects that when there is trust, academics may be willing to share their tacit knowledge (knowledge in the human brain) to support HEIs transformation and inculcation of insights that could boost academic growth. The identified variables "sharing tacit knowledge and trust" buttressed in this context become significant in the present knowledge economy where both entities are imperative for the sustainable development of HEIs.

This paper aims to understand how trust could be used as a determining factor in tacit knowledge sharing among academics in HEIs. To develop the study further, two research objectives were used to address the study, namely: to establish the role of trust in tacit knowledge sharing, and to explore factors that may hinder not having trust in tacit knowledge sharing among academics.

In Sect. 2, the background of the study was presented where the overview of empirical studies of trust in tacit knowledge sharing was discussed, followed by Sect. 3 which addresses the method applied in the study. Section 4 entails the findings/contribution of the study, while Sect. 5 connotes the implication of the study and 6 is the conclusion of the paper.

## 2   Background

Tacit knowledge has become a key component through which academics could survive especially in this era of the fifth industrial revolution (5IR). The 5IR encompasses human interaction with machines (AI). While AI has infiltrated everywhere inclusive HEIs, the use of tacit knowledge among academics cannot be undermined. The survival strategy of academics has to do with the application of tacit knowledge for enhanced service delivery in HEIs. Tacit knowledge could assist academics in this world of uncertainty, where artificial intelligence (AI) is gradually taking over job opportunities. As academics engage in one task or the other where they discuss with each other, they share their tacit knowledge to enhance work performance and academic capability. This is also supported by [2] who attests that most activities experienced in corporate and private organizations were the effort of tacit knowledge. Sharing tacit knowledge among academics leads to innovative work performance of tasks exhibited [1]. Academics indicate that before they can share their tacit knowledge with their colleagues, there should be some level of trust. The reason that necessitates this assertion is that tacit knowledge, hidden in the human brain/mind, has become an enabler in quality service delivery in organizations. [4]

notes that Knowledge Sharing and Trust are concepts that have been explored by many researchers such as [2, 4]. [4] believed that it is important to trust someone whenever knowledge is shared. For example, when a sick person visits the doctor at the hospital regarding a certain ailment or sickness, it is believed that the knowledge that was shared between the doctor and the sick person should not be shared on the public notice of the hospital.

The reason why such knowledge should not be shared is because it is confidential knowledge similar to the tacit type of knowledge. Another example we could also learn from is interviewing respondents in a research investigation or a journalist. The tacit type of knowledge which the respondents or the journalist shared must be kept at a closed door, to maintain ethical standards, otherwise, the person seeking such information has bridged the oat that guides against knowledge protection. The information and knowledge given out to the person seeking it must be protected, except on request for concrete reasons. The cases referred to in this context are distinct and serve different purposes but the bottom line that the authors seek to drive home is the ability to trust someone whenever tacit knowledge being hidden type of knowledge or confidential knowledge is shared.

While one of the authors was working at a certain University in Africa whose identity cannot be revealed due to ethical reasons, he conceived an idea or innovation to carry out a community project in one of the communities, before writing the proposal on the community project, he decided to share the thought of the project with another colleague and during the discussion, they both discussed intellectually and laughed very well about it. Surprisingly, the other colleague who never had or planned any initiative decided to bypass the colleague who owns the original plans and submitted the same idea of the project to the necessary office for approval. When it was the turn of the earlier colleague who had the actual project, the officer in charge said you may not carry out this community project as someone had already submitted a similar project. For curiosity's sake, the colleague in question decided to ask, can I please know who has such a brilliant idea for a community project? The officer then mentioned the name of the colleague. When he saw the name of the person that submitted the proposal he became shattered and furious. He quickly went to meet him and asked why he did that, by stealing my idea for this project and even if you had such a thing in mind we could have collaborated. This attitude shows some level of distrust and betrayal among academics. As intellectuals, it is expected that there is no need to betray your colleague as trust is valuable in life, no matter the circumstance. It is on this premise the authors decided to carry out phenomenological research that understudies trust as a determining factor in tacit knowledge sharing among academics in HEIs. This study fills the existing knowledge gap of tacit knowledge sharing in the context of the knowledge management domain and the contextual paradigm of a phenomenological approach in HEIs.

## 3   Research Method

To achieve the aim of this study, the researchers employed the qualitative content analysis of documents harvested from Google Scholar and phenomenological approaches. The researchers harvested fifty research papers from Google Scholars in developing the research papers. Of the fifty research papers harvested from Google Scholar, the inclusion and exclusion criteria were applied to determine the papers most suited for consideration using the keywords "role of trust in tacit knowledge sharing", and "factors that may hinder not having trust in tacit knowledge sharing among academics. The research papers left were twenty-five, which the researchers also used in the qualitative content analysis where they internalised salient issues that have to do with the two research objectives earlier mentioned in this segment. The phenomenological research method was also considered in support of the qualitative content analysis of documents harvested from Google Scholar for the study. These methods were considered appropriate due to their efficacy in comprehending the lived experiences and insights of the researchers working in diverse HEIs. The phenomenological research approach facilitated an understanding of the lived experiences and insights the researchers have towards utilizing shared tacit knowledge in developing research papers or grant projects. It also shed light on instances where individuals were unapologetic when confronted about their behaviour. Previous studies by [5] and [6] assert that the phenomenological approach is dedicated to systematically investigating personal experiences based on individuals' lifestyles, career trajectories, and societal impacts, which can serve as references or sources of inspiration. The authors of this study chose the phenomenological research approach based on their expertise in knowledge management, where tacit knowledge holds significance.

This approach was further supported by a qualitative content analysis of empirical literature [7] sourced from the Google Scholar database [8]. Several studies, including those by [5, 9–11], and [6], have applied the phenomenological research approach, augmented by content analysis. The authors concluded that this approach, along with content analysis, offers a deeper understanding of internalized literature and the lived experiences related to various phenomena. In this study, the authors analyzed their personal lives and social environments. Their experiences regarding how trust facilitated tacit knowledge sharing in HEIs bolstered their career progression. The subsequent section discusses the findings and implications of the study, anchored in the phenomenological approach and the authors' lived experiences in HEIs, particularly their career progression track records. The emphasis is on how academics can cultivate trust among themselves to foster continued tacit knowledge sharing. This is followed by an exploration of factors that could impede trust and the role of tacit knowledge in enhancing the quality of service delivery within organizations.

## 4 Findings and Implication of the Study

This study investigated trust as a pivotal determinant of tacit knowledge sharing among academics in HEIs. This section presents the study's findings and implications regarding the roles that trust plays in tacit knowledge sharing. The findings were derived from a phenomenological approach, incorporating the authors' lived experiences and insights supplemented by a content analysis of empirical literature sourced from the Google Scholar database. The study also examined various factors that could potentially impede trust in tacit knowledge sharing among academics, such as time constraints, job security concerns, the prevalence of explicit knowledge sharing over tacit knowledge, disparities in experience levels, and insufficient time for interpersonal contact were considered in the study.

## 4.1 Role of Trust in Tacit Knowledge Sharing Among Academics

Considering who to share tacit knowledge with, trust must be established in this world of uncertainty. Many people have fallen victim to betrayal due to the knowledge they have shared with others. Therefore for academics being knowledge producers in HEIs to share their tacit knowledge with their colleagues, it is imperative to consider trust hence this study becomes significant in this context. [12] note that the levels of trust meaningfully influence the degree to which academics are eager to share and employ tacit knowledge. Affect-based trust remarkably impacts the readiness to share tacit knowledge, while perception-based trust plays a more substantial role in the willingness to utilize tacit knowledge [12].

In this segment of the paper, the term "role" pertains to the actions academics can take to foster the establishment of trust within HEIs. Trust plays a crucial role in facilitating tacit knowledge sharing among academics, as it forms the foundation upon which relationships can be built and strengthened within HEIs. Trust is believed to promote various forms of support among academics, including willingness, openness, and eagerness to share tacit knowledge. It enables academics to demonstrate love, support, mentorship, management, and service towards each other within HEIs. Importantly, trust transcends considerations of race, religion, background, class, and educational qualifications, thereby promoting diversity and inclusion, where everyone collaborates as team members. From an organizational perspective, the role of trust in tacit knowledge sharing is invaluable, as it safeguards job security, mitigates difficult situations, and simplifies complexities that could potentially endanger the organization and its staff members.

Tacit knowledge plays a pivotal role in enhancing organizational productivity. Often, academics possess a wealth of knowledge that remains concealed until they are assigned specific tasks. Through engagement in these tasks, their knowledge gradually reveals itself through their actions. One prominent framework highlighting the significance of tacit knowledge is the SECI model [13]. Trust is viewed as a fundamental aspect of human social interaction that develops over time. This concept extends across various disciplines within the social sciences [14]. In the literature, trust is recognized as a relational phenomenon that evolves through interactions between parties [15].

The SECI model [13] holds significance in this context as it facilitates academics' socialization through knowledge sharing during interactions. Another crucial aspect when dealing with the role of trust in tacit knowledge is externalization, which involves the conversion of tacit to explicit knowledge [16]. How do academics see the other external individual when it comes to building trust with such a person? Building trust could only be achieved by both external factors of willingness and continuous engagement in interaction, then the academic would come to know the person better. Additionally, it is essential to consider combination (conversion of explicit to explicit knowledge) [17], and internalization, which involves converting explicit to tacit knowledge [13]. Research [2] suggests that tacit knowledge fosters innovation, ideas, and creativity, leading to the development of innovative projects and enhancing work performance. Tacit knowledge, encompassing innovation, ideas, and creativity emerging from academic discourse, can be attributed to experiences and knowledge accumulated over the years. Once trust is established, sharing tacit knowledge becomes seamless. The global innovation witnessed in HEIs today is a result of academics collaborating as teams and the trust they have built over time, thereby transforming organizations. This reflects the authors' experience throughout their careers, where they have converted explicit knowledge to tacit and vice versa for teaching and learning, research production, collaborations, and networking with international colleagues. The authors emphasize the significance of building trust by sharing tacit knowledge acquired over the years, as this knowledge defines their expertise in their respective professions. The extent to which academics trust each other correlates with the wellness, productivity, and international recognition of HEIs.

Reference [18] discusses the reduction of uncertainty and the collective integration of organizational knowledge. It posits that tacit knowledge plays a crucial role in resolving uncertainty that would otherwise be challenging to address. The influence of organizational culture, as highlighted in [19], is paramount as it dictates the organization's potential for growth regardless of the context. In HEIs, the presence of well-cultivated academic cultures facilitates easier and more effective sharing of tacit knowledge. Reference [20] emphasizes the importance of reconciling different academic perspectives, particularly in areas of agreement or disagreement stemming from diverse beliefs, insights, and expertise. Academics leverage their beliefs, insights, and expertise to ensure the dissemination of valid and appropriate knowledge within HEIs. The significance of trust in tacit knowledge sharing becomes particularly pronounced when disagreements arise among academics regarding the terms associated with their tasks.

### 4.2 Factors that Could Interfere with Trust in Tacit Knowledge Sharing Among Academics

Certain factors such as time to share knowledge, apprehension regarding job security, the dominance of sharing explicit knowledge over tacit knowledge, differences in experience levels, lack of time for contact and interaction, poor verbal and interpersonal skills, age and gender differences, lack of social network, differences in education levels, fear of not receiving recognition, and cultural differences. These factors are fundamental in the interference of trust in tacit knowledge sharing among academics. The authors might want to ask how can academics share tacit knowledge when there is competition among each other. Competition is created in HEIs to render quality services and meet HEIs goals, most academics do not have time for each other especially those who are in their tenure track position requiring time and much effort to create substantive records in their career progression.

Tacit knowledge is key to HEIs productivity, especially when academics play their roles well. Most of what academics know (knowledge) is hidden until a certain task is given. The tasks begin to reveal the knowledge that can only be achieved when given tasks where they share what they know. For instance, attending conferences to present papers, during faculty defence of masters and doctoral students. One amazing emphasis that could last and position academics very well is revealed in the test of time through [13] tacit knowledge embedded in the SECI model [13]. [21] emphasized that when academics execute any tasks, what happens at that time is knowledge-generation and processes where they create new knowledge through their product design and service delivery. Nonaka, studies [22–24] have stood the test of time through various use of the SECI model that explains the practicality of tacit knowledge application in service delivery. The skillfulness of academics is used through tacit knowledge to accumulate every information resource used in their teaching and learning in HEIs. What about countless research papers produced today hence HEIs place much value on research, teaching and services because most of what academics do is embedded in their tacit type of knowledge. The SECI model [13] has a lot to say about how tacit knowledge is shared among academics, especially, when socializing (sharing experiences and interacting with employees through tacit knowledge) [16] externalizing (conversion of tacit to explicit) [16], combination (explicit renewed to explicit knowledge) [17], and internalization (converting explicit to tacit knowledge) [13]. [25] alludes that tacit knowledge being innovation, ideas, and creativity of academics could lead to the development of several projects.

The tacit knowledge is the innovation, ideas, and creativity that emanate from the discourse of individual expertise. It can also be attributed to experiences and knowledge acquired over the years among employees on what they know best. This has been the experience of the authors throughout their career progression having worked in different private and public organizations in Africa, where they converted explicit knowledge to tacit and vice versa. The reason the authors of this paper felt the qualitative content analysis of literature and phenomenological research approach is more appropriate in this study is aligned with where they showcase their thoughts and experiences on how tacit knowledge remains an enabler of organizational productivity. The extent to which employees can tell how much know-how they possess and have acquired reflects on knowledge application in the production of knowledge. Tacit knowledge could be used to quantify production of goods and services in this ever-changing world of uncertainty.

## 5   Implication of the Study

The implication of the study is that trust in tacit knowledge holds fundamental significance across all spheres of human endeavour. Tacit knowledge serves as the embodiment of an individual's voice within an organization, through which their capabilities and contributions are recognized. Without tacit knowledge, it becomes challenging to discern what an academic's potential is, predominantly in showcasing their talents and best practices amidst an ever-evolving HEIs landscape. In today's dynamic corporate environment, the vitality of organizations hinges on the collective know-how possessed by their employees. A deficiency in employee know-how poses a serious impediment to organizational functioning and service delivery, whether in the private or public sector. The strength of academics in HEIs is intricately linked to the knowledge carriers—i.e., the academics who demonstrate their expertise through their actions. The qualitative content analysis of documents harvested from Google Scholar and the phenomenological approaches adopted in this study has underscored the indispensable nature of tacit knowledge in organizational survival. In an era of uncertainty and escalating customer information needs, leveraging the hidden treasure of tacit knowledge becomes imperative for organizational competitiveness. One of the key roles of trust in tacit knowledge sharing identified in this study is its capacity to harness, tap into, and share among academics for future generations. This fosters confidence among HEI management in retaining the academics for future business enterprises. Quality service delivery in both public and private organizations, concerning the application of tacit knowledge, entails serving customers promptly and with utmost respect and priority. Furthermore, fostering a culture of collaboration and continuous teamwork among employees is crucial. The productivity and performance of corporate and private organizations globally are largely driven by the application of tacit knowledge in various activities and tasks. Therefore, recognizing and leveraging the role of tacit knowledge is paramount for organizational success and sustainability in today's competitive landscape.

## 6 Conclusion

The study underscores the indispensable role of trust in tacit knowledge sharing among academics in HEIs for achieving enhanced quality service delivery, a facet that cannot be overstated. In today's dynamic context, no organization can thrive without leveraging tacit knowledge across various service delivery domains. The tacit knowledge exhibited by employees varies according to their job roles and areas of expertise. The study highlights that organizational resilience heavily relies on the capabilities of employees to apply their know-how effectively in their tasks. Furthermore, the study suggests that as employees share their knowledge, they not only contribute to filtering outdated information but also acquire new insights crucial for improving service quality. In an ever-evolving economy where uncertainty prevails and customer demands escalate, organizations must devise strategic measures to endure. Harnessing the latent potential of tacit knowledge, especially in young and competitive organizations, is deemed essential for sustainability.

It is suggested that by sharing their hidden treasures of deep tacit knowledge, as identified in the study, both academics and HEIs can thrive. While emphasizing the pivotal role of trust in tacit knowledge sharing for improved service delivery in HEIs among academics, the study acknowledges contextual disparities and underscores the imperative to harness, tap into, and share the wealth of knowledge stored within employees. The study further underscores the monumental impact of tacit knowledge, attributing its contributions to the development of cutting-edge technologies prevalent today. Consequently, the study advocates for the promotion and showcasing of tacit knowledge to accomplish tasks effectively. Nonetheless, a limitation of this research lies in the scant exploration of African private and public organizations. There exists a notable gap in the literature concerning the methodological approaches and theoretical frameworks regarding the application of tacit knowledge in organizations, which this study endeavours to address. In terms of future research, acknowledging the diverse interest of building trust with non-academic staff members in higher education becomes significant considering their tacit knowledge roles in supporting activities that go on in HEIs.

## References

1. Enakrire, R.T., Smuts, H.: Efficacy of knowledge and skills in teaching and learning and research in higher education institutions. In: International Conference on Knowledge Management in Organizations, pp. 16–24. Springer International Publishing, Cham (2022)
2. Alzoubi, M.O., Alrowwad, A.A., Masa'deh, R.E.: Exploring the relationships among tacit knowledge sharing, communities of practice and employees' abilities: the case of KADDB in Jordan. Int. J. Organizat. Analy. **30**(5), 1132–1155 (2022)

3. Malik, S.: Emotional intelligence and innovative work behaviour in knowledge-intensive organizations: how tacit knowledge sharing acts as a mediator? VINE J. Info. Knowle. Manage. Sys. **52**(5), 650–669 (2022)
4. McNeish, J., Mann, I.J.S.: Knowledge sharing and trust in organizations. IUP J. Knowl. Manage. **8** (2010)
5. Tomkins, L.: Using interpretative phenomenological psychology in organisational research with working carers. In: Brook, J., King, N. (eds.), Applied Qualitative Research in Psychology, pp. 86–100. Palgrave, London (2017)
6. Noon, E.J.: Interpretive phenomenological analysis: An appropriate methodology for educational research. J. Perspect. Appl. Acad. Pract. **6**(1) (2018)
7. Given, L.M.: The SAGE encyclopedia of qualitative research methods, vols. 1–0. Thousand Oaks, CA: SAGE Publications, Inc. (2008)
8. Greening, N.: Phenomenological research methodology. Sci. Res. J. **7**(5), 88–92 (2019)
9. Smith, J.A., Flower, P., Larkin, M.: Interpretative Phenomenological Analysis: Theory, Method and Research. Qualitative Research in Psychology **6**(4), 346–347 (2009)
10. VanScoy, A., Evenstad, S.B.: Interpretive phenomenological analysis for LIS research. Journal of Documentation (2015)
11. VanScoy, A., Bright, K.: Articulating the experience of uniqueness and difference for librarians of color. Libr. Q. **89**(4), 285–297 (2019)
12. Holste, J.S., Fields, D.: Trust and tacit knowledge sharing and use. J. Knowle. Manage. **14**(1), 128–140
13. Nonaka, I.: A Dynamic Theory of Organizational Knowledge Creation, pp. 14–23. Hitotsubashi University, Kunitachi, Tokyo, Japan, Institute of Business Research (1994)
14. Möllering, G., Bachmann, R., Hee, Lee, S.: Introduction: Understanding organizational trust– foundations, constellations, and issues of operationalization. J. Manager. Psychol. **19**(6), 556–570
15. Mayer, R.C., Davis, J.H., Schoorman, F.D.: An integrative model of organizational trust Academy of Management Review, 20(3), 709–734 (1995). Gill, H., Boies, K., Finegan, J.E., Mcnally, J. 301
16. Farnese, M.L., Barbieri, B., Chirumbolo, A., Patriotta, G. Managing knowledge in organizations: A Nonaka's SECI model operationalization. Frontiers in Psychology **10**(2730) (2019). https://doi.org/10.3389/fpsyg.2019.02730
17. Nonaka, I., Toyama, R., Konno, N.: SECI, Ba and leadership: a unified model of dynamic knowledge creation. Long Range Plan. **33**(1), 5–34 (2000)
18. Oğuz, F., Elif Şengün, A.: Mystery of the unknown: revisiting tacit knowledge in the organizational literature. J. Knowl. Manag. **15**(3), 445–461 (2011)
19. Mambo, S., Smuts, H.: The impact of organizational culture on knowledge management: the case of an international multilateral organization. EPiC Series in Comp. **85**, 184–195 (2022)
20. Muñoz, C.A., Mosey, S., Binks, M.: The tacit mystery: reconciling different approaches to tacit knowledge. Knowl. Manag. Res. Pract. **13**, 289–298 (2015)
21. Nonaka, I., Byosiere, P., Borucki, C.C., Konno, N.: Organizational knowledge creation theory: a first comprehensive test. Int. Bus. Rev. **3**(4), 337–351 (1994)
22. Andreeva, T., Ikhilchik, I.: Applicability of the SECI model of knowledge creation in Russian cultural context: theoretical analysis. Knowl. Process. Manag. **18**(1), 56–66 (2011)
23. Adesina, A.O., Ocholla, D.N.: The SECI model in knowledge management practices: past, present and future. Mousaion **37**(3) (2019)
24. Canonico, P., De Nito, E., Esposito, V., Iacono, M.P., Consiglio, S.: Knowledge creation in the automotive industry: analysing obeya-oriented practices using the SECI model. J. Bus. Res. **112**, 450–457 (2020)
25. Mitchell, V.W., Harvey, W.S., Wood, G.: Where does all the 'know how' go? the role of tacit knowledge in research impact. High. Educ. Res. Dev. **41**(5), 1664–1678 (2022)

# Graphical Support for Knowledge Transfer During IT Project Implementations

Florian Schmidt, Christian Ploder[(✉)], Arno Rottensteiner, and Thomas Dilger

MCI - The Entrepreneurial School, Universitätsstrasse 15, 6020 Innsbruck, Austria
`christian.ploder@mci.edu`

**Abstract.** This paper explores a novel approach to process representation during business process modeling, emphasizing a temporal axis and additional information to improve support for ERP implementation projects. Integrating an advanced modeling tool aims to improve the reliability of planning and understanding. ERP systems play a key role in facilitating the integration and automation of business processes. While conventional BPMN-based process modeling provides a structurally rich representation, it often overlooks temporal sequence, dynamic activity characteristics, and detailed process element information - which is especially ahrd to understand for novices. Through an empirical study, this research qualitatively evaluates an innovative approach for process representaion through a focus group discussion. The result enables the visualization of a structured model that captures time-dependent process steps and their impact on the people involved. Finally, the study presents and analyses the challenges and limitations of previous model and offers potential future perspectives for process representation. Rooted in the empirical study, the research findings provide companies with a promising basis for improving IT implementation projects, fostering a better understanding and encouraging a critical examination of their process knowledge.

**Keywords:** Process Visualization · Business Process Modelling · Knowledge Transfer · Business Process Description

## 1 Introduction

ERP systems as one of the most important IT systems in a company, essential since the 1990s, streamline business processes [10]. Business Process Modeling is key to ERP implementation, but challenges arise from incorrect models and deviations [20] especially during the communication in the corresponding workshops. Very often Business Process Modeling and Notation (BPMN) is used. Knowledge management practices promote collaboration and communication among team members. This is particularly important during ERP implementation, where cross-functional teams may be involved. Collaboration platforms,

© The Author(s), under exclusive license to Springer Nature Switzerland AG 2024
L. Uden and I.-H. Ting (Eds.): KMO 2024, CCIS 2152, pp. 61–70, 2024.
https://doi.org/10.1007/978-3-031-63269-3_5

discussion forums, and real-time communication tools contribute to effective knowledge transfer [11]. The dynamic nature of BPMN raises questions about the adaptation of underlying processes. Technological advances drive constant re-evaluation of processes. Implementation challenges persist, leading academics to search for success or failure factors [8]. In addition to business process management, the goal is to prevent inaccurate modeling and ensure effective process management for business success and stakeholder satisfaction and stakeholder integration in the discussion [22]. This paper explores the integration of ERP and business process modeling to improve the effective representation of business processes. The focus is on restructured approaches and methods for modeling ERP systems based on commonly understandable business processes. Through a specific use case, the study aims to demonstrate new presentation possibilities to model business processes within an ERP system implementation and have high quality discussion in the corresponding teams.

How can an advanced graphical process representation support the knowledge transfer in the project team during an ERP implementation project?

Section 3 focuses on the methodology of the study design used to collect data in this research, after briefly presenting the theoretical background and reviewing the literature in the next section. After the presentation of the setting, the results of the study will be presented and discussed in Sects. 4 and 5. The paper concludes with a list of some of the study's limitations and an outlook for further research into process design.

## 2   Theoretical Background

In this section, the paper delves into the basic elements of the theoretical background, drawing on literature from various researchers to elucidate the central ideas of this scientific exploration and the realm of ERP implementation. To provide a clear understanding, the section thoroughly examines basic terms.

### 2.1   ERP-System Implementation

An Enterprise Resource Planning (ERP) system is a software application that streamlines and unifies various organizational business processes. It acts as a comprehensive Management Information System (MIS) comprising accounting, procurement, production, sales, and human resources modules. These modules are closely linked to facilitate a coherent data flow, ensuring efficient business processing and seamless information exchange [7, p. 6]. Schwarz outlines the six stages of ERP implementation [20]. Implementing an ERP system is a complex and costly endeavor that depends on a focused analysis of the key elements. Success in this endeavor depends on the identification of critical success factors. According to Ranjan et al. [18], implementing an ERP system involves significantly redesigning business processes. ERP systems are integrated applications that impact the entire organization [1, p. 559]. ERP implementation aims to introduce the new system seamlessly, meet deadlines, exploit new technologies, and realize additional benefits [19]. To support all of the given challenges, the authors found a gap in the BPMN literature, which should be closed by this paper about how to document better and communicate processes in ERP implementation projects.

## 2.2   Business Process Model Notification

The BPMN modeling language has become a dominant force in the business process domain, becoming the most widely used tool for mapping business process activities and reaping the benefits of project management. Recognized as a leading standard, BPMN's concepts are practical in real-world scenarios and provide an accurate reflection of individual business processes [3]. These business process models are essential for documenting daily operations and specifying software requirements during development [12]. BPMN is a tool for controlling and validating specific business processes, thus supporting implementation. The model's adaptability to new standards, laws and technologies contributes significantly to improving the quality of individual business processes and has attracted attention since its inception. It's worth noting that these steps express sequences, selections, parallel executions, and single iterations through their control logic. They form a chain of nodes connected by sequence flows or other influences [17].

BPMN anchors elements with an extension mechanism for adding attributes. This allows the representation of a new modeling language within a specific domain, extracting information from the platform-oriented concept [21]. It's a graphical notation for business process activities, describing dependencies between sub-processes and tasks [17]. Categorization facilitates presentation and understanding, allowing focus on the modeling process for more straightforward presentations with fewer errors [4].

## 2.3   Project Management with Gantt Chart

In project management, a well-planned and targeted flow of information is crucial for effectively guiding stakeholders and development participants. The widely used "Gantt chart" plays a central role in project planning and control, breaking down tasks over time and visually representing project progress [16]. This tool allows for customization and makes actions immediately visible to all involved. Although a long-standing management tool since the early 19th century, Gantt charts remain a powerful tool for visualizing information flows and identifying problems in the planning process [23]. Pankaja [15] emphasizes the need for an efficient cost-benefit and planning system, with Gantt charts providing early insight into project stages and facilitating corrective action in process design.

## 2.4   Critical Success Factors

In the field of ERP implementation and related processes, the concept of value has gained prominence and has been recognized as a critical success factor (CSF) by scholars such as Nagpal et al. [14]. Fundamentally, using ERP systems aims to increase organizational productivity and generate higher revenues. However, implementing ERP systems can pose significant financial risks and potentially threaten the viability of an organization [13]. ERP implementation involves significant change and must be carefully managed, with key factors including management commitment, process redesign, and integration of existing business information [1]. Research gaps in CSFs are identified, with Finney & Corbett [5] calling for more research and a new change management approach to minimize failure rates. Practical project and process management, characterized by a structured approach, is essential and requires experts for coordination [6].

### 2.5   Common Construct

The challenges and theoretical perspectives discussed highlight the potential for expanding project management research, particularly in business process modeling. Experts emphasize the need for innovative tools and approaches to fill gaps of classical BPMN. Quality assurance and identifying human, IT, or machine support tools are crucial. The proposed solution involves real-time mapping of BPMN model activities to facilitate the implementation and refinement of project processes and expand the understanding for novices in this area. This improves the understanding and visualization of processes for both customers and consultants. To illustrate the new concept of visualizing processes, a time-based model has been developed that integrates the core elements of Gantt, cost, time, quality, and critical factors. The focus is on the time-based progression of activities, the definition of processes, and the associated effort. An example of the direct time spent on an activity is shown in Fig. 1, where in the standard BPMN the length of the activity is based on the text and with advanced visualization the working time is coded in the length of the activity.

## 3   Study Design

This paper's study design and scientific approach was the planned methodology of a qualitative focus group discussion. This technique of collecting data through interviews with individuals or a whole group reflects a guided investigation of reality [2]. A qualitative research approach goes in-depth and tests the meaningfulness of the core constructs being researched, which already exist and are derived from the theory. The research methodology aims to be as close to reality as possible, to find a common thread in a construct, and, through an open approach. A qualitative focus group discussion in a workshop was initiated to gain insight from ERP implementation experts and to gather their perspectives on the advanced graphical process representation model. The selected group of 10 experts in ERP implementation and usability design participated in evaluating the first advanced model for business process representation derived from literature. The experts were selected by convenience sampling based on practical experience longer than 5 years in ERP Projects. Some of them are working at the

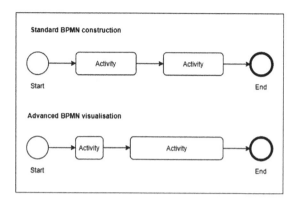

**Fig. 1.** New representation of a BPMN activity

consultants side some directly for the implementation company. The aim of the focus group session was to challenge the provided model, discuss the representation changes and get ideas for further improvements. The empirical research took place from March to May in 2023. The discussions, which were recorded and transcribed, were qualitatively analyzed using Kuckartz's [9] content analysis. Themes and patterns were coded to derive conclusions and recommendations for improving the graphic representation.

## 4   Results

The following Table 1 shows the frequency of the categories mentioned in the discussion, which are used as a basis for the design of the graphical process representation. The fixed categories are based on the theoretical background, the critical success factors, the human perception of the visual representation, and the possible distances that may arise on the part of the experts.

As can be seen from the Table 1 the quality factor is assessed with a relatively low frequency. This leads to the conclusion that the quality factor as such is difficult to define and covers too broad a spectrum. *"What I understood is the cost but not the quality. To what extent can help me here? So the costs are also about the budget I have as a consultant, but what is the quality? That is not yet completely clear to me. I would not be sure from the feeling (...) whether that helps this model at all, that quality is included as a factor in addition to the costs"* (Person 10, pos. 57). It is noticeable that cost and time, which can be equated with processing time, are still frequently mentioned as elements to be retained in the construct. *"The fact, that the development team gets this so roughly represented and on the other hand the customer can design for itself, for example, processes in such a way, that is the customer knows than with its process that this is distributed cost-technically and time technically in such a way that this can assign appropriate data even from the Controlling"* (Person 3, pos. 59). For the experts, it was essential to retain the critical success factors. The

Table 1. List of Codes were mentioned

| | Code system | Frequency | Avg.score |
|---|---|---|---|
| 1 | Costs | 55 | **9.02** |
| 2 | Time | 72 | **11.80** |
| 3 | Quality | 53 | **6.89** |
| 4 | Critical Success Factors | 91 | **14.92** |
| 5 | Human influences and perceptions | 149 | **24.43** |
| 6 | Visualization | 73 | **11.97** |
| 7 | Psychology Distance | 51 | **8.36** |
| 8 | Human Bonding | 66 | **10.82** |

high rate of human perception of a visualization and graphical representation of a process confirms that this was well received. *"Because that's how we have it now, that we have a rough project timeline. But yes, if it's generally at higher levels of the process, like Level 1 or Level 2, it's a nice overview for the development team, the project team, and management."* (Person 3, pos. 262). Therefore, the new BPMN representation of a process activity consists of the following key elements.

Only a few experts distanced themselves from the new graphical representation. *"For me, the whole thing is still a bit unclear, but costs must be included in the detail"* (Person 2, pos. 91). It can be said that they tended to relate to it, which is confirmed by the human connection factor. *"I understand the process and the idea, but I'm just very irritated by the colors and don't know what they want from me"* (Person 9, pos. 115). Therefore, critical success factors and how the people involved in the process deal with them are crucial for implementation and knowledge transfer. Documentation is recommended to facilitate further steps at deeper process levels. *"In my opinion, the only thing that can serve as an orientation is a time scale and documentation for the other measured value. Perhaps we should not deposit the values of the project, but deposit the quality, for example, later as a control value and concentrate now on the first factors and what this process costs the customer internally"* (Person 3, pos. 262). The revised business process model construct aligns with expert preferences and emphasizes detailed time and day orientation. In particular, the discussed process is now based on working days and focuses on essential factors such as working time and costs, the latter serving as processing time. *"And if I understand it correctly, we can use there, for example, a process from the customer, and we can now try to take from the upper timeline the exact time into the process planning. Until when or at what direct time can something happen"* (Person 10, pos. 55). Eliminating the complex and indefinable quality factor streamlines the model. Processes are intricately interlocked to ensure accurate day allocation within the agenda, capturing critical elements of the new process modeling. In response to expert feedback, symbols have been removed to improve visualization and sim-

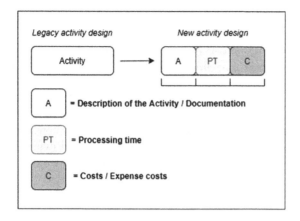

**Fig. 2.** Essential factors of activity

plicity. Activities are now grouped into three sectors, with left-side descriptions for enhanced readability, using minimal color to avoid complexity. A representative construction combining all the elements, including a Gantt chart, resulted in the following solution for a possible new process visualization (Figs. 2, 3).

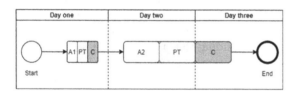

**Fig. 3.** New model combined with Gantt Chart

Top-level timeline integration provides a controlled view of the process flow, allowing detailed visualization of activity sequences, total process time, waiting time, and time between steps. The modular process view focused on individual time elements ensures controllable and predictable process cycle times, overcoming Process Time's (PT) limitations. The time-based process representation improves the understanding of process complexity and interrelationships between different levels, promoting reflection, communication, and coordination between teams. In the context of an ERP project, a time-based process representation is supportive when elements and factors are clearly defined. The refined and streamlined construct, free of confusing colors and symbols, supports ERP implementation by detailing a single process over time, facilitating faster understanding and implementation by developers and teams. *"For me, it was immediately understandable because I know BPMN, have more contact points, had it in my training, and knew roughly in its direction. But suppose you have no idea about it in general. In that case, this construct can be irritating"*

(Person 7, pos. 94). The approach has attracted interest from respondents' organizations, indicating potential acceptance and positive impact. *"In principle, I find it very interesting, but of course, I have much less experience with modeling or business process modeling, and it took me a relatively long time to get started. In retrospect, what confused me the most, in the beginning, was the mixture of everything and especially the timeline"* (Person 2, pos. 257). In summary, while supportive, the construct adheres to the principle that less complexity is more effective, mainly when supported by a robust data flow. Its cost and time-orientated nature provide a valuable starting point and overview for processes that lack comprehensive documentation and direct description.

## 5   Discussion

In supporting the new model, it was necessary to exclude the prediction of the time axis due to insufficient discussion of the origin of the data. Incomplete, incorrect, or vaguely defined existing data could compromise the validity of the process model and invite skepticism. Introducing a timeline in BPMN modeling and custom process activities can make understanding more difficult, especially when time elements such as processing time need to be accurately visualized. *"I wouldn't question BPMN modeling now because that's what the whole world uses. We don't need to discuss it because it is the best method to represent a process"* (Person 9, Pos. 115). While modeling and interaction proved successful, the lack of exploration of this aspect hindered its consideration, potentially affecting the implementation of the visualization concept. Respondents preferred fewer colors in the visualization, finding that this provided a more precise overview and enhanced the meaning of the construct. *"I found the choice of colors a little irritating at first, as I couldn't quite make out the time scale"* (Person 3, pos. 9). In terms of process applicability and efficiency, the research suggests that the construct investigated is suitable for level one process landscapes and level two processes due to their equal relevance, while detailed processes are considered too complex. The focus on project management for ERP system implementation is a practical starting point for overview and implementation. *"You can see that nicely in the model now after understanding when what step is planned in the process!"* (Person 9, pos. 220) As all the experts in the focus group discussion share the same company and perspective, the results specifically reflect the opinions within this environment. The paper focuses on the first process construct as an example, selected to provide meaningful results based on the author's theoretical and technological process knowledge. Despite these facts, the work contributes to the basic understanding of process modeling, emphasizing supporting timelines and detailed information. The intention is to provide insight into potential approaches for new process modeling techniques.

## 6   Outlook and Limitations

This paper provides a first glimpse into the potential of process modeling for implementation, representation, and ERP projects. It suggests new research avenues for improved understanding and application. To fill research gaps, additional case studies and empirical research could identify data sets and time and cost-oriented process representations that contribute to a new construct. Exploring the potential and limitations of time-axis process modeling in ERP implementation is critical to improving effectiveness. The authors suggest refining the given model by practical implementations and additional research by measuring the improvements.

# References

1. Aloini, D., Dulmin, R., Mininno, V.: Risk management in ERP project introduction: review of the literature. Inf. Manag. **44**(6), 547–567 (2007). https://doi.org/10.1016/j.im.2007.05.004
2. Baur, N., Blasius, J. (eds.): Handbuch Methoden der empirischen Sozialforschung, 2. aufl. 2019 edn. Springer, Wiesbaden (2019). https://doi.org/10.1007/978-3-658-21308-4
3. Chinosi, M., Trombetta, A.: BPMN: an introduction to the standard. Comput. Stand. Interfaces **34**(1), 124–134 (2012). https://doi.org/10.1016/j.csi.2011.06.002
4. Corradini, F., et al.: A guidelines framework for understandable BPMN models. Data Knowl. Eng. **113**, 129–154 (2018). https://doi.org/10.1016/j.datak.2017.11.003
5. Finney, S., Corbett, M.: ERP implementation: a compilation and analysis of critical success factors. Bus. Process. Manag. J. **13**(3), 329–347 (2007). https://doi.org/10.1108/14637150710752272
6. Halim, R.M.A., Arafeh, M., Sweis, G., Sweis, R.: Critical success factors for enterprise resource planning systems from the stakeholders' perspective: the case of Jordan. Mod. Appl. Sci. **13**(1), 106 (2018). https://doi.org/10.5539/mas.v13n1p106
7. Klaus, H.: What is ERP? Inf. Syst. Front. **2**(2), 141–162 (2000). https://doi.org/10.1023/A:1026543906354
8. Kouamé, S., Hafsi, T., Oliver, D., Langley, A.: Creating and sustaining stakeholder emotional resonance with organizational identity in social mission-driven organizations. Acad. Manag. J. **65**(6), 1864–1893 (2022). https://doi.org/10.5465/amj.2018.1143
9. Kuckartz, U.: Qualitative Inhaltsanalyse: Methoden, Praxis, Computerunterstützung. Grundlagentexte Methoden, Beltz Juventa, Weinheim and Basel, 4. auflage edn. (2018). http://www.beltz.de/de/nc/verlagsgruppe-beltz/gesamtprogramm.html?isbn=978-3-7799-3682-4
10. Kurbel, K.: Enterprise Resource Planning und Supply Chain Management in der Industrie: Von MRP bis Industrie 4.0, 8., vollst. überarb. und erw. auflage edn. De Gruyter-Studium, De Gruyter Oldenbourg, Berlin and Boston (2016)
11. Lemos, B., Joia, L.A.: Relevant factors for tacit knowledge transfer within organizations: an exploratory study. Gestão Prod. **19**, 233–246 (2012)
12. Leopold, H., Mendling, J., Gunther, O.: Learning from quality issues of BPMN models from industry. IEEE Softw. **33**(4), 26–33 (2016). https://doi.org/10.1109/MS.2015.81
13. Mandal, P., Gunasekaran, A.: Issues in implementing ERP: a case study. Eur. J. Oper. Res. **146**(2), 274–283 (2003). https://doi.org/10.1016/S0377-2217(02)00549-0

14. Nagpal, S., Khatri, S.K., Kumar, A.: Comparative study of ERP implementation strategies. In: 2015 Long Island Systems, Applications and Technology, pp. 1–9. IEEE (2015). https://doi.org/10.1109/LISAT.2015.7160177
15. Pankaja, P.K.: Effective use of Gantt chart for managing large scale projects: a publication of the American association of cost engineers. ProQuest Cost Eng. 14–21 (2005). https://www.proquest.com/scholarly-journals/effective-use-gantt-chart-managing-large-scale/docview/220442584/se-2
16. ProductPlan: Gantt chart: what is a Gantt chart (2023). https://www.productplan.com/glossary/gantt-chart/
17. Raedts, I., Petković, M., Usenko, Y.S., van der Werf, J.M., Groote, J.F., Somers, L.: Transformation of BPMN models and behaviour analysis: conference paper. DBLP 1–12 (2007). https://www.researchgate.net/publication/221250389_Transformation_of_BPMN_Models_for_Behaviour_Analysis
18. Ranjan, S., Jha, V.K., Pal, P.: Literature review on ERP implementation challenges. Int. J. Bus. Inf. Syst. 21(3), 388 (2016). https://doi.org/10.1504/IJBIS.2016.074766
19. Rubenstein, A.H., Harmon, R.L., Peterson, L.D., Noori, H.: Focus: Managing Technology: Managing the Dynamics of New Technology: Issues in Manufacturing Management. Managements Publications (1990). https://www.proquest.com/openview/e97dbd8dc722e074a94c525ac1c54772/1?pq-origsite=gscholar&cbl=26142
20. Schwarz, L.: 6 key phases of an ERP implementation plan. ORACLE NETSUITE (2022). https://www.netsuite.com/portal/resource/articles/erp/erp-implementation-phases.shtml
21. Stroppi, L.J.R., Chiotti, O., Villarreal, P.D.: Extending BPMN 2.0: method and tool support. In: Dijkman, R., Hofstetter, J., Koehler, J. (eds.) BPMN 2011. LNBIP, vol. 95, pp. 59–73. Springer, Heidelberg (2011). https://doi.org/10.1007/978-3-642-25160-3_5
22. Wagner, K.W.: Performance Excellence: Der Praxisleitfaden zum effektiven Prozessmanagement, 3. auflage edn. Hanser, München (2019). https://doi.org/10.3139/9783446461932
23. Wilson, J.M.: Gantt charts: a centenary appreciation. Eur. J. Oper. Res. 149(2), 430–437 (2003). https://doi.org/10.1016/S0377-2217(02)00769-5

# Knowledge in Business and Organisation

# Approach to Measuring Organizational Performance from the Perspective of Intellectual Capital

Angela Bustamante[1]([✉]), Dario Liberona[2], and Roberto Ferro[1]

[1] Universidad Distrital Francisco José de Caldas, Bogotá, Colombia
{aibustamantea,rferro}@udistrital.edu.co
[2] Seinajoki University of Applied Sciences, Seinäjoki, Finland
dario.liberona@seamk.fi

**Abstract.** Organizational performance is perceived as the performance of each member of it; aligned to the fulfillment of objectives through the application of best practices in the development of each activity within the organization [1]. This is considered one of the main factors for decision-making in favor of compliance with the strategy and definition of improvement actions [2]. For its measurement and in accordance with the environmental conditions, models are sought that integrate human potential variables such as intellectual capital since it has a strong influence on performance [3]. In accordance with the above and given that a measurement model that includes intellectual capital variables is not evident, an organizational performance measurement tool is proposed that takes these variables into account through the use of fuzzy logic. To do this, the system variables are established, based on techniques for their prioritization; The parameters of each variable and the rules for the tool are defined that are finally validated in the study organization (IT department of the Universidad Distrital Frnacisco José de Caldas). As a result, the relevance of the proposed tool is identified, concluding that through it important intangible factors are adopted in the performance of an organization, making visible specific internal conditions that affect the behavior of personnel and in this way generating improvement strategies.

**Keywords:** Organizational performance · Intellectual capital · Measurement

## 1 Introduction

The measurement of organizational performance is identified as a process of group or individual verification of the fulfillment of goals [1]. From this, development plans are proposed for improvement [4]. According to Gómez, Balkin & Cardy, performance measurement includes 3 factors: identification, measurement and management of the performance of the members of the organization [5].

Human talent is a fundamental part of the performance measurement process, which is why certain factors such as high staff turnover generate difficulties in optimal compliance with the organizational strategy [6].

© The Author(s), under exclusive license to Springer Nature Switzerland AG 2024
L. Uden and I.-H. Ting (Eds.): KMO 2024, CCIS 2152, pp. 73–85, 2024.
https://doi.org/10.1007/978-3-031-63269-3_6

There are some intangible variables that affect performance, these are related to intellectual capital that affect many areas of organizations, and have a high significance for survival, growth [7] and seek to generate value for it [8], achieving the identification of factors that must be improved within the organization [9].

Using different methodologies, tools and techniques, an attempt has been made to implement the measurement of organizational performance, depending on its dimensions, grouped into objective and subjective measurements [10]. Various studies found in the last decade use measurement tools for intangible variables such as: Kaplan and Norton balanced scorecard, CMI-IRIS methodology, performance indicators, evaluation of work performance, indicators, standard internal control model, among others [11–14].

Some measuring organizational performance studies that apply different methodologies give an idea of the diversity of techniques that can be used for this action and its success, according to the variables and environment of the organizations. Some of these are (Table 1):

**Table 1.** Applied techniques case studies organizational performance.

| Applied technique | Result |
|---|---|
| MECI internal control standard model | Aimed at optimizing human resources, strengthening the work capabilities of public servants, to guarantee the development of their professional and personal potential and the fulfillment of the objectives of the institutions, where different actors responsible for the goals of each area intervene, turning it into a strategic tool in the Comprehensive Management of Human Talent and in Public Management [4] |
| CMI-IRIS Methodology | A CMI is obtained, built from interrelated indicators, from different perspectives to measure the real situation of various aspects relevant to the success of the company [12] |
| Fuzzy logic | A relative importance of the attributes is assigned using Owa operators to identify and select a candidate for a specific job position [15] |
| Evaluation system:<br>• Performance planning<br>• Goal alignment<br>• Evaluation for development | The key points for a performance evaluation in organizations are defined, identifying progress and contributions of employees taking into account continuous improvement and impact [16] |

There is no standardized rule to identify the tool to apply, as it can be defined according to the conditions of each organization, so your choice will be defined according to the corresponding needs. Also, it is important to establish variables related to human capital that affect the performance of the organization such as satisfaction, workload, competencies, among others [17]. Therefore, having a tool that includes these variables in performance measurement will facilitate the review and improvement of these organizational aspects to propose better working conditions that improve the development of people and their performance within the organization.

Additionally, those tools must be found that integrate qualitative and quantitative variables given the characteristics of the research; Due to the above and to determine the most convenient technique to apply, advantages and disadvantages of different tools are identified to define the one that will be used (Table 2):

**Table 2.** Tools, methodologies and techniques for measurement

| Tool | Advantages | Disadvantages |
| --- | --- | --- |
| Single Management Progress Report Form | • Synthesis of performance information in a single report<br>• Generation of reporting culture | • Regulatory compliance and not efficiency<br>• Greater importance to the instrument than to the model<br>• Limited information obtained for decision making [18] |
| Job performance evaluation | • Optimization of human resources<br>• Strengthening work and behavioral skills | • It is focused on regulatory compliance and not on efficiency [19] |
| balanced scorecard | • Alignment of strategic indicators with the organization<br>• Learning tool | • Independent evaluation of defined indicators<br>• Subjective and abstract interpretations according to whoever is carrying out the evaluation<br>• The results can be complex to interpret [20] |
| Fuzzy logic | • Easy to implement<br>• Good results in processes that are difficult to model<br>• It is not necessary to know the mathematical model that governs its operation<br>• Simple way to reach a conclusion from ambiguous, imprecise or incomplete input information | • To model fuzzy sets, the opinion of experts is necessary<br>• When faced with a problem with a solution using a mathematical model, worse results are obtained [21] |
| Expert system | • Knowledge can be easily copied and stored, making it very difficult to lose it<br>• Problem resolution is fast | • When you have specific problems it can be difficult to program it<br>• Knowledge rules are difficult to extract [22] |

*(continued)*

**Table 2.** (*continued*)

| Tool | Advantages | Disadvantages |
|---|---|---|
| Binary comparisons | • Easy implementation<br>• Close to continuous level measurements | • Analysis takes a long time [23] |

From this approach of measuring performance as part of human perceptions, the use of models is required that generate quantitative results based on qualitative factors. Due to the above, it is determined to use the fuzzy logic technique for the construction of the measurement tool, since it facilitates the modeling of the qualitative information that will be treated in the research in an approximate way, by simulating the actions. of human reasoning in the organizational performance system based on knowledge, so that it can be treated quantitatively [24].

## 2 Methodology

In the development of the study, in the construction of the tool, the variables that will be part of it are identified and selected; Once designed, it is validated at the Universidad Distrital Francisco José de Caldas in the IT dependence of the Advanced Technology Research Network - RITA.

### 2.1 Information Collection

In this phase, a search and collection of information was carried out to identify the tool to use and the approaches to follow within the study of the concepts of performance and intellectual capital. It was determined to apply the fuzzy logic technique for the construction of the measurement tool, since it facilitates the modeling of the qualitative information that will be treated in the research in an approximate way, by simulating the actions of human reasoning in the organizational performance system based in knowledge, so that it can be treated quantitatively. The concept of organizational performance on which we worked was the one defined by Chávez 2014, which defines the performance of the organization as the performance of each member in terms of meeting the objectives related to the application of best practices for the development of each activity within the organization [9]. For intellectual capital, it was defined to establish an approach in relation to the Intellectus model of Bueno 2002, where it is defined as the intangible assets that organizations possess and manage and establishes three associated elements: human capital, structural capital and relational capital [25].

### 2.2 System Parameterization

For each element that makes up intellectual capital (human capital, structural capital and relational capital), cause-effect diagrams were constructed to consolidate all the possible variables involved in the study (Fig. 1).

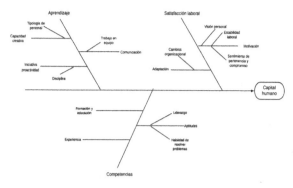

**Fig. 1.** Example human capital cause-effect diagram. (Own creation)

As a result, 49 initial variables are obtained, which were identified and defined for the study. From this list of variables and with the support of the four dependencies that are part of the Information Systems and Telecommunications Management process (GSIT) [26] of the District university, an initial prioritization was carried out, where the importance of each variable was identified in relation to organizational performance. To carry out this prioritization, a form was designed and applied to the GSIT dependencies, the objective of which was to classify the variables identified according to the degree to which each of these variables affects the performance of the members of the organization. Each of the 49 variables was rated on a scale from 1 to 4, where 1 means it does not affect organizational performance and 4 significantly affects organizational performance, according to the knowledge and experience of the experts from each dependency. According to the final consolidated grade, making a simple average of the responses obtained from each variable and, applying Pareto's law, those variables with the highest importance score were selected (Fig. 2).

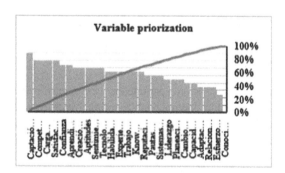

**Fig. 2.** Prioritization of variables – Pareto Diagram. (Own creation)

With the previous results, 9 initial variables are identified (Competences, Motivation, Communication, Job satisfaction, Capture and transmission of knowledge, Workload, Collaborative Learning, Trust and Internal relations between staff) and to define the final selection of variables, with support from system experts of each dependency of the GSIT process, a structural analysis is carried out to determine those influential and non-dependent variables that will be selected. This is in order to prevent the fuzzy sets that will be defined for the variables from containing other sets of the other variables.

A matrix of direct influences is created where the potential influences are identified between each of the variables through the following range:

- 0: No influence.
- 1: Weak influence.
- 2: Moderate influence.
- 3: Strong influence.

A matrix is constructed and an influence map is made using the MICMAC software (Fig. 3).

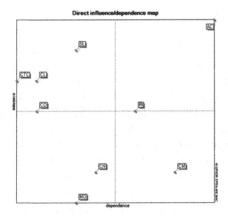

**Fig. 3.** Map of direct influences. (Own elaboration using MICMAC tool)

The variables defined to be the input in the proposed tool were the following (Table 3):

## 2.3  Tool Construction

For each defined variable, the associated parameters were determined with the help of the system experts (Linguistic value, Membership function, Measurement index) (Table 4).

To establish the value of the variables in the measurement, measurement indices were proposed that were prioritized based on a weighting identified for each one. This measurement indices proposed for each variable are presented below:

*Capture and transmission of knowledge.*

$$\frac{People\ who\ know\ procedures\ for\ capturing\ and\ transmitting\ knowledge}{Total\ number\ of\ people} \tag{1}$$

$$\frac{People\ who\ apply\ procedures\ for\ capturing\ and\ transmitting\ knowledge}{Total\ number\ of\ people} \tag{2}$$

**Table 3.** Variables defined.

| Name | Description |
|---|---|
| Capture and transmission of knowledge | Procedures through which the organization generates and transmits knowledge among its members |
| Competences | Knowledge that the person has about the things that help their work development, achieving good performance |
| Workload | Set of psychophysical requirements to which the worker is subjected throughout his or her working day |
| Work satisfaction | Degree of connection and participation in tasks, based on a good balance between personal contributions and compensations |

*Competences*

$$\frac{People\ with\ certifications\ and\ /or\ studies\ related\ to\ their\ position}{Total\ number\ of\ people} \tag{3}$$

$$\frac{People\ with\ certifications\ and\ /or\ additional\ studies\ not\ related\ to\ their\ position}{Total\ number\ of\ people} \tag{4}$$

$$\frac{People\ with\ experience\ in\ other\ sectors\ related\ to\ their\ position}{Total\ number\ of\ people} \tag{5}$$

$$\frac{People\ with\ experience\ in\ other\ sectors\ not\ related\ to\ their\ position}{Total\ number\ of\ people} \tag{6}$$

*Workload*

$$\frac{People\ who\ have\ expressed\ dissatisfaction\ with\ the\ volume\ of\ work}{Total\ number\ of\ people} \tag{7}$$

$$\frac{People\ with\ frequent\ delays\ in\ the\ delivery\ of\ their\ tasks\ or\ response\ to\ requests}{Total\ number\ of\ people} \tag{8}$$

$$\frac{People\ who\ have\ reported\ fatigue\ recurrently\ during\ the\ work\ day}{Total\ number\ of\ people} \tag{9}$$

**Table 4.** Example defined parameters variable *Capture and transmission of knowledge*

| Variable | Parameters |
|---|---|
| Capture and transmission of knowledge | **Measurement index**<br>U1 = Level of knowledge acquisition and transmission<br>**linguistic value**<br>Non-existent, Standardized, Implemented<br>**Membership function**<br>Non-existent |

$$f(x) = \begin{cases} 1, & x \leq 0,045 \\ \frac{0,45-x}{0,405}, & 0,045 \leq x \leq 0,45 \\ 0, & x \geq 0,45 \end{cases}$$

Standardized

$$f(x) = \begin{cases} 0, & x \leq 0,05 \\ \frac{x-0,05}{0,4} & 0,05 \leq x \leq 0,45 \\ 1, & 0,45 \leq x \leq 0,55 \\ \frac{0,95-x}{0,4} & 0,55 \leq x \leq 0,95 \\ 0, & x \geq 0,95 \end{cases}$$

Implemented

$$f(x) = \begin{cases} 0, & x \leq 0,55 \\ \frac{x-0,55}{0,4}, & 0,55 \leq x \leq 0,95 \\ 1, & x \geq 0,95 \end{cases}$$

$$\frac{People \ who \ have \ used \ leisure \ time \ in \ the \ development \ of \ heir \ work}{Total \ number \ of \ people} \tag{10}$$

*Work satisfaction*

$$\frac{People \ who \ feel \ comfortable \ with \ the \ activities \ they \ are \ doing \ at \ work}{Total \ number \ of \ people} \tag{11}$$

$$\frac{People \ with \ a \ feeling \ of \ stability \ and \ growth \ in \ the \ organization}{Total \ number \ of \ people} \tag{12}$$

$$\frac{People \ who \ see \ themselves \ continuing \ in \ the \ organization \ in \ the \ medium \ term}{Total \ number \ of \ people} \tag{13}$$

$$\frac{People\ feel\ comfortable\ with\ their\ work\ team}{Total\ number\ of\ people} \tag{14}$$

$$\frac{People\ feel\ comfortable\ with\ the\ working\ conditions\ of\ the\ job}{Total\ number\ of\ people} \tag{15}$$

Additionally, the structure of the fuzzy logic system and the fuzzy rules of the system are defined, based on the knowledge and expertise of the group of people who are part of the coordination of the department where the tool was validated. To define the rules, the combination of all possible linguistic values of each input variable was carried out and the result value of the output variable for each combination was defined, as seen in the example below (Fig. 4 and Table 5):

**Table 5.** Example system rules

| Capture and trans-mission of knowledge | Competences | Workload | Work satisfaction | Organizational performance |
|---|---|---|---|---|
| Non-existent | Basic | Inadequate | Low | Not satisfactory |
| Non-existent | Basic | Inadequate | Half | Not satisfactory |
| Non-existent | Basic | Inadequate | High | Not satisfactory |
| Non-existent | Basic | Adequate | Low | Not satisfactory |

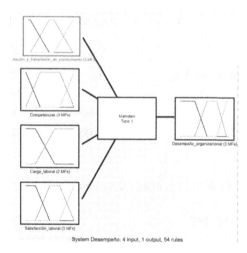

**Fig. 4.** Structure of the fuzzy logic system for organizational performance. (Own creation)

Finally, the scenarios are identified for each interval of the values resulting from the measurement (Fig. 5).

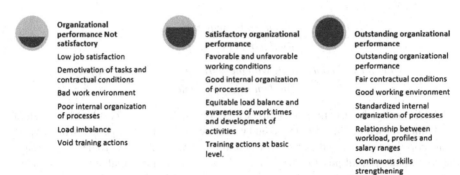

**Fig. 5.** Proposed organizational performance scenarios. (Own creation)

## 2.4 Tool Validation

The programming of the rules was carried out in the Matlab fuzzy Logic toolbox, (software provided by the Universidad Distrital Francisco José de Caldas, the institution has a full Academic Headcount (TAH) license for MATLAB, Simulink, and complementary products). To validate the tool, through a form with 15 questions associated with the proposed measurement indices of each input variable, it is applied to all members of the department (11 people) and based on their responses, the results and the values of each variable and the final performance value were established. Finally, performance improvement strategies are proposed according to the result obtained from the application (Tables 6 and 7).

**Table 6.** Initial results.

| Variable | Total | Result value |
|---|---|---|
| Capture and transmission of knowledge | 0,724 | Standardized |
| Competences | 0,705 | Necessary |
| Workload | 0,495 | Inadequate |
| Work satisfaction | 0,655 | Half |

**Table 7.** Organizational performance results.

| Organizational performance result | linguistic value |
|---|---|
| 0,654 | Satisfactory |

# 3   Results and Discussion

For the dependency, a result of 0.654 was obtained, which means that it has satisfactory organizational performance. From this result it can be inferred that in the Advanced Technology Research Network there are knowledge transfer processes known to most people, however, they are not fully implemented; The job satisfaction of the contractors is at a medium level, where satisfaction with the activities carried out in each position and the work team prevails, however, there is disagreement with the contractual conditions. On the other hand, only some people feel that they will have job stability and less than 40% project themselves to work in a dependency in the medium term. With respect to the workload, it is confirmed that there is a high volume of work for some positions and that for that same proportion there are delays in the delivery of tasks. Finally, in terms of competencies, contractors are sufficiently prepared to perform their duties at the level of knowledge and experience and additionally, there are internal initiatives to strengthen contractors' capabilities.

According to the above, some strategies are proposed to support the improvement of the results of the indices and input variables, which will generate an improvement in the final result:

- It is proposed to evaluate the existing knowledge transfer processes and additionally, include a dissemination, training and monitoring activity of said processes, since currently only some people are applying these, this will support the development of the functions and the generation of knowledge within the agency.
- It is necessary to carry out an evaluation of the loads of the roles within the department in order to establish priority activities that take more time to develop, in this way the number of resources that will be allocated can be equitably assigned. Will be required for its execution, which will support the balance of responsibilities internally, achieving a reduction in delays in the delivery of tasks and projects.
- It is important to continue with the training and development of personnel so that competencies are generated in accordance with the requirements of each position. Therefore, it is proposed to strengthen these activities with internal training actions in which each contractor can explain to their work team the activities they carry out every day so that they can rely on a member in cases where it is required and at the same time. When a retirement or change of personnel occurs for some reason, work can continue normally.

# 4   Conclusions

The selection of the technique for the development of the tool was made based on the characteristics of the study environment and validation of the tool, where qualitative variables that are related to the development of the person within the organization pre-vailed, including their satisfaction, skills, workload, among others. Due to the above, a tool was defined that will facilitate the understanding of the qualitative values of the variables in a quantitative way to facilitate their interpretation.

In the study carried out, for the identification and prioritization of variables and in the construction and validation of the tool, it is essential to have the concept and support of the system experts when the corresponding data is not available, since at the same time Not having historical data is a convenient way to model reality according to its characteristics and taking into account the appropriate variables and parameters for the measurement tool.

According to the result obtained in the validation in the Advanced Technology Research Network dependency, there is a satisfactory level of performance, so it could be inferred that there are adequate levels of the tool variables. However, carrying out a specific review of each variable index, some were found that must be studied and actions established for their improvement. For example, the issue of workload is a variable to study since it was found that there are some people who have a greater workload, causing delays in the completion of activities and projects, causing it to not be adjusted equitably. The assignment of responsibilities.

The conditions proposed for this tool are initial and can be evaluated and optimized according to different work techniques, for example, it can be validated which membership function will be appropriate to achieve the best results.

The designed and validated measurement tool is based on the measurement of organizational performance from the use of intellectual capital variables and the definition of fuzzy sets applied to IT departments of public higher education institutions, since its validation was carried out in a structure with these particularities, so it is recommended that to apply this model to any other type of organization, the defined factors appropriate to its environment be adjusted.

The measurement indices that have been used to evaluate each input variable can be validated and adjusted to the conditions of each organization, so the application form may be different.

The proposed measurement tool is based on the measurement of organizational performance with characteristics of the study organization and the results obtained are aligned with reality, so it is recommended that, to apply this model to any other type of organization, the defined factors are adjusted and appropriate to their environment.

# References

1. Chávez, A.: Performance management in educational organizations. Horizonte de la Ciencia, pp. 75–81 (2014)
2. Latin American and Caribbean Institute of Economic and Social Planning, Performance Indicators in the public sector, Santiago de Chile: ECLAC (2005)
3. Ibarra, M., Hernandez, F.: The influence of intellectual capital on the performance of small and medium manufacturing companies in Mexico: The case of Baja California. Innovar **29**, 79–96 (2019)
4. Arenas, Liévano, M.: The evaluation of the work performance of public servants in Colombia (2017). [Online]. Available: https://repository.usta.edu.co/bitstream/handle/11634/10452/Arenaspaula2017.pdf
5. Gómez Mejía, L., Balkin, D., Cardy, R.: Human Resources Management. Pearson, Madrid (2016)
6. Benavides, I.: Personnel turnover and its high impact on company productivity (2015). [Online]. Available: https://repository.unimilitar.edu.co/bitstream/handle/10654/7395/ROTACI%c3%93N%20DE%20PERSONAL%20Y%20SU%20HIGH%20IMPACTO%20EN%

20LA%20PRODUCTIVIDAD%20DE%20LAS%20EMPRESAS%20-%20Ivan%20Bena
vides..pdf?sequence=1&isAllowed=y

7. Fernández, D., Guevara, G., Dávila, T., Cruz, J.: Intellectual capital as a factor of organizational performance in Micro and Small Enterprises. Comuni@cción, vol. 13, pp. 63–73 (2022). Author, F., Author, S., Author, T.: Book title. 2nd edn. Publisher, Location (1999)
8. Rodríguez, E.R., Pedraja, L.M., Araneda, C.A., Muñoz, C.P.: Relationships between the phases of the knowledge management process in academic units. Technological Information **33**(1), 49–56 (2022)
9. Pulido, J., Muñoz, F.: Knowledge management, critical success factor in organizational performance. Criterio Libre **18**, 131–149 (2020)
10. Barradas, M., Rodríguez, J., Maya, I.: Organizational performance. A theoretical review of its dimensions and form of measurement. J. Stud. Acco. Admin. Info. Technol. **10** (2021)
11. Kaplan, R., Norton, D.: Balanced Scorecard, Harvard Business School Press (2000)
12. Matilla, M., Chalmeta, R.: Methodology for the implementation of a business performance measurement system. Technological Information 119–126 (2007)
13. Machorro, F., Romero, M.: Proposal for a Self-Assessment Instrument for Organizational Performance in Public Institutions of Higher Education in Mexico, pp. 3–10. Universidad Formación (2017)
14. Mendez, J., Mendez, M.: The balanced scorecard and its effect on the performance of organizations. Espacios **42**, 66–77 (2021)
15. Delgado, M., Cofré, F.: Proposal for a model for quantifying work performance using fuzzy logic. XII Spanish Congress on technologies and fuzzy logic 183–188 (2004)
16. Montoya, A.: Performance evaluation as a tool for the analysis of human capital. Future Vision (2009)
17. Bautista, R., Cienfuegos, R., Aguilar, E.: Job performance from a theoretical perspective. Valor Added 109–121 (2020)
18. Public function: Instructions for entering and completing the single FURAG management progress report form (2019)
19. Presidency of the Republic: Guide for the evaluation of job performance. Bogota (2020)
20. Kaplan, R., Norton, D.: Balanced Scorecard. Harvard Business School Press (2000)
21. Feltan, A., Caballero, A.: Principles of Fuzzy Logic (2016)
22. Badaró, S., Ibañez, L., Agüero, M.: Expert Systems: Fundamentals, Methodologies and Applications. Science and Technology 349–364 (2013)
23. Morosini, E.: Thurstone's Psychological Scaling (2012). [On-line]. Available: https://cupdf.com/document/escala-de-thurstone.html
24. Medina, S., Zuluaga, E., López, D., Granda, F.: Approach to the measurement of organizational intellectual capital applying fuzzy logic systems. Cuadernos de administración 35–68 (2010)
25. Bueno, E., et al.: Intellectus Model: Measurement and management of intellectual capital. Madrid (2011)
26. Universidad Distrital Francisco José de Caldas: Management of Information Systems and Telecommunications (GSIT). [Online]. Available: http://planeacion.udistrital.edu.co:8080/sigud/pa/gsit

# Food Safety Management Systems: European and Asian Approach

Roma Panwar[1] and Magdalena Marczewska[2]([⊠])

[1] Taipei Medical University, Taipei, Taiwan
[2] Faculty of Management, University of Warsaw, Warsaw, Poland
mmarczewska@wz.uw.edu.pl

**Abstract.** Food safety management systems (FSMS) aim to prevent food safety outbreaks. However, despite implementation of FSMS, food industries fail to create a food safety culture (FSC). Purpose of this study is to understand the FSMS of developing and developed countries on an example of Indian and European ready to eat food industries. Analytical research approach was adopted to understand the issues faced by industries in implementation of FSMS. Research methodology was comprised of desk research and case studies. It also includes the interviews of food safety professionals. This study highlights the need of FSC in food industries. FSMS can be implemented anywhere but effectiveness can only be guaranteed with FSC, and associated knowledge and awareness Findings emphasized the importance of transparency, knowledge and commitment from involved stakeholders to prevent the rising food safety issues.

**Keywords:** Food Safety Culture · Food Safety Management System · Quality Management System · HACCP · ISO22000 · Knowledge

## 1 Introduction

Food is imperative for life. It has a significant contribution in human existence. Safe food supply supports country's economy, trade and tourism and facilitates sustainable development. Billions of peoples' lives are in jeopardy due to rising food safety issues. Even in the 21st century, these issues have not diminished. In the past, economic disasters had happened due to the consumption of contaminated food that resulted due to deliberate or unintended personal behavior, and also government non-success to defense food safety. To protect consumers and mitigate such issues, regular monitoring and rapid detection of contaminants and pathogen is required. Safe and nutritious food strengthens the system and health of society [1]. Countries share concernment pertaining to food safety as international food commerce, travel activity of people and livestock across the border has increased. Governments world-wide are increasing their efforts to strengthen food safety standards whilst enhancing and updating regulatory standards at national and international level. However, situations in some of the emergent nations in Asia–Pacific region remains far from adequate. One of the major concerns at a global scale is to provide safe ready to eat food (RTE) in ever competitive markets. Emerging pathogens

© The Author(s), under exclusive license to Springer Nature Switzerland AG 2024
L. Uden and I.-H. Ting (Eds.): KMO 2024, CCIS 2152, pp. 86–99, 2024.
https://doi.org/10.1007/978-3-031-63269-3_7

are becoming a concern too. In the WHO European region, it was approximated that more than 23 million people fall ill from contaminated food each year, resulting in 4654 deaths. RTE foods are also classified as major cause of food borne illness and are often contaminated by food handlers. The food standard agency (FSA, UK) defines RTE as any food for consumption without further heating or processing. This definition is applicable for both pre-wrapped and open food [2]. Generally, **due to the lack of awareness, knowledge** and resources unavailability, products are exposed to several contaminants at various stages. In most of the countries, RTE street foods are manufactured in open environment with less efficient resources. RTE meals are increasing popularity among consumers due to the benefit of consumption and ease of preparation, including consumer interest components [2]. With new food products getting into market every day, list of RTEs is getting longer and longer [2, 3] and so does the threat of contamination. Developing countries struggle to enforce food safety standards despite having a legal framework in place. Factors such as rising population of working women, expanding millennial population, busy market schedules and on the go consumption habits are expected to sustain revenue growth of global RTE food products' markets.

This study was conducted to understand the differences of FSMS in developed and developing countries, with the focus on the role of knowledge, knowledge sharing, and awareness. India was chosen as a developing country and Europe was chosen as a benchmark to understand the FSMS structure of developed country and European countries' FSMS structure. This study emphasizes **that knowledge availability and sharing, awareness**, attitude, and willingness to follow safe food practices among stakeholders can influence food systems in a positive manner. Objective of this study is to understand the importance of FSMS in food industries and to present best practices for successful implementation, on the example of RTE food industries. FSMS is a crucial tool to mitigate lot of serious issues occurring in food systems, however all stakeholders have an important role to play for its successful implementation. Following research questions (RQ) are addressed in this study:

RQ1: How can food industries evaluate the effectiveness of FSMS?
RQ2: How to create FSC and what role consumers play with regards to food safety?
RQ3: How governing and maintaining FSMS helps in food security of any nation?

The next section of the paper presents a literature review on quality and food safety management and challenges of implementing food safety management systems. Then research method along with research procedure are presented followed by research results. The paper ends with an extensive presentation and discussion of research conclusions, and elaboration on practical implications and best practices.

## 2 Literature and Background

### 2.1 Quality and Food Safety Management

Quality Management is the requisite for any organization to thrive. It is the management and collection of all activities that can assist in the production of quality products within the organization. It provides complete idea how any industry should collaborate to formulate and convey plans to ensure high quality services. Any industry must adhere to a set of protocols to achieve a desired level of excellence. Protocols for quality management system (QMS) scrutinize industries' policies and shift them for advancement. A QMS should be developed, established, and implemented by every industry to achieve customer focused result. However, for food industries, FSMS is imperative which includes good hygiene practices (GHP), good manufacturing practices (GMP), and HACCP policies. Quality and food safety management systems (QFSMS) deliver customer focused products which are safe and of high quality.

Objective of QFSMS is to measure and verify each component in a timely manner and achieve success. It helps in improving quality of services and products to ensure that these are safe and of supreme quality. ISO 9001:2015 has put together few standards to evaluate the QMS of any organization [4]. Such standards assist organizations for effective implementation of various managements systems which are necessary for creating confidence among customers and for business growth. On the other hand, objective of FSMS is to provide safe food products to consumers and to ensure that food safety standards regulated by government are met at all stages of food chain. ISO 9001:2015 can help in implementation of FSMS because food safety depends on the quality of processes and products. FSMS is a comprehensive process which covers a standard review of food industry [4]. By implementing FSMS in food industries, it is easy to inspect that all food elements are of great quality and suitable for public health. Significant attribute of having FSMS in place is business protection. It also enhances productivity. Implementing and maintaining an authentic FSMS is a tedious task but quite fruitful. HACCP (Hazard Analysis Critical Control Point) is the foundation for all FSMS. It is obligatory for food industries to implement a HACCP based FSMS in Europe and India as well. Need of HACCP arose from the exigency to provide safe food for NASA's astronaut because unsafe food could have led to interruptions and disaster mission. Pillsbury participated in the space program along with NASA and Nautical Research laboratory. This project was called "Production and testing of food". Aim of the project was to develop a code of conduct by which they could control and test raw materials, environment, personnel, production process, storage, distribution. It was to ensure that final packaged product do not require any additional test beyond monitoring. HACCP helps in analyzing all possible risks pertaining to food safety and assist with control measures to diminish them. HACCP allows an efficient government oversight, as record keeping (one of the 7 principles of HACCP) helps food safety authorities to investigate how well a food industry is complying with food regulations over a period. 7 principles of HACCP are as follows [5]: hazard analysis, identification of critical control points (CCPs), establishment of critical limits, monitoring of CCPs, corrective action for CCPs, verification, record-keeping (documentation).

For HACCP implementation, there is a requirement of competent HACCP team who can lay out a plan and can describe the products and its intended use. There are various certification programs available worldwide to enhance knowledge with regard to HACCP implementation and maintenance. Process flow diagrams should be prepared and verified at each step of food chain to prevent hazards from entering into the food chain. If any deviation occurs, then cause shall be determined, control points and critical limits should be evaluated to prevent such deviations to occur in future [5].

An effective FSMS comes under the requirement of the, among others, below mentioned laws and regulations:

1) ISO22000:2018 (International Organization for Standardization) – It follows the structure and process of ISO 9001(QMS) and integrates it with food safety following the principle of HACCP, developed by Codex Alimentarius Commission (CODEX). Latest version was amended in 2018 [6].
2) BRC (British Retail Consortium) global standard for food safety – BRC was formed in January 1992. In 1998, BRC had produced the first edition of the BRC food technical standard and protocol for food suppliers. In 2016, BRC global standards were acquired by LGC (Laboratory of the Government Chemist) group so that they are no longer controlled and managed by BRC only. Since then, BRC global standards for food safety is one of the most popular certification standards and has been adopted by food manufacturers across the world [7].
3) The Food Safety Act 1990 (UK) – It provides framework for wide ranging legislation on food safety and consumer protection in Great Britain. Primarily focus of the act is that food must comply with food safety requirements, must be "of the nature, substance and quality demanded", and must be correctly labelled [8].
4) U.S. Food and Drug Administration (FDA) introduced Food Safety Modernization Act (FSMA) on January 4, 2011, which focuses on U.S. food supply to be safe by controlling or preventing contamination in food supply. Main objective of FSMA to transform the nation's food system by shifting the focus from responding to situation to prevent it [9].
5) World Health Organization (WHO) assists by developing scientific risk assessments to define safe exposure level which forms the foundation for developing international and national food safety standards to ensure safe and fair-trade practices.
6) Food Safety and Standard Authority of India (FSSAI) has been established under food safety and standards act, 2006, which integrates various acts and orders that have handled food safety related issues till now in various ministries and department. Mission of FSSAI is to achieve excellence in the formulation of food safety standards based on modern science and to regulate the food sectors in a responsive and efficient manner [10].
7) EU Food safety control policies – General Food Law i.e. (Regulation (EC) No 178/2002 of European Parliament and of the Council) formulates principles and requirements of food legislation, establishment of EFSA and procedures with regards to food safety [11].

Furthermore, ISO22000:2018 is also based on basic prerequisite programs (GMP, GHP, HACCP) required for food safety regulations in different countries across the world. ISO22000:2018 is internationally accepted as it plans out the requirement of FSMS quite clearly. It provides information how an organization can control food safety hazards and also demonstrates the ability of organizations to control food safety hazards [6].

Main objectives of ISO22000:2018 include:

1) Harmonization of requirements of FSMS globally.
2) Expedite the application of standard for implementation of FSMS (consistent with ISO9001 and 14001) [4, 5].

3) Improving the effectiveness of FSMS and customer satisfaction.

In September 2005, ISO had customized QMS within ISO 22000 by incorporating HACCP principles. ISO 22000:2005 was published in 2005 and it has been revised in 2018 (now known as ISO 22000:2018). ISO 22000:2018 has international substratum in the global market and guarantees globally food safe chain whilst adopting internationally harmonized system [13]. Earlier ISO 22000 was not recognized by Global food safety initiative but now ISO 22000:2018 comes with some refinement like detailed pre-requisite programs (PRPs). It is based on the principle of risk-based thinking [7].

FSMS established by ISO22000:2018 consists of ISO 9001 and HACCP. It contains series of internationally approved requests to fulfill the requirement of each organization within the global food chain [14].

### 2.2  Challenges of Implementing Food Safety Management Systems

Impediment in FSMS implementation diverges from one place to other. Individual businesses have different objectives and work culture. There are many obstacles needed to be overcome for effective implementation of FSMS. Most critical is lack of knowledge and awareness. For an effective FSMS, basic hygiene practices shall be in place. PRPs form the foundation of it. Food safety issues mainly occur due to the failure of PRPs, that can be solved by proper training, education, knowledge sharing and awareness.

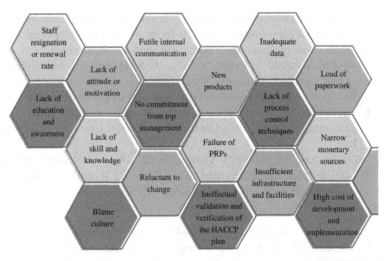

**Fig. 1.**  Challenges and barriers in FSMS implementation based [18–28].

In 2010 study Ball et al. indicated that socio-physiological factor impacts the implementation of HACCP programme [15, 16]. In 2011, Wilcock and collaborators have stated that lot of problems were encountered by owners, senior managers, food safety personnel and production workers while implementing FSMS [16, 17]. In 2015, Chen et al., have highlighted that adversities faced on implementing non-regulatory FSMS were in the area of finance and resources [18]. An extensive list of challenges and barriers in FSMS implementation is presented in Fig. 1.

For successful implementation of FSMS, every organization should try to overcome such issues regardless of their size.

## 3  Materials and Methods

This research was based on desk research and qualitative research methods, namely, case studies, interviews and surveys. Desk research was conducted to gain crucial information about food safety, ready to eat food markets and latest trend in food industries. Wilmar, Haldiram and Nestle were chosen for the case studies as units of analysis. This choice was motivated by companies' characteristics and approach towards FSMS, as well as markets on which these companies operate. Following this study focus, the purpose of case study analysis was to understand the structure of FSMS in different kind of food industries of Europe and India, especially RTE food industries. Analytical research design approach was used to understand the causes and effect of unsafe food practices. Information and data for case studies were collected from company websites, published papers, government reports and from other internet sources. Data from government websites were used to understand the food safety acts and regulations in India and Europe. Food industries' websites were reviewed to understand food safety objectives of chosen food industries.

In order to gather more information about FSMS characteristics in RTE food industries and catch differences between European and Indian systems, one semi-structured interview was conducted via Zoom with Quality Head of Wilmar, India to understand the importance of FSMS and to find out existing gaps compared with European standards, including: knowledge and awareness level, lack of resources, lack of attitude and lack of motivation. The interview was over an hour long and was recorded, transcribed and anonymized.

Moreover, questionnaires with 20 questions related to the essential aspects that are required for implementation of **FSMS (e.g., food handlers' knowledge and attitude towards food safe practices,** management commitment, availability of resources and funds for FSMS) were prepared and sent out by e-mail to experts, i.e., food safety auditor (TUV, India) and R&D head (Haldiram, India), to support and validate desk research, case studies and interviews. The research procedure is presented in Fig. 2.

All samples were chosen purposefully in order to address research questions. Basic information on selected case studies can be found below.

Case Study 1 – Haldiram is an Indian multinational company. Origins of Haldiram's can be traced back to a small namkeen shop in Bikaner founded by Ganga Bishan Agarwal. Modest shop gained popularity and augmented to meet an increasing demand for its unique tasting Bhujia. Further his grandson Mr. Agrawal navigated the business towards the heights it has reached today. First full production unit was opened to launch a delectable variety of savories, sweets, and beverages to the market.

Success of this journey led this unit expand and evolve as a brand that is an integral part of every Indian household. Goal of Haldiram is to protect the resources and relationships upon which business depends, by promoting environmental and socially

**Fig. 2.** Research procedure

responsible practices across value chain. Haldiram, India is also certified with various FSMS and QMS certifications including ISO 22000:2018, FSSC 22000.

In 2015, US FDA has rejected number of snacks imported from Haldiram snacks for the concerns over level of pesticides and bacteria. Among the products rejected, there were brand cookies, biscuits and wafers. However, important statement which was made during this incident by Haldiram was that "food safety standards are different in U.S. and India". Haldiram spokesperson emphasized in his statement that pesticides permitted in India may not be allowed in US as they ensure that all RTE products and other snacks are thoroughly checked through elaborate microbiological and chemical tests before being transferred to further processing and distribution. Such incidents highlight the importance of transparent communication and harmonization of international food safety standards and regulations [29].

Case Study 2 – Wilmar International Ltd. Was founded in 1991 and it is headquartered in Singapore. It encompasses the entire value chain of the agricultural commodity business. It operates an integrated sugar business across the entire value chain from sugar cane and beet plantations to the sweetener's aisle in supermarkets. It has over 500 plants and an extensive distribution network covering India, China and Indonesia and other 50 countries and regions. Wilmar is also processing, branding and distributing wide range of edible food products such as vegetable oils, snacks, bakery, dairy, soy proteins. Wilmar is ranked 192nd on the 2022 Fortune Global 500 by Fortune Magazine and Adani Wilmar ltd. India was awarded commendation certificate for significant achievement in the food safety C11 food safety awards in 2021 [30]. It is committed to provide products that meet the highest food safety standards, and their objective is to provide zero unsafe products, zero food safety product recalls, zero critical food safety audit findings. Wilmar is also certified with FSSC 22000 based on existing ISO standards [31].

Case study 3 – Nestle is a Swiss multinational food and drink processing corporation head quartered in Switzerland. Henri Nestle innovated an infant food in 1867 and in 1905, company merges with Anglo-Swiss to form Nestle Group. Quality and safety are Nestlé's top priority and also one of Nestlé's 10 corporate business principles. Nestlé's QMS guarantees food safety, compliance with quality standards and creating value for consumers. Internal QMS has been audited and verified by independent certification bodies to prove conformity to internal standards and regulatory requirements. At Nestle, they apply internationally recognized GMP to ensure quality and food safety. HACCP system is used to ensure food safety which is verified by external certification bodies against ISO standards. It is also certified with FSSC22000. Nestle follows codex guidelines. It has a strong presence across Europe and India as well [32].

## 4 Research Results

### 4.1 Characteristics of FSMS in Haldiram

Journey of Haldiram started back in 1937 with a sweet shop. Later they expanded their business. At that time, there were any strict food safety regulations in India. This case study sheds light on how differences in food safety regulations can be a problem at international level. This is illustrated by the situation when USA rejected all snacks and cookies imported from Haldiram, India mentioning that pesticides and microbial level is quite high in products, however as per Haldiram, it was under acceptable limit. Hence, this study focuses on importance of harmonization of food safety standards at international level. Another important characteristic of this case study is regarding the role of awareness, knowledge sharing and education in maintaining food safety. Haldiram has outlets of various sizes in different states of India and it is quite difficult to expect same level of awareness from all food handlers without training and education.

### 4.2 Characteristics of FSMS in Wilmar

Main characteristic of this case study is that it provides information about the importance of work culture within the organization. For this case study, quality head was interviewed. It was highly emphasized that without transparent communication and management commitment, successful implementation of FSMS is not possible. Effective communication can create an effective FSC. Another important characteristic highlights the association between food safety and security with Wilmar's objective of zero food safety recalls.

### 4.3 Characteristics of FSMS in Nestle

Nestle is a brand on which consumers trust blindly due to the reputation it made worldwide. However, even Nestle has been questioned about safety aspects several times.

This case study reveals that food safety risks and contamination will keep on occurring however research and innovations in food systems can provide solutions to deal with emerging concerns. This case study put light on other important aspects as well, for instance – strong FSMS also means transparency. In Nestle (instant noodles case), it was about complete information in labeling. This case study motivates food industries to understand the vital characteristics of FSMS. An effective FSMS can save the business and human lives.

All three case studies have quite common characteristics that focus on the importance of FSC. FSC talks about the attitude, belief, practices and values regarding food safety even when nobody is watching. Strong FSC can definitely help food industries to prevent non-compliances that otherwise impact quality, safety and legality [33].

### 4.4   Characteristics of FSMS in Indian Food industry

In India, according to FSSAI act, 2006, all food industries shall have FSMS plan [11]. Even if the food industry already has a food safety certification as ISO, they need to undergo FSSAI mandatory third-party audit. However, these are announced audits, which is a disadvantage for food industries. Some of the industries follow good practices, only when such audits are happening and it does not really contribute to the implementation of effective FSMS. To understand the real companies' performance, there shall be unplanned audits. In India, FSMS plan is imperative to achieve FSSAI certification. FSMS helps Indian food industries to measure the effectiveness of system and to identify the training needs of employees. However, it should be noted, that some companies are reluctance to show commitment when it is about investing money on resources and education of employees for effective FSMS. Moreover, there is an information inequality among different food industry actors in India, when it comes to knowledge about FSMS regulations and standards.

### 4.5   Characteristics of FSMS in European Food industry

In Europe, EU laws are harmonized by EFSA [12]. It covers risk assessment and transparent communication. Main characteristic of European food industries' FSMS is transparency. In European food industries, regulations are stringent as compared to developing countries. Characteristics of FSMS remains same in India and European countries but implementation differs in many states of India due to the culture of announced audits. It should be noted that FSMS are known by all types of food sector companies, including low enterprises and street food vendors in Europe.

## 5   Research Conclusions and Discussion

Due to globalization of food trade, it is imperative that every country mandates FSMS implementation. There is a need of creating FSC from farm to fork. Some of the developing countries face difficulty in accessing best practice technology and information. EU have entrenched industry standards and their focus is moved towards the communication regarding quality and safety aspects to stakeholders including consumers [34]. For developing countries, right infrastructure and support from government is required to ensure food safety. Existing studies talk about costs involved, benefits obtained, other barriers during implementation of FSMS. However, this study compares the FSMS of developed and developing countries. Comparison is necessary to emphasize that effective FSMS in developed countries alone cannot contribute to food security, safety, and sustainability. Basic food safe practices are crucial to prevent hazards including biological hazards to enter into food chains. Emerging concerns can also be mitigated via same approach. Effective implementation of FSMS can maintain a high quality and safe environment within food industries. Furthermore, it is stated by participants, that all national and internal FSMS is based on HACCP approach. If HACCP is followed, it is quite easy to implement FSMS. It is also highlighted that commitment from top management plays crucial role in maintenance of FSMS. If management is committed towards food safety, it will definitely motivate the employees to follow the same. Regarding the customer complaints, if there is FSC in place, it is just a five-finger exercise to prevent any critical food safety related issue. Customer complaints are a kind of feedback which helps in further improvement.

Food safety standards also talk about the importance of internal and external communication. For an effective and safe system, there is a need to cultivate FSC that invigorates the information in both ways for instance; internally with-in the teams and externally with different stakeholders. Also, internally information flow shall be both ways, from top to bottom workforce and from bottom to top [35].

Moreover, strength of transparent communication in between all the stakeholders of food industries should not be diminished. Transparency within the food system is essential to fix our food systems' issue. Food safety regulations in India are sufficient and precise, but enforcement via authorities and management is lacking. Enforcement is better in developed countries. For an effective FSMS, global harmonization of food safety regulations is imperative. No doubt, FSSAI has done a great job. They conduct regular inspections and mandatory audits which pushes food industries to follow regulations in India. However, some industries follow good practices for some particular days only and forget it for other days. New initiatives by FSSAI are quite focused on consumers' knowledge regarding food safety. Unsafe products can create chaos at bigger scale if safety standards are not followed. Food handlers are sometimes reluctance to follow basic hygiene measures considering it a tedious task. In such situations, motivation factors can really play a crucial role. For industries providing RTE food, it is vital that their employees must understand the importance of food safety. Once food is in distribution, hazards and pathogens cannot be controlled.

Surprisingly, many food industries are only focusing on achieving and gaining food safety certifications as a marketing tool to attract customers although in reality there is lack of willingness regarding implementation of FSMS; especially in catering sectors.

Quality and safety of food products both play a significant role in creating a healthy world. It is dependent on good FSMS because if food is not safe, it has no quality. Industries should not only implement FSMS just for the sake of achieving certifications, they shall indeed work on root cause analysis and hazard assessment. It is crucial to understand the processes because at the end, results achieved can definitely take food businesses to another level. There are multiple challenges, however these challenges can be overcome by management support, equal participation, clear communication, honest accountability, knowledge and awareness. Gap analysis and hazard assessment to be conducted by food safety and quality personnel to understand the real situation. Audit is a perfect mechanism to provide input and results should be accepted for improvement. Lastly but not least, consumers also play an important role in enhancing food safety. If they have the right awareness level with regard to food safe practices, they can ask questions regarding safety and quality of food products which also motivates industries to ensure the safety of products in order to retain their market place and business growth.

Moreover, research findings indicated that personnel involve in food handing plays most important role in maintaining FSMS, however management commitment is of supreme importance. Knowledge, awareness and resources availability are important aspects as well. There are strict food safety regulations in various countries including developing countries however enforcement of such regulations still to be worked upon. There are serious emerging concerns like antibiotic resistance pathogens that have entered into food systems and safe hygiene practices can prevent their prevalence. Food industries including RTE food industries are augmenting due to increasing consumer demands however industries and stakeholders need to be cautious and should ensure that industries follow FSMS rules and regulations diligently. Professionals in food industries must understand the consequences of not having an effective FSMS in place. Food safety professionals should have right competence level with regard to food safety issues to mitigate any harm. Investment on resources and training is also required to help medium and small-scale industries (RTE outlets) for strengthening food systems.

To implement FSMS successfully, industries shall have a food safety plan (FSP). FSP can ease the process of FSMS implementation. However, it is imperative for industries to do a risk assessment to understand strength and weakness in system. There shall be a competent HACCP and food safety team. Industries shall invest in best practices for instance: employees' training on quality management and food safety topics. No compromised shall be done on PRP requirements that includes GHP and GPP. Food industries shall understand that they need to create FSC whilst raising awareness via different training session. Food safety and good hygiene practices shall not be followed only for a particular day; however, it should be followed continually to improve the existing standard. The practical implications of this research are presented below as answers to the research questions posed in the introductory part.

RQ1: How can food industries evaluate the effectiveness of FSMS?

Effectiveness of FSMS can be evaluated by audits as industries can get itself prepared to prevent any food safety related concerns. Audits provide clarity if already existing FSMS is suitable or not. Competent FSMS team in any food industry can conduct audits and perform risk assessment. It is necessary that audit findings are recorded, and root-cause analysis is done to understand the issue. Regular monitoring and awareness check can be done in industries to understand if food handlers really understand their tasks. Results from monitoring and audits shall be recorded to see the performance level. Furthermore, FSMS effectiveness can also be evaluated by collecting feedback from customers. All stated ways add value to existing FSMS and provide an opportunity for continual improvement.

RQ2: How to create FSC? What role consumers' awareness and attitude play with regard to food safety?

Without awareness and education, it is not possible to bring perfection in any task. When it is about creating FSC, it is necessary that employees are provided training on needs and requirements. For instance, hand hygiene is the basic step to avoid cross-contamination. However, it has been observed that food handlers in many industries are not aware of correct hand washing steps. It is vital to tell them that hands carry germs like E. coli which is a pathogenic bacterium and has the ability to make people sick. Food is not always the main reason of food borne illness. There are other reasons like human contact and environmental contamination. Consumers should also be aware of right practices as once product is purchased, it's their responsibility to ensure safety of product. Additionally, consumers have complete right to know about their products in detail. With right awareness and knowledge, FSC can be cultivated as it will help food industries and public to follow best practices to prevent food borne illness as well as food wastage.

RQ3: How governing and maintaining FSMS helps in food security of any nation?

Implementation, maintenance, and continual improvement of FSMS can help in preventing food borne diseases. If there are less food safety concerns, there will be less food recalls and less food wastage. Food borne illness causes economic burden on nations. Effective FSMS and government support can help in reducing food borne illnesses. If safe and nutritious food is available to all the people, it means it is contributing towards food security.

## References

1. Fung, F., Wang, H.S., Menon, S.: Food safety in the 21st century. Biomed. J. **41**(2), 88–95 (2018). https://doi.org/10.1016/j.bj.2018.03.003
2. Patel, D., Rathod, R.: Ready-to-eat food perception, food preferences and food choice–a theoretical discussion. Worldwide J. Multi. Res. Dev. **3**(8), 198–205 (2017)
3. Fast, R.B.: Origins of the US breakfast cereal industry. Cereal Foods World **44**(6), 394–397 (1999)
4. International Organization for Standardization. (2015) Quality Management Systems – Requirements (ISO standard no. 9001:2015)
5. International Organization for Standardization (2015) Environmental management systems — Requirements with guidance for use (ISO standard no. 14001:2015)
6. Meghwal, M., Heddurshetti, U., Biradar, R.: Good Manufacturing Practices for Food Processing Industries: Purposes, Principles and Practical Applications, Applied Research and Production. In" Meghwal, M., Goyal, M.R., Kaneria, M.J. (eds.) Food Technology Vol. 11, Innovations in Agricultural and Biological Engineering, CRC Press, USA (2016)
7. International Organization for Standardization (2018) Food safety management systems — Requirements for any organization in the food chain (ISO standard no. 22000:2018)
8. British Retail Consortium (2015) Global standard for food safety, Issue-7, London.

9. Food Standards Agency (1990) The Food Safety Act 1990 – A Guide for Food Businesses
10. U.S. Government Publishing Office: An act to amend the Federal Food, Drug, and Cosmetic Act with respect to the safety of the food supply, 124 Stat. 3885 (2011)
11. Food Safety and Standards Act (2006) Food Safety and Standards Act, No. 34 OF 2006
12. European Parliament and the Council (2002) Regulation (EC) No 178/2002 of the European Parliament and of the Council
13. Panghal, A., Chhikara, N., Sindhu, N., Jaglan, S.: Role of food safety management systems in safe food production: a review. J. Food Safety **38**(4), e12464 (2018). https://doi.org/10.1111/jfs.12464
14. Chen, S.J., Liu, S.L., Chen, Y.Y., Chen, C.S., Yang, H.T., Chen, Y.S.E.: Food safety management systems based on ISO 22000:2018 methodology of hazard analysis compared to ISO 22000:2005. Accred. Qual. Assur. **25**(1), 23–37 (2020). https://doi.org/10.1007/s00769-019-01409-4
15. Ball, B., Wilcock, A., Aung, M.: Background factors affecting the implementation of food safety system. Food Prot. Trends **30**(2), 78–86 (2010)
16. Chaoniruthisai, P., Punnakitikashem, P., Rajchamaha, K.: Challenges and difficulties in the implementation of a food safety management system in Thailand: a survey of BRC certified food productions. Food Control **93**, 274–282 (2018). https://doi.org/10.1016/j.foodcont.2018.06.004
17. Wilcock, A., Ball, B., Fajumo, A.: Effective implementation of food safety initiatives: Managers', food safety coordinators' and production workers' perspectives. Food Control **22**(1), 27–33 (2011). https://doi.org/10.1016/j.foodcont.2010.06.005
18. Chen, E.C., Flint, S., Perry, P., Perry, M., Lau, R.: Implementation of non-regulatory food safety management schemes in New Zealand: a survey of the food and beverage industry. Food Control **47**, 569–576 (2015). https://doi.org/10.1016/j.foodcont.2014.08.009
19. Karaman, A.D., Cobanoglu, F., Tunalioglu, R., Ova, G.: Barriers and benefits of the implementation of food safety management systems among the Turkish dairy industry: a case study. Food Control **25**(2), 732–739 (2012). https://doi.org/10.1016/j.foodcont.2011.11.041
20. Milios, K., Zoiopoulos, P.E., Pantouvakis, A., Mataragas, M., Drosinos, E.H.: Techno-managerial factors related to food safety management system in food businesses. Br. Food J. **115**(9), 1381–1399 (2013). https://doi.org/10.1108/bfj-11-2011-0284
21. Tomasevic, I., Smigic, N., Djekic, I., Zaric, V., Tomic, N., Rajkovic, A.: Serbian meat industry: a survey on food safety management systems implementation. Food Control **32**(1), 25–30 (2013). https://doi.org/10.1016/j.foodcont.2012.11.046
22. Dora, M., Kumar, M., Van Goubergen, D., Molnar, A., Gellynck, X.: Food quality management system: reviewing assessment strategies and a feasibility study for European food small and medium-sized enterprises. Food Control **31**(2), 607–616 (2013). https://doi.org/10.1016/j.foodcont.2012.12.006
23. Karaman, A.D.: Food safety practices and knowledge among Turkish dairy businesses in different capacities. Food Control **26**(1), 125–132 (2012). https://doi.org/10.1016/j.foodcont.2012.01.012
24. Escanciano, C., Santos-Vijande, M.L.: Implementation of ISO-22000 in Spain: obstacles and key benefits. Br. Food J. **116**(10), 1581–1599 (2014). https://doi.org/10.1108/bfj-02-2013-0034
25. Escanciano, C., Santos-Vijande, M.L.: Reasons and constraints to implementing an ISO 22000 food safety management system: evidence from Spain. Food Control **40**, 50–57 (2014). https://doi.org/10.1016/j.foodcont.2013.11.032
26. Macheka, L., Manditsera, F.A., Ngadze, R.T., Mubaiwa, J., Nyanga, L.K.: Barriers, benefits and motivation factors for the implementation of food safety management system in the food sector in Harare Province, Zimbabwe. Food Control **34**(1), 126–131 (2013). https://doi.org/10.1016/j.foodcont.2013.04.019

27. Khalid, S.M.N.: Food safety and quality management regulatory systems in Afghanistan: policy gaps, governance and barriers to success. Food Control **68**, 192–199 (2016). https://doi.org/10.1016/j.foodcont.2016.03.022

28. Teixeira, S., Sampaio, P.: Food safety management system implementation and certification: survey results. Total Qual. Manag. Bus. Excell. **24**(3–4), 275–293 (2013). https://doi.org/10.1080/14783363.2012.669556

29. Haldirams: Haldirams Nagpur. Taste of tradition (2022). https://www.haldirams.com/. Accessed 10 Oct 2022

30. Wilmar: Wilmar (2022a). https://www.wilmar-international.com/. Accessed 10 Oct 2022

31. Wilmar: Wilmar Awards (2022b). https://www.wilmar-international.com/about-us/awards. Accessed 10 Oct 2022

32. Nestle: Nestle, good food, good life (2022). https://www.nestle.com/. Accessed 10 Oct 2022

33. Safe Food Alliance: Importance of food safety culture. https://safefoodalliance.com/management/the-importance-of-food-safety-culture/ (2019). Accessed 10 Oct 2022

34. Rahmat, S., Cheong, C.B., Abd Hamid, M.S.R.B.: Challenges of developing countries in complying quality and enhancing standards in food industries. Procedia Soc. Behav. Sci. **224**, 445–451 (2016)

35. Stier, R.F.: Communication is the basis of a food safety management system. Food Engineering, Food Safety (2014). https://www.foodengineeringmag.com/articles/91718-communication-is-the-basis-of-a-food-safety-management-system. Accessed 10 Oct 2022

# Enabling Knowledge Management Culture During the Pandemic: Preliminary for the Post-pandemic Effect

Shahrinaz Ismail[✉] [iD]

Asia Pacific University of Technology and Innovation (APU), Kuala Lumpur, Malaysia
shahrinaz.ismail@apu.edu.my

**Abstract.** A significant impact on the knowledge management (KM) initiatives is caused by the sudden change in working environment due to the global pandemic in 2020. The abrupt digital transformation has caused a lot of changes, impacting the KM initiatives in higher education institutions (HEIs). In addition to the hectic tasks of managing classes and attending meetings, faculty members were still required to perform well in research. For a university with diverse culture and level of commitment in research, there is a challenge to close the knowledge gap between the experienced researchers and the novices. The pandemic has made it more challenging, with the constant need to reach and motivate the researchers to be updated with knowledge through research activities. Hence, an investigation was performed to know how the KM activities affect the existing KM-enabled culture in the organization. The attributes of KM-enabled culture are explored to know whether they are affected by the KM on-going online activities during the pandemic. An exploratory factor analysis was conducted on the gathered data, resulting in four significant attributes of KM-enabled culture, observed still exist during the pandemic. The outcome is expected to give an input to future work on confirmatory factor analysis and post-pandemic effect.

**Keywords:** Knowledge Management · KM On-going Activities · KM-enabled Culture · Exploratory Factor Analysis · Structural Equation Modeling

## 1 Introduction

The sudden change in working environment due to the COVID-19 pandemic has caused a significant impact on the knowledge management (KM) initiatives in an institute of higher learning. Since the teaching environment has shifted from face-to-face to fully virtual, every faculty member is fully occupied with learning new tools, preparing the learning materials, and conducting online classes, on top of facing challenges working virtually from home. Due to the dire need to focus on teaching, the other tasks that came with the job position of faculty members, like research and innovation development, has been put aside. Despite that, the key performance indicators (KPIs) of the faculty members remain the same and none of the other tasks should be put aside.

© The Author(s), under exclusive license to Springer Nature Switzerland AG 2024
L. Uden and I.-H. Ting (Eds.): KMO 2024, CCIS 2152, pp. 100–111, 2024.
https://doi.org/10.1007/978-3-031-63269-3_8

For a university with diverse culture and level of commitment in research, it is a huge challenge to bridge the gap between the most renown researchers and those who were still taking baby steps in research. Foreseeing the need to motivate every faculty member to continue contributing to the research KPIs, action research was conducted to understand the impact of the KM activities that were implemented across the year. The identified issues relating to the KM on-going activities in 2020 are: constant identification of knowledge gaps in the organization and filling them by recruiting new organizational members and/or providing such knowledge to the organizational members along with the means necessary to attain it; acknowledgement and follow up of the evolution of the organization by designing new KM activities and re-designing/re-engineering the existing KM activities as deemed necessary; and the regular measurement of KM practices and the close following of any progress made.

Foreseeing the need to know whether KM activities during the pandemic could positively affect the KM-enabling culture within an institution or not, this research aims to determine the factors that contribute to the KM-enabling culture when KM activities are implemented. A conceptual model developed from literature review is produced to kick start the investigation, in which the its variables change tremendously during the data analysis stage. This paper presents the findings from exploratory factor analysis under the concept of structural equation modeling (SEM), to finalize the variables fit for the proposed model.

## 2   Knowledge Management Enabling Culture

Knowledge management (KM) is significant in organizations, especially in higher education institutions (HEIs). Activities that are often performed for managing knowledge include creating, acquiring, disseminating, and leveraging knowledge, mainly to attain competitive advantage [1, 2] and to achieve the vision of quality research in HEIs. In most cases, the prominent activity that is obviously seen as the most important is knowledge sharing [3, 4]. When an expert within the organization shares knowledge, other employees look up and refer to the expert as they recognize the expertise, making knowledge sharing so obvious that it may outshine other KM activities that the organization is promoting. However, this does not diminish the importance of other KM activities.

Previous research investigated the critical success factors for KM culture in organizations. KM culture is often linked to organizational culture, in which one may not be able to be sustained without the other. If organizational culture is unconsciously created from the fundamental assumptions and beliefs shared by members of the organization that defines the organization's view of itself and its environment [5], KM-enabling culture is more towards a trusting knowledge culture that is directed towards rewarding innovation, learning, experimentation, scrutiny, and reflection [6]. KM-enabling culture is important as it impacts on infrastructure and strategy, as well as the mission, vision, objectives, and goals of the organization [7].

Among the highlights of KM-enabling culture is the importance of knowledge sharing that requires trust among the members of the organization. Knowledge sharing is one of the KM activities that should be initiated among the employees, as it would further derive benefits and team spirit, motivating the knowledge workers towards more knowledge sharing and other KM activities [7]. As the spiral of cause-and-effect continues, the KM effort will bloom, which identifies a unique KM culture in the company.

An issue was raised in the scope of HEIs, which is feeling insecure to share knowledge with colleagues since knowledge is considered valuable resource or asset. Knowledge in HEIs is intensive because it is created from new research and studies, which are further documented in publications [8], in which this whole process becomes important KPI for academics globally. Hence, the problem of reluctance in sharing knowledge is understandable, as it feels as if the individual's capacity would diminish (psychologically) when it could be imitated by others, leaving the knowledge sharer to feel at a losing end, even though is it not true. Among the important factors that affect academic's behavior of unwilling to share knowledge among themselves, even via Web technology for instance, are motivation factors, IT acceptance and organizational culture [7]. Motivation is the biggest issue due to the lack of time and the high level of effort expected for knowledge sharing activities [6]. Other than trust and time availability, leadership directives and practices are also important.

Apart from the issues of trust, time and leadership, previous research highlighted the importance of commitment among employees to enable KM activity, mainly knowledge sharing. The importance of commitment from HEI employees' side is emphasized, in which willingness to commit affect their attitude, which then will reflect the KM-enabling culture [9]. In encouraging academics to voluntarily commit to sharing knowledge, for example, support from the management is required to provide the best available engagement methods [4]. This is where leadership roles and motivating atmosphere can be observed. With conducive motivating environment in the workplace, commitment can overcome the issues of employees' lack of effort that could lead to absenteeism and job turnover [10].

In supporting organizational KM initiatives, eight attributes of KM-enabling culture are suggested, which include knowledge sharing, appropriate leadership, communication quality, motivated organization members, organizational learning, positive atmosphere, role clarity and trust [7]. As reliable as it may sound, these attributes may differ in different set of environment exists in an organization.

On the other side of KM-enabling culture characteristics is the KM on-going activities. Some important issues relating to these activities are as follows [7]: i) Constant identification of knowledge gaps in the organization, then filling them by recruiting new organizational members and providing such knowledge to the members along with the means necessary to attain it; ii) Acknowledgement and follow up of the evolution of the organization by designing new KM activities and re-designing the existing KM activities as deemed necessary; and iii) Regular measurement of KM practices and the close following of any progress made.

Reflecting on the issues of KM activities pointed out by the previous authors, the KM activities could be related to the issues and classified in stages, based on the common practice in project and software engineering, which is similar to ADDIE model used in instructional design [11]. The stages are planning and analysis stage, development and implementation stage, and evaluation and improvement stage. In other words, the KM activity stages are grouped into three [7] as presented in Table 1.

**Table 1.** KM Activities Stages.

| Issues in KM On-going Activities | Activity Stages |
|---|---|
| Constant identification of knowledge gaps | Planning and Analysis stage |
| Recruiting new organizational members | |
| Provide knowledge (from the gaps) to the new recruits | |
| Acknowledgement and follow-up with the evolution (through activities) | Development and Implementation stage |
| Designing new KM activities | |
| Re-designing/re-engineering existing KM activities | |
| Regular measurement of KM practices | Evaluation and Improvement Stage |
| Close following of any progress made | |

## 3   Conceptual Model of KM-Enabling Culture

A conceptual model is proposed to kick start the investigation on the variables for KM-enabling culture. It is understood that KM-enabling culture depends on the eight attributes or characteristics, as depicted from previous literature. In addition, KM-enabling culture also depends on the KM on-going activities, because these could be a success or failure in sustaining the attributes that may or may not exist in the current organizational environment. Nevertheless, the demographic factor could also be part of the equation, as age, gender, position in the company, and years of working experience could affect the changes in the "enability" of KM culture in the company. Hence, this research proposes a conceptual model of KM-enabling culture, as shown in Fig. 1.

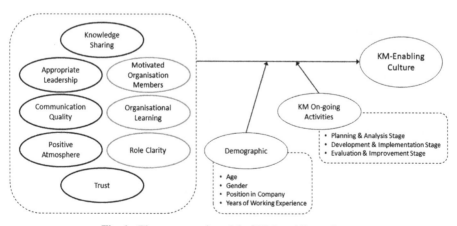

**Fig. 1.** The conceptual model of KM-enabling culture.

Figure 1 shows that, even within its own set, the characteristics of the KM-enabling culture could be a dynamic component, in which the attributes may be strong or weak, at the same time affecting one another. This dynamic condition could change drastically or sustain for certain time duration, depending on the on-going activities related to KM that happen within the company. This is the reason of having the attributes independently situated within a component entity as one variable.

On the other side, KM on-going activities include the stages of planning and analysis stage, development and implementation stage, and evaluation and improvement stage. These are to be tabulated to the real activities going on or happening within the year of this research investigation, i.e., the year the pandemic started. Among examples of activities are as shown in Table 2.

**Table 2.** KM On-going Activities in 2020 (example).

---

*Planning and Analysis Stage*

*Constant Identification of Knowledge Gaps*
- Highlight on acknowledgement importance among members participated in competitions
- The need on technical knowledge is identified and included for 2020 workshops

*Recruiting New Organizational Members*
- Share of Call-for-Paper on Scopus-indexed conferences and journal (in newsletter)
- Formed research team under new domain and shared the model for implementation

*Provide Knowledge (from the Gaps) to the New Recruits*
- Knowledge Sharing Session on research grant 2020
- Mentoring and personal guide to the participating individuals/teams

---

*Development and Implementation Stage*

*Acknowledgement and follow up with the Evolution (through activities)*
- Research Newsletter (online dissemination)
- Research Week 2020

*Designing New KM Activities*
- Research Webinar on Building Research Profile
- Organize Research Week session for Interest Groups to share knowledge

*Re-designing / Re-engineering existing KM Activities*
- Re-design Research Week as part of the newly-named "RW Series"
- Re-design the columns in newsletter from issue to issue

---

*Evaluation and Improvement Stage*

*Regular Measurement of KM Practices*
- Evaluation on 2020 is be included in 2021 newsletter

*Close Following of any Progress Made*
- Cover news on progress meetings in newsletter
- To be included in 2021 newsletter

---

# 4 Methodology

## 4.1 Research Design

This study employed a quantitative research design, in which a survey was conducted to assess the KM-enabling culture among the faculty members of a private university during the pandemic. An online questionnaire was designed and distributed to collect data on the underlying constructs proposed in the theoretical model, such as Knowledge Management On-Going Activities, Knowledge Sharing, Appropriate Leadership, Communication Quality, Positive Atmosphere, Trust, Organizational Learning, Motivated Organization Members, Role Clarity, and KM-Enabling Culture. These constructs were operationalized by multi-item measures using 5-point Likert scales, with anchors ranging from 1 for strongly disagree to 5 for strongly agree.

## 4.2 Sampling and Data Collection

This quantitative exploratory study is a small-scale investigation designed to test the feasibility of the conceptual model and method for later use on a larger scale. It is also to identify possible associations that may be worth following up in a subsequent larger study. This is due to the timing and ambiguous situation. Since this study is closely related to the KM activities implemented during the pandemic, it is necessary to conduct it while the experience from the activities is still fresh in the respondents' minds.

Due to the nature of this study, the sample size is expected to be at least 12 people [12–14], or 10% of the effective sample size for the study as a whole or the case population [15, 16]. In the case of a faculty in a private university under study, the number of faculty members is approximately 120 people, hence 12 people as sample size is considered sufficient. Anyway, the main aim for this exploratory study is to test the validity and reliability of the questionnaire, in which other results of analysis would be a bonus.

Quantitative data was collected at the end of 2020. Purposive sampling was employed, as the questionnaire was distributed to the faculty members who are part of the unit under study, i.e., a faculty under a private university. A total of 13 respondents out of 120 faculty members completed the responses to all the questionnaire items.

# 5 Results

## 5.1 Descriptive Analysis on Sample Profile

As shown in Table 3, majority of the respondents were between the age 40 to 49 years old (53.4%), and only one respondent (0.01%) fell under the age over 49 years old. Most of the respondents were female (76.9%), in which majority held the positions of lecturer (46.2%) and senior lecturer (46.2%). Despite the age, more than half of the respondents (69.2%) have worked in the case university for more than 10 years.

**Table 3.** Demographic Profile of Respondents (n = 13).

| Variable | N | Percentage (%) |
|---|---|---|
| *Age* | | |
| 30 to 39 years old | 5 | 38.5 |
| 40 to 49 years old | 7 | 53.4 |
| Over 49 years old | 1 | 0.1 |
| *Gender* | | |
| Male | 3 | 23.1 |
| Female | 10 | 76.9 |
| *Current position in the company* | | |
| Senior Lecturer | 6 | 46.2 |
| Lecturer | 6 | 46.2 |
| Assistant Lecturer | 1 | 0.1 |
| *Years of working experience in current company* | | |
| 1 to 5 years | 1 | 0.1 |
| 5 to 10 years | 3 | 23.1 |
| 10 to 15 years | 4 | 30.7 |
| More than 15 years | 5 | 38.5 |

## 5.2  Validity and Reliability of Constructs

Even though a conceptual model is drafted based on the literature review, the attempt made in this research is more on the exploratory intention. In other words, this research aims to find the relationships between constructs within the proposed model. Out of eight attributes of KM-enabling culture [7], only four attributes could be used for exploratory factor analysis, after considering the suggestion on items to be deleted to increase the reliability of the items in the constructs. These attributes are Appropriate Leadership, Role Clarity, Motivated Organization Members and Positive Atmosphere.

An Exploratory Factor Analysis (EFA) is conducted in this research, since there is no intention to confirm the existence of any existing relationship prior to the analysis of the data. However, by allowing various techniques, methods, procedures and rules, the relationship in the data is revealed. For this research, it is found that the four appropriate attributes are not sufficiently strong as separate entities, but have to be collective components of variables. Not all items under these attributes are suitable for the model, in which making them collective in new variables make them acceptably strong. Hence, the four attributes are merged into two new variables: Leadership Role consists of Appropriate Leadership and Role Clarity; Motivating Atmosphere consists of Motivated Organization Members and Positive Atmosphere.

In order to test the reliability of the constructs used in the conceptual model, Cronbach's alpha, composite reliability and average variance extracted (AVE) are calculated. Table 4 shows the results for reliability of the questionnaire design. All constructs are highly reliable, with Cronbach's alpha value above 0.90, i.e., very strong.

**Table 4.** Construct Reliability.

| Construct Reliability | Cronbach's Alpha | rho_A | Composite Reliability | Average Variance Extracted (AVE) |
|---|---|---|---|---|
| KM activity | 0.972 | 0.978 | 0.976 | 0.837 |
| KM-Enabling Culture | 0.989 | 0.989 | 0.991 | 0.957 |
| Leadership Role | 0.978 | 0.980 | 0.981 | 0.867 |
| Motivating Atmosphere | 0.982 | 0.984 | 0.985 | 0.865 |

Composite reliability is calculated to measure the internal consistency of the items under a construct. It is recommended that the reliability of a construct is at least 0.70. A high composite reliability is a very good indication that the items constantly measure the same construct. From the results in Table 4, all composite reliability values for the constructs ranges from 0.976 to 0.991, exceedingly far from 0.70. It is a clear indication that all the items consistently measure their corresponding construct.

The AVE value for each construct is listed in Table 4. Finding the AVE value for a construct would provide a knowledge of, on average, how much variations in the items can be explained by the construct or variable. For example, even though the Cronbach's alpha value for KM Activity is highly reliable with 0.972, the AVE is 0.837. This means that, on average, 83.7% of the variations in the faculty KM Activity is explained by eight items or questions. On the other hand, we recall a 16.3% error in our measurement items, which is acceptable. For adequate convergent, an AVE of at least 0.50 is highly recommended because the items explain less errors than the variance in the constructs, putting the proposed constructs of the model on the safe side.

Under construct validity, convergent validity is measured to find out whether the items are measuring a particular construct are indeed measuring them. If the items do measure a specific construct, then they need to converge. Factor loading needs to be more than 0.60 in value. Table 5 shows the list of items, with the factor loading values.

### 5.3 Structural Equation Modeling (SEM)

A multivariate technique called structural equation modeling (SEM) is performed in this research, since it uses a conceptual model with path diagram and linked regression-style equations to capture complex and dynamic relationships within the variables [17]. In SEM, regression concepts only apply in relative terms, due to the possibility of having a dependent variable becoming an independent variable in other components of the SEM system [18, 19]. This technique is applicable for exploratory purpose of finding relationship between variables that prior unforeseen possible.

SEM is also common to test a mediation model and to conduct a formal test on mediation effects [20]. The mediation effect can be specified as an indirect effect [21, 22], as the description may be depicted as "the indirect effect of an independent variable

**Table 5.** Construct Validity.

| Construct and Item | Mean (SD) | Factor Loadings | Construct and Item | Mean (SD) | Factor Loadings |
|---|---|---|---|---|---|
| KM Ongoing Activities | | | Motivated Organization Members and Positive Atmosphere | | |
| KA01 | 3.85 (1.83) | 0.83 | MM01 | 3.77 (2.12) | 0.91 |
| KA03 | 3.46 (1.78) | 0.90 | MM02 | 3.77 (1.93) | 0.92 |
| KA04 | 3.54 (1.82) | 0.94 | MM04 | 5.00 (2.22) | 0.86 |
| KA05 | 4.46 (1.78) | 0.95 | MM05 | 5.08 (2.27) | 0.87 |
| KA06 | 4.69 (1.68) | 0.94 | MM06 | 3.54 (1.82) | 0.89 |
| KA07 | 4.69 (1.68) | 0.94 | PA02 | 4.00 (1.88) | 0.95 |
| KA08 | 3.77 (1.97) | 0.92 | PA03 | 4.00 (1.80) | 0.94 |
| KA09 | 3.62 (1.78) | 0.91 | PA04 | 4.08 (1.86) | 0.98 |
| | | | PA05 | 4.00 (2.00) | 0.98 |
| | | | PA06 | 4.00 (2.00) | 0.99 |
| Appropriate Leadership and Role Clarity | | | KM-Enabling Culture | | |
| AL02 | 4.15 (1.99) | 0.94 | KC01 | 4.69 (1.81) | 0.97 |
| AL03 | 3.92 (2.06) | 0.94 | KC03 | 5.00 (1.80) | 0.97 |
| AL04 | 3.77 (1.89) | 0.93 | KC04 | 4.77 (1.80) | 0.99 |
| RC01 | 5.00 (1.80) | 0.93 | KC06 | 4.54 (1.87) | 0.98 |
| RC03 | 4.39 (2.17) | 0.94 | KC07 | 4.46 (1.78) | 0.98 |
| RC04 | 4.46 (1.74) | 0.93 | | | |
| RC05 | 3.92 (1.73) | 0.90 | | | |
| RC06 | 4.31 (2.09) | 0.94 | | | |

(X) on a dependent variable (Y) via a mediator (M)". In other words, X affects M, which in turn affects Y. Table 6 shows the relationships between constructs/variables.

**Table 6.** Total, Direct and Indirect Effects in SEM Analysis.

| Relationship | Total Effect | Direct Effect | Indirect Effect |
|---|---|---|---|
| KM activity → KM-Enabling Culture | 0.808 | NP | 0.808 |
| KM Activity → Leadership Role | 0.757 | 0.757 | NP |
| KM Activity → Motivating Atmosphere | 0.871 | 0.871 | NP |
| Leadership Role → KM-Enabling Culture | 0.508 | 0.508 | NP |
| Motivating Atmosphere → KM-Enabling Culture | 0.486 | 0.486 | NP |

*Note:* NP means not possible

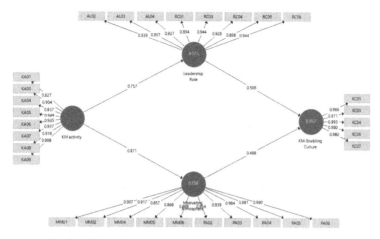

**Fig. 2.** SEM analysis on model fitness of KM-enabling culture.

The output of this analysis is a path diagram, which is a visualization of the proposed model based on the results from SEM analysis, as shown in Fig. 2. The path diagram clearly shows that there are four variables with positive relationships among them, as how the results are presented Table 6. Not shown in Fig. 2 is the indirect effect of KM Activity and KM-Enabling Culture (0.808), since the other two variables (i.e., Leadership Role and Motivating Atmosphere) become the mediating variables between them with the values determined as direct effect.

Figure 2 also shows the results of factor loadings from Table 5, illustrated in arrows between the variable nodes (blue circles) and their respective items (yellow boxes). Figure 2 also shows the values of R-squared (R2) in the respective variable nodes (blue circles). R-squared measures the proportion of the variance for a dependent variable that is explained by an independent variable or variables. It shows the goodness-of-fit for a linear regression model. As example, the R2 value for Motivating Atmosphere is 0.758, indicating that approximately 75.8% of the observed variation for KM Activity can be explained by the Motivating Atmosphere. Table 7 shows the full results.

**Table 7.** R-squared for Independent Variables.

| Variables | R Square | R Square Adjusted |
|---|---|---|
| KM-Enabling Culture | 0.952 | 0.942 |
| Leadership Role | 0.573 | 0.534 |
| Motivating Atmosphere | 0.758 | 0.736 |

In general, all dependent variables in the model can be explained by more than half of the observed variations of the respective independent variables, i.e., values are higher than 0.50. Even though a high R-squared value does not determine the best fit of the variables for the model, at least it shows the significance and possible good-for-fit in the model. To confirm this, further research with bigger sample size is necessary.

## 6 Discussion and Conclusion

The exploratory study presented here is to determine the variables for a model of KM-enabling culture. As mentioned in the Results, out of eight KM-enabling culture attributes, it is found that only four are relevant and reliable, in which their strengths in the model could only be possible if they are grouped into components. This has brought to new variables called Leadership Role, i.e., combination of Appropriate Leadership and Role Clarity; and Motivating Atmosphere, i.e., combination of Motivated Organization Members and Positive Atmosphere, as shown in Fig. 3. This does not mean that other attributes are not totally insignificant in the mode, but merely not very reliable for the current situation of the case organization, especially when the KM activities are constrained due to the pandemic.

**Fig. 3.** Finalized model with four variables and hypotheses.

In terms of limitations, this research received low response rate from the survey respondents. During the pandemic, the low response is depending on the interest among the organizational members, since being "hyper-busy" state has made them putting the task of responding to a survey their last priority. Nevertheless, since this is considered a pilot study for exploratory purpose, the number of respondents is expected to be sufficient when the next phase of questionnaire survey is conducted, with the finalized variables as determined by the results of this research.

Future work may need to check on the residual plots to ensure that the model is good-for-fit. This is achievable with real data of more than 30 responses to confirm the model, using confirmatory factor analysis (CFA). With the finalized variables, further research can be conducted on other HEIs, too. If deemed relevant, this model can be used for other companies beyond education industry, which may have some degree of KM activities performed and practiced among their employees.

KM activities are possible to be virtually implemented despite the pandemic constraints. It is highly challenging to get full commitment from everyone; efforts and initiatives put forth by the employees who feel responsible to make KM sustainable deserve a recognition. Efforts performed during the pandemic prove that KM is sustainable, as practiced in the company, and its importance is appreciated. Measuring the KM-enabling culture proves the significance of KM sustainability to the organization.

# References

1. Nicolas, R.: Knowledge management impacts on decision making process. J. Knowl. Manag. **8**, 20–31 (2004)
2. Suhaimee, S., Zaki, A., Bakar, A., Alias, R.A. Knowledge sharing culture in Malaysian public institution of higher education: an overview. In: Proceedings of the Postgraduate Annual Research Seminar, Skudai, Malaysia: Universiti Teknologi Malaysia, pp. 354–359 (2006)
3. Yu, T.K., Lu, L.C., Liu, T.F.: Exploring factors that influence knowledge sharing behavior via weblogs. Comput. Hum. Behav. **26**(1), 32–41 (2010)
4. Fauzi, M.A., Tan, C.N.L., Ramayah, T.: Knowledge sharing intention at Malaysian higher learning institutions: the academics' viewpoint. Know. Manag. E-Learn. **10**(2), 163–176 (2018)
5. Schein, E.: Organizational Culture and Leadership. Jossey-Bass Publishers, Washington (1985)
6. Allee, V.: Twelve Principles of Knowledge Management. Train. Dev. **51**(11), 71–74 (1997)
7. Stylianou, V., Savva, A.: Investigating the knowledge management culture. Universal J. Educ. Res. **4**(7), 1515–1521 (2016). https://doi.org/10.13189/ujer.2016.040703
8. Fullwood, R., Rowley, J., Delbridge, R.: Knowledge sharing amongst academics in UK universities. J. Knowl. Manag. **17**(1), 123–136 (2013)
9. Meyer, J.P., Parfyonova, N.M.: Normative commitment in the workplace: a theoretical analysis and re-conceptualization. Hum. Resour. Manag. Rev. **20**(4), 283–294 (2010)
10. Joiner, T.A., Bakalis, S.: The antecedents of organizational commitment: the case of Australian casual academics. Int. J. Educ. Manag. **20**(6), 439–452 (2006). https://doi.org/10.1108/095 13540610683694
11. Piskurich, G.M.: Rapid Instructional Design: Learning ID Fast and Right (3rd Ed.) (2015). ISBN: 978-1-118-97397-4
12. Sheatsley, P.B.: Questionnaire construction and item writing. In: Rossi, P.H., Wright, J.D., Anderson, A.B. (eds.) Handbook of Survey Research, chapter 6. Academic Press Inc, San Diego, CA (1983)
13. Sudman, S.: Applied sampling. In: Rossi, P.H., Wright, J.D., Anderson, A.B. (eds.) Handbook of Survey Research, chapter 5. Academic Press Inc, San Diego, CA (1983)
14. van Belle, G.: Statistical Rules of Thumb. John Wiley, New York (2002)
15. Saunders, M., Lewis, P., Thornhill, A.: Research Methods for Business Students, 7th edn. Pearson, Harlow (2016)
16. Dillman, D.A., Smyth, J.D., Christian, L.M.: Internet, Phone, Mail, and Mixed-mode Surveys: The Tailored Design Method. John Wiley & Sons, Inc., Hoboken, NJ (2014)
17. Gunzler, D., Chen, T., Wu, P., Zhang, H.: Introduction to mediation analysis with structural equation modeling. Shanghai Arch. Psychiatry **25**(6), 390–394 (2013). https://doi.org/10.3969/j.issn.1002-0829.2013.06.009
18. Bollen, K.A.: Structural Equations with Latent Variables. Wiley, New York, NY (1989)
19. Kowalski, J., Tu, X.M.: Modern Applied U Statistics. Wiley, New York, NY (2007)
20. Ryu, E., Cheong, J.: Comparing Indirect Effects in Different Groups in Single-Group and Multi-Group Structural Equation Models. Front. Psychol. (2017). https://doi.org/10.3389/fpsyg.2017.00747
21. Alwin, D.F., Hauser, R.M.: The decomposition of effects in path analysis. Am. Sociol. Rev **40**, 35–47 (1975). https://doi.org/10.2307/2094445
22. Bollen, K.A.: Total, direct, and indirect effects in structural equation models. In: Clogg, C.C. (ed.) Sociological Methodology, pp. 37–69. American Sociological Association, Washington, DC (1987)

# A Study on Time Series Approach Applications for Optimized Forecasting of Mega Sporting Events

Napitiporn Manoli[1]([⊠]) [iD], Masakazu Takahashi[1], and Yoshiyuki Matsuura[2]

[1] Graduate School of Sciences and Technology for Innovation, Yamaguchi University, Yamaguchi, Japan
d008wcu@yamaguchi-u.ac.jp
[2] Graduate School of Innovation and Technology Management, Yamaguchi University, Yamaguchi, Japan

**Abstract.** Hosting major sporting events, such as the FIFA World Cup, is intended to generate positive outcomes for the host country and related industries. The sports and event organizing business is highly competitive, with technology and innovation playing crucial roles. To succeed and reap the benefits of organizing such an event, businesses must possess the ability to compete technologically and respond to market needs in a timely manner. In this study, we used Robust Forecasting Models to achieve our objectives. Our analysis involved conducting a time-series analysis using the number of patent applications related to recording and monitoring technologies. The results yielded effective forecasting methods for each prediction time frame. According to the findings of the study, the seasonal exponential smoothing method demonstrated superior predictive ability when dealing with data containing a seasonal pattern, while the moving average approach showed improved prediction results when there were fluctuating data due to limited availability for training. Consequently, the results of this study can aid R&D managers in making informed decisions and predictions regarding market demand for technological advancements in sports and related sectors.

**Keywords:** Mega Sporting Events · Time Series Analysis · Exponential Smoothing · MA · ARIMA · SARIMA

## 1 Introduction

This study examines time series analysis methods for forecasting patent application numbers, which can indicate technological demand in the context of sporting events and related businesses. Given that market demand, sales, business product costs, and economic policy in different periods are highly and sensitively affected by patent applications for businesses and institutions, this study investigated methods for predicting trends using various timeframes to extract valuable information that meets business needs.

© The Author(s), under exclusive license to Springer Nature Switzerland AG 2024
L. Uden and I.-H. Ting (Eds.): KMO 2024, CCIS 2152, pp. 112–121, 2024.
https://doi.org/10.1007/978-3-031-63269-3_9

This challenge is addressed by understanding the concept of time series analysis and desired outcomes. Time series prediction is a crucial task in data mining, drawing significant interest for its ability to extract valuable insights from extensive datasets, as explained in [1–3]. In real-world scenarios, a substantial portion of the data manifests as a time series, characterized by time-dependent elements recorded at consistent intervals. This type of prediction is immensely useful across a wide range of applications, including forecasting financial returns, stock market trends, retail sales, inventory levels, environmental events, such as river flooding, and energy consumption patterns. Additionally, as mentioned in [4, 5], numerous time series prediction competitions serve as effective and credible platforms, offering empirical evaluation of various predictive methodologies.

Therefore, diverse time series methodologies with varying intervals were employed to reduce data fluctuations and improve forecast accuracy. Consequently, precise forecasting models were delineated using statistical performance data.

The remainder of this paper is organized as follows. Section 2 discusses the background and related work. Section 3 briefly summarizes the gathered data on the target publications. Section 4 describes the analytics of the data and presents analytical results. Finally, Sect. 5 gives some concluding remarks and future issues.

## 2 Background and Related Work

In this section, we provide a comprehensive overview of the research background and related work pertaining to time series analysis, exponential smoothing techniques, moving averages, and the ARIMA family of models.

### 2.1 Time Series Analysis

As Athiyarath et al. mentioned in [6], time series data comprise systematic and non-systematic components. The systematic component is consistent, recurrent, and modellable through patterns, such as level, trend, and seasonality. By contrast, the non-systematic component is characterized as a random phenomenon, which eludes direct modeling owing to its inherent unpredictability. Decomposition techniques, particularly trend and seasonal factors, are employed to isolate these elements, aiding forecast model construction. This process also includes identifying local changes and long-term effects and removing seasonal influences to clarify the trend. The level represents the series' average pattern, whereas the trend reflects its harmonic progression. Seasonality, a short-term cyclic variation, is particularly notable in the long-term data.

Time series analysis, which involves sequentially recording measurements of a particular quantity over time, is crucial in various scientific fields. Fulcher et al. [7] compared time series analysis methods to determine the empirical structure of a time series. Their findings indicate that the relationships between the data and the methods used to measure them are decisive. By representing time series and operations in this manner, a powerful framework for organizing collections of time series and operations was provided.

## 2.2 Exponential Smoothing Methods

Exponential smoothing methods are forecasting techniques that are widely used for the analysis of univariate time series owing to their simplicity and robustness as automatic forecasting procedures, as mentioned in Bermudez *et al.* [8], Gardner [9], and Hyndman *et al.* [10]. They originated in the work of Brown and Holt [11, 12] but became well known in the paper by Winters [13]. The general form of the exponential smoothing forecast function, involving a set of adaptive coefficients, was provided, possibly for the first time, by Box and Jenkins [14]. Gardner [15] explained that simple smoothing is a method of representing a time series, denoted as:

$$X_t = b + \varepsilon_t \tag{1}$$

where $\varepsilon_t$ is a random component with a mean of zero and a variance of $\sigma_b^2$. In this model, level $b$ is treated as a constant within any local segment of the series although it may exhibit gradual changes over time. Researchers have investigated the usefulness of simple smoothing. Some argue that it does not improve accuracy compared to the unweighted moving average [16], whereas others claim the opposite [17]. Simple smoothing is used for time series data without trends or seasonal variations, while Double Exponential Smoothing is applied to data with trends but no seasonality. This method enhances simple exponential smoothing by integrating two key equations: the level and trend equations.

Seasonal Exponential Smoothing is a sophisticated forecasting technique designed for time series data that exhibits both trends and seasonal variations. Corberán-Vallet *et al.* [18] discussed Linear (Holt) Exponential Smoothing, an advanced time series forecasting method that extends simple exponential smoothing to account for trends but no seasonality. The method includes a second equation to capture the trend component in addition to the level component. Damped-Trend Linear Exponential Smoothing is a modified version that introduces a damping factor into the trend component and gradually reduces its magnitude over time. This enhances the resilience of the method to overestimate future trends, particularly during extended forecast periods.

Gardner [15] introduced the Winters Method, a seasonal extension of Holt's method, with three smoothing equations for level, trend, and seasonal components. It is suitable for data with trends and seasonal patterns and can be applied in additive or multiplicative cases.

## 2.3 Moving Average and ARIMA Model Family

Numerous studies have focused on time series prediction, which can be divided into two main methodological groups, as outlined by Bowerman *et al.* [19]. One group employs statistical techniques such as Moving Average (MA), Autoregressive Moving Average (ARMA), and Autoregressive Integrated Moving Average (ARIMA) models. The second group utilizes computational intelligence approaches.

According to Hyndman [20], a moving average is a method for smoothing a time series by calculating the average of consecutive segments. This technique uses mathematical convolution and produces a new series with reduced short-term fluctuations, thereby revealing trends more effectively. Weighted averages are commonly used in conjunction with the moving average technique, which is also known as running means or rolling averages. This method continuously updates the average by excluding the oldest data point and incorporating the newest data point, progressing along the time series.

The ARMA model, as outlined in Géron [21], generates forecasts by combining weighted past values with a corrective moving average component based on a weighted sum of recent forecast errors. Differencing is a fundamental principle of the Autoregressive Integrated Moving Average (ARIMA) model [22]. According to Hung *et al.* [23], the ARIMA model incorporates differences by conducting d-rounds to stabilize the time series. The ARMA framework post-differencing enables the ARIMA model to effectively forecast. In the final step, the subtracted terms are reintroduced, resulting in a comprehensive and detailed analysis of the time series. The Seasonal ARIMA (SARIMA) model extends the ARIMA family and is specifically designed to account for seasonal variations in time series data. Similar to the standard ARIMA model, SARIMA adds a layer to model the seasonal fluctuations at specified frequencies using the ARIMA methodology.

In this study, we concentrated on implementing advanced statistical methods for time series analysis across diverse data intervals, which can lead to significant progress in the field. Especially when skilled in reducing variations and enhancing prediction accuracy, these abilities are essential for comprehending trends in sports technology patent applications. The incorporation of these diverse analytical tools will be customized to accommodate the unique characteristics of the temporal distribution of data, thereby providing a solid foundation for anticipating technological demand. This approach not only fills the existing research gap but also establishes a precedent for future studies focused on predicting technological advancements in swiftly changing fields.

## 3 Data Summary

The data collection strategy for this study involved obtaining patent information from the Tomson Reuters Derwent Innovation Index database [24]. The search strategy is presented in Table 1.

The keywords and synonyms or relevant words of monitoring and recording technology were selected, and in the initial step, we conducted a search on the patent database with the title and abstract of the document. The search generated 2,286 documents from around the world. The screening procedure was followed, and duplicated and unrelated content was removed. Finally, we analyzed time series methods using the number of patent applications divided by year as the target variable $y$ for prediction.

## 4 Analytical Results and Discussion

In this section, we investigate various analytical methodologies and present the outcomes of these analyses. This includes an in-depth examination of time series analysis and smoothing techniques, along with the application of the MA, ARIMA, and SARIMA models. These methods are utilized for constructing time series models, which are instrumental in identifying underlying patterns and predicting trends for forthcoming time intervals.

**Table 1.** Search Strategy of Patent Applications

| Retrieve Date | 18/12/2023 |
|---|---|
| Data Base | Thomson Reuters Derwent Innovation Index |
| Technology Category and Synonym or Relevant Words | T1: Monitoring control; vision, display, viewing, view, controlling, control |
| | T2: VDO; video, VDO, recording, record, HD, high-definition, high ADJ resolution, high-resolution |
| Assumption | Each document can fall into multiple categories of technology |
| Scope | All countries |
| Period of data | 1981–2023 |
| Gathering results | 2,286 patent application documents |

## 4.1   The Time Series Analysis

In this study, we conducted a comprehensive time series analysis of patent application trends across various timeframes, from monthly to annual periods, to elucidate the dynamic nature of patent filing activities.

The analysis of patent applications over the first month of each year, from 1981 to 2023, reveals fluctuations that range from sharp increases to decreases. A declining trend in the moving average suggests a potential shift in innovation trends (see Fig. 1). This shift may be influenced by changes in economic conditions, technological trends, or patent policies that affect the inclination towards patent protection. Seasonal and cyclical patterns are more apparent in the detailed monthly and annual data, whereas they appear less pronounced in the semi-annual and quarter charts because of the aggregated data. The level of detail in the data offers distinct insights into patent application trends, with short-term fluctuations more apparent in the monthly data and long-term trends, such as the recent decline most clearly seen in the annual chart due to the aggregated format.

Table 2 presents a statistical overview of patent applications gathered across various time frames. The data reveals an average of approximately 4.413 patent applications per month, quarter, and semi-annual period, and approximately 53.160 on an annual basis. The standard deviation of the patent application figures shows consistent patterns on a monthly, quarterly, and semi-annual basis, with values ranging from approximately 3.18 to 4.10. This suggests uniform variability within these timeframes. In contrast, the standard deviation of the annual data is much higher, around 36.53, owing to the broader dispersion of data points. In terms of sample size, each of the monthly, quarterly, and semi-annual categories consisted of 516 data points matching their respective collection frequencies. However, the annual category comprises 43 samples, reflecting 43 years of data from 1981 to 2023.

The Augmented Dickey-Fuller (ADF) test results, which are essential for determining the stationarity of the dataset, are categorized into three types: zero-mean ADF, single-mean ADF, and trend ADF. The negative values in these tests indicate stationarity,

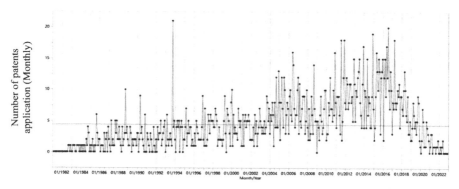

**Fig. 1.** Plot of the number of patent applications in 1981–2023.

**Table 2.** Statistical data of the time series analysis.

|  | Month | Quarter | Semi-Annual | Annual |
|---|---|---|---|---|
| Mean | 4.413 | 4.413 | 4.413 | 53.163 |
| Standard deviation | 4.105 | 3.378 | 3.183 | 36.525 |
| Number of samples | 516 | 516 | 516 | 43 |
| Zero Mean ADF | −7.787 | −2.713 | −1.391 | −0.731 |
| Single Mean ADF | −12.309 | −4.522 | −2.404 | −1.212 |
| Trend ADF | −13.851 | −5.101 | −2.255 | −0.117 |

suggesting the absence of a unit root. Intriguingly, the test results become increasingly negative from the annual to monthly datasets, implying that finer granularity enhances the statistical evidence for stationarity in patent application numbers. Stationarity is crucial in time series analysis as non-stationary data can lead to unreliable forecasting and statistical modeling. The ADF values across various timescales offer insights into the stability of the patent application process, with finer data exhibiting greater stability and reduced random walk characteristics.

## 4.2   Comparison of Time Series Forecasting Models

In this section, we compare different time series forecasting models applied to patent application data at varying time granularities: month, quarter, semi-annual, and annual. The models include Simple Exponential Smoothing, Double Exponential Smoothing, Holt's Linear Exponential Smoothing, Damped-Trend Linear Exponential Smoothing, Seasonal Exponential Smoothing, Winters Method, Moving Average (MA), ARIMA, and Seasonal ARIMA.

Table 3 compares various time series models for patent application data using Akaike's Information Criterion (AIC) and Schwarz's Bayesian Criterion (SBC) as evaluation measures. Models with lower AIC and SBC values are generally preferred, as they penalize the inclusion of excessive parameters and reduce the risk of overfitting. This implies that these models are more parsimonious and effective in capturing key trends without unnecessary complexity. As a result, models with the lowest AIC and SBC values are typically chosen as the best fit for time series analysis.

**Table 3.** Comparison of different time series forecasting models' performance

| Models | Month | | Quarter | | Semi-Annual | | Annual | |
|---|---|---|---|---|---|---|---|---|
| | AIC | SBC | AIC | SBC | AIC | SBC | AIC | SBC |
| 1. Seasonal Exponential Smoothing | 2529.695 | 2538.136 | 1761.104 | 1769.581 | 1068.940 | 1077.405 | 265.122 | 267.924 |
| 2. Damped-Trend Linear Exponential Smoothing | 2568.774 | 2581.506 | 1751.530 | 1764.262 | 1050.429 | 1063.162 | 350.892 | 356.105 |
| 3. Simple Exponential Smoothing | 2577.394 | 2581.638 | 1750.864 | 1755.108 | 1046.319 | 1050.563 | 346.892 | 348.630 |
| 4. Double (Brown) Exponential Smoothing | 2580.858 | 2585.100 | 1906.524 | 1910.766 | 1155.088 | 1159.330 | 345.303 | 347.017 |
| 5. Linear (Holt) Exponential Smoothing | 2582.447 | 2590.931 | 1756.711 | 1765.196 | 1053.644 | 1062.129 | 343.351 | 346.778 |
| 6. Winters Method (Additive) | 2756.728 | 2769.389 | 2042.584 | 2055.246 | 1048.944 | 1061.606 | 267.122 | 271.325 |
| 7. Moving Average (MA) | 2803.290 | 2811.782 | 1671.666 | 1688.651 | 970.454 | 1000.177 | 390.657 | 394.180 |
| 8. ARIMA | 2923.619 | 2927.865 | 2722.635 | 2726.881 | 2661.185 | 2665.431 | 433.457 | 435.218 |
| 9. Seasonal ARIMA | 2923.619 | 2927.865 | 2722.635 | 2726.881 | 2661.185 | 2665.431 | 433.457 | 435.218 |

After a thorough analysis of each model's performance, it became apparent that the Seasonal Exponential Smoothing model stood out for its exceptional ability to forecast both monthly and annual patent application trends. It achieved the lowest AIC and SBC values at 2529.695 and 2538.136 for monthly trends and 265.122 and 267.924 for annual trends, respectively. This model effectively captures the underlying patterns across different temporal resolutions. For quarterly and semi-annual forecasting, the Moving Average (MA) model stands out with its robust predictive performance, denoted by an AIC of 970.405 and an SBC of 1000.177 for semi-annual intervals. The model further solidifies its efficacy for semi-annual intervals, with an AIC of 1671.666 and an SBC of 1688.651 for quarterly data.

These statistics affirm the model's capacity to accurately represent temporal patterns within a framework of model parsimony, which is a critical consideration in the rigorous process of model selection for time-series analysis. However, the ARIMA and Seasonal ARIMA models have the highest AIC and SBC values across all time granularities, indicating a less optimal fit than the other models.

**Seasonal Exponential Smoothing (SES) Model Results**
The SES model exhibited remarkable accuracy in predicting monthly and annual patent

application trends. The foremost capacity of the SES model to predict trends is its ability to forecast annual patterns (see Fig. 2). The shaded area represents the prediction intervals, offering a visual range of, where future data points are likely to fall with a certain level of confidence. If the model is well-calibrated, the actual data points will mostly fall within this shaded area, and the line follows the general direction and patterns of historical data, showing both the model's responsiveness to changes in the level and its ability to capture the seasonality of the data.

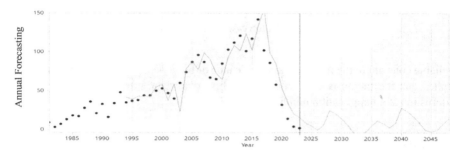

**Fig. 2.** Annual forecasting using the SES model.

Based on the findings of the SES forecasting model, it appears that the level smoothing weight is fixed at 1, which signifies that the model relies heavily on the most recent observation when adjusting the level or mean of the series. This suggests a model that responds fully to recent changes in data without applying smoothing techniques. Additionally, the seasonal smoothing weight was set to zero, suggesting that the model did not consider seasonality. While seasonality is typically a crucial aspect of an SES model, in this case, the model seems to be designed to concentrate solely on this level, disregarding any seasonal variations.

**Moving Average (MA) Model Results**

The MA model demonstrated exceptional precision in predicting semi-annual and quarterly forecasts. The primary function of the MA model lies in its capacity to predict trends, and it is particularly adept at forecasting semi-annual patterns, as shown in Fig. 3. The connection between the model's predictions and actual data is highlighted, providing valuable insights into future trends for patent applications.

In the semi-annual forecasting model, the MA model incorporates six lag terms (MA1–MA6) and an intercept value, each of which plays a significant role in the model's predictive accuracy.

For example, the first lag term, MA1, has an estimate of $-1.421$, demonstrating a notable negative impact of the previous period's application count on the current forecast. This influence is substantiated by a t ratio of $-39.92$, and a very low p-value (Prob > |t|), indicating a probability of random occurrence of less than 0.0001. The subsequent lag terms, MA2 and MA3, with estimates of $-1.431$ and $-1.444$ and t ratios of $-39.07$ and $-35.9$, respectively, are similarly significant.

The intercept, estimated at 4.365, represents the baseline number at which the series fluctuates. This is confirmed by a t Ratio of 19.4 and a p-value below 0.0001, suggesting

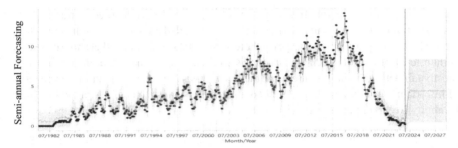

**Fig. 3.** Semi-annual forecasting using the MA model.

a reliable constant in the model. The significance of both the lag terms and the intercept implies that the model is well calibrated to historical data, effectively capturing the patterns in patent application numbers.

## 5  Concluding Remarks

This study introduces a novel methodology for forecasting technology trends within the sports event industry by utilizing global patent application data in the fields of monitoring systems and video recording technology. The content encompasses discussions of the research context, relevant prior work, research methodologies, and analytical outcomes. Additionally, the article provides a comprehensive overview of time series analysis techniques. The study results suggest that the seasonal exponential smoothing method outperforms other approaches when dealing with seasonally influenced data, whereas the moving average method demonstrates better predictive abilities in the presence of fluctuating data owing to limited training availability. Ultimately, the findings of this study can assist R&D managers in making decisions and projections regarding technological advancements in sports and related sectors.

This study presents some of the constraints. The number of patent applications has risen notably in some years, potentially caused by filing for the same patent registration across multiple countries. The accuracy of an analysis is subject to the quantity of data available, and depending solely on recording and monitoring technology has its limitations. By incorporating a larger amount of data and testing various keywords, the Time Series method may offer a more precise depiction of market needs.

Our future work includes: (1) investigating alternative comparative models, such as computational intelligence techniques, (2) enhancing prediction accuracy through the utilization of ARIMA family models with additional parameters, and (3) extending the analysis to encompass other technology categories in the sports sector.

## References

1. Palit, A.K., Popovic, D.: Computational intelligence in time series forecasting: theory and engineering applications. Springer Science & Business Media (2006)
2. Fu, T.C.: A review on time series data mining. Eng. Appl. Artif. Intell. **24**(1), 164–181 (2011)

3. Esling, P., Agon, C.: Time-series data mining. ACM Comput. Surv. (CSUR) **45**(1), 1–34 (2012)
4. McNames, J., Suykens, J.A.K., Vandewalle, J.: Winning entry of the KU Leuven time-series prediction competition. Int. J. Bifurcat. Chaos **9**(08), 1485–1500 (1999)
5. Lendasse, A., Oja, E., Simula, O., Verleysen, M.: Time series prediction competition: the CATS benchmark. Neurocomputing **70**(13–15), 2325–2329 (2007)
6. Athiyarath, S., Paul, M., Krishnaswamy, S.: A comparative study and analysis of time series forecasting techniques. SN Comput. Sci. **1**, 175 (2020)
7. Fulcher, B.D., Little, M.A., Jones, N.S.: Highly comparative time-series analysis: the empirical structure of time series and their methods. J. Royal Soc. Interface **10**(83), 20130048 (2013)
8. Bermudez, J.D., Corberán-Vallet, A., Vercher, E.: Multivariate exponential smoothing: a Bayesian forecast approach based on simulation. Mathemat. Comput. Simul. **79**, 1761–1769 (2009)
9. Gardner, E.S., Jr.: Exponential smoothing: the state of the art—Part II. Int. J. Forecast. **22**, 637–666 (2006)
10. Hyndman, R.J., Koehler, A.B., Snyder, R.D., Grose, S.: A state space framework for automatic forecasting using exponential smoothing methods. Int. J. Forecast. **18**, 439–454 (2002)
11. Brown, R.G.: Statistical Forecasting for Inventory Control. McGraw-Hill, New York (1959)
12. Holt, C.C.: Forecasting trends and seasonals by exponentially weighted averages. O.N.R. Memorandum 52/1957. Carnegie Institute of Technology (1957)
13. Winters, P.R.: Forecasting sales by exponentially weighted moving averages. Manage. Sci. **6**, 324–342 (1960)
14. Box, G.E.P., Jenkins, G.M.: Time Series Analysis, Forecasting and Control, 2nd edn. Holden-Day, San Francisco (1976)
15. Gardner, E.S., Jr.: Exponential smoothing: The state of the art. J. Forecast. **4**(1), 1–28 (1985)
16. Elton, E.J., Gruber, M.J.: Earnings estimates and the accuracy of expectational data. Manag. Sci. **18**(8), B-409 (1972)
17. Makridakis, S., et al.: The accuracy of extrapolation (time series) methods: results of a forecasting competition. J. Forecast. **1**(2), 111–153 (1982)
18. Corberán-Vallet, A., Bermúdez, J.D., Vercher, E.: Forecasting correlated time series with exponential smoothing models. Int. J. Forecast. **27**(2), 252–265 (2011)
19. Bowerman, B.L., O'Connell, R.T., Koehler, A.B.: Forecasting, Time Series, and Regression: An Applied Approach. Thomson Learning, Belmont, CA (2005)
20. Hyndman, R.J.: Moving Averages, pp. 866–869 (2011)
21. Géron, A.: Hands-on machine learning with Scikit-Learn, Keras, and TensorFlow. " O'Reilly Media, Inc." (2022)
22. Song, Q., Leland, R.P., Chissom, B.S.: A new fuzzy time-series model of fuzzy number observations. Fuzzy Sets Syst. **73**(3), 341–348 (1995)
23. Hung, C., Hung, C.N., Lin, S.Y.: Predicting time series using integration of moving average and support vector regression. Int. J. Mach. Learn. Comput. **4**(6), 491 (2014)
24. Derwent Innovation data base: https://www.derwentinnovation.com/tip-innovation/?locale=en. 18 Dec 2023

# Knowledge Management in South Australian Wineries

Graham Gordon Chant[✉]

Stewart Barr and Associates, Adelaide, Australia
graham.chant14@gmail.com

**Abstract.** This study is the first on the major wine production areas of South Australia. The aim was to investigate when, how and what information wineries gathered, was it stored, do they have management support, do they have a knowledge vision, and do they have a dedicated person who has responsibility for knowledge management? The key finding of this research was the failure of the surveyed wineries to convert more of their tacit information (conversations, phone calls and personal information) into explicit information. This study, the first experimental study of the state of knowledge management in the five largest winegrape crush areas of South Australia replicates the findings of previous researchers on this subject.

**Keywords:** knowledge management · tacit · explicit · wineries

## 1 Introduction

Stair and Reynolds [1] wrote that "knowledge is the body of rules, guidelines, and procedures used to select, organize and manipulate data to make it suitable for a specific task". Knowledge can be partitioned further into two categories, tacit knowledge and explicit (or articulate) knowledge [2]. Tacit knowledge has many definitions the one by Casonato and Harris [3] being "Tacit knowledge is the personal knowledge resident within the mind, behavior and perceptions of individuals … includes skills, experiences, insight, intuition and judgment." Explicit knowledge refers to "formalized knowledge, expressed in the form of data, formulas, specifications, manuals and procedures" [4]. In describing knowledge management (KM) Gonzales and Martins [5] observed that "the central objective of KM processes is the dissemination of knowledge for its subsequent reuse by individuals and groups and the consequent transformation of its content, generating new knowledge."

This paper will investigate when, how and what information wineries gather, is it stored, do they have management support, do they have a knowledge vision, and do they have a dedicated person who has responsibility for knowledge management?

© The Author(s), under exclusive license to Springer Nature Switzerland AG 2024
L. Uden and I.-H. Ting (Eds.): KMO 2024, CCIS 2152, pp. 122–134, 2024.
https://doi.org/10.1007/978-3-031-63269-3_10

## 2  Review of Literature

The approach of the research study was to first carry out a literature review. This enabled an understanding of the topic to be gained, what research has already been completed on it, how it has been researched, and what the key issues are. Hart [6] says this amounts to showing that the main theories in the subject area are understood, how they have been applied and developed as well as the main criticisms that have been made of work on the topic.

Giuliani [7] stated that "in spite of an existing trend towards the codification of knowledge in the wine industry, tacit knowledge persists being important." She says that tacit knowledge still plays an important role in the industry, particularly in problem-solving activities and decision-making processes. In fact 'Experience and accumulation of tacit knowledge, passed down from generation to generation, dominated grape-growers' and winemakers' practices' [7]. Furthermore, Giuliani gave an example where tacit knowledge is superior in wineries, "the sensorial dimension of wine making is still the one where most of tacit knowledge resides." Casonato and Harris [3] found that tacit knowledge "is typically shared through discussion, stories, analogies and person-to-person interaction; therefore, it is difficult to capture or represent in explicit form." Studies by Gonzalez and Martins [5] found the importance of people as an instrument for retaining tacit knowledge. In a case study carried out by Zanuzzi et.al. [8] one interviewee reported "the people of this network have been around for many years and already know a lot, so they pass it on informally, but when that person is away, the information that is with them is missing, or if that person leaves the network, they are also not taking the care to register and store the information." Ticha and Havlicek [9] found that a variety of potential channels are utilized in the transfer of knowledge, "because knowledge itself, as well as the role players, are diverse in nature".

Management support can have an impact on the ability to capture tacit knowledge. Egbu [10] listed "senior management support" as a factor that promotes knowledge sharing. Storey and Barnett, cited in Carrillo et al. [11] stated that a cause of failure of knowledge management initiatives was "top management sponsorship without active ongoing involvement". Brochner and Javidan et al., and Bresnen et al., cited in Landaeta [12] stated that "senior management involvement", and "knowledge transfer leadership" respectively, was a factor "of knowledge transfer that may affect the performance and capabilities of projects". Landaeta [12] stated that "strong commitment from the senior management is a key facilitator of knowledge transfer" and can "overcome rigid organizational barriers". For the knowledge creation process to continue to evolve there must be strong leadership from an organization's management. Nonaka et.al. [13] stated that "leaders provide the knowledge vision, develop and promote sharing of knowledge assets, create, enable and promote the continuous spiral of knowledge creation".

The knowledge vision of an organization "gives a direction to the knowledge-creating process, and the knowledge created by it ... [defining] what kind of knowledge the company should create in what domain" [13]. Van Donk and Riezebos [14] stated that an organization needs to identify what information they need to capture. Egbu [10] in listing the factors that promote knowledge sharing, stated a "link to economic performance and strategy and coherent knowledge vision" as the top factor. Egbu [10] went on to state that specifically the strategic vision "exists in the organizational culture, its embedded routines, systems, procedures and processes". Implementing a knowledge management strategy to capture production information, and "achieve the potential benefits of KM, the critical issue is to implement a coordinated KM strategy that should be aligned with the company's overall strategy and objectives" [15].

Orange et al., cited in Kamara et al. [16], stated that a common approach "to capture the learning from projects is the post-project evaluation". However, whilst they stated that post project evaluation "can be useful in consolidating the learning of people" on the current project, "there are indications that current practice does not provide an effective framework for the capture and reuse of learning" [16]. Often there was "insufficient time for post-project evaluation to be conducted effectively (if conducted at all), as relevant personnel would have moved to other projects [16]. Other reasons given is it "does not allow the current project to be improved by incorporating the lessons being learnt as the project progresses" there is a "loss of important information or insights due to the time lapse in capturing the learning" and "post project evaluation is a not very effective mechanism for the transfer of knowledge to non-project participants" [16]. The gathering of production knowledge and experiences quite often cannot occur during production because of a lack of time and budget restrictions [17]. There is also difficulty carrying this out after production ends as team members quickly disperse to other projects and other team members will retire [17] and [15]. Kamara et al., cited in Tan et al. [18], stated "there are problems with the loss of knowledge due to the time lapse in capturing the knowledge, high staff turnover, and reassignment of people".

Whilst the capturing of project knowledge is the responsibility of all team members someone must be appointed as the person responsible for ensuring this happens [17]. Some projects employ a completely independent person from outside of the project to carry out this role [17]. Kivrak et al. [15] proposed a conceptual framework to capture tacit knowledge. The most important aspect of this framework is the employment of a knowledge management team with knowledge workers and a knowledge manager. Carrillo et al. [11] stated that "if KM is to achieve organizational goals, it should have a point of responsibility or a champion with responsibility for delivering objectives of the KM strategy".

Huysman and Wulf [19] explained that organizations need to create a culture that encourages knowledge sharing. Lee and Yang [20] agreed arguing that "the most effective way to disseminate knowledge and best practices is through systematic transfer. This is to create a knowledge sharing environment."

Several researchers have written about the importance of face-to-face interactions. Choo [21], Dangelico et al. [22], Davenport and Prusak [23], Melo [24], Nonaka and Takeuchi [25], Santiago [26] and Vick et al. [27] have all stated that socialization is used to transfer knowledge to other individuals in organizations. Indeed, whilst Yakhlef [28] states that information technology media are often used for capturing and diffusing explicit knowledge and information, he found that "face-to-face interactions and the sharing of content and perspectives is still the preferred way to capture tacit information." "Face-to-face contacts and socialization between knowledge generators and knowledge consumers ... prove to be a very effective channel of tacit knowledge sharing" [29] and [30].

## 3  Design and Method

This research was based on a phenomenological approach. It started with a literature review of the issues and continued with a small-scale survey of elite respondents in senior roles at wineries. Research using a qualitative process was used to gather the required data by way of a self-administered questionnaire. Bryman [31] has stated that a self-administered questionnaire was cheaper and quicker to administer, there was an absence of interviewer affects, there was no interviewer variability, and it was convenient for respondents; rather than having a structured interview. The research involved, firstly, a literature review and then a survey questionnaire. This aim was to obtain a sample of data and opinions from senior managers and winemakers associated with the management and production of wine. As such they were elite interviewees. Their response would then be evaluated to ascertain when, how and what winery knowledge was captured, was there management support, do they have a knowledge vision, and do they have a dedicated person who has responsibility for knowledge management?

Elite respondents in winery management were the desired respondents for this survey as they were those with, or had, proximity to power. Elites can be "loosely defined as... Those with close proximity to power" [32] or with particular expertise [33]. Delaney [34] has coined the term "organizational elites" and stated that "the elite status of my interview subject is a direct consequence of holding a particular position in an organization". In that respect those who responded to the survey questionnaire could be more precisely described as "organizational elites" as they were chosen because of their organizational or occupational position. Delaney [34] has also stated that "Organizational elites, by definition, have institutional positions that are readily ascertainable."

Fifteen wineries were randomly selected from each of the five major South Australian wine growing regions. Seventy-five wineries were sent the survey questionnaire package. This package consisted of a request for assistance letter stipulating those respondents had to be in senior roles or winemakers at the winery, thus elite interviewees. The package also contained an information sheet giving the background to the study and aims and objectives, the survey questionnaire and a reply postage paid envelope for the participant to return the completed questionnaire. The involvement of each person was voluntary with participants free to withdraw from the research project at any stage without affecting their status now or in the future. Completion of the questionnaire was anonymous as neither the manager nor winemaker's name nor the name of the winery was required, nor recorded. Of the seventy-five survey questionnaire packages sent out nineteen respondents submitted usable questionnaire responses, representing a sample size of 25%.

For the purposes of the survey the questionnaire consisted of 13 multi-choice questions divided into three sections. Section one was designed to gather background information on the respondent and the winery. Section two was designed to gather information on the strategic framework aspects of knowledge management by the respondent's winery. Section three was designed to gather information about when, how and what information the winery gathers during wine production.

## 4 Discussion of Results

Of the seventy-five survey questionnaire packages sent out nineteen respondents submitted usable questionnaire responses, representing a sample size of 25%. One of the limitations of self-administered postal questionnaires is that they typically result in lower response rates than a structured interview [31].

Section one of the survey was designed to gather background information on the respondent and the winery. One respondent in answering "other" described their role in at the winery as "Managing Director" whilst two other respondents described their role in at the winery as "Manager" and "Winemaker". Adding these to those who described themselves as "Manager" (9) or "Winemaker" (6), indicates that 18 or 95% of the respondents were senior managers in their wineries, and thus elite respondents. The breakdown of the size of the wineries surveyed reveals that 73% of those wineries employed less than 40 employees.

Section two of the survey was designed to focus on the strategic framework aspects of knowledge management. In exploring the research questions in this section, five attributes were identified. Does the winery have senior management support, a knowledge management vision, procedures for sharing knowledge, a knowledge management approach to managing winery production and is there a dedicated person who has responsibility for knowledge management. More than 58% of the wineries had senior management support and a knowledge management approach, but less than 42% knowledge management procedures, a knowledge management vision and a dedicated person with responsibility for knowledge management. Table 1 records the survey findings of the size of the winery in relation to these attributes.

Section three was designed to reveal how each of the surveyed wineries manages the knowledge that they gain during wine production. In exploring the research questions in this section two main themes were identified. The first theme was when and how is production knowledge captured during winery production. The survey data in Table 2 suggests that there are primarily three times when their wineries gathered the knowledge gained during production. These were at the end of each production phase (63% of respondents), sometime after production is finished (79%) and prior to the departure of a team member as a debrief (84%). However, only 32% of wineries continuously gathered knowledge through the production life cycle, 37% at a pre-production kick-off review of lessons learnt from previous vintages and 42% at the end of production as a wrap up.

Table 2 also records the survey data for the second theme in this section, how production knowledge is gathered. It shows that the approach for 79% of participants was to capture it by interviewing each team member, 89% by formally scheduled meetings at milestones whereas only 42% by ad hoc brainstorming sessions. Surprisingly 74% of respondents said that the knowledge gathered during the production of wine was not recorded.

Table 3 records the survey data for the third theme in this section, what types of management information are gathered. This shows that there are primarily four types of explicit knowledge that are gathered and stored during production. These were risk registers and risk treatments (68% of respondents), production reviews/reports (74%), minutes of meetings (74%) and emails (79%).

# 5  Discussion

The aim of this research study was to investigate whether winery team members were able to capture tacit knowledge, convert it into explicit knowledge, store it and then reuse it in future projects. A small-scale survey of elite respondents in senior roles at wineries. Was undertaken to discover; when how and what information was gathered, do they have management support, do they have a knowledge vision, and do they have a dedicated person who has responsibility for knowledge management?

The findings reported in Table 1 found that if there is not strong and visible support for knowledge management activities by senior management then employees will not engage in capturing project information and this result supports the work of Nonaka, Toyama and Konno [13], Egbu [10], Brochner and Javidan et al., and Bresnen et al. (cited in Landaeta [12]). Sixty-eight per cent of survey respondents from all wineries reported that they had the support of senior management for the capture of production information. The finding of 68% support by senior management is at odds with the finding that only 11% of respondent wineries had a knowledge vision. This seems to indicate that whilst a fair proportion of wineries have strong management support for the capture of production information, most of the wineries have yet to see the wisdom to have a knowledge vision where the capture of production information can be more precisely targeted. Indeed, they may not be capturing production information that is useful for them.

Another interesting finding is that whilst 68% of wineries reported they had the support of senior management only 26% reported they had a dedicated person who had responsibility for knowledge management. The findings provide clear evidence that the size of a winery is a differentiating factor when considering knowledge management attributes. Wineries that had less than 10 employees and 11 to 40 employees, had senior management support (combined 71%), a knowledge management vision (combined only 7%), knowledge management procedures (combined 36%), a knowledge management approach (combined 57%) and a dedicated person who had responsibility for knowledge management (combined 21%). This may be because they have greater resources available to them to allow them to put in place the actions required to capture production knowledge. The breakup of the 19 wineries into five groups based on their size has allowed comparisons to be made between the groups.

Table 1. Size of winery in relation to KM attributes.

| Organization ID | No of Employees in Winery | | | | | Strategic Framework. Does the Winery have the following attributes? | | | | |
|---|---|---|---|---|---|---|---|---|---|---|
| | <10 | 11-40 | 41-70 | 71-100 | >101 | Senior Management Support | KM Procedures | KM vision | KM Approach | KM Responsibility |
| 1 | | • | | | | • | • | | | • |
| 2 | • | | | | | • | • | | • | • |
| 3 | | • | | | | | | | | |
| 4 | | | • | | | • | • | • | • | |
| 5 | | | • | | | • | • | | • | |
| 6 | | • | | | | • | | | • | |
| 7 | | • | | | | • | | | • | |
| 8 | | • | | | | • | • | | • | |
| 9 | | • | | | | • | • | • | • | • |
| 10 | • | | | | | • | | | | |
| 11 | • | | | | | • | | | • | |
| 12 | | • | | | | • | • | | • | |
| 13 | | | | • | | • | • | | • | • |
| 14 | | • | | | | | | | | |
| 15 | | • | | | | • | | | • | |
| 16 | | | | | • | | | | | • |
| 17 | | | | | • | | | | | |
| 18 | • | | | | | | | | | |
| 19 | • | | | | | | | | | |
| Count | 5 | 9 | 1 | 2 | 2 | No of Employees in winery | | | | |
| % | 26 | 47 | 5 | 11 | 11 | | | | | |
| Count | 3 | 7 | 1 | 2 | 0 | 13 | Senior Management Support | | | |
| % | 60 | 78 | 100 | 100 | 0 | 68 | | | | |
| Count | 1 | 4 | 1 | 2 | 0 | | 8 | KM procedures | | |
| % | 5 | 44 | 100 | 100 | 0 | | 42 | | | |
| Count | 0 | 1 | 0 | 1 | 0 | | | 2 | KM Vision | |
| % | 0 | 11 | 0 | 50 | 0 | | | 11 | | |
| Count | 2 | 6 | 1 | 2 | 0 | | KM Approach | | 11 | |
| % | 40 | 67 | 100 | 100 | 0 | | | | 58 | |
| Count | 1 | 2 | 0 | 1 | 1 | | KM Responsibility | | | 5 |
| % | 5 | 22 | 0 | 50 | 50 | | | | | 26 |

The literature review on knowledge vision in organizations revealed that an incoherent knowledge vision or the lack of ownership of a knowledge vision inhibited knowledge sharing in organizations. Not having a knowledge vision, a winery could be capturing information that is not appropriate for the winery production they are engaged in. The survey responses indicated that only 11% of respondents had a knowledge vision. There

**Table 2.** When and how does your winery gather the knowledge gained during production.

| When knowledge gathered | | Number | % of participants |
|---|---|---|---|
| Pre-production kick-off review of Lessons Learned from previous vintages | Yes | 12 | 63 |
| | No | 7 | 37 |
| | **Total** | **19** | **100** |
| At the end of each production phase | Yes | 7 | 37 |
| | No | 12 | 63 |
| | **Total** | **19** | **100** |
| Continuously through the production lifecycle | Yes | 13 | 68 |
| | No | 6 | 32 |
| | **Total** | **19** | **100** |
| Prior to departure of a team member as a debrief | Yes | 3 | 16 |
| | No | 16 | 84 |
| | **Total** | **19** | **100** |
| At the end of production as a wrap-up | Yes | 11 | 58 |
| | No | 8 | 42 |
| | **Total** | **19** | **100** |
| Sometime after production is finished | Yes | 4 | 21 |
| | No | 15 | 79 |
| | **Total** | **19** | **100** |
| How knowledge gathered | | Number | % of participants |
| Formally scheduled meetings at milestones | Yes | 2 | 11 |
| | No | 17 | 89 |
| | **Total** | **19** | **100** |
| Individual interviews with winery employees | Yes | 4 | 21 |
| | No | 15 | 79 |
| | **Total** | **19** | **100** |
| Ad hoc brainstorming sessions | Yes | 11 | 58 |
| | No | 8 | 42 |
| | **Total** | **19** | **100** |
| No recording of knowledge gained | Yes | 5 | 26 |
| | No | 14 | 74 |
| | **Total** | **19** | **100** |
| Other (please specify) | Yes | 1 | 5 |
| | No | 18 | 95 |
| | **Total** | **19** | **100** |

are two other interesting findings that involve a knowledge vision. The first is to look at the wineries who have a knowledge vision and a knowledge manager. Five per cent

**Table 3.** What management information does your winery gather.

| Types of management information | | Number | % of participants |
|---|---|---|---|
| Production reviews/reports | Yes | 14 | 74 |
| | No | 5 | 26 |
| | **Total** | **19** | **100** |
| Minutes of meetings | Yes | 14 | 74 |
| | No | 5 | 26 |
| | **Total** | **19** | **100** |
| Emails | Yes | 15 | 79 |
| | No | 4 | 21 |
| | **Total** | **19** | **100** |
| Workarounds | Yes | 0 | 0 |
| | No | 19 | 100 |
| | **Total** | **19** | **100** |
| Milestone checklists and reports | Yes | 4 | 21 |
| | No | 15 | 79 |
| | **Total** | **19** | **100** |
| Lesson Learned reports | Yes | 1 | 5 |
| | No | 18 | 95 |
| | **Total** | **19** | **100** |
| Risk registers and risk treatments | Yes | 13 | 68 |
| | No | 6 | 32 |
| | **Total** | **19** | **100** |
| Conversations/phone calls | Yes | 6 | 32 |
| | No | 13 | 68 |
| | **Total** | **19** | **100** |
| Personal generated memory joggers or an aide-mémoire | Yes | 4 | 21 |
| | No | 15 | 79 |
| | **Total** | **19** | **100** |
| Other (please specify) | Yes | 4 | 21 |
| | No | 15 | 79 |
| | **Total** | **19** | **100** |

of the surveyed wineries who had a knowledge vision stated that they had someone in the winery who had overall responsibility for knowledge management. This low finding provides support for the work by Egbu [10] that if there is a lack of a coherent knowledge vision there will not be knowledge sharing. This also supports the work of Carrillo et al. [11] that to achieve organizational goals there must be a champion with responsibility for delivering objectives. The second finding involves those who have a knowledge vision and knowledge procedures. Eleven per cent of the surveyed wineries who had a knowledge vision stated that they had knowledge procedures. This low finding provides support for the work by Egbu [10] that a winery's strategic vision exists in its procedures and processes. It is likely that if a winery does not have a knowledge management vision, then they won't have knowledge management procedures. This is also borne out by Kivrak et al. [15] that to achieve the benefits of knowledge management a knowledge management strategy must be aligned with a winery's strategy and objectives.

The literature review on when information is gathered revealed that organizations will gather project information at various stages through a project lifecycle, but invariably it will be at the end or after the project has finished. The most inconclusive finding from the survey, reported in Table 2, was that whilst 37% of respondents gathered knowledge at the end of each production phase, 68% said continuously through the production lifecycle and 58% said at the end of final production as a wrap-up. The survey questions need to be rewritten in future to get more meaningful and consistent results. However, only 16% conducted a debriefing with team members prior to the departure of a team member. So much production knowledge was lost. Twenty-one per cent of respondents endeavored to capture production knowledge sometime after the production was finished. This research supports the work of Orange et al. (cited in Kamara et al. [16]) and Kamara et al. [16] of the importance of post project evaluations or reviews. In fact, the findings for all timings of opportunities to capture production knowledge reported by respondents is no greater than 68%. This indicates a tremendous opportunity to capture production knowledge that has been lost by most of the wineries. This finding supports the work of Disterer [17] that knowledge not gained during projects risks being lost with the end of a project. Hu and He [35] have stated that new projects start with nearly zero knowledge, however this has not been borne out by the findings. Thirty-seven per cent of the participants reported that production knowledge is captured at project kick-off or from lessons learned from previous production. This finding could be colored by the survey participants' own past experiences of the beginning of production. These elite respondents are more than likely highly experienced production managers who would bring a lot of tacit knowledge into production from day one. They may have confused the amount of knowledge that they personally bring to production at kick-off, with the amount of written knowledge available at that time. A survey question about the amount of experience the participant has may have clarified this finding.

The findings reported in the second part of Table 2 list how tacit knowledge is captured. Individual interviews with team members, a good time to capture tacit information, was only utilized by 21% of wineries. An additional open question could have been added to the survey. "If individual interviews with team members were not carried out, what was the reason?" This would have allowed the works of Orange et al. (cited in Kamara et al. [16]), Disterer, [17], Kivrak et al., [15] and Kamara et al. (cited in Tan et al. [19]) to be supported or otherwise for reasons why individual interviews did not occur. These reasons could have been that personnel had moved to other projects in the winery, there was a lack of time and budget restrictions, or team members had retired. However, it got even worse, only 11% of participants stated that their wineries captured tacit production knowledge at formally scheduled milestone meetings. But on a positive note, 58% of participants said that their wineries captured tacit production knowledge at informal ad hoc brainstorming sessions. These findings support the work of Landaeta [12] that formal and informal transfer methods should be used for the transfer of knowledge.

The literature review on the conversion of tacit information to explicit information revealed that team members' personal information is quite often not captured in formal project documentation. The survey responses support the work of Landaeta [12] and Maya et al. [36]. The findings reported in Table 3 showed there was only a small proportion of participants whose wineries converted tacit knowledge to explicit knowledge. Conversations and phone calls, personal workarounds, personal generated memory joggers or an aide-mémoire and personal emails are examples of tacit information that must be captured and converted into explicit information. Personal workarounds, personal generated memory joggers or an aide-mémoire and emails are explicit information as they are written documents, but they have been considered tacit information for this research as they are usually informally exchanged between winery participants and don't get formally captured. The findings reported that 32% of participants captured conversations and phone calls, no participant captured workarounds and 21% of participants captured personal generated memory joggers or an aide-mémoire. Surprisingly, 79% of participants captured emails. Disterer, [17] stated that it is not possible to capture this type of knowledge by traditional transfer methods and Bresnen et al. [37] put forward the premise that as knowledge is often tacit, social groupings and personal networks are an important way that knowledge can be transferred. The findings in this study revealed that production reviews/reports, minutes of meetings and risk registers and risk treatments, more traditional production management explicit information, was reported as being utilized by greater than 68% of the participants. Surprisingly with milestone checklists and reports, a customary element of production was utilized by only 21% of participants. Lessons learned often considered a best practice amongst production management practitioners was only reported by 5% of survey participants as being the type of knowledge that they captured. Analyzing the responses for the "other information" category, 21% of respondents reported for the types of production knowledge that are captured, indicated that they were all explicit information by various names. The findings of this survey in relation to wineries relying on tacit knowledge at the expense of explicit knowledge supports Giuliani's findings that tacit knowledge dominated grape-growers' and winemakers' practices [7].

# 6  Conclusion and Future Work

Through this research it has been demonstrated that without senior management support employees will not engage in capturing winery production information. The research also found that 32% of wineries who didn't have a knowledge vision didn't have a knowledge manager and 58% of wineries that didn't have a knowledge vision didn't have knowledge procedures in place. Not having a knowledge vision does not allow wineries to focus on capturing information that is aligned to their winery's strategy and objectives. Indeed, they may not be capturing production information that is useful for them. Production knowledge was being lost because it was not being captured when it was generated, it was captured too late in the process if at all. Not enough importance was put on the individual interviews with team members. But perhaps the key finding of this research was the failure of the surveyed wineries to convert more of their tacit information (conversations, phone calls and personal information) into explicit information.

The timing for the issue of this study did not consider what was happening at wineries at that time. Wineries were too busy to take the time to fill in the questionnaire. Also, the deadline imposed on the wineries was not long enough. In future questionnaires will be emailed to the wineries rather than posting them.

# References

1. Stair, R.M., Reynolds, G.W.: Principles of Information Systems: A Managerial Approach, 3rd edn. Danvers Mass. U.S.A, Boyd and Fraser (1998)
2. Dampney, C.N.G., Busch, P., Richards, D.: The Meaning of Tacit Knowledge. Austr. J. Inform. Syst. 3–13 (2007)
3. Casonato, R., Harris, K.: "Can an Enterprise Really Capture "Tacit Knowledge"?: We Answer Two Top Questions on Knowledge Management from the Electronic Workplace 1999 Conference" Gartner Group Research Note Select Q&A 16th March (1999)
4. Kogut, B., Zander, U.: Knowledge of the firm, combinative capabilities and the replication of technology. Organ. Stud. 3(3), 383–397 (1992)
5. Gonzalez, R.V.D., Martins, M.F.: Knowledge management process: a theoretical-conceptual research. Manag. Product. 24(2), 248–265 (2017)
6. Hart, C.: Doing a Literature Review. Sage Publications Ltd., London (2005)
7. Giuliani, E.: The wine industry: persistence of tacit knowledge or increased codification? Some implications for catching-up countries. Int. J. Technol. Globalization 3(2/3), 138–154 (2007)
8. Zanuzzi, C., Tonial, G., Matos, F., Selig, P.: Knowledge management and interorganizational networks of the wine industry. In: Proceedings of the 24th European Conference on Knowledge Management, ECKM 2023, pp. 1491–1499. Academic Conferences International Limited, Reading, UK (2023)
9. Ticha, I., Havlicek, J.: Knowledge transfer. Agricul. Econ.-Czech 53(12), 539–544 (2007)
10. Egbu, C.O.: Managing knowledge and intellectual capital for improved organizational innovations in the constructive industry: an examination of critical success factors. Eng. Constr. Archit. Manag. 11(5), 301–315 (2004)
11. Carrillo, P.: Managing Knowledge: lessons from the oil and gas sector. Constr. Manag. Econ. 22(July), 631–642 (2004)
12. Landaeta, R.E.: Evaluating benefits and challenges of knowledge transfer across projects. Eng. Manag. J. 20(1), 29–38 (2008)
13. Nonaka, I., Toyama, R., Konno, N.: SECI, Ba and leadership: a unified model of dynamic knowledge creation. Long Range Plan. 33, 5–34 (2000)
14. Van Donk, D.P., Riezebos, J.: Exploring the knowledge inventory in project-based organizations: a case study. Int. J. Project Manage. 23(1), 75–83 (2004)
15. Kivrak, S., Arslan, G., Dikmen, I., Birgonul, M.T.: Capturing knowledge in construction projects: knowledge platform for contractors. J. Manag. Eng. 24(2), 87–95 (2008)
16. Kamara, J.M., Anumba, C.J., Carrillo, P.M., Bouchlaghem, N.: Conceptual framework for live capture and reuse of project knowledge. In: Proceedings CIB W078 International Conference on Information Technology for Construction-Construction IT: Bridging the Distance, pp. 178–185 (2003)
17. Disterer, G.: Management of project knowledge and experiences. J. Knowl. Manag. 6(5), 512–520 (2002)

18. Tan, H.C., Carrillo, P.M., Anumba, C.J., Bouchlaghem, N., Kamara, J.M., Udeaja, C.E.: Development of a methodology for live capture and reuse of project management in construction. J. Manag. Eng. **23**(1), 18–26 (2007)
19. Huysman, M., Wulf, V.: IT to support knowledge sharing in communities, towards a social capital analysis. J. Inf. Technol. **21**(1), 40–51 (2006)
20. Lee, C., Yang, J.: Knowledge value chain. J. Manag. Dev. **19**(9), 783–794 (2000)
21. Choo, C.W.: The knowledge organization: how organizations use information to create meaning, construct knowledge, and make decisions. Int. J. Inf. Manage. **16**(5), 329–340 (1996)
22. Dangelico, R.M., Garavelli, A.C., Petruzzelli, A.M.: A system dynamics model to analyze technology districts' evolution in a knowledge-based perspective. Technovation **30**(2), 142–153 (2010)
23. Davenport, T.H., Prusak, L.: Business Knowledge: How Organizations Manage their Intellectual Capital, 10th edn. Elsevier, Rio de Janeiro (2003)
24. Melo, L.: Knowledge Management: Concepts and Applications. Érica, São Paulo (2003)
25. Nonaka, I., Takeuchi, H.: Knowledge Creation in the Company, 1st edn. Elsevier, Rio de Janeiro (1997)
26. Santiago, J.R.S.: Knowledge Management: the Key to Business Success, 1st edn. Artmed, São Paulo (2004)
27. Vick, T., Nagano, M.S., Santos, F.A.: Contributions from information management to knowledge creation in innovation teams. Perspectivas em Ciência da Informação **14**(2), 204–219 (2008)
28. Yakhlef, A.: Immobility of tacit knowledge and the displacement of the locus of innovation. Eur. J. Innov. Manag. **8**(2), 227–239 (2005)
29. Hoffman, M., Lubell, M., Hillis, V.: Network-smart extension could catalyze social learning. Calif. Agric. **69**(2), 113–122 (2015)
30. Krishnan, P., Patnam, M.: Neighbors and extension agents in Ethiopia: who matters more for technology adoption? Am. J. Agr. Econ. **96**(1), 308–327 (2014)
31. Bryman, A.: Social Research Methods, 4th edn. Oxford University Press, Oxford, UK (2012)
32. Lilleker, D.G.: Interviewing the Political Elite: Navigating a Potential Minefield. Politics **23**(3), 207–214 (2003)
33. Burnham, P., Gilland, F., Grant, W., Layton-Henry, Z.: Research Methods in Politics. Palgrave Macmillan, Basingstoke, UK (2004)
34. Delaney, K.J.: Methodological Dilemmas and Opportunities in Interviewing Organizational Elites. Sociol. Compass **1**(1), 208–221 (2007)
35. Hu, W., He X.: Knowledge management strategy and approach in multiple project environments. In: 2008 International Symposium on Information Science and Engineering (ISISE 2008), vol 2, pp. 197–200 (2008)
36. Maya, I., Rahimi, M., Meshkati, N., Madabushi, D., Pope, K., Schulte, M.: Cultural influence on the implementation of lessons learned in project management. Eng. Manag. J. **17**(4), 17–24 (2005)
37. Bresnen, M., Edelman, L., Newell, S., Scarbrough, H., Swan, J.: Social practices and the management of knowledge in project environments. Int. J. Project Manag. **21**(3), 157–166 (2003). https://doi.org/10.1016/S0263-7863(02)00090-X

# Financial and Corporate Restructuring in South Korea

Suppanunta Romprasert[✉], Thanakhom Srisaringkarn, Danai Tanamee, Switchaya Singseewo, Nichathorn Nanon, and Sutthanuch Wiriyapinit

The Faculty of Economics and International College for Sustainability Studies, Srinakharinwirot University, Wattana, Bangkok, Thailand
{suppanunta,thanakhom,danait,thanakhom}@g.swu.ac.th, sutthanuch@swu.ac.th

**Abstract.** The rapid growth of South Korea's economy, fueled by technological innovation, particularly in manufacturing, has led to shifts in consumer behavior and the laundry service industry. The rise of income-led growth, driven by domestic consumption, has increased disposable income, fostering demand for laundry services. The industry's evolution, from home washing to on-demand services, aligns with busy lifestyles, emphasizing convenience. However, the ongoing impact of COVID-19 has reshaped consumer habits, intensified hygiene concerns and creating a competitive landscape. Cleantopia, a prominent laundry service company, undergoes scrutiny for financial and corporate restructuring post-pandemic. Objectives include investigating COVID-19's impact on the market, SWOT analysis of Cleantopia's strategy, and identifying efficient strategies for future growth and stability. The multifaceted corporate structure, encompassing 134 branches and 2,492 chains nationwide, requires strategic human resource management revamping. Initiatives such as standardized service training programs and uniform service standards aim to foster brand loyalty and elevate customer satisfaction. Strengthening regulatory compliance measures ensures consistency across branches, promoting a cohesive organizational culture. Productivity enhancement, involving streamlined processes and optimized resource allocation, becomes integral in adapting to the evolving landscape. Quality assurance mechanisms guarantee consistent service quality, contributing to positive customer experiences and fortifying the company's reputation. In essence, these proposed strategies seek to fortify Cleantopia's financial resilience, enable recovery, and establish a foundation for sustained growth and competitiveness in the dynamic laundry service market.

**Keywords:** Consumer Behavior · Income – Led – Growth · South Korea · SWOT Analysis

## 1 Introduction

South Korea's economy has been experiencing rapid growth, primarily driven by technological innovation, particularly in manufacturing [1]. During the early stages of industrialization, South Korea heavily relied on imported technology, especially in the development of production facilities [2]. This approach allowed the country to produce basic

© The Author(s), under exclusive license to Springer Nature Switzerland AG 2024
L. Uden and I.-H. Ting (Eds.): KMO 2024, CCIS 2152, pp. 135–157, 2024.
https://doi.org/10.1007/978-3-031-63269-3_11

goods at competitive costs and quality, ensuring both domestic and international competitiveness [3]. The term "income-led growth" has gained significance because of President Moon's election in May 2017, with domestic consumption playing a crucial role, supported by pro-labor distributional policies, such as wage increases [4]. As a result, disposable income has increased, leading to a robust demand for the laundry service market in South Korea [5]. Technological innovation has prompted producers to add innovative features to their products, enhancing performance and differentiation from competitors [6]. The laundry industry has transformed significantly in recent years, shifting from home washing to on-demand services, including pick-up and drop-off options [7]. The demand for such services has surged due to busy lifestyles, emphasizing the importance of convenience [8]. The laundry service industry's reliability and technological advancement have further contributed to its popularity, and the market is expected to grow with the increasing adoption of cashless transactions [9]. The ongoing impact of COVID-19 in 2021 has heightened hygiene concerns among consumers, leading to changes in cleaning habits and hygiene standards [10]. This situation has affected various industries, including laundry services, creating a competitive environment [11]. Companies are adapting by applying new technologies, offering new services, and adjusting their financial and business plans to remain competitive [12]. Financial and corporate restructuring activities are seen as crucial for improving financial performance, resource allocation, innovation, profitability, service quality, and overall financial system stability [13]. In this research paper, Cleantopia, one of South Korea's largest and most popular laundry service companies, serves as a case study for a detailed analysis of financial and corporate restructuring after the impact of COVID-19 [14]. The study aims to identify the factors influencing the laundry business and develop efficient strategies to enhance Cleantopia's market position and ensure growth in the future. Objectives are: 1) Examine the effects of COVID-19 on the South Korean laundry service market. 2) Evaluate Cleantopia's business approach by conducting a SWOT analysis to formulate plans for financial and corporate reorganization in the aftermath of COVID-19. and 3) Recognize effective tactics for enhancing future profitability, financial resilience, optimal resource utilization, and overall business expansion.

## 2   Literature Review

In accordance with Hirshleifers perspective, as cited in [15], the foremost objective of a firm acting as a decision-making agent is to maximize economic profit. Corporate executives and investors vehemently advocate that profit maximization constitutes the predominant impetus underpinning the foundational establishment of business entities. In practice, individuals opt to engage in economic activities and investments guided by the central principle of profit maximization. In the absence of economic incentives, the persuasion of individuals to invest their financial resources or valuable assets in endeavors or projects devoid of anticipated returns would be exceedingly challenging, if not nearly insurmountable. Firms, as posited by [15, 16], are constructively structured by contractual agreements. Even when marginal income equates to marginal cost, enterprises do not consistently attain maximal profitability. It is contended that, to achieve sustained profit maximization in the short and long term, decision-makers, i.e., management, must incorporate multifaceted considerations encompassing risk, uncertainty, and the temporal value of money. As per the tenets of the market selection hypothesis, it is reasonable to presume that all business entities operate with the primary goal of profit maximization. The alternative would entail a substantial risk of market elimination for non-profit-maximizing businesses. Thus, in a certain sense, market forces decree those businesses either fulfill their profit maximization objective or face dissolution. Hsing-chin, Hsihui, C, Anna, M.C. & Huang, L H. [17] investigated the impact of financial restructuring on Taiwan's financial performance. The findings indicated an enhancement in performance attributable to the increased operational activities in bank management, the implementation of risk management measures, and other associated benefits derived from financial restructuring. Organizational efficiency and success are inextricably linked to the effective utilization of diverse resources to achieve predetermined objectives, as articulated by Worthington Enterprises [18]. The evaluation of organizational performance can be accomplished through financial or non-financial metrics, a notion supported by [19] and [20]. Accounting-based methodologies predominantly scrutinize financial performance through the analysis of balance sheets and financial accounting reports. Additionally, non-accounting and market-based techniques are employed to assess financial performance. Osoro [21] conducted a study on the influence of financial restructuring on the overall financial performance of Kenya's commercial banks. This study employed financial restructuring approaches such as the debt-to-capital ratio, dividend-to-capital ratio, and dividend payout ratio, utilizing Return on Equity (ROE) as a financial performance metric. The research discerned that financial restructuring had a positive impact on the financial performance of Kenya's commercial banks.

Information and relationship management systems play a pivotal role in overseeing the value chain, contributing to the efficient management of organizational structure and operational processes. According to Yi-Chan Chung and friends [22], a substantial correlation exists between business value performance and quality management. Furthermore, Hall, Algiers & Levitt [23] (2018) assert that these systems facilitate coherent and coordinated actions by industry stakeholders and policymakers by emphasizing connectivity among the various stages and actors within a supply chain. In line with the insights of Gattorna and Walters [24], the value chain framework provides a systematic approach not only for scrutinizing a company's operations but also for assessing the activities of component companies within a broader pipeline or supply chain context. As delineated by Hahn & Kuhn [25], the optimization of the value chain can be instrumental in resource allocation, risk mitigation, and the provisioning of requisite services. As per the perspective of economists Hall and Hitch, the principal objective of a company should be the generation of profit. This perspective is also upheld by conventional economists. Profit maximization, as a strategy, seeks to optimize revenue by aligning the marginal cost of producing products and services with the marginal revenue, thereby enhancing earnings while minimizing costs. The pursuit of profit maximization involves the consideration of various factors. Initially, the profit can be graphically illustrated by plotting revenue against costs. The ensuing supply and demand graph exemplifies how this can be accomplished by charting income and costs as variables in relation to the output function (Fig. 1):

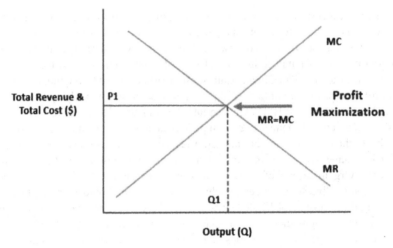

**Fig. 1.** Profit Maximization Graph. Source: [26]

To achieve profit maximization (MC = MR), it is imperative that the marginal revenue and marginal cost coincide, signifying the equilibrium point on the graph. When there exists the widest gap, or maximum disparity, between MR and MC, as well as between total revenue (TR) and total cost (TC), producers or businesses have attained this equilibrium. Based on the graph's depiction, the output quantity denoted as Q1 represents the point of intersection between MR and MC. Should the firm's output fall below the equilibrium quantity, Q1, MR will surpass MC, leading to an overall profit increase as the company generates more revenue than it incurs in production costs. At the outset, as the firm's output approaches the level of Q1, MR slightly exceeds MC. However, as output surpasses Q1, the marginal cost experiences a significant rise, overtaking marginal revenue. Consequently, the company begins to incur losses. Hence, profit maximization can only be realized within the range of Q1, as beyond this point, MC surpasses MR, leading to diminishing profits. The concept of the "Value Chain" was originally introduced by Michael Porter in his seminal work titled "Competitive Advantage: Creating and Sustaining Superior Performance" [27]. According to Porter, a company's "value chain" delineates its value-adding operations, which are intricately linked to its pricing strategy and cost structure. The company's capability to comprehensively understand both its internal competencies and the discerned needs of its customers is pivotal for the effective execution of its competitive strategy. The value chain framework comprises five key elements: the end market, the business and enabling environment, the vertical linkages, the supporting market, and the horizontal linkages. End markets, distinct from physical markets, occupy a distinctive position within the value chain structure, representing the ultimate consumers of goods and services. They play a pivotal role in the success of a product or service, exerting influence over factors such as quality, quantity, pricing, and production scheduling, thereby shaping the demand for these offerings. The interconnections among firms also exert a profound impact on the value chain of goods and services. This process of value addition is continuous, beginning with an understanding of customer needs and extending throughout the primary activities in the chain.

At each juncture, value addition is imperative to distinguish the product or service from its competitors while concurrently ensuring the highest quality standards at an optimized cost.

Michael Porter's Value Chain Model

Source: [28]

The value chain analysis framework categorizes value-adding activities into two distinct categories: primary activities and support activities. Primary activities encompass a collection of functions directly contributing to the creation of value, while support activities encompass functions and tasks designed to facilitate and bolster the primary activities. In discussion approach, researchers employ the value chain theory as a vital component in the analysis and discussion of financial and corporate restructuring. This analysis encompasses an examination of all business activities within an organization, including corporate structure, human resources management, human resources development, business strategy, product and service offerings, advertising, and delivery. This comprehensive approach involves the scrutiny of both primary and supportive activities, rendering the value chain theory a suitable framework for attribution and explanation within this report. Furthermore, researchers also utilize the theory of profit maximization, which endeavors to align the marginal cost of producing products and services with the marginal revenue, thereby enhancing profitability while minimizing costs. This approach is instrumental in analyzing the revenue trend of Cleantopia from 2017 to 2021. The objective is twofold: to gain insights into shifts in consumer behavior and to identify effective strategies for recovery from the impact of COVID-19, including measures to improve profitability and foster future business growth.

## 3  Research Methods

Two independent variables are considered within this study: the financial and corporate restructuring effects, with a focus on their influence on the change in the dependent variable, which is revenue.

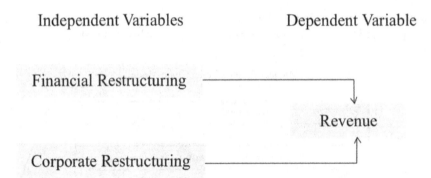

## Independent Variables Comprises of

### Financial Restructuring

This pertains to the enhancement of Cleantopia's financial strategy, necessitated by the impact of the COVID-19 situation. The process encompasses the evaluation of strategic alternatives, scrutiny of shareholder interests across different scenarios, the formulation of a restructuring plan, and the facilitation of negotiation. It is crucial for the consensus of all shareholders involved in the process that financial restructuring will fortify the company's prospects for success. The process involves an analysis of the company and its prospects, an exploration of restructuring possibilities, the development of a comprehensive restructuring plan, the determination of new cash flow requirements, and the procurement of the requisite financial resources. These sequential steps collectively contribute to the achievement of a successful financial restructuring for Cleantopia.

### Corporation Restructuring

The endeavor to enhance Cleantopia's performance following the recovery from the COVID-19 pandemic entails a multifaceted process that encompasses the reorganization of the company's management and operations. The primary aim of this restructuring effort is to bolster the company's efficiency and effectiveness. Key aspects of this process involve the strategic management of employees and human resources, including training programs aimed at skill enhancement, as well as resource allocation that entails the integration of new innovations and technologies into the company's operations. Corporate restructuring serves as a vital mechanism in elevating a company's productivity, enhancing the quality of services rendered, and, importantly, in better aligning the company to meet the diverse needs of its customers and shareholders.

### Dependent Variable Comprises of:

### Revenue

Revenue, in the context of a company, signifies the monetary inflow resulting from its operational activities. The specific method used to calculate revenue may vary depending on the chosen accounting entity or framework. This paper focuses on the calculation of revenue for the laundry service company, Cleantopia, for the period spanning 2017–2021. Revenue in this context is derived from multiple sources, including the number of consumers utilizing Cleantopia's app, patronage of stores situated within malls, and the self-laundry (coin) service. This calculated revenue is further determined by multiplying the number of consumers by the washing price, which is assessed based on the weight of general clothes laundry in kilograms.

The study investigates the influence of financial and corporate restructuring, treated as independent variables, in driving the company to augment its revenue and maximize profits. Moreover, human resources are also instrumental in the recovery process from the adverse effects of the COVID-19 pandemic. These factors collectively shape the trajectory of Cleantopia's financial performance and resilience in the face of contemporary challenges.

$$\text{Total revenue} = \text{Price per product} \times \text{Quantity}$$

$$TR = P \times Q$$

$$\text{Total revenue of Cleantopia} = \text{Number of consumers} \times \text{Washing price}$$

Note: The washing price for Cleantopia's laundry services is determined as an average cost, considering both self-service laundry and drop-off service. Specifically, the cost for one laundry cycle per consumer is set at 500 Korean Won (KRW).

| Year | Number of consumers (million) | Total Revenue (billion KRW) |
| --- | --- | --- |
| 2017 | 17.5 | 87.5 |
| 2018 | 17.9 | 89.5 |
| 2019 (during COVID-19) | 17.0 | 85.0 |
| 2020 (during COVID-19) | 16.9 | 84.5 |
| 2021 | 16.2 | 81.0 |

Source: [29].

# 4   Results and Analysis

The dry-cleaning and laundry services industry in South Korea is experiencing a surge in popularity, driven by factors such as its reliability, technological advancements within the laundry sector, and the prevailing trend of urbanization. Furthermore, the future growth of this market is anticipated to be influenced by the increasing adoption of cashless transactions, supplanting traditional coin-based services. As of 2022, the revenue in the laundry service market in South Korea has reached a substantial $1.70 billion. This market is poised for annual growth, projected at a rate of 3.52% (CAGR 2013–2022) [30]. The industry's expansion is primarily attributed to the growing consumer preference for laundry services, which offer a convenient solution at a reasonable cost. Additionally, the increasing expenditure by consumers on these services is expected to propel further market enlargement.

Even though most individuals may not relish the task of frequent laundry, the desire to wear clean and well-maintained clothing remains universal. Given the demands of modern lifestyles, many consumers are actively seeking dry-cleaning and laundry services to manage their soiled garments effectively, underscoring the industry's significance in catering to the needs of a busy and convenience-driven customer base.

Revenue in the Laundry Service Segment (billion USD)

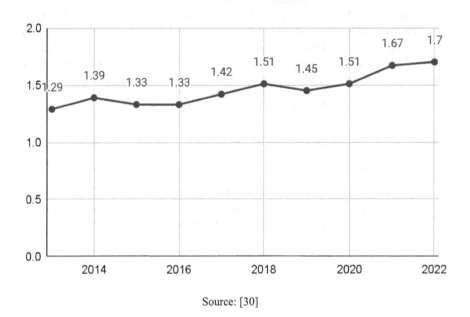

Source: [30]

**COVID-19 and the Laundry Service Market**

The South Korean laundry services market exhibited significant growth, with a compound annual growth rate (CAGR) of 12.3%, surging from $93.18 billion in 2020 to $104.65 billion in 2021. This remarkable expansion can be primarily attributed to the strategic reorganization of companies' operations and their subsequent recovery from the adverse impact of the COVID-19 pandemic. The pandemic had necessitated stringent containment measures, including social distancing, telecommuting, and the temporary closure of commercial activities, all of which had presented operational challenges to the industry [31]. The laundry services sector experienced a notable setback in 2020 due to the substantial impact of COVID-19. The demand for laundry services declined sharply during this period, owing to government-imposed lockdowns aimed at curbing the virus's spread. This downturn is expected to have a lasting impact on businesses throughout 2020 and extending into 2021. Furthermore, COVID-19 influenced consumer behavior and confidence, amplifying concerns related to hygiene. The pandemic compelled individuals to spend more time within their homes due to measures designed to mitigate virus transmission, such as remote work and online learning. Considering these shifts, the laundry service market is projected to witness increased demand in

2021, as the threat posed by the disease begins to recede. Consumers are also likely to resume activities outside their homes, including vacations. Consequently, companies in the laundry services sector must provide enhanced and valuable laundry care services to adapt to evolving consumer needs and maintain their competitiveness.

## A Case Study: Cleantopia

Cleantopia is a distinguished laundry service company that commenced its operations as South Korea's first advanced laundry shop, originating from the Seongnam Woosung branch in 1992, focusing on dry laundering business franchising. Over time, the company's concept evolved and expanded, leading to its establishment as a distinctive and highly successful enterprise in the market. Cleantopia has consistently maintained a leading position in the laundry industry through ongoing technological advancements and improvements in customer service. By 2021, Cleantopia had grown to encompass more than 134 branches and 2,492 chains across the nation, providing customers with faster and more efficient laundry services. In a significant development, South Korea's largest laundry service provider, Cleantopia Co., was acquired by Seoul-based JKL Partners in 2021 for approximately 190 billion won ($165 million) [32]. JKL Partners aims to enhance the value of the franchise operator through the introduction of mobile-based services and computer system upgrades. With 2,945 franchise locations globally, Cleantopia commands a dominant share of the laundry and dry-cleaning market, holding an 80% market share. The laundry service industry is poised for growth, driven in part by the increasing number of single-person households and dual-income families. Cleantopia is committed to leading the environmentally friendly laundry culture and serving as Korea's premier laundry service company, consistently striving to enhance the convenience and quality of life for its customers.

Cleantopia's laundry service components include a central office overseeing all divisions, Drop Stores where customers can leave items for later collection, and Multishops, which function as pickup points and self-service laundries. Notably, self-service laundries have been introduced, with over 200 such locations established in Korea by the end of 2014. Cleantopia has embarked on a venture to open 500 self-service locations in the span of five years, signifying new opportunities in the dry washing business model. The central laundry system, alongside multiple laundry drop-off and pickup points and a robust logistical network, has facilitated this expansion. The pickup and drop-off locations operate following a traditional model, with the business owner personally serving customers during standard business hours. Conversely, self-service laundries are accessible 24/7. Cleantopia has partnered with Girbau, entrusting them with nearly 2,000 machines for self-service laundries, featuring 1,500 Girbau washers and dryers operational in 245 such locations. Mr. Beom-Teak Lee, the Chairman of Cleantopia, underscores the selection of Girbau due to their exceptional reliability, competitive pricing, and robust commercial and technical support. Cleantopia has set a remarkable precedent by establishing the industry's very first cleaning school. The Cleantopia Cleaning School, recognized as one of the premier laundry schools in Korea [33], offers a comprehensive curriculum that encompasses laundering theory, practical training, and service training. These programs are designed to benefit both employees within the company and individuals aspiring to operate their own laundry businesses. The Cleantopia Cleaning School offers a range of specialized courses, including:

1. Course for Opening a Branch: Designed for individuals interested in starting their own Cleantopia branch, this program provides essential insights and guidance for launching and managing a successful laundry business within the Cleantopia franchise framework.
2. Course for Improving Quality: Focusing on the enhancement of service quality, this course equips employees and entrepreneurs with the knowledge and skills required to provide top-notch laundry services and meet or exceed customer expectations.
3. Course for Laundering Process: This program delves into the intricate details of the laundering process, offering in-depth understanding and practical training on the various steps involved in the cleaning and care of garments and textiles.
4. Course for Management: Designed for aspiring or current managers within the Cleantopia network, this course imparts critical management skills and knowledge, empowering individuals to effectively oversee laundry operations and drive business success.
5. Course for Customer Satisfaction: Recognizing the centrality of customer satisfaction, this course focuses on customer service excellence and strategies to ensure that customers' needs, and expectations are met or exceeded.

The Cleantopia Cleaning School plays a pivotal role in equipping individuals with the expertise and proficiency necessary to excel in the laundry industry, thereby contributing to the company's continued success and the delivery of high-quality services to its valued customers.

The research institution dedicated to enhancing laundry services is steadfast in its commitment to advancing laundry quality and promoting eco-friendly laundry practices through an array of experiments and technical exchanges with developed nations. The institution's core focus areas encompass:

1. Development of Specialized Laundry Service: The institution is at the forefront of developing and pioneering specialized laundry services that cater to unique customer needs and preferences. These services are designed to set new industry standards and deliver exceptional laundry quality.
2. Research on Textile, Stain, and Detergent: The institution actively engages in research to better understand textiles, stains, and detergents, with the aim of improving laundry processes and outcomes. This research informs the development of more effective cleaning methods and solutions.
3. Technical Exchange with Developed Countries: To remain on the cutting edge of laundry technology and best practices, the institution fosters collaborative exchanges with developed countries. These interactions facilitate the transfer of knowledge, expertise, and innovative laundry techniques.
4. Thorough Dry-Cleaning Solutions Management: The institution places a strong emphasis on managing dry-cleaning solutions with precision and care. Ensuring that cleaning solutions are both effective and environmentally responsible is a critical part of their mission.

Through its comprehensive approach to research and development, the institution is actively contributing to the enhancement of laundry services, the promotion of eco-friendly practices, and the continuous improvement of laundry quality, benefiting both the industry and its environmentally conscious customers.

Cleantopia is firmly committed to promoting eco-friendliness, safeguarding customers' health, and protecting the environment through innovative practices. The Cleantopia R&D Center has conducted rigorous performance tests and has successfully implemented a cutting-edge solvent-retrieve dryer across all its stores. This significant step underscores Cleantopia's dedication to delivering eco-friendly laundry services while maintaining reasonable pricing and prioritizing public health and hygiene. Key environmental initiatives by Cleantopia include:

1. Use of Environmentally Friendly EM Detergents: Cleantopia employs environmentally friendly EM detergents that can break down organic materials such as fiber debris and effectively eliminate odors from clothing. This approach contributes to both improved laundry quality and reduced environmental impact.
2. Adoption of Powder-Coat Hangers: In contrast to vinyl-coated hangers commonly utilized by most dry cleaners, Cleantopia has opted for powder-coat hangers. This choice aligns with environmental protection by minimizing the generation of hazardous substances during the recycling process, enhancing safety and sustainability.
3. Utilization of Recyclable Packaging Vinyl Bags: Cleantopia is dedicated to eco-conscious packaging by exclusively using recyclable vinyl bags for its laundry services. Furthermore, these bags can be given a second life as other plastic products when separately collected for recycling, further reducing waste, and promoting sustainability.

Cleantopia's holistic approach to eco-friendly laundry practices demonstrates a strong commitment to preserving the environment, safeguarding public health, and delivering high-quality services that are mindful of both customers and the planet.

## Financial Strategy and Corporation Structure

Cleantopia's remarkable success, boasting an impressive 80% market share in South Korea [35], is underpinned by a comprehensive and innovative management approach. The company's commitment to its core principles and continuous innovation has been pivotal in achieving and sustaining this dominant position. To implement its management philosophies, Cleantopia has deployed an array of effective marketing strategies, actively engaged in technological exchanges with developed countries, and fostered strong ties through industrial-academic cooperation. Key factors contributing to Cleantopia's success, as outlined by Mr. Beom-Teak Lee, include:

1. Pricing: Cleantopia's success is partially attributed to its highly automated and technology-driven approach, allowing for extremely competitive pricing compared to other competitors in the market. The company leverages technology to optimize efficiency and cost-effectiveness, ultimately offering value to its customers.

2. Product/Service Excellence: Cleantopia places a strong emphasis on ensuring the efficient operation of the company and providing exceptional customer service. The company provides guidance and training to all franchisees, ensuring that high standards are consistently upheld across its network.
3. Advertising: Cleantopia invests significantly in advertising, including national television commercials, especially during popular series broadcasts, as well as sponsorships of sporting events, newspaper, and radio advertisements, and more. These marketing efforts raise brand visibility and attract customers.
4. Delivery Service: Cleantopia offers a robust logistics service, with linen collection and delivery occurring three times a day. This commitment to timely service ensures that customers are consistently satisfied, with the Cleantopia logistics network playing a pivotal role in this regard.
5. Expansion Across Various Locations: Cleantopia recognizes that accessibility and availability of services are crucial to business success. To meet customer needs, the company extends its service hours and establishes a wide distribution network across the country, ensuring convenient access for customers.

Cleantopia's success story highlights the significance of a multifaceted approach that encompasses pricing, product and service quality, strategic advertising, efficient logistics, and an expansive presence, all aligned with its core management principles. This approach has not only secured its leading position but also fostered a positive impact on the laundry service industry in South Korea.

Cleantopia offers a comprehensive range of services to cater to diverse customer needs, including three special care services that focus on specific cleaning requirements:

1. **Special Cleaning Service:** This specialized service targets the removal of stubborn stains such as mold, blood, ink, and others that are challenging to eliminate with conventional washing methods. It addresses specific stain-related concerns, including yellow stains on white blouses, sweat removal for Y-shirts, summer t-shirts, men's pants, and light-colored jackets.
2. **Royal Cleaning Service:** Cleantopia's Royal Cleaning Service involves separate management by laundry specialists. It prioritizes meticulous ironing and stain removal, proactively prevents potential issues, and offers active compensation. The service includes high-quality non-woven felt bag packaging and caters to special garments such as expensive suits, luxury items, and delicate silk clothing.
3. **Same-Day Laundry Service:** For customers in need of quick laundry solutions, Cleantopia provides a same-day laundry service. This service is ideal for individuals-facing unexpected laundry needs, such as meetings or forgetting to wash work attire. In addition to these specialized services, Cleantopia entices customers with various benefits to encourage the use of their services, including:

**Discounts**

"Cleaning Day": Enjoy a 7% discount every Wednesday. "Bedclothes Day": Benefit from a significant 30% discount every Saturday and Wednesday. And the "Birthday": Receive a generous 20% discount as a birthday treat.

1. **Stamp Coupon:**

- Collect one stamp with each purchase exceeding 5,000 won.
- Upon accumulating 12 stamps, customers automatically receive 3,000 won in laundry coupons, with the stamp collection process restarting.

2. **Membership:**

- GOLD Membership: For those who make an annual payment of over 300,000 won.

    - Benefit 1: Receive a monthly 1,000 won laundry coupon.
    - Benefit 2: Enjoy special discounts for membership customers.

- VIP Membership: Available to customers who make an annual payment exceeding 600,000 won.

    - Benefit 1: Receive a monthly 5,000 won laundry coupon (equivalent to 60,000 won per year).
    - Benefit 2: Enjoy exclusive discounts for membership customers.

3. **Cleantopia App:** Cleantopia offers a user-friendly app that enhances the convenience of customers. The app provides several key features, including:

- **Laundry Status:** Allows customers to check the real-time status of their clothing in the cleaning process.
- **My Stamp:** Manages the stamp collection and redemption process.
- **Check Store Information:** Provides information about Cleantopia store locations.
- **Events/Promotions:** Keeps customers informed about ongoing events and promotions, ensuring they never miss out on special offers.

Cleantopia's comprehensive services, coupled with these customer-focused benefits and the user-friendly app, contribute to the company's reputation for delivering high-quality, convenient, and customer-centric laundry solutions.

### Discussion

The analysis of Cleantopia laundry service company in the context of financial strategy and corporate structure is a comprehensive study that encompasses several key aspects. It is organized into chapters to systematically evaluate and understand various dimensions of the company's operations and performance. Below is an overview of the structure and content of each chapter. In this chapter, the researchers outline the methodology and approach used to analyze Cleantopia. The key components of this chapter include:

**SWOT Analysis:** The researchers conduct a SWOT analysis to assess Cleantopia's strengths, weaknesses, opportunities, and threats. This analysis provides valuable insights into the company's internal and external factors that influence its financial and corporate structure.

1. **Impact of COVID-19 Pandemic:** The chapter discusses the impact of the COVID-19 pandemic on Cleantopia's operations. It explores how the pandemic affected the

laundry service industry and the specific challenges and opportunities it presented to the company.
2. **Main Impacting Factors:** The researchers identify and discuss the main factors that have influenced Cleantopia's financial strategy and corporate structure. This includes factors such as market trends, customer behavior, competition, and regulatory changes

### Results and Discussion

This chapter presents the results of the analysis conducted in the previous chapters and offers a comprehensive discussion of the findings. The key components of this chapter include:

1. **SWOT Analysis Conclusions:** The researchers draw conclusions from the SWOT analysis, summarizing Cleantopia's strengths, weaknesses, opportunities, and threats. These insights provide a basis for strategic recommendations.
2. **Financial and Corporate Restructuring:** The chapter delves into the analysis of financial and corporate restructuring at Cleantopia. It explores how the company has adapted its financial strategy and corporate structure to address challenges and leverage opportunities, particularly in the context of the COVID-19 pandemic.
3. **Total Revenue Analysis (2017–2021):** The researchers calculate and analyze Cleantopia's total revenue for the years 2017 to 2021. This analysis provides a clear picture of the company's financial performance and growth over this period. Overall, this structured analysis provides a holistic understanding of Cleantopia's financial strategy, corporate structure, and performance, including the specific impact of the COVID-19 pandemic. The SWOT analysis and revenue analysis help identify key areas of strength and areas that may require strategic attention, while the discussion on financial and corporate restructuring offers insights into the company's adaptability and resilience in the face challenges.

### SWOT Analysis

**Strengths:** The self-service laundries provided by Cleantopia are open around the clock, 24 h a day, seven days a week. This accessibility ensures that customers have the flexibility to utilize these services at any time that suits their schedule, contributing to the convenience and customer-centric approach of Cleantopia's laundry offerings. Cleantopia operates a central laundry facility that is supported by an extensive network of drop-off and pick-up points, complemented by a robust and efficient logistics structure. This integrated approach allows the company to manage laundry operations with the utmost effectiveness and ensure seamless collection and delivery of customers' clothing and textiles. Cleantopia's central laundry and logistical capabilities play a pivotal role in delivering high-quality laundry services and maintaining customer satisfaction. Customers benefit from the convenience of the Cleantopia application, which provides several valuable features, including the ability to check their clothing's status, monitor their stamp collection progress, and access information about laundry coupons. This mobile application offers customers the flexibility to stay informed and engaged with Cleantopia's services, enhancing their overall experience and convenience. Cleantopia's laundry service stands out due to its high level of automation and integration of technology at every stage of the process. This technological advantage enables the company to offer highly competitive pricing compared to other competitors in the market. By optimizing efficiency and reducing manual labor, Cleantopia is able to provide cost-effective services without compromising on quality. This competitive pricing contributes to the company's success and customer satisfaction.

**Weaknesses:** Managing a widespread network of franchises, such as Cleantopia's numerous locations across the country, can indeed pose significant challenges. It can be complex to control and standardize employee practices and maintain consistent equipment standards, particularly when dealing with a large and geographically dispersed operation. However, addressing these challenges is crucial for maintaining service quality and brand reputation.

To mitigate these challenges, Cleantopia may consider implementing centralized management and quality control mechanisms, providing comprehensive training programs for employees, and setting up regular equipment maintenance protocols. This way, the company can maintain a high standard of service quality and operational consistency across its extensive network of franchises. Effective management and quality assurance practices are essential for ensuring customer satisfaction and the continued success of the business. The absence of online payment options or QR code functionality at all franchises can indeed lead to inconvenience for customers, especially in an era where digital payment methods are widely used and expected. Cleantopia may benefit from implementing a more uniform and comprehensive online payment system across all of its franchises to enhance customer convenience.

To address this issue, Cleantopia could consider the following steps:

1. **Standardization of Payment Systems:** Work towards standardizing the payment systems and options available at all franchises. This can include accepting major credit cards, digital wallets, and popular payment apps, as well as offering QR code-based payment methods.
2. **Digital Integration:** Invest in digital solutions that can be easily integrated into the operations of all franchises. This ensures a consistent and seamless experience for customers when it comes to online payments and QR code scanning.
3. **Employee Training:** Provide training and support to franchise owners and employees to ensure they are proficient in handling digital payment methods and QR code transactions.
4. **Regular Updates:** Keep the payment systems and technology up to date to ensure they remain secure, efficient, and compatible with evolving customer preferences.

By addressing these concerns and improving the convenience of digital payment options, Cleantopia can enhance the overall customer experience and keep pace with modern payment trends, which is increasingly important in today's competitive business landscape. Addressing software performance issues, particularly during peak usage times, is crucial to ensuring a seamless and satisfactory customer experience with the Cleantopia app. To enhance the app's functionality and responsiveness, Cleantopia may consider the following steps:

1. **Performance Optimization:** Invest in software optimization to enhance the app's performance during high-traffic periods. This may involve code improvements, server capacity upgrades, and load balancing to ensure smooth operations.
2. **Scalability:** Ensure that the app can scale up to handle increased user load without degradation in performance. Scalability improvements may involve cloud-based solutions or server upgrades.
3. **User Feedback:** Encourage customers to provide feedback on their app experience and actively use this feedback to identify and address performance issues.
4. **Testing:** Conduct rigorous testing to identify and resolve any bottlenecks or performance constraints within the app and test it under conditions that simulate peak usage.
5. **Regular Updates:** Commit to regular app updates and maintenance to keep the software running smoothly and to incorporate any necessary fixes or enhancements.

By investing in these improvements, Cleantopia can provide a more reliable and responsive app experience for its customers, especially during rush hours or when high volumes of users are accessing the app simultaneously. This can lead to increased customer satisfaction and loyalty.

**Opportunities:** Cleantopia's annual campaign to provide free uniform laundry services to schools is a commendable initiative aimed at reducing the economic burden on parents and promoting student participation in the sharing campaign. This campaign offers various benefits, including:

1. **Economic Relief:** By providing free uniform laundry services, Cleantopia lightens the financial load on parents who may otherwise have to bear the cost of maintaining school uniforms.
2. **Community Engagement:** The campaign encourages students to actively participate in a shared cause, fostering a sense of community and social responsibility among the youth.
3. **Supporting Education:** Offering free laundry services to schools contributes to a more conducive learning environment by ensuring students have clean and well-maintained uniforms.
4. **Time Efficiency:** It saves time for parents and guardians who might otherwise be responsible for washing and maintaining school uniforms.

Cleantopia's selection of schools based on specific criteria and purpose reflects a thoughtful and strategic approach to ensure the campaign's impact aligns with its intended goals. Such initiatives not only benefit the community but also enhance Cleantopia's corporate social responsibility and community engagement efforts.

**Threats:** The COVID-19 pandemic has had a significant impact on various market sectors, including the laundry service industry. Cleantopia, like many businesses, experienced a decrease in consumer demand during the pandemic due to changing consumer behaviors and heightened concerns about cleanliness and hygiene. Key observations related to these effects include:

1. **Increased Hygiene Standards:** With the ongoing pandemic, people became more conscious of cleanliness and hygiene. This led to heightened expectations for laundry

services, as individuals sought to ensure their clothing and textiles were thoroughly cleaned and sanitized.

2. **Consumer Concerns:** Some consumers may have been hesitant to use laundry services during the pandemic, as they were concerned about potential exposure to the virus through contaminated textiles.

3. **Change in Cleaning Habits:** The pandemic led to changes in cleaning habits, with some individuals choosing to launder their clothing more frequently and adopting more rigorous cleaning practices at home.

4. **Impact on Consumer Behavior:** The pandemic altered consumer behavior and priorities, impacting businesses like Cleantopia. Consumers may have reduced their reliance on laundry services during certain periods of heightened concern.

It's important for Cleantopia to adapt to these changing market dynamics by ensuring that their services align with the evolving needs and expectations of consumers. This may involve implementing enhanced sanitation measures, promoting the safety of their services, and offering flexibility to cater to changing customer preferences. Additionally, clear and transparent communication about hygiene practices can help rebuild trust among customers and address any concerns related to the pandemic's impact on the laundry service market. The laundry service market's ease of entry and similarity among competitors can present challenges and opportunities for businesses like Cleantopia. Key observations related to this competitive landscape include:

1. **Low Barrier to Entry:** The laundry service market's low barrier to entry means that new competitors can easily establish similar businesses. This can lead to increased competition and potential market saturation.

2. **Similar Services:** Many laundry service providers offer similar services, making it challenging to differentiate one business from another based solely on the type of service provided.

3. **Standardized Business Strategies:** The laundry service market may exhibit standardized business strategies, where competitors tend to follow similar operational models and pricing structures.

In such a competitive environment, Cleantopia may consider several strategies to stand out and maintain its market position:

- **Differentiation:** Focus on aspects that set Cleantopia apart from the competition, such as quality, customer service, or innovative technology.
- **Customer Experience:** Emphasize an exceptional customer experience, from convenient app features to prompt and reliable service.
- **Marketing and Branding:** Invest in effective marketing and branding to create a unique and recognizable identity in the market.
- **Continuous Improvement:** Continuously seek ways to enhance services, whether through technology, sustainability efforts, or customer benefits.
- **Strategic Alliances:** Explore opportunities for partnerships or collaborations that can provide unique value to customers.

By addressing these considerations, Cleantopia can better navigate the competitive landscape in the laundry service market and remain a preferred choice for customers. The exigencies of the COVID-19 pandemic necessitated, governmental imposition of stringent lockdown measures, resulting in the complete cessation of business operations. This has, in turn, engendered a decline in the demand for dry cleaning and laundry services, as the suspension of operations and restrictions on external mobility precluded the transportation of garments to cleaning facilities. Concomitantly, a perceptible shift in individual hygiene practices has transpired, manifesting in an augmented emphasis on cleanliness. The populace, cognizant of the virus's transmissibility, exhibits a predilection for a cashless societal milieu to mitigate the risk of contagion. In response to this paradigm shift, commercial entities are compelled to embrace innovative technologies, such as online and cashless payment modalities, to furnish enhanced convenience to their clientele. An array of salient factors significantly impacts the landscape of laundry and dry-cleaning services, thereby shaping their trajectory. Firstly, in response to the exigencies of the contemporary lifestyle characterized by time constraints, modern consumers exhibit a willingness to remunerate for laundry services. The development of cost-effective, reliable, and convenient laundry services is pivotal, as these attributes stand poised to exert a substantial influence on the demand for such services in the foreseeable future. Moreover, the confluence of burgeoning workforce demographics and the persistent need for cleaning and washing services is anticipated to sustain the demand for these services. The escalating costs associated with clothing and cleaning further underscore the continued relevance of laundry and dry-cleaning services within the socio-economic milieu.

Additionally, the ascendancy of on-demand laundry services is noteworthy, driven by a comprehensive strategy encompassing mobile bookings, seamless collection, cleaning, and timely delivery. This model not only aligns with the preferences of contemporary consumers but also fosters an informed clientele, as customers gain real-time insights into the status and delivery schedule of their laundered items through smartphone connectivity. Furthermore, the ubiquity of online laundry services is poised to accelerate the growth trajectory of mobile applications, smartphones, and internet utilization. Leveraging online platforms enables businesses to deploy an effective marketing strategy, thereby positioning themselves advantageously in the evolving landscape of on-demand laundry services. As the on-demand economy burgeons, enterprises are intensifying their efforts to deliver sophisticated mobile laundry software, thereby enhancing their competitiveness and responsiveness to evolving consumer preferences.

In accordance with Methodology, the calculation of Cleantopia's total revenue spanning the years 2017 to 2021 is executed through a systematic approach. The quantitative assessment involves the aggregation of the company's annual revenue figures for each fiscal year within the specified timeframe. The methodology employed encompasses the extraction of Cleantopia's audited financial statements, annual reports, or any other authoritative financial documentation for the years under consideration. Subsequently, the total revenue for each individual year is identified and collated. The summation of these annual revenues yields the comprehensive total revenue for Cleantopia over the stipulated period, thereby facilitating a holistic understanding of the company's financial performance and trajectory during the specified interval. This methodological framework ensures a rigorous and transparent analysis of Cleantopia's financial data, forming a foundational basis for subsequent evaluative considerations.

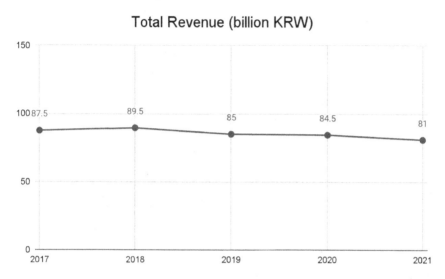

In the observed period from 2017 to 2021, Cleantopia's total revenue exhibited a notable trajectory. Commencing at 87.5 billion won in 2017, there was an incremental ascent to 89.5 billion won in 2018. However, the subsequent years witnessed a downturn, with revenues decreasing to 85 billion won and 84.5 billion won in 2019 and 2020, respectively, attributed to the impact of the COVID-19 pandemic. The trend persisted with a further decrease to 81 billion won in 2021. Considering the Profit Maximization Theory, which posits that firms aim to optimize profits by balancing marginal revenue and marginal cost, Cleantopia confronts the challenge of diminishing revenues from 2019 through 2021. Consequently, it becomes imperative for the company to implement robust and intelligent strategies to bolster its profitability. The forthcoming section, Financial and Corporate Restructuring, is dedicated to the formulation of effective strategies and recommendations aimed at enhancing Cleantopia's financial standing and resource maximization. These strategic interventions aspire to fortify the company's profitability, ensure financial stability, and optimize resource allocation. The researchers aim to proffer insightful recommendations in pursuit of the overarching objectives of profit improvement, financial stability, and resource optimization.

**Financial and Corporate Restructuring**
Considering the SWOT analysis presented in Sect. 4.4.1, the researchers advocate for strategic restructuring guided by the theory of value chain analysis. The following recommendations are posited to fortify Cleantopia's market position, enhance competitiveness, and navigate the challenges identified:

1. **Financial Strategy:** Develop a comprehensive financial plan that allocates resources judiciously. This involves earmarking funds for organizational recovery from the

repercussions of the COVID-19 situation, investing in organizational development such as employee salaries and infrastructure repair costs, allocating resources for future innovation and technological advancements in laundry equipment, and establishing an emergency fund to address unforeseen phenomena or disasters.

2. **Corporate Structure:** Implement a robust human resources management plan, especially considering the widespread presence of franchises across the country. Standardize training processes to ensure uniform service quality in every franchise, thereby enhancing efficiency, customer satisfaction, and potentially fostering brand loyalty.

3. **Cleanliness:** Prioritize cleanliness throughout the entire laundry service process. Explore the integration of additional sanitizing capabilities, such as ozone gas, into existing laundry equipment to eliminate germs and viruses, thereby assuring consumers of the safety and hygiene of their laundered items.

4. **Investment Diversification:** Allocate funds for investments in diverse industries to augment capital and reserves. This diversification strategy acts as a risk mitigation measure in case of potential challenges within the laundry service market.

5. **Online Laundry Service on Mobile Application:** In response to the evolving needs of modern consumers, enhance the online laundry service through a user-friendly mobile application. Develop software capable of supporting a high volume of users concurrently and streamline the booking and delivery process to provide added convenience.

6. **Payment Options:** Adapt to the increasing preference for cashless transactions by diversifying payment options beyond coin-based systems. Incorporate QR code or credit/debit card payments to simplify transactions, reflecting the changing post-COVID-19 consumer behavior.

7. **Advertising and Promotion:** Implement targeted advertising on various social media platforms and offer promotions or discounts to stimulate demand for laundry services. Introduce a loyalty card program to encourage repeat business and reward customers with gifts upon accumulating full points.

8. **Competitor Analysis:** Recognize the influx of new competitors in response to market growth. Regularly monitor and analyze the competitive landscape to stay abreast of emerging trends and consumer preferences, enabling Cleantopia to proactively adjust its strategies and offerings.

By aligning these recommendations with the principles of value chain analysis, Cleantopia can systematically enhance its operational efficiency, customer satisfaction, and overall competitiveness within the dynamic landscape of the laundry service market.

## 5 Conclusion

**Financial Restructuring**

The imperative for financial restructuring arises in response to the COVID-19-induced decline in Cleantopia's total revenue from 85 to 81 billion won between 2019 and 2021. To mitigate these challenges and bolster financial resilience, Cleantopia should design a meticulous financial plan. This plan should delineate the allocation of funds across various crucial areas, including:

1. **Organizational Development:** Allocate resources for the ongoing development of the organization, encompassing considerations such as employee salaries and expenses for repairing and maintaining equipment. This ensures the sustained functionality and quality of services.

2. **Recovery from COVID-19 Situation:** Devote a portion of the funds to recovery initiatives, such as promotional campaigns designed to attract more customers. This targeted approach aims to stimulate demand and recuperate revenues impacted by the pandemic.

3. **Future Development:** Allocate resources for future development endeavors, specifically directed toward innovations and technological advancements in washing machines and other tools. This forward-looking investment enhances Cleantopia's competitiveness in the evolving market landscape.

4. **Emergency Fund:** Establish an emergency fund to address unforeseen phenomena or disasters. This reserve provides the company with a financial buffer, ensuring preparedness for unexpected challenges and facilitating swift response mechanisms.

# 6  Corporate Restructuring

The multifaceted corporate structure of Cleantopia, comprising 134 branches and 2,492 chains nationwide, necessitates a strategic revamping of human resource management practices, particularly in the wake of the challenges posed by the COVID-19 situation. To enhance control, efficiency, and standardization across the organization, Cleantopia should consider the following corporate restructuring measures:

1. **Service Standards and Training:** Develop and enforce uniform service standards across all branches. Implement standardized training programs for employees to ensure consistency in service quality, thereby building brand loyalty and elevating customer satisfaction levels.

2. **Regulatory Compliance:** Strengthen regulatory compliance measures to ensure that all branches adhere to company policies and standards. This will not only streamline operations but also foster a cohesive organizational culture.

3. **Productivity Enhancement:** Corporate restructuring should target productivity improvement initiatives, enhancing the overall efficiency of operations. This may involve streamlining processes, leveraging technology, and optimizing resource allocation.

4. **Quality Assurance:** Implement robust quality assurance mechanisms to guarantee that each branch maintains the same level of quality in service delivery. This uniformity contributes to a positive customer experience and bolsters the company's reputation.

In tandem, these financial and corporate restructuring strategies are poised to fortify Cleantopia's financial position, enable recovery from the impact of COVID-19, and establish a solid foundation for sustained growth and competitiveness in the dynamic laundry service market.

# References

1. Smith, R.: The benefits of business restructuring (2020). https://www.forbesburton.com/ins ights/corporate-and-business-restructuring. Retrieved 12 Oct 2022
2. Kim, S.Y., et al.:. Stochastic electrograms selectively enhances the transport of highly electro mobile molecules. PNAS. Retrieved from: (99+) Kim et al 2015.pdf | Meg McCue – Academia.edu (2015)
3. Choi, J., Kim, I.: The relationship between local employment growth and regional economic growth: evidence from Korea. In: Hosoe, M., Kim, I., Yabuta, M., Lee, W. (eds.) Applied Analysis of Growth, Trade, and Public Policy: Ten Years of International Academic Exchanges Between JAAE and KEBA, pp. 35–43. Springer Singapore, Singapore (2018). https://doi.org/10.1007/978-981-13-1876-4_3
4. Park, S., Kim, J., Jeon, J., Park, H., Oh, A.: Toward dimensional emotion detection from categorical emo-tion annotations, arXiv preprint arXiv:1911.02499, p 11 (16) (PDF) Transformer models for text-based emotion detection: a review of BERT-based approaches (2019). https://www.researchgate.net/publication/349145342_Transformer_mod els_for_text-based_emotion_detection_a_review_of_BERT-based_approaches. Accessed 16 Mar 2024
5. Lee, D.S., et al.: The contribution of global aviation to anthropogenic climate forcing for 2000 to 2018. Atmospheric Env. **244**, 117834 (2021). https://doi.org/10.1016/j.atmosenv.2020.117834
6. Kang, M., Park, I.: Korea's trade policy and performance in turbulent times. World Econ. **45**(11), 3384–3391 (2022)
7. Am, H.S.:. On-demand Laundry Service Market Size, Growth, Forecast 2023–2030. Medium (2023). https://medium.com/@half.skull.am/on-demand-laundry-service-market-size-growth-forecast-2023-2030-6fb4ab885a02
8. Chowdhury, R.: Impact of perceived convenience, service quality and security on consumers' behavioral intention towards online food delivery services: the role of attitude as mediator. SN Bus Econ. **3**(1), 29 (2023)
9. Verified Market Reports: Cashless Commercial Laundry Machine Market Size, Trends Evaluation: Evaluating Share, Tends, and Growth Forecast for 2024–2031 (2024)
10. Das, D., Sarkar, A., Debroy, A.: Impact of COVID-19 on changing consumer behaviour: lessons from an emerging economy. Int. J. Consumer Stud. **46**(3), 692–715 (2022)
11. Shaw, R.W.: Investment and competition from boom to recession: a case study in the processes of competition – the dry-cleaning industry. J. Ind. Econ. **21**(3), 308–324 (1973)
12. Day, G.S., Schoemaker, P.: ResearchGate. **58**(4), 59–77 (2016)
13. Tam, N.D.T., Thanh, H.P., Tien, H.N.: J. Asian. Finance **7**(9), 5–84 (2020)
14. Kim, J., Lee, K.: Success story of professional laundry service in Korea. In: International Textile and Apparel Association Annual Conference Proceedings, vol. 75, issue 1 (2018)
15. Maurer, T.A., Tran, N.K.: The Hirshleifer Effect in a Dynamic Setting. SSRN 1–59. (2015)
16. Wang, N.: Coase on the nature of economics. Cambridge J. Econ. **27**(6), 807–829 (1998)
17. Hsiao, H.C., Chang, H., Cianci, A.M., Huang, L.H.: J. Bank. Finance **34**(7), 1461–1471 (2010)
18. Bozic, V., Poola, I.: Measuring organizational performance. ResearchGate (2023). https://www.researchgate.net/publication/369281495_Measuring_organizational_performance
19. Gutterman, A.S.: Organizational Performance and Effectiveness. Organizational Performance and effectiveness (2023). https://www.researchgate.net/publication/372935897_Org anizational_Performance_and_Effectiveness
20. Henri, J.F.: Performance measurement and organization effectiveness Bridging the gap. Manag. Finance **30**(6), 93–123 (2004)

21. Odula, E.O.:. The Effect of Restructuring on the Performance on the Performance of Financial Institution in Kenya. Thesis from School. Bf Business (2015)
22. Han, S.L., Sung, H.S.: Industrial brand value and relationship performance in business markets – A general structural equation model. Ind. Market. Manag. **37**(7), 807–818 (2008)
23. Hall, D.M., Algiers, A., Levitt, R.E.: Identifying the role of supply chain integration practices in the adoption of systemic innovations. J. Manag. **34**(6), 04018030 (2018)
24. Gattorna, J.L., Walters, D.W.: Managing the Supply Chain: A Strategic Perspective. MacMillan, London (1996)
25. Hahn, G.J., Kuhn, H.: Value-based performance and risk management in supply chains: a robust optimization approach. Int. J. Product. Econ. **139**(1), 135–144 (2011)
26. Wallstreetmojo Editorial Team: Profit Maximization Graph (2018)
27. Porter, M.E.: Competitive Advantage: Creating and Sustaining Superior Performance. Hardcover – Illustrated (1998)
28. Business Research Methodology. Primary Activities (2017)
29. KED Global – The Korea Economic Daily Global Educ The pandemic had necessitated stringent containment measures, including social distancing, telecommuting, and the temporary closure of commercial activities, all of which had presented operational challenges to the industry ation (2021).
30. Statista. Laundry Care – South Korea. (n.d.). Laundry Care – South Korea.
31. Kaushik, M.: The Impact of Pandemic COVID-19 in Workplace. European J. Bus. Manag. (2020)
32. Min, J.H.: S. Korea's top laundry franchise cleantopia sold to PEF. The Korea Economic Daily (2021). https://www.kedglobal.com/mergers-acquisitions/newsView/ked202108100 017#:~:text=South%20Korea's%20largest%20laundry%20service,services%20and%20c omputer%20system%20upgrades
33. Girbau Laundry Equipment. Cleantopis (Korea), An Overwhelmingly Successful Business Model (n.d.)

# Innovation and Knowledge Creation

# The Impact of Sensemaking Due to Cognitive Gaps Between Supervisors and Subordinates

Takashi Hongo[✉] and Dai Senoo

Department of Industrial Engineering and Economics, Tokyo Institute of Technology, Tokyo, Japan
{hongo.t.ab,senoo.d.aa}@m.titech.ac.jp

**Abstract.** In today's uncertain and complex environment (VUCA), modern corporations are required to continuously innovate and adapt to globalization. Globally successful companies have expanded their service range. Particularly for innovation, it is crucial to embrace diversity to bring different perspectives. In this era, modern managers, as 'Knowledge Engineers', are actively involved in knowledge creation and innovation. They are also expected to foster cooperative problem-solving and new sensemaking between supervisors and subordinates.

This study explores the relationship between cognitive gaps and sensemaking among supervisors and subordinates, specifically using 360-degree evaluation data from the IT company. Traditionally, it has been considered beneficial in supervisor-subordinate relationships to have no cognitive gap from the perspective of information processing. However, this study introduces the notion that cognitive gaps can be both negative and positive. It suggests that under certain conditions, a larger cognitive gap may actually enhance the process of sensemaking. Additionally, as one of the factors influencing sensemaking, this study constructs a theoretical framework of cognitive gaps and sensemaking that specifically incorporates subordinates' self-evaluation into the model. It proposes four types of relationships in sensemaking: 'dissatisfaction or disconnection,' 'Stability or Indifference,' 'Active Cooperation,' and 'Blind Trust or Emergent'.

**Keywords:** Knowledge Creation · Sensemaking · 360-Degree Evaluation · Feedback Assessment · Subjectivity · Cognitive Gap · Dialogue · Social Constructivism

## 1 Introduction

In the era of Volatility, Uncertainty, Complexity, and Ambiguity (VUCA), businesses are required to pursue relentless innovation. Additionally, companies that have successfully adapted to economic globalization have managed to expand their service offerings. On the other hand, companies unable to break away from existing business models or remain cocooned in local economic zones will likely face increasingly difficult situations. Innovation creation and global responsiveness are among the highest priorities for all businesses.

© The Author(s), under exclusive license to Springer Nature Switzerland AG 2024
L. Uden and I.-H. Ting (Eds.): KMO 2024, CCIS 2152, pp. 161–174, 2024.
https://doi.org/10.1007/978-3-031-63269-3_12

One of the recent corporate initiatives in response to this challenge is diversity management. According to Fleming (2004), team diversity tends to decrease the value of innovation on average, but it also holds the potential for producing outstanding innovations [1]. Bresman and Edmondson (2022) found that diversity and team performance have a negative relationship, but teams with high psychological safety show a positive relationship [2]. From these perspectives, Diversity & Inclusion are said to be important for innovation.

However, while the importance of Diversity & Inclusion at the organizational level is as stated above, looking at the structure and units of organizations, as represented by Likert's (1961) concept of linking pins, the role of managers has been the nodal points in the command system of top management. In such hierarchical operations, less cognitive gap between managers and subordinates enables sharing context with minimal communication, thus executing business operations efficiently. Subordinates understand and act according to the supervisor's context without creating their own or sharing meanings with the supervisor. Even now, many managers tend to think that a smaller cognitive gap is better, due to a strong management mindset from an information processing perspective.

On the other hand, nowadays, managers are expected to be actively involved in developing new businesses and services. Nonaka (2022) stated, 'Competent middle managers in knowledge-creating companies fulfill the typical function of 'Knowledge Engineers,' facilitating knowledge conversion.' He describes the role of managers as 'Middle-Up-Down Management,' where they integrate the tacit knowledge of many organizational members by creating mid-level concepts of businesses and products, clarifying and embodying them into new products and technologies while discerning 'what is' and 'what should be' [3].

Taking all this into account, modern middle managers, who play a role in creating innovations, are required to adopt a working style that fosters collaborative problem-solving and emergent innovation with subordinates, creating value within their relationship. Supervisors and subordinates need to build their own contexts from their respective values and perspectives, and through mutual dialogue, they should exchange contexts and collaboratively create new meanings. Sensemaking in the supervisor-subordinate relationship is essential.

This research poses the research question 'How does the cognitive gap affect sensemaking between supervisors and subordinates?' and aims to construct and propose a theoretical framework.

## 2   Literature Review

### 2.1   SECI Model (Nonaka & Takeuchi)

The SECI model, proposed by Nonaka and Takeuchi, is a model that explains the knowledge creation process within organizations. It consists of the following four processes [4]:

1. Socialization: A process of sharing tacit knowledge through experiences. At this stage, unarticulated knowledge and experiences are shared through face-to-face interactions and collaboration.

2. Externalization: A process of transforming tacit knowledge into explicit knowledge. In this phase, individual knowledge and experiences are articulated and made understandable to others.

3. Combination: A process of creating new knowledge by combining different types of explicit knowledge. At this stage, documented knowledge is categorized, added to, and restructured to generate new knowledge.

4. Internalization: A process of converting explicit knowledge into tacit knowledge and accumulating it as experience. In this stage, explicit knowledge is incorporated into individual behavior and habits and internalized as new tacit knowledge.

This model demonstrates that knowledge creation occurs not only at the individual level but also as a continuous process throughout the organization. The SECI model is widely used, particularly in organizational knowledge management and innovation strategies.

From the perspective of the SECI model and relationships, Shinhee Jeong examined organizational knowledge creation and its association with employee expertise and the quality of interpersonal relationships, as well as the moderating role of transformational leadership. Organizational knowledge creation was found to be positively influenced by the quality of interpersonal relationships and transformational leadership, while transformational leadership showed a negative moderating effect on the relationship between organizational knowledge creation and the quality of interpersonal relationships [5]. Furthermore, Mariama et al. explained how the relationship between Lee and Choi's individual-level variables and SECI, extended to team-level factors such as trust and intrinsic motivation, demonstrates the SECI model acting as a mediating variable between individual creativity and team-level factors, illustrating the crucial role of team and individual interactions in the knowledge creation process [6, 7].

As described above, there are research that delves deeper into knowledge creation theories from the perspectives of leadership and relationships. This study explores the conditions under which knowledge creation through sense-making activities can occur, based on typologies of the dyadic relationship in supervisor-subordinate relationships, albeit without direct reference to the SECI model.

## 2.2 Sensemaking in Supervisor-Subordinate Relationships

Sensemaking, as proposed by Karl Weick, is a theory regarding the process by which individuals or organizations interpret uncertain situations or ambiguous information to form understanding. The basics of sensemaking consist of the following seven elements [8].

1. Identity: This element emphasizes the role of identity and identification in shaping how people interpret events and enact roles within their context. It suggests that our sense of who we are significantly influences our actions and interpretations.

2. Retrospective: This aspect highlights the importance of looking back at past events to make sense of them. The timing of this retrospection can greatly influence what people notice and thus affect the sensemaking process.

3. Enactment: This element involves the ways in which people create their environment through dialogues and narratives. As individuals engage in these activities, they shape their understanding and control of events.
4. Social: Sensemaking is described as a social activity where stories are shared, retained, or altered. It also includes the concept that the act of sensemaking is not just outward but also inward, as individuals are also an audience to their narratives.
5. Ongoing: The ongoing nature of sensemaking is emphasized, where individuals are continuously engaged in shaping and responding to their environments. This process involves a feedback loop of learning and adaptation.
6. Extracted Cues: This involves the selection of certain cues from the context to determine relevant information and form acceptable explanations. These cues serve as reference points in the broader network of meaning.
7. Plausibility: The final element underlines a preference for plausibility and sufficiency in understanding events and contexts, rather than striving for complete accuracy. This approach is more practical and useful in a complex and ever-changing world.

In organizations, sensemaking is particularly important during times of change or crisis. Organizations need to form a shared understanding to respond quickly and effectively in highly uncertain situations.

In the realm of organizational management, particularly within supervisor-subordinate relationships, two key discursive activities—engaging in conversation and establishing the context—are pivotal for middle managers as they navigate sense-making to fulfill their strategic duties. These activities rely on middle managers' capacity to utilize symbolic and verbal expressions and are influenced by the socio-cultural frameworks to which they belong [9].

Sensemaking involves interpreting information and coordinating actions in the face of uncertainty. Middle managers confront paradoxes and contradictions that arise during organizational changes, particularly through 'performing', 'belonging', and 'organizing' to grasp how they construct meaning and manage change effectively. These managers are pivotal in bridging the gap between organizational objectives and personal identity during periods of change [10]

From an interpersonal sensemaking viewpoint regarding work meaning, it contends that a portion of it arises from evaluations by a varied group encountered in the workplace. This perspective regards work meaning as an emerging facet of the social environment of work, stressing the roles of employees in actively generating meaning through interpersonal interactions. The objective of this process is to reveal the relational underpinnings of what were previously perceived as individual processes, bringing attention to a fresh comprehension of others' roles within the workplace and the substantial contribution employees make to shaping the meaning of work [11].

Existing research on sensemaking has largely been centered on discourse analysis from interviews. This study narrows its focus to the supervisor-subordinate dynamic and examines the seven elements of sensemaking actions from the perspective of cognitive gaps, using quantitative data analysis with 360-degree evaluations.

## 2.3   Recent Trends in 360-Degree Evaluation Research

The 360-degree evaluation has been introduced primarily in the United States since the mid-20th century as a method to avoid the influence of personal bias in unidirectional evaluations of subordinates by supervisors. Companies have adopted it to bring fairness to evaluations from supervisors, or for talent development purposes, visualizing skills and designing talent development programs based on this data. In the case of companies using it for talent development, they visualize the gap between self-evaluation and evaluation by others and introspect on feedback comments from evaluators to improve daily behavior.

This study uses 360-degree evaluation as a tool to measure cognitive gaps. Therefore, it's important to understand recent trends in research on 360-degree evaluation. Research on the reliability of evaluation scores in personnel evaluations, such as the study on system noise by Scullen, Mount and Gold (2000), has been the mainstream, focusing on how to improve evaluation reliability [12].

However, Taylor & Bright (2011) note that traditional 360-degree feedback assessments, where supervisors ask subordinates for an assessment to get a 360-degree view and then interpret the feedback with a coach, tend to center on the self, making one aware of their deficiencies [13]. This often strengthens defensive instincts and loses opportunities for learning by expanding self-awareness, diverting from the human-centered approach that is the focus of organizational development.

Taylor & Bright advocate comparing others' predictions about self-assessment with their evaluations as a solution. This allows exploring the relationship between self and others in multiple contexts by using predictions about how evaluators will score a supervisor's actions instead of self-assessment. This new direction, exploring self-awareness within relationships with others, is emerging, and organizations are using 360-degree evaluations to facilitate sensemaking.

However, to the author's knowledge, no prior research has studied the relationship between cognitive gaps and sensemaking methods in supervisor-subordinate relationships. As a similar study on relationships, Kyungsub S. Choi (2007) researched productivity based on the personality types of colleagues paired in software development projects, but this was a static study on combinations of personality traits and based on an empirical worldview [14].

# 3   Research Methods

## 3.1   Research Framework

This study investigates the relationship between the gap in self-evaluations by supervisors and evaluations of supervisors by subordinates. The research hypothesis is presented in Fig. 1. E1 represents self-evaluations by supervisors, E2 represents self-evaluations by subordinates, and E3 represents evaluations of supervisors by subordinates. The cognitive gap, defined as CG, is calculated as the average difference between E1 and E3 for each question.

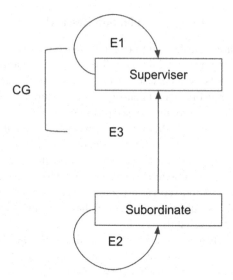

**Fig. 1.** Research Framework

### 3.2 Sample and Questionnaire

The subjects are employees in a supervisor-subordinate relationship with evaluation connections, working for the IT company headquartered in Tokyo, Japan. The data were obtained from the results of a 360-degree evaluation online survey conducted by the HR department in 2023 for the purpose of employee mutual feedback. In this company, there are 32 types of supervisor-subordinate relationships, and a 100% response rate was achieved from supervisors and subordinates in these relationships. The survey was measured using a 5-point Likert scale ranging from 1 to 5. The design of the 360-degree evaluation questionnaire was based on Katz's (1955) Three-Skill Model, setting up three categories: task-oriented skills, interpersonal skills, and attitude towards work (base mind) [15]. Each category consisted of four subcategories, resulting in a total of 30 questions. The subcategories included: (1) task thinking and (2) task execution for task-oriented aspects; (3) communication and (4) organizational contribution for interpersonal aspects; and (5) base mind as an attitude. Six questions were created for each of the subcategories (1) to (5), making a total of 30 questions used in the survey.

## 4   Results and Analysis

### 4.1   Overview of the Data

Table 1 shows the numerical results of the 360-degree evaluation implemented at company A. It presents the self-evaluation scores by supervisors, evaluation of supervisors by subordinates, and self-evaluation of subordinates. E1, E2, and E3 represent the total scores of all 30 questions in the questionnaire. For example, in the first line of Relationship 1, the subordinate's self-evaluation score is 98, the supervisor's self-evaluation is 107, and the evaluation of the supervisor by the subordinate is 106.

CG is calculated for each question by taking the difference between the evaluation scores given to supervisors by subordinates and the self-evaluation scores of the supervisors, and then calculating the average of these differences across all 30 questions (Table 1). CG is used to observe the average evaluation gap for each questionnaire item. CG for the 32 supervisor-subordinate relationships plotted on a number line is shown in Fig. 2.

**Table 1.** Evaluation Scores and CG

| | E1 | E2 | E3 | CG |
|---|---|---|---|---|
| Relationship 1 | 107 | 98 | 106 | -0.43 |
| Relationship 2 | 107 | 112 | 143 | 0.80 |
| Relationship 3 | 107 | 108 | 99 | 0.25 |
| Relationship 4 | 107 | 67 | 109 | -0.33 |
| Relationship 5 | 98 | 117 | 120 | 0.03 |
| Relationship 6 | 98 | 99 | 114 | -0.17 |
| Relationship 7 | 94 | 110 | 105 | -0.11 |
| Relationship 8 | 110 | 70 | 140 | 0.70 |
| Relationship 9 | 119 | 110 | 106 | -0.18 |
| Relationship 10 | 119 | 97 | 96 | -0.77 |
| Relationship 11 | 119 | 112 | 130 | 0.37 |
| Relationship 12 | 119 | 101 | 143 | 0.80 |
| Relationship 13 | 97 | 95 | 98 | -0.70 |
| Relationship 14 | 97 | 94 | 125 | 0.20 |
| Relationship 15 | 97 | 116 | 111 | 0.00 |
| Relationship 16 | 97 | 108 | 104 | -0.50 |
| Relationship 17 | 97 | 101 | 106 | -0.43 |
| Relationship 18 | 97 | 106 | 136 | 0.57 |
| Relationship 19 | 107 | 104 | 107 | -0.40 |
| Relationship 20 | 107 | 113 | 139 | 0.67 |
| Relationship 21 | 107 | 120 | 142 | 0.93 |
| Relationship 22 | 99 | 100 | 100 | -0.63 |
| Relationship 23 | 99 | 109 | 109 | -0.33 |
| Relationship 24 | 99 | 117 | 117 | -0.07 |
| Relationship 25 | 101 | 107 | 140 | 1.30 |
| Relationship 26 | 101 | 102 | 82 | -0.63 |
| Relationship 27 | 101 | 65 | 52 | -1.59 |
| Relationship 28 | 101 | 98 | 110 | 0.41 |
| Relationship 29 | 101 | 122 | 116 | 0.50 |
| Relationship 30 | 101 | 110 | 133 | 1.07 |
| Relationship 31 | 123 | 107 | 87 | -0.78 |
| Relationship 32 | 123 | 105 | 123 | 0.13 |

**Fig. 2.** Score of Cognitive Gaps in Supervisors-Subordinates

## 4.2 Correlations Analysis

From the above, |E3-E1| has a strong negative correlation with E1. This indicates that the higher a supervisor rates themselves, the smaller the perception gap tends to be between them and their subordinates. Conversely, when a supervisor has a lower self-evaluation, the tendency is for the perception gap with their subordinates to increase.

**Table 2.** Correlations among Variables

| Variable | E1 | E2 | E3 | E3-E1 | IE3-E1I | CG | ICGI |
|---|---|---|---|---|---|---|---|
| E1 | 1 | | | | | | |
| E2 | −.04 | 1 | | | | | |
| E3 | .19 | .36* | 1 | | | | |
| E3-E1 | −.19** | .37* | .93** | 1 | | | |
| IE3-E1I | .04 | −.07 | .25 | .24 | 1 | | |
| CG | −.17 | .43* | .91** | .97** | .22 | 1 | |
| ICGI | −.05 | −.03 | .29 | .31 | .97** | .31 | 1 |

*Note*: Listwise excluded, * p < .05 and ** < .01, two-tailed.

Furthermore, a strong correlation is observed between E3 and CG. This means that when subordinates rate their supervisors highly, the cognitive gaps with the supervisor's self-evaluation tends to be larger, and when they rate them lowly, the gaps with the supervisor's self-evaluation tends to be smaller.

From the above, it is evident that there is no relation between the self-evaluation of supervisors and the evaluation they receive from subordinates. However, a weak positive correlation is observed between the self-evaluation of subordinates and the evaluation they give to their supervisors and the correlation between E2 and CG has a mild positive correlation.

This indicates that a supervisor's self-evaluation is almost unrelated to the cognitive gap with subordinates. Specifically, regardless of whether a supervisor rates themselves highly or poorly, it does not correlate with the evaluation they receive from subordinates.

Conversely, when subordinates have a high self-evaluation, there tends to be a larger cognitive gap with their supervisors. Specifically, subordinates with high self-evaluations tend to have larger cognitive gaps with their supervisors, while those with low self-evaluations tend to have smaller gaps.

### 4.3  Cluster Analysis

To classify cognitive gaps and subordinates' self-evaluations, cluster analysis was conducted. The optimal number of clusters, determined by the Elbow method, appears to be either 3 or 4. Therefore, classification into 4 clusters was carried out (Fig. 3).

## 5  Discussion

### 5.1  Cognitive Gaps in Supervisor-Subordinate Relationships

Based on Fig. 2, there are both positive and negative gaps in the cognitive gaps, indicating cases where subordinates rate their supervisors higher than the supervisors' self-evaluations, as well as cases where they rate them lower. In other words, there are both positive and negative cognitive gaps.

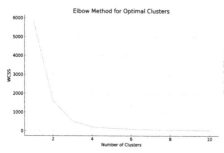

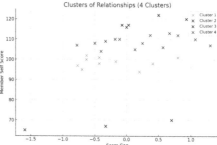

**Fig. 3.** WCSS and number of clusters

**Fig. 4.** Cognitive Gaps and Subordinates' Self-Evaluation Cluster Diagram (Cluster Analysis K-Means)

A positive cognitive gap, where subordinates rate their supervisors higher than the supervisors' self-evaluation, can be seen as a state influenced by a certain positive bias. A larger cognitive gap in hierarchical relationships might increase the possibility of discovering more cues. However, there is also the potential risk of excessive respect or trust towards the supervisor, leading subordinates to overly align with the context narrated by the supervisor based on the cues they discover, rather than exploring the meanings of their own cues. Nonetheless, when this gap is bridged, it can be advantageous in terms of the strength and speed at which enactment occurs.

Conversely, a negative cognitive gap represents the opposite situation. Although the gap itself might be large, leading to the potential discovery of more cues, if the cues discovered by the supervisor do not align with the subordinate's interpretation, it may lead to dismissal of all cues as incorrect, or doubts about the supervisor's capabilities. This situation could hinder further social progress. In such cases, if supervisors and subordinates proceed with their respective interpretations, it poses a risk of disrupting the execution of organizational tasks, as both parties operate on different understandings.

## 5.2 Cognitive Gaps and Sensemaking

Revisiting sensemaking, let's interpret them from the elements of sensemaking, the following can be considered in the context of supervisor-subordinate relationships. Table 3 summarizes the relationship between subordinates' self-evaluation and cognitive gaps in the supervisor-subordinate context.

With a positive cognitive gap, both scenarios a and b, as mentioned in the table above, are possible.

a. A relationship where both parties are mutually independent.
b. A relationship influenced by excessive respect or consideration for the supervisor, leading to unconscious influence by the supervisor's interpreted context, or a relationship where consideration is consciously given.

Let us delve into a comprehensive examination of the sensemaking processes that manifest within supervisor-subordinate relationships amidst the presence of a positive

**Table 3.** Cognitive Gaps and Sensemaking

| | Negative Cognitive Gap | Neutral Gap | Positive Cognitive Gap | |
|---|---|---|---|---|
| 1.Identy | Individual identity remains | Individual identity remains | a. | Ambiguous identity while acquiring a newly constructed identity in a new context |
| | | | | or |
| | | | b. | Performing roles presumed to be expected by the supervisor |
| 2.Retrospective | No change from ambiguous interpretation | Meditation needed to share new context | a. | Sharing newly acquired context |
| | | | | or |
| | | | b. | b. Aligning with the supervisor's retrospective interpretation |
| 3.Enactment | No progress in execution within the same context | Meditation needed for execution in the same context | a. | Strong progress in execution within the same context |
| | | | | or |
| | | | b. | Acting in a way to gain favor with the supervisor. |
| 4.Social | No progress in aligning interpretations | Meditation needed for aligning interpretations | a. | Strong progress in aligning interpretations |
| | | | | or |
| | | | b. | Aligning with the supervisor's context |
| 5.Ongoing | No continuity | Ordinary continuity | a. | Strong continuity |
| | | | | or |
| | | | b. | Pretense of continuity |
| 6.Extracted Cues | Possible ambiguous interpretations | Similar interpretations | a. | Possible ambiguous interpretations |
| | | | | or |
| | | | b. | Acquiring cues through roles expected by the supervisor |
| 7.Plausibility | No sense of satisfaction | Somewhat dissatisfying | a. | Sense of satisfaction |
| | | | | or |
| | | | b. | Misbelieving in own sense of satisfaction |

cognitive gap. When there is a significant positive cognitive gap between superiors and subordinates, from the perspective of the relationship between superiors and subordinates in organizational management, it may be possible to see things from multiple perspectives. However, there is also the risk of simply following the superior's thoughts. Additionally, concerning the obtained cues, in terms of whether to add new meaning to the ongoing context for both parties, it is anticipated that the social aspect will progress, but there is also the possibility that excessive respect for the superior may lead to leaning too much towards the superior in the context. Furthermore, at the execution stage, while possessing a stronger sense of conviction rather than accuracy may lead to smoother and more robust execution capabilities, if there is too much trust in the superior, it may lead to the superior either assuming the expected role or convincing oneself of having conviction, as well (3. Enactment, 7. Plausibility).

Even in cases where there is a significant positive cognitive gap, the quality of the relationship between both parties may result in different actions. There may be adjusting variables that influence this possibility, and this paper considers one of them to be the subordinate's self-assessment. Self-assessment is not only the subordinate's identity but also relates to the three elements of motivation's self-determination theory: autonomy, competence, and relatedness. Henceforth, exploring the subordinate's self-assessment as one of these adjustment factors.

## 5.3  Cognitive Gaps and Subordinates' Self-evaluation

As discussed, we have debated the potential effects of cognitive gaps between supervisors and subordinates on sense-making, specifically regarding subordinate evaluations of their supervisors and the supervisors' self-evaluations. However, as noted in Table 3, even within a Positive Gap, the relationship between the supervisor and subordinate could lead to different actions by both parties. What conditions or situations might dictate these outcomes? Factors such as the personalities of the supervisor and subordinate, the length of time they have worked together, mutual trust elements, and the presence or absence of psychological safety are all considered relevant. This paper uses only the element of subordinate self-evaluation, which showed a weak correlation, to conduct a limited analysis and lay the groundwork for future research.

As observed in the data overview in Sect. 4.1, there is a tendency for cognitive gaps between supervisors and subordinates to decrease when subordinates lack confidence in themselves, as they are more inclined to view their supervisor's statements and actions as correct. Conversely, the more confidence subordinates have, the more likely they are to question their supervisors' statements and actions, potentially leading to larger cognitive gaps.

This can be interpreted as an indication of the subordinates' confidence. When subordinates have a low self-evaluation, they tend to agree more with their supervisor's actions and statements, leading to a smaller gap in self-evaluation with their supervisor. Conversely, as subordinates hold higher self-evaluations, they gain more confidence in themselves, providing a foundation to question the supervisor's words and actions. This scenario is likely to result in a more apparent cognitive gap.

From the cluster analysis in Fig. 4, the relationship between the self-awareness gap of supervisors and the self-evaluations of subordinates can be classified into the following four clusters:

1. Cluster 1 (Red): Stable or Indifference Relationship

   This group represents relationships with slightly negative cognitive gaps and moderate self-evaluation scores of subordinates. The small cognitive gap between supervisors and subordinates suggests a potential for shared cognition and an average self-evaluation in terms of performance, leading to a conflict-free, stable relationship. Although the exchange and sensemaking of meanings could advance with catalysts such as creating opportunities for dialogue, generating new meanings might be difficult considering the minimal cognitive gaps.

2. Cluster 2 (Blue): Blind Trust or Emergent Relationship

   This group reflects relationships with positive cognitive gaps and high self-evaluation scores. Subordinates have a favorable view of their supervisors and hold high self-esteem. The significant cognitive gap, coupled with high self-esteem, allows subordinates to convey their interpretations and opinions to their supervisors, facilitating sensemaking and the discovery and construction of new meanings. However, there is also a possibility that the high evaluation is blind faith, where subordinates might conform to the supervisor's interpretation of meanings.

3. Cluster 3 (Green): Discontented and Disconnected Relationship

   This group shows a large negative score gap and low self-evaluation scores. It indicates substantial dissatisfaction with the supervisor-subordinate relationship and possibly low self-esteem among subordinates. In this group, the large cognitive gap combined with the subordinates' low self-evaluation does not facilitate sensemaking.

4.  Cluster 4 (Purple): Active Cooperation Relationship

This group shows relationships with relatively positive score gaps and moderately high self-evaluation scores. Subordinates generally evaluate their supervisors positively and have a relatively high self-evaluation. The reasonably positive cognitive gap allows for different perspectives to be acknowledged, and a certain level of self-evaluation suggests a potential for proactive cooperation with supervisors, leading to sensemaking.

Considering the above, the relationship between cognitive gaps and sensemaking in supervisor-subordinate dynamics could potentially be as depicted in Fig. 5. Negative cognitive gaps do not promote sensemaking. Moreover, positive cognitive gaps might lead to excessive blind faith or anticipation, but strong self-efficacy in subordinates could lead to an emergent relationship. This sense of self-efficacy might also be a factor in promoting mutual sensemaking in relationships with moderate cognitive gaps or no cognitive gaps.

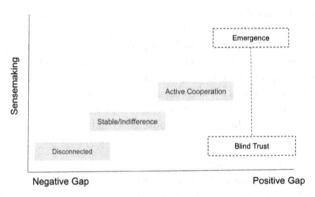

**Fig. 5.** Type of Relationship in Sensemaking

# 6   Conclusion

This study, focusing only on 32 supervisor-subordinate relationships at the company, has resulted in a limited discussion due to the small data volume. Traditionally, the absence of cognitive gaps was deemed beneficial for increasing productivity in organizations, where uniformity in values and contexts was emphasized, and individuals not conforming were often excluded. The idea that no cognitive gap is better primarily served the purpose of information processing in supervisor-subordinate relationships.

In this study, focusing specifically on supervisor-subordinate relationships, we proposed a theoretical framework as a hypothesis, examining the relationship between cognitive gaps and sensemaking using data from the IT company. According to this framework, in supervisor-subordinate relationships with a positive cognitive gap, depending on the nature of the relationship, there's a possibility of enabling multiple interpretations, fostering the creation of context and interpretation, and thereby strongly advancing enactment. For instance, supervisors are capable of not only respecting and accepting differing opinions from subordinates but also actively advocating for them. This enables subordinates to confidently articulate their own perspectives and translate novel ideas into practice, thereby exerting influence on the external environment and facilitating the process of enactment. However, it was also shown that the presence of excessive respect or consideration could potentially hinder sensemaking. Conversely, in cases of a negative cognitive gap, while there's a potential for multiple interpretations, dissatisfaction could impede further sensemaking. This challenges the traditional view that a large cognitive gap is detrimental due to its hindrance to information processing efficiency. By categorizing cognitive gaps as positive or negative, it was demonstrated that sensemaking can advance even in the presence of cognitive gaps, given certain conditions are met.

These conditions include the possibility that a subordinate's high self-evaluation, as a sense of self-efficacy, could promote active engagement with the supervisor, and that introducing appropriate catalysts (e.g., time for dialogue, diversity training) in stable or indifferent relationships could also facilitate sensemaking.

In this paper, as an additional consideration, it was mentioned that even in relationships between supervisors and subordinates with the same Positive Gap, multiple actions could occur. One potential condition or situation for this involves utilizing subordinates' self-evaluations from a perspective of self-affirmation. It was then demonstrated that, based on subordinates' self-esteem and cognitive gaps, there could be four types of relationships between supervisors and subordinates: 'dissatisfaction or disconnection,' 'Stability or Indifference,' 'Active Cooperation,' and 'Blind Trust or Emergent'.

In this paper, as an additional consideration, it was mentioned that even in relationships between supervisors and subordinates with the same Positive Gap, multiple actions could occur. One potential condition or situation for this involves utilizing subordinates' self-evaluations from a perspective of self-affirmation. It was then demonstrated that, based on subordinates' self-esteem and cognitive gaps, there could be four types of relationships between supervisors and subordinates: 'dissatisfaction or disconnection,' 'Stability or Indifference,' 'Active Cooperation,' and 'Blind Trust or Emergent'.

Finally, the challenges and future directions are addressed. This analysis was confined to 32 relationships at the company. Verification with a larger set of relationship data is necessary, which could reveal specifics related to corporate and industry-specific relationships.

Moreover, while this study focused on subordinates' self-evaluations as a factor of self-efficacy, exploring other variables is crucial. Potential factors include tenure, duration of relationships, frequency of online vs. offline interactions, number of conversations, and more subjective aspects like personality traits and value alignment. Lastly, observing and analyzing sensemaking and knowledge creation methods in each group is essential. The presence or absence of cognitive gaps could lead to different conversation methods and patterns, necessitating analysis of these conversational structures.

These explorations aim to delve into the mechanisms by which the exchange of subjectivities in supervisor-subordinate relationships fosters sensemaking and intersubjective innovation.

# References

1. Lee Fleming, Perfecting Cross-Pollination, Harvard Business Review, Vol.82, Issue 9, September (2004)
2. R Likert, New Patterns of Management (1961)
3. Nonaka, Current Status of Future Prospects of Knowledge-Creating Companies (2022)
4. Nonaka, I., Takeuchi, H.: The Knowledge-Creating Company: How Japanese Companies (1995)
5. Jeong, S.: A cross-level analysis of organizational knowledge creation: how do transformational leaders interact with their subordinates' expertise and interpersonal relationships? Human Res. Dev. Quarterly **32**, 111–130 (2021)
6. Lee, H., Choi, B.: Knowledge management enablers, processes, and organizational performance: an integrative view and empirical examination. J. Manag. Inform. Syst. **20**(1), 179–228 (2003)
7. Mariama, et al.: SECI driven creativity: the role of team trust and intrinsic motivation. J. Knowl. Manag. **22**(8), 1688–1711 (2018)
8. Karl E Weick, Sensemaking in Organizations (1995)
9. Rouleau, L., Balogun, J.: Middle managers, strategic sensemaking, and discursive competence. J. Manag. Stud. **48**, 5 (2011)
10. LüScher, L.S., Lewis, M.W.: Organizational change and managerial sensemaking: working through paradox. Acad. Manag. J. **51**(2), 221–240 (2008). https://doi.org/10.5465/amj.2008.31767217
11. Wrzesniewski, A., Dutton, J.E., Debebe, G.: Interpersonal sensemaking and the meaning of work. Res. Organ. Behav. **25**, 93–135 (2003). https://doi.org/10.1016/S0191-3085(03)25003-6
12. Scullen, S.E., Mount, M.K., Goff, M.: Understanding the latent structure of job performance ratings. J. Appl. Psychol. **85**(6), 956–970 (2000). https://doi.org/10.1037/0021-9010.85.6.956
13. Taylor, S.N., Bright, D.S.: Open-mindedness and defensiveness in multisource feedback processes: a conceptual framework. J. Appl. Behav. Sci. **47**(4), 432–460 (2011)
14. Kyungsub. S.C., et al.: Exploring the underlying aspects of pair programming: The impact of personality. Inform. Softw. Technol. **50**(11), 1114–1126 (2008)
15. Katz, R.L.: Skills of an effective administrator. Harvard Bus. Rev. **1955**, 33–42 (1995)

# Research on Knowledge Creation Over Time Using Network Analysis: SiC Power Device from Research to New Business

Hideki Hayashida[1]([✉]) and Hiroki Funashia[2]

[1] Tokyo University of Agriculture and Technology, Tokyo 1848588, Japan
hideki-hayashida@go.tuat.ac.jp
[2] Kindai University Technical College, Nabari 5180459, Japan
funashima@ktc.ac.jp

**Abstract.** The research on knowledge creation over time through network analysis holds significant importance in the domains of knowledge management and innovation. Specifically, when applied to the Research and Development (R&D) sector, analyzing the changes over time using network analysis can offer a visual representation of how knowledge creation evolves. This visualization can be invaluable in making informed decisions regarding R&D strategies within organizations. The results of overlaying the time-series network analysis of jointly filed patents and the market report show that as R&D progresses and the market grows, it is becoming increasingly concentrated in groups of several companies that have a large market share, which is interpreted by the companies that research and develop SiC other than the leading R&D group. The results of the report suggest that the companies that are researching and developing SiC other than the leading R&D clusters cannot expect to expand their own business earnings unless they form alliances with any of these clusters.

**Keywords:** Network analysis · R&D strategy · SiC Power device

## 1 Introduction

Research on knowledge creation over time through network analysis holds significant importance in the domains of knowledge management and innovation. This research has the potential to significantly benefit organizations by providing deeper insights into the processes of knowledge creation, distribution, and evolution within their structures. When applied to the Research and Development (R&D) sector, analyzing changes over time using network analysis visually represents how knowledge creation evolves. This visualization is invaluable for making informed decisions regarding R&D strategies within organizations. Essentially, understanding the dynamic nature of knowledge creation over time empowers organizations to develop strategies for rapid adaptation and innovation. Ultimately, this strategic approach enhances competitiveness and bolsters success in the ever-evolving marketplace. This research focuses on the development of the next-generation power device, SiC power devices. Presently, power devices are

© The Author(s), under exclusive license to Springer Nature Switzerland AG 2024
L. Uden and I.-H. Ting (Eds.): KMO 2024, CCIS 2152, pp. 175–182, 2024.
https://doi.org/10.1007/978-3-031-63269-3_13

indispensable in consumer electronics, power electronics, automotive industry, renewable energy, telecommunications, space and aerospace, medical devices, data centers, IoT and edge computing, quantum computing, and beyond. While most power electronics use Si power devices, SiC has recently found applications in various fields.

## 2 Literature Review

### 2.1 Power Device Development Review

The imperative for enhanced efficiency, reduced size, and heightened performance across diverse sectors such as electronics, power electronics, and renewable energy has spurred a vigorous surge in research and development towards next-generation power devices. Notably, significant attention has been directed towards silicon carbide (SiC) power devices. SiC presents numerous advantages over traditional silicon counterparts, including elevated breakdown voltage, enhanced temperature tolerance, and diminished switching losses. A pivotal milestone occurred in 1993 when a particular research group published a comprehensive theoretical analysis [2], marking the commencement of focused efforts toward optimizing SiC material quality, device architecture, and manufacturing methodologies. Consequently, the fruition of these endeavors culminated in the development of SiC Schottky diodes and SiC metal-oxide-semiconductor field-effect transistors (MOSFETs).

### 2.2 Network Analysis Review

In the realm of network analysis, seminal contributions have been made by Watts and Strogatz [3–5], who expound upon the concept of small-world networks, delineating the correlation between clustering coefficients and average path lengths. Barabási [6–9] proposes a random network model that exhibits the properties of scale-free networks, which describes in detail the statistical dynamic properties of complex networks. Dorogovtsev and Mendes [10] provide a comprehensive review encompassing research on network evolution, delving into pivotal phenomena such as the "small-world phenomenon" and "scale-free networks". Newman [11] further elucidates the intricate nature of complex networks, elucidating their constituent elements (nodes) and interactions between them (edges), along with characteristic features like degree distribution, clustering coefficient, and average path length. Scott et al. [12–14] offer a comprehensive exposition on social network analysis, encapsulating fundamental concepts and applications about network structure, dynamics, and influence metrics.

Moreover, Ortiz-Arroyo [15] introduces methodologies for identifying key players within social networks leveraging entropy measures, while Burt [16] underscores the significance of structural holes in fostering innovation and information diffusion. Uzzi and Spiro [17] accentuate the optimal balance between interaction among specialized experts and interdisciplinary collaboration for fostering creative outcomes. Borgatti et al. [18] advocate for applying network analysis in social sciences, propounding methodologies for analyzing networks across diverse scales and layers, validated through empirical investigations.

# 3 Methodology

## 3.1 Research Framework

This study used the Database of Chinese Granted, Chinese Granted Patents for Utility Models, Chinese patent Applications, Chinese Utility Model Applications, European Granted Patens, European Patent Applications, French Granted Patents, French Patent Applications, German Gebauchsmusters (Utility Model), German Granted Patents, German Patent Applications, Great Britain Granted patents, Great Britain Patent Applications, Japanese Granted Patents, Japanese Granted Patents for Utility Model, Japanese Patent Abstracts, Japanese Patent Application, US Granted Patents, US Patent Applications, and WIPO PCT Publications to analyze jointly applied patents related to SiC (Silicon Carbide) power device. Of the patent information using the word "organoid" in the full text of the patents, 244,693 patents that were made known after 1971, when the SiC device was started to be studied.

## 3.2 Network Analysis

In this work, we derived three different concepts of centrality to estimate network properties. The first one is eigenvector centrality. The simplest form of centrality is the degree at a node. However, the degree is an extremely crude measure of centrality. In effect, it gives one "centrality point" for each neighborhood a node has. However, not all neighbors are necessarily equal. Often a node's importance in a network is increased by having connections to other nodes that are themselves important. We can the eigenvector centrality using node's several points proportional to the centrality score of its neighbors rather than one point for each neighbor in the network it has. The graded equation is given as

$$u(t + 1) = Au(t) \tag{1}$$

where A and $u(t) \equiv (u_1, u_2, \ldots, u_n)^T$ are the neighbor matrix and the vector aligned centrality $u_i$ of the node $v_i$ respectively.

   Interpreting the above equation as the influence $u_i$ of a node is the sum of $u_j$ over adjacent points, we can regard variable t as the index of updates for the iteration. Since the above equation is an incremental equation with t as the index, we consider repeating it to find the centrality at each vertex. In general, however, it is not possible to find the number of updates for $u_1, u_2, \ldots, u_N$ diverges. Therefore, we impose a bound condition each time such that the sum of $u_1, u_2, \ldots, u_N$ is equal to 1, and iterate. The linear algebra show us that these iterations are shown to be maximal eigenvectors of A if there is at least one closed odd angle in the network. Therefore, if the largest eigenvalue of A is $\lambda_N$, eigenvector centrality is given as

$$Au = \lambda_N u \tag{2}$$

With eigenvector centrality defined in this way, a node can achieve high centrality by having many neighbors with modest centrality or a few neighbors with high centrality (or both). This situation is natural. The node can influence by knowing many nodes or the node can influence by knowing a few nodes.

Second, we evaluated the closeness centrality. The closeness centrality is defined that how close on average, the node is from itself to others. Mathematically, the closeness centrality is defined as

$$\frac{N-1}{\prod_{j=1,\,j\neq i}^{N} d(v_i, v_j)} = \frac{1}{L_i} \tag{3}$$

where $d(v_i, v_j)$ is the distance between nodes $v_i$ and $v_j$. $L_i$ is the average distance from node $v_i$ to other nodes.

The betweenness centrality is the degree to bridge and control the flow of information in a network for the nodes. Mathematically, betweenness centrality is defined as

$$b_i = \frac{\sum_{i_s=1,i_s\neq i}^{N} \sum_{i_t=1,i_t\neq i}^{i_s-1} \frac{g_i^{(i_s,i_t)}}{N_{i_s,i_t}}}{(N-1)(N-2)/2} \tag{4}$$

where $g_i^{(i_s,i_t)}$ is the number of vertices in the shortest path going from the start point $v_{i_s}$ to the endpoint $v_{i_t}$. $N_{i_s,i_t}$ is the number of shortest paths from the start point to the endpoint.

## 4   Results and Discussion

A feasibility study was conducted on SiC power device technology development and market trends by analyzing information using jointly applied patents and network analysis. The results of the patent analysis showed that the number of patent applications relating to SiC power device epitaxial growth is increasing exponentially since 2000. In the 2020 the number of jointly applied patents reached at 5236 as peak number.

Table 1 lists the results of the network analysis. The number of nodes and edges has increased with time, and the order has increased accordingly. As for the network structure, the maximum cluster coefficient is around 0.7, suggesting that the nodes in the network have relatively high local ties and form strong clusters.

Table 1 lists the results of the network analysis. The number of nodes and edges has increased with time, and the order has increased accordingly. As for the network structure, the maximum cluster coefficient is around 0.7, suggesting that the nodes in the network have relatively high local ties and form strong clusters.

The time series variation of the entire network is shown in Fig. 1. The evolution of R&D is clear. It can be seen that the 1970s to 1980s was the initial stage of research; in the 1990s, it entered the mass production sample evaluation stage; in the early 2000s, development toward commercialization began, and from the late 2000s to the early 2010s, development progressed at a rapid pace. In the latter half of the 2010s, however, R&D activities reached a plateau, and the focus shifted from R&D to production technology development.

The decrease in the number of nodes indicates this. In the 1970s, 1980s, and 1990s, nodes with structural holes can be seen between large clusters. Strategically, contact

**Table 1.** Result of Network Analysis

| Year | Number of Nodes | Number of edges | Cluster Coefficient | Average Degree |
|------|-----------------|-----------------|---------------------|----------------|
| 1975–1979 | 43 | 88 | 0.545 | 4.093 |
| 1980–1984 | 116 | 320 | 0.695 | 5.517 |
| 1985–1989 | 274 | 1155 | 0.731 | 8.431 |
| 1990–1994 | 401 | 1096 | 0.732 | 5.466 |
| 1995–1999 | 1072 | 4308 | 0.756 | 8.037 |
| 2000–2004 | 2457 | 9049 | 0.749 | 7.366 |
| 2005–2009 | 5,080 | 36,848 | 0.796 | 14.507 |
| 2010–2014 | 4,863 | 32,575 | 0.772 | 13.397 |
| 2015–2019 | 2,215 | 7,184 | 0.626 | 6.487 |
| 2020–2023 | 1,307 | 2,514 | 0.517 | 3.847 |

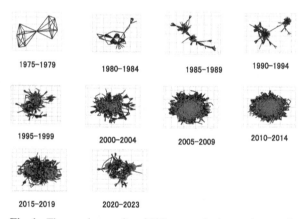

**Fig. 1.** Time-series results of SiC power device total network.

with these nodes is advantageous for obtaining R & D information. Next, in Fig. 2, the analysis results for betweenness centrality and eigenvector centrality concerning proximity centrality are presented. The left side of the figure displays a graph depicting eigenvector centrality in relation to proximity centrality, while the right side illustrates a graph representing betweenness centrality in relation to proximity centrality. Upon examining the time series changes in the graphs for proximity centrality, betweenness centrality, proximity centrality, and eigenvector centrality, a clear right-hand-upward trend is observed in the late 1990s.

Moreover, during the 2000s, the graphs unmistakably depict characteristics resembling those of a scale-free network. The time-series change in the numbers of joint applications, number of nodes, and the number of edges are shown in Fig. 3.

Nodes and edges are decreasing from late 2000s on the other hand, jointly applied patents are increasing. Also, from 2005 to 2014 the total network shows one big cluster.

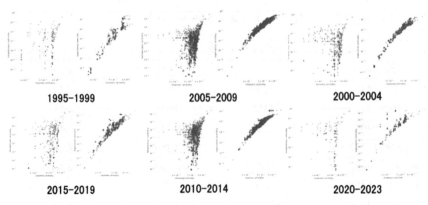

**Fig. 2.** Network analysis result of centrality (1995–2023)

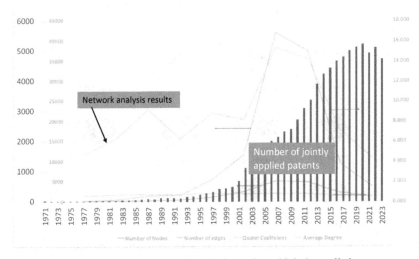

**Fig. 3.** Superimpose of Network analysis result, and jointly applied patents

However, even though jointly applied patens are exponentially increasing, In the late 2010s SiC power device development shows making new clusters. In 2020s, network cluster started grouping as three or four big cluster as shown in Fig. 1.

However, even though jointly applied patens are exponentially increasing, In the late 2010s SiC power device development shows making new clusters. In 2020s, network cluster started grouping as three or four big cluster as shown in Fig. 1.

Figure 4 presents a juxtaposition of the time-series data illustrating changes in the number of nodes and the number of joint patent applications with the market size data for SiC power devices. The figure clearly demonstrates that the growth in the number of joint patent applications has been proportional to the expansion of the market size. However, an evident decline in the number of nodes indicates that, beginning in the late

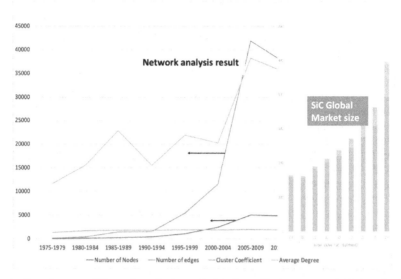

**Fig. 4.** Superimpose of Network analysis result, jointly applied patents, and Market size [21].

2010s, some companies either scaled back or withdrew their R&D efforts despite the expanding market size. This divergence can be interpreted as a discernible distinction between successful and less successful players. The market is anticipated to experience steady growth after 2023. In this context, several strategic options can be considered:

1) For those contemplating entry into the SiC power device market, viable choices include forming alliances with industry leaders, adopting technology transfer initiatives, or pursuing mergers and acquisitions (M&A). This is particularly relevant as the number of nodes and edges in networks has been steadily declining since the late 2000s.

2) For companies already engaged in their own R&D efforts, a thorough analysis of the competitive landscape is essential. Decisions can then be made on whether to maintain the current R&D strategy, collaborate through joint ventures with competitors, or embark on an M&A strategy.

It's imperative to note that a standalone, in-house R&D approach may not be the most suitable course of action.

## 5 Conclusion

The results of the study suggest that the companies that are researching and developing SiC other than the leading R&D clusters con not expect to expand their own business earnings unless they that from alliances with any other these clusters. The network analysis and market forecast data provided suggestions for the direction of R&D strategy formulation. In the future, it is expected that many actual cases will be examined to see if this SiC power device is not a unique case but a versatile method.

# References

1. US Patent US-3566262A MOLECULAR SPECTROMETER USING POINT TUNNELING IBM THOMPSON WILLIAMA (1971)
2. Baliga, B.J.: Power semiconductor device figure of merit for high-frequency applications. IEEE Electron Device Lett. **10**, 455 (1989)
3. Bhatnagar, M., Baliga, B.J.: Comparison of 6H-SiC, 3C-SiC, and Si for power devices. IEEE Trans. Electron Devices **40**, 645 (1993)
4. Watts J.D., Strogatz Steven H.: Collective dynamics of 'small-world' networks. Nat. **393**(6684), 440–442 (1998)
5. Watts, D.J.: Networks, Dynamics and the Small-World Phenomenon. Am. J. Sociol. **105**(2), 493–527 (1999)
6. Watt, D.J.: Small Worlds: The dynamic of Networks between Order and Randomness. Princeton University Press (1999)
7. Barabási, A.L., Albert, R.: Emergence of scaling in random networks. Sci. **286**(5439), 509–512 (1999)
8. Albert, R., Barabási, A.L.: Statistical mechanics of complex networks. Rev. Mod. Phys. **74**(1), 47–97 (2002)
9. Barabási, A.-L.: Network Science Cambridge University Press, United Kingdom (2016)
10. Dorogovtsev, S.N., Mendes, J.F.: Evolution of networks. Adv. Phys. **51**(4), 1079–1187 (2002)
11. Newman, M.E.: The structure and function of complex networks. SIAM Rev. **45**(2), 167–256 (2003)
12. Scott, J.: Social Network Analysis Sociology **22**(1), 109–127 (1988)
13. Knoke, D., Yang, S.: Social Network Analysis 3$^{rd}$ ed., Sage (2019)
14. Wasserman, S., Faust, K.: Social Network Analysis: Methods and Applications Cambridge University Press (1994)
15. Abraham, A., Hassanien, A.-E., Snázel, V. (eds.): Computational Social Network Analysis. CCN, Springer, London (2010). https://doi.org/10.1007/978-1-84882-229-0
16. Burt, R.S.: Structural holes: The social structure of competition. Harvard University Press (1992)
17. Uzzi, B.,, Jarret, S.: Collaboration and Creativity: the Small World Problem. Am. J. Sociol. (2), 447–504 (2005)
18. Borgatti, S.P., Mehra, A., Brass, D.J., Labianca, G.: Network analysis in the social sciences. Sci. **323**(5916), 892–895 (2009)
19. Mucha, P.J., Richardson, T., Macon, K., Porter, M.A., Onnela, J.P.: Community structure in time-dependent, multiscale, and multiplex networks. Sci. **328**(5980), 876–878 (2010)
20. Baum J., Cowman, R., Jonard, N.: Network-independent partner selection and the evolution of innovation networks UNU-MERIT Working paper series, **22,** 1–26 (2009)
21. Fujikeizai.: Current status and future outlook of the semiconductor materials market 2020 Fujikeizai ( 2020)

# KM and Education

Law and Education

# Data-Driven Student Recruitment Strategies in Private Higher Educational Institutions

Kallychurn Dooshyant Rai[1], Vinothini Kasinathan[1(✉)], and Aida Mustapha[2]

[1] School of Computing and Technology, Asia Pacific University of Technology and Innovation, 57000 Kuala Lumpur, Malaysia
{dooshyant,vinothini}@apu.edu.my
[2] Faculty of Applied Sciences and Technology, Universiti Tun Hussein Onn Malaysia, 86400 Panchor, Johor, Malaysia

**Abstract.** This research advocates for the integration of data analytics as a pivotal strategy for private higher education institutions (HEI) to navigate the dynamic landscape of student recruitment and marketing strategies. By leveraging insights derived from data, institutions can not only streamline their processes but also foster a more targeted and personalized approach that resonates with the preferences and expectations of today's diverse student population. The study focuses on descriptive and predictive analytics and proposes an interactive dashboard and a machine learning model as outcomes. The findings of this study contribute to the intersection of data analytics and higher education, providing actionable insights for HEIs aiming to thrive in an increasingly competitive environment.

**Keywords:** Knowledge Management · Data Analytics · Student Recruitment

## 1 Introduction

In recent decades, the higher education industry has been known to have an enormous expansion globally, and students have become the core of higher education market and its profit centers. The exponential growth is related to an increase in the diversification of higher education [1]. New types of institutions have emerged with the process of offering a diversified type of advanced education. Concurrently, the political economy was embedded with this expansion that has increasingly driven market forces which has led to growing privatization and competition in the higher education sector.

This research is carried out in Malaysia in particular, as it houses a diverse system of secondary education and higher education. Malaysia has more than 30 years of experience in international higher education and has been thriving ever since. The country has a well-structured, unique higher education system that provides opportunities to local and foreign students to pursue an international qualification at competitive rates. Currently, higher education in Malaysia is booming at an exponential speed and the peninsula, hosts over 500 private and public higher education institutions which includes branches of reputable foreign universities. While public universities are predominantly subsidized by the local government, private universities have a relatively different revenue stream

© The Author(s), under exclusive license to Springer Nature Switzerland AG 2024
L. Uden and I.-H. Ting (Eds.): KMO 2024, CCIS 2152, pp. 185–197, 2024.
https://doi.org/10.1007/978-3-031-63269-3_14

which is fueled by the number of students enrolled. As such, private universities are amidst fierce competition, both in the local and international market. Malaysia tertiary education has 467 private learning institutions of which 104 are universities [2]. Private universities hold the lion's share of the market and the increasing competition amongst them has forced these organizations to look for areas of competitive advantages and attract potential students across international borders.

Student enrolment is one of the main challenges that private universities are currently facing. There has been a significant one-off impact on student registrations in the preceding academic years post pandemic, particularly the international students' market, mostly because of deferments and offer cancellations. Furthermore, with travel bans, marketing and recruitment events were halted that has dampened international enrolments for the cycle of 2022 and upcoming ones. Consequently, as international competition reduced, competition for domestic students has exacerbated [3].

At present, digital revolution has paved the way for technologies that are leveraged by data and artificial intelligence [4]. In the higher education sector, leaders of institutions are acknowledging that incorporating advanced analytics such as prediction models can significantly transform the current way of working by exploring new perspectives to engage current and prospective students, increase student enrolments, improve student retention and completion rates [5]. Predictive analytics models analyze historical data on student characteristics, academic performance, and demographic factors to predict future enrollment patterns and inform targeted interventions [6].

Nonetheless, even though data analytics provides an excellent platform for strategizing students enrollment, higher education institutions may face challenges in two perspectives. First, high-quality data relevant to student enrollment, especially in the aftermath of the pandemic may be limited. Second, the pandemic has likely influenced student demographics and preferences, leading to shifts in enrollment patterns. Data-driven strategies may struggle to capture and adapt to these evolving trends, particularly if historical data does not adequately reflect post-pandemic realities. This, in turn, may hinder the accuracy and reliability of predictive models [7].

Henceforth, this research investigates the potential benefits for incorporating data analytics within the marketing and recruitment department of higher educational institutions and its impact to boost student enrolments, focusing on Asia Pacific University of Technology and Innovation (APU) as a case study. To achieve the objectives, a Business Intelligence dashboard is developed to provide insights on Malaysian student recruitment of APU. The framework also employs predictive analytics [8] so the recruitment team will be able to identify and follow-up with the most potential applicants to be accepted as students. This eventually assists in understanding the target market, enhance marketing strategies, optimize resource allocations, and brand positioning.

## 2    Materials and Methods

This study proposes a framework that incorporates descriptive and predictive analytics based on which data-driven marketing strategies are created. The technologies used are Microsoft Power BI for descriptive analytics and Python programming to create the machine learning models for predictive analytics. The following are characteristics of the proposed business analytics framework:

- To create a visualization that provide insights on the number of enquiries APU has received from each state in Malaysia.
- To create a visualization that provides insights on the popularity of courses offered at pre-university level, undergraduate level, and postgraduate level independently.
- To create a visualization that identifies the anomalies and trends in a time series data.
- To create a visualization that identifies the popularity of courses based on each state.
- To develop a dashboard that will accommodate all the visualizations.
- To conduct an analysis on each visualization created.
- To extract business intelligence from the analysis derived from the visualizations based on three predictive models: Logistic Regression (LR), $K$-Nearest Neighbor (KNN), Artificial Neural Networks (ANN).
- To analyze and select the most accurate model.

## 2.1 Descriptive Analytics

To perform the descriptive analysis, a Business Intelligence Dashboard is developed as shown in Fig. 1. The dashboard is developed via the Extract, Transform, and Load (ETL) process, where data is extracted, transformed, and loaded into an output data container [9]. In this work, the data obtained is sourced from a Microsoft questionnaire that is then exported as a spreadsheet. After data has been extracted, a data transformation process is performed to clean and to normalize the raw data into standardized data structures and types. Once the transformation has been completed, the structured and cleaned data is loaded into Power BI.

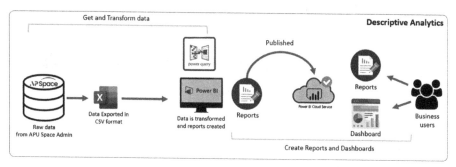

**Fig. 1.** Implementation of descriptive analytics.

## 2.2 Predictive Analytics

In preparing for predictive analytics, the implementation deals with three machine learning algorithms that would be used to predict the chances of enrolment. The process starts by importing the relevant data and libraries and continues with a process named data pre-processing to figure out if there are any observations which are missing or require any special attention. The available data will then be visualized and analyzed to understand the importance of each independent variable and the dependent variable. Figure 2 shows the implementation of the predictive analytics.

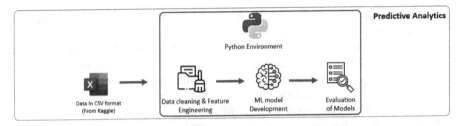

**Fig. 2.** Implementation of predictive analytics.

In this study, no observations have been found with a missing value in the dataset. Once the data pre-processing stage has been completed, the following step is to explore the data to assess on how well the values are distributed among the variables, variances, correlations between them, outliers, and other necessary information regarding the metadata. Figure 3 shows the general statistics of each variable displayed including their mean, standard deviation, minimum, maximum and other relevant information.

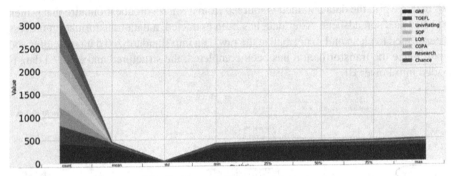

**Fig. 3.** Pictorial diagram of dataset.

The heat map in Fig. 4 visualizes the correlation of the independent variables and the dependent variable. While the heatmap is color coded to understand the correlation of variables, another way to better understand the correlation is to get the correlation values against the target variable (chance).

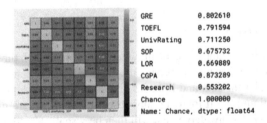

**Fig. 4.** Correlation plot and correlation values.

Based on the distribution plot in Fig. 5, we can see that the data is normally distributed for all the highly correlated variables with the target variable. This shows that there are no outliers and the models that will be built with this dataset would be generalized as good as possible and we would not run the risk of overfitting.

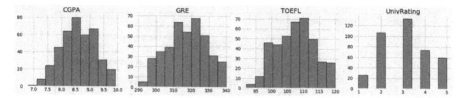

**Fig. 5.** Distribution plot.

Next, the data will be partitioned into a training set and a testing set. The training set will be used to develop the model and the testing set will be used to determine the accuracy of the models. During implementation, the relevant libraries are imported under Python 3 environment, including the machine learning algorithms libraries, which are Logistic Regression, $K$-Nearest Neighbor, and Artificial Neural Networks.

- **Logistic Regression.** Logistic Regression (LR) predicts binary results. In the dataset, the column Admit was created earlier where applicants with score > 70 has a chance of getting admitted (1) and score < 70% has less chance of getting admitted (0). It has been seen from the feature importance section that CGPA and the GRE Score have the highest influence on the chance of admission. Hence, when developing an LR, the values of CGPA and GRE score will be used to predict the enrolment.
- **K-Nearest Neighbor.** K-Nearest Neighbor (KNN) is a supervised machine learning algorithm that works by grouping objects into $k$ groups according to their characteristics by minimizing the total of the distances between each object and the group, or the cluster centroid. The algorithms begin with initializing the centroid, followed by assigning the objects to the centroids and centroids update. The algorithm selects the number $K$ of the neighbors and calculates the Euclidean distance of $K$ number of neighbors. It then takes the $K$ nearest neighbors as new category data members.
- **Artificial Neural Networks.** Artificial Neural Network (ANN) is an information processing technique that functions similar to the human brain where a large number of connected processing units work hand in hand to process information. ANN is organized into three layers; input, hidden and output. The neurons keep learning to improve the performance of the model and this adaptive learning capability of the model is advantageous for developing highly accurate predictive models [2].

## 3   Results and Analysis

### 3.1   Descriptive Analytics

Figure 6 shows the Business Intelligence Dashboard developed to understand the enquiry of students from year 2021 to 2022. There are four critical factors as follows:

- Number of enquiries by state of origin
- Number of enquiries by programme name
- Number of enquires by how did you know about APU?
- Number of enquiries by level of study

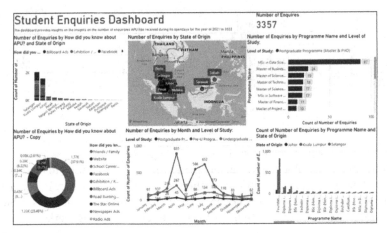

**Fig. 6.** Business Intelligence Dashboard.

Figure 7 shows the state in Malaysia from which students came to enquire on open days at APU between 2020 to 2022, with Selangor and Kuala Lumpur accounting for the highest number of enquiries with 2082 and 1586 respectively. States such as Sabah, Kelantan, Putrajaya, Terengganu, and Perlis recorded the least number of enquiries. In light of the analysis, the marketing department of APU has to increase the number of adverts in states with lesser enquires. Therefore, the university can better distribute its finance for advertisements more efficiently based on the market demand and avoids the saturation of advertisement in only one geographical location.

Next, Fig. 8 shows the popularity of different courses at pre-university level. It can be noted from the chart that the 3 most popular pre-university courses are the Foundation (1,781 enquiries), Diploma in Information Communication and Technology with a Specialism in Software Engineering (393 enquiries), and Diploma in Information Communication and Technology (380 enquiries). The three least selling courses are Diploma in International Studies (7 enquiries), Diploma in Design & Media (7 enquiries), and Diploma in Electrical and Electronic Engineering (4 enquiries).

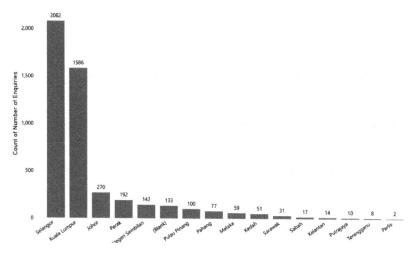

**Fig. 7.** Number of students enquires from each state of Malaysia.

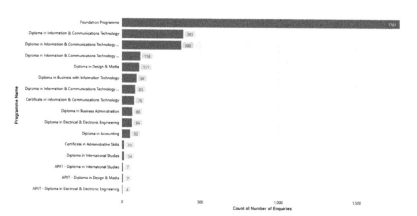

**Fig. 8.** Popularity of different courses at pre-university level.

Figure 9 shows the popularity of different courses at undergraduate level. Note that the 3 most popular courses in descending order that were enquired on were BSc. in Computer Science (160 enquiries), BSc. in Software Engineering (122 enquiries), and BSc. in Information Technology (106 enquiries). The courses with the least enquiries are BA in Tourism Management (3 enquiries), BSc. of Petroleum Engineering and BSc. in Information Technology (2 enquiries each), and BA in Accounting & Finance (1 enquiry).

Figure 10 shows the popularity of different courses at postgraduate level. Note that the 3 most popular courses in descending order that were enquired on were MSc. in Data Science and Business Analytics (87 enquiries), Master of Business Administration (24 enquiries), and MSc. in Artificial Intelligence (19 enquiries). The least enquired courses

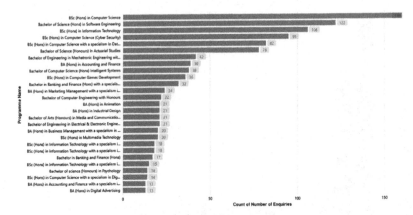

**Fig. 9.** Popularity of different courses at undergraduate level.

are MA in Finance, MSc. in Computing, MSc. in International Business Communication and PhD in Technology with 1 enquiry each.

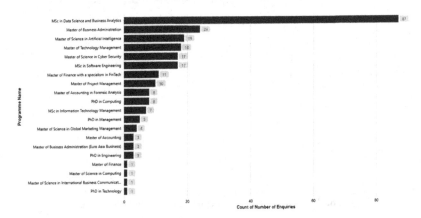

**Fig. 10.** Popularity of different courses at postgraduate level.

Figure 11 shows the time series data of the number of enquires APU has received over the year of 2020 to 2022.

Across the level of study, Pre-University programme had the most steep and interesting trend compared to the other two. The Pre-University programme started trending in 2020 and has been rising by 694.3% (2076) in 2 years. The undergraduate programme started trending in 2020 and has been rising by 499.3% (744) in 2 years. Meanwhile, the postgraduate programme started trending in 2020, rising by 174.5% (82) in 2 years. The trend has been going up exponentially since the lockdown of 2020. It is expected that the trend remains constant from the year 2022 to the year 2023. A spike in the trend for 2023 may be a double-edged sword for the organization. While increasing numbers

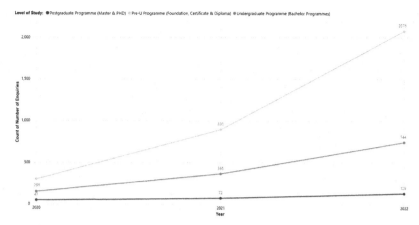

**Fig. 11.** The number of enquires APU has received over the year of 2020 to 2022.

can be tempting to increase revenue, at the same time the resources available should be able to meet the demand.

Next, the line chart in Fig. 12 shows the time series data of the number of enquires APU has received for the year 2022. Note that the first anomaly detected is in the number of enquiries where Pre-U programme had a high of 855 and a high for Undergraduate programme of 267 on April 2022. The trend detected is across the study level, which Pre-U started trending down on July 2022, falling by 87.42% (570) in 5 months. The deepest decline was between July 2022 to December 2022, dropping from 652 to 82 while the trend for postgraduate programs has been fairly constant.

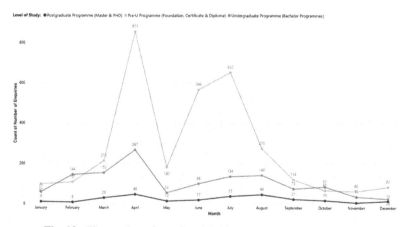

**Fig. 12.** The number of enquires APU has received for the year 2022.

The undergraduate programme experienced a down trend from April to May and did not picked up a steep increase in the trend during July 2022, unlike pre-university programme. April and July are the busiest months because these are the two period where grade 10/SPM/IGCSE results are released. Hence, the resources during these months need to be prepared including the number of counsellors, number of brochures and other materials have to be in stock to be able to cater for the huge influx of students. While the trend of pre university and undergraduate started off in a similar manner, it is noticed that the undergraduate trend did not increase during the month of July and August which are normally when the 12th grade/A-level results are out. This is an issue that has to be addressed through certain marketing strategies to attract more enquiries regarding undergraduate courses during the period of July and August.

Figure 13 shows that the majority of the enquiries come from Friends/Family (37.91%) and Website (28.46%). School Career Fairs, Facebook, Exhibitions/Roadshows and Billboards are also huge contributors in terms of converting school graduates to potential enquiries for APU programs. Power BI also provides the drill-down capability. When filtered by states, all of the high enquiry states are almost similar in terms of proportion to each other as shown in Fig. 14. Most of the enquiries by states have Friend/Family as the way on how they found out about APU. Next is through websites, school career fair, Facebook, Exhibitions/Roadshows and Billboards.

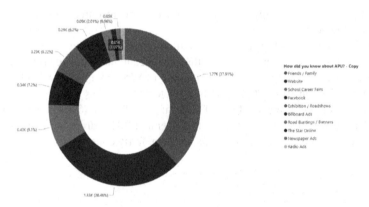

**Fig. 13.** The number of enquiries and how did they know about APU.

As website is seen to be a popular medium through which potential students have found out about APU, it is of upmost importance that the university should keep up the reach of its website to as many potential students as possible. This can be done by implementing digital marketing strategies such as Search Engine Optimization (SEO), social media advertisement and the enhancement of the UI and UX of the current website. Also, it has been noticed that APU has been excessively investing in billboard advertisement, but the data showed that enquiries who came from billboard adverts is relatively lower compared to the website.

The insights derived from the dashboard are useful for APU marketing department to understand the popularity of each course at different level of study and to invest more in the most efficient way of marketing. Analysis on popular courses helps APU to understand the number of enrolments and allocate the resources in terms of lecturers and classroom. Moreover, courses with the least number of enquiries can be investigated upon whether there is still a demand on the market for these courses or otherwise. The decision should be to either boost the marketing or to discontinue the courses.

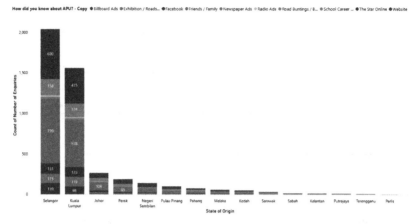

**Fig. 14.** Drill down the different ways enquiries with the state they are from.

## 3.2 Predictive Analytics

The three predictive models developed; Logistic Regression, K-Nearest Neighbor, and Artificial Neural Network are evaluated based on four evaluation metrics, which are Accuracy, Precision, Sensitivity, and Specificity.

- **Accuracy.** Accuracy is a metric employed to assess the model's performance. It is determined by calculating the proportion of correct instances out of total instances.
- **Precision.** Precision is a metric that evaluates the accuracy of positive predictions made by a model. It is calculated as the ratio of true positive predictions to the total number of positive predictions generated by the model.
- **Sensitivity.** Sensitivity is a metric used in a confusion matrix to assess how well a model can correctly identify positive instances. It is calculated as the ratio of true positive predictions to the sum of true positive and false negative predictions.
- **Specificity.** Specificity is a measure that determines how well a model can correctly identify negative instances. It is calculated as the ratio of true negative predictions to the sum of true negative predictions and false positive predictions.

Based on the evaluation metrics, the summary of results shown in Table 1 concludes that ANN has the highest accuracy amongst all the models tested. As such, based on the experiment carried out, the ANN is the best suited algorithm for this project compared to the other two models. From the commercial perspective, the management of Asia Pacific University will be able to better understand their leads and get insights on students' registration success rate. This will lead to rigorous follow-up, thus creating a higher possibility of enrolling more students by focusing on more potential applicants.

**Table 1.** Summary of results.

| Algorithms | Accuracy | Precision | Sensitivity | Specificity |
|---|---|---|---|---|
| LR | 0.80 | 0.83 | 0.69 | 0.89 |
| KNN | 0.81 | 0.80 | 0.73 | 0.87 |
| ANN | 0.91 | 1.00 | 0.81 | 1.00 |

## 4  Conclusions

Data analytics in higher education is a new topic. There has been limited progress in harnessing extremely rich data that flows through higher education systems for the purpose of acquiring actionable insights for students, lecturers, administrators, and other stakeholders. The findings and knowledge of this project will provide leverage to the APU marketing department to carry out marketing campaigns, recruitment drives and resource allocation effectively and efficiently. Consequently, capital and resource investment will be allocated based on an on-demand manner of the market and according to its analytics. The recruiter will be able to identify leads and follow up with the prospective student. The marketing department will also be able to strategize and understand potential students before venturing into untouched markets.

In order to generalize the findings in this case study to all universities in Malaysia, a more comprehensive and representative research approach would be needed, such as a multi-institutional study or a national survey of higher education institutions. This would allow for a broader understanding of the implications of data analytics in student recruitment across all universities in Malaysia and help identify common trends, challenges, and best practices for the higher education sector as a whole.

Implementing data analytics in student recruitment for private higher education institutions in Malaysia also has several policy implications. Organizations should prioritize data privacy and protection, whereby policy frameworks need to be established to ensure the ethical collection, storage, and use of student data in compliance with data protection regulations. Finally, policies should promote collaboration and knowledge sharing among all higher educational institutions, government agencies, industry stakeholders, and regulatory bodies to foster innovation and best practices in data analytics for student recruitment. This will help build a supportive data-driven ecosystem in higher education.

**Acknowledgments.** This project is supported by Asia Pacific University of Technology and Innovation.

## References

1. Teixeira, P.N., Silva, P.L., Biscaia, R., Sá, C.: Competition and diversification in higher education: Analysing impacts on access and equity in the case of Portugal. Eur. J. Educ. **57**(2), 235–254 (2022)

2. Tapsir, S. H.: Harmonising public and private institutions. The New Straits Times, https://www.nst.com.my/opinion/columnists/2019/05/488452/harmonising-public-and-private-higher-education, last accessed 2024/01/25
3. Hockley, T., Nesfield, W., Ho, H.: Impact on the Higher Education Sector. PwC, https://www.pwc.com/sg/en/publications/a-resilient-tomorrow-covid-19-response-and-transformation/higher-education.html, last accessed 2024/01/25
4. Javaid, M., Haleem, A., Singh, R. P., Suman, R.: Significant applications of big data in Industry 4.0. Journal of Industrial Integration and Management, **6**(04), 429–447 (2021)
5. Hossain, M., Dwivedi, Y.K., Rana, N.P.: Predictive Analytics for Enrolment Management: a Systematic Literature Review. Info. Systems Frontiers **22**(6), 1517–1541 (2020)
6. Kasinathan, V., Mustapha, A., Rai, K. D., Tham, H. C.: Washroom Occupancy Tracking and Hygiene Monitoring System Using IoT in Universities. In: International Conference on Knowledge Management in Organizations, pp. 375–386. Springer Nature (2023)
7. Tan, C.S., Tan, H.C., Ng, C.G.: The impact of higher education and globalization on Malaysia's talent competitiveness. Higher Education, Skills and Work-Based Learning **6**(2), 203–219 (2016)
8. Krawitz, M., Law, J., Sacha, L.: How higher-education institutions can transform themselves using advanced analytics. McKinsey & Company (2018)
9. Gandhi, R., Khurana, S., Manchanda, H.: ETL Data Pipeline to Analyze Scraped Data. In: International Conference on Information Technology, pp. 379–388. Springer (2023)

# Strategic Integration of Knowledge and Talent Management: Enhancing Academic Operations in Higher Education Through Enterprise Architecture Implementation

Amarmeet Kaur[1], Nur Liana Ab Majid[2], Nur Azaliah Abu Bakar[1](✉),
Surya Sumarni Hussien[3], and Hasimi Salehuddin[4]

[1] Faculty of Artificial Intelligence, Universiti Teknologi Malaysia, Kuala Lumpur, Malaysia
`azaliah@utm.my`
[2] National Institutes of Health, Ministry of Health Malaysia, Setia Alam, Selangor, Malaysia
[3] Computing and Mathematical Sciences Centre of Studies, Universiti Teknologi MARA, Shah Alam, Malaysia
[4] Faculty of Information Science and Technology, Universiti Kebangsaan Malaysia, Bangi, Malaysia

**Abstract.** This paper presents an approach to align a higher education institution's data, applications, and IT infrastructure with its business objectives. It employs the Zachman Framework to develop an Enterprise Architecture (EA) solution tailored for academic management within a higher education institution. The proposed 'To-Be' solution advocates for the establishment of a centralised and automated system for recruitment and retention, the integration of a dedicated collaboration platform, and the automation of administrative processes through an integrated HR management system. The paper underscores the significance of data integration and centralisation, technology infrastructure upgrades, and implementing change management strategies. The primary objective of this paper is to furnish a comprehensive roadmap for implementing the EA solution, leveraging the Zachman Framework to align academic management with the institution's strategic goals. Through the adoption of this solution, the institution aspires to augment efficiency, foster collaboration, and streamline administrative processes.

**Keywords:** Enterprise Architecture · Higher Education Institution · Knowledge Management · Talent Management

## 1 Introduction

Academician management has arisen due to the increasing importance of academic research and development, particularly in the education industry. Academician management's purpose is to assist organisations in efficiently managing academic research and development projects, with the ultimate goal of developing new information and ideas that can be used to generate creative products and services. Academics are recognised

© The Author(s), under exclusive license to Springer Nature Switzerland AG 2024
L. Uden and I.-H. Ting (Eds.): KMO 2024, CCIS 2152, pp. 198–210, 2024.
https://doi.org/10.1007/978-3-031-63269-3_15

as intellectual leaders for societal growth. Their key responsibilities include teaching, learning, and publication [1]. Higher Education Institutes (HEI) or universities, on the other hand, are knowledge-driven organisations that develop and transmit knowledge to students and society [2]. Concurrently, the technological improvement brought about by the Industrial Revolution 4.0 has entered HEIs, compelling institutions to grapple with a digital revolution in every facet [3–5]. Previous research indicates that academics are eccentric, hesitant to share knowledge, and more concerned with their accomplishments than with accomplishing university goals [5, 6]. Numerous studies provide information on the impediments to knowledge sharing in higher education [7, 8].

HEI encountered Knowledge Management (KM) hurdles such as a lack of centralised knowledge repositories, inefficient knowledge-sharing practices, limited knowledge capture and documentation, siloed KM, inadequate knowledge discovery and retrieval, limited knowledge governance, and a lack of focus on knowledge-sharing culture [7, 9–11]. This is a quandary for educational knowledge management and dissemination. Meanwhile, Talent Management (TM) in HEI challenges include a lack of strategic alignment, inconsistent talent identification and assessment, limited succession planning, insufficient talent development programmes, poor knowledge transfer and retention, limited visibility and utilisation of talent, and insufficient talent analytics [12–14]. Harnessing knowledge within universities can provide institutions with significant competitive advantages with a synergy of TM and KM in reaching the HEI vision and mission statement.

KM and TM are major disciplines with tremendous potential to drive innovation and economic progress in academic management. Effective management, on the other hand, necessitates careful consideration of factors such as communication, collaboration, resource allocation, and risk management, as well as the use of frameworks such as enterprise architecture to ensure that academic research and development projects are effectively integrated into the organisation's broader strategic goals and operations.

Digital transformation is a force that is driving change in many organisations [15]. It uses digital technologies to transform business operations, processes, and models to improve efficiency, productivity, and customer experience. Three essential forces drive digital transformation strategy: adopting a digital-first mindset, creating a digitally literate culture, and using data to ensure continuous evolution [16].

Enterprise Architecture (EA) serves as a strategic approach that integrates business and technological solutions into a unified blueprint. It encompasses the process of translating a company's vision and strategy into practical enterprise transformation by defining and refining key requirements, principles, and models that outline the organization's future state and facilitate its progression [17]. Essentially, EA provides a conceptual roadmap or blueprint for enterprises to follow in order to realize their desired future states as outlined by their strategic objectives [18]. By comprehensively tracking all business components and evaluating their configuration and performance, EA enables organizations, including Higher Education Institutions (HEIs), to assess whether these components contribute to or hinder progress towards achieving corporate strategy. HEIs and other organizations can derive various benefits from EA, including improved decision-making, increased revenues, reduced costs, and alignment of business and IT operations. Through this alignment, EA facilitates the effective achievement of strategic objectives.

KM stands as a pivotal component within EA, offering organizations the means to effectively manage their knowledge assets. KM involves the creation, sharing, and utilization of knowledge and information within an organization [19, 20]. By harnessing KM practices, organizations can enhance their decision-making processes, decrease operational costs, and boost revenue generation. Similarly, Talent Management (TM) emerges as another vital aspect of EA, enabling organizations to effectively manage their human resources. TM encompasses activities such as recruitment, development, and retention of employees possessing the requisite skills and competencies to fulfill the organization's strategic objectives [15]. Leveraging TM practices allows organizations to enhance workforce productivity, reduce employee turnover rates, and foster greater employee engagement.

While EA principles and practices are commonly applied across various industries, their implementation within HEIs presents unique challenges and considerations. Unlike typical industry companies, HEIs operate within a distinct organizational structure characterized by academic hierarchies, faculty tenure systems, and research-driven objectives. Consequently, the application of EA within academia requires tailored approaches that acknowledge and accommodate these differences. For example, the management of knowledge assets in HEIs extends beyond traditional organizational knowledge to include academic research outputs, scholarly publications, and intellectual property rights. Similarly, Talent Management strategies within HEIs must address the complexities of faculty recruitment, tenure evaluation, and professional development initiatives tailored to academic career trajectories. Therefore, while EA offers valuable frameworks for enhancing operational efficiency and strategic alignment, its implementation in academia necessitates careful adaptation to the unique institutional context and academic culture.

Organisations can create a holistic approach to managing their resources by combining knowledge management and talent management with EA. This approach can help organisations to align their business and IT strategies, improve their decision-making processes, and achieve their strategic objectives effectively. Therefore, this paper analyses the existing challenges in KM and TM in HEI, follows by proposing an EA solution focusing on developing strategies to resolve the issues highlighted. The EA will focus on optimising recruiting and retaining high-quality academic talent, enhancing collaboration and communication between faculty and staff, and streamlining administrative processes. Additionally, the solution outlines a plan for effectively integrating existing data and applications into a centralised system for academician management and developing and implementing new technology solutions as needed to support the institution's long-term goals and objectives. The architectural requirements, the approach and the methodology for the EA implementation will adopt the Zachman ADM framework as the tools.

# 2   Literature Review

Academics are acknowledged as intellectual leaders for societal growth. Their key responsibilities are teaching, learning, and publishing [1]. Furthermore, universities and HEIs are knowledge-intensive organisations that develop and spread knowledge to students and society. In parallel, HEIs have been infiltrated by the technical advancements of the Industrial Revolution 4.0, compelling establishments to contend with a digital revolution in all dimensions [3].

## 2.1   Enterprise Architecture

Enterprise Architecture (EA) has recently gained increased interest from industry and academics. EA is defined as a formal description of an organisation's current and future state(s) and managed change between these states to achieve the aims of the organisation's stakeholders and to add value to the organization [17, 19]. EA is defined as a well-defined practice for conducting enterprise analysis, design, planning, and implementation, using a comprehensive approach at all times, for the successful development and execution of strategy. It explains how EA uses architectural principles and practices to lead organisations through the business, information, process, and technological changes required to carry out their strategies [21]. These practices use numerous business components to identify, motivate, and implement these improvements. EA distinguishes between the present and prospective future states of an organisation's processes, capabilities, application systems, data, and information technology infrastructures and gives a course of action for achieving the desired future state from the existing state.

## 2.2   Issues and Challenges in Knowledge and Talent Management System

Knowledge Management (KM) focuses on developing, utilising, disseminating, and transferring knowledge within organisations, enhancing decision-making by facilitating the discovery of relevant information [9, 21]. Knowledge management has become a pivotal area of study in academia, particularly as sharing expertise and skills among organisational members improves workforce efficiency and fosters innovation. Strategies are essential to prevent knowledge loss, especially during staff turnover, requiring efficient knowledge and talent management for successful organisational outcomes [7, 10, 11].

Talent Management (TM) encompasses the complete spectrum of human resource management involving attracting and retaining top individuals [12, 14]. TM maximises the potential of existing talents to meet organisational goals, incorporating recruitment, talent development, training, and retention efforts [13, 14, 20]. Talent is defined as a person's cumulative attributes contributing to work, with previous studies highlighting the positive impact of competitive pay, conducive working environments, and training on employee motivation in Higher Education Institutions (HEIs) [13, 20].

Identified gaps in both Knowledge and Talent Management systems within Higher Education Institutions can be addressed by implementing Enterprise Architecture (EA). These gaps include the absence of centralised knowledge repositories, inefficient knowledge-sharing practices, and inconsistent talent identification. EA offers a comprehensive framework aligning people, processes, and technology to enhance KM practices, streamline information flow, and improve overall knowledge-sharing effectiveness. Additionally, EA provides a holistic view of TM processes, enabling strategic alignment, standardised talent practices, robust succession planning, comprehensive talent development, knowledge transfer mechanisms, enhanced talent visibility, and data-driven TM decisions [19].

### 2.3 Enterprise Architecture Framework for Higher Education Institutions

There are approximately 57 Enterprise Architecture (EA) frameworks, including ISO - Enterprise Architecture, TOGAF, Zachman, FEAF, IAF, and EAP. The Zachman ADM framework, created by John Zachman in the 1980s, provides a structured categorisation of an organisation's components. It employs conceptual representations such as business, logical system, and engineering models in a matrix with 6 rows and 6 columns, each representing a specific stakeholder perspective. Unlike TOGAF, the Zachman framework focuses on describing the anticipated future architecture rather than providing a technique for building it.

Previous studies, such as the ITI-GAF framework in Vietnam, have applied EA to Higher Education Institutions (HEIs), incorporating academician management as a business service support. Another research effort proposed a hybrid information structure for HEIs, emphasising big data processing and knowledge management through an educational data warehouse (EDW). As a growing field, EA aims to enhance the administration and operation of complex businesses and associated information systems, believing that it can contribute to creating future enterprises Query[20, 22]. Figure 1 illustrates the Zachman Framework for EA, showcasing its role in providing a comprehensive perspective on organisational components and their relationships.

The Zachman Framework provides a structured view of an enterprise, featuring six rows and six columns. The rows represent different perspectives, covering the entire scope, business objectives, system and technology requirements, detailed specifications, and implemented system monitoring. The columns address data, functionality, network infrastructure, stakeholder roles, timelines, and motivations for academic management processes within a Higher Education Institution (HEI). This holistic framework ensures effective management and decision-making by considering multiple viewpoints.

In academic management in an HEI context, the Zachman Framework involves key stakeholders such as academic leaders, faculty, administrative staff, HR personnel, and IT professionals. Their engagement is vital throughout the EA process, which includes Identification, Definition, Representation, Specification, and Implementation and Control phases, each catering to various aspects of academician management.

Following the structured phases of the Zachman Framework enables the EA solution to address recruitment and retention optimisation, collaboration enhancement, and streamlining administrative processes within the HEI. The comprehensive approach ensures the integration of all relevant perspectives and architectural aspects, leading to a successful implementation that enhances the efficiency and effectiveness of academician management in the institution.

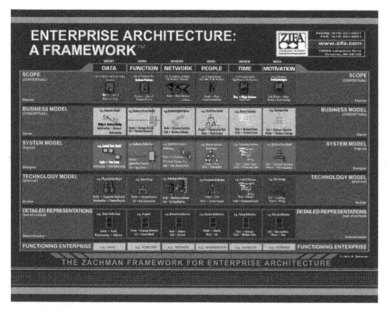

**Fig. 1.** Zachman Framework for Enterprise Architecture

# 3 Methodology Applied

Maintaining a leading edge, especially in academic management, is imperative in the dynamic landscape of higher education. Our goal is to present a tailored EA solution for Higher Education Institutions (HEIs) that optimises academic talent recruitment and retention, enhances collaboration, and streamlines administrative processes. Using qualitative methods, including a thorough document review and interviews with key personnel from academic management and information technology departments, we gain comprehensive insights into the current state of academician management and its technological infrastructure. This approach informs the design and implementation of the proposed EA solution, ensuring its robustness, efficiency, and alignment with the institution's specific needs and goals.

## 3.1 Scenario-Based Analysis of Proposed EA Solution

Situated in Malaysia, this prominent HEI specialises in engineering and technology, earning global recognition for its commitment to Sustainable Development Goals (SDGs). It holds the top spot worldwide for SDG7 - Affordable and Clean Energy and ranks 37th in Asia for SDG9 - Industry, Innovation, and Infrastructure. With three campuses offering diverse academic and student experiences, the institution is known for its mobility programs, research opportunities, and robust community and alumni relations. Despite its global standing, the HEI encounters operational challenges. Recruitment and retention issues include the need for effective talent management practices and strategies for retaining skilled employees. Collaboration hurdles, particularly in research, involve trust issues, lack of peer support, and technology reliability. Administrative processes face compliance challenges with government regulations related to finance and positions. Despite these obstacles, the institution remains committed to excellence in academic and research pursuits.

### 3.2 Steps in Developing an EA Solution

The Zachman Framework organises and represents an organisation's information assets from multiple perspectives, including data, functions, and motivation. It facilitates classifying and categorising information, making it valuable for knowledge and talent management across various disciplines in an institution. Particularly suitable for larger higher education institutions with diverse needs, its strength lies in handling complexity and capturing different stakeholder perspectives. The framework provides a structure for integrating knowledge and talent management processes, roles, and information across the organisation, guiding the development of an EA solution through step-by-step scenario analysis, as illustrated in Fig. 2.

**Fig. 2.** Scenario Analysis Steps through EA approach.

Crafting an EA solution for academician management starts with defining business requirements and future objectives in collaboration with key stakeholders. The EA team then develops a tailored conceptual architecture, covering elements like data, applications, technology, and business. After establishing the conceptual architecture, the team identifies existing systems and data for seamless integration, employing strategies like data integration and middleware solutions. The final step involves constructing a detailed implementation roadmap with specific steps, timelines, provisions for piloting, comprehensive training, and a phased transition to ensure a systematic evolution towards the envisioned academician management architecture.

## 4   Results and Discussion

Analysing academic management in higher education institutions highlights recruitment, collaboration, and administration challenges. The proposed 'To-Be' solution addresses these issues through a centralised and automated knowledge and talent management system, data integration, technology upgrades, and change management strategies. Implementing these changes will enhance efficiency and collaboration and streamline administrative processes, fostering improved academic management.

### 4.1 The As-Is Findings of Scenario

This institution faces a critical challenge in academician management, recognising the imperative need for an EA solution. The goals of the EA solution include examining existing systems, identifying gaps, redundancies, or inefficiencies, and fostering better collaboration and communication among faculty and staff. The institution also emphasises the importance of streamlining administrative processes related to academician management, aiming for efficiency in payroll, benefits, leave, and other HR-related processes. The overall sentiment reflects a reluctant acknowledgement of the need for change as the institution grapples with implementing an EA solution to address identified challenges in academic management, as shown in Fig. 3 using EA Archimate notation.

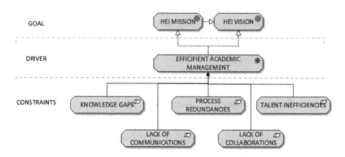

**Fig. 3.** The As-Is Findings of Scenario

These findings are categorised under four subtopics: Recruitment and Retention Processes, Collaboration and Communication, Administrative Processes, and Data Management. The following is a breakdown of the identified gaps and challenges.

**Recruitment and retention processes** at this institution lack strategic alignment with overall organisational objectives, causing a misalignment between talent needs and workforce skills. The unoptimised standardised talent identification and assessment process practice leads to subjective evaluations, biases, and inconsistent decisions. Inadequate succession planning practices leave critical positions vacant or filled with unprepared individuals when key employees depart. Additionally, the institution lacks comprehensive talent development programs, hindering career growth, limiting employee engagement, and leaving employees unprepared for future challenges.

The institution grapples with disorganised knowledge repositories, hindering access and sharing of information across departments. The absence of standardised **collaboration and communication** processes and tools leads to inconsistencies, duplication, and difficulty finding accurate information. Valuable knowledge within individuals or teams is inadequately captured and shared, resulting in critical knowledge loss during employee transitions. The presence of separate knowledge management systems or practices among departments hampers collaboration and cross-functional learning. Additionally, the institution faces challenges in the visibility and utilisation of talent, lacking the ability to identify and leverage employees' full potential due to limited insight into their capabilities, skills, and aspirations.

Insufficient knowledge in **administrative processes and data management** governance causes inconsistencies, outdated information, and challenges in ensuring quality and accuracy in shared knowledge. The lack of emphasis on fostering a knowledge-sharing culture hampers effective KM, leading to a loss of collective knowledge within the institution. Academic administrative processes, such as payroll, benefits, leave management and performance evaluations, may be disjointed and time-consuming. Additionally, the institution faces difficulties gathering and analysing talent-related data, impeding informed decision-making in workforce planning, talent acquisition, performance management, and career development.

## 4.2 The Proposed To-Be Solution for the Scenario

The proposed solution addresses the identified gaps and improves academic management processes, data management, collaboration, and administrative efficiency. The proposed to-be solutions based on the scenario are explored below:

The institution will develop a TM strategy aligned with its objectives, ensuring that **recruitment, development, and retention** efforts support its long-term goals. This strategy will involve implementing standardised talent identification and assessment processes to ensure fair and objective evaluations of employees across the institution. A robust succession planning program will also be established to identify and develop potential future leaders, ensuring a smooth transition for critical positions. The institution will also design and implement comprehensive talent development programs that enhance employees' skills, knowledge, and capabilities, fostering career growth and increasing employee engagement1. These measures will improve the institution's[1] capacity to attract and retain excellent academic personnel while aligning the workforce with the institution's long-term success strategy.

To enhance **collaboration and communication**, the institution will establish a centralised knowledge repository for easy access and sharing of relevant information. Standardised processes and tools will be implemented to ensure efficient knowledge dissemination. Knowledge capture and documentation will be incentivised, and collaborative culture will be fostered by breaking down silos and promoting cross-functional learning. Mechanisms will be introduced to enhance talent visibility and utilisation. These initiatives will create a collaborative environment that optimises knowledge sharing, improves collaboration, and maximises talent utilisation.

The institution will establish **clear ownership and governance** structures for KM to improve **administrative processes,** ensuring accountability and quality control over shared knowledge. This will promote efficient KM practices and prevent inconsistencies and outdated information. A knowledge-sharing culture will be cultivated by promoting and rewarding employee knowledge-sharing behaviours, fostering collaboration and collective learning. Additionally, implementing data-driven talent analytics capabilities will enable the effective gathering and analysis of talent-related data, providing valuable insights for workforce planning, talent acquisition, performance management, and career development. These comprehensive solutions will streamline administrative processes, enhance knowledge governance, foster a culture of knowledge sharing, and enable data-driven decision-making for effective TM.

The institution will develop a robust strategy to **integrate and centralise existing data and applications** related to academician management, prioritising data accuracy, consistency, and accessibility. Technology solutions, including KM systems and data analytics tools, will be leveraged to support the institution's long-term goals in academic management. Staff members will receive training and resources on data management best practices to ensure data integrity and effective utilisation for decision-making purposes. By implementing these solutions, the institution will enhance data management practices, streamline information access, and empower staff members with the necessary tools and knowledge to make informed decisions based on reliable data.

The **Technology Infrastructure** solution aims to upgrade and implement an optimised technology infrastructure that supports the institution's knowledge and talent management objectives. This includes hardware and software upgrades, cloud-based solutions, and scalable systems to accommodate future growth. The various systems and applications used for knowledge and talent management will be integrated into a unified and interoperable platform, ensuring seamless access, sharing, and information retrieval. These improvements will enhance the HEI's capabilities in managing knowledge and talent effectively, enabling streamlined processes and supporting its long-term objectives.

The **Change Management** solution aims to implement new knowledge and talent management practices and technologies. It includes a comprehensive plan, training, and employee support, establishing effective communication channels to promote continuous learning and improvement. This ensures a smooth adoption of new systems, addresses resistance, and enhances academician management processes, collaboration, communication, administrative efficiency, and data-informed decision-making. The solution optimises recruitment and retention, contributing to the institution's long-term success and competitiveness. Figure 4 and Fig. 5 summarises findings from the As-Is analysis and proposes a To-Be solution for addressing KM and TM issues through an EA approach.

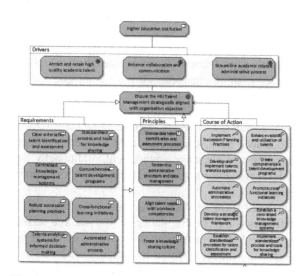

**Fig. 4.** As-Is analysis for KM and TM needs in HEI using EA

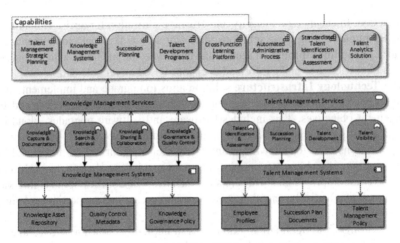

**Fig. 5.** To-Be analysis for KM and TM needs in HEI using EA

## 5   Conclusion

In conclusion, using the EA Zachman Framework for academician management provides a structured method to address current issues. The analysis revealed fragmented recruitment, ineffective collaboration, and time-consuming tasks. The proposed solution involves centralizing systems, enhancing collaboration, and automating processes. Continuous monitoring, governance, and exploring new technologies are crucial for ongoing success. Academic leaders focus on strategic goals, faculty members use collaboration tools for teaching and research, while administrative staff seek streamlined processes. The IT department handles technical infrastructure implementation and maintenance.

The Higher Education Institution (HEI) recognizes the need for a tailored EA solution to improve academician management. Their goals include optimizing recruitment and retention, enhancing collaboration, and streamlining administration. The solution should cover key areas like assessing existing systems, improving collaboration, and simplifying administrative tasks. However, implementing the EA Zachman Framework has limitations. Resistance from stakeholders used to traditional methods could slow down progress, requiring careful change management. Additionally, the effectiveness of the solution depends on available resources and the institution's commitment to ongoing monitoring and governance.

Future research could focus on addressing these limitations and refining the proposed EA solution. This could involve strategies to overcome stakeholder resistance and increase buy-in for EA implementation. Additionally, exploring the long-term sustainability and adaptability of the solution to evolving academic management needs is crucial. In summary, while the EA approach offers promising solutions, addressing its limitations and ongoing refinement through further research are essential to ensure successful implementation in higher education institutions.

**Acknowledgements.** This work is supported by Universiti Teknologi Malaysia under research grant PY/2023/00782.

# References

1. Alvesson, M., Lee Ashcraft, K., Thomas, R.: Identity matters: Reflections on the construction of identity scholarship in organization studies. Organization **15**(1), 5–28 (2008)
2. Akgün-Özbek, E., Özkul, A.E.: E-transformation in higher education and what it coerces for the faculty, in Research Anthology on Remote Teaching and Learning and the Future of Online Education. IGI Global. p. 1086–1111 (2023)
3. Alenezi, M.: Digital Learning and Digital Institution in Higher Education. Educ. Sci. **13**(1), 88 (2023)
4. Kaputa, V., Loučanová, E., Tejerina-Gaite, F.A.: Digital Transformation in Higher Education Institutions as a Driver of Social Oriented Innovations. In: Social Innovation in Higher Education, pp. 61–85. Springer (2022)
5. Coral, M.A., Bernuy, A.E.: Challenges in the Digital Transformation Processes in Higher Education Institutions and Universities. Int. J. Inf. Technol. Syst. Approach (IJITSA) **15**(1), 1–14 (2022)
6. Marks, A., Al-Ali, M.: Digital transformation in higher education: a framework for maturity assessment. In: COVID-19 Challenges to University Information Technology Governance, pp. 61–81. Springer (2022)
7. Jones-Esan, L.J., Nadda, V., Albright, K.S.: Knowledge Management and Research Innovation in Global Higher Education Institutions. IGI Global (2022)
8. Leal Filho, W., et al.: Governance and sustainable development at higher education institutions. Environ. Dev. Sustain. **23**(4), 6002–6020 (2021)
9. Hidayat, D.S., Sensuse, D.I.: Knowledge management model for smart campus in Indonesia. Data **7**(1), 7 (2022)
10. Tooranloo, H.S., Saghafi, S.: Investigating the Impact of Using Knowledge Management on Organisational Agility through Competitive Intelligence and Strategic Thinking. J. Inf. Knowl. Manag. **18**(02), 1950016 (2019)
11. Osama, F.A.-K., El-Haddadeh, R., Eldabi, T.: The role of organisational climate in managing knowledge sharing among academics in higher education. (2019)
12. Yuliana, R., Senen, S.H.: A Systematic Literature Review of Organizational Performance through Talent Management Strategies. West Sci. J. Econ. Entrepreneurship **1**(12), 490–500 (2023)
13. Ahuja, K., Ranga, P.: Impact of talent management practices on the motivation of academic employees in selected private universities in Haryana India. . Int. J. Health Sci. **6**, 664–674 (2022)
14. Al Hashimi, A.S.A., Azmin, A.A., Junoh, M.Z.M.: Talent Management in Higher Education: A Critical Review. Int. J. Educ. Psychol. Couns. (IJEPC), 2021. **6**(44), 155–166
15. Meneses-Ortegón, J.P., Gonzalez, R.A.: Knowledge management in enterprise architecture projects. in Knowledge Discovery, Knowledge Engineering and Knowledge Management: 8th International Joint Conference, IC3K 2016, Porto, Portugal, November 9–11, 2016, Revised Selected Papers 8. 2019. Springer (2016)
16. Pettey, C.: 5 Talents Needed for a Successful Enterprise Architecture Team. (2018)
17. Kotusev, S., et al.: The Structuring of Enterprise Architecture Functions in Organizations: Towards a Systematic Theory. Business & Information Systems Engineering, p. 1–24 (2023)
18. Nayeem, A., Dilnutt, R., Kurnia, S.: Enterprise Architecture Practice and Challenges in Achieving Sustainable Digital Transformation in Developing Countries (2023)
19. Möhring, M., et al.: Digitalization and enterprise architecture management: a perspective on benefits and challenges. SN Bus. Econ. **3**(2), 46 (2023)

20. Hussain, T.A.R.: Enterprise Architecture in Higher Education Institutions: a Preliminary Review (2023)
21. van de Wetering, R., Kurnia, S., Kotusev, S.: The Role of Enterprise Architecture for Digital Transformations. Multidisciplinary Digital Publishing Institute. p. 2237 (2021)

# Evaluating the Adoption of Enterprise Architecture in Universiti Teknologi MARA, Malaysia

Noor Syazwani Binti Muhammad Yani[1], Surya Sumarni Binti Hussein[1(✉)], Nur Azaliah Abu Bakar[2], and Anitawati Lokman[1]

[1] College of Computing, Informatics, and Mathematics, Universiti Teknologi MARA, Shah Alam, Malaysia
suryasumarni@uitm.edu.my
[2] Faculty of Artificial Intelligence, Universiti Teknologi Malaysia, Kuala Lumpur, Malaysia
azaliah@utm.my

**Abstract.** In today's dynamic landscape, organisations face unprecedented challenges stemming from societal, business, and technological shifts. Amidst this complexity, Enterprise Architecture (EA) emerges as a critical tool for enhancing the efficiency of information systems. However, the adoption of EA in higher education, notably at Universiti Teknologi MARA (UiTM), encounters delays. This study investigates the factors influencing EA adoption at UiTM, employing a quantitative approach with data collected from 160 responses across UiTM campuses in Malaysia. The findings reveal significant pressure factors hindering EA adoption at UiTM, offering actionable insights for effective implementation and decision-making enhancement by the management. The study identifies future research opportunities to enrich perspectives on EA adoption, including cross-institutional comparisons. Recommending a mixed research methodology to ensure robust conclusions, the study highlights that the investigated variables significantly contribute to explaining 76.1% of the variances in factors influencing EA adoption within UiTM. In conclusion, this research underscores the pivotal role of EA in higher education, particularly at UiTM, providing valuable insights into adoption influencers. The outlined recommendations lay the groundwork for further research, fostering a deeper understanding of EA adoption dynamics.

**Keywords:** Enterprise Architecture · Higher education institution · Quantitative research · Pressure factor · Adoption

## 1 Introduction

In the dynamic landscape of contemporary education, institutions are navigating a profound shift towards digitalization, technological investment, innovative pedagogy, and data-driven decision-making. This transformative wave, driven by imperatives such as enrollment enhancement, retention optimization, and revenue growth, accentuates the critical role of enterprise architecture (EA) in higher education. EA serves as a strategic

© The Author(s), under exclusive license to Springer Nature Switzerland AG 2024
L. Uden and I.-H. Ting (Eds.): KMO 2024, CCIS 2152, pp. 211–222, 2024.
https://doi.org/10.1007/978-3-031-63269-3_16

framework, guiding institutions in prioritizing digital initiatives aligned with overarching objectives while deferring those that do not align. Essentially, EA delineates an institution's current and envisioned future states [1].

Furthermore, EA provides a roadmap for transitioning between these states and offers visual representations of the institution's structure at varying levels of abstraction [2]. However, the intricate nature of the higher education ecosystem necessitates the integration of enterprise architecture. The implementation of EA in this context presents notable challenges, emphasizing the need for meticulous planning tailored to the unique needs of educational institutions [3]. Consequently, the limited adoption of EA in the education sector impedes the advancement of higher education institutions [4, 13].

The primary objective of this study is to gain a deeper understanding of enterprise architecture, particularly in the context of higher education institutions, and to pinpoint the factors conducive to the adoption of EA. In this research, we leverage the conceptual framework of institutional theory to evaluate the prerequisites necessary for the effective adoption of EA.

This study's focal point is the adoption of Enterprise Architecture (EA) in higher education institutions, with a specific focus on UiTM Malaysia. This focus is particularly pertinent to UiTM's ongoing digital transformation journey. As UiTM endeavors to enhance operational efficiency, educational quality, and stakeholder experiences through the integration of technology, comprehending the factors influencing EA adoption assumes the utmost significance. The insights garnered from this study can serve as invaluable guidance for UiTM's leadership and management, enabling them to make informed decisions concerning the strategic implementation and utilization of EA. This, in turn, will ensure a more seamless and effective digital transformation process aligned with the institution's overarching objectives.

## 2 Method

This section details the methodology employed to evaluate the impact of pressure variables on the adoption of Enterprise Architecture (EA) in higher education institutions, with a specific emphasis on UiTM Malaysia.

The study utilizes a quantitative research design following the model established by Ahmad et al. [5]. It explores normative, coercive, and mimetic pressures as independent variables influencing the adoption of EA, depicted in Fig. 1.

The study actively engaged 160 participants from various stakeholders in higher education. By employing a survey questionnaire, participants rated normative, coercive, and mimetic pressures on EA adoption using a Likert-type scale. Electronic dissemination via email and WhatsApp facilitated efficient data gathering, ensuring a diverse range of perspectives were captured and analyzed.

For rigorous examination, SPSS was utilized to analyze the collected data. This analytical tool enabled in-depth exploration of response patterns and statistical significance, uncovering underlying trends and relationships within the dataset. Through meticulous analysis, the study aimed to extract nuanced insights into the dynamics of EA adoption in the context of higher education.

Grounded in a structured approach, the research process encompasses data collection, analysis, and interpretation. Each phase is intricately linked, fostering a comprehensive understanding of EA adoption factors. By adhering to empirical evidence and employing analytical techniques, the study seeks to make substantive contributions to the discourse surrounding EA implementation in academic environments. Figure 2 shows the research process described.

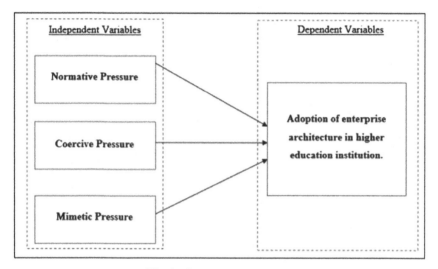

**Fig. 1.** Conceptual Framework

**Phase One: Project Initiation and Classification:**  During the initial phase, the study identified challenges associated with EA adoption in higher education institutions. Drawing from previous research, a deep understanding of both higher education institutions and EA concepts was developed. Additionally, the conceptual framework was established, pinpointing factors influencing EA adoption in alignment with the first research objective.

**Phase Two: Data Collection:**  The focus shifted to data collection, with a survey questionnaire distributed via Google Forms. The questionnaire was designed based on Institutional theory, as adapted from Ahmad et al. [6] and Adullah et al. [14], ensuring alignment with the study's objectives. Prior to distribution, a pilot test was conducted to assess its effectiveness, following Ahmad et al.'s [6] recommendation to ensure content validity.

**Phase Three: Data Analysis:**  In the final phase, data analysis took center stage, facilitated by the Statistical Package for Social Science (SPSS). Through transformation and rigorous statistical procedures, insights into various aspects of the situation were extracted. This phase served the second research objective, delving into the analysis of factors impacting EA adoption in higher education institutions.

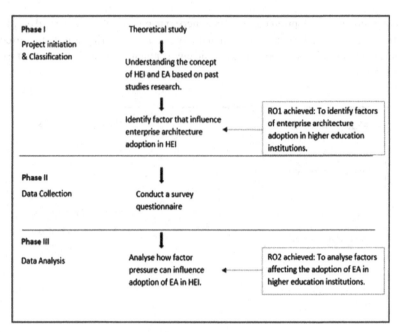

**Fig. 2.** Research Process

# 3 Results and Discussion

## 3.1 Research Process

The study encompassed personnel from all UiTM campuses across Malaysia, spanning the main campus and 34 state campuses. With a workforce of 17,488 academic and non-academic staff members and offering over 500 programs from foundation to postgraduate levels, UiTM represents a diverse educational landscape. Utilizing Google Form questionnaires, the study garnered 160 responses.

According to Raosoft Inc.'s sample size calculator, this sample size ensures an 80% confidence level with a margin of error of 5.04%. Notably, deviations from normal data distribution are inconsequential with sufficiently large sample sizes, typically exceeding 30 or 40 [7]. Parametric statistical approaches remain applicable even when data deviates from normal distribution, supported by the central limit theorem, which suggests that the sampling distribution tends toward normality with large samples regardless of the original data shape [8]. In essence, the number of respondents in this survey is deemed sufficient and reliable for the study's objectives.

## 3.2 Demographic Profile

In this study, demographic variables such as gender, employment sector, educational attainment, occupational position, and years of professional experience were analyzed using descriptive analysis and frequency distribution techniques.

The age distribution of participants revealed that the majority, comprising 33.9% and 32.1% of the sample, fell within the age range of 25 to 44 years. Individuals aged below 24 constituted a smaller fraction at 6.1%, while those aged 45 to 54 made up 24.8%. Respondents above 54 years of age represented approximately 3% of the sample. Furthermore, the study differentiated between respondents from UiTM's academic and management sectors, with 55.2% engaged in the academic sector and 44.8% in management roles.

Analysis of educational levels showed that 46.7% of respondents held a master's degree, making it the most prevalent qualification. Bachelor's degrees were held by 36.4% of respondents, while individuals with a Diploma represented 10.9%, and those with a PhD comprised approximately 6.1%. This distribution underscored the prevalence of advanced educational qualifications among participants. Job positions varied, with 3% holding positions at grade 54, 33.9% in the grade range of 44–41, and 16.4% and 18.2% in grades 52–51 and 48, respectively.

In terms of professional experience, the distribution was relatively even, with the highest percentages in the categories of "Less than 2 years" and "2–4 years," each accounting for 22.4% of the sample. The group with "5–7 years" of experience closely followed at 25.5%, while 10.3% reported having "8–10 years," and 18.8% had "More than 10 years" of experience.

### 3.3 Normality Test

Analyzing the data presented in Table 1, it is evident that all variables investigated in this study demonstrate a normal distribution. For instance, the skewness of normative pressure stands at −0.987, with a corresponding kurtosis of 1.202. These values fall within the acceptable range of −2 to 2 for skewness and kurtosis, indicating a normal distribution pattern for normative pressure. Similarly, mimetic pressure exhibits a normal distribution, with a skewness of −0.746 and a kurtosis of 0.802.

Moving on to the third independent variable, coercive pressure, it also conforms to a normal distribution, as evidenced by its skewness value of −0.649 and kurtosis value of −0.167. These findings validate the normal distribution pattern for coercive pressure. Lastly, considering the dependent variable—adoption of enterprise architecture in higher education institutions—it also follows a normal distribution. The skewness value is recorded at −1.037, while the kurtosis value is 1.626, further supporting the assertion of normal distribution for this variable.

**Table 1.** Normality Test

| Variables | Skewness Value | Kurtosis Value | Mean | Decision |
|---|---|---|---|---|
| Factor Normative Pressure | -0.987 | 1.202 | 3.8323 | Normally Distributed |
| Factor Mimetic Pressure | -0.746 | 0.802 | 3.8949 | Normally Distributed |
| Factor Coercive Pressure | -0.649 | -0.167 | 3.5172 | Normally Distributed |
| Adoption Of EA In HEI | -1.037 | 1.626 | 3.8606 | Normally Distributed |

### 3.4 Relationship Between Independent Variables and Dependent Variables

Utilizing a data analysis approach, this section investigates the association between variables using a two-tailed Pearson product-moment correlation coefficient analysis. The statistical measure employed is Pearson's product-moment correlation coefficient ('r'), which evaluates the magnitude and direction of the relationship between two variables. The coefficient's scale ranges from $-1$ to $+1$, indicating the direction of the relationship. Table 2 outlines the degree of correlation strength based on the Guilford Rule of Thumb [9].

**Table 2.** Correlation Strength based on Guilford Rule of Thumb [9]

| Correlation Coefficient | Interpretation |
|---|---|
| $r < 0.20$ | Very Weak |
| $0.20 < r < 0.40$ | Weak |
| $0.40 < r < 0.70$ | Moderate |
| $0.70 < r < 0.90$ | Strong |
| $r > 0.90$ | Very Strong |

**The First Research Objective Aims to Identify the Factors Influencing the Adoption of Enterprise Architecture in Higher Education Institutions.** This objective seeks to uncover the various elements that play a role in the decision-making process regarding the implementation of enterprise architecture within these academic settings. The hypothesis associated with this objective is structured as follows: the null hypothesis (Ho1) states that the identified factors do not exert an influence on the adoption of enterprise architecture in higher education institutions, while the alternative hypothesis (Ha1) suggests that these factors do indeed impact the adoption of enterprise architecture within such institutions. Through rigorous analysis and empirical investigation, this study seeks to validate or refute these hypotheses, shedding light on the critical factors that drive or inhibit the adoption of enterprise architecture in the higher education sector.

In summary the hypotheses are:

**Ho1: The identified factors did not influence the adoption of enterprise architecture in higher education institutions.**
**Ha1: The identified factors influence the adoption of enterprise architecture in higher education institutions.**

#### 1) Factor: Normative Pressure
Analyzing the data provided in Table 3 reveals a substantial and positive relationship between normative pressure and the adoption of Enterprise Architecture (EA) in UiTM, as indicated by an r-value of 0.829 and a p-value of 0.00. The acceptance of the alternative hypothesis (Ha1) is based on the low p-value, suggesting a significant relationship between these variables. The r-value, or correlation coefficient, quantifies the strength

and direction of this relationship, with a high r-value of 0.829 indicating a strong positive correlation between normative pressure and EA adoption. This implies that an increase in normative pressure is associated with a higher likelihood of EA adoption.

**Table 3.** Relationship between normative pressure and the adoption of EA in HEI

| Variables | r value | p value | Decision |
|---|---|---|---|
| Relationship between normative pressure and the adoption of EA in HEI | 0.829 | 0.00 | Ha2 is accepted |

Moreover, the extremely low p-value of 0.00 signifies a high level of statistical significance, indicating that the observed relationship is highly unlikely to occur by chance. Therefore, the null hypothesis is confidently rejected in favor of the alternative hypothesis (Ha1), confirming the presence of a significant relationship between normative pressure and EA adoption in UiTM.

**2) Factor 2: Coercive Pressure**
In this study, coercive pressure denotes the external influence on higher education institutions (HEIs) by regulatory bodies, government mandates, or accrediting agencies. The observed r-value of 0.532 indicates a moderate positive correlation between coercive pressure and the adoption of EA in UiTM. While not as robust as the correlation associated with normative pressure, this finding still suggests a meaningful connection between the two variables. The significance of this relationship is further underscored by the low p-value of 0.00, indicating a minimal likelihood of the observed connection occurring by chance alone. Consequently, the null hypothesis is rejected, and the alternative hypothesis (Ha1) is supported, affirming a significant relationship between coercive pressure and EA adoption in HEIs (Table 4).

**Table 4.** Relationship between coercive pressure and the adoption of EA in HEI

| Variables | r value | p value | Decision |
|---|---|---|---|
| Relationship between coercive pressure and the adoption of EA in HEI | 0.532 | 0.00 | Ha3 is accepted |

It is important to note that coercive pressure can manifest in various forms within HEIs. Governments may enact legislation mandating specific IT governance practices or data security standards, accrediting organizations may impose particular IT governance criteria, or stakeholders may exert pressure on institutions to improve their overall effectiveness and performance.

**3) Factor 3: Mimetic Pressure**
The final independent variable examined is mimetic pressure. According to Table 5, there is a notably strong positive correlation between the adoption of enterprise architecture in higher education institutions and mimetic pressure, as indicated by the Pearson

correlation coefficient (r) of 0.827. This positive trend suggests a significant increase in the adoption of Enterprise Architecture alongside mimetic pressure. The low p-value (0.00) further confirms the statistical significance of this association, indicating that it is unlikely to be a random occurrence. With substantial positive correlation between the variables, there is ample evidence to reject the null hypothesis (Ho4) and accept the alternative hypothesis (Ha4). In conclusion, the data affirm a robust positive correlation between mimetic pressure and the adoption of enterprise architecture in HEIs, supporting the stated hypothesis.

**Table 5.** Relationship between mimetic pressure and the adoption of EA in HEI

| Variables | r value | p value | Decision |
| --- | --- | --- | --- |
| Relationship between mimetic pressure and the adoption of EA in HEI | 0.827 | 0.00 | Ha4 is accepted |

To summarize the Pearson correlation analysis, all three variables exhibit positive correlation coefficients. This implies that as each type of pressure intensifies, so does the adoption of Enterprise Architecture in HEIs.

The analysis reveals varying strengths in the relationships between normative, coercive, and mimetic pressures and the adoption of EA in higher education institutions. Normative and mimetic pressures exhibit a robust positive correlation with EA adoption, while coercive pressure demonstrates a moderately positive correlation. Significantly low p-values (0.00) indicate the statistical significance of these correlations, ruling out the possibility of chance associations. The acceptance of the alternative hypothesis for all three relationships confirms the existence of a significant positive correlation in each case.

Overall, the findings underscore the influential role of normative, coercive, and mimetic pressures in driving EA adoption in higher education. Despite their collective impact, the strength of influence varies, with mimetic pressure showing the strongest correlation and coercive pressure demonstrating a moderate correlation. Thus, the accepted hypothesis (Ha1) reaffirms the identified factors' influence on EA adoption within the higher education landscape.

### 3.5  Multiple Regression Analysis

As a statistical method, Multiple Regression Analysis enables the examination of the interplay between multiple independent variables and a dependent variable. In this research, Multiple Regression Analysis served as a crucial tool to explore the intricacies of Enterprise Architecture (EA) adoption within UiTM. The primary objective was to gain profound insights into the factors shaping this adoption process, with a specific focus on normative pressure, coercive pressure, and mimetic pressure as potential catalysts or barriers to EA adoption. The results of the Multiple Regression Analysis are delineated below:

**Research Objective 2 Aims to Analyse the Factors Affecting the Adoption of Enterprise Architecture (EA) in Higher Education Institutions.** The hypotheses formulated for this objective are as follows:

**Ho2: Normative pressure negatively influences the intention to adopt EA in higher education institutions.**
**Ha2: Normative pressure positively influences the intention to adopt EA in higher education institutions.**
**Ho3: Coercive pressure negatively influences the intention to adopt EA in higher education institutions.**
**Ha3: Coercive pressure positively influences the intention to adopt EA in higher education institutions.**
**Ho4: Mimetic pressure negatively influences the intention to adopt EA in higher education institutions.**
**Ha4: Mimetic pressure positively influences the intention to adopt EA in higher education institutions.**

**Table 6.** Result of Multiple Regression Analysis

| Variables | Unstandardized Beta | Standardized Beta | t-value | p-value |
|---|---|---|---|---|
| Factor Normative Pressure | 0.349 | 0.419 | 5.808 | 0.000 |
| Factor Coercive Pressure | 0.111 | 0.147 | 3.324 | 0.001 |
| Factor Mimetic Pressure | 0.355 | 0.406 | 5.649 | 0.000 |

| | |
|---|---|
| $R^2$ | 0.761 |
| F-Value | 171.149 |
| P-Value | 0.00 |
| Durbin-Watson | 1.95 |

Table 6 provides an in-depth examination of the relationship between three primary independent variables—normative pressure, coercive pressure, and mimetic pressure—and their influence on the intention to adopt EA within UiTM. The analysis offers valuable insights into the factors shaping this adoption decision. Specifically, the results highlight the significant impact of normative pressure on the intention to adopt EA in higher education institutions. This is evidenced by a remarkably low p-value of 0.00, well below the conventional significance level of 0.05. Furthermore, the standardized beta coefficients underscore these influences, with normative pressure exhibiting the highest coefficient at 0.419, indicating its substantial effect. Mimetic pressure follows closely with a coefficient of 0.406, further underscoring its relevance in the adoption decision. In contrast, coercive pressure demonstrates a weaker impact, with a coefficient of 0.147.

In summary, normative pressure emerges as a critical driver in fostering the adoption of enterprise architecture within higher education institutions, with a particular emphasis on UiTM. This underscores the pivotal role of normative pressure in instigating transformative changes in the higher education sector. Moreover, the results from the analysis demonstrate that all the independent variables considered significantly contribute to elucidating 76.1% of the variances in the factors influencing the adoption of enterprise architecture within UiTM. This statistical model holds substantial significance, as indicated by the F-value of 171.149 with a p-value of 0.00, well below the conventional significance threshold of 0.05.

### 3.6 Knowledge Sharing and EA Adoption

Knowledge-sharing mechanisms within higher education institutions play a crucial role in amplifying normative pressure for enterprise architecture adoption. These mechanisms foster collaboration and shared understanding among stakeholders by promoting the exchange of knowledge and best practices [10]. Consequently, this shared understanding cultivates a common set of norms and expectations regarding EA adoption, creating a sense of social obligation and peer pressure to conform [11]. Moreover, knowledge sharing disseminates information about the benefits and success stories of EA adoption, further reinforcing the normative pressure to adopt. Additionally, by facilitating the sharing of lessons learned and challenges faced during adoption, these mechanisms offer guidance and support to institutions, mitigating perceived risks and uncertainties and increasing the likelihood of successful implementation [12].

## 4  Conclusion

In this study, the focus was on investigating the adoption of Enterprise Architecture (EA) within Higher Education Institutions, with a specific emphasis on UiTM across Malaysia. The primary objectives were to gain a comprehensive understanding of EA in the higher education context, identify the factors influencing its adoption, and analyze the interrelationships among these factors. Data was collected from participants across all UiTM campuses in Malaysia, resulting in a dataset comprising 160 responses gathered through a Google form questionnaire. Analytical techniques such as Descriptive Analysis, Multiple Regression Analysis, and Pearson Product-Moment Correlation Coefficient were employed, revealing positive associations between independent variables and EA adoption in higher education institutions.

Despite the robustness of the findings, several limitations were encountered during the study. One notable limitation was the potential for response bias in the survey data, as responses were based on self-reporting and subjective perceptions. Additionally, the study was limited to participants within the UiTM system, which may limit the generalizability of the findings to other higher education institutions. Future research could address these limitations by employing more diverse sampling techniques and including a broader range of institutions to enhance the external validity of the findings.

Looking ahead, there are several avenues for future research in this area. One potential direction is to conduct longitudinal studies to track the long-term effects of EA adoption in higher education institutions. Additionally, qualitative research methods such as interviews and focus groups could provide deeper insights into the factors influencing EA adoption and the challenges encountered during implementation. Furthermore, comparative studies across different countries or regions could offer valuable insights into the cultural and contextual factors that shape EA adoption in higher education. Overall, future research endeavors have the potential to further enrich our understanding of EA adoption and its implications for organizational effectiveness in higher education settings.

**Acknowledgement.** The author gratefully acknowledges the financial grant 600-RMC 5/3/GPM (040/2022) provided by the University Technologi MARA and the College of Computing, Informatics and Mathematics, Universiti Teknologi MARA, Malaysia, for all support and resources.

# References

1. Robl, M., Bork, D.: Enterprise architecture management education in academia: an international comparative analysis. Complex Syst. Inform. Model. Q. **31**, 29–50 (2022)
2. Farshadi, R., Nazemi, E., Abdolvand, N.: A framework for ranking critical success factors of business intelligence based on enterprise architecture and maturity model. Interdiscip. J. Inf. Knowl. Manag. **17** (2022)
3. Ahmad, N.A., Drus, S.M., Bakar, N.A.A.: Adoption of enterprise architecture from technology-organisation-environment and pressure perspectives: a conceptual model. J. Adv. Res. Dyn. Control Syst. **10**(11), 126–134 (2018)
4. Bourmpoulias, S., Tarabanis, K.: A systematic mapping study on enterprise architecture for the education domain: approaches and challenges. In: 2020 IEEE 22nd Conference on Business Informatics (CBI). IEEE (2020)
5. Ahmad, N.A., Bakar, N.: Moderating effect of organisation size in measuring the technology organisation environment and pressure (TOEP) in enterprise architecture adoption (2019)
6. Ahmad, N.A., et al.: Assessing content validity of enterprise architecture adoption questionnaire (EAAQ) among content experts. In: 2019 IEEE 9th Symposium on Computer Applications & Industrial Electronics (ISCAIE). IEEE (2019)
7. Li, M., et al.: Checking normality of model errors under additive distortion measurement errors. J. Nonparametr. Stat. 1–30 (2024)
8. Mustafy, T., Rahman, M.T.U.: SPSS. In: Mustafy, T., Rahman, M.T.U. (eds.) Statistics and Data Analysis for Engineers and Scientists. TCSN, pp. 135–180. Springer, Singapore (2024). https://doi.org/10.1007/978-981-99-4661-7_4
9. Ranatunga, R.V.S.P.K., Priyanath, H., Megama, R.: Methods and rules-of-thumb in the determination of minimum sample size when applying structural equation modelling: a review. J. Soc. Sci. Res. **15**(2), 102–109 (2020)
10. Dang, D., Pekkola, S.: Institutional perspectives on the process of enterprise architecture adoption. Inf. Syst. Front. **22**(6), 1433–1445 (2020)

11. Daud, R., Hussein, S.S., Rahim, N.Z.A., Ibrahim, R., Ya'acob, S., Bakar, N. A. A.: Knowledge communication in government ICT projects: a cross-case analysis study. In: Uden, L., Ting, I.H., Feldmann, B. (eds.) KMO 2022. CCIS, vol. 1593, pp. 79–90. Springer, Cham. (2022). https://doi.org/10.1007/978-3-031-07920-7_7

12. Hussein, S.S., Alfiansyah, M.W., Daud, R., Ya'acob, S., Lokman, A.M.: Developing an effective ICT strategic framework for higher education institutions: a case of Mataram University. In: Uden, L., Ting, I.H. (eds.) KMO 2023. CCIS, vol. 1825, pp. 210–221. Springer, Cham (2023). https://doi.org/10.1007/978-3-031-34045-1_18

13. Isa, W.W.M., Suhaimi, A.I.H., Noordin, N., Harun, A.F., Ismail, J., Teh, R.A.: Factors influencing cloud computing adoption in higher education institutions. Indones. J. Electr. Eng. Comput. Sci 17(1), 412–419 (2019)

14. Abdullah, N., Ab Malik, A.M., Shaadan, N., Lokman, A.M.: Developing an effective online based training questionnaire for higher education training provider: a pilot analysis. Asian J. Univ. Educ. 18(4), 1010–1023 (2022)

# KM Process and Model

# Building a Halal Food Traceability Model for Kuwaiti Halal Ecosystem from Stakeholders' Perspectives

Laila A. H. F. Dashti[1](✉), Tom Jackson[1], Andrew West[2], and Lisa Jackson[3]

[1] Department of Business and Economics, Loughborough University, Loughborough, UK
L.dashti@lboro.ac.uk
[2] Wolfson School of Engineering, Loughborough University, Loughborough, UK
[3] Aeronautical and Automotive Engineering Department, Loughborough University, Loughborough, UK

**Abstract.** Traceability systems are crucial in halal and agri-food industries due to their tracking and tracing capabilities for halal food integrity. It is difficult to create a traceability system for the halal food supply chain because of differing requirements and complex stakeholders' needs. Gaining a thorough grasp of stakeholders' viewpoints on the creation of a process-based model that can be adopted and implemented for halal food traceability in Kuwait's halal food industry was the main goal of this study. A qualitative research design was adopted to address the aim, involving interviews with 4 halal processor and 5 government officials in the halal food sector. The data were analysed using thematic analysis. The qualitative study found that farm-related processes, supplier-related processes and processors-based processes are critical components to be included in the model of the traceability system along with the application of innovative technologies (e.g., blockchain, internet-of-things). It was also noted that streaming the certification system and collaboration among stakeholders for designing an adoptable and implementable system is needed. Based on these perspectives of the halal food processors and government agencies in Kuwait, a process-based model of halal meat traceability was constructed, using Anylogic software, involving the farmers, suppliers and food processors-based processes which need to be integrated into a potential halal food traceability system. These results add to a larger body of research that aims to create a framework for traceable stakeholder requirements by using "business process modelling" to create a unified model.

**Keywords:** Supply chain · traceability system · halal food · stakeholders' requirements

## 1 Introduction

The emphasis on adherence to Islamic dietary laws by Muslim consumers propels the demand for halal-certified products. The importance placed on religious observance, particularly in Muslim-majority regions, solidifies the foundation for sustained market

© The Author(s), under exclusive license to Springer Nature Switzerland AG 2024
L. Uden and I.-H. Ting (Eds.): KMO 2024, CCIS 2152, pp. 225–236, 2024.
https://doi.org/10.1007/978-3-031-63269-3_17

growth [1–3]. In 2022, the halal food industry captured a share of US$2,221.3 billion in the global food market industry [4]. Not only is halal food consumed by Muslims, but its popularity is also rising in non-Muslim countries due to its high quality and safety standards during manufacturing [5].

Due to the lack of proper checks and procedures and the traceability systems for the halal food supply chain, there is prevalence of unethical practices, such as the fabrication of halal food ingredients during sourcing, mixing, and manufacturing processes. There have even been reports of manufacturers displaying fake halal food certificates on products in Muslim countries [6, 7]. Implementing a food traceability system provides hope for consumers and governments to regulate the halal food industry, ensuring the integrity of halal food by increasing transparency regarding processing, manufacturing, and distribution [5].

Many players are involved in the halal food supply chain (HFSC) including government, brokers, suppliers, farmers, processors and distributors [7]. Without understanding the key processes of the HFSC along with the needs and requirements of stakeholders in the HFSC, building an effective traceability system becomes jeopardized. Incorporating halal food processes into traceability systems can ensure their adoption within halal food networks [8, 9]. For example, communication between suppliers and manufacturers about the processes relating to farming, slaughtering, storing, packaging and processing of halal meat products can contribute valuable data on the integrity of halal food, which can be traced and tracked by governments and consumers to verify the integrity of ingredients used in processing and manufacturing of the halal meat products [8]. Gaining the understanding of processes involved in halal meat products is essential for ensuring adherence to Islamic dietary laws, which prescribe specific guidelines for permissible (halal) and impermissible (haram) food consumption [10].

The role of governments in regulating the HFSC is crucial for ensuring the authenticity, integrity, and compliance of halal products, which may range from provision of legal frameworks, standardization, certification processes, and enforcement mechanisms to stakeholders in the HFSC [10]. The global halal food market has witnessed significant growth, necessitating stringent measures to ensure the authenticity and traceability of halal products [11, 12]. Governments, as regulatory authorities, play a pivotal role in fostering the implementation and adoption of effective halal food traceability systems. This analysis elucidates the multifaceted strategies through which governments can contribute to the promotion of halal food traceability [13, 14]. Successful execution and implementation of traceability systems in both Muslim and non-Muslim countries require willingness of governments to enforce the traceability regime in the HFSC [7].

Kuwait, situated in the Arabian Peninsula, is a Muslim country with a population of approximately 4.45 million Muslims [15]. The Kuwaiti market faces significant challenges, including the presence of fake certificates and the sale of halal food products containing non-halal ingredients. These issues arise due to the absence of a fully operational and effective traceability system mandated by the government or voluntarily adopted by halal manufacturing firms. Without a clear understanding of processes of halal food which are important for different stakeholders in the halal supply chain, a robust and comprehensive traceability system is not possible [8]. Therefore, this study attempts to gain an insight into processes of halal meat supply chain along with stakeholders' needs in Kuwaiti halal food market, which are considered important and must be included while establishing or developing a traceability system. It lays the groundwork for building halal food traceability system for the Kuwaiti halal industry.

The remaining sections of this paper are divided into five main parts: a literature review, research methods, results and discussion, and conclusion.

## 2 Literature Review

The development of robust halal food traceability models poses several challenges stemming from the intricate nature of the halal supply chain, diverse certification practices, and the imperative to align with Islamic dietary laws. This scholarly examination aims to elucidate key challenges encountered in building halal food traceability models, drawing insights from literature and industry practices. The halal supply chain exhibits notable diversity in certification practices and standards across different regions and countries [1]. Achieving standardization in traceability becomes challenging due to the need to accommodate varying certification procedures and interpretations of Islamic dietary laws.

The absence of standardized protocols and interoperable systems hinders seamless communication and data exchange between diverse stakeholders in the halal supply chain [16]. Inefficiencies, errors, and delays in traceability processes may result from challenges in integrating disparate systems used by different entities [17]. The global nature of halal supply chains introduces complexities in tracking and verifying the halal status of products across international borders. Ensuring consistent halal compliance becomes challenging due to varying regulatory frameworks and certification requirements in different countries [18].

Halal traceability models must address the challenge of preventing fraud and ensuring the authenticity of halal claims [2]. Implication, detection and prevention of unauthorized substitutions or adulteration are essential to maintain consumer trust in halal products, necessitating sophisticated authentication mechanisms [14]. The absence of universally accepted halal certification standards contributes to the complexity of traceability. Therefore, achieving standardized traceability models requires concerted efforts to establish consensus on halal requirements and practices among certifying bodies. The implementation of advanced traceability technologies, such as blockchain and IoT, may incur high upfront costs [19]. Addressing financial barriers, especially for small and medium-sized enterprises (SMEs), is crucial for widespread adoption of traceability models across the halal food industry [14].

Ensuring consumer awareness and understanding of the significance of halal traceability is vital. Transparent communication about traceability practices is essential to enhance consumer trust and promote informed choices in the selection of halal products [20, 21]. Models utilizing blockchain and other data-intensive technologies may raise concerns related to data privacy and security. The decentralized nature of blockchain may present challenges in aligning with data protection regulations, and the potential for unauthorized access or manipulation of sensitive information remains a concern [19].

The implementation of robust food traceability models is imperative for ensuring the halal food integrity, which has become possible through an array of tools and technologies has emerged to facilitate the development of effective traceability systems. For instance, blockchain, due to its decentralized and immutable nature, ensures the integrity of data, making it an ideal solution for documenting and validating the entire journey of food products [19]. Radio frequency identification (RFID) technology is another technology that offers real-time tracking of activities in the halal food supply chain [22]. RFID enhances accuracy and speed in data capture, contributing to a more streamlined traceability process [23]. Internet of Things (IoT) and Geographic information system (GIS) tools serve as models for tracking and tracing halal food in the supply, however, these technologies still need to be refined and tested in the halal food industry, which prevents their widespread applications in the industry [18–24, 25].

In conclusion, the challenges inherent in building halal food traceability models underscore the need for concerted efforts in standardization, interoperability, and technological innovation. Addressing these challenges requires collaboration among industry stakeholders, certifying bodies, and governments to establish uniform practices and promote awareness. Ongoing research and development efforts are crucial for creating adaptive and scalable halal food traceability models that align with the dynamic and globalized nature of the halal industry. Moreover, the above-discussed tools for building traceability systems represent a diverse toolkit for building effective food traceability models, nevertheless, the integration of blockchain, RFID, IoT devices, GIS, and data analytics platforms were rarely shown by other studies. Though the studies described in the literature emphasized the tracking and inclusion of the food quality data with all stakeholders including farmer, suppliers, manufacturers, distributors, and governmental agencies however, no practical traceability system with interests from all stakeholders was presented in the domain of the halal food industry, especially in the context of Kuwait.

## 3   Research Methods

### 3.1   Qualitative Research Design

This research adopted the qualitative research design. The qualitative research helps the researchers to collect an in-depth information about social phenomenon under investigation with the aim of having a deeper understanding of the experiences of the people with knowledge about the research problem [26]. As this research work aims to understand the issues in the halal food industry, and to gain the in-depth insight into the requirements and needs of the consumers for the modelling the traceability system for halal market in Kuwait. Therefore, the qualitative research design is the most optimal approach for addressing the research questions posed in this study.

### 3.2   Qualitative Interviews

The purpose of the interview is to gather the maximum data from respondents, so that all objectives of the study are satisfied [27]. This study was conducted with the aim to gain preliminary data regarding the research problem under discussion, allowing the development of more refined approach and data to model the traceability system. Therefore, initially 5 interviewees (participants P1-P5) occupying the managerial positions in the supply chain management from the Kuwaiti food processor/manufacturer – Al-Khazan firm and 4 interviewees (participants PG1-4) from the government agencies (Food Authority Kuwait) having a role in verification and authentication of the halal food status of the food products were selected for this study. The interviews were conducted using Zoom and face-to-face meetings with a set of questions relating to the traceability, strengths and weaknesses of existing traceability systems and the focus on further development needs. Participation was through curiosity driven motivation to provide information without influence of the interviewees [28]. Clarification of all questions was given, where the prompted questions had the intention to gather in-depth understanding of their experiences in halal industry and importance of the traceability system. The interviews lasted for 45 min approximately, and the list of topics recommended by the researcher and the respondent were thoroughly discussed. The strength of the semi-structured interview is that it helps researchers to devise as many prompt questions or sub-topics which are deemed to be necessary for addressing the research issue [29]. This helped the investigator to collect as much data as was important for answering the research questions raised in this study.

### 3.3 Data Analysis

Thematic analysis, a commonly used technique for analysing qualitative data, including textual or interview data, was used to analyse the interview data [30]. It enables researchers to spot recurring themes and patterns of subjects and concepts in the textual data [31]. The theme analysis was carried out using the subsequent protocol [32]. To fully comprehend the contents, the textual data from the interviews was reviewed and reread. Sentences or phrases with a broad meaning were categorized as codes and recorded in the code and theme notebook. The codes produced in the second stage underwent a thorough comparison; codes that were similar were grouped together, and each group retained a distinct theme/note. The development of the broader themes enabled the researcher to describe and interpret the findings. The themes and codes developed and recorded were cross-checked by the participants in order to ensure that interpretation and themes from data were precise and correct as intended by the participants.

### 3.4 Construction of Process-Based Model for Halal Food Traceability System

The Anylogic software (version 8.3.4) was employed to construct the 2D process-based model of the halal food traceability system. The data gathered from the interviewees were fed into Anylogic to construct a process-based conceptual model of traceability system. The Anylogic was employed due to its benefits of allowing researchers to construct, simulate and evaluate model of halal food traceability system.

# 4 Results and Discussion

## 4.1 Interviews with Food Processors in Kuwait

**Halal Farming:** The halal framing is imperative in the halal food industry as voiced by all participants from the halal food manufacturing industry. There is no traceability system in place to keep track of farming practices implemented by the farmers in the halal food supply chain.

*We believe that there is a gap in the halal food supply chain in terms of tracking the farming practices implemented by the farmers. The suppliers do not have record of how the halal animals were reared at farmhouses, which actually compromises the halal meat integrity.* [P2]

These data indicated that halal meat industry values the implementation of the Islamic beliefs in the context of rearing and feeding animals in Islamic manner and looking after the animals with respect and sympathy for animals [17]. Producing halal meat in accordance with the moral and ethical principles ingrained in Islamic teachings can be made possible by adhering to proper animal welfare procedures, which subsequently guarantees the integrity of the halal meat [33].

**Data about Slaughtering Practices from Suppliers Limited:** Three out of four participants acknowledged the imperative of cooperation and collaboration among stakeholders. They observed that the existing level of cooperation is limited and insufficient in maintaining a high-quality traceability system for halal food products. For example, P5 said:

*The important processes in slaughtering of halal animals involve the use of the knife, point of slaughtering on the body of animal, method of slaughtering, and reading of invocation at the time of slaughtering. The integration of data regarding the aforementioned processes will help manufacturers of the halal food to authenticate integrity of the halal meat.*

P2 and P3 emphasized on keeping record of all events during slaughtering and post-slaughtering phases for future references and cross-checking. From the above comments from the participants P2 and P3, it is clear that sharing of data about various steps involved in slaughtering and post-slaughtering processes between the suppliers and manufacturers of the halal food in Kuwait is limited, and emphasized that construction of a traceability system which can accommodate the issues and concerns from all processes relating to slaughtering and post-slaughtering phases at suppliers' slaughterhouses [8, 9].

**Innovative Technologies in Building Traceability Systems:** The respondents highlighted the limited utilization of innovative technologies in record-keeping practices. P1 said:

*The firm used the basic record-keeping software for storing the data, which must be replaced with some good quality software which not only store but also analyses the data with enhanced security measures.*

Participant 4 (P4) agreed to the views of P1. From the above data, it is evident that innovative technologies are needed by production firms, an important stakeholder in the halal food industry in Kuwait. Importance of the innovative technologies for traceability systems are acknowledged by many studies, which corroborate the findings of this study. Some other practitioners and academics in the field of traceability in halal food sector recommended the application of internet of things for enabling faster and better communication among the stakeholders in the halal food traceability [18–34].

**Data about Halal Meat Processing:** Most of respondents (P2, P3 and P4) argued that potential traceability system must focus on inclusion of data about the halal meat processing and methods for avoiding the contamination. One of the participants said like that:

*We believe that data should be recorded and stored from the point meat enters the processing site till the packaging is done.* [P1]

P3 and P4 supported the views of P1. From these data, it can be concluded that key processes to be focussed on while constructing traceability model are storage frying process, and methods for avoiding the contamination. Rejeb et al. in [18] also reported similar findings from the Malaysian halal food industry, showing the inclusion of data in traceability system about the meat processing and packaging served to strengthen the authenticity of the halal food products. Many other studies have stress on the importance of meat processing and packaging data to be critical for retaining consumers and certification from the government agencies [4–14].

### 4.2   Interviews with Government Agencies in Kuwait

**Kuwaiti Government in Favour of Establishing Traceability Framework:** All participants from the government agencies in Kuwait voiced their favour in building traceability framework which can be used by government agencies and other stakeholders to verify the halal integrity of the meat being imported in Kuwait from other countries.

*The Kuwaiti government in the process of consultations with major stakeholders in the halal food industry to develop and implement the traceability framework which can be monitored by all stakeholders and input from all stakeholders will be appreciated to improve the quality of the traceability system.* [PG2]

The views of PG2 were supported by PG3, and PG4. These data indicate that Kuwait government is determined in developing and enforcing comprehensive regulatory frameworks that delineate the requirements for halal food traceability. Clear regulations are more likely provide a legal foundation for traceability systems to the major players in the halal meat industry in Kuwait, defining the roles, responsibilities, and standards to be adhered to by stakeholders [1]. Additionally, the imposition of penalties for noncompliance serves as a deterrent against fraudulent practices, reinforcing the gravity of adherence to traceability standards.

**Standardization and Certification:** Standardization efforts contribute to consistency and interoperability, ensuring that traceability systems operate uniformly across the halal supply chain. Participant 2 described the significance of acquiring government-supported accreditation for building the traceability system in this way:

*Government-backed accreditation of halal certification bodies crucially important for enhancing the credibility of traceability processes, instilling confidence in consumers and facilitating international trade. Farmers and suppliers' positive attitude towards getting the certification can put a positive impact on the image and reputation of the concerned businesses in the Kuwaiti halal food market.* [PG2]

From the afore-mentioned data, it is evident that collaboration between governments, industry stakeholders, and relevant authorities is crucial for the development of national halal traceability standards [16]. Adherence of stakeholders to standardization and certification procedures contribute to consistency and interoperability, ensuring that traceability systems operate uniformly across the halal supply chain. The emphasis of the participants on the Government-backed accreditation of halal certification bodies is indicative of the fact certifications for different processes in the halal meat supply chain can contribute to increasing the integrity of halal meat in the Kuwaiti halal food industry [35].

**Support for Research and Development:** Most of participants echoed the support for conducting the appropriate research and development activities at both industry and government level in order to construct a viable, adoptable and implementable traceability system. For instance, PG3 said:

*Building a traceability system is not an easy process. The complexity of the traceability system arises from a variety of technologies available, utilities of the technologies in different processes and the integration of stakeholders' need into the traceability system. Given the needs of industry, stakeholders and fitting the technologies based on needs requires investment in research and development for building a traceability system.* [PG3]

Participant 4 and 5 recorded similar views as of PG3. In line with data, several other researchers in the field of halal supply chain and traceability system highlighted in agreement of data reported by this study that governments can stimulate advancements in halal traceability technologies by investing in research and development initiatives [12]. This involves supporting innovative solutions such as blockchain, RFID, and IoT, which enhance the transparency, efficiency, and security of traceability systems [19].

**Provision of Training and Incentives for Capacity Building:** Half of participants from the government emphasized on the skilling and upskilling of the workforce at the meat processing sites in Kuwait for understanding and using the traceability structures in place within organizations. Participant 3 said:

*The government is committed to provide all necessary training for employees in the governmental agencies and manufacturers of the halal meat food in relation to preserve the halal food integrity, record data about all steps in the supply chain and feed into the traceability system. Trained employees and professional can ensure improvements in halal food supply chain.* [PG3]

Participants 1 and 4 agreed with the views of participant 3. These data indicate that commitment of government in training and skilling employees and professional paves the way for building an adoptable and implementable traceability system. The manufacturers and processors of the halal food in Kuwait may join hands with the government to seek funding and support for training their employees in handling the halal food while processing and packaging at the factories as suggested by [1] and [16].

# 5   Process-Based Model of the Halal Food Traceability System

Based on data gathered from the manufacturers of the halal food and the government agencies in Kuwait regulating the halal food market, as described in the results section, the process-based model for tracking the halal meat food was developed, the details of the farming, slaughtering and processing and packaging processes to be tracked and traced for efficient traceability system are described in the subsequent subsections.

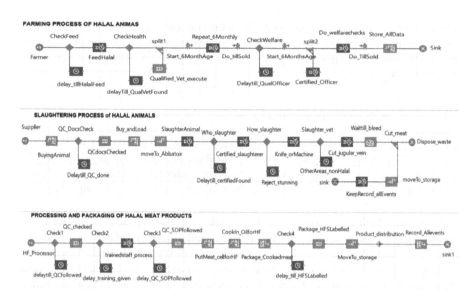

**Fig. 1.** The process-based model for tracking the halal meat food showing the farming, slaughtering and processing and packaging processes to be tracked and traced for efficient traceability system.

## 5.1   Farms-Related Processes

The farm-related processes are divided into two phases, feed store supplying feeds and the farms where the animals are reared. The feed store may offer different feed options to the farmers. The farmers check whether the feed options are halal or haram. If the feed options are haram, then the feed options are rejected, otherwise accepted. In the event of halal food options, they are recommended and offered to farmers interested in rearing animals in the halal way (see Fig. 1). The halal animals are reared using halal feed. A vet checks the health of all animals regularly, and keeps a record which is accessible to the farmers, the suppliers (purchasers) of the halal animals, halal regulatory authorities, and manufacturers of the halal meat products. This sets the tone of the monitoring mechanism right from the level of feeding and farming the halal animals which gives assurance to customers about the 'halal' status of the meat to be purchased at retailing points within the local community.

## 5.2 Supplier-Related Processes

The supplier of the halal meat/food must ensure they get animals with halal status by checking the vet records and feed records maintained at the farms of halal animals. If the vet and feed records are not available, then suppliers would reject to purchase the animals due to uncertainties about feed provided and history of diseases related to a particular animal (see Fig. 1). If the records held at the animal farm confirm the halal status of the animals, the decision to transact with the farmer is made by suppliers; the animals are transferred to slaughtering houses, where the animals are slaughtered using sharp knife or machine by a certified and trained Muslim staff by pronouncing invocation. The post-slaughter treatments are described with respect to the waste management and meat storage. The waste is disposed of appropriately and meat are cut into pieces and stored at 4 °C (see Fig. 1).

## 5.3 Halal Food Processors-Related Processes

The food processors should check the halal certification, and gain access to data about animal feed, farming, feeding and breeding data at the suppliers' warehouse. Food processors may decide to buy the meat based on examination. Meat items are transported from suppliers' warehouse to the company's warehouse where meat quality should be checked on reception, meat is handled according to halal standards, cooking is done based on halal conditions and hygienic principles. The ready-to-use products are packaged and labelled along with halal certificates and related information such as ingredients of food and stored at 4 °C. Finally, meat products are distributed to the distributors and retailers (see Fig. 1). The above-described conceptual process-based model of traceability of halal meat in Kuwait will undergo verification and validation through simulation experiments to show its effectiveness in tracking key processes in the halal meat supply chain.

# 6   Conclusion and Future Work

In conclusion, the promotion of halal food traceability systems necessitates a holistic and collaborative approach by governments. By establishing clear regulatory frameworks, supporting standardization, investing in research, and fostering international collaboration, governments contribute significantly to the credibility of halal products, consumer trust, and the sustainable growth of the global halal industry.

The main theoretical contribution to the literature gained through data analysis included the incorporation of the stakeholders' interests, especially the transparency in halal food processes in potential traceability systems as demanded by all stakeholders can increase the adoption and promotion of the halal food traceability systems within the halal food industry. This study further increased our understanding about the commitment of both government and manufacturers in integrating the key processes within the proposed model of traceability system for ensuring the increased trust of consumers in the halal food products. The process model is the first step, enabling future novel contributions in simulation of these processes, in determining critical traceability points and in determining required transparency levels in the processes at framing, slaughtering, processing and packaging levels within the halal food supply chain.

This study employed a qualitative approach, the outcomes of which cannot be generalized to other contexts of the halal food. The model provided by this study may undergo further improvements in the testing phase with the concerned stakeholders in future research work. The future studies will consider the simulation experiments on the proposed model to test the capability and efficacy of the model in fulfilling the requirements of the stakeholders involved in this study.

# References

1. Hew, J.J., Wong, L.W., Tan, G.W., Ooi, K.B., Lin, B.: The blockchain-based Halal traceability systems: a hype or reality? Supply Chain Manag.: Int. J. **6**, 863–879 (2020)
2. Abdul-Muhmin, A.G., Nordin, M.S., Abdulkareem, S.: Integrating blockchain technology for halal food traceability: a review. J. Islam. Mark. **4**, 1106–1127 (2019)
3. Al-Turjman, F.M., Qureshi, K.N., Khan, S.: Blockchain-enabled halal food traceability system. Comput. Mater. Continua **2**, 1907–1923 (2020)
4. Impactful Insights: Halal food market: Global industry, trends, share, size, growth, opportunity and forecast 2023–2028 (2023). https://www.imarcgroup.com/halal-food-market#:~: text=The%20global%20halal%20food%20market%20was%20valued%20at%20US%24% 202%2C221.3,10.8%25%20during%202023%2D2028. Accessed 07 Apr 2023
5. Iranmanesh, M., Mirzaei, M., Parvin Hosseini, S.M., Zailani, S.: Muslims' willingness to pay for certified halal food: an extension of the theory of planned behavior. J. Islam. Mark. **1**, 14–30 (2020)
6. Randeree, K.: Challenges in halal food ecosystems: the case of the United Arab Emirates. Br. Food J. (2019)
7. Poniman, D., Purchase, S., Sneddon, J.: Traceability systems in the Western Australia halal food supply chain. Asia Pac. J. Mark. Logist. **2**, 324–348 (2015)
8. Samsi, S.Z.M., Ibrahim, O., Tasnim, R.: Review on knowledge management as a tool for effective traceability system in halal food industry supply chain. J. Res. Innov. Inf. Syst. **1**, 78–85 (2012)
9. Kadir, M.H.A., Ras, R.Z.R.M., Omar, S.S., Manap, Z.I.A.: Halal supply chain management streamlined practices: issues and challenges. IOP Conf. Ser.: Mater. Sci. Eng. **160**, 012070 (2016)
10. Ahmad Tarmizi, H., Kamarulzaman, N.H., Abd Rahman, A., Atan, R.: Adoption of internet of things among Malaysian halal agro-food SMEs and its challenges. Food Res. **4**, 256–265 (2020)
11. Fuseini, A.: Halal food certification in the UK and its impact on food businesses: a review in the context of the European Union. CABI Rev. 1–7 (2017)
12. Haleem, A., Khan, M.I.: Towards successful adoption of Halal logistics and its implications for the stakeholders. Br. Food J. **1**, 60–78 (2017)
13. Charlebois, S., Sterling, B., Haratifar, S., Naing, S.K.: Comparison of global food traceability regulations and requirements. Compr. Rev. Food Sci. Food Saf. **13**(5), 1104–1123 (2014)
14. Verbeke, W., Rutsaert, P., Bonne, K., Vermeir, I.: Credence quality coordination and consumers' willingness-to-pay for certified halal labelled meat. Meat Sci. **4**, 790–797 (2013)
15. WorldMeters. Kuwait Population (Live) (2023). https://www.worldometers.info/world-population/kuwait-population/. Accessed 07 Apr 2023
16. Hassan, M.M., Shafiq, M., Al-Turjman, F.M., Alelaiwi, A.A.: A comprehensive survey on blockchain-based halal food traceability. Sensors **22**(2), 418 (2022)

17. Supian, K., Ab Rashid, N.: The role of supplier, top management and government in halal practices integrity of Malaysian food business. Int. J. Asian Soc. Sci. **8**, 549–559 (2018)
18. Rejeb, A., Rejeb, K., Zailani, S., Treiblmaier, H., Hand, K.J.: Integrating the Internet of Things in the halal food supply chain: a systematic literature review and research agenda. Internet Things **13**, 100361 (2021)
19. Makhlouf, M., Talaei-Khoei, A., Ghapanchi, A.H.: Blockchain technology in the food industry: a review. Int. J. Prod. Econ. **221**, 107476 (2020)
20. Talib, M.S., Ai Chin, T., Fischer, J.: Linking Halal food certification and business performance. Br. Food J. **7**, 1606–1618 (2017)
21. Vanany, I., Rakhmawati, N.A., Sukoso, S., Soon, J.M.: Indonesian halal food integrity: blockchain platform. In: International Conference on Computer Engineering, Network, and Intelligent Multimedia (CENIM), pp. 297–302. IEEE (2020)
22. Vlachos, I.P., Tsatsoulis, C., Petrounias, I.: A review of RFID applications in food traceability. J. Food Eng. **144**, 103–114 (2019)
23. Ahamed, N.N., Vignesh, R., Alam, T.: Tracking and tracing the halal food supply chain management using blockchain, RFID, and QR code. Multimed. Tools Appl. 1–26 (2023)
24. Wang, J., Li, P., Gao, H.: An IoT-based traceability system for food safety in the cold chain. Food Control **82**, 69–79 (2017)
25. Chang, J.: A GIS-based traceability system for the food supply chain. J. Food Eng. **271**, 109760 (2020)
26. Hennink, M., Hutter, I., Bailey, A.: Qualitative Research Methods. Sage (2020)
27. Wilson, V.: Research methods: interviews. Evid Based Libr Inf Pract **2**, 96–98 (2012)
28. Rosenthal, M.: Qualitative research methods: why, when, and how to conduct interviews and focus groups in pharmacy research. Curr. Pharm. Teach. Learn. **4**, 509–516 (2016)
29. Knox, S., Burkard, A.W.: Qualitative research interviews. Psychother. Res. **4–5**, 566–575 (2009)
30. Braun, V., Clarke, V.: Thematic Analysis. American Psychological Association (2012)
31. Clarke, V., Braun, V., Hayfield, N.: Thematic analysis. In: Qualitative Psychology: A Practical Guide to Research Methods, vol. 3, pp. 222–248 (2014)
32. Peterson, B.L.: Thematic analysis/interpretive thematic analysis. In: The International Encyclopedia of Communication Research Methods, pp. 1–9 (2017)
33. Zainuddin, N., Saifudin, A.M., Deraman, N., Osman, A.A.: The effect of halal traceability system on halal supply chain performance. Int. J. Supply Chain Manag. **9**, 490–498 (2020)
34. Najmi, A., Ahmed, W., Jahangir, S.: Firm's readiness for halal food standard adoption: assessing the importance of traceability system. J. Islam. Account. Bus. Res. **5**, 5–19 (2023)
35. Abdallah, Rahem, M.A., Pasqualone, A.: The multiplicity of halal standards: a case study of application to slaughterhouses. J. Ethnic Foods **1**, 61–81 (2021)

# Automatic Generation of a Business Process Model Diagram Based on Natural Language Processing

Madline Mößlang, Reinhard Bernsteiner$^{(\boxtimes)}$ ⓘ, Christian Ploder ⓘ,
and Stephan Schlögl ⓘ

MCI The Entrepreneurial School, Universitaetsstrasse 15, 6020 Innsbruck, Austria
`reinhard.bernsteiner@mci.edu`

**Abstract.** Business Process Management is essential for businesses to adapt to changing requirements and stay relevant in the market. It manages chains of activities, the people involved, systems, artifacts, and information to support business processes. A Business Process Model is a visual representation of a business process. Business Process Model and Notation Version 2.0 (BPMN 2.0) is one of the most commonly used specifications. Thus, it is used in this paper.

The manual gathering of information about business processes and the following modeling phase, usually conducted by experts, is very time-consuming.

This work presents a software-based tool to support generating business process models based on a narrative in natural language. Natural Language Processing (NLP) methods are applied to create the corresponding process model in BPMN 2.0. NLP deals with the automated processing of human language, allowing machines to analyze and understand the meaning of natural language.

This paper presents the first results of the evaluation of this prototype. Two different business processes have been automatically generated based on the description of persons who execute these processes. These results show that this approach accelerates the process modeling phase differently.

**Keywords:** Natural Language Processing · Business Process Modelling · BPMN 2.0 · Software Prototype · Python

## 1 Introduction

Companies are under constant competitive pressure and must be able to adapt their business processes to new requirements quickly and advantageously [1]. Modeling business processes is helpful to show the essential aspects of a domain, departments, and the link between them and to obtain the current situation of all functional activities of a relevant process [2].

Gathering correct and complete process information can be cumbersome and time-consuming. This is because the knowledge about a process can be scattered over multiple domain experts, who usually do not have enough knowledge about Business Process

© The Author(s), under exclusive license to Springer Nature Switzerland AG 2024
L. Uden and I.-H. Ting (Eds.): KMO 2024, CCIS 2152, pp. 237–247, 2024.
https://doi.org/10.1007/978-3-031-63269-3_18

Modelling (BPM). These domain experts are typically process participants or external participants like suppliers, partners, or customers [3].

As the domain experts often lack the training in modeling business processes, a process analyst takes on this job. This analysis, however, often results in a high effort for all relevant persons. This includes mining existing documentation, running interviews with the domain experts, documenting the interviews, extracting the relevant information about the process, creating a business process model, and validating the developed model. The project's central aim is to verify the feasibility of an automatically generated business process model based on an auditive description. NLP methods are used to generate the BPMN 2.0 model.

Relevant information should be extracted from an unstructured text converted from a voice recording. This information is to be extracted in a way that it can be mapped and converted to a business process model using BPMN 2.0. This tool should enable faster and more automated modeling of processes to reduce the time spent manually designing and drawing a business process by a dedicated business process analyst. Consequently, the tool should also be usable by people who do not have enough experience in designing and drawing business process models.

The following section two outlines the theoretical basis of the concepts and approaches needed to develop the prototype. Section three presents the defined requirements along with the technology stack. Section four describes the method and the use cases used to evaluate the prototype together with the evaluation results. The paper ends with a conclusion, limitations, and an outlook for further research.

## 2 Theoretical Background

This chapter gives an overview of this paper's most relevant topics and concepts.

### 2.1 Business Process Management and Modelling

Business Process Management can be seen as an essential asset of an organization. It supports software, techniques, and methods to develop, implement, control, and analyze operational processes involving people, applications, documents, and other sources of information to support business processes [4].

Business processes require a defined input and can produce information as an output [5]. The input data can be categorized into business information and process information. Business information refers to information with a lower degree of process abstraction, such as the product description, quantities, or prices. Process information describes artifacts as the name of the activity or the sequence of activities [5].

This categorization distinguishes the technical aspect from the business aspects of processes to get a clearer view of the business objectives of an organization's processes [6]. BPM is a method to make business processes more understandable as it is a graphical representation of the activities and sequence flows performed in a business process [7]. It is a vital tool to describe the process characteristics and distinguish process participants, departments, and the link between them to represent them with greater transparency [8]. BPM aims to link business process design and implementation phases [9].

A formal graphical notation is the most used method for expressing a process representation. This graphical notation must be syntactically correct (ensuring consistency with the represented process) and has to have the same meaning as the textual (typically natural language-based) description of the process [7].

The availability of different business process modeling notations is quite extensive, thus making it difficult for analysts to make a suitable choice [8]. For this project, the chosen modeling language is BPMN 2.0. This notation is a widely accepted language that provides a metamodel and an extension mechanism for additional attributes and elements [10].

BPMN 2.0 was introduced as an international standard in December 2010 and was updated in December 2013 by the Object Management Group (OMG). BPMN 2.0 is a graph-based [11], general-purpose language, independent from specific industries or domain-specific features and can be applied to various application areas [12]. Furthermore, it is not connected to a particular vendor or company.

According to the OMG definition, BPMN 2.0 models can be represented as a unified XML schema that allows models to be shared between different applications [13]. BPMN 2.0 has improved the definition by including formal execution semantics based on Petri networks and several file formats, making it useful for process design and enactment [9]. BPMN 2.0 consists of three basic diagram types: processes, collaborations, and choreographies [13].

Since it is a first prototype, this work is limited to the following elements: flow objects (events, activities, and gateways) and connecting objects (sequence flows). These objects are part of process diagrams and are often seen as the most popular BPMN vocabulary subsetsed in actual practice [14].

A comprehensive presentation of these objects can be found or example in Zur Muehlen and Recker [13, 14].

## 2.2 Natural Language Processing

As an aspect of artificial intelligence, NLP allows machines to learn, understand, and categorize human language [15].

NLP enables computers to interact with humans through human language. It equips computers with the capacity to comprehend and interpret text and speech. NLP is a multidisciplinary field integrating principles from computational linguistics and computer science, striving to bridge the divide between human and computer communications [16]. NLP deconstructs language into smaller, fundamental units known as tokens (such as words, periods, etc.) to grasp the connections and associations between these tokens [17].

Analyzing a natural text in the context of understanding and extracting information usually happens in three steps [18]:

- Morphological analysis: This analysis concentrates on word structure and studies how morphemes, the minor units of meaning in a text, form a word.
- Syntactic analysis: This examines the relationship between the words in a sentence or phrase and determines which classification each word falls under based on grammar and syntax, also called parsing.

- Semantic analysis: This analysis is based on the two previous steps and seeks to determine the meaning of words and sentences based on understanding their structure, relationships, and role.

### 2.3 NLP in the Context of Business Process Modeling

NLP concepts can be applied to the textual description, but further information is required to generate the model. The goal is to establish logical rules to extract data from the description that can be automatically mapped to the model's elements, such as activities or gateways. When extracting such knowledge from text, the following four phases are pursued [19]:

1. The textual description is the input that can be fed into the system. This textual description is derived from personal interviews with people executing the processes daily. This text serves as the basis for the NLP analysis.
2. Domain-independent extraction describes the NLP techniques, which do not require a domain-specific context but are based on the semantics and grammar of the language used.
3. Domain-specific extraction requires special rules to detect relevant information based on the domain used, in this case, the syntax of BPMN 2.0.
4. The extracted model represents the result of the knowledge extraction, in this case, an intermediate data structure that can be mapped to a BPMN 2.0 model.

Some research has already be done in this field. A comprehensive literature based comparision of different NLP tools can be found in [20]. [21] propose NLP-based approaches to automatically extract business process redesign suggestions from end-user feedback. They conducted experiments to evaluate the effectiveness of the used approach. [22] address converting textual requirements to BPMN diagrams in software requirements engineering. They propose a method to convert textual requirements to BPMN diagrams for measuring functional software size. The experiments resulted in a suitable BPMN diagram with higher accuracy compared to other methods.

## 3   Implementation of the Prototype

This section gives a short description of the implemented prototype.

### 3.1   Requirements and System Design

The application can be used without previous knowledge in designing and drawing Business Process Models with BPMN 2.0. A web application has been developed to facilitate the implementation and to avoid unnecessary installations. The following functional requirements are defined for the prototype:

- The language of the audio and textual input is German.
- The input of the chronological process description is provided either as an audio file (based on the process discovery interview) or based on a textual description.

- The process description should be done from the active first-person narrative perspective, which means that the person performing the process explains the process steps in chronological order.
- The prototype should automatically recognize the BPMN 2.0 elements (start and end events, activities, and exclusive gateways) and display them in a correct sequence flow.
- It should be possible to manually intervene in each application step and adjust the generated data.
- The automatic generation of the BPMN model should be faster than if it had been drawn manually.
- The generated model should be exportable as an XML file (.bpmn file extension). The file's structure must comply with the standard of BPMN 2.0 so that it can be imported into other applications.
- Due to a database connection, the application should be able to save the stored process descriptions per user.

### 3.2 Technology

The Python programming language is used to process textual or numerical data. Standard Python libraries are used since they provide many classes and functions to transfer the input data into a usable and machine-readable form [23]. Python also offers several NLP libraries provided by third parties, which is another reason to use this programming language for this prototype. The following figure shows the technology stack with the related libraries (Fig. 1):

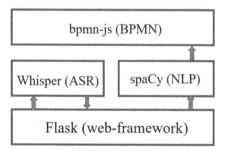

**Fig. 1.** Technology stack

For a smooth integration with the other Python-based extensions, the web framework Flask [24] was used. Flask is a well-documented, lightweight framework that leaves freedom to structure an application based on its simplicity and flexibility. It is also written in Python. This is especially advantageous when developing a prototype. To integrate the voice-to-text part of this work, the automatic speech recognition system (ASR) Whisper [25] from the company OpenAI is integrated. For this prototype, version "20230314" of Whisper and the language model "medium" was used for the German language, as the system was still in the beta phase when this prototype was developed. To display the finished BPMN 2.0 XML file as a diagram, the online modeler bpmn-js from bpmn.io by Camunda [26] was used. It allows editing the automatically generated diagram directly on the website afterward.

The open-source Python library spaCy [24] from the German company Explosion was chosen for the NLP analysis. SpaCy provides pre-trained processing pipelines that can be individually configured and trained in over 66 languages, including German, which is particularly relevant for this prototype. The largest German model used for this work has been trained on news and media articles.

### 3.3 Main Functions of the Prototype

The following functions have to be implemented to convert an oral process description into a valid BPMN 2.0 model:

1. Convert the recorded audio file to written text
2. Textual process description acquisition
3. Text-level analysis and sentence-level analysis
4. Generate the process steps and flow
5. Generate the related XML file
6. Display the generated process model in BPMN 2.0 notation

## 4   Evaluation of the Prototype

This section aims to show the prototype's evaluation results based on actual use cases.

### 4.1   Input Data

As already mentioned, the input data of the prototype is a recorded audio narrative of the process through unstructured interviews with employees from a defined specialist domain. In this case, logistics processes are used. The target group for the interviews is persons who carry out specific business processes on a daily basis, e.g. picking a customer order.

The interviews can be subdivided into two phases: an introduction and a process description. In the introduction phase, the participant is given information about the communication criteria and the overall idea of the prototype. The central part of the interview is about the detailed description of the process steps. The process flow can be derived based on the chronological order of the process steps.

### 4.2   Test Cases

Two intralogistics processes were selected as test cases. The first test case deals with the moving and posting of an item in a warehouse. The second process describes the picking and shipping of a customer's order. In both processes, the employee uses a mobile scanner in some process steps.

Two different employees performed the tests. Both recorded the process auditorily. These audio files are the basis for generating the BPMN 2.0 model using the prototype's web interface.

The following textual description represents test case one: At the start, the system assigns me a stock transfer order. The mobile scanner then shows me the item, the quantity and the source storage bin for the order. I then go to the source storage bin, and if the source storage bin is empty, I search for the goods in the warehouse manually. Then I search for the storage bin label. If the source storage bin is not empty, I scan the source storage bin. Next, I scan the article or EAN code. Then I confirm the quantity. The system then shows me the destination storage bin. Then I take the goods to the destination storage bin. If the destination storage bin is already occupied, I let the system suggest a new one. The system calculates a new destination storage bin. If the bin is empty, I scan the destination storage bin. The system then automatically posts the goods to the target storage bin.

## 4.3 Reference Process Model

A dedicated process analyst transforms the process descriptions from the interviews into the most suitable BPMN 2.0 model. This model is to serve as a basis to evaluate the machine-generated model. It should be noted that the choice of words from the interviews is to be retained, and little personal interpretation is allowed when designing the model. This is to facilitate the later comparison of the two test case models. The manually drawn model will be created with the same software as the BPMN modeler in the prototyping tool - BPMN.IO [26].

This facilitates a valid comparison since the BPMN 2.0 components look the same. The time the business analyst needs to draw the BPMN 2.0 diagram, based on the description, is also recorded and evaluated.

## 4.4 Evaluation of the Generated Models

The assessment of the results is based on the accuracy and the time needed for the generated models.

### Accuracy of the Generated Models

To determine the accuracy of the generated models, the number of automatically recognized BPMN 2.0 elements is compared to the manually designed and drawn model. For this purpose, the count of events, activities, gateways, and sequence flows are recorded. Tables 1 and 2 show the results for test cases one and two, respectively.

**Table 1.** Test case 1 – moving an item.

| Element type | Automatically generated | Manually designed |
|---|---|---|
| Event | 2 | 2 |
| Activities | 12 | 12 |
| Gateways | 2 | 2 |
| Sequence Flows | 19 | 19 |

**Table 2.** Test case 2 – picking a customer order

| Element type | Automatically generated | Manually designed |
|---|---|---|
| Event | 2 | 2 |
| Activities | 11 | 11 |
| Gateways | 1 | 1 |
| Sequence Flows | 15 | 15 |

As seen from both tables, the same number of BPMN 2.0 elements was detected for each automatically generated diagram, just as in the manually drawn diagrams. This shows that the prototype has 100% accuracy in detecting the number of BPMN 2.0 elements for these test cases. Dedicated business process analysts also compared these models to review their semantic correctness. The author of the manually generated BPMN 2.0 model compared the model with the existing test data and the generated model. Since there is also a margin for semantics and accuracy for manually drawn BPMN 2.0, the same process can be defined as BPMN 2.0 "correctly" in several variants. This may also depend on the personal style of the author. However, the labels of the compared BPMN 2.0 elements did not wholly coincide in both models, but their meaning stayed the same, and no process-relevant information was left out. As this analysis is more based on the sentiment of a person, it was not included as a metric but is still relevant for the overall result.

**Time Gain with the Generation Approach**
The main issue to be investigated with the prototype is time-saving in designing and drawing the model. A deeper insight into how much time per test case can be saved by using the software is given.

The following table depicts the times required for manual and automatic design and presentation of the business processes, as well as the time saved for both test cases.

**Table 3.** Comparison of times.

| Description | Duration |
|---|---|
| Test case 1 - automatically generated | 2:45 min |
| Test case 1 - manually designed | 7:05 min |
| Test case 1 - time gained | 4:20 min |
| Test case 2 - automatically generated | 3:31 min |
| Test case 2 - manually designed | 5:25 min |
| Test case 2 - time gained | 1:54 min |

As seen in Table 3, considerable time savings could be achieved using the prototype in both test cases. For test case one, the overall gained time was 04:20 min when using the prototype. The gain was lower but still relevant for test case two, with 01:54 min saved. This results in an overall time-saving of 61% for test case one and 35% for test case two compared to the manual approach. Added together, this accounts for a saving of approximately 48%. This means the prototype was about two times as fast as a business analyst drawing the models.

## 5  Conclusion, Limitations, and Outlook

As the results show, using the developed prototype is beneficial in three ways. First, the accuracy of the generated model compared to the model designed by a specialist is very good. The second benefit is time savings in using such an approach. The test cases show an average gain of about 48% for a similar acceptable result. The third benefit is undoubtedly that the tool can be used by people who have limited or no experience in Business Process Modeling.

Nevertheless, this approach comes with several limitations. The approach used to generate the BPMN 2.0 model is primarily built on a rule-based concept. This means grammatical and semantical rules were defined to extract information from the transcribed interviews. As German is a more complex language compared to e.g. English (German has more cases, gendering, more irregular verb conjugation, compound words, etc.), many explicit grammatical rules had to be integrated into the program code. This extensive task requires a broad knowledge of the language itself.

More advanced techniques could be used for the prototype as well. One option would be transformer neural networks, in which an algorithm has been trained to predict and calculate the output without establishing grammatical rules beforehand. A further research stream is to use Large Language Models (LLMs) like ChatGPT, Bard or Gemini.

The processes selected for the test cases are relatively simple, and not all options provided and sometimes needed to define and visualize processes are used. Only one employee was asked to describe the process steps and flows. Additional participants should express the same processes to get more robust results.

## References

1. Rusinaite, T., Kalibatiene, D., Vasilecas, O.: Requirements of dynamic business processes - a survey. In: 2015 IEEE 3rd Workshop on Advances in Information, Electronic and Electrical Engineering (AIEEE), pp. 1–4 (2015)
2. Climent, C., Mula, J., Hernández, J.E.: Improving the business processes of a bank. Bus. Process. Manag. J. (2009). https://doi.org/10.1108/14637150910949452
3. Dumas, M., La Rosa, M., Mendling, J., Reijers, H.A.: Fundamentals of Business Process Management. Springer, Heidelberg (2018)
4. van der Aalst, W.M.P., ter Hofstede, A.H.M., Weske, M.: Business process management: a survey. In: van der Aalst, W.M.P., Weske, M. (eds.) BPM 2003. LNCS, vol. 2678, pp. 1–12. Springer, Heidelberg (2003). https://doi.org/10.1007/3-540-44895-0_1
5. vom Brocke, J., Rosemann, M.: Handbook on Business Process Management 1. Introduction, Methods, and Information Systems. INFOSYS. Springer, Heidelberg (2015). https://doi.org/10.1007/978-3-642-45100-3

6. Naytah, A.H., Alkazemi, B.Y.: Exploring the characteristics of business process modeling solutions in the Saudi market. JSEA (2018). https://doi.org/10.4236/jsea.2018.1111031
7. Chinosi, M., Trombetta, A.: BPMN: an introduction to the standard. Comput. Stand. Interf. (2012). https://doi.org/10.1016/j.csi.2011.06.002
8. Entringer, T.C., Da Ferreira, A.S., de Nascimento, D.C.O.: Comparative analysis of the main business process modeling methods: a bibliometric study. Gest. Prod. (2021). https://doi.org/10.1590/1806-9649-2020v28e5211
9. García-Domínguez, A., Marcos, M., Medina, I.: A comparison of BPMN 2.0 with other notations for manufacturing processes. In: The 4th Manufacturing Engineering Society International Conference (MESIC 2011), Cadiz, Spain, 21–23 September 2011, pp. 593–600. AIP (2012). https://doi.org/10.1063/1.4707613
10. Stroppi, L.J.R., Chiotti, O., Villarreal, P.D.: Extending BPMN 2.0: method and tool support. In: Dijkman, R., Hofstetter, J., Koehler, J. (eds.) BPMN 2011. LNBIP, vol. 95, pp. 59–73. Springer, Heidelberg (2011). https://doi.org/10.1007/978-3-642-25160-3_5
11. Dijkman, R., Dumas, M., van Dongen, B., Käärik, R., Mendling, J.: Similarity of business process models: metrics and evaluation. Inf. Syst. (2011). https://doi.org/10.1016/j.is.2010.09.006
12. Zerbato, F., Oliboni, B., Combi, C., Campos, M., Juarez, J.M.: BPMN-based representation and comparison of clinical pathways for catheter-related bloodstream infections. In: 2015 International Conference on Healthcare Informatics (ICHI), Dallas, TX, USA, 21–23 October 2015, pp. 346–355. IEEE (2015). https://doi.org/10.1109/ICHI.2015.49
13. von Rosing, M., White, S., Cummins, F., de Man, H.: Business process model and notation—BPMN. In: The Complete Business Process Handbook, pp. 433–457. Elsevier (2015)
14. Muehlen, M., Recker, J.: How much language is enough? Theoretical and practical use of the business process modeling notation. In: Bubenko, J., Krogstie, J., Pastor, O., Pernici, B., Rolland, C., Sølvberg, A. (eds.) Seminal Contributions to Information Systems Engineering, pp. 429–443. Springer, Heidelberg (2013). https://doi.org/10.1007/978-3-642-36926-1_35
15. Ferrari, A., Zhao, L., Alhoshan, W.: NLP for requirements engineering: tasks, techniques, tools, and technologies. In: 2021 IEEE/ACM 43rd International Conference on Software Engineering: Companion Proceedings (ICSE-Companion), Madrid, ES, 25–28 May 2021, pp. 322–323. IEEE (2021). https://doi.org/10.1109/ICSE-Companion52605.2021.00137
16. Sintoris, K., Vergidis, K.: Extracting business process models using natural language processing (NLP) techniques. In: 2017 IEEE 19th Conference on Business Informatics (CBI), Thessaloniki, Greece, 24–27 July 2017, pp. 135–139. IEEE (2017). https://doi.org/10.1109/CBI.2017.41
17. Rodrigues, M., Teixeira, A.: Advanced Applications of Natural Language Processing for Performing Information Extraction. BRIEFSSPEECHTECH. Springer, Cham (2015). https://doi.org/10.1007/978-3-319-15563-0
18. de Almeida Bordignon, A.C., Thom, L.H., Silva, T.S., Dani, V.S., Fantinato, M., Ferreira, R.C.B.: Natural language processing in business process identification and modeling. In: Proceedings of the XIV Brazilian Symposium on Information Systems. SBSI 2018: XIV Brazilian Symposium on Information Systems, Caxias do Sul Brazil, 04–08 June 2018, pp. 1–8. Association for Computing Machinery, New York (2018). https://doi.org/10.1145/3229345.3229373
19. Neustein, A.: Text Mining of Web-Based Medical Content. Speech Technology and Text Mining in Medicine and Healthcare, vol. 1. De Gruyter, Berlin, Boston (2014)
20. Maqbool, B., Azam, F., Anwar, M.W., Butt, W.H., Zeb, J., Zafar, I., Nazir, A.K., Umair, Z.: A comprehensive investigation of BPMN models generation from textual requirements—Techniques, tools and trends. In: Kim, K.J., Baek, N. (eds.) ICISA 2018. LNEE, vol. 514, pp. 543–557. Springer, Singapore (2019). https://doi.org/10.1007/978-981-13-1056-0_54

21. Mustansir, A., Shahzad, K., Malik, M.K.: Towards automatic business process redesign: an NLP based approach to extract redesign suggestions. Autom. Softw. Eng. (2022). https://doi.org/10.1007/s10515-021-00316-8

22. Sholiq, S., Sarno, R., Astuti, E.S.: Generating BPMN diagram from textual requirements. J. King Saud Univ. - Comput. Inf. Sci. (2022). https://doi.org/10.1016/j.jksuci.2022.10.007

23. Hirschle, J.: Deep Natural Language Processing. Einstieg in Word Embedding, Sequence-to-Sequence-Modelle und Transformer mit Python. Hanser eLibrary. Hanser, München (2022)

24. Ronacher, A.: Flask. Pocoo (2023)

25. Whisper. Robust Speech Recognition via Large-Scale Weak Supervision. OpenAI

26. Camunda: BPMN.IO - bpmn-js. Camunda Services GmbH (2023)

# The CIPPI Saen Saeb Canal Model for Community Planning and Improvement

Thanakhom Srisaringkarn, Suppanunta Romprasert[✉], Polpat Kotrajarras, and Wichuta Adulwattanakul Khunrath

Faculty of Economics, Srinakharinwirot University, Bangkok, Thailand
{thanakhom,suppanunta,polpat}@g.swu.ac.th

**Abstract.** This research has two objective (1) to survey the level of satisfaction of people who use piers in the Saen Saeb canal at 3 piers, i.e., NaNa Nuea pier, Asoke Bridge pier and SWU Prasarnmit pier and their opinions about the operation of Khlong Saen Saeb Saad within the two-year project and (2) to explore the public relations media that affects the perception of information on Khlong Saen Saeb Saad within the two-year project of the people who use the piers in the Saen Saeb canal area. In this study, only focusing on context evaluation and product evaluation of CIPPI model. In which each dimension will evaluate all 3 aspects, namely, the water quality, the scenery and the readiness and safety of rescue equipment and buildings in the Saen Saeb Canal area. The study found that for the context evaluation, there was a moderate level of satisfaction in two of three aspects, i.e. The project was able to achieve its objective of managing the readiness and safety of rescue equipment and buildings in the Saen Saeb Canal area ($\overline{x} = 2.59 \pm 1.16$), The project was able to achieve its objective of managing the scenery around Saen Saeb Canal to make it more beautiful ($\overline{x} = 2.59 \pm 1.17$).By the way, managing the water quality in Saen Saeb Canal ($\overline{x} = 2.42 \pm 1.14$) have the level of satisfaction at low level. Including with, product evaluation, found that most of them had the level of satisfaction at a moderate level as well. However, the most problem was that managing foreign objects such as garbage or food scraps in the Saen Saeb Canal area ($\overline{x} = 2.34 \pm 1.15$) that is still being a current problem. For the public relations media that affects the perception of information about the Khlong Saen Saeb Saad within two-year project, it was found that most of respondents received the information through online media, i.e., Facebook, Google and Line, respectively.

**Keywords:** Saen Saeb Canal · Project Assessment · Public relation · The CIPPI model

## 1 Introduction

Saen Saeb Canal has been significant in Thailand historically for 200 years. It served as an essential role in the way of life of Bangkok citizens. Water in Saen Saeb Canal was used for consumption by households, agriculture, and transportation, including being a relaxation area and enhancing the beautiful landscape for the community.

© The Author(s), under exclusive license to Springer Nature Switzerland AG 2024
L. Uden and I.-H. Ting (Eds.): KMO 2024, CCIS 2152, pp. 248–260, 2024.
https://doi.org/10.1007/978-3-031-63269-3_19

The development of the economy and the expansion of urbanization in Bangkok, such as the increasing of industrial areas, construction, and civilization, affect the deteriorated water quality and surrounding environment of Saen Saeb Canal because they release the residual waste into Saen Saeb Canal, so it negatively affect to the physical environment [1]. The study of Kasemnet [2] found that polluted water was a chronic problem for a long time. This problem also deteriorated the role of Saen Saeb Canal from having many useful purposes canal to only being a canal for transportation purposes because people could not use water from this canal in daily life, as same as in the past.

The Government is still concerned about the water pollution and environmental problems around the Saen Saeb Canal. Hence, they had decided to launch the plan "Khlong Saen Saeb Saad within two-year project (from 2015 to 2017)" which the objectives were to enhance safety for water travelling, improve the landscape scene around Saen Saeb Canal, and solve the problem of pollution and water quality in the Saen Saeb Canal area. Also, this plan focused on solving the water pollution problem around Saen Saeb Canal to enhance the water quality and increase drainage efficiency around Saen Saeb Canal, including with developing transportation systems and water safety.

Hence, this study wants to survey the people's opinion on the implementation of Khlong Saen Saeb Saad within two-year project. To use the study results for guiding the plan implementation "Saen Saeb Canal rehabilitation development plan for 11 years (From 2021 to 2031)". This plan is a continuous plan of "Khlong Saen Saeb Saad within two-year project (from 2015 to 2017)". These are for precisely implementation of the plan objectives and adjusting the plan to be efficient in the future.

Moreover, this study wants to survey the public relations media that affect the perception of information about the Khlong Saen Saeb Saad within two-year project. It is the one way to provide the plan's information to people, including with understanding the objectives and the purpose of the plan in the same direction. These will promote environmental saving and preservation for people around Saen Saeb Canal.

For the contributions of the study are that researchers can assess the improvement of Khlong Saen Saeb Saad within two-year project whether what are differences between before and after implementing the project and should the government continue the next phase of project in the future. These are very important for making decision to launch policies and adjust policies to be proper with the current situations of Saen Saeb canal.

## 2 Literature Review

### 2.1 Theoretical Framework for Project Assessment

This study uses a theoretical framework for assessing the Khlong Saen Saeb Saad within two-year project with the CIPPI model by Stuffle Beam. It is for easy understanding of the context, can understand with systematical, and more trustful. Moreover, these results can be used for implementation and suggestions for future projects.

Stufflebeam [3] explained that the CIPPI model was applied in many studies and broad areas such as assessing the projects and plans, etc. The CIPPI assessment is a tool for project assessment by separating into sub-contexts from various perspectives. Thus, the assessment using the CIPPI model is very trustworthy. The data used for analysis in this model differs depending on its context or the project's objective. It is why the CIPPI model can respond to the researcher who wants to take the study results by using CIPPI to use them for most advantage.

In conclusion, the CIPPI assessment is the most significant part of the project for making it more believable and standardized. The head of the project cannot know whether these projects are efficient enough or they can solve the correct mistakes or not. Hence, the assessment with the CIPPI model will make the head of the project find advantages and drawbacks of the project, which can lead to the most efficient project.

Watanasuntorn [4] said the CIPPI model, by Stuffle Beam, is a dynamic assessment because components of the model include various significant indicators for assessing the project's quality and also use them for making decisions when they want to launch, edit, or suspend the project. So, the CIPPI model includes four types of assessment indicators, and each indicator is used for different objectives and different phases of the project. The details will be explained in the following sections.

1. Context Evaluation (C): Using for assessing plans or policies implemented, goals, economic and social conditions, and the organization's needs in that project. Thus, these can show whether this project can respond and solve the root cause of problems or not.
2. Input Evaluation (I): Using for assessing the amount of the project's resources before launching the project whether they have enough resources or not. This is for assessing the activities strategies and whether they are suitable or not.
3. Process Evaluation (P): This assessment happen between ongoing processes used for assessing the project's advancement. The outcomes from this process will be used to improve the efficiency of the project.
4. Product/ Impact Evaluation (P or I): Assessing after the project is finished. This process can assess whether we should continue, expand, or abort the project.

This study is assessing the Context and Product/Impact Evaluation (C and P or I) in CIPPI model because Khlong Saen Saeb Saad within two-year project was the project that finished since 2017. Hence, this study tries to evaluate the context and product or impact that occur from the project. The study results from this part of CIPPI model can be used for policies planning and adjusting the policies mechanism in the future whether the government should continue the next phase project in the case that the study results is better or suspend the project in the case that the study results is worst. These results can help the government for making decision to do the better policies movement in the future.

## 2.2 Public Relations

Public relations are the communication between an organization and various public groups. Including listening to opinions and referendums that the public has about the organization. Public relations have a purpose of building trust, knowledge, and a good attitude toward the organization [5].

### 2.2.1 The Importance of Public Relations

Public relations are of great value to society because public relations results in social responsibility for both government agencies and the private sector, and public relations also represents a good organization for contacting various groups of people. It also helps to build good relationships between organizations and society by promoting mutual adaptation and results in a common goal that benefits society. Public relations is a process that helps organizations gain helpful information to be used for setting organizational policies and goals [6].

### 2.2.2 Public Relations and Social Media

Department of Environmental Quality Promotion [7] said that the media can be considered a stimulus or a type of motivating factor in the form of knowledge, information, or even experience because the media can broadcast images of real or virtual events. It will have an effect on a person's thoughts and feelings, which will lead to behavior change and human actions.

Social Media refers to digital media that is a tool for social operations (Social Tool) for communicating with each other in social networks through websites and various applications on media that are connected to the internet by emphasizing that users are both the sender and receiver of the message, participating in producing their own content in the form of information, images, and sound. Therefore, social media is a channel that people like to use for exchanging information, opinions, experiences, and perspectives on various matters with each other [8].

## 3    Research Methods

This study is a survey research with the objective is to survey the level of opinion on the satisfaction of people who use the pier in the Saen Saeb Canal, all three piers, namely, Nana Nuea Pier, Asoke Bridge Pier, and SWU Prasarnmit Pier that had an impact on project operations of "the Khlong Saen Saeb Saad within two-year project" by using a questionnaire as a tool to collect data. The researcher had conducted the study in the following steps:

### 3.1    Defining the Population and Sample

**Population**
The population in this research was people in Bangkok who used the pier in the Saen Saeb Canal area, all three piers include Nana Nuea Pier, Asoke Bridge Pier, and SWU Prasarnmit Pier, about 5,527,994 people [9].

**Sample Selection**
This research determined the sample size that would be representative of the population. To explore the level of opinion on satisfaction with the Khlong Saen Saeb Saad within two-year project by using Yamane's formula [10].

Therefore, the sample group in the public opinion survey in Bangkok that used the passenger pier in the Saen Saep Canal area, all three piers include Nana Nuea Pier, Asoke Bridge Pier, and SWU Prasarnmit Pier, had a sample size of 451 people.

## 3.2   Research Tools

Using a survey questionnaire created by the researcher. By dividing the questions into five parts as follows:

Part 1: Questionnaire regarding general information of respondents

Part 2: Questionnaire regarding the behavior of the use of the passenger pier in the Saen Saeb Canal area

Part 3: Questionnaire about perception of basic information about the Khlong Saen Saeb Saad within two-year project

Part 4: Questionnaire regarding opinions on the Khlong Saen Saeb Saad within two-year project, with questions divided into 3 contexts: Water quality in Saen Saeb Canal, the Scenery around Saen Saeb Canal area and the readiness and safety of rescue equipment and buildings in the Saen Saeb Canal area after the operation of the Khlong Saen Saeb Saad within two-year project. This part of the questionnaire would use a 5-level Likert Scale: Strongly Agree, Agree, Neither Agree nor Disagree, Disagree, Strongly Disagree, set the criteria for interpreting the average value. This study had set the criteria for scoring the weight of the answers as follows:

1) Opinion level 1.00–1.49 means people responding to the questionnaire have an opinion level of satisfaction at the lowest level.
2) Opinion level 1.50–2.49 means people responding to the questionnaire have an opinion level of satisfaction at a low level.
3) Opinion level 2.50–3.49 means people responding to the questionnaire have an opinion level of satisfaction at a moderate level.
4) Opinion level 3.50–4.49 means people responding to the questionnaire have an opinion level of satisfaction at a high level.
5) Opinion level 4.50–5.00 means people responding to the questionnaire have an opinion level of satisfaction at the highest level.

Part 5: Questionnaire regarding additional opinions or suggestions from the people towards the the Khlong Saen Saeb Saad within two-year project, which will be an open-ended question.

### How to Assess Research Tool's Quality

1. The questionnaire of this research had passed the validity check, which has a value (Item-objective Congruency Index: IOC) equal to 0.857, indicating that the questionnaire was consistent with the research objectives.
2. The questionnaire of this research had passed the test (Pre-test) by analyzing the confidence value using Cronbach's Alpha to calculate the coefficient (Coefficient Alpha) for a total of 30 sets from the questionnaire test (Pre-test). It found that the value of the confidence was equal to 0.944, which was a confidence value that could be used as a tool for data collection.

**Data Analysis**
This study is a survey research, a quantitative data analysis, using questionnaires to collectdata. The statistics used in data analysis are descriptive statistics such as percentage, mean, and standard deviation (S.D).

# 4  Results and Analysis

The statistic results from the sample of the passenger pier at three piers around Saen Saeb Canal, namely, Na Na Nuea Pier, Asoke Bridge Pier, and SWU Prasarnmit Pier about 451 samples found that almost respondents are female (51.88%), aged between 20–30 years old (32.37%), having bachelor's degree (62.75%), being student (49.44%), income level is 15,000 baht/month (45.01%) and currently live in Bangkok (80.49%) (Table 1).

**The Behavior of Using Passenger Pier in the Saen Saeb Canal Area**
The statistic result of The Behavior of using passenger pier in the Saen Saeb Canal area by using a survey questionnaire from the sample of the passenger pier at three piers around Saen Saeb Canal, namely, Na Na Nuea Pier, Asoke Bridge Pier, and SWU Prasarnmit Pier about 451 samples found that the highest frequency used pier that almost respondents had ever used was SWU Prasarnmit Pier (49.53%), followed by Asoke Bridge Pier (34.83%) and Na Na Nuea Pier (15.64%), respectively.

For the frequency of using the passenger pier in the Saen Saeb Canal area, it found that most respondents used the Saen Saeb pier service less than 5 days/week (60.31%), followed by using the Saen Saeb pier service 5 days/week (31.04%) and 7 days/week (8.65%), respectively.

For the period of using the passenger pier in the Saen Saeb Canal area, it found that most respondents used the Saen Saeb pier service for more than or equal to 1 year (58.98%), followed by using the Saen Saeb pier service for less than 1 year (41.02%).

For the purpose of using the passenger pier in the Saen Saeb Canal area found that most respondents used the Saen Saeb pier service for traveling to tourist attractions (36.59%), followed by for traveling to educational institutions (26.16%), traveling for work (25.50%), traveling to home/resident (10.86%) and other purposes (0.89%), respectively.

The reason why they chose the passenger pier in the Saen Saeb Canal area for traveling was because the pier is located near the destination (30.35%). Secondly, the service is convenient, flexible, and fast (27.21%). Thirdly, short traveling time (22.79%), fourthly, the convenient procedure (10.91%), the next is less passenger (4.64%), followed by safety (2.70%) and other (1.40%), respectively (Table 2).

**The Perception of the Information of the Khlong Saen Saeb Saad Within Two-Year Project**
The statistical results of The perception of the information of the Khlong Saen Saeb Saad within two-year project found that most respondents got information about the project from online media (85.71%). The first three online media that respondents were interested in i.e. Facebook (28.92%), Google (26.48%) and Line (9.76%), respectively.

**Table 1.** General information of respondents (n = 451)

| General Information | Frequency | Percentage |
|---|---|---|
| Gender | | |
| Male | 217 | 48.12 |
| Female | 234 | 51.88 |
| **Total** | **451** | **100.00** |
| Age | | |
| Below 20 years old | 131 | 29.05 |
| 20–30 years old | 146 | 32.37 |
| 31–40 years old | 87 | 19.29 |
| 41–50 years old | 60 | 13.31 |
| 51 -59 years old | 25 | 5.54 |
| More than 60 years old | 2 | 0.44 |
| **Total** | **451** | **100.00** |
| Educational level | | |
| Primary education | 9 | 2.00 |
| Junior high school | 7 | 1.55 |
| High school / Vocational Certificate | 101 | 22.39 |
| Diploma/ High Vocational Certificate | 19 | 4.21 |
| Bachelor's degree | 283 | 62.75 |
| Higher than Bachelor's degree | 32 | 7.10 |
| **Total** | **451** | **100.00** |
| Occupation | | |
| Government officer | 22 | 4.88 |
| State enterprise employees | 22 | 4.88 |
| Private company employees | 105 | 23.28 |
| private business | 63 | 13.97 |
| Student | 223 | 49.44 |
| Etc | 16 | 3.55 |
| **Total** | **451** | **100.00** |
| Income level | | |
| Less than 15,000 baht/month | 203 | 45.01 |
| 15,001–20,000 baht/month | 77 | 17.07 |
| 20,001–25,000 baht/month | 79 | 17.52 |
| 25,001–30,000 baht/month | 51 | 11.31 |
| More than 30,001 baht/month | 41 | 9.09 |
| **Total** | **451** | **100.00** |
| Current address | | |
| Bangkok | 363 | 80.49 |
| Metropolitan area (Samutprakarn, Nontaburi, Patumthani Etc.) | 58 | 12.86 |
| Other provinces | 30 | 6.65 |
| **Total** | **451** | **100.00** |

**Table 2.** The Behavior of using passenger pier in the Saen Saeb Canal area (n = 451)

| The Behavior of using passenger pier in the Saen Saeb Canal area | Percentage |
|---|---|
| Which passenger piers have you used the service? | |
| – Na Na Nuea Pier | 15.64 |
| – Asoke Bridge Pier | 34.83 |
| – SWU Prasarnmit Pier | 49.53 |
| **Total** | **100.00** |
| How often do you use the passenger pier around Saen Saeb Canal (per week)? | |
| – 7 days/week | 8.65 |
| – 5 days/week | 31.04 |
| – Less than 5 days/week | 60.31 |
| **Total** | **100.00** |
| How long have you used the passenger pier around Saen Saeb Canal? | |
| – Less than 1 year | 41.02 |
| – More than or equal 1 year | 58.98 |
| **Total** | **100.00** |
| What is your purpose in using the passenger pier service in the Saen Saeb Canal area? | |
| – For travelling to work | 25.50 |
| – For travelling to home | 10.86 |
| – For travelling to tourist attractions such as department store, street market, park etc | 36.59 |
| | 26.16 |
| – For travelling to educational institutions such as school, college, university etc | 0.89 |
| – other | **100.00** |
| **Total** | |
| What was the reason for choosing to use the passenger pier around Saen Saeb Canal? | |
| – Convenient, Flexible, and Fast | 27.21 |
| – Convenient procedure | 10.91 |
| – Less passengers | 4.64 |
| – Safety | 2.70 |
| – The pier is located near the destination | 30.35 |
| – Short travelling time | 22.79 |
| – Other | 1.40 |
| **Total** | **100.00** |

Followed by the mass media, namely, Television and radio (11.50%), finally was print media, namely, newspaper (2.79%) (Table 3).

### The Level of Opinion on the Satisfaction of the Khlong Saen Saeb Saad Within Two-Year Project

For the survey of the level of opinion on the satisfaction of the people who have use the 3 passenger piers in Saen Saeb Canal areas, namely Na Na Nuea Pier, Asoke Bridge Pier and SWU Prasarnmit Pier that affected to the operation of the Khlong Saen Saeb Saad within two-year project by using the framework of CIPPI model. Especially, in

**Table 3.** The perception of the information of the Khlong Saen Saeb Saad within two-year project

| Type of media | The perception of the information of the Khlong Saen Saeb Saad within two-year project |
|---|---|
| | Acknowledge person (percentage) |
| **Print Media** | |
| Newspaper | 8(2.79) |
| **Total** | **8(2.79)** |
| **Mass Media** | |
| Radio | 3(1.05) |
| Television | 30(10.45) |
| **Total** | **33(11.50)** |
| **Online Media** | |
| Google | 76(26.48) |
| E-mail | 7(2.44) |
| Line | 28(9.76) |
| Facebook | 83(28.92) |
| Instagram | 23(8.01) |
| Youtube | 25(8.71) |
| Other | 4(1.39) |
| **Total** | **246(85.71)** |
| **Total** | **(100)** |

this study focused on context evaluation and product evaluation which each aspect was assessed with 3 topics, namely, water quality in Saen Saeb Canal, the scenery around Saen Saeb Canal area and the readiness and safety of rescue equipment and buildings in the Saen Saeb Canal area. The results were as follows.

Context evaluation found that in almost all contexts, the level of opinion on satisfaction in moderate level, namely, the readiness and safety of rescue equipment and buildings in the Saen Saeb Canal area ($\bar{x} = 2.59 \pm 1.17$) and the scenery around Saen Saeb Canal area ($\bar{x} = 2.59 \pm 1.17$) that had the level of opinion on satisfaction at moderate level. The water quality in Saen Saeb Canal ($\bar{x} = 2.42 \pm 1.14$) had a low level of opinion on satisfaction (Table 4).

For the Product Evaluation, it found that almost all products had the level of opinion on satisfaction at a moderate level when they were considered in each aspect.

- Water quality around Saen Saeb Canal found that the management of aquatic weeds and other aquatic plants in the Saen Saeb Canal area ($\bar{x} = 2.51 \pm 1.14$) was almost better. On the other hand, other sub-products were still problems, namely, the problem in managing the quality of water in the Saen Saeb Canal area, such as the smell, color, and turbidity of the water ($\bar{x} = 2.39 \pm 1.13$) and the most severe was the problems with managing foreign objects such as garbage or food scraps in the Saen Saeb Canal area ($\bar{x} = 2.34 \pm 1.15$).

**Table 4.** Context Evaluation (n = 451)

| Contexts | Population Sample | | Level of opinion on satisfaction |
|---|---|---|---|
| | Mean | Standard Deviation (S.D.) | |
| The project was able to achieve its objective of managing the quality of water in the Saen Saeb Canal area to be cleaner | 2.42 | 1.14 | Low level |
| The project was able to achieve its objective of managing the scenery around Saen Saeb Canal to make it more beautiful | 2.59 | 1.17 | Moderate level |
| The project was able to achieve its objective of managing the readiness and safety of rescue equipment and buildings in the Saen Saeb Canal area to be more prepared | 2.59 | 1.16 | Moderate level |

- The scenery around San Saeb Canal found that the managing shady areas around tree lines and the walking area along Saen Saeb Canal ($\bar{x} = 2.81 \pm 1.21$) and the managing the cleanliness of walkways, bicycle paths, and piers ($\bar{x} = 2.54 \pm 1.15$) were almost better. For the managing garbage shelters along the canal and keeping garbage as clean as possible ($\bar{x} = 2.43 \pm 1.13$) was still a problem.
- The readiness and safety of rescue equipment and buildings in the Saen Saeb Canal area were almost better in all products, namely, the availability of safety equipment on the pier, such as rubber rings, life jackets, and signs recommending the use of the pier ($\bar{x} = 2.62 \pm 1.18$) was the most better. Followed by port repair and improvement management ($\bar{x} = 2.59 \pm 1.17$) and Improving the walkway along the dam and the walkway bridge across the canal that is damaged and unusable ($\bar{x} = 2.57 \pm 1.14$), by respectively (Table 5).

**Table 5.** Product Evaluation (n = 451)

| Products | Mean | Standard Deviation (S.D.) | The level of opinion on satisfaction |
|---|---|---|---|
| Water quality in Saen Saeb Canal | | | |
| – Managing the quality of water in the Saen Saeb Canal area, such as the smell, color, and turbidity of the water | 2.39 | 1.13 | Low level |
| – Managing of aquatic weeds and other aquatic plants in the Saen Saeb Canal area | 2.51 | 1.14 | Moderate Level |
| – Managing foreign objects such as garbage or food scraps in the Saen Saeb Canal area | 2.34 | 1.15 | Low level |
| Scenery around Saen Saeb Canal area | | | |
| – Managing garbage shelters along the canal and keeping garbage as clean as possible | 2.43 | 1.13 | Low level |
| – Managing the cleanliness of walkways, bicycle paths, and piers | 2.54 | 1.15 | Moderate Level |
| – Managing shady areas around tree lines and the walking area along Saen Saeb Canal | 2.81 | 1.21 | Moderate Level |
| The readiness and safety of rescue equipment and buildings in the Saen Saeb Canal area | | | |
| – Port repair and improvement management | 2.59 | 1.17 | Moderate Level |
| – Improving the walkway along the dam and the walkway bridge across the canal that is damaged and unusable | 2.57 | 1.14 | Moderate Level |
| – The availability of safety equipment on the pier, such as rubber rings, life jackets, signs recommending the use of the pier | 2.62 | 1.18 | Moderate Level |

# 5 Conclusion

The analysis result of the Khlong Saen Saeb Saad within two-year project assessment by using the CIPPI model, particularly Context Evaluation and Product Evaluation, found that almost all respondents had a moderate level of opinion on satisfaction with the project when it was considered in each aspect, the results of the study were as follows.

Context Evaluation found that almost all respondents assessed that the Khlong Saen Saeb Saad within two-year project achieved the project objectives at a moderate level because more than half of respondents have the level of opinion on satisfaction with the project's objectives, namely, the project was able to achieve its objective in managing the readiness and safety of rescue equipment and buildings in the Saen Saeb Canal area to be more prepared and the project was able to achieve its objective in managing the scenery around Saen Saeb Canal to make it more beautiful at a moderate level. By the way, the last project's objective was that the project was able to achieve its objective of managing the quality of water in the Saen Saeb Canal area to be cleaner which had the level of opinion on satisfaction in the project's operation at a low level. The last context that had a low level of respondent satisfaction might occur that the project has been launched only two years. Hence, people cannot observe the difference between before the project started and at present. However, the government has a plan called "the Saen Saeb Canal rehabilitation development plan for 11 years (from 2021 to 2031), which is the consecutive operational project from the Khlong Saen Saeb Saad within two-year project. This project is a plan to improve Saen Saeb Canal continuously in the long run.

For the Product Evaluation from the results of the Khlong Saen Saeb Saad within two-year project assessment by using the CIPPI model found that all products had the level of satisfaction at a moderate level, which led to the project's product achieving the objective at a moderate level, too. When they were considered in each aspect, it found that.

- Firstly, water quality in Saen Saeb Canal found that the managing of aquatic weeds and other aquatic plants in the Saen Saeb Canal area were trend to be better. By the way, the managing foreign objects such as garbage or food scraps in the Saen Saeb Canal area was still problems, followed by the managing the quality of water in the Saen Saeb Canal area, such as the smell, color, and turbidity of the water, respectively.
- Secondly, scenery around Saen Saeb Canal area found that the managing shady areas around tree lines and the walking area along Saen Saeb Canal and the managing the cleanliness of walkways, bicycle paths, and piers were trend to be better. By the way there was still problems at the managing garbage shelters along the canal and keeping garbage as clean as possible.
- Thirdly, the readiness and safety of rescue equipment and buildings in the Saen Saeb Canal area found that it was better in all products, namely, the availability of safety equipment on the pier, such as rubber rings, life jackets, signs recommending the use of the pier, including with, the port repair and improvement management and improving the walkway along the dam and the walkway bridge across the canal that is damaged and unusable were trend to be better respectively.

Moreover, this study also surveyed the public relations media that affected the perception of the information about the Khlong Saen Saeb Saad within two-year project of the respondents who have used the passenger pier at Saen Saeb Canal, then found that almost all respondents got information about the project from online media. The first three online media that respondents are interested in, i.e., Facebook, Google, and Line, respectively. Pulsawad [11] found that the most popular social media in Thailand was Facebook, and the next was Google and Line, respectively. Hence, the government can benefit from these public relations media for advertising the project in the next phase, which might increase the accessibility to the project's information of stakeholders.

# References

1. Areerachakul, S.: Comparison of Adaptive neuro-fuzzy inference system and Artificial neural network for estimation of Biochemical Oxygen Demand parameter in surface water: a case study of Saen Saep canal. Suan Sunandha Rajabhat University (2012). http://58.181.147.16/bitstream/ssruir/610/1/001-55.pdf
2. Kasemnet, L., Thongpukdee, P.J.T., Boonprakob, P.: Life-style and water resource conservation behavior of people in the Saen Saeb canal community. J. Behav. Sci. (2003). http://bsris.swu.ac.th/journal/80544/file/45.pdf
3. Stufflebeam, D.L.: The CIPP model for evaluation. In: Stufflebeam, D.L., Madaus, G.F., Kellaghan, T. (eds.) Evaluation Models: Viewpoints on Educational and Human Services Evaluation. EEHS, vol. 49, pp. 279–317. Springer, Dordrecht (2000). https://doi.org/10.1007/0-306-47559-6_16
4. Watanasuntorn, K.: Application of Stufflebeam's CIPP model for educational project evaluation. Suranaree J. Soc. Sci. 2(1), 67–83 (2008)
5. Swasdiampairaks, P.: Unit 8 Marketing Promotion: Public Relations (n.d.d.)
6. Kleechaya, P.: Public relations performance evaluation framework: a conceptual proposal. J. Public Relat. Advert. 1(2), 81–99 (2018)
7. Department of Environmental Quality Promotion: How do people make decisions for the environment? Department of Environmental Quality Promotion, Ministry of Natural Resources and Environment (2015)
8. Pawichai, S.: Public relations strategies in utilizing social media. e-jodil 7(2), 1–13 (2017)
9. Administrative Strategy Division: Population in Bangkok 2021 classified by age and area (2021). https://webportal.bangkok.go.th/pipd/page/sub/23329/สถิติกรุงเทพมหานคร-2564
10. Yamane, T.: Statistics: An Introductory Analysis-3. Harper & Row, New York (1973)
11. Pulsawad, A., Sardtraruji, K.: Public relations under social media trends. Journal of Public Relat. Advert. 6(2) (2013)

# Information and Knowledge Management Systems

# Building a Sustainable Knowledge Management System from Dark Data in Industrial Maintenance

Keyi Zhong[1(✉)], Tom Jackson[1], Andrew West[2], and Georgina Cosma[3]

[1] Business School, Loughborough University, Epinal Way, Loughborough LE11 3TU, UK
K.Zhong@lboro.ac.uk
[2] School of Mechanical, Electrical and Manufacturing Engineering, Loughborough University, Epinal Way, Loughborough LE11 3TU, UK
[3] School of Computer Science, Loughborough University, Epinal Way, Loughborough LE11 3TU, UK

**Abstract.** As digitalization exponentially generates vast data volumes, concerns about its environmental impact have surged. Dark data, characterized by being stored but underutilized, not only presents challenges to organizations but also aligns with the imperative of digital decarbonization. Notably, the manufacturing domain lacks prior exploration of addressing dark data issues. In response, this study introduces a knowledge management perspective to tackle the challenge through the construction of a Knowledge Management System (KMS). The proposed KMS is built upon the foundation of a Knowledge Graph (KG). Data ingestion analysis reveals that the identified data sources are sparse and incomplete, prompting the application of data scraping and enrichment techniques. Data from various sources is integrated, and knowledge is extracted from the enriched datasets. A fault KG containing the physical level and the failure level is manually constructed to ensure enhanced accuracy and reliability. The proposed KMS framework, grounded in the power of KGs, serves as a comprehensive solution to the challenges posed by dark data in the manufacturing sector, and provides industrial maintenance applications such as fault analysis and decision-making guidance, to improve knowledge reuse and promote digital decarbonization.

**Keywords:** Dark Data · Knowledge Management Systems (KMS) · Digitalization · Industrial Maintenance

## 1 Introduction

Digitalization involves the process of converting information, processes, activities, and other aspects of various domains into a digital format [1, 2]. This transformation has led to the generation of vast amount of data by leveraging the advantages of digital technology. Although various organizations have accumulated and harnessed the power of data, a substantial portion of data remains unexplored, preventing the uncovering of valuable insights. An astonishing statistic reveals that 2.5 quintillion bytes of data

© The Author(s), under exclusive license to Springer Nature Switzerland AG 2024
L. Uden and I.-H. Ting (Eds.): KMO 2024, CCIS 2152, pp. 263–274, 2024.
https://doi.org/10.1007/978-3-031-63269-3_20

are produced each day, yet 55% of this data remains underutilized [3, 4]. Moreover, a multitude of datasets originates from different sources, comes in varying formats, and sometimes suffers from issues like sparsity and incompleteness. These challenges make it more difficult for humans to harness the full potential of the data. Consequently, organizations fail to unlock the latent value of data, giving rise to the concept of "dark data".

Effectively addressing the challenges associated with dark data is crucial for unlocking its potential and deriving meaningful insights, especially within the manufacturing domain. The fourth industrial revolution, known as Industry 4.0, introduces a new paradigm that integrates digital and physical systems, enabling customized production and intelligent industrial systems [5]. Industry 4.0 technologies emphasize the utilization of data, including artificial intelligence, big data analytics, the industrial internet of things, and more [6–8]. Therefore, it can be concluded that the presence of dark data poses significant obstacles to the advancement of Industry 4.0. Unlocking the value of dark data is particularly important for manufacturing companies. However, limited studies have investigated how to explore dark data and convert it into useful information. This suggests a research gap regarding the processing and application of dark data within the context of manufacturing.

Data streams from various machines/parts within industrial systems come in different formats, including numerical data, graphical data, text data, etc., covering the entire lifecycle of production lines. In terms of text data, manufacturing companies typically maintain a repository of maintenance reports or maintenance work orders, aiding technicians in processing maintenance tasks such as fault analysis. However, these maintenance datasets held by companies often face challenges related to sparsity and incompleteness, characterized by missing or unknown data points, which can be categorized as dark data. The management of maintenance texts containing dark data remains an unexplored avenue.

Several studies have explored the integration of knowledge management (KM) and digital transformation [9, 10], including IoT applications [11], data management [12], and more. Existing literature has highlighted the importance for manufacturing companies to cultivate and oversee new knowledge essential for organizational decision-making and the attainment of business objectives [13]. Hence, it is noteworthy to investigate whether KM could play a role in addressing dark data in maintenance text datasets. In this context, a knowledge management system (KMS) can be considered a pivotal tool for managing maintenance text datasets within the realm of KM.

The effective utilization of dark data can also contribute to reducing the environmental impact of manufacturing companies. According to a report from Normative (2023) [14], the manufacturing and production sector is responsible for one-fifth of global carbon emissions and consumes 54% of the world's energy. Mitigating carbon emissions from the manufacturing sector plays a crucial role in achieving global climate targets [15]. Consequently, "sustainability" has garnered increasing attention, necessitating manufacturers to find a balance between their activities and their impact on the natural environment.

In light of this, this study aims to develop a sustainable KMS framework to process dark data, that is both incomplete and of low quality for the purpose of industrial maintenance. The goal is to enhance decision-making within the production system while simultaneously contributing to the reduction of data carbon emissions. The main contributions are summarized as follows:

1) An overall framework is proposed to detail how to process dark and incomplete data and construct a KMS.
2) A Knowledge graph (KG) model containing the physical and the failure level is introduced to integrate diverse data sources.
3) A case study from a global automotive manufacturer (we will call AM) is conducted, and sparse and incomplete maintenance text datasets are utilized to construct a KMS.

The rest of this paper is organized as follows. Section 2 reviews the literature. Section 3 illustrates the methods of this study, encompassing the overall framework and the case study details. Section 4 concludes the paper and provides the future research directions.

## 2 Literature Review

### 2.1 Dark Data: A Big Challenge for Organizations

#### 2.1.1 Digitalization and Data Management

In recent years, the evolution of cutting-edge information technology has spearheaded profound transformations across various sectors, notably manufacturing, which is currently immersed in the revolutionary wave known as Industry 4.0 [6, 16, 17]. The new industrial stage is accompanied by the prevalence of buzzwords such as the Internet of Things (IoT), smart manufacturing, and digital twins 18. It provides a new development paradigm for businesses and results in higher productivity of production processes [19, 20].

Digitalization has engendered an unprecedented deluge of data which is organized and harnessed by companies. Effectively navigating, organizing, and harnessing extensive and often unwieldy data reservoir has become an indispensable mission for these enterprises. These datasets emanate from diverse sources, exhibit varying formats, and frequently encompass substantial segments that remain inapplicable to human usage. Moreover, they often grapple with issues of sparsity and incompleteness, necessitating preprocessing before they can be effectively employed. As such, the task of data management has evolved into a progressively intricate endeavor.

#### 2.1.2 Dark Data: The Definition and Why Data Fall into Dark Data

Despite the monumental volume of data that accumulates daily, a disconcerting proportion of it fails to yield meaningful insights for organizations. Each passing day witnesses the generation of approximately 2.5 quintillion bytes of data, yet a substantial 55% of this data languishes in underutilization [3, 4]. Astonishingly, Dell Technologies Corporation's report from 2013 [21, 22] paints a bleak picture where merely 22% data of the digital universe held utility, with less than 5% undergoing comprehensive analysis—a disheartening loss of valuable information. In essence, organizations amass and retain data with the intent of capitalizing on it, but they fail to unlock its latent value, thereby contributing to the emergence of what we term "dark data". Gartner's definition [23] of dark data aptly encapsulates this phenomenon as information amassed and stored by organizations for business purposes that ultimately languishes, untapped and unexamined.

Several factors underlie the transformation of data into "dark" enigma. Foremost among them is the considerable time and expense required for processing and analyzing data, deterring its utilization [24]. Moreover, data is inherently heterogeneous, originating from various formats and diverse sources, rendering its value extraction a formidable challenge. Even as machine learning and deep learning make significant strides, their efficacy wanes when confronted with highly heterogeneous data that defies analysis without human intervention, thus perpetuating the cycle of dark data. Furthermore, datasets held by organizations often suffer from sparsity and incompleteness, marked by missing or unknown data points. Such datasets tend to be ignored as they offer little in the way of meaningful insights, exacerbating the prevalence of dark data.

Companies, in their relentless pursuit of critical information, grapple with the pervasive menace of dark data. Recent advancements in digitalization technology rely heavily on the availability of substantial, high-quality datasets to create effective models that bolster decision-making. However, the presence of dark data casts a shadow over the quality of these requisite datasets, eroding the accuracy of models and potentially steering organizations toward misguided decisions. Consequently, the effective management and exploitation of dark data loom large as a pivotal task for businesses.

### 2.1.3 Dark Data in Manufacturing

While dark data has recently started receiving scholarly attention, its study within the manufacturing domain remains relatively sparse. A systematic literature review [21] has taken the pioneering step of framing a specific definition within the manufacturing sector. Within this context, dark data materializes as information that is captured and preserved during routine business operations, often in an unstructured or uncatalogued form, languishing unanalyzed due to the dearth of appropriate analytical tools. This review underscores the significance of dark data within the manufacturing domain and advocates for manufacturing companies to unearth the latent value concealed within these enigmatic datasets.

However, based on the analysis of existing literature, limited studies have delved into the implications of dark data on the manufacturing sector. Moreover, as far as our knowledge extends, there is a noticeable gap in research regarding the methods for processing and leveraging dark data within the manufacturing context. This highlights a promising avenue for future research and directs us toward a more in-depth exploration of the subject, offering potential insights into the utilization of dark data in manufacturing.

## 2.2  Knowledge Management for Dark Data

### 2.2.1  Knowledge Management (KM) and Knowledge Management Systems (KMS)

Numerous papers have emphasized the pivotal role of knowledge management (KM) within organizations, highlighting it as an increasingly crucial capability [12, 25]. KM facilitates the creation, capture, organization, access, and utilization of intellectual assets, thereby fostering long-term sustainability and providing a strategic advantage [26–28]. Moreover, effectively managing this information exchange can usher in transformative changes advantageous to the organization. Through adept KM practices, companies can seamlessly integrate insights from varied sectors and diverse employee groups, positioning themselves for strategic success [29].

A practical approach to realizing KM is through the formulation and implementation of Knowledge Management Systems (KMS). KMS are specialized information systems tailored to oversee and optimize organizational knowledge processes. Their primary role is to bolster the creation, retrieval, dissemination, and application of knowledge within an organization [9]. According to Alavi and Leidner [30], KMS have predominant purposes: (i) Codification and sharing of best practices with the focus of internal knowledge transfer; (ii) Construction of knowledge directories to identify, classify and codify the knowledge that remains concealed and unstructured; and (iii) Formation of knowledge networks, enabling users to communicate swiftly and effortlessly.

### 2.2.2  Digital Carbonization and Sustainable KMS

With the recent surge in data proliferation, the landscape of KMS is rapidly evolving. Modern KMS are harnessing an array of cutting-edge digital technologies to enhance their efficiency and refine decision-making processes. However, while digital technology has offered profound benefits and bestowed unparalleled convenience upon humans, its environmental impacts cannot be overlooked.

According to one report in 2022 [31], digitalization account for 4% of greenhouse gas emissions, with its energy consumption escalating by 9% annually. The technological progress has enabled the generation of vast amounts of data. For instance, the data volume associated with IOT is predicted to reach 79 zettabytes worldwide by 2025 [3, 4]. Processing, analyzing, and storing such immense quantities of data necessitate extra energy, thus contributing to the increasing production of carbon emissions. These carbon emissions generated through the utilization of digital technologies, services, and processes are defined as "digital carbon footprints".

Recently numerous organizations have incorporated the reduction of digital carbon footprints as an integral component of their sustainability strategy. This sustainability strategy is aspired by the ambitious net-zero goals of governments globally, like "Industrial decarbonization strategy" in the UK or "net-zero emissions by 2050" in the US. Nevertheless, while the spotlight is increasingly on digital decarbonization, striking a harmonious balance between minimizing carbon footprints and utilizing the strength of technological advancement remains a substantial challenge for organizations.

Given this, there arises a pressing need to optimize KMS, namely sustainable KMS. Such systems can help organizations navigate the complexities of modern-day challenges, enabling them to make informed decisions that respect both environmental sustainability and technological progression. By integrating environmental considerations into knowledge management practices, organizations can develop a roadmap that guides their digital transformations in a way that aligns with sustainability goals. This approach not only helps in achieving operational efficiencies but also positions organizations as responsible stewards of the environment in the eyes of stakeholders and the wider community.

### 2.2.3  Sustainable KMS Embracing Dark Data

The ecological standpoint gained the insight into the paramount necessity of building sustainable KMS. Within the realm of industrial maintenance, a vast number of datasets—predominantly those in natural language form—are notably sparse, often missing numerous data points, which is categorized as "dark data" according to the definition. To the best of our knowledge, there was no research on constructing KMS to utilize dark data and model the relationships between dark data.

To develop a KMS leveraging such dark data, the primary step is data enrichment. The raw data, once considered inadequate or unrefined, undergoes a transformation process. Initially, the enriched data is converted into valuable and meaningful information. This information is then synthesized and channeled into actionable knowledge. Such knowledge is not just a random assortment; it is systematically organized, interconnected, and made easily accessible to users [32].

Furthermore, a KMS designed using dark data not only maximizes the utility of existing knowledge but also promotes its effective reuse. By doing so, it diminishes the prevalence of dark data. This approach not only streamlines the knowledge management process but also serves as an environmentally conscious and sustainable strategy. In the longer run, organizations can benefit immensely from such systems by ensuring that every piece of data, no matter how trivial it might seem initially, contributes to informed decision-making and optimal operations.

## 3  Research Methods

This paper aims to develop a sustainable decision-support KMS by utilizing dark datasets, with a specific focus on enhancing industrial maintenance processes. To achieve the research objectives, a case study at AM a global automotive manufacturing company was conducted. The real-world investigation not only sheds light on the challenges and opportunities in processing sparse maintenance texts but also serves a practical model to address similar issues encountered by other industries. Furthermore, our research paves the way for constructing a comprehensive framework tailored to converting dark data into information and knowledge.

### 3.1  Overall System Framework

The overall system framework for this research is shown as Fig. 1. The process initiates with the data ingestion phase, where raw data is meticulously gathered and organized.

Given the incompleteness and sparsity of maintenance text data, very little meaningful information can be obtained by direct knowledge extraction. As a result, the primary focus is to enrich these data. Efforts were made to manually scrape missing data from the web and integrate it with the existing maintenance text data. Here, additional information is also incorporated based on human understanding. Once the data undergoes through pre-processing, knowledge extraction will be performed revolving bestowing meaning and upon the data and weaving connections among these data. Subsequently, a knowledge graph (KG) will be built to construct the KMS. Employing this approach, the KMS harnesses collective knowledge from multiple sources after integrating information from dark data, not only empowering maintenance technicians with valuable insights and solutions for maintenance problems, and saving time and costs simultaneously.

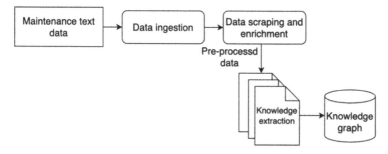

**Fig. 1.** Overall system framework.

In this case study conducted at AM, the focus was on critical components within the car assembly line, specifically the table lifters. The primary objective of this study was two-fold: firstly, to integrate maintenance text data and extract hidden information from the reports which has become "dark data"; and secondly, to establish relationships among all the collected information, ultimately leading to a more sustainable KMS. Recognizing the potential of KG method as a powerful tool for effectively integrating maintenance data and extracting valuable insights, this study embarked on creating a Fault KG specific to the operation and maintenance of table lifters. The goal was to structure and organize this knowledge effectively. The KMS leveraged the structured knowledge within the KG to provide solutions to various maintenance problems.

## 3.2 Data Ingestion

Data ingestion serves as the first step of the proposed framework. Data ingestion pertains to the transformation of raw data into reusable information. Such raw data usually originate from heterogeneous sources and vary in different sizes and formats [33].

Table 1 illustrates the maintenance textual datasets related to the AM table lifter components, providing essential information crucial for this study. These datasets encompass various aspects, including table lifter logic, maintenance plans, fault history, and maintenance reports. These reports were generated after the car production line had stopped due to a faulty manufacturing component. After their creation these reports were used once or never at all, putting them into the category of dark data.

It is important to note that, like many datasets in manufacturing companies, the maintenance text data suffer from a significant amount of missing information. Additionally, the fault history records are relatively sparse, which presents challenges in capturing useful insights for this study.

**Table 1.** Maintenance textual datasets.

| Table lifter maintenance data | Information contained | Data formats |
| --- | --- | --- |
| AM table lifter logic | Running process of table lifters | Images and videos |
| Maintenance plan | Components (physical level) on assembly lines and maintenance information | Tables |
| Fault history | Fault details, causes and actions | Excel spreadsheet |
| Maintenance reports | Fault details, causes and actions | PowerPoints or files |

### 3.3 Data Scraping and Data Enrichment

As previously mentioned, dealing with incomplete and sparsely populated maintenance datasets presents challenges when attempting to extract valuable insights. To overcome these limitations, a data scraping process was initiated to enhance the maintenance records, with a primary focus on the fault history records. Within these records, there are a total of 236 entries, but 78 of these entries lack information regarding failure descriptions and failure actions. Thus, the need for data scraping and enrichment becomes imperative.

The data enrichment process began by extracting keywords from each entry to guide the scraping effort. Expanding datasets using these keywords enhances knowledge accumulation, strengthening the Fault Knowledge Graph (Fault KG). Missing information was generated using these keywords and ethically searched for on the web. External data were integrated with existing maintenance text, and additional details were added based on human expertise to ensure dataset comprehensiveness and accuracy.

### 3.4 Data Integration and Knowledge Extraction

After data scraping, the critical step involved integrating data and extracting knowledge to form a Knowledge Management System (KMS). Data integration, a complex process prone to inconsistencies, can impact accuracy. Natural Language Processing (NLP) techniques help address this, normalizing textual variations like capitalizations and abbreviations.

Knowledge Graphs (KGs) are essential for industrial maintenance, unlocking latent potential and guiding decision-making. Figure 2 illustrates the process of transforming raw data into valuable insights using KGs, starting with attributing significance to data. The resulting knowledge structure, comprising entities and relations, facilitates insightful analysis and informed decision-making, showcasing the core functionality of KMS in extracting actionable insights from complex datasets.

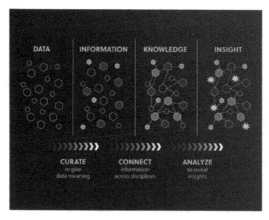

**Fig. 2.** Transforming raw data into valuable insights through the utilization of KGs [32].

## 3.5 KG Construction

While automated KG construction methods have demonstrated their effectiveness, the importance of ensuring accuracy and reliability has been recognized due to the presence of dark data, promoting us to adopt a manual approach for the initial KG construction. The procedure of constructing KG is illustrated in Fig. 3.

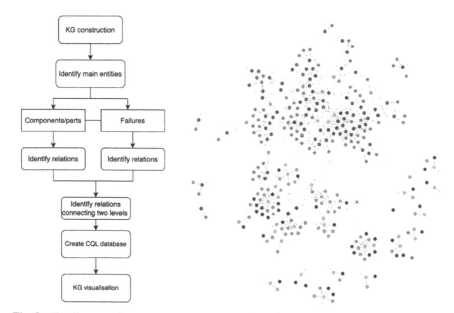

**Fig. 3.** The diagram of constructing KG.

**Fig. 4.** An overview of KG.

To begin the KG construction process, the first step involves identifying entities and relations. Considering the available data sources, the fault KG can be structured into two levels: the physical level and the failure level. Accordingly, two fundamental categories of entities emerge: the components or parts of table lifters and the failures that have occurred over the past years. Specifically, the failure level encompasses fault causes, potential solutions, and other fault details.

Next, we identify relations based on these two levels. At the components/parts level, several relations are established, such as "location", "check criteria", "check content", "use", "category", "assembled part" and more. These relations can be connected to other entities within the KG. Similarly, at the failure level, relations such as "failure description", "possible causes", "action", and "related failure" are confirmed.

Furthermore, we identify relations that connect the physical level and the failure level, which are crucial for capturing important insights in the KG. These connections are established through the "checked parts" relation. Additionally, to further enhance the connectivity of entities, we create a few special relations. Enriched datasets were utilized to construct the KG by selecting information from both the physical level and the failure level. To achieve the construction of the KG, we create CQL sentences, enabling us to represent and organize the entities and relations effectively.

A total of 213 CQL sentences were created to construct the source database for KG. Leveraging the Neo4j platform, a graph database service, we successfully visualized the fault KG. By using Python to interact with Neo4j, the CQL source database was effectively transformed into a comprehensive KG, consisting of 491 nodes and 684 relationships (a total of 18 different types of relationships). An overview of KG was shown in Fig. 4. This KG can be regarded as a KMS that links crucial knowledge such as components/parts, failures, failure causes, and potential solutions. It enables organizations to retrieve relevant knowledge, guides decision-making analysis, and promotes knowledge reuse.

## 4 Conclusion

This study addresses the critical challenge of dark data within the manufacturing sector, particularly in the context of industrial maintenance. Leveraging the power of Knowledge Management Systems (KMS) and Knowledge Graphs (KG), we proposed a sustainable framework to process and extract valuable insights from incomplete and sparse maintenance text datasets. Our research contributes to the existing knowledge by introducing a comprehensive approach to handling dark data and we demonstrated the practical application of our proposed framework, shedding light on the challenges and opportunities associated with processing sparse maintenance texts.

The integration of data scraping and enrichment techniques, combined with human knowledge, enabled us to construct a Fault KG that captures both the physical and failure levels of critical components, such as table lifters. This KG, forming the foundation of our KMS, facilitates the organization and accessibility of knowledge, offering solutions to maintenance problems and empowering technicians with valuable insights.

Furthermore, our study highlights the potential environmental benefits of sustainable KMS. By effectively utilizing dark data, organizations can reduce their digital carbon footprint, aligning with global sustainability goals. The integration of environmental considerations into knowledge management practices provides a pathway for organizations to navigate the complexities of modern challenges while demonstrating responsible stewardship of the environment.

In conclusion, our research not only addresses the research gap regarding dark data in manufacturing but also provides a practical framework for organizations to enhance decision-making in industrial maintenance processes. The proposed sustainable KMS framework, grounded in the effective utilization of dark data, offers a valuable contribution to the intersection of knowledge management, digital transformation, and environmental sustainability. Future research directions may include testing and validating the constructed KMS and exploring broader applications of this framework on diverse industries facing similar challenges associated with dark data.

# References

1. Parviainen, P., Tihinen, M., Kääriäinen, J., Teppola, S.: Tackling the digitalization challenge: how to benefit from digitalization in practice. Int. J. Inf. Syst. Proj. Manag. **5**, 63–77 (2022)
2. Legner, C., et al.: Digitalization: opportunity and challenge for the business and information systems engineering community. Bus. Inf. Syst. Eng. **59**, 301–308 (2017)
3. Jackson, T.W., Hodgkinson, I.R.: Keeping a lower profile: how firms can reduce their digital carbon footprints. J. Bus. Strateg. **44**, 363–370 (2023)
4. Statista. Data volume of internet of things (IoT) connections worldwide in 2019 and 2025 (2020). https://www.statista.com/statistics/1017863/worldwide-iot-connected-devices-data-size/
5. Carvalho, T.P., et al.: A systematic literature review of machine learning methods applied to predictive maintenance. Comput. Ind. Eng. **137**, 106024 (2019)
6. Dalenogare, L.S., Benitez, G.B., Ayala, N.F., Frank, A.G.: The expected contribution of Industry 4.0 technologies for industrial performance. Int. J. Prod. Econ. **204**, 383–394 (2018)
7. Bai, C., Sarkis, J.: Improving green flexibility through advanced manufacturing technology investment: modeling the decision process. Int. J. Prod. Econ. **188**, 86–104 (2017)
8. Bai, C., Dallasega, P., Orzes, G., Sarkis, J.: Industry 4.0 technologies assessment: a sustainability perspective. Int. J. Prod. Econ. **229**, 107776 (2020)
9. Di Vaio, A., Palladino, R., Pezzi, A., Kalisz, D.E.: The role of digital innovation in knowledge management systems: a systematic literature review. J. Bus. Res. **123**, 220–231 (2021)
10. Cabeza-Pullés, D., Fernández-Pérez, V., Roldán-Bravo, M.I.: Internal networking and innovation ambidexterity: the mediating role of knowledge management processes in university research. Eur. Manag. J. **38**, 450–461 (2020)
11. Azad, P., Navimipour, N.J., Rahmani, A.M., Sharifi, A.: The role of structured and unstructured data managing mechanisms in the Internet of things. Cluster Comput. **23**, 1185–1198 (2020)
12. Ghanbari, Z., Jafari Navimipour, N., Hosseinzadeh, M., Darwesh, A.: Resource allocation mechanisms and approaches on the Internet of Things. Cluster Comput. **22**, 1253–1282 (2019)
13. Abubakar, A.M., Elrehail, H., Alatailat, M.A., Elçi, A.: Knowledge management, decision-making style and organizational performance. J. Innov. Knowl. **4**, 104–114 (2019)
14. Zmicier, V., McCreesh, J., Farbstein, E.: How manufacturers can reduce carbon emissions. Normative (2023)
15. Mehmood, S., Zaman, K., Khan, S., Ali, Z., Khan, H.U.R.: The role of green industrial transformation in mitigating carbon emissions: exploring the channels of technological innovation and environmental regulation. Energy Built Environ. **5**, 464–479 (2024)

16. Li, L., Lei, B., Mao, C.: Digital twin in smart manufacturing. J. Ind. Inf. Integr. **26**, 100289 (2022)
17. Ghobakhloo, M.: Industry 4.0, digitization, and opportunities for sustainability. J. Clean Prod. **252**, 119869 (2020)
18. Sharma, P., Dash, B.: The digital carbon footprint: threat to an environmentally sustainable future. Int. J. Comput. Sci. Inf. Technol. **14**, 19–29 (2022)
19. Jeschke, S., Brecher, C., Meisen, T., Özdemir, D., Eschert, T.: Industrial internet of things and cyber manufacturing systems. In: Jeschke, S., Brecher, C., Song, H., Rawat, D.B. (eds.) Industrial Internet of Things. SSWT, pp. 3–19. Springer, Cham (2017). https://doi.org/10.1007/978-3-319-42559-7_1
20. Brettel, M., Friederichsen, N., Keller, M., Rosenberg, M.: How virtualization, decentralization and network building change the manufacturing landscape: an industry 4.0 perspective. Int. J. Mech. Ind. Aerosp. Sci. **8** (2014)
21. Corallo, A., Crespino, A.M., Vecchio, V.D., Lazoi, M., Marra, M.: Understanding and defining dark data for the manufacturing industry. IEEE Trans. Eng. Manag. **70**, 700–712 (2023)
22. Hopkinton, M.: Digital Universe Invaded By Sensors (2014). https://www.dell.com/en-us/dt/corporate/newsroom/announcements/2014/04/20140409-01.htm
23. Gartner. Dark Data (2022). https://www.gartner.com/en/information-technology/glossary/dark-data
24. Munot, K., Mehta, N., Mishra, S., Khanna, B.: Importance of dark data and its applications. In: 2019 IEEE International Conference on System, Computation, Automation and Networking (ICSCAN), pp. 1–6. IEEE (2019). https://doi.org/10.1109/ICSCAN.2019.8878789
25. Al Ahbabi, S.A., Singh, S.K., Balasubramanian, S., Gaur, S.S.: Employee perception of impact of knowledge management processes on public sector performance. J. Knowl. Manag. **23**, 351–373 (2019)
26. Al Saifi, S.A.: Positioning organisational culture in knowledge management research. J. Knowl. Manag. **19**, 164–189 (2015)
27. Hussinki, H., Kianto, A., Vanhala, M., Ritala, P.: Assessing the universality of knowledge management practices. J. Knowl. Manag. **21**, 1596–1621 (2017)
28. Martins, V.W.B., Rampasso, I.S., Anholon, R., Quelhas, O.L.G., Leal Filho, W.: Knowledge management in the context of sustainability: literature review and opportunities for future research. J. Clean Prod. **229**, 489–500 (2019)
29. Nisar, T.M., Prabhakar, G., Strakova, L.: Social media information benefits, knowledge management and smart organizations. J. Bus. Res. **94**, 264–272 (2019)
30. Alavi, M., Leidner, D.: Knowledge management systems: issues, challenges, and benefits. Commun. Assoc. Inf. Syst. **1** (1999)
31. Workfavor (2022). https://blog.worldfavor.com/the-growing-carbon-footprint-of-digitalization-and-how-to-control-it
32. Jennifer, S.: Dark data in R&D: how knowledge management can uncover hidden value (2022). https://www.cas.org/resources/cas-insights/digital/dark-data-knowledge-management
33. Yu, W., Dillon, T., Mostafa, F., Rahayu, W., Liu, Y.: A global manufacturing big data ecosystem for fault detection in predictive maintenance. IEEE Trans. Ind. Inform. **16**, 183–192 (2020)

# Product-Service System for the Foundry Sector

Mariusz Salwin[1]([✉]) [iD], Dominika Strycharska[2] [iD], and Andrzej Kraslawski[3] [iD]

[1] Faculty of Mechanical and Industrial Engineering, Warsaw University of Technology, 85 Narbutta Street, Warsaw, Poland
mariusz.salwin@onet.pl

[2] Department of Production Management, Faculty of Production Engineering and Materials Technology, Czestochowa University of Technology, 19 Aleja Armii Krajowej, Czestochowa, Poland

[3] School of Engineering Science, Industrial Engineering and Management (IEM), LUT University, Lappeenranta, Finland

**Abstract.** Product-Service System (PSS) is a concept that combines products and services that aim to satisfy specific customer needs. This is an approach that helps build a competitive advantage for enterprises and supports sustainable development. In the area of PSS design and industrial practice, there are no examples of the application of this concept in the foundry sector. This paper aims to create a conceptual PSS model for the foundry sector. This example was developed based on workshops conducted in a company specializing in the production of fittings. By developing a conceptual PSS model that is based on the actual problems, needs and service expectations of the enterprise, we intend to draw attention to many important issues. The developed PSS model provides foundries with tools in the form of services that are aimed at solving production problems, increasing production efficiency, minimizing the negative impact of printing activities on the environment and extending the life cycle of the machine.

**Keywords:** Product-Service System · Product-Service System Design · Foundry Sector

## 1 Introduction

Changes in the structure of the economy, which lead to manufacturing companies moving away from exclusive production to offering products enriched with services, constitute a significant evolution [1–4]. This process is closely related to the global trend of the growing share of the service sector in national economies. In 2021, the services sector accounted for an impressive share of global GDP, amounting to over 64.43%. In a service-based economy, a key role is played by meeting the individual needs of customers, who are less and less interested in purchasing or owning a product and more focused on the benefits and opportunities that the product can provide [5]. These changes have a significant impact on the area of Product-Service System (PSS) research, which reflects the new economic reality [6–8].

© The Author(s), under exclusive license to Springer Nature Switzerland AG 2024
L. Uden and I.-H. Ting (Eds.): KMO 2024, CCIS 2152, pp. 275–291, 2024.
https://doi.org/10.1007/978-3-031-63269-3_21

PSS comes from Scandinavia [1, 9]. This is an important approach that responds to changes in today's industry, which is evolving from traditional production towards a more integrated model combining products and services [10, 11]. PSS contributes to optimizing the use of resources, reducing costs and increasing the competitiveness of enterprises [12]. Moreover, it allows us to provide customers with more comprehensive and personalized solutions, which promotes sustainable development and customer satisfaction [13–17].

Environmental protection is an extremely important issue for the foundry sector. Casting processes often require large amounts of energy and raw materials, which can generate greenhouse gas emissions and other pollutants. That's why foundries are increasingly focusing on sustainable production practices and responsible waste management. Environmental protection is becoming not only an obligation, but also an opportunity to create more nature-friendly and effective solutions in this sector [18–21].

A unique feature of foundry products is their ability to take on various shapes and forms depending on the customer's needs and specifications and the ability to choose different materials for the production of castings. The casting process allows you to create parts with complex shapes that often would not be possible to obtain using other manufacturing techniques. Therefore, castings are often used to produce parts with unusual shapes that fulfill specific functions in various industrial fields [18–21].

Foundry is a unique production sector that includes foundry services, machines, devices, raw materials and materials used in the production process. Throughout history, this industry has played an important role in the development of many other sectors and the scientific revolution, contributing to the emergence of a modern knowledge-based economy and its distribution. Over the years, foundry has undergone significant evolutions, and in the industrial era its development accelerated. In today's foundry, we distinguish several basic techniques and machines used in each of them [18–21].

The paper focuses on developing the PSS concept for foundry machines as an innovative approach to production and sales. The authors emphasize the numerous benefits of implementing PSS for both manufacturers and foundries. The transition from the traditional form of selling foundry machines to offering comprehensive service solutions that will adapt foundry machines to the individual needs of foundries appears to be a strategic element of the evolution of this industry. Additionally, PSS can significantly contribute to sustainable development by optimizing the use of resources and materials. The presented example was created as a result of workshops conducted in a manufacturing company and is part of research on the company's new offer.

The PSS model developed in the article brings a new quality to the foundry sector, bringing a number of innovations compared to traditional sales models. PSS is no longer just about selling the machine or product itself, but about providing comprehensive solutions based on products and services. This approach allows for the personalization of the offer, tailored to the individual needs of the client. Importantly, customers no longer have to invest significant funds in the purchase of machines or devices, but only pay for their use, which minimizes initial costs. Additionally, PSS promotes long-term cooperation, offering ongoing support, service, training and continuous process improvement. It is also a path towards sustainable development, enabling the reduction of the impact on the natural environment and the efficient use of resources. Therefore,

PSS is becoming an attractive and future-proof approach in the foundry sector, bringing benefits to both suppliers and customers.

The paper is structured as follows: the first part is the introduction. The next part presents the research methodology. The third part contains the literature analysis. The next part presents the results. The last part is the conclusions.

## 2  Research Methodology

This paper aims to create a Product-Service System (PSS) model dedicated to the foundry sector. This article posed two main research questions:

- Are there any possibilities of using PSS in the foundry sector?
- What specific benefits can the use of the PSS model bring to manufacturers of foundry machines, their users and the natural environment?

The analyzes conducted in the article provide a number of suggestions for the implementation of PSS in the foundry sector. These solutions aim to increase production efficiency and at the same time reduce the impact on the natural environment. The article presents the potential of implementing the PSS model in the foundry industry and explains the specific benefits that may result from it both for foundry machines, their users and the natural environment.

The methodology adopted in this article includes several research stages:

1. Literature review: In the first stage, a systematic literature review was conducted using renowned scientific databases such as Science Direct, Springer Link, Scopus, Web of Science, Informs PubsOnLine, JSTOR and others. The term "Product-Service System in industry" and its synonyms were searched. The time range covered the years 2000–2022, and the language of publication was English. The result of this step was the finding of 150 works related to PSS in the context of various industrial sectors. In parallel, an analysis of available PSS design methods was carried out. The term "Product-Service System design" and its equivalents were searched in the same databases and in the same years (2000–2022). As a result, 70 different PSS design methods were found in 74 scientific papers.
2. Analysis of the foundry industry. This stage was based on the analysis of foundry machine manufacturers and their users. This stage of the research was based on industry reports.
3. Industrial workshops - The workshop on the development of PSS for foundry machines was conducted as a multi-stage process in which various stakeholder groups participated. They were attended by representatives of the machine manufacturer, employees of a company specializing in the production of fittings and academic experts. The workshops took place as follows:

- The study of a company specializing in the production of fittings - included the analysis of problems and needs related to the foundry machine and the identification of needs for additional services. In order to identify the main problems generating significant losses and costs for the company, Pareto-Lorentz analysis was used.

- The next stage was to conduct a brainstorming session during which the company's main service needs were identified. Based on these findings, a survey questionnaire was created, which included proposals for services to solve problems and meet the company's needs. The services in the questionnaire were divided into 6 categories. From each category, the company's employees chose those that they considered the most important from their perspective.
- Construction of the PSS model - based on the analysis of literature, the foundry industry and the results of research conducted in the company, a PSS model dedicated to foundry machines was created. The new PSS model includes services that showed the greatest interest and were at the same time most beneficial from the enterprise's perspective.

This comprehensive methodology allowed for the collection of a wide range of information regarding PSS, the foundry sector, and the problems and needs of machine users, which formed the basis for the PSS developed in the paper.

## 3   Literature Review

### 3.1   Product-Service System Design Methods and Product-Service System in Industrial Practice

The literature reviewed provides many examples of case studies in which various PSS design methods have been used in real life [22–24]. Not all of these methods were strictly assigned to specific industries. Therefore, in this study we assigned specific methods to appropriate economic sectors (Fig. 1).

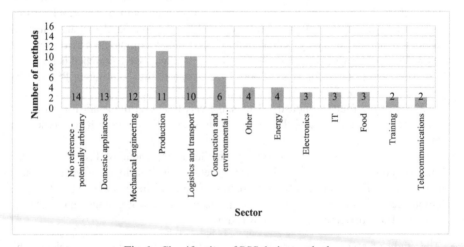

**Fig. 1.** Classification of PSS design methods.

It is worth noting that some of these methods are intended for different industries. The largest share, i.e. 14 methods, are not strictly assigned to any specific industry, which suggests their universality and potential for use in various sectors of the economy. Nevertheless, as many as 13 PSS design methods are addressed to the domestic appliances, consumer electronics and other equipment sectors, and 12 to the mechanical engineering sector. An interesting observation is the lack of PSS design methods dedicated to foundry available in the literature.

The next stage of the literature analysis was the analysis of industrial PSS cases. Key examples include: Rolls-Royce TotalCare, Caterpillar Cat® Connect, GE Power Digital, Siemens Healthineers, Schneider Electric EcoStruxure, IBM Watson IoT, ABB Ability™, Komatsu Smart Construction, FANUC FIELD system and John Deere Precision Ag. The tested PSS models were born in renowned companies and are adapted to various industry sectors. It is also worth noting that they are characterized by high value, advanced technology and a long life cycle. It is worth emphasizing that among the analyzed PSS models we did not find a solution dedicated to foundry.

### 3.2  Foundry Industry

The foundry sector is of key importance for many industries. It supplies essential components and products that are used in the production of various consumer and industrial goods. A unique feature of foundry products is their ability to take on various shapes and forms depending on the customer's needs and specifications and the ability to choose different materials for the production of castings. The casting process allows you to create parts with complex shapes that would often be impossible to obtain using other manufacturing techniques. Therefore, castings are often used to produce parts with unusual shapes that fulfill specific functions in various industrial fields [18–21] (Figs. 2 and 3).

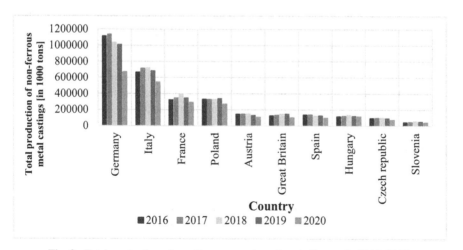

**Fig. 2.** Total production of non-ferrous metal castings in Europe in 2016–2020.

The most important foundry markets in the world include China, the USA, India and the countries of the European Union. In Europe, the industry is a significant source of employment and has a rich history. This sector is strongly linked to other industries [18].

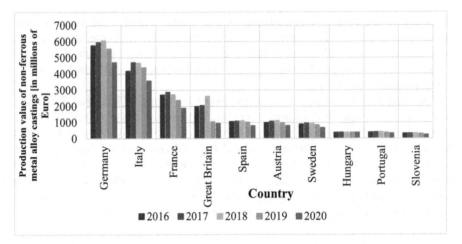

**Fig. 3.** Value of production of castings from non-ferrous metal alloys in Europe in 2016–2020.

In the European Union countries in 2020, the value of production of castings from non-ferrous metal alloys [in millions of euros] amounted to 16,017.1 million euros, and the total production of castings from non-ferrous metals [in 1,000 tons] amounted to 5,751,764. At that time, there were 2,320 foundries employing 113,026 people [18].

The sector of machinery used in foundry is a key industry branch that provides the necessary equipment for the processes of casting metals and other materials. They are characterized by durability, advanced technologies and a long life cycle. There are induction furnaces, metal melting furnaces, foundry molds, die casting machines, foundry presses and industrial robots. They are often equipped with automation systems, which increases the efficiency and precision of casting processes. Occupational safety and process optimization are other key aspects of this sector, taking into account the risks associated with working at high temperatures and heavy materials.

Currently, the main manufacturers (including IMR, Bühler, DISA, Frech) offer on the market various types of casting machines in various versions of equipment along with standard services (i.e. training, installation, maintenance).

## 4    Results

### 4.1    Characteristics of the Analyzed Company

The analyzed company specializes in the production of high-quality, innovative sanitary fittings for households and public buildings. The company has over a century of experience in providing safe, convenient and sustainable water access solutions. Since its establishment, it has focused on high-quality products that present user-friendly technical solutions that contribute to water and energy savings.

Currently, the company is a powerful European supplier of sanitary fittings. It has three production plants employing approximately 1,400 people. The production of fittings is based on low pressure die casting. The analyzed company uses fully electric

IMR BPC155 E foundry machines. The company's mission is to make the use of water easy and ecological, and its vision is to become the European leader in advanced sanitary fittings.

## 4.2  Company Problems and Needs

### Company Problems

As mentioned earlier, the company enjoys an established position on the market. Nevertheless, it still faces various challenges. In the analyzed case, Pareto-Lorentz analysis was applied to identify these challenges (Fig. 4). Although the company systematically takes steps to reduce them, they still generate significant costs for the company. In 2022, the key issues included: difficulties in machine calibration, complex foundry process settings, frequent mechanical and electrical failures, problems with precise machine setup, difficulties in diagnosing and locating faults, complexity of replacing worn or damaged parts, time-consuming commissioning and process testing processes. All the above-mentioned factors are interconnected and contribute to financial losses for the company.

In the analyzed company, the greatest losses are caused by: difficulties in calibrating machines, complicated settings of the foundry process, frequent mechanical and electrical failures, problems with precise machine setting, difficulties in diagnosing and locating faults. Together they constitute 80.00%. Therefore, the company should focus on solving these problems, because by eliminating them, it can significantly improve efficiency, reduce costs and increase production quality.

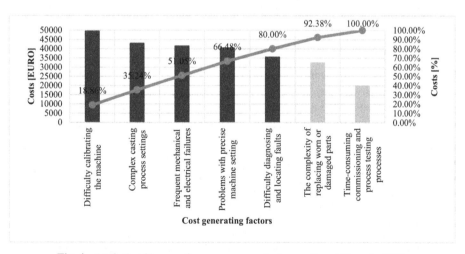

**Fig. 4.** Analysis of losses of a company producing sanitary fittings in 2022.

**Company Needs**

The workshops led to the identification of the main needs related to the following areas:

- Training - retraining of employees operating the machines is required in connection with the purchase, modernization or extension of options and tools available on the machine.
- Low-pressure casting process - selection of appropriate proportions of raw materials (brass, graphite, zinc, water), analysis and selection of optimal process parameters (average sand fraction, shot time, sintering time, sintering temperature, cleaning of equipment, precise settings of machines and tools, monitoring and control quality, elimination of deficiencies, appropriate molds.
- Operation and service - parts replacement and repair are not instantaneous, so the company may need technical support and service to ensure adequate resources to handle calls and repairs. Constant access to spare parts is also necessary to quickly repair or replace damaged elements.
- Die molds – design, manufacturing, gating systems, maintenance, storage.
- Sustainable development - focus on activities aimed at reducing the impact on the environment, more ecological production, analysis of access to solutions and technologies that increase energy efficiency and reduce the impact on the environment, waste management - the low-pressure casting process may generate waste that must be properly processed and disposed of.

The above factors significantly reduce the efficiency of the machine, which ultimately leads to financial losses. Additionally, they are associated with an environmental burden related to unnecessary consumption of energy and water, as well as the lack of waste and the need to dispose of waste that does not meet quality standards.

### 4.3 The Service Needs of the Company

In the next stage of the workshops, proposals for services within the PSS model for foundry machines were developed. These services were created in response to specific problems and needs of the analyzed enterprise, ensuring that the new PSS model will meet the expectations set by the company. The proposed services are divided into groups:

- Low pressure foundry machine services
- Low pressure die casting services
- Services related to the low-pressure casting process
- Quality management
- Sustainable development
- Additional services

Then the company's management board, middle management, foremen and employees of production and other departments of the company had the opportunity to choose from among the services of each group those that they considered the most important from their perspective. Table 1 presents the results of this selection for the most relevant services in each of these groups.

The implementation of these services into the PSS model is an effective solution to problems and meets the needs related to the low-pressure casting process, contributing to increasing the efficiency of the company. Thanks to this, the company can achieve higher production quality, strengthen its competitiveness on the market and increase the level of customer satisfaction.

**Table 1.** Services selected by employees of a company dealing in low-pressure casting of sanitary fittings with expandable areas.

| | Management board | Middle management | Production workers | Other workers |
|---|---|---|---|---|
| Low pressure casting machine services | Delivery, installation and commissioning of the machine | Machine monitoring and diagnostics | Machine operation training | Guarantee |
| | Machine update | Machine operation training | Diagnostics and troubleshooting | Spare parts delivery |
| | Software | Rent | Cleaning | Rent |
| | Spare parts delivery | Spare parts delivery | Software | Financial services |
| | Rent | Analysis of the causes of failure | Spare parts delivery | Software |
| Low-pressure die casting services | Planning of production and demand for molds | Engineering and design services | Installation of cores, cooling systems and other necessary elements | Engineering and design services |
| | Software and software training | Testing and validation | Analysis of the causes of failure | Data reporting and analysis |
| | Selection of materials to suit the requirements and specificity of the cast batch | Planning of production and demand for molds | Regeneration, renovation, repair, maintenance | Financial services |
| | Engineering and design services | Analysis of the causes of failure | Supply and maintenance of tools | Storage |
| | Execution | Software and software training | Storage | Strength analyses |
| Services related to the low-pressure casting process | Health and safety services | Foundry machine parameter settings | Changeover optimization | Risk management |

*(continued)*

**Table 1.** (*continued*)

|  | Management board | Middle management | Production workers | Other workers |
|---|---|---|---|---|
|  | Process automation and optimization | Preparing reports and analyzing production data | Design of arrangement of workstations | Optimization of production processes |
|  | Setting up the casting process | Production planning and coordination | Analysis of the causes of failure | Market and competition analysis |
|  | Technical consultancy | Changeover optimization | Health and safety services | Process improvement |
|  | Casting process analysis | Technical advice and support | Supervision of the casting process | Health and safety services |
| Quality management | Product quality control | Customer complaint management | Quality control training | Improving quality processes |
|  | Quality control of supplied raw materials | Qualitative data reporting and analysis | Quality control of the casting process | Supply of raw materials and materials |
|  | Adaptation to regulations and industry standards | Supply of raw materials and materials | Product quality control | Adaptation to regulations and industry standards |
|  | Laboratory tests and examinations | Product quality control | Monitoring the casting process | Monitoring the casting process |
|  | Quality certifications and accreditations | Laboratory tests and examinations | Quick response to quality incidents | Quality certifications and accreditations |
| Sustainable development | Waste management and recycling | Take-back | Waste management and recycling | Supply chain management |
|  | Adaptation to environmental regulations | Development of environmentally friendly products | Monitoring energy and raw material consumption | Energy management |
|  | Energetic audit | Implementation of sustainable production certificates | Implementation of sustainable production certificates | Legal and regulatory support |

(*continued*)

**Table 1.** (*continued*)

|  | Management board | Middle management | Production workers | Other workers |
|---|---|---|---|---|
|  | Environmental risk assessments | Monitoring energy and raw material consumption | Training | Consulting |
|  | Analysis of access to solutions and technologies increasing energy efficiency | Ecological evaluation of production processes | Analysis of access to solutions and technologies increasing energy efficiency | Monitoring emissions of harmful substances |
| Additional services | Maintenance of infrastructure and facilities | Inventory and materials management | Noise reduction | Operational cost management |
|  | Supply chain management | Security and normative compliance | Training in new technologies | Warehouse management |
|  | Financial services | Resource management | Diagnostics and troubleshooting | Consulting |
|  | Insurance | Technology and automation support | Engineering consulting | Legal and regulatory support |
|  | Training | OEE analysis and optimization | Training | Project management support |

At this stage, the company expressed its interest in renting a machine and services that would improve machine operation and the casting process. Additionally, the analyzed company showed greater interest in the monthly subscription fee for using the machine than in purchasing it.

### 4.4 Product-Service System for Foundry Sector

Using the PSS-based approach and the acquired knowledge regarding the problems and needs of the enterprise, the next stage of the workshops was the development of the PSS model. In the analyzed system, the key participants are the machine manufacturer and the customer. Within this model, the main components are a low-pressure casting machine and services that are of interest to a company producing high-quality, innovative sanitary fittings (Table 2).

The company specializing in the production of low-pressure casting machines provides these machines to customers, along with a complete package of services (Fig. 5, Table 3). The manufacturer charges a fee per hour of machine operation and a fixed

**Table 2.** Service bundles in Product-Service System for foundry sector.

| Service bundles | Basic Bundle of Services | Standard Bundle of Services | Extended Bundle of Services | Professional Bundle of Services | Advanced Bundle of Services |
|---|---|---|---|---|---|
| Machine | Delivery and installation | Machine operation training | Spare parts delivery | Machine update | Machine monitoring and diagnostics |
| | Guarantee | Cleaning | Software | Rent | Financial services |
| | Startup of the machine | Regeneration, renovation, repair, maintenance | Diagnostics and troubleshooting | Insurance | Analysis of the causes of failure |
| Casting die | Engineering and design services | Execution | Software | Software training | Data reporting and analysis |
| | Supply and maintenance of tools | Regeneration, renovation, repair, maintenance | Installation of cores, cooling systems and other necessary elements | Selection of materials to suit the requirements and specificity of the cast batch | Planning of production and demand for molds |
| | Storage | Strength analyses | Testing and validation | Financial services | Analysis of the causes of failure |
| Process | Setting up the casting process | Technical advice and support | Process automation and optimization | OEE analysis and optimization | Preparing reports and analyzing production data |
| | Health and safety services | Changeover optimization | Supervision of the casting process | Optimization and improvement of production processes | Simulations and analyzes of the casting process |
| | Noise reduction | Training in the casting process | Technology and automation support | Monitoring the casting process | Production planning and coordination |
| Quality | Supply of raw materials and materials | Product quality control | Adaptation to regulations and industry standards | Quality control of the casting process | Quality certifications and accreditations |
| | Quality control of supplied raw materials | Customer complaint management | Laboratory tests and examinations | Qualitative data reporting and analysis | Quick response to quality incidents |
| | Quality control training | Inventory and materials management | Supply chain management | Security and normative compliance | Improving quality processes |

*(continued)*

**Table 2.** (*continued*)

| Service bundles | Basic Bundle of Services | Standard Bundle of Services | Extended Bundle of Services | Professional Bundle of Services | Advanced Bundle of Services |
|---|---|---|---|---|---|
| Sustainable development | Take-back | Environmental risk assessments | Legal and regulatory support | Ecological evaluation of production processes | Development of environmentally friendly products |
| | Waste management and recycling | Monitoring energy and raw material consumption | Monitoring emissions of harmful substances | Implementation of sustainable production certificates | Analysis of access to solutions and technologies increasing energy efficiency |
| | Training | Energetic audit | Energy management | Adaptation to environmental regulations | Consulting |
| Additional services | Engineering consulting | Market and competition analysis | Financial services | Design of arrangement of workstations | Project management support |
| | Training in new technologies | Risk management | Insurance | Maintenance of infrastructure and facilities | Supply chain management |
| | Warehouse management | Resource management | Simulations | Operational cost management | Certificates and accreditations |

monthly subscription fee. It is worth noting that ownership rights to the machine remain with the manufacturer and are not transferred to the user. The customer's primary concern is using the low-pressure casting machine as many castings as possible, rather than owning, managing and maintaining it. After a certain period of use, the machine can be replaced with a new one.

An approach based on the PSS concept brings many benefits to all parties to the transaction. The client can focus on its core business, i.e. low-pressure casting and foundry development. He does not have to worry about service, repairs or spare parts of the machine. An additional advantage is avoiding the need to train employees and purchase specialized equipment needed for these activities, which saves time and resources. It is also important that in the event of a failure, the manufacturer is obliged to quickly repair the machine, because its interest depends on the continuous operation of the device. Thanks to this approach, the client can increase the number of orders processed and at the same time reduce its operating costs.

An additional advantage of PSS in the analyzed case may be the use of the Internet of Things (IoT). IoT in PSS for low-pressure casting machines and dies is an innovative approach. By placing advanced sensors on machines, we collect data on performance, temperature and energy consumption. This data is sent to a management system that

**Table 3.** Table captions should be placed above the tables.

| Ownership | The manufacturer is the owner | | | | |
|---|---|---|---|---|---|
| Sale | Subscription | Fee per hour worked | Fee for the cast made | | |
| Service bundles | Basic Bundle of Services | Standard Bundle of Services | Extended Bundle of Services | Professional Bundle of Services | Advanced Bundle of Services |
| Benefits for the customer | Focusing on core business | Savings on investment costs | Reduction of costs related to the gradual wear of machines | Optimizing performance and efficiency | Risk minimization |
| Benefits for the manufacturer | A permanent source of income | Recognition | Long-term relationships with customers, which translates into greater loyalty | Increasing competitiveness | Adjust machine parameters to the optimal level of operation |
| Environmental benefits | Less impact on the environment | Waste minimization | Extending the life cycle of the machine | Optimization of raw material consumption | Reduction of energy consumption |

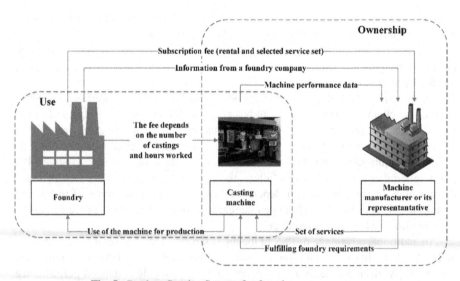

**Fig. 5.** Product-Service System for foundry sector - concept.

enables real-time monitoring and early failure detection. This allows you to plan maintenance and reduce downtime. Additionally, IoT enables remote control of machines and optimization of production processes in real time. All this leads to increased efficiency, cost reduction and increased product quality. For customers, this means minimized downtime and improved product quality. As a result, the company becomes more competitive and more environmentally friendly, saving energy and raw materials.

## 5  Discussion

PSS is a comprehensive solution that aims to satisfy the needs and requirements of customers. An important aspect of the research conducted on a global scale is the practical implementation of theoretical PSS concepts into industrial reality. In this paper, a design workshop on PSS was conducted, focusing on the foundry sector. As a result of these workshops, the main challenges and needs of a company using foundry machines were identified and a set of services was created that effectively meet them. The low-pressure casting machine, integrated with the actual needs of the enterprise, was incorporated into the comprehensive PSS system.

Based on the conducted design workshop, the following conclusions can be drawn:

- An important element is understanding the needs of users: the workshops allowed for a deeper understanding of their needs and priorities in terms of low-pressure foundry machines. Active participation of users allows for direct knowledge of their needs, priorities and expectations. It is crucial to deliver PSS solutions that truly meet customer needs.
- PSS design should take into account the flexibility of solutions to adapt to changing customer needs. Services must be grouped into baskets so that the customer can choose those that are necessary for him at a given moment of using the machine
- A subscription model can be an attractive option, allowing customers to use machines without a large upfront investment. It may be particularly attractive in conditions of high inflation and rising interest rates, which will prevent the inhibition of new investments among enterprises. Additionally, it eliminates fees related to the gradual wear and tear of machines.
- By properly tailoring services to users, solutions tailored to individual needs can be created, which allows for better optimization of production processes and increased machine efficiency.
- Services related to the casting process constitute a new offer for foundries that has not been available on the market before.
- Leaving ownership rights with the manufacturer allows him to constantly control the operation of the machine. In this way, the manufacturer is able to identify weak points and machine elements that can be improved in future generations.
- The developed PSS concept contributes to the optimization of raw material and energy consumption. By better managing machinery and production processes, it can help reduce the waste of raw materials, which in turn reduces the burden on natural resources. Services related to the energy efficiency of machines will help reduce electricity consumption, which is beneficial for the natural environment and leads to lower consumption of fossil fuels.

- A challenge for the manufacturer may be to create a service network that, in addition to direct contact, should be based on remote assistance.

Additionally, design workshops conducted in a foundry specializing in the production of high-quality fittings constitute a solid basis for the development and implementation of the PSS model for foundry machines. They clearly indicate what aspects you need to pay attention to and what elements you need to focus on when creating a PSS model fully tailored to the client's needs.

# References

1. Goedkoop, M., van Haler, C., te Riele, H., Rommers, P.: Product Service-Systems, Ecological and Economic Basics (1999)
2. Morelli, N.: Designing product/service systems: a methodological exploration. Des. Issues **18**, 3–17 (2002). https://doi.org/10.1162/074793602320223253
3. Musial, D., Szwaja, M., Kurtyka, M., Szwaja, S.: Usage of converter gas as a substitute fuel for a tunnel furnace in steelworks. Materials **15**, 5054 (2022). https://doi.org/10.3390/ma1 5145054
4. Bala-Litwiniak, A., Musiał, D., Nabiałczyk, M.: Computational and experimental studies on combustion and co-combustion of wood pellets with waste glycerol. Materials **16**, 7156 (2023). https://doi.org/10.3390/ma16227156
5. Statista: Distribution of gross domestic product (GDP) across economic sectors worldwide from 2007 to 2018, Distribution of gross domestic product (GDP) across economic sectors worldwide
6. Mont, O.K.: Clarifying the concept of product–service system. J. Clean. Prod. **10**, 237–245 (2002). https://doi.org/10.1016/S0959-6526(01)00039-7
7. Manzini, E., Collina, L., Evans, S.: Solution Oriented Partnership, How to Design Industrialised Sustainable Solutions. Cranfield University, Place of Publication not Identified (2004)
8. Tischner, U., Ryan, C., Vezzoli, C.: Product-service systems. In: Crul, M.R.M., Diehl, J.C., Ryan, C. (eds.) Design for Sustainability: A Step-by-Step Approach, pp. 95–102. UNEP, DTIE, Sustainable Consumption and Production Branch. Delft University of Technology, Paris, Delft (2009)
9. Salwin, M., Gladysz, B., Santarek, K.: Technical product-service systems—A business opportunity for machine industry. In: Hamrol, A., Ciszak, O., Legutko, S., Jurczyk, M. (eds.) Advances in Manufacturing. LNME, pp. 269–278. Springer, Cham (2018). https://doi.org/10.1007/978-3-319-68619-6_26
10. Boucher, X., Medini, K., Fill, H.-G.: Product-service-system modeling method. In: Karagiannis, D., Mayr, H.C., Mylopoulos, J. (eds.) Domain-Specific Conceptual Modeling, pp. 455–482. Springer, Cham (2016). https://doi.org/10.1007/978-3-319-39417-6_21
11. Boukhris, A., Fritzsche, A., Möslein, K.: Co-creation in the early stage of product-service system development. Proc. CIRP **63**, 27–32 (2017). https://doi.org/10.1016/j.procir.2017.03.316
12. Aas, T.H., Breunig, K.J., Hellström, M.M., Hydle, K.M.: Organising development processes: the case of product–service systems. Int. J. Innov. Manag. 2350030 (2023). https://doi.org/10.1142/S1363919623500305
13. Salwin, M.: Design of Product-Service Systems in Printing Industry (2021). https://lutpub.lut.fi/bitstream/handle/10024/163257/Mariusz%20Salwin%20A4.pdf?sequence=1&isAllo wed=y

14. Andriankaja, H., Boucher, X., Medini, K.: A method to design integrated product-service systems based on the extended functional analysis approach. CIRP J. Manuf. Sci. Technol. **21**, 120–139 (2018). https://doi.org/10.1016/j.cirpj.2018.02.001
15. Tukker, A.: Eight types of product–service system: eight ways to sustainability? Experiences from SusProNet. Bus. Strat. Environ. **13**, 246–260 (2004). https://doi.org/10.1002/bse.414
16. Kopytowski, A., Świercz, R., Oniszczuk-Świercz, D., Zawora, J., Kuczak, J., Żrodowski, Ł: Effects of a new type of grinding wheel with multi-granular abrasive grains on surface topography properties after grinding of Inconel 625. Materials **16**, 716 (2023). https://doi.org/10.3390/ma16020716
17. Pałęga, M.: Application of the job safety analysis (JSA) method to assessment occupational risk at the workplace of the laser cutter operator. Manag. Prod. Eng. Rev. (2023). https://doi.org/10.24425/mper.2021.138529
18. Sobczak, J., Dudek, P.: Aktualny stan odlewnictwa na tle gospodarki światowej. Postcovidowe prognozy. Przegląd Odlewnictwa **71**, 602–615 (2021)
19. DeGarmo, E.P. (ed.): Materials and Processes in Manufacturing. Wiley, Hoboken (2003)
20. Beeley, P.R.: Foundry Technology. Butterworth Heinemann, Oxford, Boston (2001)
21. Campbell, J., Campbell, J., Campbell, J.: Castings Principles: The New Metallurgy of Cast Metals. Butterworth Heinemann, Burlington (2003)
22. Salwin, M., Lipiak, J., Kulesza, R.: Product-service system – a literature review. Res. Logist. Prod. **9**, 5–14 (2019). https://doi.org/10.21008/j.2083-4950.2019.9.1.1
23. Salwin, M., Jacyna-Gołda, I., Kraslawski, A., Waszkiewicz, A.E.: The use of business model canvas in the design and classification of product-service systems design methods. Sustainability **14**, 4283 (2022). https://doi.org/10.3390/su14074283
24. Salwin, M., Kraslawski, A., Lipiak, J.: State-of-the-art in product-service system design. In: Panuwatwanich, K., Ko, C.-H. (eds.) The 10th International Conference on Engineering, Project, and Production Management. LNME, pp. 645–658. Springer, Singapore (2020). https://doi.org/10.1007/978-981-15-1910-9_53

# The Design of AI-Enabled Experience-Based Knowledge Management System to Facilitate Knowing and Doing in Communities of Practice

Wen-Cheng Shen[iD] and Fu-Ren Lin[✉][iD]

Institute of Service Science, National Tsing Hua University, Hsinchu City, Taiwan 300,
Republic of China
{gildshen,frlin}@iss.nthu.edu.tw

**Abstract.** This research aims to propose an experience-based knowledge management (EBKMS) to facilitate knowledge activities in a community of practice (CoP). Based on the capabilities offered by conversational AI and a large language model (in general, called foundation models), the proposed EBKMS is equipped with natural language processing, understanding, and reasoning abilities to facilitate humans to communicate with their personal knowledge assistant (K-assistant) to interact with other members in their CoPs. We design the structure and operations of the EBKMS to elaborate on how they can fulfill the SECI process by integrating human and AI. The proposed framework will be developed and tested in a real-world CoP for practitioners mainly from small and medium-sized enterprises (SMEs) to update their practices and enable them to cooperate for problem-solving to enhance their resilience in facing unanticipated but urgent challenges for their sustainability. This research lays a foundation for developing conversational AI-enabled knowledge management systems to enhance human and AI collaboration.

**Keywords:** Experience-Based Knowledge Management System (EBKMS) ·
Conversational AI · Community of Practice (CoP) · Knowledge Management
(KM) · Foundation Models

## 1 Introduction

### 1.1 Research Background

Foundation Models like GPT-4, Gemini, and Mistral have significantly advanced, offering functionalities in language, vision, robotics, reasoning, creativity, deduction, interaction, and understanding philosophy [1, 2]. These advancements extend their roles to software development, literature, mathematics, and more, marking a transformative shift in organizational knowledge management [3]. This paradigm shift in AI technology enhances knowledge exchange performance, improving the conversion of tacit to explicit knowledge. AI's growth complements human intelligence (HI), fostering collaborative

© The Author(s), under exclusive license to Springer Nature Switzerland AG 2024
L. Uden and I.-H. Ting (Eds.): KMO 2024, CCIS 2152, pp. 292–303, 2024.
https://doi.org/10.1007/978-3-031-63269-3_22

intelligence [4, 5]. However, the research on AI and HI collaboration in knowledge management is still emerging, leading to the study's first research question: "How can AI and HI effectively collaborate to advance knowledge management?" To answer our research question, we aim to develop a knowledge management system using Foundation Models to create an AI agent as a knowledge assistant, enhancing knowledge activities like extraction, transformation, distribution, and integration. We anticipate that natural language interaction between humans and AI-embedded knowledge assistants will significantly improve collaborative relationships in these activities. Prior research shows that foundation models can augment HI, enhancing human capabilities in various contexts. This leads to conceptualizing the AI agent as a "knowledge digital twin," representing a new paradigm in AI use. Our research explores the cooperative function of HI and AI as a unified "knowledge entity," reflecting a shift in AI application. These adaptable foundation models are expected to boost knowledge exchange performance, especially in converting tacit to explicit knowledge [1]. Therefore, the second research question in this study, we ask "How to design a system with a foundation model that aids humans in knowledge activities marking a significant advancement in knowledge management?" As AI becomes more integral to daily life, the idea of individually owned knowledge entities is increasingly plausible, where AI assists in knowledge co-creation with humans and among various entities. This trend could significantly impact knowledge generation and dissemination across domains. Adopting the Service-Dominant (S-D) Logic [6], we can term such a collaborative environment a "knowledge co-creation ecosystem." Our research aims to explore AI's role in assisting HI in accessing and synthesizing knowledge from various entities, particularly within social networks. We focus on how AI-HI collaboration within a CoP accelerates knowledge accumulation, organization, dissemination, and collaborative actions, and how knowledge sharing within a CoP enhances HI via AI, forming a cyclical process of knowledge enhancement. This represents a major shift in learning and doing in an AI-facilitated human knowledge network. Therefore, we ask the third research question, "How will AI facilitate knowledge co-creation in communities of practice that benefit humans?" We also consider how knowledge is transformed and disseminated through knowledge networks in a CoP, focusing on the collaborative knowledge management between AI and HI during the SECI process (socialization, externalization, combination, and internalization). With AI's evolving role, there's an opportunity to revisit and possibly update this model, especially after 30 years since its inception. We question if the SECI model will be renovated with the integration of AI agents in the knowledge creation process and which aspects of human knowledge creation cannot be replaced by AI [7]. This leads us to our fourth question: "In the era of AI, how will the SECI model be updated through the knowledge co-creation process between human and AI agent?" This question aims to explore the evolution of the SECI model in the dynamic context of an AI-enhanced knowledge management system.

## 1.2  Research Motivations

To address the research questions specified in Subsect. 1.1, we plan to develop a system that transforms human experience (tacit knowledge) into explicit knowledge. We refer to this system as the EBKMS. Concurrently, we aim to investigate a CoP that embodies the concept of knowledge co-creation. This CoP will apply EBKMS in various knowledge activities, including knowledge extraction, transformation, organization, transfer, integration, internalization, and execution. In doing so, we seek to echo the essence of Yangming's doctrine: "The inner knowledge and the exterior action as one". By bridging this philosophical concept with upfront IT technologies, this research strives to harness the potential of Foundation Models (e.g., Large Language Models, LLMs) and Knowledge Graphs (KGs), to synergistically integrate AI with HI. From the perspective of S-D Logic, the goal of this research is to propose a novel framework for the integration of HI and AI. This framework will evolve the SECI model from a human-to-human (H2H) interaction paradigm to a more Human-AI as a loop format. This new paradigm seeks to foster a community of practice facilitated by HI-AI knowledge co-creation agents, which we coin it a "HAI Community for Practice". To demonstrate the applicability of the EBKMS to a CoP, we intend to develop this HAI CoP concept to a CoP called the Academy of Resilience (AOR), which accommodates members mainly from SMEs in Taiwan, who are interested in exchanging their knowledge to innovate and strengthen their business capabilities.

## 2 Literature Review

### 2.1 Knowledge Management and SECI Model

Experience is recognized as tacit knowledge, a form integral to knowledge creation and management. Chinese philosopher Yangming Wang highlighted its significance with Wang's principle of "The inner knowledge and exterior action as one" influencing Asian scholarship. Polanyi labeled experience as tacit knowledge, vital for learning and skill acquisition [8]. It links to "Phronesis" or practical wisdom [9]. Teece et al.'s dynamic capabilities theory, emphasizing sensing, seizing, and transforming capabilities, underlines its importance for SMEs in adapting to changes, involving knowledge management and exploitation [10–13]. However, converting tacit knowledge to explicit form poses challenges, such as enigmatic knowledge diffusion, diverse communication modes, and the need for translating varied domain knowledge [14, 15]. The SECI Model, introduced by Nonaka in the 1990s, maps knowledge conversion into four modes: socialization, externalization, combination, and internalization. It was later refined to include dialectic thinking, viewing knowledge creation as a dialectical process [16]. This model represents a continuous, dynamic spiral of knowledge transformation and includes the concept of 'Ba' as a knowledge-creating space. It illustrates how organizational knowledge creation is a social and dynamic process [7, 17, 18].

### 2.2 Knowledge Networks in Organizations or Virtual Organizations

Lin and Lin's 2001 [19] study offers a comprehensive framework for knowledge management in organizations, particularly in virtual ones (VOs), using the SECI model. It proposes a model for learning in VOs, crucial for performance in the e-commerce era. Central to this model is the Transactive Memory System (TMS), featuring Knowledge

Maps, Social Networks, and Mnemonic Functions. A case study of a teachers' community illustrates TMS's role in knowledge sharing across school boundaries. Knowledge Maps are tools that identify, organize, and share organizational knowledge, aiding in understanding members' expertise and facilitating collaboration. Social Networks within organizations enhance information circulation, crucial in VOs for trust-building and cooperation among dispersed members. Mnemonic Functions help in recalling and applying knowledge, supporting individual and collective memory, especially with complex data. The VOL model underscores the importance of double-loop learning in TMS interactions, transitioning from single-loop learning, which alters behavior, to double-loop learning which revises methods, goals, or assumptions for deeper organizational changes. TMS in VOs accelerates learning, aiding in knowledge map development and adapting to changing team dynamics, fostering profound organizational transformation [19].

### 2.3 Service-Dominant (S-D) Logic, Service Innovation and AI

This research adopts Service-Dominant (S-D) Logic, developed by Vargo and Lusch, as its theoretical framework. S-D Logic shifts marketing from a goods-centric to a service-centric perspective, focusing on resource integration by actors for value creation and exchange. In this view, resources are tools for actors, extending the concept of exchange. Services are actions involving specialized competencies for mutual benefit, central to a service ecosystem. This ecosystem is described as a self-regulating network of actors, unified by shared institutional logic, engaging in collaborative value creation [6, 20]. Knowledge, initially a primary resource in S-D Logic, is now seen as both part of the institutional structure and an operant resource. In service ecosystems, innovation intermediaries are key, integrating resources from various actors into innovative solutions [21]. They act as agents or brokers in the innovation process, facilitating interactions between parties [22]. Their roles include knowledge brokers [23], matchmakers [24], and network orchestrators [25], bridging gaps and fostering innovation. AI emerges as an influential intermediary, enhancing information sharing, system integration, and knowledge exchange. It facilitates experiential learning and strengthens organizational capabilities in assimilating and utilizing external knowledge, acting as a "knowledge broker" to promote effective knowledge sharing among stakeholders and collaborative efforts within the ecosystem.

### 2.4 A Paradigm Shift on HI and AI with Foundation Models

The AI era is marked by advancements in LLMs, leading to a paradigm shift. Multimodal LLMs now offer enhanced functionality in various applications, mimicking human-like integration, and application of knowledge across diverse domains [26]. In this research, we use "foundation models" defined by Stanford's Center for Research on Foundation Models (CRFM). These models, trained on extensive data, can be adapted to a range of tasks [1]. Our research employs pivotal AI techniques, including Natural Language Processing (NLP), which processes user inputs for better understanding through data cleaning, feature extraction, and tokenization. Natural Language Understanding (NLU) focuses on intent identification and entity recognition. Natural Language Generation

(NLG) creates responses based on context and information retrieval [27]. Natural Language Reasoning (NLR) advances logical thinking and addresses hallucination issues in LLMs through fine-tuning and Chain of Thoughts (CoTs) methods [28, 29]. Data storage utilizes various databases, each tailored to specific data types, including traditional, graph, document, and vector databases. Retrieval Augmented Generation (RAG) and fine-tuning overcome LLMs' limitations, with RAG providing quick but variable-precision data access and fine-tuning offering specialized, domain-specific adaptation, although it requires more time and resources [30, 31]. Digital technologies, including AI, significantly enhance knowledge sharing in digital work environments, fostering "hybrid teams" of humans and AI [3, 32, 33]. Jarrahi et al. (2023) highlight AI's role in various KM aspects, from knowledge creation using predictive analytics to knowledge sharing and application, enhancing organizational learning and decision-making processes [4]. AI's evolving role in KM necessitates new perspectives for effective human-AI collaboration, augmenting rather than replacing human roles.

## 3   Research Methodology

Using the design science approach, this research aims to create an information system artifact that integrates HI and AI to support knowledge management in a CoP. We adopt the Action Design Research (ADR) approach, which combines action research and design science, to involve knowledge workers actively in developing the service ecosystem. ADR has proven effective in designing information and service systems [34, 35], with its evolutionary process and iterative cycle particularly suitable for creating a user-engaged, value co-created service ecosystem. The collaborative relationship between HI and AI and among actors in knowledge management practices justifies using ADR. We aim to shape a CoP through HI and AI integration for effective knowledge management, progressing through ADR stages. In the Diagnosis Stage, we'll identify engagement gaps among CoP knowledge workers, tackling issues like converting tacit to explicit knowledge and understanding members' motivations and barriers through interviews for EBKMS solutions. The Design Stage will focus on developing a service ecosystem tailored to knowledge exchange, involving knowledge workers, AI, and service blueprints, with iterative design and testing. The Implementation Stage includes deploying the EBKMS with AI technologies and ensuring continuous assessment and improvement for value co-creation. Finally, the Evolution Stage will adapt to user engagement, dynamically updating the EBKMS to enhance knowledge transformation and collaborative actions.

## 4   Knowledge Service Ecosystem Development

We're crafting a knowledge service ecosystem for CoP, underpinned by AI and the EBKMS, to transform tacit into explicit knowledge. Knowledge workers use K-assistants, embedded with NLU, for extracting experiences, sharing knowledge, and coordinating actions. These assistants, integrating human and artificial intelligence, manage a Transactive Memory System (TMS) and support learning processes. They are proficient in natural language processing, knowledge, and memory management.

EBKMS's tech includes LLMs, ontology engineering, and knowledge graphs, interfaced through tools like LINE Chatbot. Leveraging the LangChain framework, the development emphasizes dynamic adaptability, and stakeholder involvement, and incorporates both commercial and freemium services, ensuring privacy and task accuracy with RAG techniques. The TMS structure comprises user interfaces, NLP, knowledge management, and memory systems, all detailed in Fig. 1 and the following sections.

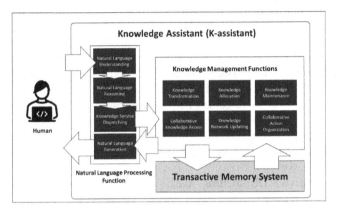

**Fig. 1.** Technical features of a K-assistant

## 4.1 Human User Interface

In our research, human users engage with Knowledge Assistants (K-assistants) through conversational AI, including chatbots and virtual agents for natural language dialogues, interpreting text, emoticons, and emojis to gauge user emotions [27]. These multimodal agents blend text and visuals for improved intent recognition. K-assistants handle diverse communication forms such as text, voice, photos, PDFs, and videos, enabling varied knowledge-sharing interactions. Their multimodal dialogue systems offer flexibility, reduce cognitive load, and enhance speech recognition error handling [36, 37]. Integrating Taiwan's popular LINE messaging service with K-assistants, this research utilizes the LINE API for seamless communication, allowing knowledge expression in various formats and ensuring a stable, low-maintenance communication platform.

## 4.2 Natural Language Processing Function

The development of the K-assistant's Natural Language Processing function encompasses Natural Language Understanding (NLU), Reasoning (NLR), and Generation (NLG) modules, each with specific roles as follows.

- **Natural Language Understanding (NLU):** NLU in conversational AI involves a series of processes starting with user input, which can be text, objects, or actions. This input is preprocessed to filter out irrelevant or insecure messages, ensuring relevance and security. The NLU module then interprets and analyzes the filtered input to understand the user's context and intent, which is crucial for generating appropriate responses. It determines actions like generating replies or querying databases. Further post-processing may refine the message for specific responses or format adjustments. The final output is prepared using language generation or data structuring. The NLU process also involves information extraction tasks like intent identification, sentimental understanding, and entity recognition, utilizing a pre-defined ontology database. This ensures that the conversational AI agent accurately interprets and responds to user inputs, maintaining contextual understanding and security throughout the interaction.

- **Natural Language Reasoning (NLR):** NLR in LLMs involves various information extraction tasks that structure information. As detailed by Wang (2023), these tasks include Named Entity Recognition, identifying entities in text; Relation Extraction, classifying relationships between entities [38]; and Event Extraction, augmenting events extracted from text [38–41]. Post-extraction, the system moves to reasoning tasks. The prompts of CoTs guide LLMs in explicit reasoning, fostering systematic problem-solving. KGs structured using Neo4j graph databases, represent knowledge as graphs, aiding LLM interpretation and offering an interface for ontology updates. An inference engine uses KGs to enhance LLM inferencing, supporting and refining reasoning processes [29].

- **Knowledge Service Dispatching:** Based on the user's intent and preferences, it selects the most suitable knowledge service. Through the LangChain framework, agents can determine the most effective actions and their sequence. These actions can be executed using one or several tools, defined as a series of chains. A chain is a function that operates using LLMs. It will store the results obtained from the knowledge service, and then forward the outcome to the NLG module.

- **Natural Language Generation (NLG):** The K-assistant generates natural language responses, starting with context and conversation history analysis for coherence. It integrates insights from NLU for user intent understanding and employs RAG for efficient information retrieval. Response generation involves personalizing responses, formulating candidate responses, re-ranking for coherence, and regulatory compliance, and finally presenting the response in a suitable format.

### 4.3   Knowledge Management Functions

A collection of knowledge management functions is proposed to equip K-assistants with knowledge management capabilities to facilitate knowledge activities between its master and the other knowledge entities (the unit consisting of a human user and K-assistant) on the knowledge networks. *The Knowledge Transformation (KT)* function efficiently converts tacit knowledge into explicit knowledge by codifying information according to domain ontologies, resulting in two primary representations: concepts aligned with the domain ontology, realized through graph databases, and various knowledge object formats like.pdf,.doc,.ppt,.jpg, indexed in file repositories. Implemented through seven modules, KT begins with augmenting existing knowledge by integrating personalized insights, ensuring context relevance. Conceptualization of augmented knowledge collates and reshapes data into coherent concepts, forming a unified knowledge base. Synthesis of candidate knowledge refines concepts for expert review. Reinforcement with human knowledge validates these candidates, involving human experts for practical applicability. Grounding into fundamental concepts distills knowledge for clarity and comprehension, while conversion to essential formats transforms it for widespread application. Finally, storing in the TMS enables efficient future retrieval. *Knowledge Allocation* (*KA*) involves the strategic allocation of incoming knowledge to appropriate destinations for optimal retention and accessibility. *Knowledge Maintenance* (*KMT*) updates both ontology and knowledge objects post-transactions, ensuring database relevance. *Collaborative Knowledge Retrieval* (*CKR*) matches inquiries with embedded vectors for efficient retrieval. *Knowledge Network Updating* (*KNU*) updates the network post-knowledge activities to enhance knowledge sharing. Lastly, *Collaborative Action Organization* (*CAO*) integrates domain knowledge to form task forces for specific actions, identifying participants and designating roles for targeted action.

### 4.4 Transactive Memory Management System (TMMS)

A K-assistant accesses and manages a TMS, crucial for knowledge management. This system comprises elements described as follows. *General Databases* store the indices of knowledge objects and connections to other entities in the knowledge network, using relational tables and SQL for data manipulation. *Document Repositories* hold documents in various formats (.pdf, .doc, .txt, .ppt, etc.) and are suitable for managing unstructured and semi-structured data, accessed typically through NoSQL-like systems. *Graph Database* (Neo4j) is designed: for storing domain ontology in a graph structure with nodes and edges, utilizing the Neo4j graph database and Cypher query language for node and edge manipulation. *Vector Databases* (Milvus) store the embedded vector space data based on LLMs and can be accessed using vector operations like cosine similarity to find similar vectors. The TMMS also manages knowledge networks, providing capabilities, such as *Collaborative Knowledge Retrieval* for efficient and effective information exchange among users in knowledge networks, *Data Security, and Privacy Protection* to ensure control of the proper management of sensitive data and privacy, including regular backups and data recovery to prevent data loss. These components collectively enable the K-assistant to handle complex knowledge management tasks, balancing efficient data handling with security and privacy considerations.

## 5  Knowledge Service Scenarios of an EBKMS for a CoP

Building on the foundations laid in Sects. 4 and 5 regarding the introduction to the EBKMS with its knowledge entity definition and knowledge management functions, this section aims to demonstrate the application of EBKMS within a CoP. We integrate the data structure and knowledge management functions and present several essential knowledge service scenarios. Firstly, for community member registration, a K-assistant is assigned to each new user. This K-assistant utilizes transactive memory, creating an initial domain ontology based on the user's profile and forming an initial knowledge network from the user's acquaintances. The new member can allocate knowledge objects to the transactive memory, and the K-assistant facilitates various knowledge activities. When searching for knowledge objects within the CoP, the K-assistant enacts the CKR function after discerning the user's intent through the NLU and NLR functions. Following this, the KMT and KNU functions are used to update the user's domain ontology and knowledge networks in the transactive memory. For storing newly acquired knowledge, the K-assistant activates the NLU and NLR functions to identify intended knowledge objects to retain. The KA function then determines whether to store these objects or distribute them through the user's knowledge networks to other people. The KMT and KNU functions finalize the knowledge storing process. In forming a task force for joint action, the EBKMS harnesses social capital from CoP participants. The NLU and NLR functions first define objectives and outcomes, followed by the CKR function identifying potential domain experts. The CAO function then organizes the task force for the joint action. When a participant decides to leave the CoP, they instruct their K-assistant to terminate their community connections. The NLU and NLR functions recognize this intention, triggering the KMT function to freeze the user's transactive memory and the KNU function to send a farewell message to acquaintances, indicating the user's departure. Finally, for a member rejoining the CoP, the previously frozen transactive memory facilitates the resumption of relationships. The KMT and KNU functions are activated to update the user's status as active in the community. These scenarios illustrate the versatility and functionality of the EBKMS in managing knowledge within a CoP, highlighting its capacity to facilitate effective communication, knowledge sharing, and collaboration.

## 6  Discussions

This article outlines the development of a K-assistant, an AI agent embedded with natural language processing and transactive memory management capabilities, designed to facilitate knowledge activities within a CoP. The EBKMS, underpinned by foundation models, aims to transform tacit knowledge into explicit form, enhancing collaboration. Adopting the ADR approach, the EBKMS's design and implementation align with the formation and evolution of a CoP, fostering collaboration between humans and AI. Using the Community of Resilience as a case study, the development team offers a prototyping service during the design stage, allowing members to interact with a K-assistant beta. Feedback from these interactions informs subsequent improvements in EBKMS functions. This iterative process of development and refinement continues throughout the evolution stage, enhancing the effectiveness of knowledge activities in the AoR. For practitioners in the AoR, the K-assistant facilitates connections and knowledge exchange, thereby boosting the community's social capital. The EBKMS development team focuses on ensuring transparency and trust in AI decisions, crucial for building a strong relationship between users and their K-assistants. Researchers in resilience use the AoR as a knowledge network, contributing to the development of resilience theories. The K-assistant serves as a practical example of conversational AI and LLMs in supporting societal well-being, offering insights for technological innovation. However, the deployment of EBKMS faces challenges related to participant motivation and the sustainability of the technical platform. The willingness of members to share knowledge and the trust developed through K-assistants influence the depth and breadth of shared knowledge. Sustaining the EBKMS platform to maintain long-term relationships between users and their K-assistants is critical for the evolving knowledge networks in the CoP. Future research should include an action plan addressing these constraints, incorporating insights from behavior science and community development. This collaborative effort aims to sustain the CoP, ensuring that the AoR realizes the well-being of human societies through AI-facilitated knowledge networks.

# 7 Conclusion

This research aimed to design an AI-facilitated knowledge management service that enables human intelligence to collaborate with AI to enhance knowledge activities, taking a community of practice as the target domain. We proposed an AI agent, called K-assistant, to realize this intention by illustrating the constituent components and operations for the SECI process. The resulting knowledge service system, called EBKMS, emphasizes natural language processing and knowledge transformation to facilitate the transformation of tacit knowledge to be codified and stored into a transactive memory system. The action design research approach will be employed to realize the EBKMS embedded with K-assistant in the Academy of Resilience, a CoP for practitioners in SEMs. This research contributes to the advancement of knowledge management service integrated with conversational AI capabilities and transactive memory management, which is novel and executable in the era of human-centered AI.

# References

1. Bommasani, R., et al.: On the Opportunities and Risks of Foundation Models. arXiv (Cornell University) (2021). https://doi.org/10.48550/arxiv.2108.07258
2. Bubeck, S.: Sparks of Artificial General Intelligence: Early experiments with GPT-4 (2023). arXiv.org. https://arxiv.org/abs/2303.12712
3. Dwivedi, Y.K., et al.: Opinion Paper: "So what if ChatGPT wrote it?" Multidisciplinary perspectives on opportunities, challenges and implications of generative conversational AI for research, practice and policy. Int. J. Inf. Manage. **71**, 102642 (2023). https://doi.org/10.1016/j.ijinfomgt.2023.102642
4. Jarrahi, M.H., Askay, D.A., Eshraghi, A., Smith, P.G.: Artificial intelligence and knowledge management: a partnership between human and AI. Bus. Horiz. **66**(1), 87–99 (2023). https://doi.org/10.1016/j.bushor.2022.03.002
5. Sanzogni, L., Guzmán, G., Busch, P.: Artificial intelligence and knowledge management: questioning the tacit dimension. Prometheus (St. Lucia) **35**(1) (2017). https://doi.org/10.1080/08109028.2017.1364547
6. Lusch, R.F., Nambisan, S.: Service innovation: a service-dominant logic perspective. Manag. Inf. Syst. Quart. **39**(1), 155–175 (2015). https://doi.org/10.25300/misq/2015/39.1.07
7. Ichijo, K.: Synthesis of human knowledge creation and artificial intelligence. In Routledge eBooks (pp. 140–152) (2022). https://doi.org/10.4324/9781003112150-12
8. Polanyi, M.: Personal knowledge: towards a Post-Critical philosophy. Br. J. Educ. Stud. **8**(1), 66 (1959). https://doi.org/10.2307/3119338
9. Nonaka, I., Toyama, R., Hirata, T., Bigelow, S.J., Hirose,A., Kohlbacher, F.: Managing flow. In Palgrave Macmillan UK eBooks. (2008).https://doi.org/10.1057/9780230583702
10. Teece, D.J.: Explicating dynamic capabilities: the nature and microfoundations of (sustainable) enterprise performance. Strateg. Manag. J. **28**(13), 1319–1350 (2007). https://doi.org/10.1002/smj.640

11. Teece, D.J., Pisano,G.P., Shuen, A.: Dynamic capabilities and strategic management. Strat. Manag. J. **18**(7) (1997). https://doi.org/10.1002/(sici)1097-0266(199708)18:7

12. Khurana, I., Dutta, D.K., Ghura, A.S.: SMEs and digital transformation during a crisis: the emergence of resilience as a second-order dynamic capability in an entrepreneurial ecosystem. J. Bus. Res. **150**, 623–641 (2022). https://doi.org/10.1016/j.jbusres.2022.06.048

13. Christofi, M., Khan, H., Zahoor, N., Hadjielias, E., Tarba, S.Y.: Digital transformation of SMES: the role of entrepreneurial persistence and market sensing dynamic capability. IEEE Trans. Eng. Manag. 1–18https://doi.org/10.1109/tem.2022.3230248

14. Qiao, T., Shan, W., Zhang, M., Liu, C.: How to facilitate knowledge diffusion in complex networks: the roles of network structure, knowledge role distribution and selection rule. Int. J. Inf. Manage. **47**, 152–167 (2019). https://doi.org/10.1016/j.ijinfomgt.2019.01.016

15. Eraut, M.: Learning contexts. Learn. Health Soc. Care **5**(1), 1–8 (2006). https://doi.org/10.1111/j.1473-6861.2006.00115.x

16. Nonaka, I., Toyama, R.: The Knowledge-creating theory revisited: knowledge creation as a synthesizing process. Knowl. Manag. Res. Pract. **1**(1), 2–10 (2003). https://doi.org/10.1057/palgrave.kmrp.8500001

17. Nonaka, I., Takeuchi, H.: The Knowledge-Creating Company. Oxford University Press (1995).https://doi.org/10.1093/oso/9780195092691.001.0001

18. Takeuchi, H.: The Wise Company: How Companies Create Continuous Innovation (2019)

19. Lin, F., Lin, S.: A conceptual model for virtual organizational learning. J. Organ. Comput. Electron. Commer. **11**(3), 155–178 (2001). https://doi.org/10.1207/s15327744joce1103_02

20. Vargo, S.L., Lusch, R.F.: Institutions and axioms: an extension and update of service-dominant logic. J. Acad. Mark. Sci. **44**(1), 5–23 (2015). https://doi.org/10.1007/s11747-015-0456-3

21. Randhawa, K., Wilden, R., Akaka, M.A.: Innovation intermediaries as collaborators in shaping service ecosystems: the importance of dynamic capabilities. Ind. Mark. Manage. **103**, 183–197 (2022). https://doi.org/10.1016/j.indmarman.2022.03.016

22. Howells, J.: Innovation intermediaries in a digital paradigm: a theoretical perspective. Technovation **129**,102889 (2024). https://doi.org/10.1016/j.technovation.2023.102889

23. Verona, G., Prandelli, E., Sawhney, M.: Innovation and virtual environments: towards virtual knowledge brokers. Organ. Stud. **27**(6), 765–788 (2006). https://doi.org/10.1177/0170840606061073

24. Blanka, C., Traunmüller, V.: Blind date? Intermediaries as matchmakers on the way to start-up—industry coopetition. Ind. Mark. Manage. **90**, 1–13 (2020). https://doi.org/10.1016/j.indmarman.2020.05.031

25. Schepis, D., Purchase, S., Butler, B.: Facilitating open innovation processes through network orchestration mechanisms. Ind. Mark. Manage. **93**, 270–280 (2021). https://doi.org/10.1016/j.indmarman.2021.01.015

26. Dhar, V. (2023). The paradigm shifts in artificial intelligence. arXiv (Cornell University). https://doi.org/10.48550/arxiv.2308.02558

27. Kusal, S., Patil, S., Choudrie, J., Kotecha, K., Mishra, S., Abraham, A.: AI-based conversational agents: a scoping review from technologies to future directions. IEEE Access **10**, 92337–92356 (2022). https://doi.org/10.1109/access.2022.3201144

28. Gutiérrez, C., Sequeda, J.F.: Knowledge graphs. Commun. ACM **64**(3), 96–104 (2021). https://doi.org/10.1145/3418294

29. Wen, Y., Wang, Z., Sun, J.: MindMap: Knowledge Graph prompting sparks graph of thoughts in large language models. arXiv (Cornell University) (2023). https://doi.org/10.48550/arxiv.2308.09729

30. Gao, Y., et al.: Retrieval-augmented generation for large language models: a survey. arXiv (Cornell University) (2023). https://doi.org/10.48550/arxiv.2312.10997

31. Kandpal, N., Deng, H., Roberts, A., Wallace, E., Raffel, C.: Large language models struggle to learn Long-Tail knowledge. arXiv (Cornell University) (2022). https://doi.org/10.48550/arxiv.2211.08411
32. Deng, H., Duan, S.X., Wibowo, S.: Digital technology driven knowledge sharing for job performance. J. Knowl. Manag. **27**(2), 404–425 (2022). https://doi.org/10.1108/jkm-08-2021-0637
33. Shen, W.-C., & Fu-Ren Lin. (2023, January 3). What Drives Workers to Learn Online during COVID-19 Pandemics? https://hdl.handle.net/10125/103415
34. Sein, H., Purao, S., Rossi, C., Lindgren, R.: Action design research. Manag. Inf. Syst. Q. **35**(1), 37 (2011). https://doi.org/10.2307/23043488
35. Su, C.-H.: Action Design Research with Human-AI Collaboration: Introducing SDGs to University. National Tsing Hua University, Master Htesis (2021)
36. Oviatt, S., Schuller, B.W., Cohen, P.R., Sonntag, D., Potamianos, G., Krüger, A.: The Handbook of Multimodal-Multisensory Interfaces, Volume 1: Foundations, User Modeling, and Common Modality Combinations (2017)
37. McTear, M.F.: Conversational AI: dialogue systems, conversational agents, and chatbots. Synth. Lect. Hum. Lang. Technol. **13**(3), 1–251 (2020). https://doi.org/10.2200/s01060ed1v01y202010hlt048
38. Wang, X.: InstructUIE: multi-task instruction tuning for unified information extraction (2023). arXiv.org. https://arxiv.org/abs/2304.08085
39. Wan, Z.: GPT-RE: in-context learning for relation extraction using large language models (2023). arXiv.org. https://arxiv.org/abs/2305.02105
40. Wang, X.: Code4Struct: code generation for few-shot event structure prediction (2022). arXiv.org. https://arxiv.org/abs/2210.12810
41. Yuan, S.: Generative entity typing with curriculum learning (2022). arXiv.org. https://arxiv.org/abs/2210.0291

# Digital Decarbonization in Manufacturing Supply Chains: Addressing the Environmental Impact of the Data Industry

Marios Georgiou[1], Thomas Jackson[2(✉)], Ian R. Hodgkinson[2], Lisa Jackson[1], Steve Lockwood[2], and Keyi Zhong[2]

[1] Aeronautical and Automotive Engineering, Loughborough University, Loughborough, Leicestershire, UK

[2] Loughborough Business School, Loughborough University, Loughborough, Leicestershire, UK

t.w.jackson@lboro.ac.uk

**Abstract.** This research emphasizes the growing importance of addressing the environmental impact of the data industry, often overlooked in discussions about achieving net-zero targets. While industries like construction, aviation, and energy are commonly associated with greenhouse gas (GHG) emissions, the digital sector is increasingly recognized as a significant contributor. The paper introduces the concept of "digital decarbonization" to tackle the carbon footprint associated with digital knowledge practices, highlighting that these practices are not inherently carbon neutral. Ultimately, this integrative review sets the stage for future research on digital decarbonization in supply chains, aiming to address this critical issue in the quest for a sustainable, net-zero future.

**Keywords:** dark data · knowledge management system (KMS) · digitalization

## 1 Introduction

It is crucial for the field of knowledge management to introspect and assess its own supply chain, considering the potential environmental implications. The relentless pursuit of knowledge relies on processing the ever-expanding volume of data, transforming it into information, and eventually evolving into knowledge. This paper initiates an exploration of this realm, seeking to quantify the escalating volume of data and comprehend its environmental footprint within the context of the supply chain domain. Industries targeted for net-zero goals include construction, aviation, and energy, with the emerging data industry also gaining attention due to its significant carbon footprint. Jackson and Hodgkinson emphasize the necessity of accounting for the digital carbon footprint, introducing the concept of digital decarbonization [1]. Teuful and Sprus report that digitalization contributes to 4% of greenhouse gas (GHG) emissions, with data centers, particularly hyper data centers, having a substantial carbon footprint estimated at 200TWh/year across supply chains [2]. Research on measuring the digital carbon footprint reveals varied standards globally [3, 4]. Existing approaches often focus on primary

© The Author(s), under exclusive license to Springer Nature Switzerland AG 2024
L. Uden and I.-H. Ting (Eds.): KMO 2024, CCIS 2152, pp. 304–315, 2024.
https://doi.org/10.1007/978-3-031-63269-3_23

processes, neglecting secondary emissions from infrastructure, hardware, and software. This oversight extends from cloud data centers to personal devices, impacting GHG costs, especially with data replication and redundancy.

While digital innovations are seen as tools for decarbonization, their own emissions are often overlooked. Itten et al. and Yann et al. highlight the need to assess emissions associated with transitioning from physical to digitized processes [5, 6]. This integrative review employs the 4R's model (Recovering, Recycling, Reusing, Remaining useful life) to comprehensively analyze the challenges faced by supply chains in digital decarbonization. The integrative literature review synthesizes existing knowledge on digital decarbonization, providing a foundation for future research. Following Elsbach and van Knippenberg's approach, the review outlines the context, scope, and guiding principles before detailing the search strategy and article selection [7]. Thematic analysis identifies common threads across diverse literature, and the article concludes by presenting key research avenues for future investigations into digital decarbonization across supply chains.

## 2  Background

## 3  Setting the Scene: Supply Chain Data Growth

Efforts to track greenhouse gas (GHG) emissions across supply chains face challenges, particularly in sectors like transportation where only 13% of Nationally Determined Contributions (NDCs) record freight emissions. Despite the growth in data capture and usage across industries, little attention has been given to the GHG emissions from digital data, which is poised to expand significantly over the next decade. The escalating demand for data, housed in various data centers, including hyper and traditional cloud, entails energy-intensive processes, resulting in GHG emissions. Predictions based on factors like instructions per second, joules per transistor, and transistors per instruction indicate a substantial growth in energy consumption by 2030 [8, 9]. The Industry 4.0 trend and the rise of sensor-enabled data further contribute to this data surge, impacting cloud computing's energy consumption and environmental effects. Concerns about 'dark data,' which remains unused or dormant, highlight inefficiencies in data storage, draining energy without extracting its potential value. However, there is a lack of studies focusing on the manufacturing supply chain or the specifics of dark data generated within it. Understanding this aspect is crucial for effective metadata use and data standardization, promoting accessibility and understanding [10]. Models for data artifacts, such as Building Information Modeling (BIM) in the Steel construction industry, show promise in incorporating GHG emission-related data. However, challenges include making information freely available across platforms and ensuring syntactic and semantic interoperability. The current lack of a data-centric approach throughout all stages of the manufacturing supply chain calls for attention and development. In the context of knowledge management, understanding the complexities of GHG emissions in data usage and storage is vital for informed decision-making, sustainable practices, and the development of standardized approaches for data handling in various industries.

## 4 Methodology

The integrative review centers on comprehensive data from all stages of the manufacturing supply chain, encompassing scopes 1 and 2, and where applicable, scope 3 greenhouse gas (GHG) emissions. The focus is solely on hyper and local data centers, as illustrated in the system context diagram, omitting consideration for the unpredictable usage and emissions associated with processing data on local devices. Utilizing the 4Rs framework (Recovering, Recycling, Reusing, Remaining useful life) as a guide, the review delves into the challenges and opportunities at each stage of the supply chain, emphasizing sustainable data practices. The paper acknowledges the efficiency improvements in hyper data center infrastructure but highlights the need for a deeper understanding of data requirements to effectively manage the projected data growth and associated emissions. In developing the search strategy, the team employed various academic search platforms, with Google Scholar as a primary focus. A set of broad yet pertinent keywords, such as data decarbonization, dark data, digital carbon footprint, Greenhouse Gas Emissions, supply chain, and data centers, guided the exploration. The review's inclusive approach, incorporating diverse literature types, including editorials and commentaries, ensures a comprehensive understanding of the evolving landscape of digital decarbonization.

A meticulous article selection process involved filtering through citations and relevance scores, leading to the inclusion of 71 papers. The timeline chosen for the review (2000–2022) aligns with the increased scholarly focus on decarbonization, particularly in supply chain emissions, data center growth, and dark data generation. Figure 1 illustrates a notable surge in publications, emphasizing the growing significance of digital decarbonization in recent years.

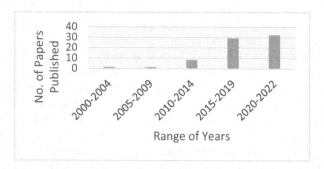

**Fig. 1.** Frequency analysis between 2000–2022

To give some insights into the distribution of publications across various journals, the *Journal of Sustainability* was the most prevalent platform with a total of 5 publications. This was followed by the *Journal of Cleaner Production* with 4 and *Renewable and Sustainable Energy Reviews* and *Nature Climate Change* each with 2. The remaining sources, including journals such as *Supply Chain Management; Transactions on Consumer Electronics; Building Automation; Resources, Conservation and Recycling;*

*Nordic Digital Business Summit, Science and Engineering Investigations*; and *Transactions on Power Systems,* each providing a single publication on the topic. The diverse range of sources underscores the interdisciplinary nature of the topic, necessitating an integrative review to consolidate the fragmented knowledge base. The frequency analysis depicted in Fig. 1 further confirms the escalating attention to digital decarbonization, culminating in the highest number of publications in 2022. This trend reinforces the relevance and timeliness of the integrative review in synthesizing existing knowledge and fostering a deeper understanding of this emerging and crucial field.

## 5 Thematic Analysis

From the investigative review we identified several key themes, which are outlined and discussed in turn below:

**Data Centres and Workloads.** To effectively address GHG emissions associated with data, it is crucial to gain a comprehensive understanding of how data centres manage their operations. Valuable insights into the challenges of attributing GHG emissions workloads within data centres and the presentation of a high-level data model that delineates the physical components contributing to GHG emissions within these centres has been presented [11], as depicted in Fig. 2. Figure 2 underscores the intricacy of power consumption within a data centre, making it evident that identifying the power associated with supply chain processes is a similarly intricate task. This model provides an initial framework for comprehending data centre operations.

Furthermore, it is worth considering the potential to enhance this model by incorporating virtualization of computing resources such as storage, processing, memory, and bandwidth. This addition would offer a more nuanced view of data centre operations, facilitating a deeper understanding of energy consumption and GHG emissions. Exploring the availability of commercial tools designed to assist businesses in quantifying their emissions resulting from overall workloads could also be beneficial.

Numerous research papers have endeavoured to monitor and verify GHG emissions throughout the entire supply chain of various industries. However, it is highlighted that a significant challenge: the existing GHG Protocol may not accurately determine data centre emissions for customers of hyper data centres, as either the data is unavailable to them or is incomplete [11, 12]. This limitation underscores the need for improved transparency and data sharing within the industry to effectively address GHG emissions associated with data centres and their role in supply chain processes.

The primary contributors to direct energy consumption in data centres are servers and cooling systems, along with additional demands from storage drives and network devices. Even though digital operations are often concealed within vast data centres, their environmental impact cannot be ignored. According to Jones [13], the data centre sector currently accounts for approximately 0.3% of global carbon emissions, and this figure is expected to show a considerable upward trend in the foreseeable future. It is essential to measure and comprehend the environmental impact of these workloads to foster sustainable growth and development of digital technologies and opportunities. Unless efficiency measures are significantly improved, it is projected that nearly 20% of all electricity will be consumed by the digital ICT sector by 2025, resulting in approximately

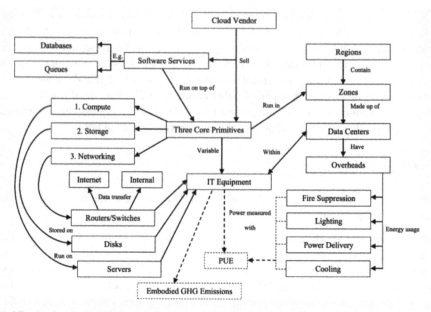

Public cloud components

**Fig. 2.** Data Model of data centre assets

5.5% of the world's carbon emissions; this would surpass the emissions of all but three countries: the US, China, and India [14].

Some improvements have been made in the transition from data centres to cloud as well as in the processing power which led to an improvement on the growth of consumption [15]. Investigations have found that if a firm takes better consideration to the accuracy of their generated carbon emissions data, they can lower their emissions [16]. An evaluation index for big data centre sustainability and a guidance tool that can help to construct a sustainable data centre has been devised by [17]. The model is using multiple criteria along with decision making tools to evaluate the sustainability, which is based on the TOPSIS technique (fuzzy technique for order preference by similarity to an ideal solution) and the analytic network.

The development of big data has led to high energy consumption, high carbon emissions and high costs which have become common problems for every business, organisation, and country [18]. A report from Google in 2011 showed how keeping an email on the local server can cause around 100kg of $CO_2$ per user per year [19]. A rough estimation on converting this to $CO_2$ emissions is around 30 kg of $CO_2$ per TB of data per year. At the same time though, with the arrival of augmented and virtual reality as well as the increase of big data, the data footprint will likely increase. Research suggests that for every data centre, the waste heat must be used to reduce heating costs [20]. Data centres that are in cold areas can benefit and meet the energy demands easier. All these methods can contribute to an effective operation of a data centre that could save money as well as contribute to lower GHG emissions. The huge data volume is the raw material of data centres and are most generated by the government, commerce, healthcare and social networks. Research developed by [21], for example, describes data centres as the backbone for computational services (by any company), data computing, communication, cloud services and many more. In 2016, it was found that the distribution of energy consumption for data centres was mainly caused by the storage of data and the refrigeration system [18]. The energy consumption from those two aspects was around 35% from each, resulting in 70% of energy consumption which is a clear indication these are the main contributors of energy consumption. The data service sector has been continuously growing in the past decade driven by multiple activities such as by sharing file documents, by storing data on to local or cloud servers and data mining. In data centres, water is extensively used for generation of electricity and by water cooling the equipment which this impacts the environmental sustainability.

**Dark Data.** The prevalence of dark data in data centres and the issues in identifying whether it has any use has been identified [10]. They define dark data as data not used or very rarely used, and suggest the creation of a new role, the scientific data officer within a company identifying and exploiting this data if possible. Data is descrivved in 3 categories: "Business critical data – this is data identified as vital to the ongoing operational success of our organization [22]. The organizations need to protect and pro-actively manage Business Critical data. Redundant, Obsolete and Trivial (ROT) data – this is data identified as Redundant, or duplicate, data, Obsolete, no longer having business value, and Trivial data (ROT) with little or no business value. These definitions are very useful to our understanding and can be used alongside the 4R's proposed in this study to identify data sets in a more structured manner.

Clearly companies and organisations are generating enormous amounts of data from their activities. Data generated from various systems such as sensors, demand side digitalisation sensors, machines, controllers, enterprises systems and so on, may be transformed into multiple formats such as critical data, dark data and ROT data. Such data are the scarcity of information that had been used only once by the organisation and stored among the data assets [23]. A recent report by Statista, states that the prevalence of spam emails is notable, as they accounted for more than 45% of all emails sent in December 2021 [24]. Streaming services, such as Netflix, also contribute significantly to carbon emissions. Watching half an hour of Netflix content results in about 1.6 kg of $CO_2$, equivalent to driving four miles. It is worth noting that Netflix streaming services collectively consume around 370 Terawatt hours (TWh) per year, which surpasses the combined figure for data centres worldwide [25].

The integration of big data, data science, and AI with IoT could offer a smart future, such as agriculture, logistics, smart grids, cities, and homes [26]. Additionally, these technologies can aid in optimizing energy consumption for heating and lighting in buildings, leading to more efficient and environmentally friendly energy use. Which then has the potential to reduce carbon emission in the future. Many firms have successfully reduced their footprints from harnessing large amounts of data. Research conducted in Disney World have found that there was an energy management program which was done to collect hourly information of different consumptions such as water, electricity etc. It was found that those data would turn to dark data and affect the footprint of the organisation. By collecting that information and sharing them with the stakeholders, Walt

Disney World have been able to control the electricity consumption as well as to reduce the generation of their dark data [27]. Data collection can help organizations for better decisions, design much better materials and by controlling climate change will have an impact on the supply chains and on organisations [28].

The role of automatic metadata extraction to better tag data before it becomes dark and suggests unstructured data sources (emails, video, sound, social media) have been considered as areas currently not well understood [10, 29]. Undoubtedly large data sets in unstructured data formats could be found if systematically searched for, this could cover items such as, shipping data documents, documents of understanding, certificates of source authenticity. This area lends itself to Natural Language Processing (NLP) techniques to extract meaningful content from documents, emails, possibly even images to enhance the data gathered to support understanding of GHG emissions. In addition, sensor-based data probably is being collected and never used, indeed it may even be poorly classified, so its use is limited. Finally, there is likely 'forgotten' data residing in databases that could be useful or if not, archived or even deleted as applicable.

**Industry 4.0 and IoT Sensors.** The IoT stands for the everyday objects (devices) that are connected to the internet and covers wearable devices to home appliances, transportation vehicles and electric cars. IoT has increased the data generated by using those devices. While the IoT applications are commonly known as smart technology, they mainly focus on using data/AI to optimise energy usage. This phenomenon has given rise to a significant and continuous expansion of the internet. The rapid development of IoT and cloud computing, machine learning and data mining can improve the data driven strategies [30]. However, the backbone of digitalisation (data centres) are high energy users with high service demands making it difficult to support clean development. IoT technology has proven to be a successful tool in enhancing energy efficiency, particularly within the Information and Communication Technology (ICT) sector, including data centres. One compelling example of its application is the use of IoT in optimizing air conditioning systems, resulting in reduced energy consumption and the promotion of sustainable practices. Major retail giants like Carrefour and Walmart have harnessed Industry 4.0 tools to provide detailed information about product origins, locations, and production processes, contributing to greater transparency and sustainability in their supply chains. In addition to these achievements, companies like Ener-go utilize smart meters to measure clean energy transactions, while General Motors employs Industry 4.0 technologies to optimize their operations. Notably, General Motors has achieved a remarkable 40% reduction in CO2 emissions and a nearly 35% decrease in energy consumption [31]. However, it is essential to recognize that while IoT offers the potential for energy-saving measures and consumption reduction, it raises valid concerns regarding the vast amounts of data collected. Many IoT devices collect substantial volumes of personal and private data, giving rise to critical questions about data privacy and security.

**Artificial Intelligence and Blockchain.** AI is poised to exert a profound influence on the future of supply chains [32]. An illustrative application can be found in agriculture, where AI-driven technologies, such as facial recognition, empower farmers to gather valuable insights from large animal herds. This allows them to enhance milk production, achieving performance levels comparable to those managing smaller herds—a feat that would be impractical to achieve manually, has been demonstrated [33]. Moreover, AI stands out as a leading digital technology with the potential to play a pivotal role in advancing the pursuit of net-zero goals [34].

Blockchain, on the other hand, represents a decentralized algorithm designed to circumvent reliance on centralized authorities. While it has gained prominence in decentralized financial systems and cryptocurrencies, its applicability within the supply chain domain merits consideration. However, it's essential to acknowledge that blockchain's energy consumption is notably high. The algorithm's reliance on extensive replication leads to redundant computations, resulting in substantial energy consumption [35]. It has been reported that blockchain technology can improve key objectives within supply chain management like the quality, sustainability, flexibility, risk reduction, dependability, cost and speed [36]. A case study for blockchain in healthcare: "MedRec" prototype for electronic health records, medical research data and payment systems can rapidly improve the accountability and transparency within the supply chain management and develop sustainable indicators for better understanding and measurement [37]. Blockchain have 5 strengths in supply chain managements which includes the resilience, automation, aggregation, visibility and validation. Smart systems provide a connection through a digital device application that mainly rely on user's control to manage or maintain energy consumption by creating alerts on pricing information, energy consumption & generation. Such systems are providing decision making solutions that can help to develop a sustainable household with much better energy efficiency [38]. Those elements are gathered through the IoT, which is a network that all devices are connected to communicate multiple data for analysis. A study showed that the annual electricity requirements for the blockchain algorithm in cryptocurrencies is around 70TWh in 2020 alone which is equivalent of powering around 8 million households associated with $44MtCO2$ of footprint. Due to inefficiency of the operation of the algorithm, a single transaction can cost around 800 kWh, which is enough power to operate 25 households for a whole day [39]. Nevertheless, if blockchain is used effectively, it can have an important role in supply chain management which can ensure sustainability.

**Data Usage in Supply Chains.** The 4R framework necessitates a comprehensive dataset to determine the utility of data based on defined criteria. Accurate mapping of this data for future use is pivotal. The presence of robust metadata, encompassing various aspects such as business and technical metadata, security, context, value, and lifecycle, is of paramount importance. While some research has delved into these aspects [29], it remains an area in supply chains that warrants more attention. The ever-expanding volume of data projected for use necessitates a straightforward framework for comprehending data utility and making decisions regarding its relevance. Such a framework is essential for achieving a comprehensive understanding of GHG emissions in manufacturing supply chains.

Visualizing this framework as a two-axis model, where data is categorized as either known or unknown and useful or useless, four distinct quadrants emerge. The first two quadrants, known and useful, and unknown and useless, are self-explanatory. The other two, known but useless, and unknown but potentially useful, present opportunities for deriving new insights or appropriately classifying and migrating data to less resource-intensive platforms, which can translate to cost savings and reduced GHG emissions. To make this approach effective, an initial data audit across all platforms, focusing on critical datasets, is essential. Often, companies have core datasets that they regularly review, such as master data related to people, places, and products. These datasets can serve as a starting point for gradually constructing a map of data utility within the relevant processes. Clearly known, useful data should be exploited as much as possible, shared as much as possible (legal and competitive requirements not withstanding). Where data are unknown but useful this needs to be discovered and a 'light shone upon it' to convert that dark data into useful data. Also note that useful data may become useless over time and vice versa. The model above could easily be extended to other sectors (retail, pharmacy, banking etc.,) if it shows value.

Without a complete data framework for capture and subsequent collation, standardisation, and contextualisation of the data then data will be poorly stored, difficult to identify and potentially not used, used incorrectly, or become dark. This is not a slight undertaking, and this theme merely highlights a starting point, but without a rigorous, repeatable approach it is difficult to understand how data elements (as they are ingested from say, takeovers, new systems) can be accurately brought into the environment and used to its maximum potential. Data will need to be shared and collaborated where appropriate, there is also the requirement to trust the data gathering and ensure its security. A novel approach here could be the use of blockchain to support the data flows, ensuring all have a 'stake' in the quality, timeliness, and security of the data.

## 6 Discussion, Future Research and Conclusions

As nations strive for net-zero targets, the digital industry, particularly data centres, is increasingly recognized as a significant contributor to global greenhouse gas (GHG) emissions. The concept of "digital decarbonization" emerges to tackle carbon emissions from digital practices. The exponential surge in data and the prevalence of "dark data" present challenges in understanding and mitigating GHG emissions. This review advocates for a data-centric approach across supply chain stages, emphasizing transparency and emission reduction, especially in hyper and local data centres.

Exploring GHG emissions and associated data requirements, costs, and emissions tied to data storage, maintenance, processing, and utilization is a novel research area. While current data center emissions may seem minor, the rise of new data capture methods, particularly sensor and unstructured data, is expected to increase energy consumption and emissions. Without clear rules and tools, data may accumulate without purpose, leading to rising costs. Our argument is that despite advancements in various data management aspects, there's no comprehensive end-to-end approach to track supply chain data emissions. In conclusion, addressing the digital carbon footprint in manufacturing supply chains is vital for achieving net-zero goals. Future research will play a pivotal role in devising strategies, standards, and tools to reduce GHG emissions related to data practices, ensuring a more sustainable and environmentally responsible digital future.

## References

1. Jackson, T. Ian Hodgkinson, R.: Is there a role for knowledge management in saving the planet from too much data?. Knowl. Manag. Res. Pract. 21(3), 427–435 (2022)

2. Teuful, B., Sprus, C.M.: How digitalization acts as a driver of decarbonization (2020). www.ey. com/en_ch/decarbonization/how-digitization-acts-as-a-driver-of-decarbonization. Accessed on 27 Feb 2022
3. Singh N., Longendyke L.: A global look at mandatory greenhouse gas reporting programs (2015). https://www.wri.org/insights/global-look-mandatory-greenhouse-gas-report ing-programs
4. Freitag C., Berners-Lee M., Widdicks K., Knowles B., Blair G., Friday A.: The real climate and tranformative impact of ICT: a critique of estimates, trends, and regulations. Patterns **2**(9), 100340 (2021). https://doi.org/10.1016/j.patter.2021.100340
5. Itten R., et al.: Digital transformation—life cycle assessment of digital services, multifunctional devices and cloud computing. Int. J. Life Cycle Assess. **25**(10), 2093–2098 (2020). https://doi.org/10.1007/s11367-020-01801-0
6. Yann, D., Hardy, S.: Climate change and trade facilitation: estimating greenhouse gas emission savings from implementation of cross-border paperless trade in Asia and the Pacific. J. Asian Econ. Integr. **3**(2), 190–210 (2021). https://doi.org/10.1177/26316846211035567
7. Elsbach, K., van Knippenberg, D.: Creating high-impact literature reviews: an argument for integrative reviews. J. Manage. Stud. **57**(6), 1277–1289 (2020). https://doi.org/10.1111/joms. 12581
8. Andrae Anders, S.G.: Prediction studies of electricity use of global computing in 2030. Int. J. Sci. Eng. Invest. **8**(86), 27–33 (2019). https://www.researchgate.net/profile/Anders-Andrae/ publication/332111132_Prediction_Studies_of_Electricity_Use_of_Global_Computing_in_ 2030/links/5ca37a56299bf1b86d5fb384/Prediction-Studies-of-Electricity-Use-of-Global-Computing-in-2030.pdf
9. Andrae Anders, S.G.: Hypotheses for primary energy use, electricity use and CO2 emissions of global computing and its shares of the total between 2020 and 2030. WSEAS Trans. Power Syst. **15**(4), 50–59 (2020). https://www.researchgate.net/profile/Anders-Andrae/publication/ 339900068_Hypotheses_for_Primary_Energy_Use_Electricity_Use_and_CO2_Emissions_ of_Global_Computing_and_Its_Shares_of_the_Total_Between_2020_and_2030/links/5e6 b48eba6fdccf321d93c6a/Hypotheses-for-Primary-Energy-Use-Electricity-Use-and-CO2-Emissions-of-Global-Computing-and-Its-Shares-of-the-Total-Between-2020-and-2030.pdf
10. Schembera, B., Duran, J.M.: Dark data as the new challenge for big data science and the introduction of the scientific data officer. Philos. Technol. **33**, 93–115 (2020). https://doi.org/ 10.1007/s13347-019-00346-x
11. Mytton D.: Assessing the suitability of the Greenhouse Gas Protocol for calculation of emissions from public cloud computing workloads. J. Cloud Comput. **9**, 45 (2020). https://doi. org/10.1186/s13677-020-00185-8
12. Mytton, D.: Hiding greenhouse gas emissions in the cloud. Nat. Clim. Change **10**(701) (2020). https://doi.org/10.1038/s41558-020-0837-6
13. Jones, N.: The information factories. Nature **561**, 163–167 (2018). https://datacenters.lbl.gov/ sites/default/files/nature.pdf. Accessed on Aug 2023
14. Andrae Anders, S.G.: Total consumer power consumption forecast **10**, 69 (2017). https:// www.researchgate.net/publication/320225452_Total_Consumer_Power_Consumption_For ecast. Accessed on 2023
15. Pihkola H., Hongisto M., Apilo O. and Lasanen M.: Evaluating the energy consumption of mobile data transfer-from technology development to consumer behaviour and life cycle thinking. Sustainability **10**(7), 1–16 (2018)
16. Melville, N.P., Saldanha, T.J., Rush, D.E.: Systems enabling low-carbon operations: the salience of accuracy. J. Clean. Prod. **166**, 1074–1083 (2017)
17. Zhang, Q., Yang, S.: Evaluating the sustainability of big data centres using the analytic network process and fuzzy TOPSIS. Environ. Sci. Pollut. Res. **28**(14), 17913–17927 (2021). https:// doi.org/10.1007/s11356-020-11443-2

18. Rong, H., Zhang, H., Xiao, S., Li, C., Hu, C.: Optimizing energy consumption for data centers. Renew. Sustain. Energy Rev. **58**, 674–691 (2016)
19. Google, "Google's green computing: Efficiency at scale," Google (2011). https://static.goo gleusercontent.com/media/www.google.com/en//green/pdfs/google-green-computing.pdf
20. Haywood, A., Sherbeck, J., Phelan, P., Varsamopoulos, G., Gupta, S.K.S.: Thermodynamic feasibility of harvesting data center waste heat to drive an absorption chiller. Energy Convers. Manage. **58**, 26–34 (2012)
21. Weihl, B., Teetzel, E., Clidaras, J., Malone, C., Kava, J., Ryan M.: Sustainable data centers. XRDS: Crossroads. ACM Magazine Assoc. Comput. Mach. **17**, 8–12 (2011)
22. Dimitrov, W., Сярова, C., Petkova, L.: Types of dark data and hidden cyber-security risks. Tech. Rep. (2018). https://doi.org/10.13140/RG.2.2.31695.43681
23. Nagorny K., Lima-Monteiro P., Barata J., Colombo A.W., Big data analysis in smart manufacturing: a review. Int. J. Commun. Network Syst. Sci. **10**(3), 31–58 (2017)
24. Kaspersky Lab, "Statista - Global spam volume as percentage of total e-mail traffic from 2011 to 2022" (2022a). https://www.statista.com/statistics/420400/spam-email-traffic-share-annual/. Accessed on 08 2023
25. Kamiya, G.: Factcheck: What is the carbon footprint of streaming video on Netflix? (2020b). https://www.carbonbrief.org/factcheck-what-is-the-carbon-footprint-of-streaming-video-on-netflix/. Accessed 08 2023
26. Al-Ali, A.R., Zualkernan, I.A., Rashid, M., Gupta, R., AliKarar, M.: A smart home energy management system using IoT and big data analytics approach. IEEE Trans. Consum. Electron. **63**(4), 426–434 (2017)
27. Allen, P.: HPAC engineering - how Disney saves energy and operating costs (2005). https://www.hpac.com/building-automation/article/20927761/how-disney-saves-ene rgy-and-operating-costs
28. National Academy of Sciences: Big Data in Materials Research and Development: Summary of a Workshop. The National Academies Press, Washington DC (2014)
29. Schembera, B.: Like a rainbow in the dark: metadata annotation for HPC applications in the age of dark data. J. Supercomput. **77**, 8946–8966 (2021). https://doi.org/10.1007/s11227-020-03602-6
30. Bharany, S., et al.: Energy efficient fault tolerance techniques in green cloud computing: a systematic survey and taxonomy. Sustain. Energy Technol. Assess. **53**, 1–15 (2022)
31. Kouhizadeh, M., Sarkis, J.: Blockchain practices, potentials, and perspectives in greening supply chains. Sustainability **10**(10), 1–16 (2018)
32. Olsen, T.L., Tomlin, B.: Industry 4.0: opportunities and challenges for operations management. Manuf. Serv. Oper. Manag. **22**(1), 113–122 (2019)
33. Koeleman, E.: Facial recognition of dairy cows (2016). https://www.dairyglobal.net/general/facial-recognition-of-dairy-cows/. Accessed on 08 2023
34. Speaker, T., O'Donnell, S., Wittemyer, G., Bruyere, B., Loucks, C., Dancer, A.: A global community-sourced assessment of the state of conservation technology. Conserv. Biol. **36**, 1–13 (2022)
35. Mora, C., et al.: Bitcoin emissions alone could push global warming above 2C. Nat. Clim. Chang. **8**, 931–933 (2018)
36. Kshetri, N.: Blockchain's roles in meeting key supply chain management objectives. Int. J. Inf. Manage. **39**, 80–89 (2018)
37. Ekblaw, A., Azaria, A., Halamka, J.D., Lippman A.: A case study for blockchain in healthcare: "MedRec" prototype for electronic health records and medical research data. In: Proceedings of the 2nd International Conference on Open and Big Data, pp. 1−13 (2016). https://www.semanticscholar.org/paper/A-Case-Study-for-Blockchain-in-Health care-%3A-%E2%80%9C-%E2%80%9D-for-Ekblaw-Azaria/56e65b469cad2f3ebd560b3a 10e7346780f4ab0a?p2df

38. Shaw-Williams, D.: The expanding role of home energy management ecosystem: an Australian case study. Elsevier Behind and Beyond the Meter: Digitalization, Aggregation, Optimization, Monetization, Sioshansi, F. (Ed.), pp. 157–176 (2020)
39. Monrat, A.A., Schele, N.O., Andersson K.: A survey of blockchain from the perspectives of applications, challenges, and opportunities. IEEE Access 7, 117135–117151 (2019)

# AI, IT and New Trends in KM

# Increasing Interpretability in Outside Knowledge Visual Question Answering

Max Upravitelev[1]([✉]), Christopher Krauss[1], and Isabelle Kuhlmann[2]

[1] Fraunhofer Institute for Open Communication Systems FOKUS,
Kaiserin-Augusta-Allee 31, 10589 Berlin, Germany
{max.upravitelev,christopher.krauss}@fokus.fraunhofer.de
[2] University of Hagen, Universitätsstraße 11, 58097 Hagen, Germany
isabelle.kuhlmann@fernuni-hagen.de

**Abstract.** The field of Visual Question Answering (VQA) bridges the disciplines of vision- and language-based reasoning by combining scene understanding and the answering of arbitrary questions regarding a given image. The number of questions that can be answered is limited by the visual information given in an image, but it can be expanded by utilizing external knowledge from different sources. Recently, the Outside Knowledge Visual Question Answering (OK-VQA) task was introduced to facilitate research in this field. Several current state-of-the-art solutions incorporate Graph Neural Networks (GNNs) for this task. Like other Neural Network-based architectures, GNNs usually behave as black boxes. The interpretability of the reasoning behind predictions from GNNs is, however, a desirable property. Especially in the context of Knowledge Management within organizations, it can be important (and in some cases, is also required by law) to know how the reasoning behind decisions made by utilizing GNNs came to be. Nonetheless, increasing the interpretability can come at the cost of decreasing the overall performance of a model. The following investigation concludes that this does not have to be the case in every scenario by evaluating a GNN-based model developed for the OK-VQA task and a selection of proposed updates to this model, which are based on the attention mechanism. Furthermore, potential interpretation techniques are explored, which focus on considering the attention values.

**Keywords:** Interpretability · Visual Question Answering · Graph Neural Networks

## 1 Introduction

Visual Question Answering (VQA) aims at analyzing a scene within an image so that arbitrary questions about this scene can be answered. The number of questions that can be handled is limited by the visual information provided in an image but can be extended by incorporating external knowledge sources.

© The Author(s), under exclusive license to Springer Nature Switzerland AG 2024
L. Uden and I.-H. Ting (Eds.): KMO 2024, CCIS 2152, pp. 319–330, 2024.
https://doi.org/10.1007/978-3-031-63269-3_24

Recently, a first dataset (OK-VQA [12]) was proposed to provide an evaluation benchmark for approaches to solve this novel task.

One common approach to the OK-VQA task within current solutions is the utilization of end-to-end trained models based on Graph Neural Networks (GNNs). A challenge to further improve the results of this approach is the interpretability of these models. The need for interpretability becomes increasingly crucial as several governmental bodies worldwide (e.g., the European Union) discuss its implementation within real-life applications. This affects organizations utilizing Neural Network (NN)-based architectures within their knowledge management strategies. Interpretability is also a desirable property within the development of new models, as it could highlight which cases the models have the most difficulty with. Yet, an increase in interpretability has to take into account a possible trade-off between interpretability and accuracy, where increasing one factor could lead to a decline in the other (as described in [2], for example).

The following investigation focuses on the question of whether this trade-off has to be a consequence in every case. This is explored on an example architecture chosen from the OK-VQA domain. This domain is suitable for the investigation since it deals with data from different modalities and allows for models that incorporate attention-based approaches, which can increase interpretability. The attention mechanism is a famous part of the Transformer architecture and was popularized in [18] as such. It was also applied to other types of data beyond textual data, like image and graph data. The model chosen for the investigation is KRISP-GCN, a configuration of the KRISP (Knowledge Reasoning with Implicit and Symbolic rePresentations) model from [11]. The investigation focuses on two proposed updates: (1) Swapping out the original Graph Convolutional Network (GCN) architecture with a Graph ATtention Network (GAT) architecture and (2) expanding the Knowledge Graph (KG) representation by augmenting chosen node representations with vectors representing visual features.

The accuracy metric on the OK-VQA benchmark is used for evaluating the performance of the model and the proposed updates. The evaluation of the increase in interpretability is, however, less straightforward. Despite the fact that interpretability is usually referred to as a degree, no common framework of how its increase can be quantified exists to the best of our knowledge. Hence, the interpretability is considered within two case studies in a qualitative manner. In addition, the possibility of a new metric for comparing GAT-based models is discussed here, which is based on interpretable attention scores and could allow for measuring which model is "more wrong".

## 2   Background and Related Work

### 2.1   The OK-VQA Task

Over the last years, several datasets were proposed for benchmarking progress on different VQA tasks (an overview can be found in [20]). The first dataset devoted specifically for the OK-VQA task was the eponymous dataset introduced in 2019 [12]. An example from the dataset can be seen in Fig. 1. Since the answer

**Fig. 1.** Question: What fruit is this beverage made of? Answer: "grapes"

"grapes" is neither in the image nor in the question, the given data has to be somehow connected with an outside knowledge source that, for example, contains the knowledge triplet (wine, madeFrom, grapes). The OK-VQA dataset contains 14,055 open-ended questions and corresponding images like this example, which are split into different categories and over two parts of the dataset: A training dataset that contains 9,009 image/question pairs and a test dataset that serves as the dataset for the actual evaluation and contains 5,046 image/question pairs, while human annotators provided the corresponding answers.

## 2.2 Related Work

OK-VQA approaches often deal with three types of data, namely textual, image, and graph data. Most of the current approaches are built with submodules that use the attention mechanism at some point within their pipeline and can be divided into text-centric and graph-centric strategies.

Text-centric strategies consider the task as a Natural Language Processing (NLP) task and focus on generating verbose image captions [5] or textual representations of knowledge triples [1]. Like Question Answering (QA) strategies in the NLP domain, this approaches are centered on providing a given context to a given question and generating an answer based on this information.

Other approaches focus more on the representation of the constructed graph data. MUCKO [21] constructs modal-specific subgraphs that are processed within submodules of the overall model representing visual, semantic and fact-based graph data. At the center of the MuKEA [4] approach is the goal of learning multi-modal knowledge triples to construct a KG that correlates visual objects, internal knowledge, and external knowledge in the form of (visualInformation, relation, textLabel). The resulting KG is used to directly infer an answer corresponding to a given image/question pair, which can be seen as predicting the tail from the accumulated knowledge triples. Similarly to MUCKO, MSG-KRM [8] constructs a multi-modal KG (MMKG) by building three separate KGs for integrating knowledge from the three sources above, introducing both symbolic and non-symbolic nodes in the process. Unlike within the MUCKO architecture, information on the type of edges is also evaluated by the utilized GNN, which itself is based on GAT. This allows for increased interpretability of the model, which, like in MUCKO, considers the intermediate layers handling the modal-specific KGs. However, the output from these layers is passed to a further layer in both cases, which hinders the interpretability of how the final predictions came to be.

The KRISP (Knowledge Reasoning with Implicit and Symbolic rePresentations) model was introduced in 2021 [11]. Due to its significance within this investigation, the details of the model are considered in the following sections. Here, the goal is to contextualize the KRISP approach in the general OK-VQA field to give reasons why it was chosen as a baseline model:

- KRISP considers internal and symbolic knowledge and can be understood as a representative example of approaches that follow this strategy due to its popularity and good results on the OK-VQA benchmark.
- KRISP is not interpretable by design, but the interpretability can be improved by updates proposed in this paper.
- The component that handles graph data within KRISP is one of its last layers within the overall architecture, so the results generated here can be considered to be representative of the final predictions.

## 3    Methodology

### 3.1    An Overview of the KRISP Approach

There are several possible sources for retrieving knowledge within the OK-VQA task. A common differentiation is to distinguish between implicit and explicit/symbolic knowledge. **Implicit knowledge** can be retrieved from pre-trained NN-based models. It is non-symbolic, meaning that only the trained weights of an NN represent some sort of knowledge. However, these weights are not interpretable for humans out of the box, since they are available only as a large set of numerical values. Another source of knowledge is explicit knowledge, or **symbolic knowledge**, which consists of unstructured or structured knowledge, such as in the form of excerpts of publicly available KGs. The original KRISP [11] model presented a novel approach to combine the two sources of external knowledge representations. The source for implicit knowledge was the pre-trained and transformer-based language model BERT [3], which is used within the utilized VisualBERT [10] architecture. The symbolic knowledge was represented by a KG, which was constructed from excerpts from several publicly available knowledge bases and processed by a GNN.

The processing and combination of these sources can be summarized as follows:

1. A question/image pair is processed by a Faster R-CNN [15] object detector and textual processors.
2. The VisualBERT submodule receives a preprocessed question/image pair.
3. The output of the last layer of the VisualBERT submodule, $z^{implicit}$, is returned.
4. The prediction $y^{implicit}$ is calculated from $z^{implicit}$.

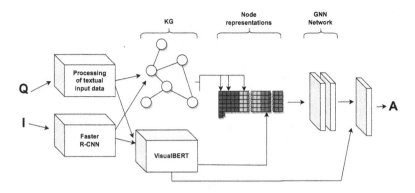

**Fig. 2.** Overview of the general KRISP approach.

5. $z^{implicit}$ is compressed from a vector of 768d to 128d and is passed to the GNN-based submodule together with the pre-processed question/image pair.
6. In the GNN-based submodule, all nodes that correspond to the question/image input data are activated based on preprocessed KG data.
7. The compressed $z^{implicit}$ vector is concatenated to every activated node, which is the first strategy to integrate internal and symbolic knowledge in KRISP.
8. The updated KG is passed to a GNN-based submodule, which returns $z^{symbolic}$.
9. The prediction of the GNN-based submodule, $y^{symbolic}$, is calculated by multiplying $z^{implicit}$ and $z^{symbolic}$. This is the second strategy of integrating the two knowledge sources within KRISP, which is called "late fusion".
10. The two vectors containing the predictions scores $y^{implicit}$ and $y^{symbolic}$ are concatenated.
11. The final answer predictions correspond to the highest score values within the concatenated prediction vector.

A visualization of the summarized steps can be seen in the model overview in Fig. 2. More information on KRISP as well as the original training details like hyperparameter settings can be found in the original paper [11].

### 3.2 Preparation of the GNN Input Data

The construction strategy of KRISP can be divided into two parts: (a) Constructing a KG based on excerpts from existing KGs like ConceptNet [16] during data preprocessing steps, and (b), adding dimensions representing information about the node.

The KG representation in (b) is built as a 433d vector with the following elements:

1. Element 0: A binary value indicating if the concept appears in the question.
2. Elements 1–4: Probabilities between 0 and 1 from each of the 4 classifiers, indicating the probability of a concept being detected in the image.

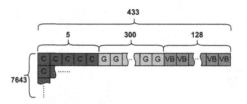

**Fig. 3.** Node feature construction within the KRISP approach (resulting in a 7643 × 433 matrix)

3. Elements 5–304: A 300d GloVe representation of the concept label.
4. Elements 305–432: $z^{implicit}$ from the VisualBERT submodule, compressed to 128 elements.

During the pre-processing step, the KG representation is constructed with a vector of 305d which is added to each node, where the first five elements correspond to (1) and (2) and are set to 0 at the beginning. Additionally, a 300d GloVe representation (3) is added to every node. GloVe (Global Vectors for Word Representation) [14] is a pre-trained model for acquiring word embeddings. During the actual training, information about the nodes related to each question/image pair is gathered from preprocessed data, specifically information regarding (1) and (2). In this way, the nodes are "activated" to indicate the relevant nodes within the KG for further processing. All other node representations are set to 0 within (1) and (2) while the GloVe representation remains. Finally, (4) is concatenated as a version of $z^{implicit}$, which was compressed from 768d to 128d by passing it through a linear transformation layer and a subsequent ReLU activation for efficiency reasons. The resulting matrix is visualized in Fig. 3.

### 3.3 The Baseline Model and the Proposed Updates

**KRISP-GCN: The Baseline Model Configuration.** The model that was chosen as the baseline within this investigation is a configuration of the general KRISP approach. While there are other configurations discussed in the original paper regarding the architecture of the GNN submodule, the reason for choosing GCN was the question of scope: One goal of this investigation is to improve the interpretability of a baseline model by utilizing an attention-based counterpart.

**KRISP-GAT: Replacing GCN with GAT.** The first update to the baseline model KRISP-GCN focuses on the utilized architecture within the GNN-submodule: The GCN-based network is replaced with GAT. One reason for this update is the expectation that the performance of the model could improve, since GAT often performs better than GCN, as concluded by findings like in [13]. The other reason for this choice is the utilization of the attention mechanism. While the structure of node surroundings is reflected by considering the node degrees in GCN, the so-called "normalization coefficients" remain static values during the learning process. These coefficients become learnable parameters in GAT

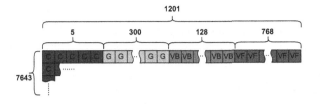

**Fig. 4.** Node feature construction within the proposed KRISP-GAT-VF update (resulting in a 7643 × 1201 matrix)

called attention scores [9] – values that are interpretable by humans, since they are normalized between 0 and 1 and correspond to the calculated importance of the relation between two nodes.

**KRISP-GAT-VF: Augmenting the KG with Visual Features.** Within KRISP, the vector representing each node's features has 5 classifier elements representing the visual content of the image, 300 elements representing the GloVe embedding of the textual label of the node, and 128 elements representing the output of the VisualBERT module. Although the GloVe vector is the largest chunk of each node vector, the evaluations in the KRISP paper [11] indicate that its influence is rather small: Its ablation results in a drop in accuracy of only 0.36%. On the other hand, the representation of the visual content is represented by only five elements that do not contain any visual features, but probabilities regarding whether a concept is present in the image or the question. The Faster R-CNN object detector considers the region around a detected object, marked by a bounding box. This cut-out of the image is further processed and is compressed to a 2048d feature vector in the process. This vector is the same vector that represents a visual embedding and is processed within the VisualBERT submodule, where it is further compressed to 768d. As a second update within this paper and as visualized in Fig. 4, the augmentation of the input vectors of the nodes by this compressed vector is proposed. In this way, the initial node representations are enriched by the actual representation of a visual concept in the image.

## 4   Evaluation

### 4.1   Presentation and Discussion of Accuracy Results

A way of calculating accuracy on the VQA task was introduced within the family of VQA datasets [6] with Accuracy(ans) = $\min\left(\frac{human_{ans} \cdot ans}{3}, 1\right)$, where $human_{ans} \in \mathbb{N}_0$ is the number of humans who provided the same answer within the annotation, as the given answer $ans$. Table 1 displays the results of the baseline evaluation and the evaluation of its updates, where KRISP-GAT corresponds to the results of the first update proposed in this paper, and KRISP-GAT-VF to the second. For a better comparison, the two updates were also trained with the GCN architecture from the baseline. Since there are several randomized factors that could influence the outcome during the training of a model, each configuration was trained in three separate runs. The results indicate that the goal of maintaining the level of accuracy while increasing the interpretability has been reached with the first proposed update. Here, switching out the GCN architecture with an architecture that includes attention scores did lead to an increase in accuracy. However, the results also indicate that the proposed update of KG construction did not improve the results. In fact, while the KRISP-GCN-VF yielded the best results (which could indicate that the general node construction strategy is promising), its counterpart KRISP-GAT-VF yielded the worst. Thus, it can be concluded that increasing the interpretability alongside the accuracy can actually be achieved – but not across every scenario.

### 4.2    Increasing the Interpretability

Currently, there is no consensus on a definition of interpretability or explainability within the literature, and both terms are often used interchangeably. In [9], the current discussions are summarized in regard to a model that can be "interpretable" or "explainable". It is deemed "interpretable" if it is understandable to humans by design, like a decision tree (or, in our case, a knowledge graph). "Explainable", on the other hand, is attributed to models whose results can only be understood post-hoc by applying explainability methods. In [19], the utilization of attention scores for interpretability is compared to post-hoc explanations of model predictions, while there is also a significant difference: The attention scores are a fundamental part of the overall model; they are not computed post-hoc for explanatory reasons. Their interpretation can be seen as considering a byproduct for interpretability purposes, so in terms introduced above, it could be understood as a partially human-readable model, but only if some specific parts of the model are considered after the prediction.

Furthermore, while interpretability is often referred to as a "degree", there is currently no framework available to measure, for example, how much a model update actually changed the degree. Since, for now, only a binary interpretability measure that represents whether a model prediction is interpretable, or not, is applicable, interpretability will be defined qualitatively (based on [19]): The interpretability of a model is given when a human observer can interpret the cause of a decision. The following case studies were conducted to showcase the enhanced interpretation.

**Table 1.** Level of Accuracy on the OK-VQA benchmark

| Model | Run 1 | Run 2 | Run 3 | mean | std |
|---|---|---|---|---|---|
| KRISP-GCN | 0.3095 | 0.3159 | 0.3126 | 0.3127 | 0.0032 |
| KRISP-GCN-VF | 0.3272 | 0.3189 | 0.3214 | 0.3225 | 0.0043 |
| KRISP-GAT | 0.3167 | 0.3222 | 0.3205 | 0.3198 | 0.0028 |
| KRISP-GAT-VF | 0.3097 | 0.3132 | 0.3112 | 0.3114 | 0.0018 |

**Table 2.** Top 3 predictions returned by the model and its VisualBERT and GNN submodules for the target node "grape". Note: Due to the construction strategy of the answer vocabulary some answers can be predicted twice.

|                    | 1              | 2                | 3                   |
|--------------------|----------------|------------------|---------------------|
| Overall GCN        | grape, 0.9999  | grape, 0.9992    | purple, 0.0049      |
| Overall GAT        | grape, 0.9168  | grape, 0.2772    | wine, 0.2051        |
| VisualBERT in GCN  | grape, 0.9993  | wine, 0.0024     | vitamin c, 0.0.0019 |
| VisualBERT in GAT  | grape, 0.9168  | wine, 0.0207     | glass, 0.0192       |
| GNN in GCN         | grape, 0.9999  | purple, 0.0049   | green, 0.0034       |
| GNN in GAT         | grape, 0.2772  | wine, 0.2051     | bottle, 0.1187      |
| Target             | grape          |                  |                     |

## Case 1: Right Answer in KRISP-GCN and KRISP-GAT

In Table 2, we can see that the resulting predictions for both, the original KRISP-GCN baseline model and the proposed KRISP-GAT update, correspond to the correct target answer with high confidence scores. When considering the results of KRISP-GCN, the prediction values are the only information that can be interpreted concerning the computation of the results. For example, we can see that in this particular case, the confidence of the prediction is so high that the next scored prediction is only at 0.0049. This seems to indicate a difference in the calculation within the GAT architecture, where the other probable answers within the top 5 results are all above 0.1. Also, the VisualBERT representation within the node vectors seems to have a weaker influence on GAT than GCN, since the results from the GAT submodule are more present in the overall scores. Although the information about the final predictions can already be somewhat interpreted about how it came to be, this is all the information we have in the case of GCN. With GAT, attention scores can be considered for further interpretability. The difference becomes apparent in Table 3: Since we are working with a KG, we can consider the final target node and its relations to its neighbors to interpret the result. With GCN, we can speculate that the most important relation for the result follows the intuition that we are looking for a knowledge triple with "wine" as the head and "grape" as the tail, but we do not know for sure. With GAT, we can consider the attention scores of the edges and see that, in fact, "wine" is considered to be the most important neighbor.

**Table 3.** Attention scores for the top 5 neighbors of the target node.

| Path               | Attention Score |
|--------------------|-----------------|
| wine – grape       | 0.8012          |
| water – grape      | 0.0496          |
| melon – grape      | 0.0403          |
| chardonnay – grape | 0.0154          |
| plant – grape      | 0.0147          |

**Table 4.** Top 3 predictions returned by the model and its VisualBERT and GNN submodules.

|                       | 1                | 2                | 3                           |
| --------------------- | ---------------- | ---------------- | --------------------------- |
| Overall GAT           | usa, 0.3675      | walmart, 0.2221  | macintosh, 0.1849           |
| Overall GAT-VF        | england, 0.8848  | china, 0.8597    | china, 0.67169              |
| VisualBERT in GAT     | england, 0.105   | disney, 0.0780   | theodore roosevelt, 0.0764  |
| VisualBERT in GAT-VF  | england, 0.8848  | china, 0.6716    | france, 0.2238              |
| GNN in GAT            | usa, 0.3675      | walmart, 0.2220  | macintosh, 0.1849           |
| GNN in GAT-VF         | china, 0.8598    | europe, 0.5159   | england, 0.3935             |
| Target                | germany          |                  |                             |

**Case 2: Wrong Answers in KRISP-GAT and KRISP-GAT-VF.** Inspired by the field of Inconsistency Measurement [7], the goal of the second case study is to explore the possibility of interpreting attention scores to quantify the wrongness of a prediction by investigating the example in Fig. 5. As seen in Table 4, both models that were proposed within this investigation yield wrong results. In both cases, the target "germany" is not only not predicted, but is also not present in the top 3 predictions (and also not in the top 15, actually). In both cases, the predicted result is wrong across all submodules. It is, however, notable that the top-scoring predictions are countries. In fact, the predicted nodes and the target node are 1-hop neighbors of the node "country" in our KG. Even without interpreting attention scores, this opens up the strategy of counting the hops between the predictions and the targets based on the KG to get a quantification of how far away a prediction is from a target. An additional strategy could be to incorporate the attention scores on the paths between the activated nodes and the targets. In this case, the sum in KRISP-GAT results in 1.4063, while the sum in KRISP-GAT-VF results in 0.7445. This sum of the attention scores across selected paths could indicate that KRISP-GAT-VF is "more wrong" than KRISP-GAT, where a higher scored value could indicate that the model is closer in confidence to the target prediction. An inconsistency measure based on this sum could also be computed for all wrong answers on a dataset and thus be explored as another metric for the evaluation of a model, in addition to accuracy.

**Fig. 5.** Question: Which country are these souvenirs from? Answer: "germany"

# 5  Conclusion and Outlook

The results within the quantitative evaluation indicate that it is possible to improve the accuracy and the interpretability of a model simultaneously by utilizing an attention-based GNN architecture, like in the case of replacing a GCN architecture with a GAT architecture. The findings also suggest that this is not a universal occurrence in all situations. This was especially surprising regarding the second proposed update of this paper, the augmentation of the constructed node features with visual features representing the detected object. While this update did lead to a comparably large improvement when used together with a GCN architecture, it failed to do so when used together with GAT.

The purpose of the case studies was to investigate how attention scores increase the interpretability of a model. One first approach was to consider the actual attention scores in regard to correctly predicted answers. When considering the surroundings of a target node with GCN, there might be an intuition of which neighbors might have been considered the most important ones for the result. With the GAT architecture, it seems to be possible to know for sure. The biggest takeaway from the case studies, however, is that attention scores could make models comparable beyond prediction probabilities. This remains to be investigated systematically in future work, but some first pointers could be concluded from the case studies. The main idea here was that attention scores could be used to investigate how wrong a model is compared to a model with correct predictions or to compare two models with wrong predictions to evaluate which of the models actually could have gotten closer to a correct result. Thus, attention scores could be used not only in the interpretation of a correct prediction of a model but perhaps also for the formulation of additional metrics besides accuracy. For future work that utilizes GNNs, it could be considered to move away from the binary view of the wrong and right answers and toward a quantification of the wrongness of the answers, similar to the field of Inconsistency Measurement [17]. Especially within GNNs, this could lead to new measurements of how wrong a model actually is, since the attention scores can be compared alongside specific paths within the utilized graphs. This opens up new possibilities for comparing and interpreting the outcome of GNN-based architectures.

# References

1. Chen, Z., et al.: LaKo: knowledge-driven visual question answering via late knowledge-to-text injection. arXiv (2022)
2. DeLong, L.N., Mir, R.F., Whyte, M., Ji, Z., Fleuriot, J.D.: Neurosymbolic AI for reasoning on graph structures: a survey. arXiv (2023)
3. Devlin, J., Chang, M.W., Lee, K., Toutanova, K.: BERT: pre-training of deep bidirectional transformers for language understanding. In: Proceedings of the 2019 Conference of the North American Chapter of the Association for Computational Linguistics: Human Language Technologies. Association for Computational Linguistics, Minneapolis (2019)

4. Ding, Y., Yu, J., Liu, B., Hu, Y., Cui, M., Wu, Q.: MuKEA: multimodal knowledge extraction and accumulation for knowledge-based visual question answering. In: 2022 IEEE/CVF Conference on Computer Vision and Pattern Recognition (CVPR), pp. 5079–5088. IEEE, New Orleans (2022)

5. Gao, F., Ping, Q., Thattai, G., Reganti, A., Wu, Y.N., Natarajan, P.: A thousand words are worth more than a picture: natural language-centric outside-knowledge visual question answering. arXiv (2022)

6. Goyal, Y., Khot, T., Summers-Stay, D., Batra, D., Parikh, D.: Making the V in VQA matter: elevating the role of image understanding in visual question answering. In: Conference on Computer Vision and Pattern Recognition (CVPR) (2017)

7. Grant, J.: Classifications for Inconsistent Theories, vol. 19, pp. 435–444. Duke University Press (1978)

8. Jiang, L., Meng, Z.: Knowledge-based visual question answering using multi-modal semantic graph. Electronics **12**(6), 1390 (2023)

9. Labonne, M.: Hands-On Graph Neural Networks Using Python. Packt Publishing Ltd., Birmingham (2023)

10. Li, L.H., Yatskar, M., Yin, D., Hsieh, C.J., Chang, K.W.: VisualBERT: a simple and performant baseline for vision and language (2019)

11. Marino, K., Chen, X., Parikh, D., Gupta, A., Rohrbach, M.: KRISP: integrating implicit and symbolic knowledge for open-domain knowledge-based VQA. In: 2021 IEEE/CVF Conference on Computer Vision and Pattern Recognition (CVPR), pp. 14106–14116. IEEE, Nashville (2021)

12. Marino, K., Rastegari, M., Farhadi, A., Mottaghi, R.: OK-VQA: a visual question answering benchmark requiring external knowledge. In: Proceedings of the IEEE/CVF Conference on Computer Vision and Pattern Recognition (CVPR) (2019)

13. Pal, A., Murugan, S., Sankarasubbu, M.: MAGNET: multi-label text classification using attention-based graph neural network, pp. 494–505 (01 2020)

14. Pennington, J., Socher, R., Manning, C.: GloVe: global vectors for word representation. In: Proceedings of the 2014 Conference on Empirical Methods in Natural Language Processing (EMNLP), pp. 1532–1543. Association for Computational Linguistics, Doha (2014)

15. Ren, S., He, K., Girshick, R., Sun, J.: Faster R-CNN: towards real-time object detection with region proposal networks. In: Advances in Neural Information Processing Systems, vol. 28. Curran Associates, Inc. (2015)

16. Speer, R., Chin, J., Havasi, C.: ConceptNet 5.5: an open multilingual graph of general knowledge (2018)

17. Ulbricht, M., Thimm, M., Brewka, G.: Handling and measuring inconsistency in non-monotonic logics. Artif. Intell. **286**, 103344 (2020)

18. Vaswani, A., et al.: Attention is all you need. In: Guyon, I., et al. (eds.) Advances in Neural Information Processing Systems, vol. 30. Curran Associates, Inc. (2017)

19. Wu, L., Cui, P., Pei, J., Zhao, L. (eds.): Graph Neural Networks. Springer, Singapore (2022). https://doi.org/10.1007/978-981-16-6054-2

20. Wu, Q., Wang, P., Wang, X., He, X., Zhu, W.: Visual Question Answering. Springer, Singapore (2022). https://doi.org/10.1007/978-981-19-0964-1

21. Zhu, Z., Yu, J., Wang, Y., Sun, Y., Hu, Y., Wu, Q.: Mucko: multi-layer cross-modal knowledge reasoning for fact-based visual question answering. arXiv (2020)

# Application of Open AI in Small and Medium-Sized Enterprise (SME) Risk Assessment and Financial Analysis System

Chia-Chun Kang[✉], Li-Jie Zhang, Jie-Mie Wang, and Chi-Hsu Lin

Shu-Te University, Kaohsiung City, Taiwan
{kcc0211,s21113107,s21113123,s21113109}@stu.edu.tw

**Abstract.** In recent years, with the rapid development of technology, artificial intelligence (AI) has also been growing rapidly. From widely known applications like Apple's Siri to the recent highly popular Chat-GPT, people are leveraging AI for entertainment, learning, creative endeavors, and more. This project aims to utilize the widely acclaimed ChatGPT to create risk assessment and financial analysis tools tailored for small and medium-sized enterprises (SMEs), thereby facilitating business growth.

**Keywords:** Artificial Intelligence · Small and Medium-sized Enterprise · SME · OpenAI · Risk Assessment · Financial Analysis

## 1 Introduction

In today's business environment, small and medium-sized enterprises (SMEs) face various challenges, particularly in the areas of financial management and risk assessment. Many SME operators and finance professionals often lack the utilization of publicly available information as a reference for evaluating the risk of counterparties [7]. Typically, they rely on industry information or intuitive judgments to decide whether to engage in business transactions with a particular party.

In these enterprises, financial decisions are often made directly by the owner or their spouse, and transactions are conducted through corporate online banking or in-person at the counter. However, before entering into transactions, these businesses often do not conduct thorough market information queries and risk assessments on the counterparty, which may lead to unnecessary financial crises [3].

To address this issue, our team has developed a financial and market risk assessment system. This system aims to assist SMEs in more effectively assessing the risk of potential counterparties, providing comprehensive market information and data analysis. Through this system, businesses can obtain detailed reports on the financial condition, credit history, and market performance of their trading partners, enabling them to make more informed financial decisions.

© The Author(s), under exclusive license to Springer Nature Switzerland AG 2024
L. Uden and I.-H. Ting (Eds.): KMO 2024, CCIS 2152, pp. 331–340, 2024.
https://doi.org/10.1007/978-3-031-63269-3_25

# 2   Literature Review

## 2.1   AI in Finance

AI in finance, the application of artificial intelligence in the financial domain, has become a crucial component of Financial Technology (FinTech) in recent years. The core of AI in finance lies in utilizing technologies such as machine learning, deep learning, natural language processing, and others to analyze and process large volumes of financial data, thereby providing more precise and efficient financial services [2].

In the current era of digitization and rapid technological advancement, the application of artificial intelligence (AI) in the financial sector has emerged as a significant research topic [6]. AI in finance refers to the process of leveraging AI technologies, such as machine learning, deep learning, natural language processing, to enhance the efficiency and quality of financial services [4]. This article explores the applications of AI in the financial sector, including its advantages, challenges, and future development trends.

Firstly, AI plays a crucial role in risk management and fraud detection [10]. By learning from historical transaction data, AI can identify abnormal transaction patterns, issue timely warnings, and prevent financial fraud and credit card scams. For instance, Visa employs an AI system that analyzes each transaction, identifying potential fraudulent activities within milliseconds.

Secondly, in the realm of asset management and investment advisory, AI demonstrates significant potential [8]. Through big data analysis and predictive models, AI can provide personalized investment advice to investors [4]. For example, robo-advisors automatically construct and adjust investment portfolios based on users' risk preferences and investment goals.

Additionally, AI plays a key role in enhancing the efficiency of banking operations [6]. AI can handle vast amounts of repetitive tasks, such as answering common customer service queries and conducting data analysis during the credit assessment process. This not only improves work efficiency but also allows employees to focus on more valuable tasks [5,10].

However, the development of AI in finance also faces challenges, with data privacy and security being the most prominent [1]. As AI systems increasingly rely on personal and corporate data, protecting this data from misuse becomes a significant challenge. Furthermore, the transparency and interpretability of AI decision-making processes are crucial issues. Many AI models, such as deep learning models, are considered black box models, making their decision-making processes difficult to interpret, leading to potential regulatory compliance issues [5].

In conclusion, AI in finance is gradually transforming the traditional financial industry, providing more intelligent, efficient, and personalized financial services. In the future, with technological advancements and improved regulations, AI in finance is expected to play a more significant role in areas such as risk control, asset management, and customer service [10].

## 2.2   The Applications of AI in Finance

1. Risk Management: AI technology can effectively analyze large volumes of data to predict and manage credit risk and market risk. Through machine learning models, financial institutions can more accurately assess customer credit scores [3,7].
2. Algorithmic Trading: Leveraging AI for high-frequency trading, automatic execution of trading strategies based on market data and trends. AI can analyze market changes in real-time and make rapid decisions [4,8].
3. Customer Service: Utilizing chatbots and virtual assistants to provide 24-hour customer service. AI can handle common queries, enhancing the overall customer experience [6].
4. Fraud Detection: AI systems can identify abnormal transaction behavior, effectively preventing and reducing financial fraud. Through pattern recognition, AI assists in real-time alerts and blocking suspicious transactions [2,10].

## 2.3   The Advantages of AI in Finance

1. Efficiency Enhancement: AI can process a large volume of transactions and conduct data analysis, significantly improving work efficiency, reducing human errors, and enhancing the accuracy of decision-making [4,5].
2. Optimized Customer Experience: Personalized financial products and services tailored to meet individual customer needs, providing faster and more convenient financial services to enhance the overall customer experience [5,6].
3. Innovation: AI drives innovation in financial products and services, paving the way for new business models, fostering the development of financial technology, and leading industry transformations [9].

## 2.4   Challenges Faced

1. Data Security and Privacy: Dealing with large volumes of data necessitates ensuring the security and protection of customer privacy. Compliance with regulations and effective data management become crucial issues [8].
2. Technology Integration and Adaptation: Financial institutions need to adapt to new technologies and integrate them into existing systems. Employees must cultivate relevant skills to cope with the application of AI technology [6].

## 2.5   Future Trends

1. Application of Deep Learning and Reinforcement Learning: It is anticipated that there will be increased utilization of deep learning and reinforcement learning technologies in the financial sector. This is expected to further enhance the predictive capabilities of models and the quality of decision-making [3].

2. Integration of Blockchain and AI: The combination of blockchain technology and AI is expected to enhance data security and transparency. This integration is likely to drive the development of smart contracts and decentralized finance [9].

In summary, the application of AI in the financial sector is rapidly evolving, bringing forth numerous opportunities and challenges. In the future, with technological advancements and the refinement of relevant regulations, AI is poised to play an even more critical role in the financial industry.

# 3    The Proposed Risk Assessment and Financial Analysis System

Some businesses lack relevant information about their trading partners before entering into transactions [4]. Often, they only discover financial issues with their counterparts, such as the inability to make payments, through information provided by industry peers. This situation can lead to financial crises or even bankruptcy for small and medium-sized enterprises.

Furthermore, when it comes to self-assessment of company finances, many business owners are not clear about the financial condition of their own companies. They may be unable to perceive the financial health of their companies through financial statements. Through the system developed in this research, business owners can have a more convenient way to examine the financial condition of their companies.

## 3.1    The Concept of the System

In the rapidly evolving digital business environment of today, small and medium-sized enterprises (SMEs) face increasingly complex market challenges, especially in fund management and risk assessment [5]. To assist these enterprises in addressing these challenges more effectively, our team has developed an innovative financial and market risk assessment system. This system utilizes web scraping technology written in the Python language, combined with advanced artificial intelligence analysis (such as ChatGPT), and is presented through a user-friendly web interface. The aim is to provide SMEs with a convenient and powerful data analysis tool.

The core functionality of this system is to facilitate effective coordination between SMEs and their trading partners in terms of the supply of funds. Through our system, users can easily access key market and financial risk information, carefully selected and analyzed from public market data and various financial resources. This enables business owners and financial decision-makers to make informed financial decisions based on more comprehensive and accurate information, ensuring the long-term stability and development of their businesses.

## 3.2    The Risk Assessment System

The Risk Assessment System is a tool designed specifically to enhance the decision-making quality of small and medium-sized enterprises (SMEs) in business transactions. The core functionality of this system involves utilizing web scraping technology to retrieve and analyze relevant information about specific companies from public resources, followed by a risk assessment based on a set of scoring criteria.

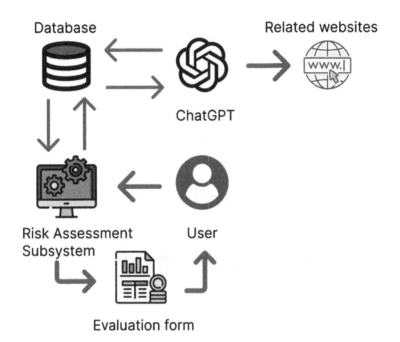

**Fig. 1.** The Process of Risk Assessment

Figure 1 is the main features and functionalities of the system and the details are discussed below.

1. Data Input: Users only need to provide the target company's unified business number and full name, and the system will automatically conduct data retrieval.
2. Web Scraping Technology: Advanced web scraping technology is employed to gather information from various public databases and websites, including government announcements, financial databases, and news reports.
3. Risk Scoring Criteria:
   - Capital Changes: Assess the stability of the company's capital structure.
   - Address Changes: Check if the company frequently changes its business location or expands its operations.

- Personnel Changes: Observe the stability of the company's management, such as frequent changes in leadership.
- Invoice Issuance Status: Examine the company's financial transparency and compliance.
- Operational Status: Confirm whether the company is operating normally.
- Litigation Records: Check if the company is involved in significant legal cases.
- Labor Law Penalties: Verify if the company has records of violating labor standards.
- Environmental Penalties: Assess whether the company complies with environmental regulations.
- Asset Setup: Analyze the company's financial liabilities and mortgage status.

4. Risk Report: The system generates a detailed risk assessment report based on the collected data and scoring for each criterion.
5. Application Value:
   - Decision Support:Provides comprehensive risk assessment to aid businesses in making informed and strategic decisions.
   - Risk Management: Timely identification of potential business risks to reduce the risk of unfavorable investments or collaborations.
   - Efficiency Enhancement: Automated data collection and analysis significantly save time and resources.

In summary, the Risk Assessment System offers SMEs a powerful tool to better understand and manage risks associated with business transactions, promoting stability and sustained growth for businesses.

### 3.3   The Financial Analysis System

The Financial Analysis System is a tool specifically designed for small and medium-sized enterprises (SMEs), aiming to provide in-depth and intuitive financial data analysis. This system utilizes advanced data processing techniques to extract key financial data from the provided income statements and balance sheet PDF files, offering interactive query functionality.

Figure 2 shows the main features and functionalities of the system and the details are discussed below.

1. Data Extraction: Users upload PDF files of income statements and balance sheets, and the system automatically identifies and extracts key financial data such as revenue, expenses, assets, and liabilities.
2. Data Organization and Analysis: Extracted data is organized and transformed into an easily understandable format. The system performs preliminary analysis, providing an overview of the financial health.
3. Interactive Queries: Users can pose specific financial-related questions to the system, and the system answers these questions based on the provided financial statement data.

4. Intelligent Responses: The system employs advanced natural language processing technology to understand and respond to user queries, with a focus on the data from the provided income statements and balance sheets
5. Application Value:
   (a) In-depth Analysis: Assists users in gaining a deep understanding of the company's financial condition, including profitability, asset-liability structure, and cash flow.
   (b) Decision Support: Provides real-time financial data analysis to help users make more informed decisions.
   (c) Time Savings: The automated data extraction and analysis process significantly save time and effort compared to manual analysis.
   (d) User-Friendly: A user-friendly interface and interactive query system make it easy for non-professionals to use.

In conclusion, this Financial Analysis System provides businesses with a powerful and convenient tool to better understand and analyze their financial statements, facilitating wiser business decisions and financial management.

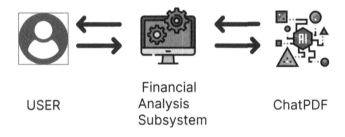

| USER | Financial Analysis Subsystem | ChatPDF |

**Fig. 2.** The Process of Financial Analysis

### 3.4   Carbon Credit Calculation

Calculating carbon credits involves assessing the amount of carbon dioxide an organization, project, or individual reduces or avoids emitting. Carbon credits are tradable units typically representing the right to reduce or avoid one metric ton of carbon dioxide or other greenhouse gas emissions.
   Here are the main features and functionalities of the system:

1. Data Input: Users input relevant data such as energy consumption, transportation methods, production processes, etc.
2. Baseline Setting: The system sets baseline emission levels based on industry standards or historical data.
3. Actual Emission Calculation: Calculates the actual $CO_2$ emissions based on the input data.

4. Emission Reduction Assessment: Automatically calculates emission reductions and converts them into carbon credits.
5. Report Generation: Generates detailed carbon credit reports, including emission reduction effectiveness and corresponding carbon credit quantities.
6. Monitoring and Analysis: Continuously monitors emission levels, provides trend analysis, and offers improvement recommendations.
7. Application Value:
   - Carbon Footprint Management: Assists businesses or individuals in effectively managing and reducing their carbon footprint.
   - Compliance and Reporting: Helps businesses comply with environmental regulations and accurately report emissions.
   - Environmental Responsibility Fulfillment: Demonstrates an organization's environmental responsibility through emission reduction.
   - Financial Opportunities: Carbon credits can be traded as financial assets, providing additional income for businesses.

In summary, this system is a comprehensive carbon credit calculation and management tool designed to help users effectively measure, manage, and reduce their carbon emissions while capitalizing on opportunities in the carbon trading market (Fig. 3).

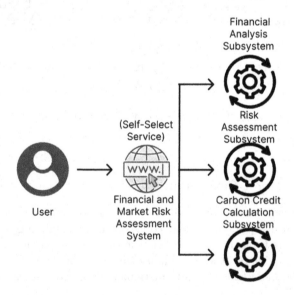

**Fig. 3.** The Process of Risk Assessment and Financial Analysis

# 4   Conclusion and Future Research Suggestions

The Financial Analysis and Market Risk Assessment System is an innovative and versatile tool designed to provide comprehensive financial analysis and market risk assessment for small and medium-sized enterprises (SMEs). This system integrates various functions such as risk assessment, financial analysis, and carbon credit calculations, allowing businesses to conduct all-encompassing financial and market assessments on a unified platform. Through this system, companies can more effectively manage their financial risks, make informed decisions supported by information, and thus maintain competitiveness in a fiercely competitive market environment.

About technological innovation, the development of the system demonstrates the potential application of technology in the fields of financial and risk management. The automation of data analysis and processing significantly enhances efficiency and accuracy.

With the continuous changes in the market environment, the demand from SMEs for tools that can help them understand and manage risks is increasing. The development of this system is a response to this market demand.

Through the carbon credit calculation feature, the system assists companies in assessing and managing their environmental impact. This is a crucial step towards achieving sustainable development goals, highlighting that businesses can take on environmental responsibility while pursuing economic interests.

About future development, With advancements in technology and shifts in the market, there is potential for further development of this system, including the integration of more advanced analytical tools and algorithms. Future exploration may involve expanding the system into additional sectors and markets to meet broader user requirements.

# References

1. Koessler, L., Schuett, J.: Risk assessment at AGI companies: a review of popular risk assessment techniques from other safety-critical industries. Cornell University (2023)
2. Chehri, A., Fofana, I., Yang, X.: Security risk modeling in smart grid critical infrastructures in the era of big data and artificial intelligence. Sustainability 13, 3196 (2021)
3. Mhlanga, D.: Financial inclusion in emerging economies: the application of machine learning and artificial intelligence in credit risk assessment. Int. J. Financ. Stud. 9, 39 (2021)
4. Melnychenko, O.: Is artificial intelligence ready to assess an enterprise's financial security? J. Rick Financ. Manag. 13, 191 (2020)
5. Berdiyeva, O.: Artificial intelligence in accounting and finance: meta-analysis. NUST Bus. Rev. 3, 56–79 (2021)
6. Ren, C.: Assessing the efficacy of ChatGPT in addressing Chinese financial conundrums: an in-depth comparative analysis of human and AI-generated responses. Comput. Hum. Behav.: Artif. Hum. 1, 100007 (2023)

7. Yu, L.: An AI approach to measuring financial risk. Singapore Econ. Rev. **68**, 1529–1549 (2023)
8. Wang, N.: Application of artificial intelligence and big data in modern financial management. IEEE Xplore (2020)
9. Kazachenok, O.P.: Economic and legal approaches to the humanization of FinTech in the economy of artificial intelligence through the integration of blockchain into ESG Finance. Humanit. Soc. Sci. Commun. **10**, 1–9 (2023)
10. Rane, N.: Blockchain and artificial intelligence (AI) integration for revolutionizing security and transparency in finance. SSRN (2023)

# An Initial Insight into Measuring Quality in Cloud-Native Architectures

Vasilka Saklamaeva[✉], Tina Beranič, and Luka Pavlič

Faculty of Electrical Engineering and Computer Science, University of Maribor,
Koroška Cesta 46, 2000 Maribor, Slovenia
{vasilka.saklamaeva,tina.beranic,luka.pavlic}@um.si

**Abstract.** Cloud-native architectures represent a shift in the IT landscape by delivering ICT services "as a service" and necessitating additional emphasis on the aspects of quality as organizations migrate applications to these environments. This paper presents the findings of an initial review examining quality models, metrics, and thresholds within the domain of cloud-native architectures. The study encompassed 41 relevant publications, offering insights into the evolution of research trends over the years. Extracting key data from these studies, we analyzed facets such as the focus on quality dimensions, research types, contribution types, and citation rates. Our results reveal a prevalence of solution proposals and opinion papers, concentrating on metrics, models, methods, and tools. Notably, the peak of significant publications occurred in 2020. Most studies concentrated on investigating performance-related quality aspects, followed closely by Quality of Service (QoS), monitoring, and scalability. The presented overview provides a valuable reference and starting point for researchers and practitioners navigating the landscape of quality considerations in cloud-native architectures.

**Keywords:** cloud · cloud-based · cloud-native · quality · model · metric

## 1 Introduction

In the continuously evolving domain of IT, the emergence of cloud-native architectures has brought a paradigm shift in the methodologies employed for the information systems design, development, and deployment. Cloud computing is a paradigm in which ICT services are provided on a demand basis and "as a service". [1] This model involves dynamically adjusting resources to accommodate fluctuating workloads [1, 2]. As organizations progressively transition their applications to cloud environments, ensuring the quality of these dynamic and distributed systems becomes of utmost importance.

Several research papers have addressed the domain of defining quality models and metrics in cloud-native architectures. The research gap this paper endeavors to bridge pertains to the presentation of novel insights via a review of quality within cloud-native architectures. We were curious to explore the variations of these findings across diverse settings, with the final goal of enhancing our understanding of this area of interest. The aim of this paper is to highlight some insights within our research into the quality

© The Author(s), under exclusive license to Springer Nature Switzerland AG 2024
L. Uden and I.-H. Ting (Eds.): KMO 2024, CCIS 2152, pp. 341–351, 2024.
https://doi.org/10.1007/978-3-031-63269-3_26

dimensions within cloud-native architectures. Given the rising adoption of cloud-native practices, understanding the quality attributes inherent in these architectures takes a pivotal role in realizing effective digital transformations.

At the beginning of our research, we formulated a research question to enhance our understanding of the research area presented above. It serves as a guiding inquiry, directing our efforts and providing a structured path to address the complexities and nuances of our chosen area of research.

***RQ1: What are the Primary Types of Quality Models, Metrics, and Thresholds Used in Cloud-Native Architectures?***

Our initial research question was broken into sub-questions, aiming to establish a landscape of the basic characteristics of the identified studies. Within the purview of RQ1 supplementary data was sought, exposing the formation of the following sub-questions:

***RQ1.1:*** *How does the distribution of publications appear over the years?*
***RQ1.2:*** *Which authors are the most influential in this area?*
***RQ1.3:*** *In which scholarly venues do researchers disseminate their findings?*
***RQ1.4:*** *To which facets of quality does the study direct its focus?*
***RQ1.5:*** *What typology characterizes the research conducted in the study?*
***RQ1.6:*** *What primary type of contribution does the study offer?*
***RQ1.7:*** *What is the magnitude of citations acquired by the studies?*

The rest of the paper is structured as follows. Section 2 provides a review of current literature within the domain of quality in cloud-native architectures, accompanied by a presentation of the literature review. Section 3 describes the outcomes of our initial study, and in Sect. 4 we discuss the knowledge we found. In Sect. 5, we draw conclusions, encapsulating the key findings derived from our research questions, and provide directions for future research.

## 2 Literature Review

### 2.1 Related Work

To further understand our designated research area, we examined related works within the realm of quality in cloud-native architectures. Odun-Ayo et al. [3] conducted a systematic mapping study that centered on three dimensions: topic (architectures, cloud migrations, development, implementation, security, and application), research, and contribution. In contrast to their emphasis on cloud-native architectures, our research diverges as it exclusively concentrates on the quality aspects inherent in cloud-native architectures.

Ravi et al. [4] conducted an in-depth examination centered on analytics, specifically exploring two aspects: analytics in and for cloud. Their review encompassed an analysis of 88 research articles published between 2003 and 2017, which differs from our focus on the intersection between quality and cloud-native computing. Scheuner et al. [5] undertook a multivocal examination of FaaS performance through a comprehensive literature review. Their analysis encompassed 112 studies sourced from both academic and grey literature. The study brought to light existing gaps in the literature, but only focusing on FaaS.

## 2.2  Review Methodology

To investigate the defined research question along with its associated sub-questions outlined in Sect. 1, we followed a few sequential steps:

1. **Initial Search**: Employing the predefined search strings, we explored the designated digital libraries while adhering to the specified inclusion and exclusion criteria.
2. **Duplicate Removal**: A removal of duplicate entries from the initial set of literature resulted in a refined collection of unique hits.
3. **Title-Based Screening**: In this phase, potential irrelevant literature was excluded based on title and in alignment with the specified inclusion and exclusion criteria.
4. **Abstract-Based Screening**: After an examination of abstracts in accordance with the established criteria, 169 papers were excluded, leaving a selection of **168** papers.
5. **Content-Based Screening**: As the conclusive step, a content-based screening was executed, resulting in the exclusion of 127 papers. This process also encompassed data extraction and mapping, with the outcomes presented in Table 1. The final refined selection comprised **41** papers.

The identification of primary sources was conducted in December 2023. To augment the comprehensiveness of our findings, we executed searches across five digital libraries, namely IEEE Xplore, ScienceDirect, SpringerLink, ACM Digital Library, and Web of Science. In these digital libraries, we employed five specific search strings to retrieve relevant literature, which are shown in the list below.

- **SS1:** "cloud AND native AND (architectur* OR *aaS) AND (quality OR model* OR metric* OR performance OR secur* OR scal* OR cost*)"
- **SS2:** "cloud AND native AND (tool* OR assist* OR application OR techniq* OR agent*)"
- **SS3:** "cloud AND native AND quality AND (challeng* OR difficult* OR problem* OR threat* OR issue* OR setback* OR obstacle*)"
- **SS4:** "(custom* OR tailored OR personalized) AND (quality model* OR metric*) AND cloud AND native AND (trend* OR advance* OR new OR emerging)"
- **SS5:** "(best practice* OR trend* OR recommend*) AND (quality model* OR metric*) AND cloud AND native"

To regulate the quality of the retrieved information from the chosen digital libraries, we established specific inclusion and exclusion criteria to refine the set of identified literature. The inclusion criteria comprised aspects such as the requirement for papers to be written in English and their pertinence to topics encompassing cloud-native computing, quality assessment, metrics, and performance within cloud-native architectures. In contrast to that, the exclusion criteria encompassed considerations such as the lack of relevance to cloud-native architectures or applications, non-alignment with the defined research questions, absence of peer-reviewed status (including books, papers from editorials, slides, presentations, etc.), non-affiliation with the fields of computer science and IT, and its inaccessibility.

An aspect we mapped in our research involved categorizing the contribution type for each examined paper. To achieve this, we established a set of six distinct categories, with their respective descriptions outlined in Table 1.

**Table 1.** Contribution type values [3]

| CONTRIBUTION TYPE | DESCRIPTION |
|---|---|
| Model | The creation or proposal of conceptual or architectural frameworks that outline the structure, behavior, or design principles of cloud-native systems |
| Metric | The identification, establishment, or assessment of quantitative or qualitative measures used to evaluate various aspects of cloud-native architectures |
| Method | The introduction or analysis of specific approaches, methodologies, or processes for designing, developing, deploying, or managing cloud-native architectures |
| Tool | The development, improvement, or evaluation of software tools, frameworks, platforms, or technologies specifically designed to support, enable, or enhance cloud-native architectures |
| Process | The definition, analysis, or improvement of workflows, procedures, or systematic approaches related to the lifecycle of cloud-native systems |
| Other | Other types of contributions that are not covered by the categories above |

The complete collection of all mapped data elements for each reviewed research paper encompassed the publication year, research and contribution type, and similar attributes. Table 2 shows all the extracted data elements.

**Table 2:** Data mapping overview

| DATA ITEM | VALUE | PREDEFINED VALUES | RQ |
|---|---|---|---|
| Study ID | Integer | / | |
| Study title | Title of the Research | / | |
| Year of publication | Calendar year | / | 1.1 |
| Author names | Sets of author names | / | 1.2 |
| Venue | Title of publication venue | / | 1.3 |
| Domain aspect | Specific focus of research | / | 1.4 |
| Research type | Research type employed | Opinion paper Experience paper Conceptual paper Solution proposal Validation research Evaluation research | 1.5 |

*(continued)*

**Table 2:** (*continued*)

| DATA ITEM | VALUE | PREDEFINED VALUES | RQ |
|---|---|---|---|
| Contribution type | Nature of the research's contribution | Model<br>Metric<br>Method<br>Tool<br>Process<br>Other | 1.6 |
| Citation number | Number of citations | / | 1.7 |

# 3  Preliminary Results

In this Section, we will investigate the responses to the research question and its associated sub-questions introduced in Sect. 1. This inquiry has been undertaken through a cautious examination of the literature, as detailed in Sect. 2. By examining specific aspects of the identified literature, we have acquired some valuable information that enhances our comprehension and explanation of key aspects within the realm of quality in cloud-native architectures.

Our review comprises of 41 initial papers. Through their review, we observed a progressive exploration of quality considerations in cloud-native architectures dating back to 2010. The trajectory of this exploration showed a steady rise, culminating in a plateau in 2020, during which we identified 7 publications dedicated to addressing this specific aspect. The findings are graphically presented in Fig. 1.

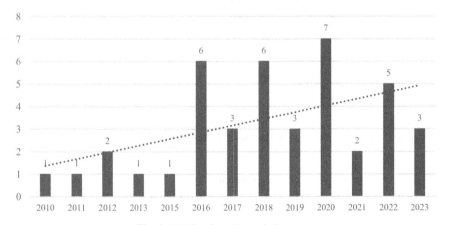

**Fig. 1.** Publications through the years.

Concerning the response to RQ1.2, which investigates the most influential authors in the designated area, we extracted relevant data from the compiled literature. Upon thorough examination, it was observed that while certain author names recurred, there was no noticeable pattern of repeated occurrences. This implies that, to the best of our knowledge, there does not appear to be a specific individual or group actively engaged in systematic exploration within our identified area of interest. Building upon this context, in addressing RQ1.3, no noteworthy venues emerged where authors disseminated their findings more than twice.

In our mapping process, we delved into the quality aspects emphasized by the papers under consideration. Despite a considerable degree of overlap, we systematically categorized these aspects, identifying 17 quality dimensions that have been investigated at various points in time. The graphical representation of these findings is illustrated in Fig. 2. According to the visualization on the referenced graph, most identified aspects address the domain of performance (10), Quality of Service (7), scalability, and monitoring (6 each). Lesser shares are apportioned to optimization, data management, and cost analysis (4 each), while security, resource management, and elasticity each receive a share of 3. Additionally, there are infrequently addressed aspects in the "other" category, such as anomaly detection, adaptability, architectural styles, dependability, observability, resilience, prediction, provisioning, virtualization, analytics, architectural implications, bad practices, maturity model, modelling, root cause analysis, scheduling, heterogeneity, fault-tolerance, privacy, load-balancing, reusability, anti-patterns, and bad smells.

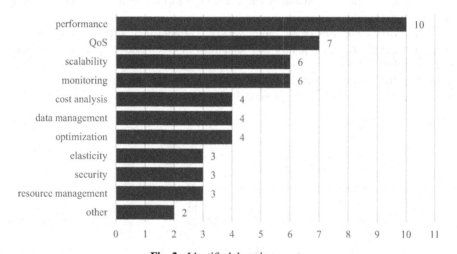

**Fig. 2.** Identified domain aspects.

RQ 1.5 pertained to the research types encompassed in the papers obtained through our review. The criteria for exploring this research question were established by Wieriga et al. [6], as we adhered to the predefined values they advocated for mapping this axis.

Significantly, a noteworthy proportion (20) of the papers fell within the "solution proposal" category (a presentation of an innovative method or enhancement to an existing approach, along with justification for its significance, without comprehensive validation [6]), closely followed by the "opinion paper" category with 15 papers (the articulation of the author's viewpoint on the merits or flaws of something, as well as guidance on how to approach it [6]). Smaller proportions are distributed among the "validation research," "experience paper," and "conceptual paper" categories. Additionally, we did not identify any evaluation research studies. The observed prevalence of opinion papers and solution proposals, particularly in comparison to other classifications, may be attributed to our findings suggesting a multitude of propositions for new tools to monitor quality in cloud-native architectures. Additionally, authors of various research works expressed their opinions on specific issues and proposed solutions. The distribution of papers across these categories is visually illustrated in Fig. 3.

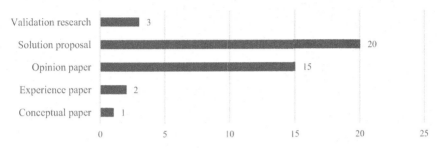

**Fig. 3.** Identified research types.

During our research, we recognized various types of contributions, addressed with RQ1.6. We defined a set of six predetermined variables outlined in Table 1: model, metric, method, tool, process, and other, acknowledging that a single paper may contribute to multiple categories within this set of values but a minimum of one. The findings of this analysis are presented in Fig. 4. Illustrated on the graph is the prevalence of the "metric" category (18 studies in total, e.g. [7–10]) in the identified literature, closely followed by the "model" category (17 in total, e.g. [4, 11, 12]), "method" category (16 in total, e.g. [7, 13, 14]), and "tool" category (14 in total, e.g. [7, 8]). A smaller proportion was allocated to the "process" category (9 overall, e.g. [12, 14]) and the "other" category (7 in total, e.g. [15, 16]), encompassing miscellaneous types of contributions beyond the specified classifications.

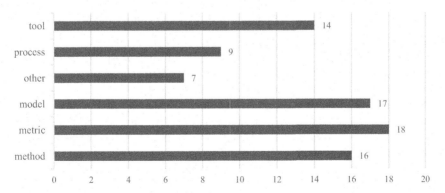

**Fig. 4.** Identified contribution types.

The final dimension explored in our study involves the citation numbers associated with each examined paper. The corresponding results are visually represented in Fig. 5. The citation numbers in the graph pertain to January 2024. Notably, Shahard et al.'s [14] paper garnered the highest citation count, totaling 100 citations. Following closely, Scheuner et al. [5] received 66 citations, Pahl et al. [12] received 54 citations and Thalheim et al. [17] accrued 52 citations. It is noteworthy that all other papers received comparably lesser shares of citations ranging from 34 to 0.

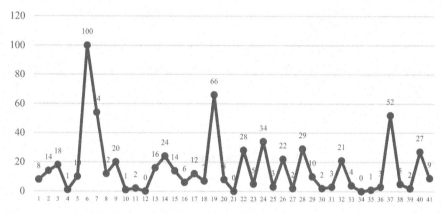

**Fig. 5.** Citation rates of the literature set.

## 4  Discussion

This paper presents preliminary research into quality aspects of cloud-native architectures. Through the literature review presented, we have identified and underscored several noteworthy findings. While our primary objective was to unveil the primary types of quality models, metrics and thresholds used in cloud-native architectures, we deconstructed this objective by systematically mapping diverse aspects. This approach allowed us to form a better understanding of the research domain under consideration.

*RQ1.1:* *How does the distribution of publications appear over the years?*
Our review revealed a continuous exploration of quality aspects in cloud-native architectures since 2010, peaking in 2020 with 7 publications.
*RQ1.2:* *Which authors are the most influential in this area?*
Data extracted from the compiled literature revealed no noteworthy pattern of repeated occurrences among certain author names. This suggests a lack of specific individuals or groups exploring the identified area of interest to the best of our knowledge.
*RQ1.3:* *In which scholarly venues do researchers disseminate their findings?*
Our research indicated the absence of significant venues (be it journals, conferences, or workshops) where authors shared their research findings on more than two occasions.
*RQ1.4:* *To which facets of quality does the study direct its focus?*

Through our research process, we analyzed the quality aspects highlighted in the considered papers, identifying 17 dimensions investigated over time. Our results show a predominant focus on performance, Quality of Service, scalability, and monitoring. Less emphasis is placed on optimization, data management, and cost analysis. The least frequently addressed aspects based on our results include virtualization, prediction, anomaly detection and similar.

*RQ1.5:* *What typology characterizes the research conducted in the study?*

We followed the criteria established by Wieriga et al. [6] and observed a considerable number of papers falling into the "solution proposal" and "opinion paper" categories. Minimal representation was found in the "validation research," "experience paper," and "conceptual paper" categories, with no identified evaluation research studies.

*RQ1.6:* *What primary type of contribution does the study offer?*

We defined six predetermined variables, acknowledging that a paper may contribute to multiple categories but at least one. Figure 4 illustrates the prevalence of metric (18 studies), followed by model (17), method (16), and tool (14) categories, with smaller proportions allocated to the process (9) category and other (7).

*RQ1.7:* *What is the magnitude of citations acquired by the studies?*

The final dimension of our study explores citation numbers. Our results show that Shahard et al.'s [14] paper led with 100 citations, followed by Scheuner et al. [5] with 66, Pahl et al. [12] with 54, and Thalheim et al. [17] with 52, while other papers received citations ranging from 34 to 0.

## 5   Conclusion

Our research embarked on an initial exploration of quality aspects in cloud-native architectures. Analyzing 41 papers, we conducted a preliminary overview of valuable characteristics, using a structured mapping template as our guide. The data mapping served as the foundation for evaluating responses to our research questions, covering aspects such as publication year, citations, and contribution type. While conducting the literature review, we set specific inclusion and exclusion criteria as delineated in Sect. 2.2. We acknowledge that, as a limitation, the corpus of literature identified may not encapsulate the entirety of relevant studies, which is an issue we intend to address in future works.

Examining publications over the years, our findings revealed a peak in 2020, which addressed quality aspects such as performance, followed by QoS, scalability, and monitoring. Solution proposals garnered the largest literature set, with opinion papers following closely behind. The nature of contributions was another significant revelation, with metrics, models, methods, and tools taking precedence, followed by process and others.

The initial research provides valuable insights into the cloud-native architectures quality aspects, serving as a foundational steppingstone for potential future research. Our future research endeavors will involve an improvement of these findings through the incorporation of an additional methodological step, known as snowballing. Given that our initial investigation showed a significant corpus of literature addressing metrics within cloud-native architectures, our targeted focus will therefore be on the exploration of various metrics, their intended purposes, and the depth of insights they offer. We believe that this preliminary work serves as a foundational work for future investigations.

This, in turn, is anticipated to enhance our understanding of this dynamic and rapidly evolving domain. Through this process, we aspire to contribute to the ongoing discussion and advancements in the field of cloud-native architectures.

**Acknowledgments.** The authors acknowledge the financial support from the Slovenian Research Agency (Research Core Funding No. P2-0057).

# References

1. Herbst, N., et al.: Quantifying cloud performance and dependability: taxonomy, metric design, and emerging challenges. ACM Trans. Model. Perform. Eval. Comput. Syst. 3(4) (2018). https://doi.org/10.1145/3236332
2. Mell, P., Grance, T.: The NIST definition of cloud computing. Gaithersburg, MD (2011). https://doi.org/10.6028/NIST.SP.800-145
3. Odun-Ayo, I., Goddy-Worlu, R., Ajayi, L., Edosomwan, B., Okezie, F.: A systematic mapping study of cloud-native application design and engineering. J. Phys. Conf. Ser. **1378**(3), 32092 (2019). https://doi.org/10.1088/1742-6596/1378/3/032092
4. Ravi, K., Khandelwal, Y., Krishna, B.S., Ravi, V.: Analytics in/for cloud-an interdependence: a review. J. Netw. Comput. Appl. **102**, 17–37 (2018). https://doi.org/10.1016/j.jnca.2017.11.006
5. Scheuner, J., Leitner, P.: Function-as-a-Service performance evaluation: a multivocal literature review. J. Syst. Softw. **170**, 110708 (2020). https://doi.org/10.1016/j.jss.2020.110708
6. Wieringa, R., Maiden, N., Mead, N., Rolland, C.: Requirements engineering paper classification and evaluation criteria: a proposal and a discussion. Requir. Eng. **11**, 102–107 (2006). https://doi.org/10.1007/s00766-005-0021-6
7. Henning, S., Hasselbring, W.: A configurable method for benchmarking scalability of cloud-native applications. Empir. Softw. Eng. **27**(6) (2022). https://doi.org/10.1007/s10664-022-10162-1
8. HoseinyFarahabady, M., Lee, Y.C., Zomaya, A.Y., Tari, Z.: A QoS-aware resource allocation controller for function as a service (FaaS) platform. In: Maximilien, M., Vallecillo, A., Wang, J., Oriol, M. (eds.) Service-Oriented Computing, Cham. Springer International Publishing, 2017, pp. 241–255 (2023). https://doi.org/10.1007/978-3-319-69035-3_17. Accessed on 13 Dec 2023
9. Malawski, M., Figiela, K., Gajek, A., Zima, A.: Benchmarking heterogeneous cloud functions. In: Heras, D., et al. (eds.) Euro-Par 2017: Parallel Processing Workshops, Cham. Springer International Publishing, pp. 415–426 (2018). https://doi.org/10.1007/978-3-319-75178-8_34. Accessed on 13 Dec 2023
10. Andrikopoulos, V., Strauch, S., Fehling, C., Leymann, F.: CAP-oriented design for cloud-native applications. In: Ivanov, I.I., van Sinderen, M., Leymann, F., Shan, T. (eds.) Cloud Computing and Services Science, Cham. Springer International Publishing, pp. 215–229 (2013). https://doi.org/10.1007/978-3-319-04519-1_14. Accessed on 13 Dec 2023
11. Dürr, K., Lichtenthäler, R.: An evaluation of modeling options for cloud-native application architectures to enable quality investigations. In: 2022 IEEE/ACM 15th International Conference on Utility and Cloud Computing (UCC), pp. 297–304 (2022). https://doi.org/10.1109/UCC56403.2022.00053
12. Pahl, C., Jamshidi, P., Zimmermann, O.: Architectural principles for cloud software. ACM Trans. Internet Technol. **18**(2), SI, (2018). https://doi.org/10.1145/3104028

13. Muñoz-Escoí, F.D., Bernabéu-Aubán, J.M.: A survey on elasticity management in PaaS systems. Computing **99**(7), 617–656 (2017). https://doi.org/10.1007/s00607-016-0507-8
14. Shahrad, M., Balkind, J., Wentzlaff, D.: Architectural implications of function-as-a-service computing. In: Proceedings of the 52nd Annual IEEE/ACM International Symposium on Microarchitecture, in MICRO '52. New York, NY, USA. Association for Computing Machinery, pp. 1063–1075 (2019). https://doi.org/10.1145/3352460.3358296
15. Gundu, S.R., Panem, C.A., Thimmapuram, A.: Hybrid IT and multi cloud an emerging trend and improved performance in cloud computing. SN Comput. Sci. **1**(5), 256 (2020). https://doi.org/10.1007/s42979-020-00277-x
16. Niedermaier, S., Koetter, F., Freymann, A., Wagner, S.: On observability and monitoring of distributed systems – an industry interview study. In: Yangui, S., Bouassida Rodriguez, I., Drira, K., Tari, Z. (eds.) Service-Oriented Computing, Cham. Springer International Publishing, pp. 36–52 (2019). https://doi.org/10.1007/978-3-030-33702-5_3. Accessed on 13 Dec 2023
17. Thalheim, J., et al.: Sieve: actionable insights from monitored metrics in distributed systems. In: Proceedings of the 18th ACM/IFIP/USENIX Middleware Conference, in Middleware 2017. New York, NY, USA. Association for Computing Machinery, pp. 14–27 (2017). https://doi.org/10.1145/3135974.3135977

# KP-Cartographer: A Lightweight SLAM Approach Based on Cartographer

Linjie Li$^{(\boxtimes)}$, Ran Tao$^{(\boxtimes)}$, Xiaohui Lu, and Xin Luo

School of Compute Science and Technology, Donghua University, Shanghai 201620, China
1728082979@qq.com, taoran@dhu.edu.cn

**Abstract.** Cartographer is a simultaneous localization and mapping (SLAM) app-roach proposed by Google, capable of creating maps and localization from point cloud data obtained from LiDAR. In order to perform localization and mapping on mobile devices with lower computational power, suitable for scenarios such as fire-fighting and rescue, we designed a laser point cloud feature extraction algorithm and a personnel localization algorithm. We integrated them into the Cartogra-pher method, proposing a lightweight SLAM method named KP-Cartographer. To validate the effectiveness of our method, we constructed five laser point cloud datasets with different characteristics and conducted multiple comparative exper-iments. Qualitative experimental results demonstrate that the KP-Cartographer method proposed in this paper surpasses A-LOAM and LeGO-LOAM in map completeness and clarity. Compared to Cartographer, it effectively identifies small obstacles and accurately captures differences between glass and window frames. Quantitative experimental results indicate that, compared to Cartographer, 1) The KP-Cartographer method proposed in this paper reduces the volume of laser point cloud data to within 6% of the original data, with a maximum CPU utilization reduction of 21.96%. 2) The maximum Absolute Trajectory Error (ATE) of the KP-Cartographer method proposed in this paper is 0.0308, and the maximum Rel-ative Pose Error (RPE) is 0.0068. This achieves lightweight processing with no significant difference in accuracy.

**Keywords:** SLAM · Point Cloud · Feature Extraction · Mapping · Localization

## 1 Introduction

Localization technology involves determining a person's position using technologi-cal methods. Traditional indoor positioning methods like Bluetooth [1], WIFI [2, 3], radio frequency identification (RFID)[4], and ultra-wideband, require pre-installation of equipment in the positioning environment [5, 6, 7]. However, traditional indoor posi-tioning methods are not applicable to certain specific scenarios, such as firefighting and rescue operations. Firefighters operate in high-risk environments involving smoke, flames, and structural hazards. When these methods are used for firefighter positioning, they face numerous challenges: inaccuracies due to fire and smoke, the risk of equipment damage during firefighting and rescue [8], and the efficiency of the positioning methods.

© The Author(s), under exclusive license to Springer Nature Switzerland AG 2024
L. Uden and I.-H. Ting (Eds.): KMO 2024, CCIS 2152, pp. 352–362, 2024.
https://doi.org/10.1007/978-3-031-63269-3_27

In firefighting and rescue scenarios, not only is precise localization capability required, but also detailed environmental maps depicting building structures and obstacles are necessary to ensure the safety of firefighters. Given these challenges, the high-precision ranging and anti-interference capabilities of laser radar make it a suitable choice for precise localization and mapping in many specific scenarios.

With the emergence of lidar and SLAM [9], we can use sensors to obtain geometric information about the environment, combine their own motion data, generate environmental maps in real-time, and locate. Laser SLAM mainly includes SLAM based on filtering[10, 11], graph-based SLAM [12, 13], extended with LOAM [14, 15, 16] and multi-sensor fusion [17, 18, 19, 20]. The Cartographer [13] is the most representative. However, The Cartographer uses the voxel filtering method to process the point cloud, which has two defects: (1) it struggles with non-standard point clouds due to occlusion or measurement errors. (2) lacks focus on environmental characteristics. Thus, lightweight feature extraction from point clouds based on environmental characteristics is essential. There are three main ways to extract features: skeleton-extraction, statistical methods, and geometric methods. Skeleton-extraction is used in medical imaging and isn't suitable for mapping. Statistical methods, being random, may overlook key features. Thus, our paper focuses on geometric methods. In [21], statistical data was used to filter abnormal data, however, resulting in errors due to lost geometric features. [22] proposed a noise classification and denoising algorithm for point cloud models, but sensitive to parameter adjustments.

To tackle these challenges, we propose a KP-Cartographer, a lightweight mapping and localization algorithm based on the Cartographer. Using key point clouds to matching greatly simplifies parameters, improves algorithm efficiency. The main contributions of this paper include:

(1) In this paper, we designed a laser point cloud feature extraction algorithm and a personnel localization algorithm. We integrated them into the Cartographer method, proposing a lightweight SLAM method named KP-Cartographer.
(2) Using the RS-LiDAR-16 laser radar to construct five datasets with different characteristics, which can be used for mapping and localization experimental tests.
(3) In this study, we performed qualitative and quantitative experiments on five custom datasets. For qualitative experiment, KP-Cartographer surpasses A-LOAM and LeGO-LOAM in map completeness and clarity. Compared to Cartographer, it effectively identifies small obstacles and accurately captures differences between glass and window frames. Quantitative experimental results indicate that, compared to Cartographer, The KP-Cartographer reduces the volume of laser point cloud data to within 6% of the original data, with a maximum CPU utilization reduction of 21.96%, the maximum ATE is 0.0308 and the maximum RPE is 0.0068. This achieves lightweight processing with no significant difference in accuracy.

## 2 Method

### 2.1 The Proposed KP-Cartographer Approach

In order to reduce the computational complexity of Cartographer and apply it to mobile scenarios such as fire rescue, we design two algorithms to optimize it, and propose a KP-Cartographer method, as shown in Fig. 1.

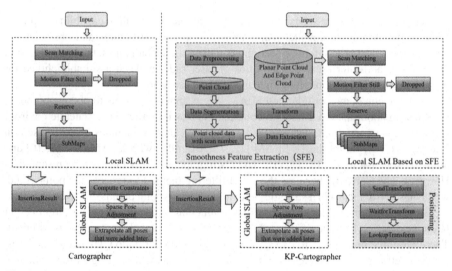

**Fig. 1.** Compared to Cartographer, KP-Cartographer integrates the SFE algorithm to reduce computation and employs the Positioning algorithm for real-time localization access.

As shown in Fig. 1, the flowcharts on the left and right depict the processes of Cartographer and KP-Cartographer, respectively. Cartographer comprises two main modules: Local SLAM and Global SLAM. To reduce point cloud data computation, KP-Cartographer integrates the SFE algorithm within the Local SLAM module. SFE evaluates the local surface smoothness of the point cloud to extract plane and edge point clouds. After Global SLAM, KP-Cartographer integrates a Positioning algorithm that facilitates real-time localization by broadcasting information from each coordinate system. In the following sections, we provide detailed descriptions of our proposed SFE and positioning algorithms.

## 2.2 Smoothness Feature Extraction Algorithm

To reduce computation, we designed the SFE algorithm to extract plane and edge point clouds with environmental features, as shown in Fig. 2.

The conventional Cartographer employs voxel filtering to downsample point clouds, followed by matching computations for all point cloud data of each laser scan frame. However, voxel filtering does not specifically capture the intrinsic characteristics of the environment. Therefore, in the KP-Cartographer approach, we utilize the SFE algorithm to extract plane point clouds and edge point clouds. Using these point clouds for calculations can significantly reduce computational workload. The feature extraction algorithm SFE is shown in Algorithm 1.

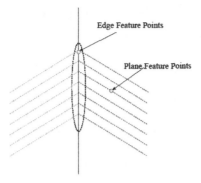

**Fig. 2.** Plane and edge feature points.

---

**Algorithm 1: SFE**

**Input:** Complete Point Cloud Data $P_k$ , LIDAR Scan Number $scan$

**Output:** Feature Point Cloud Data $I_k$

1  for each point $p_j$ in $P_k$ do
2     Obtain the coordinate $(X_j, Y_j, Z_j)$ of $p_j$;
3     if $X_j, Y_j, Z_j \neq null$ then
4        Calculate the distance $E_j^O$ from the projection
5        point of $p_j$ on the horizontal plane to the origin O
6        $SNum_j \leftarrow \arctan (Z_j, E_j^O)$ ;
7     end
8     else throw;
9  end
10  Identifies the Point Cloud with the scan number $P_k'$;
11  for each point $p_j$ on the same scan line do
12     if $p_j \neq null$ then
13        if $Distance \geq mi$ then
14           Calculate the Euclidean distance $D_j$
15           from the point $p_j$ to the origin O
16           if $e * D_j < ldiff_j$ && $rdiff_j$ then
17              if $i * D_j < ldiff_j$ && $rdiff_j$ then
18                 calculate the the smoothness of the local surface $C_j$ ;
19                 $sort(C_j)$;
20                 Select 16 planar feature points with smaller $C_j$ and
21                 8 edge feature points with larger $C_j$ as the
22                 feature point cloud $I_k$;
23              *end*
24              else throw Occluded Point Cloud;
25           *end*
26           else throw Parallel Point Cloud;
27        *end*
28        else throw;
29     end
30  end
31  return $I_k$;

---

As shown in Algorithm 1, Let $P_k = \{p_1, p_2, ...p_j..., p_n\}$ be the point cloud acquired at time k, where $p_j$ is a point in $P_k$. . The number of laser beam scan is used as input. For each point that is not a point NAN (Not a Number), which projected to the horizontal plane $\alpha$ is $p_j{}'$, The scan number of the point cloud $p_j$ is calculated according to Eq. 1.

$$\text{SNum}_j = \arctan \frac{Z_j}{E_j^O} \tag{1}$$

where $E_j^O$ is the Euclidean distance from $p_j{}'$ to origin $O$, and $Z_j$ is the z-axis coordinate of $p_j{}'$. Then we can obtain point cloud $P_k{}'$ marked with scan number, and for the point cloud on the same scan line, we filter and calculate the smoothness of the local surface. We discard the point as occluded when it is perceived as a parallel point, and the $ldiff_j$ and $rdiff_j$ satisfy Eq. 2, with $e = 0.02$. When $e$ is set to 0.3, and satisfy Eq. 2, we consider it as an occluded point and discard it.

$$\begin{cases} rdiff_j > e * D_j \\ ldiff_j > e * D_j \end{cases} \tag{2}$$

where $ldiff_j$ and $rdiff_j$ respectively represent the left and right depth difference of $p_j$, and the $D_j$ is Euclidean distance to the origin. After removing unreliable point clouds, we evenly divide the remaining point clouds into four sub regions, which are: $\beta_1, \beta_2, \beta_3, \beta_4$. For each scanning point $P_j\beta_\eta$ in the subregion $\beta_\eta(1\eta4)$, the local surface smoothness $C_j$ is calculated based on Eq. 3.

$$C_m = \frac{1}{|S|\left\| X_{(k,m)}^L \right\|} \left\| \sum_{n\in S, n\neq m} (x_{(k,m)}^L - x_{(k,n)}^L) \right\| \tag{3}$$

where $mP_k$, $S$ represents the set of points around the central point m within the same scan. Based on the smoothness of the local curve surface $C_j$, select 16 planar feature points with higher local curve surface smoothness and 8 edge feature points with lower local curve surface smoothness from each region as feature point clouds. The pose of the LiDAR in the world coordinate system is denoted as $P_L(x_l, y_l, \theta)$. The coordinate of $p_j$ in the lidar coordinate system is $(x_{Pk}^j, y_{Pk}^j, z_{Pk}^j)$. By using Eq. 4, we can obtain the mapped coordinates $(x_w, y_w)$ of the point cloud P in the submap.

$$\begin{pmatrix} x_w \\ y_w \end{pmatrix} = \begin{bmatrix} \cos\theta & -\sin\theta \\ \sin\theta & \cos\theta \end{bmatrix} \begin{pmatrix} x_{Pk}^j \\ y_{Pk}^j \end{pmatrix} + \begin{pmatrix} x_l \\ y_l \end{pmatrix} \tag{4}$$

## 2.3 Positioning Algorithm

Cartographer can obtain highly accurate positional relationships, but it does not directly output real-time coordinates, which is not conducive to embedded development. Therefore, we propose a positioning algorithm that can directly and conveniently obtain real-time personnel positioning information based on coordinate transformations. The positioning algorithm is illustrated in Algorithm 2.

---

**Algorithm 2: Positioning**

**Input:** Coordinate system name $TF_i$, $TF_j$

**Output:** Coordinates $X$, $Y$, $Z$

1 Determine the $Transform$, $Listener$;

2 Reading solid-state coordinate relationships in $urdf$;

3 Wait for $Transform$;

4 Look up $Transform$;

5 Get $TF_i$ and $TF_j$ relationship;

6 Calculate the coordinates $X$, $Y$, $Z$;

7 **return** Coordinates $X$, $Y$, $Z$;

---

As shown in Algorithm 2, the positioning algorithm determines the coordinate system to be monitored based on the input coordinate system's name such as $TF_i$, $TF_j$. Initially, when there is input of point cloud data $P_k = \{p_1, p_2, ...p_j..., p_n\}$, the algorithm combines the imported solid urdf with the calculated coordinate system transformations to obtain all coordinate relationships and stores them in a tree structure to preserve the transformation relationships. Subsequently, by waiting for the transformation relationships of the input coordinate system and listening to them, Finally, the positioning algorithm computes the real-time $X$, $Y$, $Z$ coordinates based on the obtained relationships.

## 3 Experiment and Analysis

### 3.1 LiDAR, Environment and Dataset Establishment

At present, due to the lack of LiDAR datasets for indoor localization needs, such as whether the dataset contains continuous obstacles, structurally similar corridors, etc., we built five different datasets across various scales and environments with the use of a RS-LiDAR-16 lidar as a sensor. The RS-LiDAR-16 LiDAR uses the TOF method for ranging, with a measurement distance of up to 150 m and a measurement accuracy of ±2 cm. The number of output points can reach 300000 points/second, and the horizontal measurement angle is 360°. The time required to complete one round of launch is 55.5 us. RS-LiDAR-16 LiDAR integrates 16 laser transceiver components and is defined as 16 channels. When the LiDAR is working, the corresponding relationship between the channels and the true vertical angle is shown in Fig. 3.

We collected datasets with five different characteristics using the aforementioned LiDAR inside a loop-shaped building containing structurally similar corridors, two different staircases, continuous small obstacles, and a glass walkway. These datasets are referred to as *Circular Building, Containing Obstacles, Inside of the Room, Without Obstacles, Glass Corridor*. The starting point of each dataset and the structure inside the building are illustrated in Fig. 4.

As shown in Fig. 4, the starting point of the *Circular Building* is the staircase on the right, passing through continuous obstacles on the right, similar corridors above, the glass corridor on the left, and circling around the building back to the starting point. The collection route for the *Containing Obstacles* is part of *Circular Building*, with the endpoint being the similar corridors above. *Inside of the Room* includes more details

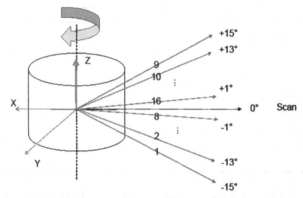

**Fig. 3.** The RS-LiDAR-16 Pitch Angle Definition. During data collection, we designated the forward direction as the positive x-axis, the leftward direction as the positive y-axis, and the upward direction as the positive z-axis.

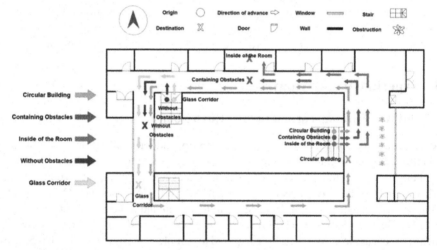

**Fig. 4.** The architectural layout of the structures within datasets, along with the initial positions, final positions, and forward directions of the experiment participants.

inside the room compared to *Containing Obstacles*. *Without Obstacles* and *Glass Corridor* start from the staircase above, with the latter including the glass corridor in addition to the former. The dataset's details are outlined in Table 1.

Our experiments were conducted on Ubuntu 18.04, employing the Melodic version of the ROS. For the model-building process, we utilized C++ and Python.

### 3.2 Qualitative Experiment

As shown in Fig. 5, we conducted qualitative experiments on four algorithms: Cartographer, KP-Cartographer, A-LOAM, and LeGO-LOAM, using the Circular Building dataset (Fig. 5(a-d)).

**Table 1.** Introduction to the characteristics of five datasets.

| Name | The Main Scenes Characteristics | | | | |
|------|-------|-----------|------------------|-----------------|---------------|
| | Sence | Obstacles | Similar Structure | Inside the Office | Glass Corridor |
| Circular Building | Big | √ | √ | / | √ |
| Containing Obstacles | Small | √ | √ | / | / |
| Inside of the Room | Small | √ | √ | √ | / |
| Without Obstacles | Small | / | / | / | / |
| Glass Corridor | Small | / | √ | / | √ |

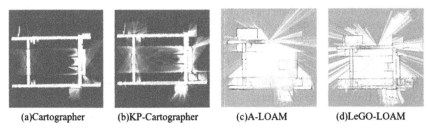

(a)Cartographer    (b)KP-Cartographer    (c)A-LOAM    (d)LeGO-LOAM

**Fig. 5.** Using the *Circular building* dataset, the results for Cartographer, KP-Cartographer, A-LOAM, and LeGO-LOAM are shown in (a) to (d), respectively.

KP-Cartographer (Fig. 5(b)) outperforms A-LOAM (Fig. 5(c)) in terms of map completeness and LeGO-LOAM (Fig. 5(d)) in terms of map clarity. Meanwhile, LeGO-LOAM has limitations in distinguishing features like obstacle clusters on the east side and window frames versus glass on the west side. Therefore, in the subsequent qualitative experiments, we will not compare A-LOAM, LeGO-LOAM.

We evaluate Cartographer and KP-Cartographer using four small scene datasets: *Containing Obstacles, Inside of the Room, Without Obstacles, Glass Corridor*. The results are compared in Fig. 6 (a-h).

Figure 6(a-b) utilized the *Containing Obstacles* dataset. Comparing the right side of Fig. 6(b) to that of Fig. 6(a), KP-Cartographer demonstrated excellent performance in identifying continuous obstacles near staircases. Figure 6(c-d) employed the *Inside of the Room* dataset. In comparison to Fig. 6(c), the upper part of Fig. 6(d) captured details within the room effectively. Figure 6(e-f) utilized the *Without Obstacles* dataset, with Fig. 6(f) exhibiting clearer map construction compared to Fig. 6(e), devoid of gray shadows. Figure 6(g-h) employed the *Glass Corridor* dataset, in Fig. 6(g) and 6(h), the left sections of both images demonstrate the success of KP-Cartographer over

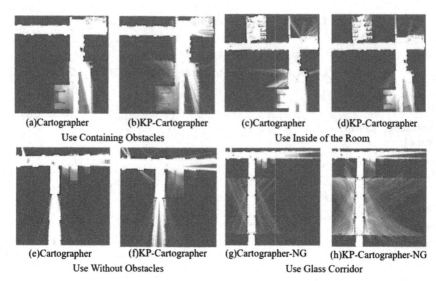

(a)Cartographer     (b)KP-Cartographer          (c)Cartographer     (d)KP-Cartographer
Use Containing Obstacles                     Use Inside of the Room

(e)Cartographer     (f)KP-Cartographer     (g)Cartographer-NG     (h)KP-Cartographer-NG
Use Without Obstacles                          Use Glass Corridor

**Fig. 6.** (a) to (h) illustrate the mapping results of Cartographer and KP-Cartographer using four small scene datasets with different environmental characteristics *Containing Obstacles, Inside of the Room, Without Obstacles, Glass Corridor*.

Cartographer in accurately depicting stair structures and distinguishing between glass and window frames in the corridors.

### 3.3 Quantitative Experiment

We conducted quantitative experiments using four small scene datasets: *Containing Obstacles, Inside of the Room, Without Obstacles*, and *Glass Corridor* to evaluate Cartographer and KP-Cartographer in terms of ATE, RPE, Point Cloud Computation, and CPU Utilization Reduction. ATE and RPE are defined in the TUM dataset and are widely used to evaluate the performance of SLAM algorithms. "Point Cloud Computation" refers to the proportion of point cloud computation per frame compared to Cartographer. "CPU Utilization Reduction" indicates the reduction in CPU utilization when using KP-Cartographer compared to Cartographer on the same machine. The experimental results are shown in Table 2.

As indicated in Table 2, KP-Cartographer achieves a maximum ATE of 0.0308 and RPE of 0.0068 compared to Cartographer during mapping and localization processes. The difference in accuracy is not significant. Moreover, it ensures that the proportion of point cloud computation per frame does not exceed 6% of the original point cloud data, while the CPU utilization is reduced by up to 21.96%, achieving lightweight processing and enhancing its usability, thus promoting embedded development. Additionally, in Table 2, due to the smaller size and lack of multiple obstacles in the Without Obstacles dataset scene, the CPU utilization only decreases by 2.68% compared to experiments based on other datasets, which is considered normal.

**Table 2.** The comparative results of quantitative experiments between the KP-Cartographer and Cartographer on four different datasets.

| Dataset | ATE | | RPE | | Point Cloud Computation | CPU Utilization Reduction |
|---|---|---|---|---|---|---|
| | RMSE | SD | RMSE | SD | | |
| Containing Obstacles | 0.0308 | 0.0156 | 0.0045 | 0.0026 | 4.98% | 11.30% |
| Inside of the Room | 0.0165 | 0.0089 | 0.0043 | 0.0022 | 5.16% | 18.28% |
| Without Obstacles | 0.0139 | 0.0053 | 0.0040 | 0.0019 | 5.16% | 2.68% |
| Glass Corridor | 0.0275 | 0.0139 | 0.0068 | 0.0040 | 4.70% | 21.96% |

# 4 Conclusion

In this paper, we propose a lightweight laser SLAM algorithm called KP-Cartographer based on Cartographer. The algorithm includes a laser point cloud feature extraction algorithm, SFE, and a personnel positioning algorithm. Compared to the original Cartographer, KP-Cartographer maintains mapping quality and localization accuracy while reducing computation, making it suitable for embedded development. We conducted multiple comparative experiments on five self-built datasets with different characteristics. Qualitative results show that KP-Cartographer constructs maps more clearly and comprehensively than A-LOAM and LeGO-LOAM and effectively identifies small obstacles and distinguishes between glass and walls better than Cartographer. Quantitative experimental results indicate that, compared to Cartographer, The KP-Cartographer reduces the volume of laser point cloud data to within 6% of the original data, with a maximum CPU utilization reduction of 21.96%, the maximum ATE is 0.0308 and the maximum RPE is 0.0068. This achieves lightweight processing with no significant difference in accuracy. KP-Cartographer can play a significant role in scenarios with low computational resources, such as firefighting scenarios. It helps commanders provide real-time guidance to firefighters during rescue operations, aiding them in avoiding obstacles and selecting appropriate entry points, potentially improving safety and efficiency in firefighting scenarios. Future research will integrate multi-sensor data to improve mapping accuracy and reduce computational complexity, making it suitable for embedded platforms and real-time localization.

# References

1. Sheng, Z., Pollard, J.K.: Position measurement using Bluetooth IEEE Trans. Consum. Electron. **52**(2), 555–558 (2006)
2. Yang, Q., Pan, S.J., Zheng, V.W.: Estimating location using Wi-Fi IEEE 2007 ICDM Contest. IEEE Intell. Syst. **23**(1), 8–13 (2008)
3. Li, Q., et al.: Fingerprint and assistant nodes based WiFi localization in complex indoor environment. IEEE Access **4**, 2993–3004 (2017)
4. Lin, C.J., et al.: Application of intelligent agent and RFID technology for indoor position: safety of kindergarten as an example. In: International Conference on Machine Learning & Cybernetics, IEEE, pp. 2571–2576 (2010)

5. Saad, M.M.: High-accuracy reference-free ultrasonic location estimation. Trans. Instrum. Measur. **61**(6), 1561–1570 (2012)
6. Huang, S., Chen, J., Jiang, H.: UWB indoor location based on improved least square support vector machine considering anchor anomaly. In: 2020 IEEE 16th International Conference on Control & Automation (ICCA) IEEE (2020)
7. Wen, K., et al.: A new quaternion kalman filter based foot-mounted IMU and UWB tightly-coupled method for indoor pedestrian navigation. IEEE Trans. Veh. Technol. **PP**(99), 1 (2020)
8. Li, J., et al.: An automatic and accurate localization system for firefighters. In: International Conference on Internet-of-Things Design and Implementation (2018)
9. Dissanayake, G., et al.: Estimating uncertain spatial relationships in robotics. IEEE Trans. Robot. Autom. **17**, 229–241 (2001)
10. Grisetti, G., Stachniss, C., Burgard, W.: Improved techniques for grid mapping with rao-blackwellized particle filters. IEEE Trans. Rob. **23**(1), 34–46 (2007)
11. Kohlbrecher, S., et al.: A flexible and scalable SLAM system with full 3D motion estimation. In: IEEE International Symposium on Safety IEEE (2011)
12. Konolige, K., et al.: Efficient sparse pose adjustment for 2D mapping. In: 2010 IEEE/RSJ International Conference on Intelligent Robots and Systems, 18–22 October 2010, Taipei, Taiwan IEEE (2010)
13. Hess, W., et al.: Real-time loop closure in 2D LIDAR SLAM. In: 2016 IEEE International Conference on Robotics and Automation (ICRA) IEEE (2016)
14. Zhang, J., Singh, S.: LOAM: lidar odometry and mapping in real-time. In: Robotics: Science and Systems Conference (2014)
15. Zhang, J., Singh, S.: Low-drift and real-time lidar odometry and mapping. Auton. Robots 401–416 (2017)
16. Shan, T., Englot, B.: LeGO-LOAM: lightweight and ground-optimized lidar odometry and mapping on variable terrain. In: 2018 IEEE/RSJ International Conference on Intelligent Robots and Systems (IROS) IEEE (2019)
17. Koide, K.: A Portable 3D LIDAR-based system for long-term and wide-area people behavior measurement. Int. J. Adv. Rob. Syst. **16**(2) (2019)
18. Engel, J., Koltun, V., Cremers, D.: Direct Sparse Odometry. IEEE Trans. Pattern Anal. Mach. Intell. IEEE, 1 (2016)
19. Huang, K., Xiao, J., Stachniss, C.: Accurate direct visual-laser odometry with explicit occlusion handling and plane detection. In: 2019 International Conference on Robotics and Automation (ICRA) IEEE (2019)
20. Han, Y., Amir A.M., Shaozhang, X.: Novel cartographer using an OAK-D smart camera for indoor robots location and navigation. In: Journal of Physics: Conference Series, vol. 2467, no. 1. IOP Publishing (2023)
21. Rusu, R.B., et al.: Towards 3D point cloud based object maps for household environments. Rob. Auton. Syst. **56**(11), 927–941 (2008)
22. Chaochuan, et al.: A new fast filtering algorithm for a 3D point cloud based on RGB-D information. PloS One **14**(8), e0220253 (2019)

# Artificial Intelligence to Elevate Knowledge Management in Malaysian Public Sector: An Overview

Rohaizan Daud[1]([✉]), Norasyikin Shaikh Ibrahim[1]([✉]), and Min Hui Leow[2]([✉])

[1] National Institute of Public Administration (INTAN), Kuala Lumpur, Malaysia
{rohaizan,syikinibrahim}@intanbk.intan.my
[2] Universiti Teknologi MARA (UiTM), Pulau Pinang, Malaysia
leowminhui@uitm.edu.my

**Abstract.** Studies show that the capabilities of Artificial Intelligence (AI) significantly elevate Knowledge Management (KM), allowing employees to swiftly access information and make real-time informed decisions. This paper attempts to offer a thorough synthesis of the literature on AI and KM, with a particular focus on examining the extent to which AI can benefit organisations with their endeavours to effectively handle information and manage knowledge. Although conventional KM has evolved over time, documentation has remained as its foundation. The essential aspect of both KM and AI is knowledge. KM facilitates the comprehension of knowledge, while AI enables users to expand, apply, and innovate knowledge in a wide variety of ways. To effectively utilize their artificial partners for KM, humans must cultivate their perspectives, abilities, and work habits. It is important to do so while being cautious of the potential drawbacks of automation, such as becoming intellectually lazy or developing a resistance towards algorithms. Organisations benefit from such preparations as they enable the practical use of AI's distinct capabilities in KM. These capabilities can only be fully utilized and realized through efficient and mutually beneficial cooperation between knowledge workers and intelligent systems.

**Keywords:** Artificial intelligence · Knowledge Management · public sector · job/work rotation · professionals

## 1 Introduction

It is an evident trend in global economic shifts that Knowledge Management (KM) has gained considerable attention as a valuable asset for organisations in the 21st century. This recognition is particularly notable in nations where economic progress hinges on knowledge and information [1]. Technological advancements have given rise to new employment patterns and business processes geared toward enhancing KM. Simultaneously, within the framework of Industry 4.0, Artificial Intelligence (AI) emerges as a key technological advancement expected to streamline managerial tasks, facilitating smoother processes for manual workers and boosting efficiency. A knowledge-centric

© The Author(s), under exclusive license to Springer Nature Switzerland AG 2024
L. Uden and I.-H. Ting (Eds.): KMO 2024, CCIS 2152, pp. 363–377, 2024.
https://doi.org/10.1007/978-3-031-63269-3_28

economy emerges as a competitive advantage for organisations and countries showcasing innovation through the establishment of new connections, as well as the development of novel processes and procedures. In the digital age, there is a pressing need for businesses and organisational structures to cultivate inventive and problem-solving approaches to facilitate the dissemination of knowledge concerning the digitisation of business operations.

The potential and advantages offered by AI are vast. As suggested, akin to how the second industrial revolution brought about electrification, the fourth revolution is anticipated to be characterized by 'Cognification' [2]. We are approaching a realm dominated by data and insights, emphasising the need to explore the connection between AI and KM for a more impactful integration of AI. Understanding the connection between AI and KM requires an initial acknowledgment of how businesses utilize knowledge [3]. According to a survey conducted by the National Institute of Public Administration (INTAN) among 2940 government employees, 11% of respondents anticipate facing family issues such as long-distance marriage in 2022. As a result, 30% of respondents contend that their present place of work prevents them from spending quality time with their families, resulting in decreased job performance. Hence, job transfers emerge as a solution, necessitating the transfer and sharing of employees' knowledge. Thus, effective KM becomes crucial for organisations as each knowledge process demands proper management. The success and competitiveness of organisations depend on their maturity in executing critical tasks within their industry. Both KM and AI revolve extensively around 'knowledge' [4]. AI provides tools for machines to learn, interpret, and apply information, contributing to enhanced decision-making. KM ensures a comprehensive understanding of knowledge, while AI empowers the enlargement, utilisation, creation, and unlocking of knowledge in unprecedented ways [5]. Despite being overlooked by some KM practitioners, AI stands as an essential cornerstone for the development and advancement of KM [6].

AI in education predates KM, establishing a strong foundation in computing over decades and finding extensive application across various domains [7]. In line with Dalkir [8], KM involves processes like identification, collection, and reinforcement of knowledge. Mao et al. [9] define KM as a domain that methodically improves content and expertise to boost an organisation's responsiveness, competency, efficacy, and innovation over time. Additionally, Jimenez-Jimenez et al. [10] emphasize that KM revolves around controlling information flow to ensure people receive relevant information at the right time. Shannak et al. [11] highlight that KM, as deduced from these definitions, involves embedding knowledge in services, processes, and products, and presenting it in documents and databases.

Recent technological advancements have rendered KM more affordable, standardized, widespread, and successful in meeting individual requirements. The capabilities of AI significantly elevate KM, allowing employees to swiftly access information and make real-time informed decisions. Businesses benefit by enhancing process and record tracking, and AI extends its impact by extracting knowledge from vast amounts of data, predicting future corporate trends. Consequently, AI technologies are extensively employed to enhance the performance of KM systems in modern businesses, ultimately improving overall efficiency.

This paper attempts to offer a thorough synthesis of the literature on AI and KM, with a particular focus on examining the extent to which AI can benefit organisations with their endeavours to effectively handle information and manage knowledge. Despite the fact that this study's scope was limited to the public sector, we believe its findings would also be useful to other industries with related areas of interest.

# 2 Review of Literature

## 2.1 Knowledge Management and Job Rotation

Knowledge workers manage their jobs based on their knowledge and expertise. Whereas knowledge management refers to an organisation's initiatives to gather, store, share, and apply the knowledge and expertise to improve organisation's performances and achievements. Existing literature distinguishes the KM phases into the acquisition of knowledge, the development of knowledge, knowledge exchange, knowledge encoding, the application of knowledge, and the preservation of knowledge [12]. Knowledge acquisition and development are the fundamental phases that include searching, recognising, selecting, compiling, and mapping information [13]; the process develops and generates new concepts or solutions for organizational activities that facilitate innovation and idea production. Knowledge exchange or sharing is a way to encourage the integration of information and the spread of knowledge to sustain work efficacy and competitive advantage [14].

An organisation must adopt the codification strategy to record individual employee's professional knowledge or information in a searchable KM system so that other employees can easily access and apply it for the benefit of the company. On that note, job rotation has an impact on organizational knowledge loss. Job rotation, moving laterally within and between functional groups, is a career development strategy that has a positive correlation with promotion, organizational integration, work satisfaction, networking, commitment, technical development, administrative, personal development, and so on [15]. Job rotation provides functional employees with the chance to learn about various work procedures or aspects of different working sectors [16]. However, when a member of staff leaves an organisation or a certain department, professional records of that individual may be lost if not properly managed. The loss of knowledge during job rotation is linked to the maintenance or preservation of knowledge.

Job-related knowledge refers to the knowledge that someone knows about the tasks they are performing. Job-related knowledge is the most important knowledge that needs to be shared and preserved in an organisation for sustainable growth. Job-related knowledge may be tacit or explicit. Tacit knowledge is knowledge hidden from the consciousness of the knower and cannot be easily captured or codified [17]; explicit knowledge is the knowledge that can be articulated in formal language and easily transmitted amongst individual [18].

## 2.2 Relationships Between Knowledge Management and Artificial Intelligence

Although conventional KM has evolved over time, documentation has remained as its foundation. The essential aspect of both KM and AI is knowledge. KM facilitates the comprehension of knowledge, while AI enables users to expand, apply, and innovate knowledge in a wide variety of ways. However, the shift to remote and hybrid working has brought to light the flaws in the way knowledge is handled in the present KM procedures [19]. AI is the capacity of a system to adapt in response to particular knowledge inputs, in order to perform particular jobs [20]. To that extent, Taherdoost and Madanchian [19] summarized the advantages of adopting AI technology in KM, as if enhancing knowledge delivery, usage, sharing, and capturing; improving the flexibility of knowledge presentation; enforcing intellectual capital; and assisting problem-solving through a real-time knowledge system.

Relating to the preservation of job-related knowledge due to job rotation, the crucial role of KM is to sustain an organisation's memory via effective knowledge storage and retrieval approaches. Given the constitutive relationship that exists between AI and big data, the use of AI in KM is most apparent in improving the knowledge storage and retrieval [21]. Data that was previously thought to be cumbersome and hard to interpret can now be harvested, classified, organized, stored, and retrieved owing to data-driven and self-learning algorithms [22]. Furthermore, AI builds more interconnected coordination systems by uniting workers who work on related issues but are separated by different boundaries [23]. In this case, AI contributes to collaborative intelligence that effectively overcomes knowledge loss, which is harder to achieve with conventional database systems [24].

When opportunities arising from AI are appropriately managed, organisational practice of KM will reach to a higher level. This suggests that AI-assisted solutions may be applied at every phase of a KM process, allowing stakeholders to act appropriately or accomplish tasks more rapidly, successfully, and efficiently [25].

## 3  Methodology

This section delineates the search strategy and criteria applied in this study. Three research databases were queried for journals or articles published from 2016 to the current year (2024) without indicating a particular study design or methodology. It can be either qualitative, quantitative, mixed-method or maybe not recorded. The databases were Emerald, JStor and Wiley Web Online. The search strategy formulation involved the use of Boolean operators "AND" and "OR" at the executing stage. The aim was to identify research related to AI and KM in the public sector. The keywords used are "artificial intelligence" AND/OR "knowledge management" AND/OR "public sector" AND/OR "job rotation" anywhere in the articles. Two hundred and five (205) works of literature were identified by using the search keywords as shown above. Subsequently, any redundancy in article titles and DOIs were eliminated for further review, following the filtration process based on the title and abstract. It then followed by selecting relevant literature through a pragmatic screening process, resulting in a total of seven (7) remaining articles. The search was broadened by conducting a manual exploration on the Google Scholar database, and the "snowball" concept was implemented to ensure the inclusion of literature that may not be indexed in libraries. Seven more pieces of literature were discovered through the Google Scholar database, resulting in a final count of fourteen (14) pieces of literature (see Table 1). Quality criteria were applied to screen papers on artificial intelligence, knowledge management, and the public sector. This assessment aimed to evaluate the value, relevance, credibility, and comprehensiveness of the selected papers, following the guidelines by [26].

All papers obtained from digital libraries must be written in English. Any papers that do not adhere to the specified inclusion criteria were excluded. Finally, articles that meet these criteria are included in the review synthesis. Fundamentally, there are three main factors in which AI can assist organisations in their efforts to successfully manage information and knowledge. The factors are (i) increasing human knowledge, (ii) physical facilities and structures, and (iii) procedures. Based on the result obtained, a mixed qualitative and quantitative approach were employed. Quantitative data were collected using the OPQOL and TAM questionnaires, while qualitative data were gathered through semi-structured interviews. The cross-sectional study, focused on employees in the Malaysian Public Sector, utilized a questionnaire with two sections: (i) demographic information and (ii) factors through which AI can enhance KM in the Malaysian Public Sector. The questionnaires are in Malay. Given the diverse backgrounds of respondents, face-to-face interviews were conducted instead of self-administered surveys. The interviewer ensured accurate recording by presenting and repeating responses to the interviewees.

## 4   Results and Discussion

Based on the findings, the merging of AI and KM in the public sector has resulted in significant interest and research. There are three factors in which AI may increase KM to sustain knowledge because of particular needs (work rotation, long-distance marriage, etc.).

### 4.1   Elevate Humans in KM

Metaphors like "human-in-the-loop" AI or "the last mile problem" in AI-empowered automation do not fully capture the significant contribution that workers may make. These formulations often depict people as an insignificant consideration, as an extension of the technical AI system, or as an obstacle to complete automation. On the contrary, we advocate for a mutually beneficial partnership that acknowledges the indispensable contributions of people to knowledge work and endeavors to innovate and enhance their function. The personnel who incorporate AI into their work practices are crucial for the success of AI implementation inside organisations.

AI can enhance the capabilities of knowledge workers by providing opportunities for reskilling and upskilling. By making human talents and actions more apparent to AI systems, organisations may utilize this information to offer focused training and development opportunities. EdCast utilizes AI to customize training programmes for people by assessing their existing capabilities and aligning them with anticipated labour market demands [41]. Introducing AI into organisations may require the involvement of knowledge workers, such as knowledge scientists and AI champions, who may take on new roles within the organisation. In the subsequent sections, we delve into the roles of knowledge scientists and AI champions.

**Table 1.** The included literatures

| Author/Year | Title | Source |
|---|---|---|
| De Carvalho Botega & da Silva (2020) [27] | An artificial intelligence approach to support knowledge management on the selection of creativity and innovation techniques | Journal of Knowledge Management |
| Trunk et al. (2020) [28] | On the current state of combining human and artificial intelligence for strategic organizational decision making | Business Research |
| Khatib & Falasi (2021) [29] | Effects of artificial intelligence on decision making in project management | American Journal of Industrial and Business Management |
| Nguyen & Malik (2021) [30] | Impact of knowledge sharing on employees' service quality: the moderating role of artificial intelligence | International Marketing Review |
| Ogbeibu et al. (2021) [31] | Green talent management and turnover intention: the roles of leader STARA competence and digital task interdependence | Journal of Intellectual Capital |
| Anshari et al. (2022) [32] | Fourth industrial revolution between knowledge management and digital humanities | Information |
| Asokan et al. (2022) [33] | Socially responsible operations in the Industry 4.0 era: post-COVID-19 technology adoption and perspectives on future research | International Journal of Operations & Production Management |
| Leoni et al. (2022) [34] | The mediating role of knowledge management processes in the effective use of artificial intelligence in manufacturing firms | International Journal of Operations & Production Management |
| Odugbesan et al. (2022) [35] | Green talent management and employees' innovative work behavior: the roles of artificial intelligence and transformational leadership | Journal of Knowledge Management |

(*continued*)

**Table 1.** (*continued*)

| Author/Year | Title | Source |
|---|---|---|
| Olan et al. (2022) [36] | Artificial intelligence and knowledge sharing: Contributing factors to organizational performance | Journal of Business Research |
| Bukartaite & Hooper (2023) [37] | Automation, artificial intelligence and future skills needs: an Irish perspective | European Journal of Training and Development |
| Gravili et al. (2023) [38] | Big data and human resource management: paving the way toward sustainability | European Journal of Innovation Management |
| Stewart et al. (2023) [39] | Attitudes towards artificial intelligence in emergency medicine | Emergency Medicine Australasia |
| Wotschack et al. (2023) [40] | Learning via assistance systems in industrial manufacturing. An experimental study in an Industry 4.0 environment | Journal of Workplace Learning |

## 4.2 Educate Individuals in the Field of Knowledge Science

The emergence of explainable AI (XAI) and neural-symbolic learning has led to the recognition of new positions, such as knowledge scientists and data scientists. These professionals are responsible for gathering and organising datasets for the training of machine learning algorithms [42]. Knowledge scientists may enhance the integration of symbolic AI and statistical AI by constructing knowledge graphs that reflect foundational information and augment training data. These graphs serve as a means to combine classical methodologies with neural networks. Knowledge graphs can enhance the explainability and transparency of AI agents' decision-making by expressing rules and their corresponding explanations. In this approach to explainable AI, both knowledge scientists and machine learning algorithms collaborate and operate as crucial elements [43].

Knowledge scientists play a crucial role in expressing the reasons behind knowledge, to some extent, due to their comprehension of the KM environment and their extensive involvement with the AI system. This statement can act as the initial stage in convincing various stakeholders whose agreement is necessary for the effective execution of any choices influenced by the KM system. The ability to gather support from both internal and external sources is a deeply inherent human skill [44].

### 4.3    Identify Individuals Who Are Highly Skilled and Knowledgeable in the Field of Artificial Intelligence

AI champions play a crucial role in promoting a different perspective that highlights the enhancement of knowledge workers rather than their replacement. This perspective focuses on the anticipated enhancement of the specific activities performed by knowledge workers. AI champions are those who bridge the gap between unique AI capabilities and specific KM demands and tasks. These individuals are not only knowledgeable and enthusiastic about AI, but they also have extensive expertise in certain fields, strong business skills, and effective communication abilities. They can effectively explain how AI can enhance knowledge processes and use people's capabilities.

Although there are instances where new individuals must be recruited based on their cognitive abilities and analytical expertise, it is typically necessary to provide training and retraining to present employees in order for them to fill these new roles. According to Davenport and Mahidhar [45], the essential talents of these personnel include not just improved data and technological skills, but also the capacity to analyse business challenges and choose which technologies are suitable to solve them. In addition to the above particular positions, it is expected that all knowledge workers would need to acquire AI literacies, which are crucial for achieving success in knowledge-intensive employment.

### 4.4    Promote a High Level of Understanding and Proficiency in Artificial Intelligence

With the automation of monotonous and repetitive jobs by AI, workers must acquire the skills to engage with intelligent systems instead of relying on human interaction for these tasks. Proficiency in AI is an essential element required for enhancing the skills of both managers and workers who engage with AI systems. Knowledge workers must have a deeper understanding of AI systems, algorithmic capabilities [46], and new analytical skills focused on data interpretation to effectively comprehend AI-driven judgements. Know-why involves providing justification for these judgements, as well as adopting a critical viewpoint. Bersin and Zao-Sanders [47] contended that in order to possess data literacy, it is important for contemporary professionals to comprehend the process of questioning the outcomes generated by algorithms, rather than blindly accepting the infallibility of system judgements. Decision makers must cultivate an attitude of curiosity, actively questioning and critically engaging with algorithmic outcomes. They can also offer feedback that can serve as a dynamic training platform for the AI system.

### 4.5    Physical Facilities and Structures

Infrastructural preparedness refers to the state of both data and algorithmic systems that rely on data and enhance knowledge processes.

#### 4.5.1    Organize and Arrange the Data

The increased potency of the next iteration of AI may be attributed, in part, to the copious amount of data created inside modern organisations [48]. Deep-learning methods need substantial amounts of training data to get dependable results. Therefore, the quality and quantity of data play a crucial role in determining the performance of deep-learning systems. While it is true that AI systems may assist organisations in overcoming silos, the robustness of AI solutions is really derived from the dispersed nature of the data across these silos. Effective integration of data into AI systems for KM necessitates intentional cross-functional endeavours and collaboration among various stakeholders within the organisation, provided that the data possesses an optimal blend of quality and quantity. The reliable data is derived via a data value chain that encompasses systematic processes of collecting, cleansing, storing, managing, analysing, and safeguarding data [49]. In order to enhance the training of AI models, it is necessary to integrate internal data sources with external data sources that provide information about the current competitive environment. This will create a comprehensive environment for conducting AI-driven analysis.

### 4.5.2 Enhance the Ability to Understand and Explain, as Well as Ensure Responsibility and Transparency

AI technology must be customized for use within an organisation. Several AI capabilities created in academic and industrial laboratories may not be suitable for implementation in knowledge practices because to concerns around interpretability and accountability. Supervised learning models remain the most common machine-learning models used in organisations today. This is mostly due to the fact that the labelling of their training data improves the model's interpretability and accountability. An important expense that enterprises must bear while generating these models is the labor-intensive process of cleaning and preparing proprietary data to deploy a minimum viable AI product [50]. Effective utilisation of data for supervised learning models requires a united and cross-functional endeavour to accurately tag the data in a granular manner.

### 4.5.3 Construct Knowledge Graphs

A significant obstacle in using knowledge lies in the continuous generation of data in real-time, with the majority of this data being unstructured. This creates obstacles to prompt and significant analysis enabled by AI. Knowledge graphs are a nascent method that organisations may utilize to leverage this data. Knowledge graphs oversee the fundamental ideas, terminology, and entities, as well as their interconnections, within the firm. A knowledge graph facilitates the comprehension of connections among data elements, enabling intricate integration, exploration, and examination. For instance, a knowledge graph may be created to comprehend the intricate connections among geographies, weather conditions, expenses, and production, enabling the company to ascertain the effects of severe weather on the cost of a component manufactured in Texas.

A significant number of firms are currently utilising knowledge graphs for AI-powered KM. AstraZeneca use knowledge graphs to enhance drug development by investigating an interconnected system of established connections among chemical compounds, chemicals, illnesses, and biological entities [51]. AI systems rely on knowledge graphs and play a crucial role in establishing meaningful connections between different data points inside these graphs. Knowledge graphs have the ability to surpass the constraints posed by dynamic, unstructured, and diverse data sources commonly found in organisations [52]. Knowledge graphs are very advantageous for KM due to their ability to use their comprehension of the connections between entities in order to elucidate the rationales behind their suggestions.

### 4.5.4 Ethical Considerations of Artificial Intelligence Integration in Knowledge Management

The integration of AI in KM raises significant ethical considerations that necessitate careful examination [53]. One key concern is the potential bias inherent in AI algorithms, which might inadvertently perpetuate and amplify existing biases present in the training data. Addressing issues of fairness and equity in decision-making processes is crucial to ensure that AI-powered KM systems do not inadvertently discriminate against certain groups. Additionally, privacy concerns emerge as AI systems often involve the processing of vast amounts of sensitive information. Striking a balance between leveraging AI for knowledge enhancement and safeguarding individuals' privacy becomes a critical ethical consideration. Transparency and accountability in AI decision-making processes are essential to engender trust among users and stakeholders. As organizations increasingly rely on AI in KM, it becomes imperative to establish robust ethical frameworks, guidelines, and continuous monitoring mechanisms to ensure responsible and ethically sound integration of AI in the realm of KM.

### 4.6 Procedures

An essential supplementary investment for achieving effective AI implementation is harmonising operational practices with AI. Adopting a process-centered strategy entails transitioning from a perspective of utilising AI for process automation to recognising it as a chance to enhance or completely transform processes.

### 4.6.1 Establish Cross-Functional Teams

The utilisation of AI skills may be employed to restructure current organisational processes, with the implementation of process redesign to facilitate cooperation between AI and knowledge workers [54]. Algorithmic systems rely on extensive data that encompass several units. Facilitating the provision of this data for AI systems necessitates actions that include the entire organisation. Interdisciplinary and cross-functional teams can help to promote these projects and bridge the gap between business domain expertise and computational skills. These teams offer a combination of expertise and viewpoints that are essential for the successful execution of AI systems. The teams consist of AI and analytics specialists collaborating closely with topic experts, operational personnel, and frontline workers.

The process of redesigning processes, such as digitalization, datafication, and quantification, and determining how algorithms might enhance different knowledge activities necessitates an ongoing dialogue and agreement between technology experts and domain specialists. The implementation of such a process cannot be executed hierarchically. AI will have an impact on many processes and individuals [48]. Knowledge workers possess a distinct viewpoint on their fundamental tasks and, consequently, should be given the authority to make judgments, determine the way to include algorithms, and subsequently establish confidence in their applications.

### 4.6.2 Revamp to Automate and Enhance

Contrary to popular belief, automation does not inherently oppose human enhancement and can instead promote it [55]. To enhance the capabilities of individuals, organisations must actively seek ways to automate laborious and repetitive tasks, therefore liberating knowledge workers. A portion of this monotonous labour can be assigned to intelligent assistants, which learn and automate routines through the observation of knowledge workers and team collaborations (e.g., by organising meetings). These intelligent systems can expand their capabilities to include exception management. AI can detect invoices that lack order numbers and determine discrepancies in quantities, thereby enabling finance personnel to prioritize more strategic and significant responsibilities [56].

During the process redesign, organisations must also concurrently evaluate possibilities for enhancement. Organisations may use procedures wherein both AI and humans concurrently make choices, followed by a comparison of the resulting results. Alternatively, the decision-making process might be sequential, where one party, usually the human, verifies the choice made by the other side. These processes present chances for reciprocal learning; by employing explainable AI and interactive machine learning approaches, both parties can develop an understanding of the fundamental reasoning.

## 5   Conclusion

The objective of KM is to facilitate the connection between knowledge workers and the appropriate information resources or individuals, at the optimal moment, to enhance decision-making [57]. The increasing capabilities of AI and its promising aspects may need new methods of dividing tasks between human workers and intelligent machines, distinct from those observed in previous organisational structures. These emerging positions necessitate people to acquire a fresh array of talents and abilities, as well as demand intelligent computers to adopt new design mindsets.

The implementation of AI in KM processes is not without its challenges and barriers for organizations. One prominent issue is the potential resistance from employees who might be wary of adopting AI technologies or resistance towards algorithms [58]. This resistance can stem from various factors, including a fear of job displacement or changes in job roles due to automation. The reluctance to embrace AI technologies may be driven by a lack of understanding, unfamiliarity with the technology, or a perceived threat to job security. The implementation of AI in KM processes may also inadvertently contribute to intellectual laziness within organizations [59]. As AI systems automate and streamline knowledge-related tasks, there is a potential risk that employees may become overly reliant on these technologies, leading to a diminished inclination for critical thinking and active engagement with information. To successfully integrate AI into KM processes, organizations must navigate these challenges by fostering a culture of adaptability, addressing technical issues, critical thinking, and prioritizing ethical considerations throughout the implementation journey.

To effectively utilize their artificial partners for KM, humans must cultivate their perspectives, abilities, and work habits. It is important to do so while being cautious of the potential drawbacks of automation. Organisations benefit from such preparations as they enable the practical use of AI's distinct capabilities in KM. These capabilities can only be fully utilized and realized through efficient and mutually beneficial cooperation between knowledge workers and intelligent systems.

# References

1. Jallow, H., Renukappa, S., Suresh, S.: Knowledge management and artificial intelligence (AI). In: 21$^{St}$ European Conference on Knowledge Management (ECKM 2020), pp. 1–9. Academic Conferences and Publishing International Ltd (2020). http://hdl.handle.net/2436/623359
2. Lei, Z., Wang, L.: Construction of organisational system of enterprise knowledge management networking module based on artificial intelligence. Knowl. Manage. Res. Pract. 1–13 (2020). https://doi.org/10.1080/14778238.2020.1831892
3. Pereira, T., Santos, H.: The matrix of quality dimensions of knowledge management: knowledge management assessment models review. Knowl. Manage.: Int. J. **12**, 33–41 (2013). https://doi.org/10.18848/2327-7998/cgp/v12i01/50839
4. Liebowitz, J.: Knowledge management and its link to artificial intelligence. Expert System with Applications **20**, 1–6 (2001). https://doi.org/10.1016/S0957-4174(00)00044-0
5. Goncharova, A., Murach, D.: Artificial intelligence as a subject of civil law. Knowl. Educ. Law Manage. **1**, 153–159 (2020). https://doi.org/10.51647/kelm.2020.3.1.26
6. Wu, I.-L., Hu, Y.-P.: Open innovation based knowledge management implementation: a mediating role of knowledge management design. J. Knowl. Manag. **22**, 1736–1756 (2018). https://doi.org/10.1108/JKM-06-2016-0238
7. Sanzogni, L., Guzman, G., Busch, P.: Artificial intelligence and knowledge management: questioning the tacit dimension. Prometheus **35**, 1–20 (2017). https://doi.org/10.1080/08109028.2017.1364547
8. Dalkir, K.: Knowledge management in theory and practice. Taylor & Francis, Abingdon-on-Thames (2013). https://doi.org/10.4324/9780080547367
9. Mao, H., Liu, S., Zhang, J., Deng, Z.: Information technology source, knowledge management capacity, and competitive advantage: the moderating role of resource commitment. Int. J. Inf. Manage. **36**, 1062–1074 (2016). https://doi.org/10.1016/j.ijinfomgt.2016.07.001
10. Jimenez-Jimenez, D., Martínez-Costa, M., Sanchez Rodriguez, C.: The mediating role of supply chain collaboration on the relationship between information technology and innovation. J. Knowl. Manag. **23**, 548–567 (2019)
11. Shannak, R., Masa'deh, R., Al-Zu'bi, Z., Obeidat, B., Alshurideh, M., Altamony, H.: A theoretical perspective on the relationship between knowledge management systems, customer knowledge management, and firm competitive advantage. Eur. J. Soc. Sci. **32**, 520–532 (2012)
12. Md Ratan, A., Mohammad Shahriar, H., Khatun, M.: The impact of knowledge management process on job satisfaction and employee retention. Int. J. Manage. Account. **2**, 119–130 (2020)
13. Pinho, I., Rego, A., Cunha, M.: Improving knowledge management processes: a hybrid positive approach. J. Knowl. Manag. **16**, 215–242 (2012). https://doi.org/10.1108/13673271211218834

14. Diab, Y.: The concept of knowledge sharing in organizations (studying the personal and organizational factors and their effect on knowledge management). Manage. Stud. Econ. Syst. (MSES) **6**, 91–100 (2021)
15. Gowsalya, R.S., Jijo, F.J.: A study on employee job rotation. Int. J. Res. Trends Innov. **2**, 205–210 (2017)
16. Yu, J., Zhang, J.: A market design approach to job rotation. Games Econom. Behav. **120**, 180–192 (2020). https://doi.org/10.2139/ssrn.3275841
17. Wong, W.L.P., Radcliffe, D.F.: The tacit nature of design knowledge. Technol. Anal. Strat. Manag. **12**, 493–512 (2000). https://doi.org/10.1080/713698497
18. Koulopoulos, T.M., Frappaolo, C.: Smart Things to Know About Knowledge Management. Capstone Publishing, Oxford (1999)
19. Taherdoost, H., Madanchian, M.: Artificial intelligence and knowledge management: Impacts, benefits, and implementation. Computers **12**, 1–18 (2023). https://doi.org/10.3390/computers 12040072
20. Haenlein, M., Kaplan, A.: A brief history of artificial intelligence: on the past, present, and future of artificial intelligence. Calif. Manage. Rev. **61**, 5–14 (2019). https://doi.org/10.1177/0008125619864925
21. Brynjolfsson, E., McAfee, A.: The business of artificial intelligence. Harvard Business Review (2017). https://hbr.org/2017/07/the-business-of-artificial-intelligence
22. Paschen, J., Wilson, M., Ferreira, J.: Collaborative intelligence: how human and artificial intelligence create value along the B2B sales funnel. Bus. Horiz. **63**, 403–414 (2020). https://doi.org/10.1016/j.bushor.2020.01.003
23. Jarrahi, M.H., Philips, G., Sutherland, W., Sawyer, S., Erickson, I.: Personalization of knowledge, personal knowledge ecology, and digital nomadism. J. Am. Soc. Inf. Sci. **70**, 313–324 (2019). https://doi.org/10.1002/asi.24134
24. Jarrahi, M.H., Askay, D., Eshraghi, A., Smith, P.: Artificial intelligence and knowledge management: a partnership between human and AI. Bus. Horiz. **66**, 87–99 (2023). https://doi.org/10.1016/j.bushor.2022.03.002
25. Alani, E., Kamarudin, S., Alrubaiee, L., Tavakoli, R.: A model of the relationship between strategic orientation and product innovation under the mediating effect of customer knowledge management. J. Int. Stud. **12**, 232–242 (2019). https://doi.org/10.14254/2071-8330.2019/12-3/19
26. Okoli, C., Schabram, K.: A guide to conducting a systematic review of information systems research. SSRN Electron. J. **37**, 879–910 (2011). https://doi.org/10.2139/ssrn.1954824
27. De Carvalho Botega, L.F., da Silva, J.C.: An artificial intelligence approach to support knowledge management on the selection of creativity and innovation techniques. J. Knowl. Manag. **24**, 1107–1130 (2020). https://doi.org/10.1108/JKM-10-2019-0559
28. Trunk, A., Birkel, H., Hartmann, E.: On the current state of combining human and artificial intelligence for strategic organizational decision making. Bus. Res. **13**, 875–919 (2020). https://doi.org/10.1007/s40685-020-00133-x
29. Khatib, M.E., Falasi, A.A.: Effects of artificial intelligence on decision making in project management. Am. J. Ind. Bus. Manag. **11**, 251–260 (2021). https://doi.org/10.4236/ajibm.2021.113016
30. Nguyen, T.-M., Malik, A.: Impact of knowledge sharing on employees' service quality: the moderating role of artificial intelligence. Int. Mark. Rev. **39**, 482–508 (2021). https://doi.org/10.1108/IMR-02-2021-0078
31. Ogbeibu, S., Jabbour, C.J.C., Burgess, J., Gaskin, J., Renwick, D.W.S.: Green talent management and turnover intention: the roles of leader STARA competence and digital task interdependence. J. Intellect. Cap. **23**, 27–55 (2021). https://doi.org/10.1108/JIC-01-2021-0016

32. Anshari, M., Syafrudin, M., Fitriyani, N.L.: Fourth industrial revolution between knowledge management and digital humanities. Information **13**, 1–12 (2022). https://doi.org/10.3390/inf o13060292
33. Asokan, D.R., Huq, F.A., Smith, C.M., Stevenson, M.: Socially responsible operations in the Industry 4.0 era: Post-COVID-19 technology adoption and perspectives on future research. Int. J. Oper. Prod. Manage. **42**, 185–217 (2022). https://doi.org/10.1108/IJOPM-01-2022-0069
34. Leoni, L., Ardolino, M., Baz, J.E., Gueli, G., Bacchetti, A.: The mediating role of knowledge management processes in the effective use of artificial intelligence in manufacturing firms. Int. J. Oper. Prod. Manag. **42**, 411–437 (2022). https://doi.org/10.1108/IJOPM-05-2022-0282
35. Odugbesan, J.A., Aghazadeh, S., Qaralleh, R.E.A., Sogeke, O.S.: Green talent management and employees' innovative work behavior: the roles of artificial intelligence and transformational leadership. J. Knowl. Manag. **27**, 696–716 (2022). https://doi.org/10.1108/JKM-08-2021-0601
36. Olan, F., Arakpogun, E.O., Suklan, J., Nakpodia, F., Damij, N., Jayawickrama, U.: Artificial intelligence and knowledge sharing: contributing factors to organizational performance. J. Bus. Res. **145**, 605–615 (2022). https://doi.org/10.1016/j.jbusres.2022.03.008
37. Bukartaite, R., Hooper, D.: Automation, artificial intelligence and future skills needs: an Irish perspective. Eur. J. Train. Develop. **47**, 163–185 (2023). https://doi.org/10.1108/EJTD-03-2023-0045
38. Gravili, G., Hassan, R., Avram, A., Schiavone, F.: Big data and human resource management: paving the way toward sustainability. Eur. J. Innov. Manag. **26**, 552–590 (2023). https://doi.org/10.1108/EJIM-01-2023-0048
39. Stewart, J., et al.: Attitudes towards artificial intelligence in emergency medicine. Emergency Medicine Australasia, 1–14 (2023). https://doi.org/10.1111/1742-6723.14345
40. Wotschack, P., Vladova, G., de Paiva Lareiro, P., Thim, C.: Learning via assistance systems in industrial manufacturing. An experimental study in an Industry 4.0 environment. J. Workplace Learn. **35**, 235–258 (2023). https://doi.org/10.1108/JWL-09-2022-0119
41. Caine, M., Firth-Butterfield, K.: How AI can train workers for the jobs of the future (2020). https://www.weforum.org/agenda/2020/10/ai-jobs/
42. Doran, D., Schulz, S., Besold, T.R.: What does explainable AI really mean? A new conceptualization of perspectives (2017). https://ceur-ws.org/Vol-2071/CExAIIA_2017_paper_2.pdf
43. Blumauer A.: Explainable AI: the rising role of knowledge scientists. Forbes (2019). https://www.forbes.com/sites/forbestechcouncil/2019/12/30/explainable-ai-the-rising-role-of-kno wledge-scientists/#428c9b8603f0
44. Von Krogh, G.: Artificial intelligence in organizations: new opportunities for phenomenon-based theorizing. Acad. Manage. Discov. **4**, 404–409 (2018). https://doi.org/10.5465/amd.2018.0084
45. Davenport, T.H., Mahidhar, V.: What's your cognitive strategy? MIT Sloan Management Review (2018). https://sloanreview.mit.edu/article/whats-your-cognitive-strategy/
46. Jarrahi, M.H., Sutherland, W.: Algorithmic management and algorithmic competencies: Understanding and appropriating algorithms in Gig work. In: Taylor, N., Christian-Lamb, C., Martin, M., Nardi, B. (eds.) Information in contemporary society. iConference, vol. 11420, pp. 578–589. Springer, Cham. https://doi.org/10.1007/978-3-030-15742-5_55
47. Bersin, J., Zao-Sanders, M.: Boost your team's data literacy. Harvard Business Review, Boston (2020)
48. Paschen, U., Pitt, C., Kietzmann, J.: Artificial intelligence: building blocks and an innovation typology. Bus. Hor. **63**, 147–155 (2020). https://doi.org/10.1016/j.bushor.2019.10.004
49. Joshi, A., Wade, M.: The building blocks of an AI strategy (2020). https://sloanreview.mit.edu/article/the-building-blocks-of-an-ai-strategy/

50. Davenport, T., Seseri, R.: What is a minimum viable AI product? MIT Sloan Management Review (2020). https://sloanreview.mit.edu/article/what-is-a-minimum-viable-ai-product/

51. Dhuri, S.: How AstraZeneca is using Netflix like knowledge graph to discover new drugs. Medium (2020). https://siddhuri.medium.com/how-astrazeneca-is-using-netflix-like-knowle dge-graph-to-discover-new-drugs-a6cd187e5b10

52. Elnagar, S., Weistroffer, H.R.: Introducing knowledge graphs to decision support systems design. In: Information Systems: Research, Development, Applications, Education, pp.3-11. Springer, Cham, Switzerland (2019).

53. Vidu, C., Zbuchea, A., Mocanu, R., Pinzaru, F.: Artificial intelligence and the ethical use of knowledge. In: Conference: Strategic 2020, Bucharest (2020)

54. Wilson, H.J., Daugherty, P.R.: Human + Machine: Reimagining Work in the Age of AI. Harvard Business Review Press, Boston, MA (2018)

55. Raisch, S., Krakowski, S.: Artificial intelligence and management: the automation-augmentation paradox. Acad. Manag. Rev. **46**, 1–48 (2021). https://doi.org/10.5465/amr.2018. 0072

56. Dan, W., Elliot, T., Noga, M.: Eight ways machine learning is improving companies' work processes. Harvard Business Review (2017). https://hbr.org/2017/05/8-ways-machine-learning-is-improving-companies-work-processes

57. O'Dell, C., Davenport, T.: Application of AI for knowledge management. CIOReview (2019). https://knowledgemanagement.cioreview.com/cxoinsight/application-of-ai-for-knowledge-management-nid-30328-cid-132.html

58. Li, C., Ashraf, S.F., Amin, S., Safdar, M.N.: Consequence of resistance to change on AI readiness: Mediating – moderating role of task-oriented leadership and high performance work system in the hospitality sector. SAGE Open, **13** (2023). https://doi.org/10.1177/215 82440231217731

59. Khogali, H.O., Mekid, S.: The blended future of automation and AI: examining some long-term societal and ethical impact features. Technol. Soc. **73**, 1–12 (2023). https://doi.org/10. 1016/j.techsoc.2023.102232

# A Study on the Factors Affecting the Use of Smartphone Payment Services in Japan

Kazunori Minetaki[1]($\boxtimes$) and I.-Hsien Ting[2]

[1] Department of Business, Kindai University, Higashi-Osaka, Japan
kminetaki@bus.kindai.ac.jp
[2] Social Networks Innovation Center, National University of Kaohsiung, Kaohsiung, Taiwan
iting@nuk.edu.tw

**Abstract.** This study aims to investigate the factors that affect smartphone payment services. Previous studies have often used PLS-SEM. However, PLS-SEM has been criticized in recent years, and therefore, we analyzed this theme utilizing machine learning and deep learning. The target variable is the satisfaction of the smartphone payment service, and the main explanatory variables are (1) Reliability, (2) Responsiveness, (3) Ease of use/usability, (4) Security, (5) Web design, and (6) Point-rewarding based on the conceptual framework of e-SQ. First, we calculated the accuracy using machine learning and deep learning (CNN, Convolutional Neural Network) to assess our model. The highest accuracy was obtained in CNN. Second, we conducted Shapley Additive explanations (SHAP) to calculate the contribution of each explanatory variable, and we found that Ease of use/usability, Point-rewarding, and Reliability contributed to customer satisfaction. Third, exploiting the text data by Natural Language Processing, and we conducted Latent Dirichlet Allocation (LDA), the topic model. Its result suggested that Responsiveness and Point-rewarding were observed in word-of-mouth. Security was not detected in both analyses, implying a low awareness of security among the Japanese.

**Keywords:** Smartphone Payment Services · Machine Learning · Deep Learning · Shapley Additive explanations (SHAP) · Latent Dirichlet Allocation (LDA)

## 1 Introduction

Apple launched the first iPhone in 2007, which triggered the popularization of smartphones. The iPhone featured a touch screen and app store, providing intuitive and versatile functionality. The proliferation of high-speed Internet connections such as 3G, 4G, and 5G has also facilitated the spread of smartphones. Mobile payment is "any transaction on a mobile handset where ownership of money changes hands" [1]. Smartphones utilize near-field communication (NFC) and short-range communication technology to exchange data between smartphones and receiving devices such as POS terminals. NFC and QR codes enable users to perform a time-saving and contactless transaction. In financial transactions by Smartphone, tokens are utilized instead of actual credit or debit card

© The Author(s), under exclusive license to Springer Nature Switzerland AG 2024
L. Uden and I.-H. Ting (Eds.): KMO 2024, CCIS 2152, pp. 378–393, 2024.
https://doi.org/10.1007/978-3-031-63269-3_29

numbers. Tokens are employed to protect users' card information and enhance security securely.

Today, smartphones dominate the mobile handsets market, so we analyze smartphone payment services. Mobile payment, m-payment, and digital wallet are considered synonymous in analyses regarding smartphone users. Security, cost, and convenience are three main factors smartphone users consider when making a mobile payment [2]. Most studies on mobile payment adoption have been based on the Technological Acceptance Model (TAM) [4–6], the Unified Theory of Acceptance (UTAUT) [9, 11, 12], or UTAUT2 [7, 8, 10]. E-SQ is the most popular method of investigating consumer satisfaction and quality of service, such as e-shopping or mobile payment [2, 7, 15].

PLS-SEM has frequently been used for these analyses. Although PLS-SEM has traditionally been studied with small samples, it is revealed that PLS-SEM should not be used for small sample sizes [3]. We conducted machine learning and deep learning, especially Shapley Additive explanations (SHAP). The results suggested the magnitude of each explanatory variable on the satisfaction of financial transactions using a smartphone. SHAP does not assume a specific probability distribution. Conventional studies on mobile payment exclusively depend on statistical analysis with questionnaires. We also exploited word-of-mouth using natural language processing and obtained meaningful results using Latent Dirichlet Allocation (LDA), the topic model. We should gain more robust results by utilizing various types of data.

## 2 Literature Review

We summarize the conceptual framework to identify factors that may impact customer satisfaction by using mobile payment. According to [13], e-SQ(Electronic Service Quality) broadly encompasses all phases of a customer's interactions with a Website, such as the extent to which a Website facility is efficient and effective in shopping, purchasing, and delivery. The e-SQ dimensions are described in Table: (1) Reliability, (2) Responsiveness, (3) Access, (4) Flexibility, (5) Ease of navigation, (6) Efficiency, (7) Assurance/trust, (8) Security/privacy, (9) Price knowledge, (10) Site aesthetics, (11) Customization/personalization.

The conceptual framework of e-SQ dimensions varies depending on the literature. One conceptual and methodological limitation of developing e-SQ measurement is the lack of a rigorous validation process [14] (Table 1).

[14] is a literature review related to e-SQ that presented six consistent dimensions as follows: (1) reliability/fulfillment, which is also one of the prominent dimensions in the traditional SERVQUAL instrument, refers to the performance of a promised service in an accurate and timely manner, (2) responsiveness, which refers to a willingness to help users, prompt responses to customers inquiries and problems, and the availability of alternative communication channels, (3) Ease of use/usability refers to user-friendliness, especially with regard to searching for information, (4) privacy/security refers to the protection of personal and financial information and the degree to which consumers perceive the site as being safe from intrusion, (5) web design refers to aesthetics features and content as well as structure of online catalogs, (6) information quality/benefit, refers to the adequacy and accuracy of the information users get when visiting a web site (Table 2).

**Table 1.** Dimension of e-SQ [13]

| (1) | Reliability | Correct technical functioning of the site and the accuracy of service promises (having items in stock, delivering what is ordered, delivering when promised), billing, and product information |
|---|---|---|
| (2) | Responsiveness | Quick response and the ability to get help if there is a problem or question |
| (3) | Access | Ability to get on the site quickly and to reach the company when needed |
| (4) | Flexibility | Choice of ways to pay, ship, buy, search for, and return items |
| (5) | Ease of navigation | The site contains functions that help customers find what they need without difficulty, has good search functionality, and allows the customer to maneuver easily and quickly back and forth through the pages |
| (6) | Efficiency | The site is simple to use, properly structured, and requires the customer to input a minimum of information |
| (7) | Assurance/trust | The confidence the customer feels in dealing with the site is due to the reputation of the site and the products or services it sells, as well as the clear and truthful information presented |
| (8) | Security/privacy | The degree to which the customer believes the site is safe from intrusion and personal information is protected |
| (9) | Price knowledge | The extent to which the customer can determine the shipping price, total price, and comparative prices during the shopping process |
| (10) | Site aesthetics | Appearance of the site |
| (11) | Customization/personalization | How much and how easily the site can be tailored to individual customers' preferences, histories, and ways of shopping |

The most frequently used technology acceptance research models are the Technology Acceptance Model (TAM) and the Unified Theory of Acceptance and Use of Technology (UTAUT) [7].

TAM suggests that three factors (perceived ease of use, perceived usefulness, and attitude toward using the technology) influence users' motivations and determine their intentions to use the new technology [15].

UTAUT is a general model of technology adoption and has four factors (performance expectancy, effort expectancy, social influence, and facilitating conditions) that influence behavioral intentions to use a technology [16]. Here, performance expectancy is defined

**Table 2.** Dimension of e-SQ [14]

| (1) | Reliability/fulfillment |
|-----|-------------------------|
| (2) | Responsiveness |
| (3) | Ease of use/usability |
| (4) | Privacy/security |
| (5) | Web design |
| (6) | Information quality/benefit |

as the degree to which using technology will provide benefits to consumers in performing certain activities; effort expectancy is the degree of ease associated with consumers' use of technology; social influence is the extent to which consumers perceive that important others (e.g., family and friends) believe they should use a particular technology; and facilitating conditions refer to consumers' perceptions of the resources and support available to perform a behavior[16].

UTAUT2 integrated hedonic motivation, price value, and experience and habit into UTAUT to tailor it to the context of consumer technology use [17]. Hedonic motivation is defined as consumers' cognitive tradeoff between the perceived benefits of the applications and the monetary cost for using them, and it has been shown to play an important role in determining technology acceptance and use. Price value is defined as the fun or pleasure derived from using technology. Experience and habit reflect an opportunity to use a target technology and are typically operationalized as the passage of time from the initial use of technology by an individual.

In the subsequent introduction to the previous literature, we focus on mobile payment, m-payment, digital wallet, and m-wallet.

We introduce representative prior studies, explicitly targeting smartphone users. Security, cost, and convenience are three main factors smartphone users consider when making a mobile payment [2], which adopted the ANOVA test and regression analysis. [7] extended the UTAUT2 model with new constructs of credibility (CR) and service smartness (SS) constructs using PLS-SEM. Multiple regression analysis investigated factors affecting customer satisfaction, ease of use, security and privacy, information presentation, and convenience [18]. [19] based on the Technology Acceptance Model (TAM) examined the factors influencing the intention to use smartphone banking. Results by conducting path analysis showed that the key factors (i.e., perceived ease of use and perceived usefulness) have a greater impact on account check than account transfer and trust has a greater impact on account transfer transactions than account check transactions in smartphone banking[19].

Next, other mobile, payment m-payment, digital wallet, and m-wallet analyses are introduced. [20] conducted PLS-SEM, and the results pointed out that behavioral and organizational factors significantly impact consumers' trust, which, in turn, influences mobile payment system adoption. [21] was the study based on the Technology Acceptance Model (TAM) by performing PLS-SEM: predictor variables are Perceived value (PA), Compatibility (CO), Perceived enjoyment (PE), and Social Influence (SI); and mediating variables are Service Satisfaction (SS) and Service Trust (ST). Its results showed a significant positive relationship between and within predictor variables (PA, CO, PE & SI) and mediating variables (SS & ST) [21]. [22] combined UTAUT2 and Diffusion of Innovation (DOI), perceived security, and intention to recommend the technology constructs. Data was analyzed using SEM, and it was found that compatibility, perceived technology security, performance expectations, innovativeness, and social influence have significant direct and indirect effects on mobile payment adoption and the intention to recommend this technology [22]. The results by SEM suggested that point rewarding enhances users' need to satisfy core service, whereas point exchanging increases users' perceived value of additional value-added service and user loyalty [23].

## 3 Research Methodology

### 3.1 Conceptual Framework

As we reviewed previous studies, many approaches exist to analyzing mobile payments. Our conceptual framework is based on e-SQ because our target variable is customer satisfaction, which e-SQ has mostly researched. The framework of e-SQ is relatively robust. Considering the characteristics of financial transactions by smartphone in Japan, the variable of point rewarding, which is mainly examined in [23], is added to the explanatory variables. Therefore, we investigate the effects of six dimensions: (1) Reliability, (2) Responsiveness, (3) Ease of use/usability, (4) security, (5) web design, and (6) point-rewarding on customer satisfaction of the financial transaction by using a smartphone payment service.

### 3.2 Data Set

This study uses the "Oricon dataset" questionnaire, including smartphone payments in Japan [24] in Sects. 3.3 and 3.4. This dataset provides satisfaction with using smartphone payment services and related variables. Table 3 describes the variable list to be analyzed in the following section. Number of correspondents is 5500. Mean, S.D., Maximum, and minimum are shown. The target variable is Q1, "Overall, how satisfied are you with your experience? " The explanatory variables are Q2_1~Q2_20, Q10, SQ7, SQ8, SEX, and AGE.

The accuracy of the results obtained by machine learning and deep learning is calculated by the target variable and explanatory variables in Sect. 3.3. The marginal contribution of each explanatory variable by SHAP is Sect. 3.4. The subsets are categorized by frequency (SQ7) and age.

Also, this study uses the "Minhyo Review Dataset" provided by meisterstudio, Inc. Via the IDR Dataset Service of the National Institute of Informatics, including word-of-mouth related to smartphone payment service, with a sample size of 1673, in Sect. 3.5 [25]. One of our contributions is using not only the questionnaire but also text data of word-of-mouth to analyze the factors related to financial transactions by smartphone.

**Table 3.** Variable list

| variable | content | range or unit | N | Mean | Std. Dev. | Min | Max |
|---|---|---|---|---|---|---|---|
| Q1 | Overall, how satisfied are you with your experience? | 1 point: very dissatisfied — 10 points: very satisfied | 5,550 | 7.937 | 1.456 | 1 | 10 |
| Q2_1 | Ease of account registration | 1 point: very dissatisfied — 10 points: very satisfied | 5,550 | 7.640 | 1.616 | 1 | 10 |
| Q2_2 | Smoothness from registration to start of use | 1 point: very dissatisfied — 10 points: very satisfied | 5,550 | 7.761 | 1.596 | 1 | 10 |
| Q2_3 | Full range of deposit (balance charge) and payment methods (bank account linkage, credit card, cash charge, etc.) | 1 point: very dissatisfied — 10 points: very satisfied | 5,550 | 7.806 | 1.681 | 1 | 10 |
| Q2_4 | Smooth payment process | 1 point: very dissatisfied — 10 points: very satisfied | 5,550 | 8.117 | 1.569 | 1 | 10 |
| Q2_5 | Full range of supported stores | 1 point: very dissatisfied — 10 points: very satisfied | 5,550 | 7.366 | 1.785 | 1 | 10 |
| Q2_6 | Full range of functions other than payment (e.g., checking statement history, money transfers, bill payments, etc.) | 1 point: very dissatisfied — 10 points: very satisfied | 5,550 | 7.216 | 1.702 | 1 | 10 |
| Q2_7 | Ease of viewing and using the application | 1 point: very dissatisfied — 10 points: very satisfied | 5,550 | 7.586 | 1.652 | 1 | 10 |
| Q2_8 | Good design of the application (colors, layout, etc.) | 1 point: very dissatisfied — 10 points: very satisfied | 5,550 | 7.410 | 1.596 | 1 | 10 |
| Q2_9 | Legibility of text in the application (font size, font type, etc.) | 1 point: very dissatisfied — 10 points: very satisfied | 5,550 | 7.550 | 1.567 | 1 | 10 |
| Q2_10 | Readability of text in the application (line spacing, text layout, etc.) | 1 point: very dissatisfied — 10 points: very satisfied | 5,550 | 7.528 | 1.566 | 1 | 10 |
| Q2_11 | System stability (e.g., fewer application glitches and communication failures) | 1 point: very dissatisfied — 10 points: very satisfied | 5,550 | 7.494 | 1.662 | 1 | 10 |
| Q2_12 | Full range of campaigns (including point campaigns) | 1 point: very dissatisfied — 10 points: very satisfied | 5,550 | 7.043 | 1.906 | 1 | 10 |
| Q2_13 | Campaign content (is the campaign content appealing to you?) | 1 point: very dissatisfied — 10 points: very satisfied | 5,550 | 6.924 | 1.929 | 1 | 10 |
| Q2_14 | Ease of understanding of the campaign (e.g., campaign eligibility requirements) | 1 point: very dissatisfied — 10 points: very satisfied | 5,550 | 6.847 | 1.914 | 1 | 10 |
| Q2_15 | Ease of accumulating points (point redemption rate, balance crediting rate, etc.) | 1 point: very dissatisfied — 10 points: very satisfied | 5,550 | 7.023 | 1.988 | 1 | 10 |
| Q2_16 | Ease of using points (e.g., length of point expiration) | 1 point: very dissatisfied — 10 points: very satisfied | 5,550 | 7.349 | 1.887 | 1 | 10 |
| Q2_17 | Ease of understanding for inquiries in case of trouble (Q&A, call center, chat) | 1 point: very dissatisfied — 10 points: very satisfied | 5,550 | 6.495 | 1.832 | 1 | 10 |
| Q2_18 | Ease of understanding security measures | 1 point: very dissatisfied — 10 points: very satisfied | 5,550 | 6.528 | 1.789 | 1 | 10 |
| Q2_19 | Enhanced security measures (two-step verification, facial recognition, compensation programs, etc.) | 1 point: very dissatisfied — 10 points: very satisfied | 5,550 | 6.630 | 1.785 | 1 | 10 |
| Q2_20 | Reliability of service | 1 point: very dissatisfied — 10 points: very satisfied | 5,550 | 7.286 | 1.637 | 1 | 10 |
| Q10 | Average amount paid per payment. | 100yen-150000yen | 5,550 | 2264.813 | 6450.33 | 100 | 150000 |
| SQ7 | Please indicate the frequency of use. | 1 point: very dissatisfied — 10 points: very satisfied | 5,550 | 2.915 | 0.954 | 1 | 4 |
| SQ8 | Please indicate the length of time you have been using the service. | 1point~ less than 1 month ~ 7 point: More than 3 years | 5,550 | 5.280091 | 1.332 | 2 | 7 |
| SEX | sex | male:1, female:2 | 5,550 | 1.435676 | 0.496 | 1 | 2 |
| AGE | age | 18 years old - 83 years old | 5,550 | 47.891 | 13.224 | 18 | 83 |

## 3.3 Methodology of Data Analysis

As mentioned, many previous studies have used PLS-SEM with a small sample. One of the criticisms of PLS-SEM is this point. Misconceptions surrounding the supposedly superior ability of PLS to handle small sample sizes and non-normality [3]. Furthermore, it is addressed that our broader review and analysis of the available evidence makes it clear that PLS is not useful for statistical estimation and testing [3]. SEM, which utilizes maximum likelihood, is distorted with a small sample and non-normality; therefore, PLS-SEM is often used instead of SEM. The problem with PLS, however, is that it cannot test systems of equations causally (i.e., overidentifying restrictions cannot be tested) nor can it directly estimate standard errors of estimates [26]. SEM and PLS-SEM are not appropriate when the explanatory variables may have endogeneity.

Our study adopts SHAP (SHapley Additive exPlanations), which does not assume a particular stochastic distribution and causality among variables and calculates the marginal contribution of each explanatory variable. SHAP is a cooperative game theoretic approach that explains the output of any machine learning model. It connects optimal credit allocation with local explanations using the classic Shapley values from game theory and their related extensions. We calculate the accuracy using machine learning and deep learning (CNN, Convolutional Neural Network) to assess our model, where the target variable is customer satisfaction, and the explanatory variable is six dimensions based on e-SQ, as shown in Table 4.

## 3.4 Assessment of Accuracy by Machine Learning and Deep Learning

To assess our model, we calculate the accuracy using machine learning and deep learning. We adopt machine learning and deep learning to analyze the relationship between the degree of customer satisfaction and explanatory variables. SVM (Support Vector Machine), Decision Tree, Random Forest, and KNN (K-Nearest Neighbor method) are

**Table 4.** Categories of main explanatory variables

| | |
|---|---|
| Reliability | System stability (e.g., fewer application glitches and communication failures) |
| | Reliability of service |
| Responsiveness | Ease of understanding for inquiries in case of trouble (Q&A, call center, chat) |
| Ease of use/usability | Ease of account registration |
| | Smoothness from registration to start of use |
| | Full range of deposit (balance charge) and payment methods (bank account linkage, credit card, cash charge, etc.) |
| | Smooth payment process |
| | Full range of supported stores |
| | Full range of functions other than payment (e.g., checking statement history, money transfers, bill payments, etc.) |
| | Ease of understanding security measures |
| Security | Enhanced security measures (two-step verification, facial recognition, compensation programs, etc.) |
| Web design | Ease of viewing and using the application |
| | Good design of the application (colors, layout, etc.) |
| | Legibility of text in the application (font size, font type, etc.) |
| | Readability of text in the application (line spacing, text layout, etc.) |
| Point-rewarding | Full range of campaigns (including point campaigns) |
| | Campaign content (is the campaign content appealing to you?) |
| | Ease of understanding of the campaign (e.g., campaign eligibility requirements) |
| | Ease of accumulating points (point redemption rate, balance crediting rate, etc.) |
| | Ease of using points (e.g., length of point expiration) |

used as machine learning methods, and for deep learning, CNN (Convolutional Neural Network) is conducted. SVM is a model for classification in which boundaries are drawn to maximize the margin and the distance between the boundary and the data to prevent misclassification as much as possible. A decision tree divides data step by step and analyzes them as a tree branches off. Decision trees are easy to interpret because the flow of data segmentation can be grasped. Random Forest creates multiple decision trees in parallel and makes predictions based on the majority vote of the output of each decision tree. K-Nearest Neighbor method is a non-parametric, supervised learning classifier that uses proximity to make classifications or predictions about the grouping of an individual data point.

CNN (Convolutional Neural Network) is a feed-forward neural network composed of the input layer, the multiple hidden layers, and the output layer, processing data with a grid-like topology. Data is allocated 70% for training and 30% for testing. The target variable of the overall satisfaction of smartphone payment is categorized into 3°: the rate of 10 and 9 is 2, the rate of 2 and 1 is 0, and the other rate is 1. The assessment of the above-mentioned machine learning methods is described in the confusion matrix, which summarizes accuracy, precision, recall, and f1-score (See Table 5). The performance of Random Forest is best. The deep learning method CNN shows better accuracy than machine learning (See Fig.1). The results of several machine learning methods, including CNN (Convolutional Neural Network), which is deep learning, suggest that the explanatory variables are effective for predicting the degree of customer satisfaction.

**Table 5.** The confusion matrix

| Model | Accuracy | Precision | Recall | F1 Score |
|---|---|---|---|---|
| SVM | 0.8306 | 0.8268 | 0.8306 | 0.8267 |
| Decision Tree | 0.7574 | 0.7619 | 0.7574 | 0.7594 |
| RandomForest | 0.8408 | 0.8372 | 0.8408 | 0.8381 |
| KNN | 0.8216 | 0.8198 | 0.8216 | 0.8117 |

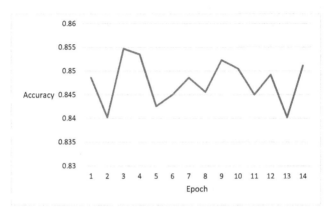

**Fig. 1.** Accuracy by CNN

## 3.5 Data Analysis by SHAP (SHapley Additive exPlanations)

One of the weaknesses of traditional machine learning and deep learning is the "black box nature". We can't know which factor is the most crucial to the target variable because of the "black box nature." To adopt SHAP (SHapley Additive exPlanations) solves this problem.SHAP (SHapley Additive exPlanations) is a game theoretic approach that explains the output of any machine learning model. It connects optimal credit allocation with local explanations using the classic Shapley values from game theory and their related extensions. The target variable is overall satisfaction with smartphone payment, and the explanatory variables are described in the section. The mean of SHAP value by each explanatory variable is shown in Fig. 2.

The top 5 in order of largest mean of SHAP value expressed in absolute values are Smooth payment process (Q2_4), Ease of viewing and using the application(Q2_7), Ease of account registration (Q2_1), which are both included in Ease of use/usability, Ease of accumulating points (Q2_15) included in Point-rewarding, and reliability of service (Q2_20) included in Reliability.

Generally, Ease of use/usability is more effective in increasing customer satisfaction with smartphone payment services. Nevertheless, reliability of service (Q2_20) is listed in the top 5 rankings. Security (Q2_19) has less impact on satisfaction with smartphone payment services.

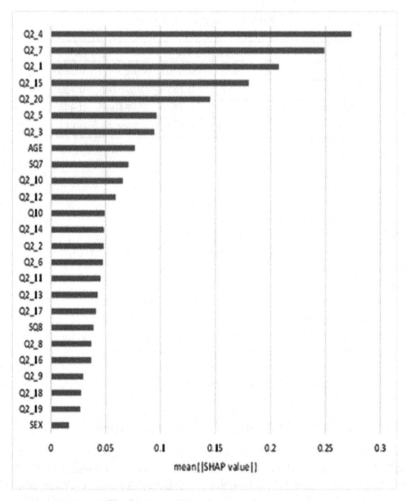

**Fig. 2.** Mean of SHAP value of total case

Furthermore, we conducted the same detailed analyses based on the degree of frequency and age.

Figure 3 illustrates the case of a lower frequency of smartphone payment service (under 4 or 5 days). The top 5 in order of largest mean of SHAP value expressed in absolute values are Smooth payment process (Q2_4), Ease of accumulating points (Q2_15), Ease of account registration (Q2_1), Reliability of service (Q2_20), and Full range of supported stores (Q2_5).

Low-frequency users care for reliability and seek many stores where smartphone payment services can be available.

The result of the high-frequency case is shown in Fig. 4. The top 5 in order of largest mean of SHAP value expressed in absolute values, in the case that frequency of using financial transactions is over 2 or 3 days per week, are Smooth payment process

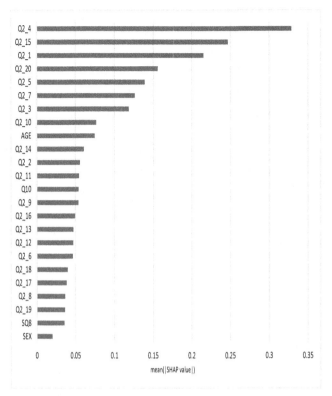

**Fig. 3.** Mean of SHAP value in the case that frequency of using financial transactions by smartphone: under 4 or 5 days per week

(Q2_4), Ease of viewing and using the application (Q2_7), Ease of accumulating points (Q2_15), Ease of account registration (Q2_1), and Full range of campaigns (including point campaigns) (Q2_13).

High-frequency users seek Point-rewarding and Web design. Also, high-frequency users take less care of Reliability.

We compare the case of 50 years old and over (Fig. 5) and the case of under 50 years old (Fig. 6). The top 5 in order of largest mean of SHAP value expressed in absolute values are Smooth payment process (Q2_4) which is by far larger than other factors, Ease of accumulating points (Q2_15), Full range of deposit (balance charge) and payment methods (bank account linkage, credit card, cash charge, etc.) (Q2_3). Ease of account registration (Q2_1) and reliability of service (Q2_20).

The remarkable characteristic is that people 50 years old and over seek a smooth payment process.

In the case of those under 50 years old, the top 5 in order of largest mean of SHAP value expressed in absolute values are Ease of account registration(Q2_1), Ease of viewing and using the application(Q2_7), Smooth payment process (Q2_4), reliability of service (Q2_20) and Ease of accumulating points (Q2_15).

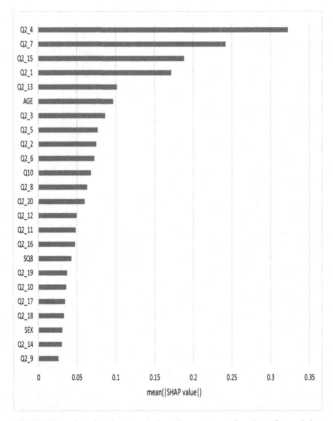

**Fig. 4.** Mean of SHAP value in the case that frequency of using financial transactions by smartphone is over 2 or 3 days per week

They attach importance to Web design, such as the Ease of viewing and using the application, compared to people 50 years old and over.

### 3.6   Analysis of Word-of-mouth by Latent Dirichlet Allocation (LDA)

Word-of-mouth indicates what users are and are not satisfied with. We adopt Latent Dirichlet Allocation (LDA), the topic modeling. Topic modeling is a technique in natural language processing (NLP) and machine learning used for discovering hidden thematic structures in a collection of documents or texts. It is particularly useful for organizing, summarizing, and understanding large unstructured text datasets.

One of the most popular algorithms for topic modeling is Latent Dirichlet Allocation (LDA), which is a generative probabilistic model that aims to discover hidden thematic structures in a collection of documents. We must decide the optimal number of topics in Latent Dirichlet Allocation (LDA); therefore, we use the Perplexity and Coherence score (see Fig. 7). Perplexity is a statistical measure that can be used to evaluate the quality of a topic by predicting a sample or a set of data, given its estimated probabilities. Lower perplexity values indicate a better model fit to the data. Coherence measures assess the

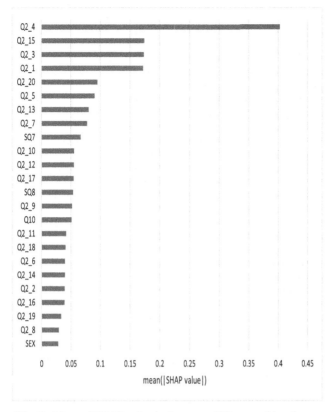

**Fig. 5.** Mean of SHAP value in the case of 50 years old and over

semantic coherence of topics by examining the relatedness of top words within a topic. Higher coherence scores typically indicate better-defined topics.

To calculate the Perplexity and Coherence scores, we use five topics. Table 6 shows five topics categorized by Latent Dirichlet Allocation (LDA). It suggests topics related to (1) bank account and payment, (2) telephone correspondence, (3) evaluation when using the free market, and (4) point accumulation.

We focus on (2) telephone correspondence and (4) point accumulation. Telephone correspondence is included in the Responsiveness category in Table 4, which was not noticed in the SHAP analysis. Point-rewarding is observed in both SHAP and LDA.

## 4   Discussion

Our study adopts machine learning and deep learning in analysis of the customer satisfaction of smartphone payment. SHAP can provide the marginal contribution of each explanatory variable. We will compare the results obtained by IV (instrumental variable), which is statistical analysis, and SHAP in further study. Also we should find out why the contribution of Responsiveness is low in the analysis SHAP.

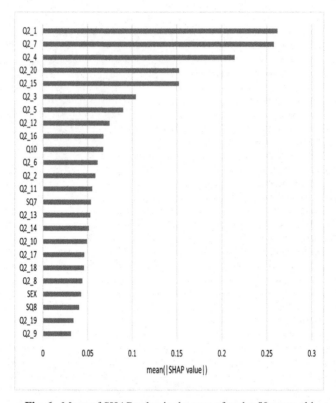

**Fig. 6.** Mean of SHAP value in the case of under 50 years old

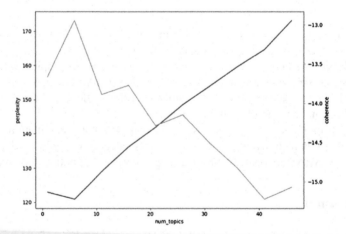

**Fig. 7.** Perplexity and Coherence score

**Table 6.** Result by Latent Dirichlet Allocation (LDA)

| Topic 1 | Bank | 0.0172 | Account | 0.0123 | Pay | 0.0119 | Payment | 0.0115 | Yen | 0.0105 |
|---|---|---|---|---|---|---|---|---|---|---|
| Topic 2 | Correspondence | 0.0196 | What | 0.0136 | Yen | 0.0133 | Day | 0.0116 | Phone | 0.0093 |
| Topic 3 | Listing | 0.0434 | Buy | 0.0409 | Evaluating | 0.0329 | Products | 0.0179 | Free market | 0.0176 |
| Topic 4 | PayPay | 0.0336 | Store | 0.0166 | Phone | 0.0131 | Card | 0.0119 | Payment | 0.0111 |
| Topic 5 | Use | 0.0199 | PayPay | 0.0153 | Point | 0.0143 | Yen | 0.0126 | Payment | 0.0107 |

## 5  Conclusions

This study identifies the factors affecting satisfaction with smartphone payment based on e-SQ. Assessment of our model shows enough accuracy, especially in CNN (Convolutional Neural Network).

The SHAP results indicate that ease of use/usability, such as ease of account registration, ease of viewing and using the application, and smooth payment process, contribute to customer satisfaction with smartphone payment largely as a whole. Secondly, point-rewarding, such as ease of accumulating points, campaign content, and reliability, contribute highly. Security affects less satisfaction with smartphone payment services.

Furthermore, the SHAP results grouped by frequency of use and generation are meaningful. High-frequency users seek point-rewarding and web design but care less about reliability. On the other hand, low-frequency users care about reliability and seek many stores where smartphone payment services are available. The contribution of a smooth payment process is prominent in the old generation, while the younger generation values web design.

This study utilizes both questionnaire and text data, such as word-of-mouth. The results of LDA, one of the topic models, suggest that point-rewarding and responsiveness are observed in word-of-mouth. Both SHAP and LDA analyses can confirm the importance of point-rewarding. Responsiveness is found in word-of-mouth by LDA but not detected by SHAP.

We found that the Japanese pay little attention to the security of smartphone payments. As a result, they are vulnerable to malware or fraud; hence, urgent countermeasures are needed.

**Acknowledgment.** In this paper, Kazunori Minetaki exclusively used both "Oricon Dataset" provided by oricon ME, Inc. And "Minhyo Review Dataset" provided by meisterstudio, Inc. Via IDR Dataset Service of National Institute of Informatics.

I (Kazunori Minetaki) thank oricon ME, Inc., meisterstudio, Inc., and IDR Dataset Service of National Institute of Informatics.

## References

1. Pope, M., et al.: Mobile payments: the reality on the ground in selected Asian countries and the United States. International Journal of Mobile Marketing **6**(2), 88–104 (2011)

2. Shin, S., Lee, W.J., Odom, D.O.: A Comparative study of smartphone users perception and preference towards mobile payment methods in the U.S. and Korea. J. Appl. Bus. Res. (JABR) **30**(5), 1265–1376 (2014). https://doi.org/10.19030/jabr.v30i5.8793
3. Mikko, R., McIntosh, C.N., Antonakis, J.: On the adoption of partial least squares in psychological research: Caveat emptor. Pers. Individ. Differ. **87**, 76–84 (2015). https://doi.org/10.1016/j.paid.2015.07.019
4. Matemba, E.D., Li, G.: Consumers' willingness to adopt and use WeChat wallet: an empirical study in South Africa. Technol. Soc. **53**, 55–68 (2018)
5. Ramos-de-Luna, I., Montoro-Ríos, F., Liébana-Cabanillas, F.: Determinants of the intention to use NFC technology as a payment system: an acceptance model approach. Inf. Syst. E-Bus. Manag. **14**, 293–314 (2016). https://doi.org/10.1007/s10257-015-0284-5
6. Liébana-Cabanillas, F., Muñoz-Leiva, F., Sánchez-Fernández, J.: Behavioral model of younger users in M-payment systems. J. Organ. Comput. Electron. Commer. **25**(2), 169–190 (2015). https://doi.org/10.1080/10919392.2015.1033947
7. Shin, S., Lee, W.J.: Factors affecting user acceptance for NFC mobile wallets in the U.S. and Korea. Innov. Manag. Rev. **18**(4), 417–433 (2021)
8. Sivathanu, B.: Adoption of digital payment systems in the era of demonetization in India: an empirical study. J. Sci. Technol. Policy Manag. **10**(1), 143–171 (2019). https://doi.org/10.1108/JSTPM-07-2017-0033
9. Qasim, A., Abu-Shanab, E.: Drivers of mobile payment acceptance: the impact of network externalities. Inf. Syst. Front. **18**, 1021–1034 (2016). https://doi.org/10.1007/s10796-015-9598-6
10. Tang, C.Y., Lai, C.C., Law, C.W., Liew, M.C., Phua, V.V.: Examining key determinants of mobile wallet adoption intention in Malaysia: an empirical study using the unified theory of acceptance and use of technology 2 model. Int. J. Model. Oper. Manag. **4**(3), 248–265 (2015). https://doi.org/10.1504/IJMOM.2014.067383
11. Fitriani, F., Suzianti, A., Chairunnisa, A.: Analysis of factors that affect nfc mobile payment technology adoption (case study : telkomsel cash). In: ICTCE '17: Proceedings of the 2017 International Conference on Telecommunications and Communication Engineering, pp. 103–109 (2017). https://doi.org/10.1145/3145777.3145778
12. Junadi, S.: A model of factors influencing consumer's intention to use e-payment system in Indonesia. Procedia Comput. Sci. **59**, 214–220 (2015)
13. Zeithaml, V.A., Parasuraman, A., Malhotra, A.: A conceptual framework for understanding e-service quality: implications for future research and managerial practice. MSI Working Paper Report, No. 00-115, pp. 1–46 (2000)
14. Riadh, L.: Developing e-service quality scales: a literature review. J. Retail. Consum. Serv. **17**(6), 464–477 (2010). https://doi.org/10.1016/j.jretconser.2010.06.00
15. Davis, F.D.: Perceived usefulness, perceived ease of use, and user acceptance of information technology. MIS Q. **13**(3), 319–340 (1989). https://doi.org/10.2307/249008
16. Venkatesh, V., Morris, M., Davis, G., Davis, F.: User acceptance of information technology: toward a unified view. MIS Q. **27**(3), 425–478 (2003). https://doi.org/10.2307/30036540. 2003)
17. Venkatesh, V., Thong, J., Xu, X.: Consumer acceptance and use of information technology: extending the unified theory of acceptance and use of technology. MIS Q. **36**(1), 157–178 (2012). https://doi.org/10.2307/41410412
18. Alwi, S., Alpandi, R.M., Salleh, M.N.M., Najihah, I.B., Ariff, F.F.M.: An empirical study on the customers' satisfaction on fintech mobile payment services in Malaysia. Int. J. Adv. Sci. Technol. **28**(16), 390–400 (2019)
19. Kim, J.B., Kang, S.: A study on the factors affecting the intention to use smartphone banking: the differences between the transactions of account check and account transfer. Int. J. Multimedia Ubiq. Eng. **7**(3), 87–95 (2012)

20. Mondego, D.Y., Gide, E.: Exploring the factors that have impact on consumers' trust in mobile payment systems in Australia. J. Inf. Syst. Technol. Manag. Jistem USP **17**, e202017009 (2020)
21. Gupta, S.K., Tiwari, S., Hassan, A., Gupta, P.: Moderating effect of technologies into behavioural intensions of tourists toward use of mobile wallets for digital payments: TAM model perspective. Int. J. Hosp. Tour. Syst. **16**(1), 43–57 (2023)
22. Tiago, O., Thomas, M., Baptista, G., Campos, F.: Mobile payment: understanding the determinants of customer adoption and intention to recommend the technology. Comput. Hum. Behav. **61**, 404–414 (2016)
23. Zhang, L., Wang, Y., Anjum, M.A., Mu, J.: The impacts of point rewarding and exchanging on users' loyalty toward mobile payment applications: a dual channeling perspective. Internet Res. **32**(6), 1832–1861 (2022)
24. Oricon ME Inc. Customer satisfaction survey data. Informatics Research Data Repository, National Institute of Informatics (2023). https://doi.org/10.32130/idr.10.1
25. Meisterstudio, Inc. Minhyo Review Dataset. Informatics Research Data Repository, National Institute of Informatics (2022). https://doi.org/10.32130/idr.16.1
26. John, A., Bendahan, S., Jacquart, P., Lalive, R.: On making causal claims: a review and recommendations. Leadersh. Q.. Q. **21**(6), 1086–1120 (2010). https://doi.org/10.1016/j.lea qua.2010.10.010

# The Use of Web Scraping to Explain Donation Behavior

Christian Ploder[1]🔾, Johannes Spiess[2], Stephan Schlögl[1(✉)]🔾,
Thomas Dilger[1]🔾, Reinhard Bernsteiner[1], and Markus Gander[1]

[1] MCI | The Entrepreneurial School, Innsbruck, Austria
stephan.schloegl@mci.edu
[2] Joint Systems Fundraising & IT-Services GmbH, Innsbruck, Austria
johannes.spiess@sos-kd.org
https://www.mci.edu, https://www.sos-childrensvillages.org/

**Abstract.** The number of natural disasters has been rising for several years. The resulting damage is immense, with developing countries being hit the hardest. In order to support reconstruction, affected countries depend on donations, whose collection and re-distribution is usually coordinated by NGOs. For them to be able to collect donations in a more targeted manner, they require, among others, a better understanding of the effects different types of media have on the donation process and respective donation success. Aiming to address a part of this need, the work presented in this article examines the relationship between media exposure and donor behavior. Our goal is to investigate the extent to which media presence affects the number of donations. The paper discusses the first step in this journey, reporting on the challenges we faced when using the 2015 earthquakes in Nepal as a test-bed to automatically collect media coverage from various sources.

**Keywords:** Web Scrapping · Automatic Information Retrieval · Donation Behavior

## 1 Introduction

Primarily driven by the climate crisis, recent years have seen a sharp increase in natural disasters being recorded all over the globe [4]. In order to respond to these events, and offer necessary help in a market-oriented manner, NGOs increasingly employ modern IT tools and data analysis methods. In this paper we report on our efforts of using data collection and analysis methods to investigate a potential connection between the media presence of a natural disaster and the associated flow of donations. In other words, we aim to explore how media exposure to natural disasters is related to donor behavior. As a test-bed for our investigation we use the two earthquakes which occurred in Nepal in 2015.

Natural disasters cause immense damage in affected areas, in both material and psychological means. In addition to the billions of dollars in material damage,

© The Author(s), under exclusive license to Springer Nature Switzerland AG 2024
L. Uden and I.-H. Ting (Eds.): KMO 2024, CCIS 2152, pp. 394–403, 2024.
https://doi.org/10.1007/978-3-031-63269-3_30

it is often the psychological problems that are spreading among the population, which require even more time and money to heal. Donations can help with both the reconstruction of infrastructure and the mental health of natural disaster victims, and thus help to quickly revitalize the local economy and minimize long-term consequences [12]. For NGOs to collect these necessary donations, it is essential to understand what motivates people to donate. In addition, it is also important to target the right groups in society, as different groups in society prefer to support different causes [19].

Consequently, our work aims to investigate a potential relationship between media presence and donation income. To this end, we aim to generate insights on how media data on natural disasters can be collected, how donors react to media presence, and which other technical and organizational aspects need to be tackled to offer IT support for the donation collection process and help NGOs in recognizing donation trends more quickly. Thus, in summary, our work is guided by the following research question:

*"To what extent does the media presence of natural disasters influence respective donor behavior?"*

The work in this paper reports on a first step towards answering this question, i.e. the data collection process and its associated challenges.

## 2  Natural Disasters and Their Consequences

According to the World Health Organization (WHO), a disaster is defined as a sudden ecological phenomenon of sufficient magnitude to require external assistance [11]. These disasters are further divided into natural and artificial disasters [11] (Note: our work focuses on natural disasters and respective challenges). Natural disasters are events triggered by natural forces such as earthquakes, floods, hurricanes, fire, or weather extremes [11]. Furthermore, a distinction is made between natural disasters and so-called 'natural hazards'. There are different definitions for this subdivision. However, the United Nations Office for Disaster Reduction (UNDRR) has published standard definitions for this purpose, which are used for further guidance. According to these definitions, a natural hazard is a natural process or phenomenon that can result in death, injury, other health effects, property damage, loss of livelihoods and services, social and economic disruption, or environmental damage. A natural disaster, on the other hand, is defined as a severe disruption of the functioning of a community or society with widespread human, material, financial, or environmental losses and impacts that exceed the ability of the affected community or society to cope with its resources [4]. Natural hazards and natural disasters are furthermore sub-divided into sudden and slow-onset natural disasters. Both types can cause long-term disruptions to the environment and/or society. An example of slow-onset natural hazards is seen in droughts, which have a particularly severe impact on the agricultural sector, especially on poor farmers, who are highly dependent on rainfall. Effects may further spill over into the economic and social sectors in the form of famine, which often persists for the duration of the drought. In contrast to slow-onset, the destructive forces of sudden natural hazards are more prominent. Forces are more pronounced. An example of a sudden natural hazard is a flood. The effects of such a natural hazard are seen much more quickly than in a drought, and although the water may disappear in a rather short amount of time, the damage it causes can have severe long-term consequences and affect a wide variety of sectors [4].

Natural disasters lead to immense economic and human consequences. Usually these consequences are negative, with only sporadic cases of neutral or positive effects. Also, it has been shown that the effects of such natural disasters are highly influenced by the conditions which prevail in the region/country the disaster occurs in [12]. The country's economic development level, e.g., is one of the conditions that significantly influences its sensitivity to the impact of natural disasters. That's why most human and financial losses in past natural disasters have occurred in developing countries [12]. Another condition that influences the vulnerability of countries to natural disasters is a country's size. Countries with more land area, more population, or a higher gross domestic product have more assets that are exposed to natural disasters, which means that the resulting economic losses are higher [6]. In turn, larger countries are typically more comparatively differentiated and thus have more opportunities to conduct intersectoral or interregional reallocations, which helps in reducing damages [6]. Thus, while direct losses from natural disasters are higher in larger countries, these countries also have more resources to absorb the losses better, making them smaller relative to the size of the country. Next to country size, it is its geographical location that plays a crucial role, which means that some regions or countries have different vulnerabilities with respect to natural disasters than others. Here it is particularly small island states that are especially vulnerable [6,10]. Other determining factors include political and institutional factors. Stable democratic governance and sound property rights, e.g., reduce the impact of natural disasters [2].

The human consequences triggered by a natural disaster, on the other hand, are very much related to the level of development of the affected country or region. In recent years, the overwhelming majority of fatalities from natural disasters had lived in developing countries, especially in the Asia-Pacific region. Of the three types of natural disasters, hydrometeorological ones are the deadliest in all areas of the world [6]. And also those who survive may be subject to severe long-term health related effects. That is, people exposed to natural disasters are at increased risk of suffering from psychological problems such as depression, anxiety, or especially Post-traumatic Stress Disorder, as well as other unspecified types of stress [8]. Disruptions in the social system, losses of property as well as within the family, the inability to live one's desired lifestyle as well as the general chaos that prevails after natural disasters in the affected areas exert enormous psychological and mental pressure on the people affected [1]. Effective donation management, which allows to provide financial and humanitarian aid quickly and purposefully helps with both the economic and human consequences of natural disasters. The collection and processing of media coverage on natural disasters may help increase said effectiveness and thus significantly support the donation management process.

# 3 Challenges of Collecting Data on Natural Disasters

The online coverage of natural disasters is comprehensive, providing vast amounts of data on each and every event that occurs. Using web scraping tools the respective data may be automatically collected and prepared for analysis. That is, web scraping allows for the collection of unstructured data from the Internet, for its processing as well as its transformation. In doing so, it helps save time, as it reduces sources of error, usually works faster than a human, and eventually stores the data in a structured database which may easily be queried using standardized database tools. However, the successful scraping of specific websites takes some practice. Most predefined solutions focus on extracting product prices or weather data, or they focus on tracking changes on websites. Furthermore, we see web scraping being used for marketing and benchmarking scenarios [14]. To our knowledge, however, there is no explicit web scraping toolkit for the collection and analysis of data on natural disasters. A respective solution, which can handle the differences in available data sources and structures, thus would need to be built.

## 3.1 Technical Challenges

There are a number of technical hurdles that need to be overcome in web scraping. Many modern websites increasingly rely on dynamic programming languages such as JavaScript, making it much more difficult to perform web scraping than websites with a simple HTML structure. Web scrapers also assume that the information they need is presented in a uniform structure. If this structure changes or is not consistent, a web scraping algorithm may not function correctly [9]. Once the algorithm is adapted to the data, there may still be data access issues preventing its use. That is, website holders may introduce measures to 'protect' their website content from being automatically scrapped. In total, there are eight defenses mechanisms that can make web scraping more difficult. The first strategy is to use a *robots.txt* file. This file is attached to a web page and defines how the web page should be scraped. While it may not prevent from scraping, it lays out the rules by which scraping is granted. The second strategy is called IP ban. It blocks any IP addresses from which it notices a high number of reoccurring requests. Similar, the so-called the volume limit for IP requests, checks whether single IP addresses make requests faster or more frequently than is humanly possible. If such is detected, the respective requests are answered more slowly. Next, one may check the user agent, which defines the browser that is used to access the website. If web scraping is employed, this browser information is usually empty. Requests with blank user agent information may thus be blocked. Another strategy is banning through navigation-based detection. This involves some more sophisticated analysis of user behavior. Robot-based navigation may be detected and consequently the request be blocked. One may also use different user verification mechanisms. For example, email verification requires a user's e-mail address to be linked to an active session, whereas phone verification requires his/her phone number. Finally, access to the site may be restricted through a so-called API key [9].

### 3.2  Legal Challenges

Governments as well as businesses strive to have maximum control over their data and thus may implement legal frameworks to block web scraping on their websites. Many of these websites thus require users to accept the terms of use. In these terms of use, website providers can define that web scraping is limited or even prohibited [13]. Failure to comply with these terms of use can, in the worst case, result in legal action, with lawsuits being brought against unauthorized access and respective copyright infringement [9].

### 3.3  Ethical Challenges

The technical solutions that support web scraping are becoming constantly more sophisticating. As to how they comply with ethical rules and guidelines regarding the processing of vast amounts of data, however, is still unclear. Yet, respective rules are needed to protect the public interest and make organizations and individuals who use web scraping to help their business interest adhere to these regulations. Web scrapers need to become self-aware of the damage they can cause. For example, triggering a large number of requests in a short amount of time can overload web page servers and cause them to crash [5]. Respective rules could help move web scraping outside of core business hours to minimize the potential impact it can have on the availability of the website's content to actual visitors. Furthermore, web scraping can disrupt other people's privacy by collecting sensitive data. Here, rules could force web scrapers to anonymize the collected data before processing it further. Rules and guidelines may also define whether it is considered ethical to collect data from websites that make it intentionally difficult to do so [7,9]. Finally, they may outline considerations regarding situational and relational ethics discussing potential harm, such as crippling servers, as well as the problem of making information available in an aggregated form [17].

Despite these challenges, it may be argued that respective data collection and processing may significantly help in donation management and thus increases the effectiveness with which NGOs conduct this important part of their work.

## 4   Methodology

In order to investigate the feasibility of web scraping for the collection of data on natural disasters we focused on the two earthquakes that hit Nepal in 2015.

In this, we consider the given media presence as the total number of daily media reports related to these two earthquakes. A web scarping tool running over a defined period of time thus has the goal to collect and process as many of these reports as possible.

### 4.1  Programming Tools

We used the Python programming language including the 'BeautifulSoup' and 'Selenium' modules to build a web scraper for overnight data collection. Furthermore, we used the 'Pandas' module to sort, clean, validate and structure the collected data. Using so-called 'Pandas Dataframes', which create heterogeneous two-dimensional tables, the module allows to organize large and complex data structures [16]. Finally, the Python module 'Seaborn' was used to visualize the found data. It allows for visualizing data in different diagram types and lets users customize and export these diagrams according to people's preferences and use case needs [15].

### 4.2  Data Sources

In order to test the web scraper with international sources we used the following data sources: (1) the Austrian Newspaper 'Der Standard' (https:// www.derstandard.at); (2) the Austrian Press Agency APA (https://www. apa.com); (3) the local newspaper 'The Himalayan Times' (https://www. thehimalayantimes.com), and (4) a dedicated online search via Google News (https://news.google.com). All the scraping was done in June and August 2022. It included articles and news from April $25^{th}$, 2015, to December $31^{st}$, 2016. The starting date was chosen because the first earthquake hit Nepal on this day. The end date was set to December $31^{st}$, 2016 in order to allow for a meaningful time period while simultaneously avoiding other factors that may have influenced the donation flow, such as other natural disasters.

## 5  Results

The following paragraphs describe how the web scrapper performed on each of the tested data sources, while Fig. 1 presents an aggregation of all media counts that the it collected.

### 5.1  Der Standard

The website of the daily newspaper 'Der Standard' permits web scraping only via sitemaps. For this purpose, it creates a separate sitemap for each month containing each of its article titles. Random manual checks of these sitemaps furthermore showed that articles about the Nepal earthquakes used the keyword 'Nepal' in their title. Thus, sitemaps seemed suitable to filter out relevant articles – at least those, which referred to the earthquakes in their title. Employing the

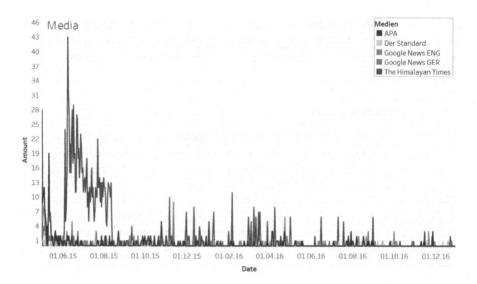

**Fig. 1.** Total media counts collected by the web scraper

'BeautifulSoup' moduel the web scraper was able to open all sitemaps from April 2015 to December 2016 and search for the keyword *"Nepal"*. For every article, which contained the keyword, the scraper then stored the link to the article, its publication date and its source (i.e., 'Der Standard') in a Pandas DataFrame. Next, all found entries were sorted by date and manually scanned so as to make sure that they reported on the earthquakes and not on other news events in Nepal. Those which referred to other news events were deleted from the collection. The final list amounted to a total of 78 articles from the 'Der Standard' dated between April 25th, 2015 and December 31st, 2016, which reported on the earthquakes in Nepal. Investigating the list of stored articles, one sees that most of the entries were published in the first few weeks after the earthquakes, when the situation there was still rather heated. In addition, some entries on the topic were published in October, when a new political leadership was elected. In 2016, relevant articles were published around the anniversary of the disaster.

## 5.2   APA

The Austria Press Agency (APA) is a central information and research platform and as such serves as Austria's largest media and specialist database [3]. It gave access to its database for 17 days to prepare this study, whereby the extraction maximum was set to a maximum of 500 data records. Since the data export was available in the .csv format, it first had to be converted to fit the Pandas DataFrame. Before inserting, the data was also cleaned, particularly with respect to empty lines. Eventually a total of 463 media articles, which were published between April 25th, 2015 and December 31st, 2016 could be collected and were consequently added to the Pandas DataFrame. With the APA dataset, a particular trend was found in an increased number of articles published in January 2016. This can be explained with the annual review on earthquakes around the world, which during this year had a dedicated focus on Nepal.

### 5.3   The Himalayan Times

In order to also include local news from Nepal in the study, we focused on 'The Himalayan Times' as it was found (1) to publish local news in English and (2) authorizes the processing of its website content through web scraping. We started by searching the website for the keyword *'earthquake'*. These initial investigations showed that a search for *'earthquake'* during the defined period produced results spread over maximum of three pages per day with a maximum of twelve entries per page. Furthermore we found that we had to use the 'Selenium' module in order to acknowledge a cookies banner when entering the website for the first time. Running the web scraper for each target day between April 25$^{th}$, 2015 and December 31$^{st}$, 2016 we were then able to collect and store a total of 1.274 validated articles on the earthquakes. Similar to other sources it can be seen that also 'The Himalayan Times' published almost daily about the earthquakes shortly after they happened with an extensive coverage in May/June/July 2015 because of the needed cleanup and the help for effected citizens. After this the number of articles slowly abated.

### 5.4   Google News

Finally, we turned to 'Google News' as an information source. It allows the processing of simple search queries via web scrapers. In Google's robots.txt, it is defined that only static searches are permitted. Thus it is necessary to store scraped data as local result pages. To collect the information we searched in English and German, using the key terms "Erdbeben Nepal" resp. "earthquake Nepal". Again we used the time period between April 25$^{th}$, 2015, and December 31$^{st}$, 2016 as a search frame. Queries were performed using a VPN service for Austria, Germany, the United Kingdom, the United States, and Canada. For each found article, we collected the article's title and subtitle, its publication date, its link, and the newspaper that published it. To do so, we had to automatically open each of the locally stored pages and extract the required information. The retrieved data was then stored in a Pandas DataFrame and subsequently reviewed and cleaned, mainly removing duplicates. This final information collection led to a total of 607 articles, 375 of which were in English and 232 in German.

## 6   Summary and Next Steps

We presented our approach to automatically collect media coverage on natural disasters via web scraping, using the 2015 earthquakes in Nepal as a sample use case and the Austrian Press Agency as well as two newspapers (one Austrian and one Himalayan) and Google News as sample data sources. These efforts aimed at providing the technical foundation for future investigations into a possible connection between the time and amount of news coverage and donor behavior. Waters conducted similar studies, looking at the 2004 Asian tsunami, the 2005 Hurricane Katrina, and the 2010 Haiti earthquake [18]. These studies found that simple news coverage had no direct impact on daily donations.

Our attempt to use web scrapping in order to connect media presence with donor behavior on a larger scale, however, looks promising. To further investigate and validate this approach, the next step on our agenda is to actually link our collected news data on the 2015 earthquakes in Nepal with information on the respective donor behavior. To achieve this we will collaborate with the SOS Peoples Village Austria, who are usually responsible for coordinating Austrian donations related to natural and humanitarian disaster.

# References

1. Abeldaño, R.A., Fernández, R.: Community mental health in disaster situations. A review of community-based models of approach. Ciencia saude coletiva **21**(2), 431–442 (2016). https://doi.org/10.1590/1413-81232015212.17502014
2. Anbarci, N., Escaleras, M., Register, C.A.: Earthquake fatalities: the interaction of nature and political economy. J. Public Econ. **89**(9–10), 1907–1933 (2005). https://doi.org/10.1016/j.jpubeco.2004.08.002
3. APA: APA-onlinemanager (AOM) | APA - Austria Presse Agentur (2022). https://apa.at/produkt/apa-onlinemanager-aom/. Accessed 18 Sept 2022
4. Banholzer, S., Kossin, J., Donner, S.: The impact of climate change on natural disasters. In: Zommers, Z., Singh, A. (eds.) Reducing Disaster: Early Warning Systems For Climate Change, pp. 21–49. Springer, Dordrecht (2014). https://doi.org/10.1007/978-94-017-8598-3_2
5. Boeing, G., Waddell, P.: New insights into rental housing markets across the united states: web scraping and analyzing craigslist rental listings. J. Plan. Educ. Res. **37**(4), 457–476 (2017). https://doi.org/10.1177/0739456X16664789
6. Cavallo, E.: Natural disasters and the economy – a survey. Int. Rev. Environ. Resour. Econ. **5**(1), 63–102 (2011). https://doi.org/10.1561/101.00000039
7. Gregory, K.: Online communication settings and the qualitative research process: acclimating students and novice researchers. Qual. Health Res. **28**(10), 1610–1620 (2018). https://doi.org/10.1177/1049732318776625
8. Ikizer, G., Karanci, A.N., Doğulu, C.: Exploring factors associated with psychological resilience among earthquake survivors from turkey. J. Loss Trauma **21**(5), 384–398 (2016). https://doi.org/10.1080/15325024.2015.1108794
9. Luscombe, A., Dick, K., Walby, K.: Algorithmic thinking in the public interest: navigating technical, legal, and ethical hurdles to web scraping in the social sciences. Qual. Quant. **56**(3), 1023–1044 (2022). https://doi.org/10.1007/s11135-021-01164-0
10. Mohan, P., Strobl, E.: The impact of tropical storms on the accumulation and composition of government debt. Int. Tax Public Financ. **28**(3), 483–496 (2021). https://doi.org/10.1007/s10797-020-09622-5

11. Noji, E.K.: Natural disasters. Crit. Care Clin. **7**(2), 271–292 (1991). https://doi. org/10.1016/S0749-0704(18)30306-3
12. Panwar, V., Sen, S.: Economic impact of natural disasters: an empirical re-examination. Margin J. Appl. Econ. Res. **13**(1), 109–139 (2019). https://doi.org/ 10.1177/0973801018800087
13. Scassa, T.: Ownership and control over publicly accessible platform data. Online Inf. Rev. **43**(6), 986–1002 (2019). https://doi.org/10.1108/OIR-02-2018-0053
14. Singrodia, V., Mitra, A., Paul, S.: A review on web scrapping and its applications. In: 2019 International Conference on Computer Communication and Informatics (ICCCI), pp. 1–6. IEEE (2019). https://doi.org/10.1109/ICCCI.2019.8821809
15. Stancin, I., Jovic, A.: An overview and comparison of free python libraries for data mining and big data analysis. In: 2019 42nd International Convention on Information and Communication Technology, Electronics and Microelectronics (MIPRO), pp. 977–982. IEEE (2019). https://doi.org/10.23919/MIPRO.2019.8757088
16. Thurner, L., et al.: Pandapower-an open-source python tool for convenient modeling, analysis, and optimization of electric power systems. IEEE Trans. Power Syst. **33**(6), 6510–6521 (2018). https://doi.org/10.1109/TPWRS.2018.2829021
17. Tracy, S.J.: Qualitative quality: eight "big-tent" criteria for excellent qualitative research. Qual. Inq. **16**(10), 837–851 (2010). https://doi.org/10.1177/ 1077800410383121
18. Waters, R.D.: Tracing the impact of media relations and television coverage on U.S. charitable relief fundraising: an application of agenda-setting theory across three natural disasters. J. Public Relat. Res. **25**(4), 329–346 (2013). https://doi. org/10.1080/1062726X.2013.806870
19. Zagefka, H., James, T.: The psychology of charitable donations to disaster victims and beyond. Soc. Issues Policy Rev. **9**(1), 155–192 (2015). https://doi.org/10.1111/ sipr.12013

# Knowledge Management and Web 3.0

Eric Kin Wai Lau[(✉)]

Lee Shau Kee School of Business and Administration, Hong Kong Metropolitan University,
Hong Kong, China
ekwlau@hkmu.edu.hk

**Abstract.** It is commonly believed that information technologies (IT) play essential role in implementing knowledge management in organizations (Franco and Mariano, 2007; Revilla, Rodríguez-Prado & Prieto, 2009; Braccini and Federici, 2010; Choo and Neto, 2010). Web 3.0 technologies provide a more open approach for knowledge conversion. The latest web development, Web 3.0 is the executable web. Powered by the semantic web technologies, artificial intelligence, natural language processing (NLP) and machine learning are possible. Autonomous information exchange and interactions with Web 3.0 may further improve organizational knowledge management processes. The purpose of this study is to gain more understanding about the relationship between knowledge management processes and the use of Web 3.0 technologies. This study attempts to analyze the current literature on knowledge management and how Web 3.0 technologies can be applied as the facilitator.

**Keywords:** Knowledge Management · Web 3.0 · SECI · knowledge management processes · web technologies · knowledge conversion

## 1 Introduction

Knowledge Management (KM) in organizations is an important topic as it helps to gain competitive advantages, enhance organization's innovation and employees' productivity [1]. Therefore, KM system must be actively implemented so as to facilitate knowledge conversions within organization. It is important to have the knowledge conversion and exchange between tacit and explicit knowledge within organization [2]. The SECI model of knowledge management proposed by Nonaka [2] focuses on socialization, externalization, internalization and combination. The heart of knowledge management is related to knowledge creation, conversion, transfer and application. Hopefully, knowledge within organization can be used and applied at the corporate level.

In the last 30 years, a lot of research efforts have been spent in the area of knowledge management (KM). It is commonly believed that KM is an importance business capability for organizations' competitive advantages [3]. Due to the complexity of organizational transformation and the radical changes therein, it is necessary to build knowledge-related capabilities, including knowledge sharing and training [4–7].

© The Author(s), under exclusive license to Springer Nature Switzerland AG 2024
L. Uden and I.-H. Ting (Eds.): KMO 2024, CCIS 2152, pp. 404–412, 2024.
https://doi.org/10.1007/978-3-031-63269-3_31

# 2 Literature Review

## 2.1 Basic Elements of Knowledge Management (KM)

Knowledge created by people. Prusak [8] stated that knowledge management involves people and the processes that people use to collect, share, transform, teach, learn and use information to achieve certain objectives. As defined by Davenport and Prusak [9, p. 5], "(knowledge) is a fluid mix of framed experience, contextual information, values and expert insight that provides a framework for evaluating and incorporating new experiences and information"

Knowledge can be represented in either tacit or explicit format [10]. Tacit knowledge is learnt from a person's experience and practice. Therefore, tacit knowledge cannot be codified in a language and is difficult to record. It makes knowledge sharing and transfer difficult [11]. For ease of knowledge management, we need to have a process to convert tacit knowledge into a codified format (i.e. explicit knowledge).

Stover [12] proposed that the process of knowledge transfer can be:

1) tacit to tacit via a socialization process;
2) tacit to explicit via a externalization process, i.e. knowledge sharing in written format, such as stories, presentation, etc.;
3) explicit to explicit via the use of information technologies, such as a database, expert system, etc.;
4) explicit to tacit as an internalization process;

As proposed by Nonaka [2], the Socialization–Externalization–Combination–Internalization (SECI) model tries to manage organizational knowledge into four main processes, i.e. socialization, externalization, combination and internalization (see Fig. 1).

Knowledge transfer and sharing within an organization are essential elements in the knowledge management process. According to Nonaka [2, p. 17], "Informal communities can provide the opportunity for nurturing the emergent properties of knowledge at each level and developing new ideas. Once this is done the organization must be able to integrate that knowledge into its own best practices. If this is done effectively, new knowledge associated with more advantageous organizational processes or technologies will be able to gain a broader currency within the organization."

## 2.2 Knowledge Management and Information Technologies

As defined by Alavi and Leidner [13, p. 106], knowledge is "information possessed in the mind of individuals: it is personalized information (which may or may not be new, unique, useful, or accurate) related to facts, procedures, concepts, interpretations, ideas, observations, and judgments". Information technologies (IT) play an essential role in implementing knowledge management in organizations [14–17]. In the case study, Franco and Mariano [16] found that effective use of information technology repositories can facilitate the knowledge management processes (i.e. knowledge storage and retrieval). They include the IT culture, the standard procedures of a single centralized IT and personal willingness to update the IT tools. Revilla et al. [17] tried to summarize the important roles of IT tools in knowledge management (see Table 1).

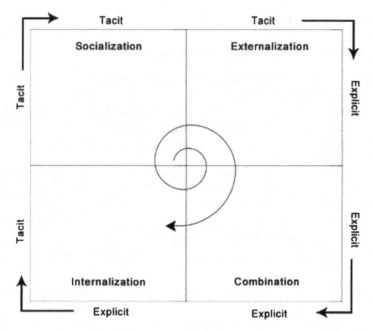

**Fig. 1.** The SECI Model [2].

**Table 1.** Important Roles of IT Tools in Knowledge Management [17]

| IT dimensions | Role and importance | IT tools |
|---|---|---|
| Convergent IT | Connect people to people Improve coordination communication and collaboration between people Point people toward special expertise Create collaboration platforms | Groupware E-mail Calendar systems Collaborative virtual environments Video-conferencing systems Electronic discussion systems Work management systems |
| Divergent IT | Connect people to explicit knowledge Have information and explicit knowledge components online Easy access and retrieval of knowledge Point people to documents that describe or store knowledge Create knowledge repositories | Office applications Integrated document management Decision support systems Data warehouse Internet, intranet Electronic libraries Yellow pages |

Another earlier study, by Martin-Niemi and Greatbanks [18], raised the importance of virtual communities in knowledge conversion. They investigated the use of computer-mediated communication as knowledge transfer. They identified ten potential enabling conditions of/in blog-based communication that facilitate knowledge conversion. They are recognition, common language use, cooperative behaviour, mutual trust, active empathy, leniency in judgement, active questioning, metaphor use, storytelling and access to help. Raudeliuniene et al. [19] tested the effects of both information technologies and social networks on knowledge management processes (i.e. knowledge acquisition, knowledge creation, knowledge storage, knowledge-sharing and knowledge application). With a sample of 210 respondents in the Middle East region, they found that both information technologies and social networks were positively correlated with the knowledge management processes.

In a recent study, Colnar, et al. [20] hypothesized information communication technologies have a moderation effect in knowledge creation and the quality level of health-care services. In a sample of 151 health-care workers in Montenegro, they concluded that information communication technologies support knowledge sharing in organizations.

## 2.3 Web Technologies and Knowledge Management Processes

Web 1.0 was the first generation of web technologies where people could download content and information from static web pages via Internet hyperlinks. Web 2.0 moved forward from "read-only" Web 1.0 technologies and allowed participative web where people could retrieve and share information [21]. Web 2.0 applications include podcasts, tagging, blogging, social networks. The latest web development, Web 3.0 is the executable web. Powered by the Semantic Web technologies, artificial intelligence, natural language processing (NLP) and machine learning are possible. Autonomous information exchange and interactions with Web 3.0 may further improve organizational knowledge management processes (Table 2). Therefore, with the help of Web 3.0 technologies, it is expected that Web 3.0 applications will further enhance organization knowledge management.

The evolution of web technologies is a kind of knowledge application. Web 1.0 and Web 2.0 focus on knowledge transfer (i.e. structured knowledge collection and knowledge sharing in the social networks). However, semantic Web 3.0 focuses on the application of human and machine data with semantic languages. In an earlier study, Razmerita et al. [19] raised the importance of Web 2.0 in knowledge management. They suggested Web 2.0 tools in social networks facilitate both individual and collective knowledge sharing. Web 3.0 is the third phase in the Internet evolution. The main characteristics of Web 3.0 are decentralization, open connection, ubiquity, machine learning and artificial intelligence. Rego et al. [22] suggested the semantic technologies in Web 3.0 further support the learning process in knowledge management.

It affects all knowledge management systems across sectors and industries. How organizations prepare for and response to the latest Web 3.0 development? A wide range of organizations including private sectors, non-profit making organizations and government agencies can adopt the models developed in this proposed project, gain insights from the findings so as to prepare for the rapid changes in business environments and cultivate the upcoming opportunities.

Adopted from What is Web 1.0, Web 2.0, and Web 3.0? Definitions, Differences & Similarities [21]. (https://www.simplilearn.com/what-is-web-1-0-web-2-0-and-web-3-0-with-their-difference-article)

**Table 2.** Major Differences between Web 1.0, Web 2.0 and Web 3.0

|  | Web 1.0 | Web 2.0 | Web 3.0 |
|---|---|---|---|
| Mode | Read-only content | Read and Write | Read, Write and Interact |
| Content Ownership | Content provider | Shared content | Consolidated content |
| Web design | Visual/interactive Web | Programmable Web | Linked data Web |
| Application | Web pages | Wikis and blogs | Waves and live streams |
| Web technologies | HTML/HTTP/URL/Portals | XML/RSS | RDF/RDFS/OWL |
| Functions | File/Web servers, search engines, e-mail, P2P file sharing, content and enterprise portals | Instant messaging, Ajax and JavaScript frameworks, Adobe Flex | Personal intelligent data assistants, ontologies, knowledge bases, semantic search functions |

## 3   Research Questions

The study explores how Web 3.0 further enhances the knowledge management process in organizations. This study tries to answer the following research questions:

- Research Question 1. How does Web 3.0 affect knowledge conversion in organizations?
- Research Question 2. To what extent does the effectiveness of knowledge management differ among Web 1.0, Web 2.0 and Web 3.0?
- Research Question 3. To what extent is there any relationship between the use of Web 3.0 and organizations' backgrounds?
- Research Question 4. To what extent is any organizational support needed to facilitate the use of Web 3.0 for organization knowledge management?

The study constructs are identified in Table 3.

## 4   The Conceptual Framework

Figure 2 illustrates the hypothesized relationships among the main constructs in the study. This study hypothesized that Web 3.0 technologies will be positively correlated with knowledge management processes and KM effectiveness. Additionally, organization backgrounds and organization support will mediate the relationships. With the conceptual framework proposed in the study, it can help to achieve:

- Introduce the application of Web 3.0 technologies and knowledge conversions in business, non-profit making organizations and governments;
- Build leading business practices for the use of Web 3.0 technologies in the knowledge management systems;
- Demonstrate how to use Web 3.0 technologies to enhance the effectiveness of knowledge management systems;

**Table 3.** Main Constructs in the Proposed Study

| Perspective | Constructs |
|---|---|
| Knowledge Management | Knowledge Conversion Processes (socialization, externalization, combination and internalization) |
| | Knowledge Management Satisfaction |
| Web Technologies | The Use of Web 1.0, Web 2.0 and Web 3.0 |
| Organization Backgrounds | Organization Size |
| | Business Nature |
| Organization Supports | Top Management Supports, Leadership, Training, Financial Incentives, Non-financial Incentives |

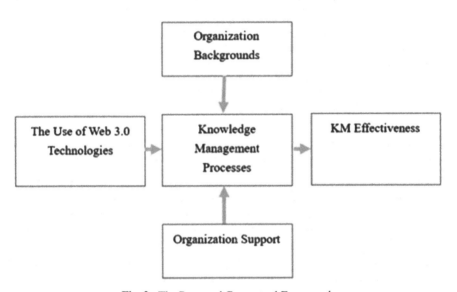

**Fig. 2.** The Proposed Conceptual Framework.

## 5  Research Design

The purpose of this study is to measure the use of Web 3.0 technologies for organizations' knowledge management in China. This study will attempt to analyse the current literature on knowledge management and how Web 3.0 technologies can be applied as its facilitator. Therefore, the study adopts both qualitative and quantitative approaches to investigate the research questions. First, in-depth interviews conducted to collect detailed descriptions of how Web 3.0 technologies can be applied for the knowledge management systems in organizations. Open-ended interviews with business executives in China on their current practices of the use of Web technologies in knowledge management systems are conducted. Quantitative studies focus on the knowledge management processes, KM effectiveness and the use of Web 3.0 technologies as knowledge management systems. A structured questionnaire developed from empirical studies and validated in an exploratory factor analysis (EFA). Next, confirmatory factory analysis (CFA) with maximum-likelihood estimation will be used to test the unidimensionality and convergent validity of the constructs. Then, structural equation modelling (SEM) will be employed. Hong Kong and Mainland organizations across different industries randomly selected from the public databases provided by the Hong Kong Trade Development Council, and the Shanghai and Shenzhen Stock Exchange Markets. Questionnaires mailed to the chief executive officers for their participation. Hopefully, the sample of both qualitative and quantitative studies represent a good cross-section of business sectors.

The study –

- To investigate of basic elements of the use of Web 3.0 technologies and knowledge management systems in organizations;
- To conduct an in-depth review of previous knowledge management studies and identify main constructs of knowledge management processes in organizations;
- To develop an instrument to test those key constructs of knowledge management processes and the effectiveness of knowledge management systems identified in the meta-analysis;
- To conduct an empirical study on the use of Web technologies as knowledge management systems in Hong Kong and China;
- To test and validate the models of knowledge management systems in different organization settings;
- To identify predictors of the effectiveness of knowledge management system from the large-scale quantitative studies in Hong Kong and China;

The main objective of the study was to examine systematically the content of statements offered by the interviewees in the first phrase, and to sort them according to the message they discuss on their knowledge management practices in their company and the use of Web 3.0 technologies. We seek to develop analytic interpretations of the qualitative data. Once collected and organized according to this dichotomy, line-by-line analysis of these scripts and then reviewed in accordance with their common thoughts of the interviewees in the message. Interviewees are conducted in China and it is expected to be completed in the middle of 2024. Afterwards, analysis of these interview scripts will reveal major conducts for the quantitative studies in China.

# 6   Conclusion

The study focuses on understanding how the applications of Web 3.0 can be deployed for organizational knowledge management. The study results of the study would be helpful for corporate decision-makers in understanding the importance of Web 3.0 in their knowledge management implementation efforts. The distinctive contribution of the study provides a systematic review of how Web 3.0 technologies facilitate knowledge management within organization; in this regard, it is the first comprehensive study about the use of Web 3.0 technologies in different industries and scale of organizations (i.e. both profit making and non-profit making organizations). In additional, the study is the first empirical study about the relationships between Web 3.0 technologies, knowledge management processes, organization backgrounds, organization supports and the effectiveness of knowledge management systems.

Empirical findings from the proposed project provide organizations with some practical knowledge and capabilities to response the application of Web 3.0 technologies. Data and insights provided by the proposed project will allow public, private and government policy makers to build sufficient technical capabilities that empower their knowledge management processes. The study provides both theoretical and managerial implications to a wide variety if stakeholders, including government officials on knowledge management, researchers in the research development of Web 3.0 technologies. Other potential interested parties include school students (both undergraduates and postgraduates), instructors and non-profit making organizations who are facilitating knowledge management in societies.

# References

1. Malhotra, Y.: Knowledge management for the new world of business. J. Qual. Particip. **21**(4), 58–60 (1998)
2. Nonaka, P.: A dynamic theory of organizational knowledge creation. Organ. Sci. **5**(1), 14–37 (1994)
3. Evanschitzky, H., Ahlert, D., Blaich, G., Kenning, P.: Knowledge management in knowledge-intensive service networks: a strategic management approach. Manag. Decis. **45**(2), 265–283 (2007)
4. Assegaff, S., Hussin, A.R.C., Dahlan, H.M.: Knowledge management system as enabler for knowledge management practices in virtual communities. Int. J. Comput. Sci. Issues (IJCSI) **10**(1), 685–688 (2013)
5. Bo, B.N.: Strategic knowledge management research: tracing the co-evolution of strategic management and knowledge management perspectives. Compet. Rev. **15**(1), 1–13 (2005)
6. Cha, J., Newman, M., Winch, G.: Revisiting the project management knowledge framework: rebalancing the framework to include transformation projects [Project management knowledge framework]. Int. J. Manag. Proj. Bus. **11**(4), 1026–1043 (2018)
7. Taghizadeh, S.K., Karini, A., Nadarajah, G., Nikbin, D.: Knowledge management capability, environmental dynamism and innovation strategy in Malaysian firms [Knowledge management capability in Malaysian firms]. Manag. Decis. **59**(6), 1386–1405 (2021)
8. Prusak, L.: Where did knowledge management come from? IBM Syst. J. **40**(4), 1002–1007 (2001). https://doi.org/10.1147/sj.404.01002
9. Davenport, T., Prusak, L.: Working Knowledge. Harvard Business School Press, Boston (1998)
10. Polanyi, M.: The Tacit Dimensions. Doubleday, New York (1966)
11. Gourlay, S. N.: Tacit knowledge, tacit knowing, or behaving?. In: Paper Presented at the 3rd European Organisational Knowledge, Learning and Capabilities Conference, Athens, 5–6 April 2002 (2002)
12. Stover, M.: Making tacit knowledge explicit: the ready reference database as codified knowledge. Ref. Serv. Rev. **32**(2), 164–173 (2004)
13. Alavi, M., Leidner, D.: Knowledge management and management systems: conceptual foundations and research issues. MIS Q. **25**(1), 107–136 (2001)
14. Braccini, A.M., Federici, T.: An IS for archaeological finds management as a platform for knowledge management: the ArcheoTRAC case. Vine **40**(2), 136–152 (2010)

15. Choo, C.W., Neto, A.R.: Beyond the BA: enabling knowledge creation in organizations. J. Knowl. Manag. **14**(4), 592–610 (2010)
16. Franco, M., Mariano, S.: Information technology repositories and knowledge management processes: a qualitative analysis. Vine **37**(4), 440–451 (2007)
17. Revilla, E., Rodríguez-Prado, B., Prieto, I.: Information technology as knowledge management enabler in product development: empirical evidence. Eur. J. Innov. Manag. **12**(3), 346–363 (2009)
18. Martin-Niemi, F., Greatbanks, R.: The ba of blogs: enabling conditions for knowledge conversion in blog communities. Vine **40**(1), 7–23 (2010)
19. Raudeliuniene, J., Albats, E., Kordab, M.: Impact of information technologies and social networks on knowledge management processes in middle eastern audit and consulting companies. J. Knowl. Manag. **25**(4), 871–898 (2021)
20. Colnar, S., Radević, I., Martinović, N., Lojpur, A., & Dimovski, V. The role of information communication technologies as a moderator of knowledge creation and knowledge sharing in improving the quality of healthcare services. PLoS One **17**(8) (2022). https://doi.org/10.1371/journal.pone.0272346
21. Terra, J.: What is Web 1.0, Web 2.0, and Web 3.0? Definitions, Differences & Similarities(2022). https://www.simplilearn.com/what-is-web-1-0-web-2-0-and-web-3-0-with-their-difference-article
22. Rego, H., Moreira, T., Morales, E., Garcia, F.J.: Metadata and knowledge management driven web-based learning information system towards Web/e-learning 3.0. Int. J. Emerg. Technol. Learn. (Online) **5**(2), 36–44 (2010)

# Healthcare

# Predictive Analytics a Silver Bullet for a Pandemic – A Systematic Literature Review

George Maramba[(✉)] [iD] and Hanlie Smuts [iD]

University of Pretoria, Pretoria, South Africa
georgemaramba@gmail.com

**Abstract.** Predictive analytics entails using historical data combined with statistical modelling, data mining and machine learning to determine the future outcome. Modern organisations are inundated with large volumes of data, which they need to learn and understand to make speedy, agile, informed and appropriate decisions to solve today's complex business problems. A sector that has not fully adopted using predictive analytics is healthcare, which was revealed by how many federal governments and healthcare providers responded to the Corona Virus Disease 2019 (COVID-19). Applying predictive analytics enables healthcare organisations and federal governments to solve and manage complex situations such as COVID-19 spontaneously and find elegant solutions that could be reused should a similar pandemic recur. This study was conducted to determine the benefits and matrices of predictive analytics essential for combatting a pandemic. The study demonstrates and asserts that predictive analytics is vital when dealing with a pandemic. Predictive analytics provide agility and performance capabilities, which strengthen strategies to improve solutions multi-fold. The study employed a systematic literature review.

**Keywords:** Predictive analytics in healthcare · e-health big data · healthcare data analysis

## 1 Introduction

The advent of healthcare information systems has contributed to the production of large data volumes for patient care, compliance and regulatory requirements (Imran et al. 2020). After several years of lagging technologically, the healthcare sector has started to acclimatise to today's digital age (Belle et al. 2015, Sheng et al. 2020). The adoption of technological tools in healthcare has attributed to the collection of various datasets, which, if analysed and understood, can be a panacea for addressing the increase of novel chronic and acute diseases discovered daily (Wang et al. 2020, Hassan et al. 2021). Predictive data analytics in healthcare play a critical role in helping determine the causes of diseases, generating effective diagnoses (Imran et al. 2020, Muneeswaran, Nagaraj et al. 2021), enhancing the quality of service guarantees by increasing the efficiency of delivery and effectiveness of treatments, providing accurate predictions,

© The Author(s), under exclusive license to Springer Nature Switzerland AG 2024
L. Uden and I.-H. Ting (Eds.): KMO 2024, CCIS 2152, pp. 415–429, 2024.
https://doi.org/10.1007/978-3-031-63269-3_32

enhance clinical care and pinpoint opportunities of cost savings (Imran et al. 2020, Muneeswaran, Nagaraj et al. 2021). The adoption and use of predictive analytics in the healthcare sector are growing enormously, and its benefits are undeniable (Hassan et al. 2021, Muneeswaran, Nagaraj et al. 2021). The application of predictive analytics informs preventative medicine practices and reduces the adverse effects of drugs and other treatments (Hassan et al. 2021).

An organisation that knows what to expect in the future based on historically collected data and current data is better prepared to manage any form of risk that might arise (Hassan et al. 2021). Pandemics are complex and difficult to manage; thus, correct decision-making is key to saving human lives (Muneeswaran, Nagaraj et al. 2021). Predictive analytics provide a complete view of different aspects that require collaboration and cohesion (Rehman et al. 2022, Subrahmanya, Shetty et al. 2022). The guiding research question for this paper is: *What role does predictive analytics play in combatting a pandemic?* In answering this research question, the paper explores the value and importance of using predictive analytics to manage and contain a pandemic such as COVID-19. This paper consists of a background, methodology, discussion of the findings and a conclusion. The next section discusses the background of the study.

## 1.1  Background

Existing studies by Bhaskar et al. (2020), Guiyang et al. (2020), Park, Kim et al. (2020), Subrahmanya, Shetty et al. (2022) and Rehman et al. (2022) undeniably reveal that federal governments and healthcare organisations battled to contain the COVID-19 pandemic. During the initial COVID-19 wave, governments and healthcare organisations approached the pandemic haphazardly (Harrison and Wu 2020, Harris 2021), neglecting the tools that could have managed the situation much better. Bolisani et al. (2021), Hassan et al. (2021) and Rehman et al. (2022) identify a lack of collaboration, poor decision-making and insufficient knowledge about the pandemic as the main reasons for the high infection and death rates in some countries. During the COVID-19 pandemic, various datasets were collected about different aspects (Bhaskar et al. 2020); however, it took longer for healthcare organisations to use them for analytics (Rehman et al. 2022). There has been an increase in studies conducted during the peak of COVID-19 on predictive analytics being considered as part of solutions to combat future pandemics (Khanra et al. 2020, Mishra et al. 2020). Predictive analytics employ algorithms such as regression analysis, machine learning, artificial intelligence, statistical models and neural networks to enable managers to cross-reference current and historical data to make predictions about future, current, and past events and trends (Wang et al. 2018).

A pandemic is resource intensive and, therefore, requires meticulous planning and strategies (Handfield et al. 2020, Rehman et al. 2022). Applying already available data to understand and find strategies to contain the pandemic would be much faster using predictive analytics (Wang and Wu 2021). We discuss the benefits of adopting and using predictive analytics to counter-act a pandemic.

### 1.1.1    Benefits of Predictive Analytics During a Pandemic

Predictive analytics models are artefacts designed to assess historical data, identify patterns, determine, observe and discover trends and deviations using data to predict future trends (Khanra et al. 2020, Hassan et al. 2021, Guo and Chen 2023). Predictive analytics might address these key application areas in the healthcare sector and diagnosing, risk prediction, decision-making, pharmaceuticals, identifying, and flagging anomalies (Alsunaidi et al. 2021). Predictive analytics provide the following benefits critical in the healthcare sector:

1. Large datasets on hospital patients and citizens enable quick identification of current health trends and early epidemics, emergencies and pandemics before they fully materialise (Alsunaidi, Almuhaideb et al. 2021, Chaturvedi and Chakravarty 2021).
2. Predictive analytics present the opportunity to monitor citizens' vital signs, thereby determining their stress levels and the health status of various age groups (Alsunaidi et al. 2021, Annolino 2022).
3. Predictive analytics enable identifying health drives and clinics, raising awareness of appropriate conditions of the populations (Alsunaidi et al. 2021, Hasan et al. 2023).
4. Predictive analytics provide a centralised visualisation across the target universe population to aid health professionals and decision-makers in making adequate facilities and resources available (Annolino 2022).
5. Predictive analytical models and scripts can be reused and further improved to provide refined results (Eltoukhy et al. 2020).
6. Predictive analytics speed up investigations, innovations and knowledge creation such that solutions and strategies can be devised within a short period (Mahalle et al. 2020).
7. Predictive analytics provide a view for identifying potential fatalities, high-risk patients, and disease spread rates and track and monitor the spread and prevalence of a pandemic (Ahmed et al. 2021, Annolino 2022).
8. Predictive analytics present opportunities to create innovative new healthcare technologies, improved health management strategies and agile procedures to administer during pandemics and diseases (Batko and Ślęzak 2022).
9. Predictive analytics realise achieving evidence-based medicine centred on clinical data and decision-making treatments (Batko and Ślęzak 2022).
10. Predictive analytics enable the identification of unnecessary procedures and repetitive processes (Batko and Ślęzak 2022).

The reviewed studies identified the importance and value of adopting predictive analytics in the healthcare sector, particularly when combatting pandemics like COVID-19 (Mahalle et al. 2020, Ahmed et al. 2021, Batko and Ślęzak 2022). The next section discusses the methodology adopted for this study.

### 1.1.2    Challenges of Predictive Analytics During a Pandemic

The previous section has elaborated on the benefits of predictive analytics during a pandemic. Even though such benefits present a positive dimension, technological artefacts are accompanied by a new set of challenges (Cohen et al. 2014). Predictive analytics raise policy, ethical, and legal challenges, particularly with healthcare data (Cohen et al. 2014). This is becoming a major hindrance to the adoption of predictive data analytics. Cohen et al. (2014) and Hassan et al. (2021) determine that federal government regulatory bodies battle to prescribe a legal framework to ensure adherence to the use of healthcare data because predictive analytics is still evolving. It is also complex to determine what is and is not private, both for researchers and healthcare practitioners (Attaran and Attaran 2019, Hassan et al. 2021). Healthcare data challenges include data privacy, intellectual property, data security, data ownership, data stewardship and governance (Cohen et al. 2014, Hassan et al. 2021).

However, the challenges do not outweigh the benefits predictive analytics bring to the healthcare sector. However, it requires prescribed policies and frameworks to manage and ensure that predictive analytics benefits are realised across all healthcare organisations (Amarasingham et al. 2014, Hassan et al. 2021). An appropriate synergy of policy, regulations, ethics, and data frameworks will ensure fewer challenges to the adoption and use of predictive analytics.

## 2   Methodology

The study was conducted in two parts: The first part comprised the execution of a systematic literature review (SLR), while the second part was the development of a predictive analytics model to be adopted when managing a pandemic.

Systematic Literature Review

The first part of this study employed an SLR. An SLR enables researchers to consolidate existing findings and knowledge about the phenomenon under study (Siddaway et al. 2019). It further supports the identification and assessment of relevant primary studies in existing literature aligned to the study, revealing how other studies have been conducted.

The search strings "*predictive analytics in healthcare*", or "*healthcare data analysis*", or "*healthcare data*" were applied to execute searches on our institutional repository. The targeted databases were *ProQuest, Springer*, and *ScienceDirect*, as they have a high impact factor. Table 1 summarises the process followed to select the final studies for review, depicted by the process and number of articles.

The SLR studies (Step 3) were filtered by date, namely, papers published after 2020. This was done to obtain the most recent studies, particularly targeting those published during and after the pandemic period. Only peer-reviewed papers published in English were eligible for consideration. In addition, we removed duplicates, resulting in a total of 75 papers. Twenty-one studies were excluded after reviewing their titles and abstracts, and another set of nineteen papers were removed during the quality assessment process. The quality assessment considered aspects of the studies, such as predictive analytics on healthcare data, possessing identified measures and key performance indicators, containing trend analysis, and supporting decision-making. Thirty-five papers were considered for the SLR analysis.

The selected papers were analysed using *Leximancer* software version 4.51. *Leximancer* is a software solution that applies unsupervised Bayesian decision theory and machine learning to analyse and visualise a corpus of work (Smith and Humphreys 2006).

**Table 1.** SLR Search Results

| Process | Number of articles |
|---|---|
| Step 1: Studies identified through database searching | 88 |
| Step 2: Additional studies identified through other sources | 0 |
| Step 3: Studies excluded due to duplication or exclusion criteria around the year of publication | 13 |
| Step 4: Studies after initial screening and duplicates removed | 75 |
| Step 5: Studies excluded based on title and abstract review | 21 |
| Step 6: Studies reviewed based on title and abstract | 54 |
| Step 7: Studies excluded based on quality assessment | 19 |
| **Studies included in final analysis** | **35** |

*Leximancer* analysis and visualisation are based on semantic and relational information extraction (Smith and Humphreys 2006). The next section discusses the findings of the SLR.

## 3 Findings

The findings are presented in two parts: The first part discusses the findings derived from the SLR, while the second part presents the developed predictive analytics model.

### 3.1 Systematic Literature Review Findings

The thirty-five studies were imported into the *Leximancer* software from which analysis was done. A high-level theme and concept map linked to the keyword, *predictive*, is presented in Fig. 1.

The themes and concepts linked to the keyword, *predictive*, were extracted and rearranged to align with the study. Two themes, *privacy* and *data*, were demoted from being themes to being concepts and *data* was allocated to learning while *privacy* was classified under risk. The identified prevalent themes and concepts from the analysed studies linked to the keyword *predictive* are summarised in Table 2, depicting the themes and concepts.

The six themes presented in Table 2 were discussed most often in the reviewed thirty-five studies selected for the SLR. It is important to note that no single study identified all the themes. The identified themes are discussed in this section in detail, starting with the learning theme.

*Learning:* This critical stage must be conducted with the utmost diligence as it feeds into the subsequent phases while learning and setting up prediction settings and parameters algorithms must be tested and calibrated (Zieba and Bongiovanni 2022). Data and information are vital inputs for an accurate predictive model; however, this is also possible if the relevant technology and tools are made available (Kumar 2021, Wang and Wu

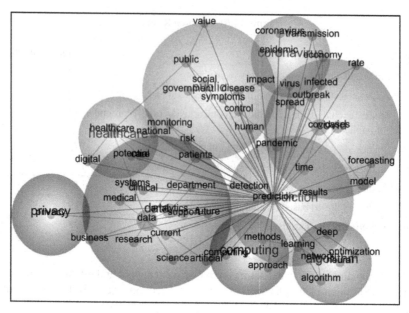

**Fig. 1.** Predictive – Themes and Concept Map

**Table 2.** Key concepts and themes

| Predictive | Theme | Concepts |
|---|---|---|
| | Learning | Algorithm, data, information, model, patients, public, neural network, time, technology, deep learning, data |
| | Symptoms | Clinical, social, disease, spread, detection |
| | Network | Model, social, healthcare, integration, transmission |
| | Risks | Infections, deaths, support, care, potential, privacy, outbreak, impact, time |
| | Monitoring | Healthcare, change, tests, future, science, research, approach, triggers, new variants, remedies, forecasting, artificial intelligence, |
| | Optimisation | Technology, analytics, networks, value, results, control |

2021). Importantly, the right model and network must be selected and the appropriate measures and metrics applied (Kamble and Gunasekaran 2020). Subjects (patients, people) under study could be segmented to gain insights and avoid incorrect generalisations (Kuvvetli et al. 2021, Fathuse et al. 2023). The learning theme enables the exploration of the domain under investigation, and thus, it is important to understand the time factors and variables of a pandemic as they can be measured to make correct predictions (Lee et al. 2022).

*Symptoms:* After learning and understanding the domain, identifying symptoms of a disease during a pandemic is a key factor in saving lives (Agbehadji et al. 2020, Tchagna

Kouanou et al. 2021). Setting up clinical matrices to measure and analyse the disease behaviour and determine its pattern of spreading is critical in containing a pandemic (Agbehadji et al. 2020). The use of predictive analytics allows for identifying disease behaviours and patterns quickly, enabling agile solutions (Tchagna Kouanou et al. 2021). Once symptoms are known, the spread of the disease can be detected easily, and data patterns can be visualised (Tchagna Kouanou et al. 2021).

*Networks:* Network metrics are a key component when fighting a complex or new phenomenon; the initial phases of pandemics always pose a great challenge, and that is when most lives are lost (Priyabrata et al. 2021) because of a disconnect between concerned stakeholders. During pandemics, medical practitioners, healthcare institutions, society, and governments need synergies (Harris 2021). Creating and reinforcing networks presents a clear sightline to visualise an entire section without missing other aspects. Measuring network metrics enables the identification of virus transmission patterns, which provides administrators and managers with various options for which direction to take (Park et al. 2020). There were challenges in the distribution of COVID-19 essentials in many countries, exacerbated by a lack of integrated, defined supply networks (Guiyang et al. 2020, Park et al. 2020).

*Risk:* An important aspect to measure; using predictive analytics to measure risk is also a risk *per se* (Hassan et al. 2021). Processes need to be checked, evaluated and refined continuously to ensure everything performs and works as intended (Subrahmanya et al. 2022). Analytical metrics need to be set on the following factors, namely infection rate, death rate, type of care required, any form of potential problems, privacy issues, and the impact of the continuity of the pandemic (Hasan et al. 2023). Understanding the risk level, together with reliable and informed potential predictions, enables managers to strategise accordingly and direct resources where they are most needed (Bhaskar et al. 2020, Queiroz et al. 2022). It is essential to be able to predict the timing of an outbreak, the probability of how long it would last and its impact (Queiroz et al. 2022). Predictive analytics must not only provide warnings but also provide the quantities of resources required.

*Monitoring:* The role of adopting predictive analytics in fighting a pandemic is to enable effective monitoring to provide informed decision-making (Govindan et al. 2020, Kuvvetli et al. 2021, Lee et al. 2022). Having adequate knowledge and a holistic view provide opportunities to strategise elegant and robust solutions to manage complex situations and also save lives during a pandemic (Konstantinos et al. 2021). Monitoring is a crucial aspect, and metrics with which to forecast and predict enable timely planning ahead of a catastrophe (Lee et al. 2022). Setting triggers to provide notifications when a deviation is detected by using defined algorithms enables early detection, which, in turn, empowers research and coordination teams to be alert and agile and take appropriate approaches (Morawiec and Sołtysik-Piorunkiewicz 2021). Monitoring variant changes and the effectiveness of adopted solutions such as drugs/vaccines enables clinical scientists to know where they need to invest more resources and which solutions are or are not working (Bolisani et al. 2021). The predictive metrics should be formulated as a knowledge base or artificial intelligence zone for the pandemic, which builds on new learnings, and further, such metrics must be dynamic (Arafatur et al. 2020, Gupta et al.

2021). Clinical tests should be conducted continually to gauge changes and the impact of the pandemic, whereby trend analysis and patterns can be closely monitored (New York Health Government Data 2022). Checking medical practitioners' stress levels is essential to ensure they are not overwhelmed and overworked (Pinzaru and Zbuchea 2020, Tchagna Kouanou et al. 2021).

*Optimisation:* Once a knowledge base and a predictive framework have been developed, these measures and settings need to be reviewed continually to enrich and optimise processes and procedures (Davahli et al. 2021). Predictive analytics could be applied to manage supply chain networks (Bhaskar et al. 2020), resource utilisation, value chain, technology integration, and results generation and to evaluate control measures (López-Torres et al. 2019, Davahli et al. 2021, Hasan et al. 2023).

The identified six themes discussed in this section make up core predictive analytics aspects that can be further deconstructed by their concepts into measures and metrics. The predictive analytics aspects are arranged and presented as a life cycle to be followed when fighting a pandemic. Figure 2 presents the predictive analytics life cycle.

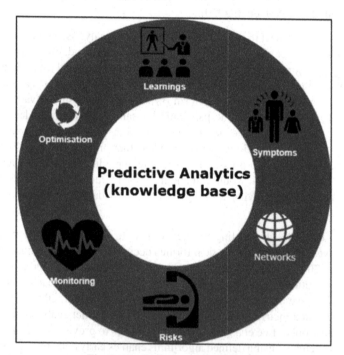

**Fig. 2.** Predictive analytics life cycle

This study identified the previously discussed core aspects of predictive analytics in the healthcare sector that are essential for fighting a pandemic. The cycle starts with the identification of and learning about the pandemic, followed by defining the symptoms, then creating and linking networks, defining metrics for potential risks, monitoring metrics and, finally, optimising both metrics and processes. All these aspects directly feed into the predictive analytics knowledge base. Predictive analytical measures provide meticulous data-driven trend analysis to help determine the direction and change of strategy to manage a pandemic. The formulated predictive analytics life cycle compares to the Cross Industry Standard Process for Data Mining (CRISP-DM) (Wirth and Hipp 2000), which has become the foundation for data analytics. *Leximancer* identified the following phases of CRISP-DM as being in line with the core aspects in Fig. 2: data understanding (learning), data preparation (symptoms), modelling (risks), and evaluation (monitoring and optimisation) (Wirth and Hipp 2000). Table 3 summarises the identified predictive analytical measures as a methodology to follow when adopting analytics to manage a pandemic.

**Table 3.** Predictive analytics process flow

| |
|---|
| Step 1: Investigate and understand the disease |
| Step 2: Define and share knowledge to identify the critical symptoms |
| Step 3: Define networks to ring-fence the pandemic |
| Step 4: Identify all possible risks attributed to the pandemic |
| Step 5: Monitor the pandemic through analytics in a real-world situation |
| Step 6: Find ways to review and optimise measures and processes |

The six steps presented in Table 3 must be deconstructed into functional, measurable attributes. The upcoming section presents these functional, measurable attributes, i.e., the proposed predictive analytics model.

### 3.2 The Proposed Predictive Analytics Model

The adoption and application of predictive analytics in healthcare have been identified as a life cycle. The set metrics should be reviewed and optimised continuously, with algorithms to keep them aligned to extract value from it. The researchers deemed it prudent to propose a comprehensive predictive analytics model that would function as a guideline for healthcare organisations. Figure 3 presents the proposed predictive analytics model for use during a pandemic.

The presented healthcare predictive analytics model is designed to enable healthcare organisations to adopt the application of analytics as a solution to manage a pandemic. The identified six aspects (themes) are the core pillars of the model; metrics and measures must be set up for each theme. Learning metrics enable the healthcare organisation to understand the pandemic and its domain, while knowledge of the symptoms is part of learning. Diseases keep evolving; therefore, continuous review and measurement of metrics is paramount (Chaturvedi and Chakravarty 2021).

After setting up learning symptoms metrics, the next stage identifies network patterns, relationships, dependencies and hierarchies. Networks encompass the administration of the pandemic resources and coordinating healthcare organisations, such as laboratories, scientists and clinicians; they need to collaborate, share data, combine and

**1. Learning**
- Quantify the domain data under study, such as patients and citizen counts.
- Calculate the time taken for the virus causing the pandemic to mature/spread.
- Identify various ways infections can spread.
- Identify conditions conducive to infections occurring.
- Identify which population is succumbing to the infections.
- Identify and quantify the most affected areas/locations.
- Identify all data sources and platforms.

**2. Symptoms**
- Identify and quantify the symptoms.
- List the symptoms.
- Categorise the symptoms to determine thresholds: minor, moderate and severe.
- Identify forms in which a disease is spreading.
- Calculate variants of the diseases and separate symptoms to provide clear analytics.

**3. Networks**
- Identify and quantify all relevant stakeholder networks.
- Quantify the services and products from other service providers.
- Generate network service trends to determine the impact of a possible service disruption.
- Set up measures to monitor the network's participant performance.
- Identify distribution metrics by service providers to determine their efficiency.

**4. Risks**
- Calculate the infection rate and predict future changes.
- Calculate recovery rate.
- Calculate death rate.
- Determine the level of support required from a medical and social perspective.
- Determine the probability of a possible outbreak.
- Calculate the impact of an outbreak.
- Calculate and predict the time to stabilise or stop the spread of the disease.

**5. Monitoring**
- Set up monitoring tools, including automatic triggers on all metrics identified in the previous core predictive analytics aspects.
- Monitoring metrics may include:
  - Number of tests being conducted (pandemic area)
  - Disease infection increases or decreases.
  - Variants of the disease
  - Strategies and approaches that are working and not working.
  - New variants, time taken for a new variant to be detected.
  - Number of remedies approved and working.
  - Number of recoveries
  - Clinical tests in progress, number of subjects under testing
  - Percentage deviation between prior and current research

**6. Optimisation**
- Rerun the predictive model several times to determine consistency and areas that require improvements.
- Continuously calibrate the model to achieve and determine the most effective processes and metrics.
- Enforce deep and machine learning.
- Compare various result sets to uncover blind spots, hot spots and critical areas.
- Identify and set up control metrics to gauge the efficiency of the model.
- Continuously review metrics, algorithms, and triggers to ensure that there is alignment and relevance.

**Fig. 3.** Healthcare predictive analytics model [*created by researchers visual*]

analyse data to gain further insights (Agbehadji et al. 2020). Risks must be known, analysed and converted into meaningful numbers that aid decision-making, such as how many beds would be required, which age group would be highly affected, which areas would be affected the most, and how many people are likely going to die. These questions need to be answered using predictive risk assessment metrics.

Monitoring and correct control are crucial to managing a pandemic successfully (Alsunaidi et al. 2021). Continuous monitoring through the rigorous verification of algorithms and rerunning metrics to determine the consistency of the setup processes must be conducted without fail (Govindan, Mina et al. 2020). The set measures to perform monitoring must be relevant, necessary and fit for purpose (Subrahmanya et al. 2022). Continuous monitoring leads to optimisation of the model and its processes, such as data access, calculations and simulations. All aspects of the model require continuous assessment and optimisation to remain relevant and efficient, particularly when accessing big datasets.

## 4 Limitations and Future Research

The identification of themes and concepts was limited only to literature that was accessed and analysed; therefore, there is a need for further investigations to encompass more aspects of the proposed model. Further research in this subject could focus on identified challenges, such as predictive analytics privacy, security, data collection and distribution legislation. In addition, there is a need for more research to develop predictive, transparent healthcare models and frameworks.

## 5 Conclusion

The knowledge base is a growing, dynamic learning centre in which knowledge creation is derived from data analytics. In the healthcare sector, predictive analytics have played a crucial role ever since the advent of big data availability. In the absence of a pandemic, predictive analytics enable improving the quality of healthcare services. It also supports medical practitioners' continuous learning, research and work. Predictive analytics enhance business and management in facilitating the effective running of healthcare organisations. The predictive data results enable users to determine various possible actions to implement, allowing for test simulation before adopting resources for the solution. The power of predictive analytics in healthcare is its ability to evaluate the effect of future decisions and inform possible outcomes before implementing decisions. It can also provide reasons why certain events might occur.

This paper has presented the benefits of predictive analytics in healthcare, which create awareness of its value. Predictive analytics enable healthcare organisations to be flexible and agile when managing pandemics such as COVID-19. Challenges such as privacy, security and legislation still impact the adoption and application of predictive analytics, which could be resolved with future research on policy frameworks. The study contributes key concepts and themes, a predictive analytics lifecycle, as well as a proposed predictive analytics model to the body of knowledge. Predictive analytics are still developing and evolving in various sectors of the economy; therefore, it will take time before it materialises fully, particularly in healthcare organisations. However, predictive analytics is undeniably a silver bullet for a pandemic.

**Acknowledgements.** The research reported in this article was supported by the South African Department of Science and Innovation (DSI) and the South African Medical Research Council (SAMRC) under BRICS JAF #2020/033. The content and findings reported or illustrated herein are the sole deductions, views and responsibility of the researcher/s and do not reflect the official position and sentiments of the funders.

# Appendix

Appendix 1: Reviewed Journal Sources

| Journal/Source | Number of Studies |
| --- | --- |
| Advances in Decision Sciences | 1 |
| Bull World Health Organ | 1 |
| Decision Analytics Journal | 1 |
| Electronics | 1 |
| Elsevier | 1 |
| Enterprise Information Systems | 1 |
| Heliyon | 1 |
| Institute of Electrical and Electronics Engineers | 4 |
| Infection, Genetics and Evolution | 1 |
| Intelligent Systems and Methods to Combat COVID-19 | 1 |
| International Journal of Computer Applications | 1 |
| International Journal of Environmental Research and Public Health | 3 |
| International Journal of Infectious Diseases | 1 |
| International Journal of Information Technology | 1 |
| Irish Journal of Medical Science | 1 |
| Jama | 1 |
| Journal of Discrete Mathematical Sciences and Cryptography | 1 |
| Journal of Healthcare Engineering | 1 |
| Mathematical Biosciences | 1 |
| Multimedia Systems | 1 |
| Nursing | 1 |
| Patterns | 1 |
| Proceedings of Innovative Data Communication Technologies and Application: 2020 | 1 |
| Sensors | 1 |

(*continued*)

(*continued*)

| Journal/Source | Number of Studies |
|---|---|
| SN Computer Science | 1 |
| Springer | 3 |
| Technological Forecasting and Social Change | 1 |
| Walailak Journal of Science and Technology | 1 |
| **Total** | **35** |

# References

Agbehadji, I.E., Awuzie, B.O., Ngowi, A.B., Millham, R.C.: Review of big data analytics, artificial intelligence and nature-inspired computing models towards accurate detection of COVID-19 pandemic cases and contact tracing. Int. J. Environ. Res. Public Health 17(15), 5330 (2020)

Ahmed, I., Ahmad, M., Jeon, G., Piccialli, F.: A framework for pandemic prediction using big data analytics. Big Data Res. **25**, 100190 (2021)

Alsunaidi, S.J., et al.: Applications of big data analytics to control COVID-19 pandemic. Sensors **21**(7), 2282 (2021)

Amarasingham, R., Patzer, R.E., Huesch, M., Nguyen, N.Q., Xie, B.: Implementing electronic health care predictive analytics: considerations and challenges. Health Aff. **33**(7), 1148–1154 (2014)

Annolino, H.: Leveraging predictive analytics to reduce influenza and COVID-19-related adverse events. Nursing **52**(3), 35 (2022)

Rahman, M.A., Zaman, N., Asyhari, A.T., Al-Turjman, F., Bhuiyan, M.Z.A., Zolkipli, M.F.: Data-driven dynamic clustering framework for mitigating the adverse economic impact of Covid-19 lockdown practices. Sustain. Cities Soc. **62**, 102372 (2020)

Attaran, M., Attaran, S.: Opportunities and challenges of implementing predictive analytics for competitive advantage. In: Applying Business Intelligence Initiatives in Healthcare and Organizational Settings, pp. 64–90 (2019)

Batko, K., Ślęzak, A.: The use of big data analytics in healthcare. J. Big Data **9**(1), 3 (2022)

Belle, A., Raghuram Thiagarajan, S.M., Soroushmehr, R., Navidi, F., Beard, D.A., Najarian, K.: Big data analytics in healthcare. BioMed Res. Int. **2015**, 1–16 (2015). https://doi.org/10.1155/2015/370194

Bhaskar, S., et al.: At the epicenter of COVID-19-The tragic failure of the global supply chain for medical supplies. Front. Public Health **8**, 562882 (2020)

Bolisani, E., Cegarra Navarro, J.G., Garcia-Perez, A.: Managing counter-knowledge in the context of a pandemic: challenges for scientific institutions and policymakers. Knowl. Manag. Res. Pract. **19**(4), 517–524 (2021)

Chaturvedi, D., Chakravarty, U.: Predictive analysis of COVID-19 eradication with vaccination in India, Brazil, and USA. Infect. Genet. Evol. **92**, 104834 (2021)

Cohen, I.G., Amarasingham, R., Shah, A., Xie, B., Lo, B.: The legal and ethical concerns that arise from using complex predictive analytics in health care. Health Aff. **33**(7), 1139–1147 (2014)

Davahli, M.R., Karwowski, W., Fiok, K.: Optimizing COVID-19 vaccine distribution across the United States using deterministic and stochastic recurrent neural networks. PLoS ONE **16**(7), e0253925 (2021)

Eltoukhy, A.E., Shaban, I.A., Chan, F.T., Abdel-Aal, M.A.: Data analytics for predicting COVID-19 cases in top affected countries: observations and recommendations. Int. J. Environ. Res. Public Health **17**(19), 7080 (2020)

Fathuse, N., Hlongwana, K.W., Ginindza, T.G.: "Why am I even here if I can't save the patients?": the frontline healthcare workers' experience of burnout during COVID-19 Pandemic in Mthatha, South Africa. Int. J. Environ. Res. Public Health **20**(8), 5451 (2023)

Govindan, K., Mina, H., Alavi, B.: A decision support system for demand management in healthcare supply chains considering the epidemic outbreaks: a case study of Coronavirus Disease 2019 (COVID-19). Transport. Res. Part E: Logist. Transport. Rev. **138**, 101967 (2020)

Guiyang, Z., Mabel, C., Christina, T.: Lessons learned from the COVID-19 Pandemic exposing the shortcomings of current supply chain operations: a long-term prescriptive offering. Sustainability **12**, 5858 (2020)

Guo, C., Chen, J.: Big data analytics in healthcare. In: Nakamori, Y. (ed.) Knowledge Technology and Systems: Toward Establishing Knowledge Systems Science, pp. 27–70. Springer, Heidelberg (2023). https://doi.org/10.1007/978-981-99-1075-5_2

Gupta, H., et al.: Data analytics and mathematical modeling for simulating the dynamics of COVID-19 epidemic—a case study of India. Electronics **10**(2), 127 (2021)

Handfield, R., Finkenstadt, D.J., Schneller, E.S., Godfrey, A.B., Guinto, P.: A commons for a supply chain in the post-COVID-19 era: the case for a reformed strategic national stockpile. Milbank Q. **98**(4), 1058–1090 (2020)

Harris, J.: Confronting legacies and charting a new course? the politics of coronavirus response in South Africa. In: Coronavirus Politics: The Comparative Politics and Policy of COVID-19, pp. 580–599 (2021)

Harrison, E.A., Wu, J.W.: Vaccine confidence in the time of COVID-19. Eur. J. Epidemiol. **35**(4), 325–330 (2020)

Hasan, I., Dhawan, P., Rizvi, S., Dhir, S.: Data analytics and knowledge management approach for COVID-19 prediction and control. Int. J. Inf. Technol. **15**(2), 937–954 (2023)

Hassan, S., Dhali, M., Zaman, F., Tanveer, M.: Big data and predictive analytics in healthcare in Bangladesh: regulatory challenges. Heliyon **7**(6), e07179 (2021)

Imran, S., Mahmood, T., Morshed, A., Sellis, T.: Big data analytics in healthcare– a systematic literature review and roadmap for practical implementation. IEEE/CAA J. Automatica Sinica **8**(1), 1–22 (2020)

Kamble, S.S., Gunasekaran, A.: Big data-driven supply chain performance measurement system: a review and framework for implementation. Int. J. Prod. Res. **58**(1), 65–86 (2020)

Khanra, S., Dhir, A., Islam, A.N., Mäntymäki, M.: Big data analytics in healthcare: a systematic literature review. Enterp. Inf. Syst. **14**(7), 878–912 (2020)

Nikolopoulos, K., Punia, S., Schäfers, A., Tsinopoulos, C., Vasilakis, C.: Forecasting and planning during a pandemic: COVID-19 growth rates, supply chain disruptions, and governmental decisions. Eur. J. Oper. Res. **290**(1), 99–115 (2021)

Kumar, S.L.: Predictive analytics of Covid-19 pandemic: statistical modelling perspective. Walailak J. Sci. Technol. (WJST) **18**(16), 15583–15597 (2021)

Kuvvetli, Y., Deveci, M., Paksoy, T., Garg, H.: A predictive analytics model for COVID-19 pandemic using artificial neural networks. Decis. Anal. J. **1**, 100007 (2021)

Lee, C.S., Cheang, P.Y.S., Moslehpour, M.: Predictive analytics in business analytics: decision tree. Adv. Decis. Sci. **26**(1), 1–29 (2022)

López-Torres, G.C., Garza-Reyes, J.A., Maldonado-Guzmán, G., Kumar, V., Rocha-Lona, L., Cherrafi, A.: Knowledge management for sustainability in operations. Prod. Plan. Control **30**(10–12), 813–826 (2019)

Mahalle, P.N., Sable, N.P., Mahalle, N.P., Shinde, G.R.: Predictive analytics of COVID-19 using information, communication and technologies. Preprints: 2020040257 (2020)

Mishra, S., Mishra, B.K., Tripathy, H.K., Dutta, A.: Analysis of the role and scope of big data analytics with IoT in health care domain. In: Handbook of Data Science Approaches for Biomedical Engineering, pp. 1–23. Elsevier, Amsterdam (2020)

Morawiec, P., Sołtysik-Piorunkiewicz, A.: Knowledge management significance in agile organization in Lights of COVID-19 pandemic changes. In: European, Mediterranean, and Middle Eastern Conference on Information Systems. Springer, Heidelberg (2021). https://doi.org/10.1007/978-3-030-95947-0_50

Muneeswaran, V., Nagaraj, P., Dhannushree, U., Ishwarya Lakshmi, S., Aishwarya, R., Sunethra, B.: A framework for data analytics-based healthcare systems. In: Raj, J.S., Iliyasu, A.M., Bestak, R., Baig, Z.A. (eds.) Innovative Data Communication Technologies and Application. LNDECT, vol. 59, pp. 83–96. Springer, Singapore (2021). https://doi.org/10.1007/978-981-15-9651-3_7

New York Health Government Data. New_York_State_Statewide_COVID-19_Testing. S. o. N. York. New York, USA (2022). https://health.data.ny.gov/

Park, C.-Y., Kim, K., Roth, S.: Global shortage of personal protective equipment amid COVID-19: Supply chains, bottlenecks, and policy implications. Asian Development Bank (2020)

Pinzaru, F., Zbuchea, A.: Adapting knowledge management strategies in the context of the COVID-19 pandemic. a preliminary overview. In: Proceedings of the 14th International Management Conference "Managing Sustainable Organizations" 5–6 November 2020 (2020)

Chowdhury, P., Paul, S.K., Kaisar, S., Moktadir, M.A.: COVID-19 pandemic related supply chain studies: a systematic review. Transport. Res. Part E: Logist. Transport. Rev. **148**, 102271 (2021)

Queiroz, M., Wamba, S., Jabbour, C., Machado, M.: Supply chain resilience in the UK during the coronavirus pandemic: a resource orchestration perspective. Int. J. Prod. Econ. **245**, 108405 (2022)

Rehman, A., Naz, S., Razzak, I.: Leveraging big data analytics in healthcare enhancement: trends, challenges and opportunities. Multimedia Syst. **28**(4), 1339–1371 (2022)

Sheng, J., Amankwah-Amoah, J., Khan, Z., Wang, X.: COVID-19 pandemic in the new Era of big data analytics: methodological innovations and future research directions. Br. J. Manag. **32**(4), 1164–1183 (2020)

Siddaway, A.P., Wood, A.M., Hedges, L.V.: How to do a systematic review: a best practice guide for conducting and reporting narrative reviews, meta-analyses, and meta-syntheses. Annu. Rev. Psychol. **70**, 747–770 (2019)

Smith, A., Humphreys, M.: Evaluation of unsupervised semantic mapping of natural language with Leximancer concept mapping. Behav. Res. Methods **38**, 262–279 (2006)

Subrahmanya, S.V.G., et al.: The role of data science in healthcare advancements: applications, benefits, and future prospects. Irish J. Med. Sci. (1971-) **191**(4), 1473–1483 (2022)

Tchagna Kouanou, A., et al.: An overview of supervised machine learning methods and data analysis for COVID-19 detection. J. Healthcare Eng. **2021** (2021)

Wang, C.J., Ng, C.Y., Brook, R.H.: Response to COVID-19 in Taiwan: big data analytics, new technology, and proactive testing. JAMA **323**(14), 1341–1342 (2020)

Wang, W.T., Wu, S.Y.: Knowledge management based on information technology in response to COVID-19 crisis. Knowl. Manag. Res. Pract. **19**(4), 468–474 (2021)

Wang, Y., Kung, L., Byrd, T.A.: Big data analytics: understanding its capabilities and potential benefits for healthcare organizations. Technol. Forecast. Soc. Chang. **126**, 3–13 (2018)

Wirth, R., Hipp, J.: CRISP-DM: towards a standard process model for data mining. In: Proceedings of the 4th International Conference on the Practical Applications of Knowledge Discovery and Data Mining, Manchester (2000)

Zieba, M., Bongiovanni, I.: Knowledge management and knowledge security—building an integrated framework in the light of COVID-19. Knowl. Process. Manag. Manag. **29**(2), 121–131 (2022)

# Covid and Emotional Intelligence – Doctors' Reflections

Chun Wai Wong[1]([✉]) and Benjamin Sutton[2]

[1] Cardiology Department, Warrington and Halton Hospitals NHS Trust, Warrington, UK
wongcw@doctors.org.uk
[2] Respiratory Department, Birmingham Queen Elizabeth Hospitals, Birmingham, UK

**Abstract.** Since the COVID-19 crisis was declared a pandemic by the World Health Organization in 2020, NHS staff have been under high levels of stress due to increased workload and patient needs. More than two-fifths of doctors in the UK say that their mental health is now worse than before the pandemic which can negatively impact the quality of patient care. Healthcare workers (HCWs) have carried a heavy burden during the COVID-19 crisis therefore supporting their psychological well-being must be a priority. This paper describes the working experiences of a junior doctor and a consultant in a hospital in UK. Our experiences show us that it would be beneficial to us if we knew about emotional intelligence (EI) in our training. In this paper, we discuss the importance and implications why emotional intelligence is essential for healthcare workers, especially during a pandemic crisis and how it should be included in the training of doctors.

**Keywords:** Emotional Intelligence · Covid · Healthcare · Doctor

## 1 Introduction

The global pandemic, COVID-19, has caused serious negative impacts on the global economy and catastrophic human consequences [1, 2]. Most countries have implemented full or partial lockdown measures to slow the spread of disease. The lockdown has slowed global economic activity substantially, many companies have reduced operations or closed down, and people are losing their jobs. Because of the lockdown, the COVID-19 pandemic has brought about many changes and challenges in business and organisation.

Since the COVID-19 crisis was declared a pandemic by the World Health Organisation on the March 11, 2020, NHS staff have been under high levels of stress due to increased workload and patient needs [3]. Healthcare workers (HCWs) had to be redeployed across all sectors to care for patients with COVID-19 whilst minimising risk for patients with other conditions with face-to-face contact reduced as much as possible. Some NHS staff needed to shield themselves, as they were at a high risk of becoming seriously ill if they had been infected with the COVID-19 virus. Consequently, HCWs are at risk of developing greater severity of psychiatric and psychological disorders. HCWs also experience negative effects due to the pandemic, especially burnout and moral injury that stem from making or witnessing changing decisions as well as dealing

© The Author(s), under exclusive license to Springer Nature Switzerland AG 2024
L. Uden and I.-H. Ting (Eds.): KMO 2024, CCIS 2152, pp. 430–443, 2024.
https://doi.org/10.1007/978-3-031-63269-3_33

with the stress and fear that comes from such a sudden, uncontrollable, and devastating event; as well as the continuous threat of future COVID-19 variants [4, 5]. Studies by researchers have shown that medical HCWs (nurses and doctors) had significantly higher levels of mental health risk in comparison to non-medical HCWs [6]. Zhang et al. [7] found that medical HCWs had significantly higher levels of insomnia, anxiety, depression, somatization and OCD symptoms in comparison to non-medical HCWs.

The handling of the pandemic was described by a cross-party select committee in October 2021 as 'one of the most important public health failures the United Kingdom has ever experienced'. The report shows that there were inadequate supplies and procurement of personal protective equipment (PPE); a test and trace system that failed to deliver; and delays in implementing public infection control measures to prevent the virus spreading [8]. The COVID-19 pandemic had brought unprecedented challenges to the world especially for the healthcare system. While we have now entered the recovery phase, it is worth reflecting on the pandemic experience to help us grow as a clinician and better prepare any future similar events. It is important to learn lessons from the pandemic so that action can be taken in the future – as the UK's health services grapple with several pressures because of the pandemic and the biggest backlog of care in their history – and to be best prepared for future pandemics and avoid repeating past mistakes.

As doctors working in the hospital during the pandemic, there were many challenges and frustrations having to cope with the physical as well as the emotional aspects of the job. How did we cope? We did our best to give the patients what we could. With hindsight, it would be better and beneficial if we have learned about emotional intelligence (EI). It is our belief that knowledge and learning about EI would have better equipped us to cope with our mental health as well as that of the patients.

This paper begins with a brief review of the current health service in UK and its problems. Next, we describe our experiences working as a junior doctor and consultant in the hospital. This is followed by a review of EI and why it is important to health care workers and how it is used in organisations to promote workers' wellbeing and how it can be incorporated in health care trainings. A list of practical recommendations for policy makers and leaders to consider when developing and assigning EI training is included. It then concludes with suggestions for further research.

## 2  Methodology

This paper is a case report with two doctors' reflections on their working experiences during the Covid pandemic.

## 3  UK Health Service and Doctors' Covid Experience

### 3.1  The Health Service in the UK During COVID-19

For a population of around 67 million, the NHS employs 1.3 million staffs including 139 thousands of doctors [9]. The healthcare systems were operating in environments of scarcity long before COVID-19 and were not in a good position to weather the storm of the pandemic [10]. As stated in the BMA Covid report, the pandemic brutally exposed critical underlying issues with too few staff, too few beds, and buildings that were unsuitable for effective infection control [10]. A better staffed and better resourced system would have been more able to deal with the acute spike in demand and high staff absence rate caused by the pandemic [11]. The BMA also pointed out that the UK government had conducted several pandemic planning exercises prior to COVID-19 and yet failed to act on some of the key recommendations, particularly those related to stockpiles of PPE [11]. Additionally, infection prevention guidance was lacking at the start. There were even concerns of spreading fear among the hospital staffs and public with wearing masks.

## 3.2 Junior Doctor Reflection

As a junior doctor (second year after graduation during the start of pandemic) working in the medical specialty, there were several challenges. First, the fear of contracting COVID-19 myself. At the start of the pandemic, there was no established treatment for COVID-19 and a significant proportion of patients who were admitted to the hospital died. Secondly, the lack of PPE both in quantity and quality raised concerns. We were wearing surgical facemask and plastic apron. In contrast, other countries' healthcare workers were wearing N95 facemask and had more protective equipment. Thirdly, the change in clinical demand. COVID-19 patients can deteriorate very easily, and prompt clinical review was required to stabilise the patient and consideration for escalation to high dependency unit or intensive care unit. The original out-of-hours staffing was not able to cope with the new demand. Fourth, there were patients dying every day. For a junior doctor who has not been in the NHS for long, it was a very difficult experience to adjust to. Lastly, it was the interaction with family and friends outside the hospital setting. Where they were worried about my health and afraid of contracting COVID-19 through me.

I was working as an NHS Foundation Year 2 doctor when the pandemic started, and the following were some of the challenges I had encountered. At the beginning, my biggest fear was contracting COVID-19 myself and becoming unwell with it. I even pictured myself dying from COVID-19. This was when we knew very little about COVID-19 with no treatment available and high mortality associated with it. To address the situation, the first step was to acknowledge my fear emotion and understanding its impact on myself. 'Amygdala hijack' happened until I decided to focus on what were within my zone of control. I maintained good hand hygiene, was using the PPE religiously, discussed my worries with my colleagues and seniors. I knew my risk of COVID-19 infection was low based on my medical history and demographic. These helped me overcome the fear of looking after COVID-19 patients. As I became more senior working through the pandemic years, I saw the same problem among the junior staffs. I could recognise that the fear of contracting COVID-19 was impacting their work performance. When it was within my capacity, I would support them to cope with it. However, if they have any significant underlying medical condition, I will signpost them to have discussion with their supervisor.

Another challenge that I encountered during the early pandemic was the high intensity of workload and high acuity of COVID-19 patients. Particularly during out-of-hours, the medical bleep would ring non-stop as multiple patients would deteriorate at the same time. Ideally the critically unwell patients should be reviewed by the medical registrar (senior clinician during out-of-hours). However, the clinical demand greatly exceeded our capacity, and the medical registrar was often occupied with other sick patients. This left me with no choice but to step in to provide the best care we could for the patients. There were steep learning curves for the following areas: clinical assessment of critically unwell patients, initial management to stabilise the patients, consideration of treatment escalation plan including Do Not Attempt Resuscitation (DNAR), discussion with the medical registrar and Intensive Care Unit (ITU), communication with patients and their worried families and above all, prioritisation skills to decide the patient review order.

The healthcare system was overwhelmed. I had imposter syndrome especially when discussing patients with the ITU directly as a Foundation Year doctor. On reflection, I had used the principles of EI to cope during that period without realising it. I was very much aware of my own emotions and limitations. But I also knew that I was the best option for the patients at that time. Before entering the ward, I took deep breaths to calm myself and proceeded to review the patients. I did my best to remain professional and projected confidence to the patients. I carried out A-to-E clinical assessment as we were taught numerous times in medical school and postgraduate. I would then discuss my management plans with the medical registrar to ensure that I have not missed out anything. If the patients were requiring more support than a medical ward can offer, I would discuss with the ITU. After each patient, I would give myself few minutes to reset my mind and then repeat the whole process. If I had a particularly challenging shift, I would request to do a debrief with the medical registrar at the end of our shift. I find it helpful to process certain thoughts and prevent burnout. Fortunately, the hospital recognised the unsustainable workload for the existing out-of-hours team and implemented an emergency COVID-19 rota few weeks into the pandemic. We saw more than quadruple increased in staffing with consultant on-site 24 h every day. The workload became much more manageable but the experience prior to emergency rota implementation made me to become a more resilient doctor.

DNAR decisions and discussions are normally performed by senior doctors such as the registrars and consultants. During COVID-19, junior doctors were often called to attend patients who were critically unwell and some even peri-arrest. For such patients, advance planning regarding resuscitation status needs to be done. The most important question was if the patient goes into cardiorespiratory arrest would resuscitation be appropriate for them. As a Foundation Year doctor who had not done many DNAR discussions, I felt uncomfortable to make the decision of DNAR. I was worried to make the wrong judgement call such as promising to resuscitate a patient who would not be an appropriate candidate or putting a DNAR on a patient who would stand a chance to survive if resuscitated. As one can imagine, either one of these outcomes would be disastrous. However, I did not avoid the DNAR topic as it represents a crucial part of the management plan. I would instead gather relevant information (such as patients' wish, their comorbidities, functional baseline and other factors) for the medical registrar to make the final decision on DNAR. After a few shifts, I escalated my concern to my supervisor who was supportive and reassured me that I did the right thing. Within the same week, a COVID-19 clerking proforma was created which included resuscitation decision to be decided by a consultant on admission.

After a short period of struggle, I adapted to the changing world and did my best to provide the care that my patients deserved. The pandemic made me a better doctor. In terms of my abilities to make clinical assessment, make fast decisions, communicate clearly, be more empathetic, be more resilient and have better situational awareness. Looking back, I had used some of the principles of emotional intelligence to cope. It is important to recognise that clinicians of different grades had different challenges during pandemic. For example, a new starter might find it difficult to assess and manage an unwell patient during the pandemic. Whereas a consultant will have no issue managing the critically unwell patient but might face challenges to keep the medical department in operation due to influx of patients and multiple rota gaps from staff sickness.

## 3.3   Consultant Experiences

As a hospital respiratory consultant, I have separated my experience of the pandemic in to professional and personal thoughts. Clearly this was an extremely busy period of work and we rapidly adapted to a new system of four twelve-hour days at work and four days off which I did intermittently for over eighteen months. A lack of clarity at the start of the pandemic meant that we all needed to rapidly adapt but often without strong evidence to know how to do this. Guidelines for non-specialists needed rapid and frequent writing and then education needed to be dispersed. The assessment and triage of patients through a large admissions unit became a daily occurrence; patients being separated into groups who were for admission to the intensive care unit or not. Strong leadership was required for both junior and senior colleagues who were understandably worried about working in an environment which could potentially threaten their own health.

Inevitably colleagues from all aspects of health care became unwell, some requiring prolonged intensive care admissions and sadly some of those not surviving. Visitors were not allowed and many breathless last minute video calls to a loved one were witnessed whilst the intensive care intubation team waited along the corridor. Professionally I concentrated on developing an understanding of the condition and doing everything we could to optimise patients care. I became proud that we recruited the largest number of patients to trials in history and within a year had developed an established treatment algorithm. I think that a strong use of emotional compartmentalisation allowed people to store some the additional negative impacts to be processed at a later stage. Being married to a fellow hospital consultant and having 2 children at school meant a fractured home life which challenged both parents and offspring. Ultimately neither myself nor my wife became unwell which was a great relief.

## 4   Emotional Intelligence

### 4.1   EI Definition

The general definition of EI is the ability of an individual to recognize, practice, and regulate emotions in oneself in positive ways to overcome issues, communicate efficiently, understand others, relieve stress and resolve conflict [12]. Cherniss et al. [13] defined EI as an ability of a person to identify emotions in oneself and others, to motivate oneself, and to handle his or her feelings in a way to express them appropriately and effectively to others. The current popularity of EI theory owes it to Daniel Goleman's book 'EI Why it can matter more than IQ' [14].

### 4.1.1  Four Main Components of EI [15]

1) Self-awareness – When one is conscious of his or her own feelings and thoughts about them. Being aware of your feelings puts you in charge, not the emotions.
2) Self-control – The amygdala, the "fight or flight section of the brain, responds rapidly to threats, real or perceived, and during a hijack can overwhelm the prefrontal cortex, the area of the brain responsible for planning and strategizing. You can train the prefrontal cortex's capacity to exert control over the amygdala.
3) Social awareness – Listen attentively to others and aware of their emotions. Awareness of all the ways in which a crisis impacts the business, people and system involved in correcting the problem.
4) Relationship management – When crisis strikes, it is essential to manage many relationships among many people. The ability through inspiring others, managing conflicts, fostering teamwork and other competencies, to moving people in the direction you desire.

### 4.1.2  Characteristics of People with a High EI [16]

1) Know what they want and make plans to achieve their goals. They are more likely to understand what gives them pleasure and why. This means they are also more likely to identify their values and know their purpose in life.
2) They can name and express their feelings and connect to their emotions and to understand and manage their responses to stimuli and events. They are able to identify root causes rather than ineffectively trying to deal with symptoms or results. They are self-aware, openly expressive, and healthily assertive.
3) They have the ability to reduce their anxiety in stressful times. People with higher-than-average EI have an excellent chance of reducing anxiety by generating alternative meanings for stressful events and taking more effective action, including advocating for themselves.
4) Learn from mistakes and criticism. Having a high EI can help the people to regulate their emotions, which makes them more able to hear negative criticism and use it to improve rather than interpret it as a personal attack.
5) People with high EI learn know that asking for help is a sign of wisdom and empowerment and not simply a sign of weakness leading to disappointment, self-belittling and rejection.
6) People with high EI can remain calm in challenging situations by expressing their feelings and recognizing their emotions, learn to manage their feelings instead of allowing their emotions to hijack their thoughts.
7) Change from taking things personally and being gratuitously judgmental to expressing their curiosity, compassion and understanding. Those with high EI see an opportunity for themselves to grow and evolve instead of dwelling on taking things personally.

8) People with high EI are able to focus on what they are capable of influencing and controlling rather than wasting their time with matters that are outside their area of control.

9) People with high EI can decode their emotions. By practice understanding the meaning of any particular emotion and, where appropriate, redirect their emotional responses to where they are more appropriate and beneficial. They are able to recognize which emotions should be encouraged and which should be reconsidered.

10) High EI people are able to recognize and follow the quiet voice of their heart, instead of only listening to the demanding and often wrong voice of their ego.

11) People with high EI are able to learn to react to or ask questions based on compassion and considerations of how they are landing rather than focusing solely on their own agenda. They practice empathy and compassionate accountability instead of telling people what to do.

### 4.1.3 Benefit of EI

According to Mayer et al. [17], our success at the workplace or in our life depends 80% on EI and only 20% on intellect. Whereas intellect help solve problems, EI allows us to be more creative and to use emotions to solve problems [18]. Much research has confirmed positive association between EI and optimal mental and physical health, overall well-being, and on-aggressive behaviours [12]. Elfenbein et al. [19] in a meta-analysis found that the accuracy of emotional recognition led to a moderate, but significant increase in workplace efficiency for different specialists, such as doctors, workers in the field of human service, teachers, school principals and business managers. According to Roman et al. [18], EI can inform us in a valuable way the understandings and interventions of the human behaviour practitioners between EI and life. Valenti et al. [20] suggested that understanding emotions helps people to be aware of their own and others' behaviours and motivations, whereas managing emotions allows the individuals to navigate their feelings constructively at work. They define EI as 'the individuals' ability to properly handle their own interpersonal and intrapersonal skills, which improves the competence in facing stressors and, consequently, enhances positive outcomes [20].

Goleman [21] argued that EI is twice as important as technical skills and more important than IQ in predicting positive outcomes at the workplace He suggested that people should be judged not according to their own intelligence or professional competence, but rather by their own behaviours toward themselves and others [21]. Therefore, it is important to consider EI in working environments, both to increase productivity and efficiency and to improve workers' wellbeing, job motivation, and job satisfaction. Soto-Rubio et al. [22] have argued the importance of EI's key role in preventing burnout among health care professionals and in improving their levels of job satisfaction. According to Goleman [21], EI and its competencies are a prerequisite for the preservation of mental health in stressful situations and lack of emotional intelligence in such an unstable environment may be the cause of a failed outcome with questionable future consequences. It becomes clear that how much EI is needed during the COVID-19 pandemic.

### 4.1.4  EI in Healthcare

Doctors are often working in a highly complex, emotionally demanding environment. The ability to manage oneself and one's relationships with others is an invaluable skill that physicians and other health care leaders must possess in order to be successful. According to James [23], physician leaders who are able to exhibit high degrees of EI, particularly in how they manage their own emotions and react to the emotions of others, demonstrate better clinical outcomes, greater professional satisfaction, increased empathy, and improved teamwork within health care organizations. On the contrary, James [23] further argues that a lack of EI skills is a source of failure as a leader. He argues that low EI results in being overly defensive, resolving conflict poorly and not connecting well with the team. Unfortunately, traditional medical schools and training programs pay little attention to this soft skill needed for effective leadership. EI skills are needed whether one is leading a team in the operating room, managing staff in a clinic, or running an executive board meeting.

The benefits of high EI in healthcare are as follows [23]:

1. Improved communication & teamwork.
2. Ability to respond well under pressure.
3. Increased empathy.
4. Better quality of care.
5. Greater career satisfaction.

### 4.1.5  Implications of Our Experience

Healthcare service often involves multiple disciplinary team members working together to care for the patients. As such, EI can help to maintain good working relationships with the wider team and improve efficiency. Rossettini et al. [24] proposed the usefulness of EI in helping heath care teams to cope with stressful situations given its capacity to promote motivation, empathy, cooperation, and good communication. During a pandemic, EI could be a resource for health care leaders to deal with the emergency as it acts as "stress buffer" helping to recover faster from stressful situations [24]. In 2020, Goleman et al. [25] published another article in the Harvard Business Review titled 'How Health care Workers Can Take Care of Themselves' with focus on EI. They highlighted that the emotional challenge could linger beyond healthcare professionals' time on the job increasing the risk of burnout. Thus, it is important for healthcare professionals to pay attention to their emotional lives to remain effective and healthy. It was supported by studies that found higher EI led to better trust among patients, higher levels of patient satisfaction and less physician burnout [25].

We think there is value of introducing EI to the doctors. The principles are simple and yet practical. They are also applicable to all grades of doctors. For individual level, reading Goleman et al. [25] article titled 'How Health care Workers Can Take Care of Themselves' with focus on EI is a good place to start. They proposed a series of questions for each component as listed below to help develop one's EI [25]:

"Self-Awareness

– Am I aware of my emotions?
– Am I aware of how I am expressing them and impacting others?

- What is the tone of my self-talk?
- Are my basic human needs being met?

### Self-Management

- Do I have effective way to navigate emotional triggers?
- What is within my zone of control?
- Am I making time for sleep, nutrition and exercise?
- Do I have a support network, and do I give permission to lean on it?
- What brings meaning and purpose to my life?

### Social Awareness

- Do I listen to others first to understand rather than rush to respond?
- Can I identify and name others' emotions accurately?
- Whose work haven't I recognised?

### Relationship Management

- Am I bringing extra patience and assuming the best about others?
- As a leader, am I being transparent with information?
- Are my communications frequent, clear and open to feedback?
- Am I going slow at key moments, including moments of thanks?"

## 4.1.6   EI and Healthcare Workers

EI in healthcare settings represents an important component of the competencies of healthcare workers and the quality of the service provided in the health institution. It is more important in the health industry because the healthcare workers deal with people who are under extreme emotional stress and may or may not be able to express these emotions. In general, emotional competence is linked to several positive outcomes and can be trained successfully in organizational settings [26, 27].

Andal [28] listed six important elements why emotional intelligence is an important quality to have for healthcare workers:

1. Intrapersonal: The ability to permanently monitor (our) feelings.
2. Interpersonal: be an empathetic person paying more attention to the feelings of others and being more capable of understanding and supporting them in any situation.
3. Adaptability: Have the ability to ruler our emotions, calm themselves down, eliminate depression, irritability or other negative emotions.
4. Stress Management: Ability to perform with positive outcomes in stressful environments and taking effective decisions without being impulsive.
5. General mood: Optimistic attitude and being happy and positive.
6. Oneself-Motivation: Self Emotional control, helping to motivating the health workers to using emotions constructively in all situations, acting like an incentive in everyday life to improve the quality in profession.

Wilkerson [29] argued that because doctors are often responsible for managing the emotions of both themselves and their patients. A doctor with high EI is better equipped to understand and empathize with their patients. This can lead to better communication and more effective treatment. Also, a doctor with high EI may be better able to manage their own emotions in high-stress situations. This can help to prevent burnout [29].

### 4.1.7  The Benefits of EI Training

According to Miao et al. [30, 31], their two meta-analyses have found that emotionally intelligent people are healthier. In an early meta-analysis by Schutte et al. [32], it was found that emotionally intelligent people have better mental health, psychosomatic health, and physical health. Sarrionandia et al. [33] in another meta-analysis confirmed that emotional intelligence is positively related to mental, psychosomatic, and physical health. Martin et al. [34] also confirms the compelling evidence of the relationships between emotional intelligence and behavioural variables associated with health. The meta-analysis also found that emotional intelligence is positively related to having a healthy diet, physical activity, sleep quality, and social support [34]. Likewise, the meta-analysis also found that emotional intelligence is negatively related to unhealthy behaviours, such as substance abuse and reckless driving [34]. Their study results imply that people with a high level of emotional intelligence should be less likely to engage in risky behaviours that expose them to a greater risk of catching COVID. Study by Aliyari et al. [35] showed that people with higher emotional intelligence are more likely to adhere to COVID-19 health protocols.

As healthcare professionals are known to experience anxiety, depression, and distress due to exceedingly high work demands and workload, it is important to psychological supports and interventions to healthcare professionals [36]. It is the authors' belief that assigning EI trainings to healthcare professionals may allow them to better manage their emotions and stresses to experience more positive feelings and less negative feelings, which may lead to less experienced anxiety, depression, and distress [36]. A longitudinal study by Persich et al. [37] examined whether emotional intelligence training could help with the anxieties surrounding the COVID-19 pandemic. The study also found that, "although mental health concerns generally increased after the start of the pandemic, individuals who completed the EI training program scored lower on depression, suicidal ideation, and state anxiety relative to individuals who had been assigned to the placebo training program [37].

According to Jena et al. [38], intelligent individuals have higher levels of self-regulation and self-control and are adaptive, flexible, and optimistic. Therefore, improving working professionals' EI via training will help them better manage the fear and anxiety caused by COVID-19, cause them to act innovatively, and lead an organization to be more forward-looking and innovative. The author concurs with Miao et al. [39] that EI can significantly alleviate burdens for healthcare organizations to ensure their normal operations because emotionally intelligent healthcare professionals are high performers who know how to get necessary job resources to handle the challenging job demands to enable their organizations to effectively function. They also argue that emotionally intelligent citizens who are less prone to contract coronavirus due to their better health status and stronger immune system may decrease their demand to visit healthcare organizations to look for check-ups and treatments which may relieve the burden for healthcare organizations [39]. Emotionally intelligent leaders are also effective leaders, and they are able to make shrewd decisions and implement effective policies to deal with COVID-19 [40].

### 4.1.8 Recommendations for EI Trainings

Two studies supported the view that EI can be trained and developed [27, 39]. According to Miao et al. [39], EI trainings can be developed as follow:

1. Depending on the nature and context of a job, EI trainings can be developed based on different EI models (ability EI versus trait EI) to fit the nature and context of a job [41].
2. To appoint an "emotional intelligence manager" to manage the emotions of employees, to provide EI trainings and feedback to employees, and to foster the formation of emotionally intelligent climate in the organization [42].
3. EI trainings should be developed and contextualized to reflect its relevance for healthcare workers such as doctors.
4. Virtual platforms may be used to deliver emotional intelligence trainings. Artificial intelligence (AI) technology may be implemented to enhance EI trainings and to track progresses of one's development and mastery of EI (e.g., using AI to detect how well a participant is managing his or her emotions in a hypothetical scenario).
5. Social media websites may also feature and run EI trainings.
6. AI machines may be developed and used to manage the emotions of people and to train one's emotional intelligence simultaneously [43]. For example, emotionally intelligent AI machines may alleviate healthcare workers' stresses and anxieties and train their emotional intelligence simultaneously via role modelling by recognizing the feelings of healthcare workers and displaying compassion, understanding, and other appropriate emotions in the actual workplace. AI may also assist individuals to properly display, perceive, and manage their emotions and help individuals to make good choices based on computer-generated information [44].

## 5 Conclusion

The Covid pandemic was a difficult period for many reasons. But it was also the period where we see the most rapid growth for healthcare workers such as doctors. As we can see, emotional intelligence is important for public healthcare systems as it can have a significant impact on the quality of care that patients receive. By providing training, resources and support for healthcare professionals, public healthcare systems can help to improve communication, better patient outcomes, and increased patient satisfaction, as well as mitigate the effects of burnout on the healthcare workforce. It is thus imperative that we provide health care workers the training they need to equip them to provide netter care. Based on the information provided, we propose that public healthcare systems incorporate a comprehensive emotional intelligence training program for their doctors and healthcare workers. Future research on developing an emotional intelligence training program specific for healthcare would be invaluable.

## References

1. Dyvik, E. H.: Impact of the coronavirus pandemic on the global economy - Statistics & Facts (2024). https://www.statista.com/topics/6139/covid-19-impact-on-the-global-economy/#topicOverview. Accessed 20 Jan 2024

2. UN News. Coronavirus update: COVID-19 likely to cost economy $1 trillion during 2020, says UN trade agency - 9 March 2020 (2020). https://news.un.org/en/story/2020/03/1059011. Accessed 20 Jan 2024

3. Handa, N., Pramanik, S.: Assessing wellbeing in foundation doctors during the COVID-19 pandemic. BJPsych Open **7**(Suppl 1), S190 (2021)

4. Chan, L.F., Sahimi, H.M.S., Mokhzani, A.R.B.: A global call for action to prioritize healthcare worker suicide prevention during the COVID-19 pandemic and beyond. Crisis **43**(3), 163–169 (2022)

5. French, L., Hanna, P., Huckle, C.: COVID-19 and healthcare staff wellbeing: is burnout really a systemic issue of morality? In: Mental Health and Wellness in Healthcare Workers: Identifying Risks, Prevention, and Treatment, pp 196–212. IGI Global (2022)

6. Lu, W., Wang, H., Lin, Y., Li, L.: Psychological status of medical workforce during the COVID-19 pandemic: a cross-sectional study. Psychiatry Res. **288**, 112936 (2020)

7. Zhang, W.R., et al.: Mental health and psychosocial problems of medical health workers during the COVID-19 epidemic in China. Psychother. Psychosom. **89**(4), 1–9 (2020)

8. Coronavirus: lessons learned to date. Sixth Report of the Health and Social Care Committee and Third Report of the Science and Technology Committee of Session 2021–2022. https://committees.parliament.uk/publications/7497/documents/78688/default/. Accessed 20 Jan 2024

9. NHS workforce statistics. https://digital.nhs.uk/data-and-information/publications/statistical/nhs-workforce-statistics/november-2023. Accessed 10 Mar 2024

10. COVID-19: Impact of the pandemic on healthcare delivery. https://www.bma.org.uk/advice-and-support/covid-19/what-the-bma-is-ng/covid-19-impact-of-the-pandemic-on-healthcare-delivery. Accessed 20 Jan 2024

11. COVID-19: How well-protected was the medical profession? https://www.bma.org.uk/advice-and-support/covid-19/what-the-bma-is-ng/covid-19-how-well-protected-was-the-medical-profession. Accessed 20 Jan 2024

12. Anand, N., Gorantla, V. R., Ranjan, R., Morcos, H.: Emotional intelligence: An important skill to learn now more than ever. F1000 Res. **12**, 1146 (2023)

13. Cherniss, C., Extein, M., Goleman, D., Weissberg, R.P.: Emotional intelligence: what does the research really indicate? J. Educ. Psychol. **41**(4), 239–245 (2006)

14. Goleman, D.: Emotional Intelligence, vol. 352. Bantam Books, New York (1995)

15. Salovey, P., Mayer, J.D.: Emotional intelligence. Imagin Cogn Pers **9**, 185–211 (1990)

16. Svetlana, W.: Why Is Emotional Intelligence Important? (2022). https://www.forbes.com/sites/forbescoachescouncil/2022/12/30/why-is-emotional-intelligence-important/. Accessed 20 Jan 2024

17. Mayer, J.D., Salovey, P., Caruso, D.R.: Emotional intelligence: theory, findings, and Implications. Psychol. Inq. **15**(3), 197–215 (2004)

18. Roman, M., Roman, V.: Emotional intelligence–what is it and why does it matter? Int. J. Commun. Res. **7**(4), 275–282 (2007)

19. Elfenbein, H.A., Foo, M.D., White, J.: Reading your counterpart: the benefit of emotion recognition accuracy for effectiveness in negotiation. J. Nonverbal Behav. **31**, 205–223 (2007)

20. Valenti, G.D., Faraci, P., Magnano, P.: Emotional intelligence and social support: two key factors in preventing occupational stress during COVID-19. Int. J. Environ. Res. Public Health **18**(13), 6918 (2021)

21. Goleman, D.: What makes a leader? Harv. Bus. Rev. **76**(6), 93–102 (1998)

22. Soto-Rubio, A., Giménez-Espert, M., Prado_Gascó, V.: Effect of emotional intelligence and psychological risks of burnout, job satisfaction, and nurses' health during the COVID-19 pandemic. Int. J. Environ. Res. Public Health **17**(21), 7998 (2020)

23. Ted, A., James, M. D.: Emotional intelligence for physician leaders, trends in medicine. Harvard Medical School (2019). https://postgraduateeducation.hms.harvard.edu/trends-med icine/emotional-intelligence-physician-leaders. Accessed 20 Jan 2024
24. Rossettini, G., et al.: COVID-19 and health care leaders: how could emotional intelligence be a helpful resource during a pandemic? Phys. Ther. **101**(9), 143 (2021)
25. Goleman, D.: How Health Care Workers Can Take Care of Themselves. Harv Bus Rev. (2020). https://hbr.org/2020/05/how-health-care-workers-can-take-care-of-themselves. Accessed 20 Jan 2024
26. Hodzic, S., Scharfen, J., Ripoll, P., Holling, H., Zenasni, F.: How efficient are emotional intelligence trainings: a meta-analysis. Emot. Rev. **10**(2), 138–148 (2018)
27. Mattingly, V., Kraiger, K.: Can emotional intelligence be trained? a meta-analytical investigation. Hum. Res. Manag. Rev. **29**, 140–155 (2019)
28. Andal, S.: Emotional intelligence among health care professionals. J. Nurs. Health Sci. **10**(1), 35–39 (2021)
29. Wilkerson, J.: The Skill Every Doctor Needs, But Most Don't Have (2021). https://jerrundwi lkerson.com/the-skill-every-doctor-needs-but-most-dont-have/. Accessed 20 Jan 2024
30. Miao, C., Humphrey, R.H., Qian, S.: A meta-analysis of emotional intelligence and work attitudes. J. Occup. Organ. Psychol. **90**, 177–202 (2017)
31. Miao, C., Humphrey, R.H., Qian, S.: A meta-analysis of emotional intelligence effect on job satisfaction mediated by job resources, and a test of moderators. Pers. Individ. Differ. **116**, 281–288 (2017)
32. Schutte, N.S., Malouff, J.M., Thorsteinsson, E.B., Bhullar, N., Rooke, S.E.: A meta-analysis investigation of the relationship between emotional intelligence and health. Pers. Individ. Differ. **42**, 921–933 (2007)
33. Sarrionandia, A., Mikolajczak, M.: A meta-analysis of the possible behavioural and biological variables linking trait emotional intelligence to health. Health Psycholol. Rev. **14**(2), 220–244 (2020)
34. Martins, A., Ramalho, N., Morin, E.: A comprehensive meta-analysis of the relationship between emotional intelligence and health. Pers. Individ. Differ. **49**, 554–564 (2010)
35. Aliyari, F., Bakhtiari, M., Kianimoghadam, A.S.: Evaluation correlations between emotional intelligence subscales and adherence to health protocols during the COVID-19 pandemic. NeuroQuantology **20**(5), 100–106 (2022)
36. Lai, J., et al.: Factors associated with mental health outcomes among health care workers exposed to coronavirus disease 2019. JAMA Netw. Open **3**, 1–12 (2020)
37. Persich, M.R., Smith, R., Cloonan, S.A., Woods-Lubbert, R., Strong, M., Killgore, W.D.S.: Emotional intelligence training as a protective factor for mental health during the COVID-19 pandemic. Depress. Anxiety **38**(10), 1018–1025 (2021)
38. Jena, L.K., Goyal, S.: Emotional intelligence and employee innovation: Sequential mediating effect of person-group fit and adaptive performance. Eur. Rev. Appl. Psychol. **72**, 100729 (2022)
39. Miao, C., Qian, S., Humphrey, R. H.: Training in emotional intelligence: a proposed solution to COVID-19 related problems that interfere with innovation management - letter from academia. J. Innov. Manag. **11**(1), I–VIII (2023)
40. Walter, F., Cole, M.S., Humphrey, R.H.: Emotional intelligence: Sine qua non of leadership or folderol? Acad. Manag. Perspect. **25**, 45–59 (2011)
41. Petride, K. V.: Intelligence, emotional. In: Neuroscience and Biobehavioral Psychology, pp. 1–6 (2017)
42. Miao, C., Qian, S., Humphrey, R. H.: Emotional intelligence training can help us manage COVID-19 anxiety. LSE Business Review (2021). http://eprints.lse.ac.uk/112004/1/busine ssreview_2021_08_06_emotional_intelligence_training_can_help_us.pdf. Accessed 20 Jan 2024

43. Schuller, D., Schuller, B.W.: The age of artificial emotional intelligence. Computer **51**, 38–46 (2018)
44. Schutte, N.S., Malouff, J.M.: Comment on developments in trait emotional intelligence research: a broad perspective on trait emotional intelligence. Emot. Rev. **8**, 343–344 (2016)

# Author Index

**B**

Bakar, Nur Azaliah Abu 198, 211
Beranič, Tina 341
Bernsteiner, Reinhard 237, 394
Bustamante, Angela 73

**C**

Chant, Graham Gordon 122
Cosma, Georgina 263

**D**

Dashti, Laila A. H. F. 225
Daud, Rohaizan 363
Dilger, Thomas 61, 394

**E**

Enakrire, Rexwhite Tega 51

**F**

Ferro, Roberto 32, 73
Funashia, Hiroki 175

**G**

Gander, Markus 394
Georgiou, Marios 304

**H**

Hayashida, Hideki 175
Hodgkinson, Ian R. 304
Hongo, Takashi 161
Hussein, Surya Sumarni Binti 211
Hussien, Surya Sumarni 198

**I**

Ibrahim, Norasyikin Shaikh 363
Ismail, Shahrinaz 100

**J**

Jackson, Lisa 225, 304
Jackson, Thomas 304
Jackson, Tom 225, 263

**K**

Kang, Chia-Chun 331
Kasinathan, Vinothini 185
Kaur, Amarmeet 198
Khunrath, Wichuta Adulwattanakul 248
Kotrajarras, Polpat 248
Kraslawski, Andrzej 275
Krauss, Christopher 319
Kuhlmann, Isabelle 319
Kumaresan, Aravind 16

**L**

Lau, Eric Kin Wai 404
Leow, Min Hui 363
Li, Linjie 352
Liberona, Dario 16, 32, 73
Lin, Chi-Hsu 331
Lin, Fu-Ren 292
Lockwood, Steve 304
Lokman, Anitawati 211
Lu, Xiaohui 352
Luo, Xin 352

**M**

Magnier-Watanabe, Remy 3
Majid, Nur Liana Ab 198
Manoli, Napitiporn 112
Maramba, George 415
Marczewska, Magdalena 86
Matsuura, Yoshiyuki 112
Minetaki, Kazunori 378
Mößlang, Madline 237
Mustapha, Aida 185

**N**

Nanon, Nichathorn 135

© The Editor(s) (if applicable) and The Author(s), under exclusive license
to Springer Nature Switzerland AG 2024
L. Uden and I.-H. Ting (Eds.): KMO 2024, CCIS 2152, pp. 445–446, 2024.
https://doi.org/10.1007/978-3-031-63269-3

## P

Panwar, Roma 86
Patabendige, Vishmi Madduma 32
Pavlič, Luka 341
Ploder, Christian 61, 237, 394

## R

Rai, Kallychurn Dooshyant 185
Romprasert, Suppanunta 135, 248
Rother, Marcel 32
Rottensteiner, Arno 61

## S

Saklamaeva, Vasilka 341
Salehuddin, Hasimi 198
Salwin, Mariusz 275
Schlögl, Stephan 237, 394
Schmidt, Florian 61
Senoo, Dai 161
Shen, Wen-Cheng 292
Singseewo, Switchaya 135
Smuts, Hanlie 51, 415
Spiess, Johannes 394
Srisaringkarn, Thanakhom 135, 248

## Strycharska, Dominika 275
Sutton, Benjamin 430

## T

Takahashi, Masakazu 112
Tanamee, Danai 135
Tao, Ran 352
Thirimanna, Dona Layani 16
Ting, I.-Hsien 378

## U

Upravitelev, Max 319

## W

Wang, Jie-Mie 331
West, Andrew 225, 263
Wiriyapinit, Sutthanuch 135
Wong, Chun Wai 430

## Y

Yani, Noor Syazwani Binti Muhammad 211

## Z

Zhang, Li-Jie 331
Zhong, Keyi 263, 304

Printed in the United States
by Baker & Taylor Publisher Services